OXFORD WORLD'S CLASSICS

OLIVE SCHREINER

From Man to Man or Perhaps Only—

Edited with an Introduction and Notes by

DOROTHY DRIVER

OXFORD
UNIVERSITY PRESS

OXFORD
UNIVERSITY PRESS

Great Clarendon Street, Oxford, OX2 6DP,
United Kingdom

Oxford University Press is a department of the University of Oxford. It furthers the University's objective of excellence in research, scholarship, and education by publishing worldwide. Oxford is a registered trade mark of Oxford University Press in the UK and in certain other countries.

Published in the United States of America by Oxford University Press
198 Madison Avenue, New York, NY 10016, United States of America

British Library Cataloguing in Publication Data
Data available

Library of Congress Control Number: 2025937234

ISBN 9780192883056

Printed and bound in the UK by
Clays Ltd, Elcograf S.p.A.

The manufacturer's authorised representative in the EU for product safety is Oxford University Press España S.A. of Parque Empresarial San Fernando de Henares, Avenida de Castilla, 2 – 28830 Madrid (www.oup.es/en or product.safety@oup.com). OUP España S.A. also acts as importer into Spain of products made by the manufacturer.

MIX
Paper | Supporting responsible forestry
FSC® C018072

OXFORD WORLD'S CLASSICS

FROM MAN TO MAN OR PERHAPS ONLY—

OLIVE SCHREINER, a major South African novelist and polemical writer—pro-feminist, anti-capitalist, anti-imperialist, anti-racist, pacifist—was born in 1855 on a mission station in the British Cape Colony to a German father and an English mother. She was raised as a Calvinist but at an early age questioned that faith. After her father was dismissed from his missionary post, she worked for a while as a governess on Karoo farms, reading voraciously, writing stories, and drafting three novels, one of which, *The Story of an African Farm* (1883), she published after arriving in England. This has been described as the first and most important of the 'New Woman' novels in Britain, and also as the first South African novel in English. She had left the Cape in 1881 to study medicine, but illness closed off that course, and instead she devoted herself to writing and sociopolitical reform, joining freethinking organizations, notably the Men and Women's Club, and forming friendships with such outstanding intellectuals as Eleanor Marx, Edward Carpenter, Karl Pearson, and Havelock Ellis. After her return to the Cape, and the publication of *Dreams* (1890), she married Samuel Cron Cronwright, collaborating with him in some polemical writing but not always cohabiting with him. She formed friendships with politically active women, notably Betty Molteno and Alice Greene, and engaged with leading intellectuals, Sol T. Plaatje and Mohandas Gandhi among them; and through letter-writing brought tireless pressure to bear on influential figures in public life. In her allegorical novella *Trooper Peter Halket of Mashonaland* (1897) she attacked the expansionist policies of Cecil John Rhodes, and in other writings urged against the looming war (the second Anglo-Boer War of 1899–1902) and the betrayal of black South Africans in the Act of Union of 1910. After publishing *Woman and Labour* (1911), famously called the Bible of the Women's Movement in England, she continued her intermittent work on *From Man to Man*, but only the first half was fully revised before she was overtaken by ill health and despair, aggravated by the outbreak of the First World War. She died of heart failure in December 1920.

DOROTHY DRIVER is Emeritus Professor at the University of Cape Town, and an adjunct professor at Adelaide University, Australia. Her literary-critical research is primarily in the field of Southern African literature written in English, with a special focus on the intersections of gender and race, and on writing by women. She has produced several journal essays, book chapters and booklets on Olive Schreiner, primarily on *From Man to Man*.

OXFORD WORLD'S CLASSICS

For over 100 years Oxford World's Classics have brought readers closer to the world's great literature. Now with over 700 titles—from the 4,000-year-old myths of Mesopotamia to the twentieth century's greatest novels—the series makes available lesser-known as well as celebrated writing.

The pocket-sized hardbacks of the early years contained introductions by Virginia Woolf, T. S. Eliot, Graham Greene, and other literary figures which enriched the experience of reading. Today the series is recognized for its fine scholarship and reliability in texts that span world literature, drama and poetry, religion, philosophy, and politics. Each edition includes perceptive commentary and essential background information to meet the changing needs of readers.

CONTENTS

ACKNOWLEDGEMENTS

Primary acknowledgements have already been made in the previous edition of *From Man to Man* (University of Cape Town Press, 2015) on which the present edition has been based. However, I would like to acknowledge, once again, the various institutions which hold the originals of the material quoted in Appendix 2, 'Genesis and Composition of the Novel', sourced through *Olive Schreiner Letters Online* (*OSLO*): these are listed on pp. 386–7, in Appendix 2. Particular thanks, again, to the Johannesburg Public Library 'for access to the 1901 manuscript and the 1911 typescript of *From Man to Man*, and to the Harry Ransom Center for access to the 1887–1889 manuscript, and the other archival material on which this edition draws. I would also like to repeat my thanks to Sue Ogterop for research assistance in my preparation of the Explanatory Notes. My belated thanks, too, to three people inadvertently left out of the 2015 Acknowledgements and who have provided further assistance: Tanya Barben in accessing material, and Jeremy Fogg and Paul Walters in matters relating to Samuel Cronwright-Schreiner. For the encouragement and support offered me in the preparation of the present edition, my thanks to Jane Bennett, Carolyn Burdett, John Coetzee, Nicholas Jose, Meg Samuelson and Sue Sheridan. The Amazwi Museum of South African Literature has been of continual help and my thanks to them, as to the University of Cape Town Special Collections, for allowing me to access the Schreiner letters I needed to quote from in order to make occasional corrections to *OSLO* as a source. Particular thanks to Lynne Grant and to Catherine Corder in this regard. Also, for speedy assistance in accessing material not held in the Barr Smith Library at Adelaide University (hitherto the University of Adelaide), I would like to thank the university's library staff, particularly Robin Secomb.

In addition to the present edition of *From Man to Man*, which is what is generally known as a readerly edition, though backed by extensive scholarly editorial work, I am also contracted with Edinburgh University Press for a scholarly edition. Acknowledgements are therefore due to Oxford University Press and Edinburgh University Press for granting permission for the two editions to be published more or less side by side. My thanks to the team—Clare Gill, Andrew van der Vlies, Carolyn Burdett (again), and Clare Charlesworth—assembled to oversee the preparation for Edinburgh University Press of scholarly editions of this and other of Schreiner's works. Discussion with team members has usefully spilled over from the 'scholarly' to the 'readerly'. I would also like to thank Clare Charlesworth for some technical assistance in this regard. My grateful acknowledgment is due, finally, to the Oxford World's Classics production team: to Tara Werger and particularly to Teresa Netzler for their efficiency and patience, to Rowena Anketell for her excellent copyediting, and to Haley Buckley for proofreading.

INTRODUCTION

READERS who do not wish to know details of the plot may prefer to read this Introduction as an Afterword.

OLIVE SCHREINER first made her name with *The Story of an African Farm*, but *From Man to Man or Perhaps Only*—may well be remembered as the greater achievement. Schreiner certainly felt it to be. 'This book is going to be awfully outspoken,' she asserted: '*An African Farm* was nothing to it in heat.'[1] 'I love my new book so,' she added later, 'a hundred times better than I ever loved *An African Farm*.'[2]

From Man to Man follows the contrasting lives of two white women, sisters born on a Karoo farm five years apart. Marriage takes Rebekah, the elder sister, to Cape Town, where she bears four children, deals with her husband's infidelities, and adopts the child born of his union with the domestic servant. Bertie, the younger sister, is seduced at the age of 15 by her tutor, and, pursued by vindictive gossip, flees the Colony and is driven to a life of prostitution in London. In myriad ways Schreiner weaves her own experiences, much transformed, into both Rebekah's and Bertie's fictional lives, most obviously in Rebekah's commitment to a life of the mind, her religious inclinations, her amateur naturalism, and her passionate desire for social reform, as well as in Bertie's poignant victimhood in a world of gossip and censure, and her relegation to childlessness.

The sisters, in different but intersecting ways, exemplify Schreiner's interest in the wasted skills and wasted lives of white English-speaking middle-class women. Her double plot conveys *From Man to Man*'s major and ultimately quite straightforward theme—the structural equivalence of marriage and prostitution, and thus the corrupted and commodified nature of desire in the modern world. The implications of Bertie's prostitution are deepened, for instance, by her being sucked into becoming the mistress of a diamond merchant whose dealings bind together the British and South African mercantile

[1] Letter to Havelock Ellis, 21 July 1884 (in Appendix 2).

[2] Letter to Havelock Ellis, 10 December 1887 (in Appendix 2).

worlds. And the black child fostered by Rebekah in Cape Town points to the possible route out of such a world. In several different ways, the African context—its landscape, its history, its mix of peoples—offered Schreiner the impetus she needed to deepen her sociopolitical inquiry and her quest for what she called in her book *Woman and Labour*, composed simultaneously with *From Man to Man*, an 'enlarged and expanded humanity'.[3]

In 1881 Schreiner submitted a first full draft to Chapman and Hall in London, under the title 'Saints and Sinners'. Asked to revise, she worked on it during much of the 1880s, and more sporadically later, rewriting, condensing, and amplifying; yet by the time of her death in 1920 the work was not completed. We know that a hand-written text had been fully, or almost fully, written out by 1913 or so, and we have the first half of the novel, in typescript, lightly revised. But the latter is all that survives of the material that her husband, Samuel Cronwright-Schreiner, edited and published in 1926. In his introduction he wrote of the confused bundle of manuscript pages—subsequently destroyed—that he had to sort through in order to establish the novel's second half (see Appendix 1). *From Man to Man* is thus an unfinished work, unfinished in the sense that parts were never revised by the author, and a final chapter started but not resumed, though Cronwright-Schreiner included in his edition an ending he remembered her recounting to him (see Appendix 3).

Recent critics, nonetheless, have hailed *From Man to Man* as 'the most mature expression of [the] New Realist aesthetic' that emerged in the late nineteenth century; as the closest of all Schreiner's writing 'to being a "New Woman" text'; as 'one of the great feminist novels' of the twentieth century; and as 'a key text for Schreiner scholarship, South African literature, and Victorian literature as a whole'.[4]

Contemporary reviewers of the novel were less complimentary, startled by its unfinished nature, and perhaps influenced by the ambivalent commentary in the biography that Cronwright-Schreiner published in 1924. They certainly noted the quality of much of the

[3] Schreiner, *Woman and Labour*, 128, in Select Bibliography, *infra*.

[4] S. Pearl Brilmyer, *The Science of Character*, 31; Carolyn Burdett, *Olive Schreiner*, 54; Liz Stanley, *Imperialism, Labour and the New Woman*, 95; Sanja Nivesjö and Heidi Barends, 'Current Perspectives on Olive Schreiner's *From Man to Man or Perhaps Only—*', 44, all in Select Bibliography, *infra*.

writing—Schreiner's extraordinary capacity to capture a scene, the poetic quality of her prose—but they objected to the unevenness and shapelessness of the whole. The novelist Arnold Bennett astutely found in the writing the signs of an over-long gestation, and went on to counsel writers to spend no more than two years on a book.[5] Yet, some seventy years later, Cherry Clayton, a South African critic more familiar than Bennett with the events of Schreiner's life, as well as the historical context and the sociopolitical issues at stake, saw in the novel's long gestation a 'courageous openness' to the author's 'evolving experience and knowledge'. 'Its very incompleteness', she added, 'is an index to the difficult transmutation of life into art'.[6]

Critics have speculated on alternative reasons for Schreiner's fatal delay in completing the novel: the pressures of political involvement and of her other writing, both abroad and at home, bouts of ill health throughout her adult life (asthma, an inherited heart condition), and disruptions—once she had started revising—to her idiosyncratic writing practice, which was to rewrite sections or chapters rather than revise them.[7] One critic, speaking with the insight of a novelist, has speculated that Schreiner's 'writer's block' was due to the very ambitiousness of her project: so 'overwhelming [a] sense of responsibility' had the novel entailed as to produce in its author an 'insurmountable awe'.[8] This makes sense. Schreiner did indeed aspire to change the world. It can also plausibly be argued that *From Man to Man* was never completed because she could not find in the novel-form of her day a vehicle adequate to her combined ambitions as a novelist and social thinker across a changing historical context.

From an early age Schreiner had felt distanced from her Christian missionary upbringing, even while retaining a profoundly religious spirit. She had also to negotiate as a teenager the male domination of her time and its discrimination against girls and women, as well as the social and cultural divisions between her own English-speaking

[5] Arnold Bennett, 'Author 34 Years Over a Novel', in *Arnold Bennett: The Evening Standard Years—'Books and Persons' 1926–1931*, ed. Andrew Mylett (London: Chatto & Windus, 1974), 24.

[6] Cherry Clayton, *Olive Schreiner*, 72, in Select Bibliography, *infra*.

[7] See Liz Stanley, 'Before', 17; see also Joyce Avrech Berkman, *The Healing Imagination*, which suggests a 'confusion over artistic aims' (209) and an 'unresolved sense of audience' (212); both in Select Bibliography, *infra*.

[8] Finuala Dowling, '"Writer's Block"', 81, in Select Bibliography, *infra*.

community and the Dutch-speaking ('Boer') people among whom she worked as a governess and to whom she felt emotionally attached. To these pressures was added an increasing awareness of racial antagonisms in a country whose indigenous peoples had only recently been overpowered by invaders from across the seas, invaders who saw them as savage and even sub-human. By the end of the 1880s, then, she had ceased to think of her mother's England as 'home', although she continued sometimes to use that term in letters to family and friends. Increasingly aware of the very different ethos built into African tribal culture, she felt that the country of her birth might become a model for the rest of the world. At odds with the increasing individualism and consumerism of European modernity, Schreiner had turned first to Boer culture for an alternative social model, but she later directed her attention to African culture in order to focus on the hospitality, mutual respect, equality of power, and reciprocity in social relations that would allow comities and civilizations to flourish. Her self-education in evolutionary theory and in the histories of the rise and fall of civilizations allowed her to pursue this line.

Bitter at her lack of formal education, as a girl, her hunger for knowledge led her to read as widely as she could in contemporary European history, philosophy and science (John Stuart Mill, Herbert Spencer, Charles Darwin, among many others) and in literature, both classical and modern (Plato, Goethe, Heine, George Sand, Robert Browning, Emerson, and others)—an ardent self-education that persisted until her death. Late in life, she advised a young aspirant writer to read 'only the best books as far as possible & above all poetry': read the Bible, read Shakespeare and 'learn some of the long passages of Milton by heart'.[9] The rhythms of her own prose attest to this discipline.

In her mid-twenties, intent upon a lifetime of fiction-writing buttressed by scientific study, Schreiner launched herself into the heady London atmosphere of a free thinking British intellectual community, feminist and socialist. Then, back in the Cape once again, after the first Anglo-Boer War and the surprising British defeat, she allowed political activism to take her main focus. Living through the second Anglo-Boer War and the lamentable Act of Union of 1910, she struggled to maintain her ideals of peace and social equality in the face of her own divided loyalties and of her increasing awareness of

[9] Letter to André Murray, 7 May 1913, in *Olive Schreiner Letters Online* (*OSLO*), in Select Bibliography, *infra*.

the moral and political implications of the exploitation by capital of a racialized labour force. What follows is a closer look at some of the key features of the transnational shifts and the philosophical and political negotiations of Schreiner's life, and the part they played in the formation of her extraordinary final novel.

* * *

Olive Schreiner was born on the border between the Cape Colony and Basutoland (now Lesotho) to a Christian missionary couple. Her father was noted for his quiet and gentle manner, and his self-sacrificing generosity; her mother—though somewhat rigid in her thinking—was so high-spirited and intellectually brilliant that, said one acquaintance, '"It would be difficult to imagine a companion more fascinating."'[10] From this background, both humble and cultivated, five of the seven surviving children rose to prominence, the youngest brother becoming prime minister of the Cape, and Olive herself gaining renown as a writer and social theorist. Such easy social mobility was of course barred to South Africans who were not white. Colonial whiteness, as it interacted with gender and with other manifestations of race and class, would emerge as a thematic in Schreiner's fiction, and particularly in *From Man to Man*.

As a child, she developed a talent for making up stories, which she would recount to herself as she paced up and down. Her own first religious experience came to her as 'a little child of five': intimations of a profound unity underlying all things, 'that they were alive, & that I was part of them'.[11] Later, 'not yet nine years old', she recalls her heart 'burning and heavy' at the thought of the suffering of convicts and 'dark-men', and at the hunting ('for pleasure') of birds and animals. She seemed 'to *see* a world in which creatures no more hated and crushed, in which the strong helped the weak, and men understood each other, and forgave each other, and did not try to crush each other but to help.'[12] Out of such moments was her own mission born.

[10] Quoted in Karel Schoeman, *Olive Schreiner*, 51, in Select Bibliography, *infra*.

[11] Letter to John T. Lloyd, 29 October 1892 (in Appendix 2).

[12] Schreiner, 'The Dawn of Civilisation: Stray thoughts on Peace and War; The homely personal confession of a believer in Human Unity', in *Olive Schreiner's The Dawn of Civilisation & Other Unpublished Wartime Writings*, ed. Liz Stanley, 40–3, in Select Bibliography, *infra*.

Between the ages of 16 and 23, her parents destitute, she worked as a household help, childminder, and governess on mostly Boer farms in the Cradock area, in the Karoo. One of her employers described her as having 'everything that makes for charm in a social gathering. Her eyes, her voice, which in laughter became music, her gay mirthfulness of disposition, the ready and easy flow of language, with ideas that seemed to come to her lips with a gladsome speed and fulness, made her conversation sparkling and suggestive. [. . .] You felt that she had *read* and she had *thought*.'[13] Along with her two older siblings, she lived for two years in a tent on the Diamond Fields diggings, where she composed part of what would become *Undine*, a work of fiction completed in 1876 but (like *From Man to Man*) not published until after her death. While governessing, she drafted 'Saints and Sinners' (revised, this would become *From Man to Man*) and wrote *African Farm*, the book that would open up her literary career.

Schreiner's initial aim was to undergo medical training (motivated, her goddaughter recalls, by a desire to ' "understand how men behaved as they did" '),[14] but this plan was abandoned on account of ill health. She instead devoted herself to writing.

This was an age of intellectual ferment in Britain, marked by scientific discoveries that led to debates about the relation between religion and science; by politically bold class and labour analyses; and by growing interest in 'the Woman Question' so central to First-Wave feminist debates. *African Farm*'s pathbreaking proto-feminism and religious scepticism gave Schreiner access to leading free-thinking intellectuals and social activists. Among them was Eleanor Marx, Karl Marx's daughter, a feminist, socialist, writer, and translator, who was concerned—as was Schreiner—with the evolving nature of sexual relations between women and men, the nature of marriage, and how to reconceptualize the place of work in women's lives. Another friend was Havelock Ellis, a physician and sexologist, author of the multi-volume *Studies in the Psychology of Sex* (1897–1910), with whom Schreiner formed a close, loving friendship that lasted a lifetime. Along with these friends, now including Edward Carpenter, a New Age philosopher and gay rights activist, she attended meetings of the Fellowship of the New Life (established in 1882; the Fabian

[13] Quoted in Schoeman, *Olive Schreiner*, 204.
[14] Olive Renier, *Before the Bonfire*, 19, in Select Bibliography, *infra*.

Society was an offshoot). To Carpenter, her spirit of freedom was refreshing: she was 'of apparently lady-like origin', he said, but she 'did not wear a veil and seldom wore gloves, and [she] talked and laughed in the streets quite naturally.'[15]

In the wake of the Contagious Diseases Acts of 1864–9 that sought to regulate female sex-work while leaving male patrons untouched, furore raged about the double moral sexual standard for women and men, a topic Schreiner had already explored in *African Farm* but would address more deeply in *From Man to Man*. '[T]he subject of my book', she told Ellis in 1884, 'is prostitution & marriage. It is the story of a prostitute & of a married woman who loves another man, & whose husband is sensual & unfaithful.'[16]

The unsettling similarity between sex-work and marriage was a topic much in the air among intellectuals in late Victorian England when Schreiner joined the newly re-formulated Men and Women's Club in 1885. Now dominated by Karl Pearson, professor of Applied Mathematics at University College London, and soon-to-be author of *The Ethic of Freethought* (1888), the club hosted frank debates on sex and gender that dealt with topics so intimate that membership was limited to twenty and guests were carefully vetted. There was broad agreement in the club that equality between women and men should be striven for and the double standard in sexual mores eliminated. However, sharp differences emerged over such matters as the nature, strength, and role of female sexual desire; the key differences between women and men, especially in relation to sexual desire; and the nature and value of what was simply called 'labour' in women's lives.

Schreiner and Pearson shared strong views on the importance of altruistic social duty. They worked amicably together and even planned joint research. There were, however, points of friction. Pearson's paper on 'The Woman's Question' (1885) was, she asserted, flawed by a severe omission: 'You have studied & thought out so deeply the position of woman, why have you not given the same thought to man?'[17] Understanding of the interaction between women and men, as well as

[15] Carpenter, *My Days and Dreams*, 227, in Select Bibliography, *infra*.

[16] Letter to Havelock Ellis, 31 October 1884 (in Appendix 2).

[17] Letter to Karl Pearson, 5 February 1888, in *OSLO*. See also Schreiner's review of Pearson's *The Ethic of Freethought* (1888) in *Pall Mall Gazette*, 29 January 1889, p. 3.

the social construction of men, was needed to deepen any social enquiry: what is it that men truly want? What is the true nature of their sexual desire? This became a key question in *From Man to Man*.

To Schreiner, the reform of social relations depended also on the reform of men. She had been encouraged by her early reading of Mill, whose *Subjection of Women* (1869) advocated 'the equality of married persons before the law'. But Mill's interest—like Pearson's, later—was in the reform of women's social position as 'the only means of rendering the daily life of mankind, in any high sense, a school of moral cultivation'.[18] Schreiner's interest, in contrast, was in the evolution—that is, the social construction—of both males and females. Moreover, Pearson's eugenic emphasis on motherhood (the breeding of stock for the British race) was helping reroute Darwin's evolutionary theory into Social Darwinism, which Schreiner abhorred for its focus on competion ('brute force') rather than co-operation and care ('mother-love'). Her central character in *From Man to Man* argues vehemently against Social Darwinism, using Pearson as an unnamed fictional interlocutor.

Schreiner had also been absorbed in Edward Gibbon's *History of the Decline and Fall of the Roman Empire*. To his argument about the importance of understanding historical change she now added the history of women—the history of their decline into dependence on men—as key to repairing the false step that modernity had taken in its evolution. For Pearson, state-supported motherhood was the sum total of women's labour, whereas, for Schreiner, the full opening-up of labour to women had a different and more expansive direction, and a considerably more beneficial and wide-ranging social effect. In Schreiner's eyes, and for other female members of the club, state support of motherhood would simply lock women into place as parasites upon men. Schreiner's models of ideal civilizations, like Gibbon's, were both Athens and Rome, at their high points, but—further than Gibbon—she saw social decline heralded not only in the position of slaves ('an unhappy condition of men', as Gibbon put it) and the corruptions of luxury in the dominant class (Gibbon's 'slow and

[18] J. S. Mill, *The Subjection of Women* (London: Longmans, Green, Reader and Dyer, 1869), 78-9. See also his 'Early Essays on Marriage and Divorce', in *Collected Works* ed. John Robson (U of Toronto, 1963-1991), vol. 21: 'The question is not what marriage ought to be, but [....] what women ought to be. Settle that first, and the other will settle itself' (26).

secret poison into the vitals of the empire')[19] but also in the history of women's decline into dependence on men.

Another turn in her thinking came with her commission in 1886 to write an introduction to a new edition of Mary Wollstonecraft's *A Vindication of the Rights of Woman*, while still revising *From Man to Man*. In her draft introduction, referring to an illuminating insight she had gained years before from a nameless Bechuana women she had met in the Northern Cape, she implicitly rejects Pearson's normative and eugenic distinction between 'primitive' and 'civilized' societies. The Bechuana woman—Schreiner calls her 'a person of genius'—had made clear to her how the very survival of an African agricultural community depended on the participation of women in the long-standing tradition of physical labour, under patriarchal control, and the quelling of any impulse to resist. In this so-called 'primitive' person, Schreiner wrote, she could witness a 'social duty' being fulfilled in full awareness of its inherent contradictoriness.[20] This was not to justify women's subordination as an evolutionary necessity; it was instead to demonstrate its historicity: Schreiner's interest in the interactive relation between the individual and the social group brought her focus onto that very moment in African history in which evolution would, ideally, start to take a different course.

If one wanted to see a truly 'primitive' social formation, Schreiner went on to aver in *Woman and Labour*, one need look no further than middle-class British families where wives depended economically on their husbands. In Schreiner's eyes a wife could be called 'civilized' only once she engaged as productively as did men in paid labour, in the social, political, cultural, and economic world outside the home. In her socialist thinking, social decline was measured both by the increasing degradation of women and by the associated ascendancy of the values of a capitalist consumerism, to say nothing of the assumed privileges of class exploitation, the twin of gender exploitation. Any possibility of social equality, cohesion, and harmony depended not

[19] Edward Gibbon, *The History of the Decline and Fall of the Roman Empire*, vol. 1 (London: John Murray, 1838), 67 and 91.

[20] See Schreiner, 'Introduction to the Life of Mary Wollstonecraft and the Rights of Woman', ed. Carolyn Burdett, *History Workshop Journal* 37/1 (1994), 193n. This is reprinted in Stephen Gray (ed.), *Words in Season* (in Select Bibliography, *infra*) but in a differently edited form. For further discussion of Schreiner's text, see Burdett's introduction, 'A Difficult Vindication: Olive Schreiner's Wollstonecraft Introduction', in Select Bibliography, *infra*.

just on the labour of women in order to adjust class relations, but also on the radical revision of gender relations—what Schreiner habitually called 'the movement of sex to sex' (her concern here was with what we would now call gender, not sex).

The central call of *Woman and Labour*—'Give us labour and the training that fits us for labour'—thus served as far more than a cry from women to break their economic dependence on men and achieve economic equality, and it did far more than simply correct Pearson's claim that childbearing adequately fulfilled women's social instinct; it also strove to halt the social degeneration of the modern world through the radical readjustment of gender relations.

In a long letter she wrote Pearson in July 1886, summarizing the novel and detailing a projected ending, Schreiner asked if she could dedicate the book to him.[21] Reading this alongside her other letters to him allows one to speculate about a relation between, on the one hand, her two fictional characters (at this point unnamed), and, on the other had, herself and Pearson: as if fictional relations and real-life relations were uncannily merging. British history had already seen such couples: Mary Wollstonecraft and William Godwin; John Stuart Mill and Harriet Taylor; and closer to her time, George Eliot and Henry Lewes. Were they in Schreiner's mind as flags to a new social order?

Later that year Schreiner was shaken to the core by what she felt to be a fatal misunderstanding, on Pearson's part, of her intentions towards him, which were—she insisted—platonic. Her distress was exacerbated by the malicious interference of a female club member who advised Pearson that Schreiner had an 'animal' sexual nature, and that this had become a matter of concern among her 'sisters' at the club.[22] Feeling doubly betrayed, Schreiner fled to Europe, where she moved restlessly from place to place (France, Switzerland, Italy) until her return to the Cape in 1889.

In insisting in her letters that her intentions towards Pearson were platonic, Schreiner may have been advocating what was at the time becoming a key topic in the 'Woman Question': celibacy for heterosexual women, in a world in which heterosexual sex seemed inevitably

[21] See Appendix 3, pp. 468–72 and Letter to Pearson, 10 July 1886 (in Appendix 2). See also Letter to Pearson, n.d. July 1886, in *OSLO*, where she refers to *From Man to Man* as 'our book'.

[22] Elisabeth Cobb to Karl Pearson, 15 December 1886; quoted by Betty Fradkin, 'Olive Schreiner and Karl Pearson', 89, in Select Bibliography, *infra*.

to bring with it problems of power. But abstinence, for Schreiner, was simply an evolutionary stage on the way to radical gender reform. (She would even go so far as to postulate the evolution of male and female into an androgynous figure that would reproduce itself, allowing 'the sexual systems' to be used simply for pleasure.)[23]

Critics like to refer to Schreiner's apparent 'problem with sex', but the complexities of the question of power—as well as what we may call a poetics of sex in her fiction—deserve more careful consideration given its centrality to the male-female relations in *From Man to Man*. On the face of it, her thinking was clear enough, if a touch deterministic, but it was supremely idealistic: a fundamental trust in the unity underlying all nature; a concomitant view of an ideal relation between body and mind (they could be divorced only artificially and discursively); and a faith in the ideal sexual union—often but not necessarily identified with the ideal marriage—where a generative fusion of body and mind was the route to a new social order. In this ideal sexual union, parental duties would no longer be gendered; the unhealthy limit society had placed on the concept of male creativity would disappear (for men were creators of children as much as were women); and society would thus cease to allot motherhood only to women, but would see men, too, as mothers and motherly; hence the focus in *From Man to Man* on 'mother-love'.

Schreiner abhorred a sexuality that divorced body and mind: she found it 'savage' or 'primitive' (her terms), and, above all, devoid of the aesthetic, the giving and the receiving of 'joy', which was the true end of sex. Drawing a connection between joyous sex and artistic 'genius', she even spoke of sexual union as achieving the heights of 'the sacred',[24] in something of the manner that Carpenter would in his *Love's Coming-of-Age* (1896).

Schreiner's correspondence with both Pearson and Ellis during the late 1880s goes over and over, tentatively and sometimes contradictorily, but passionately and assertively, this difficult uncharted terrain: the evolutionary nature of sexual desire, how it structures male-female relations, and how it may lead ultimately to social reform.

[23] See Letter to Karl Pearson, 3 July 1886 (in Appendix 2).

[24] See Letters to Havelock Ellis, 28 June 1884, in *OSLO*, and 12 December 1911 (in Appendix 2); and to W. T. Stead, n.d. ?1896, in *OSLO*.

In Europe, continuing to work on the novel and composing the short, lyrical, often allegorical texts that would be gathered and published as *Dreams* (1890) and *Dream Life and Real Life* (1897), she went back to reading Gibbon. She had by now abandoned the Wollstonecraft project. With her love of truth and her passion for social improvement, she had already—in *African Farm*—shown her interest in the historical shift from religious faith to scientific truth; now she decided to address the question of truth in another frame: how did silence on the truth of male sexual desire hinder any repair to unequal and unjust sexual and gender relations?

In the 1887–9 manuscript fragments of *From Man to Man*, specifically in Ch. 6, which in the published version becomes Ch. VII, Schreiner includes in Rebekah's diary entries a lament on the loss in the modern world of a love of truth: 'During all the intervening ages of retrogression & development which we call Christian, we find hardly a trace of it [the love of truth]'.[25] Furthermore, exploring the 'interaction of brain & sex systems' and the relation between 'strong sex feeling & genius' (where 'strong sex feeling' depended on the afore-mentioned interaction), Rebekah turns to the nub of truth she needs to hear from her promiscuous husband. In the 1887–9 fictional diary this centres on his relations with the domestic worker, named in the manuscript as Clartje. She confronts her husband for the truth about a sexual desire, that she now sees as complicated by race and class differences: 'Will you let me be a man to you, & talk to me as you talk to men?'

The turn to race was crucial. In London, in the process of exploring the nature of desire, Schreiner had sought out female sex workers, advising them and in some cases opening her home to them. She had also acted as confidante to female friends and acquaintances in distress. Pearson had admonished her for spending that time to the detriment of her writing. Now, in 1890, writing to him for the last time, she both thanked him for good advice and subtly reminded him of her own final advance on his thinking: 'Mark you, Karl Pearson, [. . .] [t]hose women taught me what I could not otherwise have learnt.'[26] What was it —in 1890—that she felt she would not otherwise have learnt? In a subsequent letter to a friend she referred to the 'sex question' as *From Man to Man*'s major theme. If this informal research had

[25] Harry Ransom Center, 'Olive Schreiner: Works', MS-3734. See Stanley, 'Before, 9', in Select Bibliography, *infra*, for the dating of much of this manuscript.

[26] Letter to Karl Pearson, 11 November 1890 (in Appendix 2).

helped her think about what sex might mean inside and outside of marriage, about the question of power in relation to sex, and about the nature of naked male desire exercised upon paid, subordinated women, now, as suggested by Clartje's presence in the 1887–9 manuscripts, Schreiner was adding racial difference to the 'sex question' in order to complicate class difference, and to draw all these into her quest for the 'truth' about social relations and the direction of social reform. Here, then, is the first manifestation in Schreiner's writing of what black American feminist scholars—almost a century later—will call the intersections of gender, class, and race.

In London, she had seen in modern, bourgeois Europe the threat of increasing social degeneration caused by the growing parasitism of middle-class women without incomes of their own in a capitalist, urbanizing, industrial world. What was to be done, she had asked herself, to resolve or halt this degeneration? Now, in Alassio, she was thinking further: about the importance of race in any exploration of sexuality and gender. Rebekah's husband's seeking out of Clartje became a key to the 'lie' buried in the white male's sexual desire. In this and other ways she heard her homeland calling. In three of the allegories she wrote as her European period came to an end, she denoted a South African setting—'Three Dreams in a Desert', 'A Dream of Wild Bees', and 'The Sunlight Lay Across My Bed'—and the last of these, she told Ellis when she was back in the Cape, had put in a nutshell all she hoped *From Man to Man* to achieve. Now, she felt sure, what 'The Sunlight' had mapped out only allegorically, her novel could realize fully, in 'objective form'.[27]

Cast in the form of a dream that turns mostly to nightmare, Schreiner's allegory takes the dreamer into a living hell: wealthy revelers drink copious amounts of red wine that turns out to be the labourers' blood. The dreamer has a glimpse of the ultimate heaven, without class or race, gender-free; but is sent back to earth: 'That which you seek is there', says the God-figure of the dream.[28]

'There', for Schreiner, was back on African soil. The allegory closes on the sound of a barrel-organ from the street below, and the sight of 'a long yellow streak of pale London sunlight'. *From Man to Man* repurposes the images to mark Bertie's longing for home. Feeling

[27] Letter to Havelock Ellis, 6 November 1890 (in Appendix 2).

[28] Schreiner, 'The Sunlight Lay', in *Dreams*, 180, in Select Bibliography, *infra*.

alone in London, a 'lost woman', Bertie longs for a world where she will no longer be shamed. The ending Schreiner recounted to her husband (see Appendix 3) has Rebekah bring Bertie's body out into the Cape sunlight. Schreiner would not write out this particular ending to the novel, but it points to her interest in disclosing what would otherwise remain shrouded in shame, via the strong African sunlight, a regenerative motif elsewhere in thc novel.

Schreiner's return to the African continent was to redirect the course of her writing. Its land, its history, and its social relations held the story she required. Despite all that she associated with British capitalist imperialism in a white-dominated colonial world—the individualism, competitiveness, envy, greed, class exploitation, cruelty, hypocrisy and self-deception made manifest in the last allegory she had penned in Europe—it was this land, her own land, that (she later asserted) would serve as a model for the wider world: 'a fairer and more healthful form of civilization than has elsewhere been reached.'[29] And it came to do so in her imagining, not via a confluence of the best of British and Boer culture, as she had first supposed, but via an inter-racial confluence. Schreiner's new understanding of race was as a seed-bed from which new thoughts about evolutionary change might grow. While she was still in England, her vision of an 'enlarged and expanded humanity' had depended on the duty of each woman to keep 'active, virile and laborious', not for themselves alone, 'but for the race', by which she meant the human race.[30] But her arrival in Africa would spur her to articulate the duty of each woman differently: again to reach 'beyond her personal life and individual interests', again to preserve the 'abiding consciousness [that] constitutes the religious element of the women's movement of our day', but now to bind together 'into one solid body the women of whatsoever race, class and nation'.[31]

* * *

In South Africa, where Schreiner lived from late 1889 to late 1913, save for an eight-month visit to England, her circle of friends was again largely defined by her political concerns, but this time with an

[29] Schreiner, 'The Psychology of the Boer' (1892) in *Thoughts on South Africa*, 272, in Select Bibliography, *infra*.

[30] Schreiner, 'The Woman Question', in Barash, *An Olive Schreiner Reader*, 98 and 65, in Select Bibliography, *infra*.

[31] *Woman and Labour*, 128.

African flavour. Here she engaged with female suffragism in its relation to race; with the shortcomings of Liberal policy in the Cape Colony as regards the exploitation of indigenous and indentured labour; with the threat of even further racial limitations to the Cape franchise; and above all with what a predatory capitalism, backed by racist ideology, was doing to deform South Africa's future.

She and Samuel Cronwright-Schreiner lived together on his farm after their marriage in 1894, but her asthma worsened to such an extent that her husband gave up farming life for the law (he subsequently entered politics). Even so, for long periods the two lived apart. Her closest South African friendships were with women. Among these were Elizabeth (Betty) Molteno (1852–1927) and her partner Alice Greene (1858–1920), who were (like Schreiner) fervently pro-Boer, anti-imperialist, and anti-racist. Molteno described Schreiner as 'an embodiment of such noble, life-giving humanity as I have not hoped in the flesh to meet.'[32] Other friends were the writer Sol T. Plaatje (1876–1932), a founding member of the South African Native National Congress, later to become the African National Congress; and John Tengo Jabavu (1859–1921), an influential journalist and a pathbreaking African-language newspaper editor, like Plaatje, mission-educated. Plaatje so admired Schreiner that he named a daughter after her. Mohandas Gandhi (1869–1948), a campaigner for political rights for Indian South Africans, as well as leader of a passive resistance movement (satyagraha), would claim what he called 'the privilege' of knowing Schreiner: 'She was a friend of the Indians equally with the Natives of South Africa'; she 'knew no difference between her Negro servants and herself'.[33]

Over the next two decades she wrote newspaper and magazine essays, using the pen-name 'A Returned South African' (these were gathered and published posthumously in *Thoughts on South Africa*), co-authored with her husband a short book, *The Political Situation* (1895), and published a booklet entitled *An English South African's View of the Situation: Words in Season* (1899), pleading for peace and warning against the damage that British imperialist expansion might

[32] Letter from Elizabeth Maria Molteno to Percy Alport Molteno, 3 July 1899, University of Cape Town Libraries, Special Collections, Molteno Murray Collection, Box 6. My thanks to Catherine Corder for furnishing me with this quotation.

[33] Mohandas K. Gandhi, *Satyagraha in South Africa* (1928); trans. Valji Govindji Desai (rev. 2nd edn., Ahmedabad: Navajivan Publishing House, 1950), 168.

do to the Boer way of life. She also published *Trooper Peter Halket of Mashonaland* (1897), a sharp allegorical attack on Cecil John Rhodes's invasion of Mashonaland and the British Chartered Company's murderous appropriation of African land and mineral wealth. In hard-hitting moments, the novella shows the takeover of indigenous land and the rape of indigenous women as two sides of the same terrorist project. Though the book found a large readership in England, and was widely translated, it was also attacked as unpatriotic and—Schreiner lamented—brought about no political change at all.

As the second Anglo-Boer War loomed, this time between both Boer republics and Britain, Schreiner engaged in a passionate attempt to avert it, through speech-making, essay writing, and corresponding with politicians whose minds she hoped to change. As a British colonial subject who took the side of the Boers, her position again became suspect, and her interventions were generally greeted with vituperation among whites, both in South Africa and in England: she was nicknamed 'Shrieker' and cartooned in *Punch*.

When war broke out she was living in the small town of Hanover, where she had found some relief from attacks of asthma. Because of her pro-Boer activities, she was ordered to remain there for the duration of hostilities, under military guard, but did manage, along with her friends Molteno and Greene, and Emily Hobhouse (1860–1926), a British humanitarian, to engage in relief work to improve conditions in the concentration camps into which Boer women and children were herded.

What, then, of *From Man to Man*? During the Hanover years, Cronwright-Schreiner typed the Prelude and subsequent six chapters. These she radically revised and in 1911 had them retyped. The differences from the 1901 version, and more particularly the emendations she made to the 1911 typescript, show how Schreiner's awareness had been changing, partly through what had occurred in Mashonaland, partly through her travel into the interior, and partly through the portents for the country's future given the British victory in the war.[34]

During her travels, two features in particular had pressed upon her attention. The first was the 'social instinct' she detected among Africans, already briefly mentioned in her Wollstonecraft essay and now awaiting her expansion; the second was what she and others of her time called

[34] See the Explanatory Notes to pp. 9, 28 and 42 for the more significant emendations.

'miscegenation'. Earlier, in trying to persuade the British public that the Boers deserved Britain's protection rather than predation, Schreiner had focused on the Boers' love of the land, their freedom from the corruptions of modern capitalism, and their 'instinctive' capacity to create new social structures both cohesive and interactive.[35] Strategically, while hoping that Boer disdain for black South Africans would change with time, she had characterized their racist, 'anti-social attitude' as less damaging to race relations than that of British South Africans, and had also associated the Boers with the 'dreamy' capacity she felt was incipient in all South Africans born to the land.[36] From here she segued into a call to European settlers, and to modern Europeans more generally, to aspire to a new sense of humanity: to drop *their* sense of racialized entitlement, and their exploitative attitude towards the colonies.

After the war, however, amid indications that the exploitation of black labour would increase under capitalist domination, she turned her protective and projective eye more fully upon the African population. She had already praised the 'solid social matrix' of the 'South African Bantu' before he was 'severed from that tribal organization with which all his most heroic virtues are connected, and subjected under the feet of a dominant race which does not understand him'.[37] But she now, in 1908, took a bold further step: 'We have only with wisdom and patient justice slowly to transfer' this social sense 'to our own larger society'.[38]

Schreiner's use of the term 'heroic virtues' comes straight from W. E. H. Lecky, who distinguished between the 'heroic virtues, the amiable virtues, and [. . .] the religious virtues [. . .] to which, in different periods, different degrees of prominence have been assigned';[39] and upon which depended differing definitions of humanity. Schreiner favours the first set of virtues, the concept offered her the image of Africa's 'heroic' age as one from which the morally degraded European present might yet draw a regenerative impulse. The idea of the 'primitive' emerges anew: the 'primitive' African 'in the land of his growth [lives] with all the instincts of the free man intact'. Colonization stunted that natural evolutionary growth, much as

[35] 'The Psychology of the Boer' (1892), in *Thoughts on South Africa*, 255.

[36] 'The Psychology of the Boer', 256, 258.

[37] Schreiner, 'The Problem of Slavery', in *Thoughts on South Africa*, 128.

[38] Schreiner, *Closer Union*, 27; see also *Words in Season*, 182, both in Select Bibliography, *infra*.

[39] W. E. H. Lecky, *The History of European Morals from Augustus to Charlemagne* sixth edition, revised (London: Longmans, Green & Co., 1884), viii.

a modern bourgeois economy elsewhere was stunting humanity's evolutionary growth to perfection.

Given her missionary upbringing, and the massive contradiction between what missionaries preached and what they practised, Schreiner's interest in a 'social sense' would certainly have harked back to her Biblical reading (Hebrews' 'Do not be forgetful to entertain strangers', for instance). The ethics of hospitality may well have been a point of discussion between her and Allen Kirkland Soga (generally known as A. K.), whom she met on her travels: Soga's father, Tiyo Soga, had published an essay in 1864 on those very ethics,[40] claiming their interruption by Christianity. The concept of African hospitality bore within it the social dictum, as is now well-known, given its widespread discussion in the South African Truth and Reconciliation Commission: a person is a social being; a person is a person by and through others. Thus was dissolved the boundary between individual and group fostered by Western discourse. Soga's essay makes clear that he is speaking not of hospitality within a group, but towards outsiders to the group.

Three major sets of references inserted into *From Man to Man* show her interest in this regard. In the first, Rebekah recounts to her children a story about what Schreiner described in 1901 as her own evolving attitude towards race, as if Rebekah—like Schreiner—has imbibed that vital impulse from Africa. In her childhood Schreiner wanted 'a wall built across Africa shutting [. . .] off' all the black people, but in her adulthood a different feeling towards the native races developed.[41] So, too, in *From Man to Man*. Says Rebekah to her children: '*They were mine and I was theirs*, and the wall I had built across Africa had slowly to fall down' (p. 339, emphasis added).

In a second set of references, Schreiner provides a glimpse of an African social instinct in the figure of a young woman warrior who is prepared to sacrifice herself for the survival of others. Her figure mirrors that of the 'Bushman woman, who similarly [. . .] shows a quality higher and of more importance to the race than [. . .] any Bismarck', so that both these allegorical figures stand for 'the root out of which

[40] See Mark Sanders' discussion (via A. C. Jordan's *Towards an African Literature*, in part) of Tiyo Soga's representation of hospitality or *ubuntu*. Sanders sees *ubuntu* as 'an artifact of African modernity' that is 'internally fractured', saving Soga, in Sanders' reading, from an 'ethno-philosophical nostalgia'. See Sanders, *Complicities*, 119, in Select Bibliography, *infra*.

[41] Introduction to *Thoughts on South Africa*, 15, 17.

ultimately the noblest blossom of the human tree shall draw its strength' (p. 144). And in a third set of references Rebekah alludes to 'ways in which a Zulu chief may be higher than a learned professor' and to the creative inspiration associated with the so-called 'Bushmen' (pp. 335 and 364).

Whether Schreiner planned to work this developing interest further into the plot of *From Man to Man* we cannot know. It is indeed hard to imagine how its narrative could have incorporated, without radical rewriting, a more extended representation of the sense of social solidarity than the instances referred to above: its South African sections were already structured around a white family in the nineteenth-century Cape Colony, with no access to their black compatriots except as servants or through historical tales. Until, that is, Sartje's entry.

Through Sartje, the matter of 'miscegenation', the second feature of South African society that had struck Schreiner on her travels, could indeed be incorporated into the existing story-line, and in a manner that called up the idea of hospitality as well.

Travelling in late 1893 and early 1894 with her sister Ettie, Schreiner met with one Eliza Brown, a 'highly cultivated & intellectual woman' whose grandfather, a missionary in the London Missionary Society, had married a Khoisan woman named Sara Valentyn.[42] For the embittered Eliza Brown, her genealogy disallowed her from claiming affiliation with either 'black' or 'white' society. In contrast, as Schreiner later recalled, A. K. Soga, also of 'mixed-race', had confidently self-defined as African, taking up his father's ethnic legacy rather than his Scottish mother's.[43] The former encounter had spurred Schreiner in her essay on 'The Problem of Slavery', written around the late 1890s, to refer to 'mixed-race' people as consumed by self-loathing and shame, their social and psychological status both complex and precarious. But the latter encounter confirmed her view that to be 'mixed-race' was unproblematic if a different kind of self-identification could be achieved. As her essay begins to imply, the 'problem' was slavery or social inequity: equality between the parents, or the originating groups, was key.[44] Hence her

[42] See Letter to John Merriman, 29 June 1890, in *OSLO*. For information about Schreiner's meeting with Eliza Brown, see Liz Stanley, 'Turning Points', 105; in Select Bibliography, *infra*.

[43] Letter to Minnie Murray, 30 August 1909, in *OSLO*.

[44] See 'The Problem of Slavery', especially 126–7, and 144–6.

inclusion in *From Man to Man* of Rebekah's adopting a 'coloured' foster-child for Rebekah: here was an 'ethics of hospitality' in action.

Around this time Schreiner had become interested in the Haitian revolutionary Toussaint L'Overture (1743–1803); she toyed with the idea of writing about him for a colonial newspaper: 'So few Colonials know that there has been at least one great man of genius who was a pure-blooded negro.'[45] In 1905, she read *The Souls of Black Folk* by the African American writer W. E. B. Du Bois, which had a more immense impact: she admired Du Bois for 'giv[ing] true expression, not to what he feels it's politic & wise to express to white men, but to what he really feels'.[46] Schreiner read no African languages and thus none of the Tswana, Xhosa, or Zulu newspapers of the time; she had also not come across Pixley ka Isaka Seme's pathbreaking lecture, delivered and published in English, on 'The Regeneration of Africa' (1906). Had she encountered his assertive statement about 'the fusing force of [. . .] the true intertribal relation', she would surely have said of his essay—as she said of other writing she admired (by Schopenhauer for example)—that she might herself have written it.[47] Still, reading Du Bois prompted her to use *From Man to Man* to provide 'the voice of what others feel & can't say'. 'If no one else will speak out for the natives I must.'[48] And, markedly, the part of his book that most impressed her was Du Bois' description of his son's '"proud" little curly head', the son 'who died before he ever learnt what he was'.

Here, then, is the specific contribution Schreiner wished her novel to make, as she explains in a decisive letter to her brother Will. With the entry into *From Man to Man* of 'a little half-coloured child who is [Rebekah's] husband's by a coloured servant', and Rebekah's adoption of the child, she could open up 'the whole question of our relation to the {. . .} darker races, & the attitude which says 'they are here for our interest [and] for our pleasure, & to hell with them when they aren't that!'[49]

[45] Letter to G. W. Cross, 21 April 1898, in *OSLO*.

[46] Letter to John X. Merriman, 31 October 1905 (in Appendix 2); emphasis in original.

[47] Pixley ka Isaka Seme, 'The Regeneration of Africa', *Journal of the Royal African Society* 5/20 (1906), 407–8; for the reference to Schopenhauer, see Letter to Havelock Ellis, 2 March 1885 (in Appendix 2). Of Du Bois's book, Schreiner wrote: 'the book makes me feel so much that sometimes I can't look at it; it seems to have come from within me'. Letter to Carpenter, 26 October 1905, in *OSLO*.

[48] Letter to Mary Brown, 1 December 1908 in *OSLO*.

[49] Letter to Will Schreiner, 4 June 1908 (in Appendix 2); emphases in original.

Out of this added plot element, Schreiner can more fully develop that new thematic strain in her writing, only hinted at in *Trooper Peter Halket*: not just that prostitution and marriage-as-prostitution are symptomatic of a damaged and damaging social order, not just that the system of racial differentiation, oppression and exploitation is symptomatic of a downward moral spiral, but also that, in what she calls 'our relation to the darker races', racist *and* sexist *and* class oppression and exploitation find their intersection in the bodies of powerless, underpaid black South African women. Sartje serves as the prophetic figure of a different kind of future.

While Schreiner's aim was to put a stop to what she called 'the evil & degrading attitude of white men towards dark women',[50] the ambiguous involvement of white women had to be addressed as well. Among the white South African community there were recurrent explosions of hysteria over purported sexual assaults by black men on white women—what Schreiner deftly disclaimed as 'the so called Black Peril'.[51] She was outraged at the use politicians made of this hysteria to justify repressive racist legislation. The true peril, she said, was both 'the white peril that hangs over every black man' and 'that peril [. . .] which exists for all dark skinned women at the hands of white men'.[52] We white women, she was later quoted as saying, have a duty both to recognize the part we play in this dynamic and to see to its repair, namely, 'one law {…} for the white woman and the black {…} I believe our power to work such a reform is greater than we think.'[53]

Schreiner had, in 1908, helped found the Women's Enfranchisement League. There was nowhere as yet any cross-racial convention of women, nor did Schreiner have the acquaintance of any black activist women. In a terrible trick of history, she had left England by the time that Charlotte Maxeke and her sister Katie Makanya arrived to sing in

[50] Letter to James Henderson, 15 July 1912, in *OSLO*; also in Stanley and Salter (eds.), *The World's Great Question*, 303.

[51] Letter to James Henderson, 26 December 1911, in *OSLO*; also in Stanley and Salter (eds.), *The World's Great Question*, 297.

[52] Letters to James Henderson, 26 December 1911; and to Will Schreiner, 25 May 1911; both in *OSLO*; also in Stanley and Salter (eds.), *The World's Great Question*, 297 and 291. The term 'white peril' was also used by Sol T. Plaatje in his essay, 'The Mote and the Beam' (1921), repr. in *English in Africa* 3/2 (1976), 92.

[53] Schreiner's letter, apparently not extant, was quoted in a speech made by her friend Mary Brown. See 'White Women to the Rescue', *Ilange Lase Natal*, 26 July 1912.

the Jubilee Choir before Queen Victoria. Charlotte Maxeke would co-found the Bantu Women's League, forerunner of the African National Congress League, though only in 1918. Always a canny political strategist, Schreiner saw how the whites-only Women's Enfranchisement League might advance, in tandem, the two causes so important to her—women's rights and the black franchise. If black women could be enfranchised, more general political reform might follow.

As it turned out, however, her fellow members from the Cape branch of the League took their lead from the openly racist Transvaal branch and pressed for the vote to be accorded to white women only. Schreiner resigned at once, as member of the league and as its Cape vice-president, scrawling angrily on one of its leaflets that by *women* she meant *all women*.

She was still, at this time, working on what she called her 'big' novel, though with diminishing optimism, describing it in 1913 as a book she 'would have liked so to finish' but could not.[54] In the early years of the twentieth century she had radically revised the first half, and in 1911 had the Prelude and Chs I-VI retyped. The emendations she made between 1901 and 1911, as well as those subsequently made to the 1911 typescript, show the extent to which she felt able to foreground the agency and consciousness of the black fictional characters, without having to re-form the entire plot. In the second half of the novel, Sartje is a new presence, not just signaling white male abuse and irresponsibility, along with the expansion of the white woman's duty, and some of the accompanying ironies, but also opening up an entirely new story-line. Moreover, Schreiner makes Sartje an age-mate to Rebekah's last-born son, named Bertie after his aunt: his figure suggests the advent of an even newer kind of New Man than Drummond. The presence of these two dreamy-eyed 5-year-olds at the story's end sets the stage for a hoped-for future story in which interracial cross-gender relations will be very different from those currently obtaining. In contrast, in the story that the novel starts to sketch for Sartje in relation to the oldest son, Charles, as the little girl's would-be companion-protector, Schreiner comes to a conclusion similar to E. M. Forster's in his 1924 novel *A Passage to India*. Are people of different races able to meet on an equal footing, asks Forster? His

[54] Letter to Emily Hobhouse, March 1913, in Cronwright-Schreiner (ed.), *Letters*, 321, in Select Bibliography, *infra*.

answer: 'Not yet.' What that future world of equality would look like, Rebekah does not know. For her, '[t]he dream ends there' (p. 328). Not so for the youngest children. Their future remains to be told.

Despair at the course that her country was following had been building up, step by step, since the 1890s. First, on top of the interconnected subordination of women and the rise of capital, she had had to witness the ravages of British imperialism, then the Anglo-Boer War with its massive destruction of life and property, then the treachery of the 1910 Act of Union and the 1913 Natives Land Act, then the prospect of war in Europe which, to her distress, both Ellis and Carpenter supported, as did Plaatje and Gandhi.

Regarding the completion of *From Man to Man*, the failure of the franchise project in 1913 had very likely been the last straw. At some point around this time, having bundled up the typescript of the rewritten Prelude and first six chapters of the 'big' novel, together with the remaining seven chapters in draft manuscript form, she mailed the package to her husband, who would open it only after her death. The earlier ambitions she had expressed for the novel—to make some women 'more tender to others', to make men 'more tender to women because they will understand them better'—may now read as over-simple in the light of the radical development in her political thinking. But she not only allows her heroine Rebekah to see to it, as far as she can, that the environment she provides for the younger generation is conducive to dreaming. She also creates Sartje as an active and imaginative young labourer alongside her labouring foster-mother. With Sartje's presence, we arrive at Schreiner's last substantial addition to the narrative. In 1912 she wrote to a friend about the importance 'of educating & influencing our young girls, [. . .] teaching them 'to desire freedom for themselves & all other women on Earth'.[55] Implicitly, figures like Sartje are included, though in her very emergence as a fictional character she herself has been an educative presence.

Towards the end of 1913 Schreiner returned to Europe, seeking treatment for her heart condition. Concerned about the looming war, she worked on her essay 'The Dawn of Civilisation' and on other pacifist writings which she hoped to gather into a book. When hostilities broke out she hastily crossed the Channel back to England. She

[55] Letter to Minnie Murray, 25 April 1912 (in Appendix 2).

met with David Lloyd George, then Chancellor of the Exchequer, and pleaded unsuccessfully for South Africa not to be asked to be implicated in a war that she saw as a solely European affair. Though dismayed by their support for the war, she met with Mohandas and Kasturbai Gandhi, as well as the delegation of the South African Native National Congress that came to London in 1916 to offer military support to the British cause. This delegation included Plaatje, who had completed *Native Life in South Africa* and was working on *Mhudi,* the first novel written in English by an African author. She went home in August 1920, alone and ill, and took up residence in a boarding house in the suburbs of Cape Town. Her letters from this period make no mention of any desire to resume work on her big novel. She died of heart failure on 10 December 1920, in bed, a book in her hand.

* * *

Schreiner described *From Man to Man* as 'womanly', deeply womanly, even though (she said) she had tried not to make it so.[56] What did Schreiner understand womanliness to be, and what was it that made her describe her book thus? Surely Rebekah, both in thought (her extensive range of references, her restless philosophizing, her radical orientation towards the future) and in action (her assertiveness, her emphatic sundering of herself from the man she married) is as far from the stereotype of the womanly woman as one can imagine.

In measuring her distance from womanliness, Schreiner seems to have in mind not some inherent womanly nature but the often unconscious complicity of women in a patriarchal system that controlled and oppressed them by pinning them to its notion of the womanly ideal, as well as encouraging their competitiveness and envy towards their fellow women. In contrast, Schreiner strives to redefine the womanly, showing what it might mean, under a different social arrangement, for a woman to be female and womanly in a new, ungendered way, and for a man to become more womanly in certain respects.

Was Schreiner thinking of this when in 1911 she decided not to use the title *From Man to Man* after all, inscribing instead the words 'Perhaps Only—' in bold pen-strokes on the typescript title page? The earlier title clearly refers to the handing-over of women from one man to another: the passage of women in the act of marriage; the

[56] Letter to Havelock Ellis, 2 February 1889 (in Appendix 2).

passage of women in commercial sex. In addition it may reflect Rebekah's never-to-be-fulfilled yearning to speak to her husband—who is decidedly not a New Man—as one human being to another, perhaps not quite 'as you would if I were another man' (p. 226) but 'as two free souls looking at each other' (p. 218). The tentative new title may refer to the future that almost opens up at the novel's end: on the one hand a future union between Rebekah and Drummond, on the other a new world for the younger generation. The final chapter also gestures provocatively towards a 'Central Africa' not yet colonised though certainly explored. At a more abstract level, there is a tantalizing set of allegorical icons that 'throb' (Schreiner's repeated word) through the novel, signifying the possible re-emergence ('perhaps only') into the present-day social order of a mode of being that has been 'selected out' (in Darwinian terms) but may in fact be retrieved. Among these are the dicynodont fossil that 'comes out into the sunshine it once loved' (p. 359); and the statue of Hercules holding a child—an image of 'mother-love'. These, along with other presences in the text, are associated with the throb that passes through the ages and is now felt as a throb in Rebekah's own hand—which is, of course, also Schreiner's writing hand.

However, the bright young woman who sketched *Saints and Sinners* in the 1870s, revised it into a different novel in the 1880s, and amended its typescripts early in the twentieth century is not the same being as the sick and exhausted woman from whose novelizing hand the pen had dropped by 1913. Schreiner herself was changing, as was the ground beneath her feet. By 1913 positive change seemed further off than ever.

A published book does not often allow readers a glimpse into the all-too-often unresolved difficulties of the material act of writing, or of the subterranean currents of historical and biographical time that flowed during the time of writing. An awareness of the progress of the text's own sometimes fraught coming-into-being, insofar as the stages of that progress can be traced, might allow us a new appreciation of the achievements and failings of Schreiner's 'big' book, and perhaps give us fresh understanding and sympathy for the author's oscillation between optimism and pessimism, triumph and despair.

Seen in this way, as a text containing and embodying a record of its own process, *From Man to Man* becomes the record of a manifold struggle with history: a struggle against British imperialism, its material and cultural dispossessions, and its colonial adventure-predations; a struggle to keep abreast of what needed to be done—and could be done—about the problems arising out of racialized social relations in her homeland; and a struggle to keep alive her own ideals regarding gender, race and class relations, sexual desire, and marriage in a new form, as the complex basis for a new social order.

In this way we can move beyond simply dismissing the novel as unfinished, and embrace its unfinishedness instead: we can attend to the act of writing as writing-in-process and writing-in-action, as if we as readers are peering over the writer's shoulder as she writes.

Furthermore, the novel is not as formally clumsy as may at first appear. The dense Chapters VII and VIII, which constitute the novel's philosophical centre, are framed by the more conventionally novelistic chapters: at one end, Chapters I–VI (Rebekah's and Bertie's daily lives before the crisis of Bertie's disappearance); at the other end, Chapters IX–XII (again their daily lives, but now treating Bertie's disappearance and her London life). These framing, realist blocks are then framed in turn by a pair of chapters in a different register: the allegorical opening constituted by the Prelude, and the philosophical closure constituted by Chapter XIII, the one explicitly focused on story-telling, the other on the act of creation, self-reflexive framing for a work of art.

One particular moment of unfinishedness intrudes disturbingly into the text, however. In the story of Bertie's predatory tutor and its aftermath, some astute readers have found a deeply embedded reference to a troubled, even traumatic, incident in Schreiner's own life. In 1872, as a 17-year-old, she let it be known that she was engaged to be married to a young businessman named Julius Gau. What happened next can be only a matter of speculation, for Schreiner's husband destroyed her journals after her death, and her surviving letters from the period are insufficiently explicit. What she had written in her journals would have 'set the Thames on fire', her husband claimed.[57] The chapters telling of Bertie's experience with her tutor, and subsequently with a would-be lover, are replete with highly charged figurative language. In a sunset portrayed red as blood, for instance, is an abortion or miscarriage being hinted at?[58] Later in the book, cast out

[57] Samuel Cronwright-Schreiner to Havelock Ellis, 10 September 1934, in Havelock Ellis Collection, Harry Ransom Center, University of Texas, Austin, TX, USA.

[58] See Bradford, 'Olive Schreiner's Hidden Agony', in Select Bibliography, *infra*.

into the streets of London, Bertie dreams of returning home. But her dreaming is interrupted by a puzzling image: 'she saw, fleetingly, pressing it from her as quickly as she could, [. . .] the little face—she could not go back! She could never go back!' (p. 310). Whose is the little face?

Schreiner's writing has rightly been criticized for its reproduction of racialized labelling and stereotyping even while at the same time its sustained undermining of the standard Victorian biases about race has been acknowledged. With its long and sporadic history of composition, *From Man to Man* covers in many ways the distance—moral and political—between Schreiner's early and her more mature thinking, a distance readers may also trace, at least in part, in the difference already suggested in this introduction between the views expressed in *Thoughts of South Africa* and in *Closer Union*.

However, no mode of reading should divert us from paying tribute to the qualities of Schreiner's writing and the allure of her plot. In her passionate engagement with the life experience of women at the turn of the twentieth century, both in England and in the colonies, we find Schreiner writing at her powerful best. The magnificently achieved 'Child's Day', serving as prelude to the novel, has been hailed more than once as the best part of the novel, but the brilliantly incisive portrayals of Veronica Grey and Mrs Drummond are equally noteworthy, crucial if painful additions to the repertoire of the New Woman novel, as is the portrayal of Bertie, in a different way, her plight allegorising at once the everyday male use and abuse of women *and* the duplicitous service of British imperialism, its extractive economy masquerading as protection and care.

Rebekah, too, is expertly realised: a mother at once intellectual and sensual, her philosophizing in no way distinct from her motherliness—her mind weaving in and out of her maternal tasks. Of particular interest, too, is the fluctuating authorial identification with, and distance from, this central character: Schreiner's rendition of the painful encounter between Rebekah and Clartje, an encounter from which Rebekah runs in shame, and other excruciating insights into the psychology of female abjection. So, too, might readers pay tribute to the powerful descriptions of landscape, especially in the Karoo farm scenes and walks into the bush, and in the expansive botanical imagery that opens out into a historically and sociologically complex world, an African, sun-drenched world of Schreiner's pathbreaking imagining..

* * *

African Farm had been modest in historical and geographical range; *From Man to Man* extended its scope from the Colony to England, taking in the Victorian and Edwardian eras, even making brief but significant reference to the anti-Jewish pogroms that erupted in Tsarist Russia between 1881 and 1884 and their repercussions in the Jewish diaspora. In both her polemics and her fiction Schreiner addressed the moral and social dangers of uneven economic modernization and the future of white rule in Britain's African colonies, to say nothing of the one big question that never went away—'the Woman Question', which she tended to see more and more as 'the Man Question'—as well as the other question—in her time called 'the Native Question', and what she herself said was 'not only South Africa's great question, but the world's great question'[59]—one that has come increasingly to the fore since the publication of her final novel. On both of these questions, *From Man to Man* stands as the first and still most important text of a white South African feminism in the process of divesting itself of its white colonial, class-bound and race-bound blinkers.

[59] Letter to Jan Smuts, 19 and 28 October 1920, in *OSLO*. Many of Schreiner's earlier letters speak of 'race' as South Africa's 'great question', but this appears to be the first time she ventured it as 'the world's great question'.

NOTE ON THE TEXT

From Man to Man was left unfinished at Schreiner's death; she left no fair copy. The first edition of the novel, edited by Samuel Cron Cronwright-Schreiner and published posthumously by T. Fisher Unwin in London in 1926, was based on two sets of materials. For 'The Prelude: The Child's Day' and the first six chapters of 'The Book: The Woman's Day', Cronwright-Schreiner based his edition on the typescript Olive Schreiner had had prepared in 1911. This typescript was later deposited in the Johannesburg Public Library, where it appears to have eluded the notice of Schreiner critics until it was discovered by the present editor. The typescript bears numerous emendations in Schreiner's hand, along with some editorial changes. For the remaining section of the novel (Chapters VII–XIII) which had not been typed in Schreiner's lifetime, Cronwright-Schreiner used what he described in his introduction to the first edition (see Appendix 1, pp. 377–83) as the somewhat confusing 'bundle [. . .] of manuscripts' left after Schreiner's death in 1920. These manuscripts have not been preserved; he destroyed them after publication.

This edition of *From Man to Man* is therefore based on two texts: the 1911 typescript for the first part of the novel, and the first edition for the last seven chapters. The first impression of the first edition included many incidental and substantive errors; only a few of these were corrected in the second impression, which appeared in the same year. A third impression, without variation, was published in 1927. Thus many of the same cluster of errors track their way through these three versions. Two examples are worth mentioning here. The first relates to some Cape Dutch dialogue which, unaccountably, Cronwright-Schreiner manually changed and rendered grammatically incorrect. This is especially notable since it is from the Prelude, which Cronwright-Schreiner claimed in his introduction to have left as it was. The second occurs in the verse fragment that the child Rebekah recites from Horatius Bonar's hymn. The first edition had 'wind' in the place of 'wing' (the fourth line was not quoted, and no one knew it should rhyme with 'spring'). This would be less important if wings did not have such a strong thematic significance in the novel as a whole.

The first US edition, published in 1927 by Harper & Brothers in New York, made a number of corrections but reproduced some existing errors and even introduced a few more. For example, Schreiner's term 'back-beat' (by which she meant evolutionary reversion) was changed to 'back-seat', making nonsense of the sentence in which it appeared. Three reprints followed, without variation, from Grosset & Dunlap (New York) in 1927, Johnson Reprint Company (New York) in 1972, and Cassandra Editions (an imprint of Academy Press, Chicago) in 1977. Each of these three US texts, then, reproduced many of Unwin's original errors and all Harper's new ones. Both the UK and US texts were also peppered with inconsistent hyphenation.

In 1931 the novel was reissued in two volumes by Ernest Benn (London), which had merged with Unwin in 1926. More errors were corrected, but several remained. Virago Press (London) brought out the first paperback edition in 1982, but—as a facsimile reprint of Unwin's first impression—it neglected to include the corrections made in the second impression. Notably, in addition to including some ungrammatical Cape Dutch and the omnipresent 'wind', the Virago text succumbed to the child Rebekah's tongue-twister, following Unwin's first impression: 'The swam swam in a silvery lake'.

The novel's first South African publication in 2004 was by Stonewall Books in Cape Town. A single bulky edition, *Karoo Moon* combined *From Man to Man*, *Undine*, and *The Story of an African Farm*. The text appears to have been based on the Harper edition, although it has, mostly, English rather than US spelling and presents a few other variations and literals (e.g. Harper's 'back-seat' now changed to 'backseat'). Oddly for a South African edition, Afrikaans terms were italicized, as in *kraal*, *kappie*, *kloof*, and so on, even when recognized as South African English. At least, though, the swan is swimming, even if God's wing still disappears under the pressure of wind.

Clearly, Schreiner's novel has not been well served, whether in the various editorial decisions or in the proofreading. In an edition prepared specifically for a South African readership and published in 2015 by University of Cape Town Press, I redressed several of Cronwright-Schreiner's dubious editorial decisions, silently corrected obvious errors and inconsistencies evident in the first edition and in subsequent reprints, and modernized most of the spelling. The present edition follows much the same procedure. For instance, I have regularized Scheiner's use of 'lay' to the standard English past tense, *laid*, and (newly) introduced consistency to her use of other past tense verbs. Spellings are left unchanged when they indicate either the slow and uneven transformation from Dutch into Afrikaans or Schreiner's creative forging of South African English. While Schreiner's punctuation is modernized for the sake of clarity or consistency, the flavour of the text is preserved through (for the most part) the retention of Schreiner's use of the dash but this edition—newly—generally dispenses with her unnecessary and distracting combination of full stops and commas alongside the dash. It also, newly, regularizes her use of gendered pronouns when they shift erratically within a passage. Hyphenation is generally modernized, following the trend set by the 2007 edition of the *Shorter Oxford English Dictionary*, where many words drop their hyphens and become either one word or two: 'dining room', for instance, rather than 'dining-room'. Schreiner herself was inconsistent, as were the published texts.

However, hyphenation rules are not stable, and where choices needed to be made, Schreiner's original hyphenation is retained when it has particular significance, whether as Schreiner's own formulation or on account of its historical resonance (especially in the South African context) as in 'fair-skins', 'Boer-goat', 'fat-candle', 'down-draught', and 'back-beat'.

Cronwright-Schreiner's failure to preserve the manuscript material made the task of establishing a new edition unduly vexing. However, even the 1911 typescript posed certain difficulties. Schreiner made manual corrections to the typing (spacing, etc.), punctuation changes, deletions, single-word emendations and additions, and several longer additions. These corrections are sometimes unclear, inconsistent, or even careless. This may have been because the author did not imagine she was finalizing a text for publication, given that the remainder of the novel had yet to be typed and checked. Cronwright-Schreiner mostly honours her changes, but he ignores several and makes others, including some rewording, reparagraphing, and repunctuation that has substantive rather than incidental effect. Some of his alterations were intended to resolve difficulties created by Schreiner's incomplete or unacceptable corrections, but others were made unnecessarily or erroneously, and on his own initiative.

In his introduction to the first edition, Cronwright-Schreiner asserts that he published the Prelude 'just as it stands', but collating it against the 1911 typescript suggests that '*much* as it stands' would have been the more appropriate phrase. In addition to the various repunctuations in the Prelude, and the alterations to Schreiner's

Cape Dutch dialogue, he changes her tense on two occasions, makes some unnecessary hyphenation ('five-years-old', for instance), and changes to 'someone' the word 'people' (as in the Afrikaans 'mense'), thereby subtly shifting both meaning and tone.

In subsequent chapters, Cronwright-Schreiner seems to have misunderstood, or was not in sympathy with, Schreiner's use of Afrikaans turns of phrase, specifically her use of *so*. For instance, in the 1911 typescript, in a passage that opens Chapter VI, the author produces a magnificent description of the wooded area in suburban Cape Town. One sentence reads, 'You might ride mile after mile on a hot summer's day and never feel the sunshine on you, so the great oak trees met over your head.' Cronwright-Schreiner replaced 'so' with 'for', and in the process obliterated Schreiner's carry-over from the Afrikaans. In Afrikaans the sentence would read something like this: *en nooit die sonskyn op jou voel nie, so kom die groot eikebome oor jou kop saam* | *so het die groot eikebome oor jou kop saamgekom* ('and never feel the sunshine on you, so closely do the great oak trees meet over your head | so closely did the great oak trees meet over your head). I have restored the word 'so'.

I have retained the occasional Afrikaans timbre of Schreiner's English in other ways too. Although her use of Cape Dutch dialogue is preserved, I have modernized the spellings of several words that have now entered South African English through Afrikaans: 'kappie' rather than 'kapje', 'koppie' rather than 'kopje', for instance. However, in order to reflect the ambivalence of her cultural affiliation, I have retained her use of anglicized Afrikaans terms: 'mealie' rather than 'mielie', and 'springbuck' rather than 'springbok'.

My decisions have often been made on a case-by-case basis, with the general intention of preserving Schreiner's text as she wrote it but without including obvious errors. My procedure involved collating the 1911 typescript with Schreiner's 1901 manuscript (also lodged in the Johannesburg Public Library, and also apparently not hitherto consulted by Schreiner critics). On occasion I derived textual authority from the 1901 manuscript. For instance, in the Prelude, the words 'Presently, as it grew quite darker' are drawn from the typescript but the 1901 manuscript reads 'it grew darker'. It appears that the word 'quite' was a typist's error, drawn up from the line below; the new edition drops it. Here and elsewhere, I have sometimes preserved what may be or seem to be a grammatical oddity—'her eyes opened widely', for instance, and that powerful assertion, '*This one*, is mine!' with Schreiner's (rule-breaking) comma, so emphatically added in her manual emendations—continually bearing in mind a major interest of Schreiner's: the production typically of a text that seems to have been created through the spoken rather than the written word. Schreiner's punctuation often follows this principle.

Schreiner left the last seven chapters unrevised and, without the manuscript as justification, there are considerably fewer editorial adjustments than in the first section. Cronwright-Schreiner bracketed those words he had to surmise (whether missing or illegible in the original he does not say), and sometimes added question marks to words he could not be sure of; he also footnoted occasions where sections were illegible or incomplete.

Original footnotes, whether Schreiner's or Cronwright-Schreiner's, are repositioned into the Explanatory Notes.

In the final chapter, Cronwright-Schreiner inserts an ellipsis into the text to signal his failure to resolve a problem with the page order in Schreiner's manuscript (he briefly discusses this in his introduction). In the first edition, this ellipsis appears in the standard form but in the US reprint it becomes a line of dots, marking a sharp separation in the text, worth mentioning here as a cautionary note: at least one critic has falsely assumed that Schreiner herself intended the separation, and has made a critical argument on that basis.

Obvious errors, whether Schreiner's or Cronwright-Schreiner's, are corrected ('cold' becomes 'could', 'philosopher' becomes 'philosophers', 'debit' becomes 'debt', and 'base' becomes 'bass', for instance), with annotation where necessary. One sentence into which Cronwright-Schreiner inserted an awkward correction '[does not prove?]' has been given a simpler correction. In Chapter XII, in the sentence, 'We are right to despise them and call them Inferior Peoples and to treat them as it would be right they should treat us,' Cronwright-Schreiner inserted '[?not]' after 'would' but he misread the logic: Rebekah imagines her interlocutor (and adversary) *accepting* the fact that people will mistreat those they feel to be inferior to them. My edition deletes that 'not'. On another occasion, too, I omit Cronwright-Schreiner's bracketed addition: 'Perhaps you will say if life has been so [cruel] to me why haven't I left you and gone home to my father?' In the Afrikaans parallel form, the word 'so' means *thus* and should not be followed by an adjective. The word 'cruel' limits or even redirects Schreiner's meaning: Rebekah has been speaking of a domestic situation considerably more complex (and preventable) than simply the 'cruelty of life'. Schreiner periodically uses this formulation in her writing, and while it is not dissimilar to the use made of it in English, South African readers will hear its Afrikaans parallel, and be reminded of the fact that the white farming community Schreiner lived among as a young woman was Afrikaans-speaking, although her home language was English.

A substantial chapter (Chapter VII) is devoted to Rebekah's development of a philosophical position for which she, like Schreiner herself, had no formal training, and which is sometimes repetitive and awkwardly articulated. While as little as possible should be done to 'correct' this, a few small changes have been made for the sake of clarity. However, in this chapter as in others, no lexical emendations are silent, given the list of variants provided in Appendix 4, pp. 474–81, along with the information about general emendations.

Any text that has been finalized without the author's personal participation must be regarded as provisional, and even in this new edition some editorial uncertainties remain. Interested readers are directed to my essay, 'On Producing a New Edition of *From Man to Man, or Perhaps Only—*', *English in Africa* 42/1 (2015), 27–48, and to the digital versions and transcriptions of Schreiner's various extant manuscripts and typescripts of *From Man to Man*: the 1887–9 manuscript (a.k.a. the 1886–7 manuscript), the 1901 manuscript and typescript, and the 1911 typescript of *From Man to Man* (with manual emendations). These are available through the UCT Libraries digital collections at University of Cape Town Special Collections.

This Note on the Text has thus far referred specifically to the editing of the novel. Two further matters remain: Cronwright-Schreiner's material, and the quotations from Schreiner's journals and letters.

Except for some reparagraphing and bracketed in-text annotations, Cronwright-Schreiner's introduction, and his account of Schreiner's projected ending (Appendix 1 and Appendix 3) have been left untouched (including his use of italics where a modern style would use quotation marks).

Schreiner's letters have already been reproduced verbatim by *Olive Schreiner Letters Online* (*OSLO*), allowing readers as unmediated a glimpse as possible of her informal writing style, misspellings and all. The extracts from Schreiner's letters that, along with her diary extracts, make up Appendix 2 ('Genesis and Composition of the Novel') are lightly edited for greater readability: see the Introduction to Appendix 2.

SELECT BIBLIOGRAPHY

Works by Olive Schreiner

BOOKS

Closer Union (Cape Town: The Constitutional Reform Association; London: Fifield, 1909).

Dreams (London: T. Fisher Unwin, 1890).

Dream Life and Real Life: A Little African Story (London: T. Fisher Unwin, 1893).

An English South African's View of the Situation: Words in Season (London: Hodder & Stoughton, 1899).

A Letter on the Jew (Cape Town: Liberman, 1906).

From Man to Man or Perhaps Only…., ed. S. C. Cronwright-Schreiner (London: T. Fisher Unwin, 1926).

From Man to Man or Perhaps Only…., ed. S. C. Cronwright-Schreiner (New York: Harper & Brothers, 1927).

From Man to Man or Perhaps Only—, ed. Dorothy Driver (Cape Town: UCT [University of Cape Town] Press, 2015).

The Political Situation, co-authored with S. C. Cronwright-Schreiner (London: T. Fisher, Unwin, 1895).

Stories, Dreams and Allegories, ed. S. C. Cronwright-Schreiner (London: T. Fisher Unwin, 1923).

The Story of an African Farm [Ralph Iron, pseudonym] (London: Chapman and Hall, 1883).

Thoughts on South Africa (London: T. Fisher Unwin, 1923).

Trooper Peter Halket of Mashonaland (London: T. Fisher Unwin, 1897).

Undine (New York: Harper & Brothers, 1928; London: Benn, 1929).

Woman and Labour. (London: T. Fisher Unwin, 1911).

MANUSCRIPTS

1887–1889 Manuscript of *From Man to Man*, by Ralph Iron. Chapters 1, 4, 5 and 6. Olive Schreiner Collection, 1884–1920. HRC.

1901 Manuscript of *From Man to Man*, with typescript section. Prelude, Chapters I–VI. Olive Schreiner Collection. JPL.

1911 Typescript of *From Man to Man*, with manuscript emendations. Prelude, Chapters I–VI. Olive Schreiner Collection. JPL.

The Literary Archive of Olive Schreiner's *From Man to Man, or Perhaps Only*—. https://digitalcollections.lib.uct.ac.za/humanitec/schreiner (digitised versions and transcriptions of items held in JPL)

LETTERS

Cronwright-Schreiner, S. C. (ed.), *The Letters of Olive Schreiner* (London: T. Fisher Unwin, 1924).

Draznin, Yaffa Claire (ed.), *'My Other Self': The Letters of Olive Schreiner and Havelock Ellis, 1884–1920* (New York: Peter Lang, 1992).

Olive Schreiner Letters Online (*OSLO*) http://www.oliveschreiner.org.

Rive, Richard (ed.), *Olive Schreiner: Letters 1871–99* (Cape Town: David Philip, 1987).

Stanley, Liz and Andrea Salter (eds.) *The World's Great Question: Olive Schreiner's South African Letters, 1889–1920* (Cape Town: Van Riebeeck Society, 2014).

COLLECTIONS

Barash, Carol (ed.), *An Olive Schreiner Reader: Writings on Women and South Africa* (London and New York: Pandora; New York: Routledge and Kegan Paul in association with Methuen, 1987). See the editor's Introduction, pp. 1–20. Contains as Afterword Nadine Gordimer's essay 'The Prison-House of Colonialism' (1980) and Schreiner's 'The Woman Question' (1899; an early version of part of *Woman and Labour*).

Gray, Stephen (ed.), *Words in Season: the public writings with her own remembrances collected for the first time* (Johannesburg: Penguin, 2005).

Krige, Uys (ed.), *Olive Schreiner: A Selection* (Cape Town: Oxford University Press, 1968).

Stanley, Liz (ed.), *Olive Schreiner's The Dawn of Civilisation and Other Unpublished Wartime Writings* (Edinburgh: X Press, 2018).

Thurman, Howard (ed.), *A Track to the Water's Edge: The Olive Schreiner Reader* (New York: Harper & Row, 1973).

Works about Olive Schreiner

BIOGRAPHIES AND SURVEYS

Brandon, Ruth, *The New Women and the Old Men: Love, Sex and the Woman Question* (London: Secker & Warburg, 1990), ch. 1 (especially 25–43) 'A Derbyshire Idyll' and ch. 2 (44–94) 'Olive Schreiner and the New Men'.

Brown, Mary, 'Memories of My Friendship with Olive Schreiner', in *The Life of Mrs John Brown, including her Recollections of Olive Schreiner*, ed. Angela James and Nina Hills (London: John Murray, 1937), 181–205.

Buchanan-Gould, Vera, *Not Without Honour: The Life and Writings of Olive Schreiner* (London: Hutchinson, 1948).

Cronwright-Schreiner, S. C., *The Life of Olive Schreiner* (London: T. Fisher Unwin, 1924).

First, Ruth and Ann Scott, *Olive Schreiner: A Biography* (London: Deutsch, 1980).

Gordon, Lyndall, *Outsiders: Five Women Writers Who Changed the World* (London: Virago, 2018), ch. 4 (179–233) 'Orator: Olive Schreiner'.

Gregg, Lyndall, *Memories of Olive Schreiner* (London: Chambers, 1955).

Harmel, Michael, *Olive Schreiner 1855–1955* (Cape Town: Real Printing and Publishing, 1955), booklet.

Hobman, D. L., *Olive Schreiner, Her Friends and Times* (London: Watts & Co., 1955).

McClintock, Anne, 'Olive (Emilie Albertina) Schreiner', in *British Writers*, ed. George Stade (New York: Charles Scribner's Sons, 1992), 435–58.

Meintjes, Johannes, *Olive Schreiner: Portrait of a South African Woman* (Johannesburg: Hugh Keartland Publishers, 1965).

Pierpont, Claudia Roth, *Passionate Minds: Women Rewriting the World* (New York: Knopf, 2001), [ch. 1] (3–31) 'A Woman's Place: Olive Schreiner'.

Schoeman, Karel, *Olive Schreiner: A Woman in South Africa 1855–1881*, trans. Henri Snijders (Johannesburg: Jonathan Ball, 1991).

Schoeman, Karel, *Only an Anguish to Live Here: Olive Schreiner and the Anglo-Boer War, 1899–1902* (Cape Town: Human & Rousseau, 1992).

Stevens, Valerie L., 'Olive Schreiner', in *Palgrave Encyclopedia of Victorian Women's Writing*, ed. Lesa Scholl and Emily Morris (London: Palgrave Macmillan, 2022), 1403–6.

Van der Vlies, Andrew, 'Olive Schreiner (1855–1920)', in *World Writers in English, Volume II: R. K. Narayan to Patrick White*, ed. Jay Parini (New York, NY: Scribner's, 2004), 625–44.

Critical Works

BOOKS AND ESSAYS MAKING SUBSTANTIAL REFERENCE TO *FROM MAN TO MAN*

Barash, Carol L., 'Virile Womanhood: Olive Schreiner's Narratives of a Master Race', *Women's Studies International Forum*, 9/4 (1986), 333–40.

Bedder, Hilary, 'Olive Schreiner's *From Man to Man*: Alternative Models of Reality and the Problematics of Human Reasoning', *English in Africa* 47/2 (2020), 99–119.

Berkman, Joyce Avrech, *The Healing Imagination of Olive Schreiner: Beyond South African Colonialism* (Amherst: University of Massachusetts Press, 1989).

Berkman, Joyce Avrech, 'Possessing Women in Olive Schreiner's *From Man to Man, or Perhaps Only*', *Journal of Commonwealth Literature* 56/1, (2021), 28–43.

Bradford, Helen, 'Olive Schreiner's Hidden Agony: Fact, Fiction and Teenage Abortion', *Journal of Southern African Studies*, 21/4 (1995), 623–41.

Brilmyer, S. Pearl, *The Science of Character: Human Objecthood and the Ends of Victorian Realism* (Chicago: University of Chicago Press, 2022), ch. 5 (180–219) 'The Intimate Pulse of Reality: Or, Schreiner's Ethological Realism' *et passim*.

Burdett, Carolyn, *Olive Schreiner* (Tavistock, Devon: Northcote House, 2013), ch. 2 (34–62) 'Sex Work: *Woman and Labour*, Stories and Allegories, *From Man to Man*'.

Burdett, Carolyn, *Olive Schreiner and the Progress of Feminism: Evolution, Gender, Empire* (Basingstoke, Hampshire & New York: Palgrave, 2001), ch. 3 (86–112) 'Capturing the Ideal: New Men and Women in *From Man to Man*'.

Casey, Janet Galligani, 'Power, Agency, Desire: Olive Schreiner and the Pre-Modern Narrative Moment', *Narrative*, 4/2 (1996), 124–41.

Chang, Mei-Fang, 'Maternal Geopolitics in Conflict: Olive Schreiner's *From Man to Man*', in *Boundary Crossing: New Visions of Instruction and Research*, ed. Jane S. Tsay (Taipei: Crane, 2010), 121–40.

Chang, Mei-Fang, 'Narrative Decomposition for Utopian (Re-) Composition: The New (Wo)Man in Olive Schreiner's *From Man to Man*', *Research in African Literatures* 44/1 (2013), 106–27.

Chrisman, Laura, 'Empire, "Race" and Feminism at the *Fin de Siècle*: the Work of George Egerton and Olive Schreiner', *Cultural Politics at the Fin de Siècle*, ed. Sally Ledger and Scott McCracken (Cambridge: Cambridge University Press, 1995), 45–65.

Clayton, Cherry, *Olive Schreiner* (New York: Twayne, 1997), ch. 4 (60–73) 'Sisterhood is Powerful: *From Man to Man*'.

Dowling, Finuala, '"Writer's Block" in Olive Schreiner's *From Man to Man or Perhaps Only—*', *English in Africa*, 47/2 (2020), 79–97.

Driver, Dorothy, 'Introduction to the New Edition (2015)', *From Man to Man or Perhaps Only—*, by Olive Schreiner (Cape Town: UCT Press, 2015), ix–xlvi.

Driver, Dorothy, 'Invoking Indigeneity: Olive Schreiner and the Poetics of Plants', *Journal of Commonwealth Literature*, 56/1 (2021), 61–76 (repeats much of similarly titled booklet below).

Driver, Dorothy, 'Olive Schreiner's *From Man to Man* and "the copy within"', *Changing the Victorian Subject*, ed. Maggie Tonkin, Mandy Treagus, Madeleine Seys and Sharon Crozier-De Rosa (Adelaide: Adelaide University Press, 2014), 123–50.

Driver, Dorothy, *Olive Schreiner's Poetics of Plants* (Makhanda: Amazwi South African Museum of Literature, 2019), illustrated booklet.

Foot, Paul, New Introduction. *From Man to Man* (London: Virago, 1982), ix–xvii.

Gounelas, Ruth Parkin, *Fictions of the Female Self: Charlotte Brontë, Olive Schreiner, Katherine Mansfield* (London: Macmillan, 1991).

Horton, Susan R., *Difficult Women, Artful Lives: Olive Schreiner and Isak Dinesen, In and Out of Africa* (Baltimore: Johns Hopkins University Press, 1995).

Heilmann, Ann. ' "Over that bridge built with our bodies the entire human race will pass": A Re-reading of Olive Schreiner's *From Man to Man*', *European Journal of Women's Studies*, 2 (1995), 33–50.

Heilmann, Ann, *New Woman Strategies: Sarah Grand, Olive Schreiner, Mona Caird* (Manchester: Manchester University Press, 2004), ch. 4 (119–54) 'Transitions and Transfigurations: *Dreams* (1890), *The Story of an African Farm* (1883) and *From Man to Man* (1926)'.

Jenkins, Elwyn. 'Little Houses and Other Children's Spaces in "The Child's Day" by Olive Schreiner and *The Chronicles of Peach Grove Farm* by Nellie Fincher', *English Academy Review*, 30/2 (2013), 42–52.

Knechtel, Ruth, 'Olive Schreiner's Pagan Feminism: An Underlying Unity', *English Literature in Transition, 1880–1920*, 53/3 (2010), 259–82.

Lovell-Smith, Rose, 'Science and Religion in the Fin-de-Siècle and a New Reading of Olive Schreiner's *From Man to Man*', *Victorian Literature and Culture*, 29/2 (2001), 303–326.

Marquard, Jean. 'Olive Schreiner's "Prelude": The Child as Artist', *English Studies in Africa*, 22/1 (1979), 1–12.

McClintock, Anne, *Imperial Leather: Race, Gender and Sexuality in the Colonial Contest* (New York: Routledge, 1995), ch. 7 (258–95) 'Olive Schreiner: The Limits of Colonial Feminism' *et passim*.

Monsman, Gerald, *Olive Schreiner's Fiction: Landscape and Power* (New Brunswick, NJ: Rutgers University Press, 1991).

Munich, Adrienne, 'Jews and Jewels: A Symbolic Economy on the South African Diamond Fields', in *'The Jew' in Late-Victorian and Edwardian Culture: Between the East End and East Africa*, ed. Eitan Bar-Yosef and Nadia Valman (Basingstoke and New York: Palgrave Macmillan, 2009), 28–44.

Munslow Ong, Jade, *Olive Schreiner and African Modernism: Allegory, Empire and Postcolonial Writing* (London: Routledge, 2018), ch. 3 (101–42) 'Evolution, Gender and Race in *From Man to Man (Or Perhaps Only…)*' *et passim*.

Nivesjö, Sanja, 'Making Space for Women's Sexual Selves in Olive Schreiner's *From Man to Man*', *English in Africa*, 48/1 (2021), 97–122.

Nivesjö, Sanja and Heidi Barends, 'Current Perspectives on Olive Schreiner's *From Man to Man or Perhaps Only—*', *Journal of Commonwealth Literature*, 56/1 (2021), 44–60.

Raiskin, Judith L., *Snow on the Cane Fields: Women's Writing and Creole Subjectivity* (Minneapolis: University of Minnesota Press, 1996), ch. 1 (17–49) ' "An English South African": Olive Schreiner's South Africa, Land and Language'; and ch. 2 (50–94) 'Schreiner's Representations of Jews, Boers and Blacks'.

Ravilious, C.P., ' "Saints and Sinners": An Unidentified Olive Schreiner Manuscript', *Journal of Commonwealth Literature*, 12/1 (1977), 1–11.

Snaith, Anna, *Modernist Voyages: Colonial Women Writers in London, 1890–1945* (Cambridge: Cambridge University Press, 2014), ch. 1 (36–66) 'Olive Schreiner: Diamonds, Prostitution and *From Man to Man*'.

Stanley, Liz, 'Before: The Avant-Textes of *From Man to Man* and Olive Schreiner's Writing Practices', *Journal of Commonwealth Literature*, 56/1 (2021): 13–27.

Stanley, Liz, *Imperialism, Labour and the New Woman: Olive Schreiner's Social Theory* (Durham: Sociology Press, 2002).

Steele, Murray, 'A Humanist Bible: Gender Roles, Sexuality and Race in Olive Schreiner's *From Man to Man*', in *Gender Roles and Sexuality in Victorian Literature*, ed. Christopher Parker (Aldershot: Scolar, 1995), 101–14.

Stevens, Valerie L., 'Human-Animal "Mother-Love" in Novels by Olive Schreiner', *English Literature in Transition, 1880–1920*', 61/2 (2018), 147–71.

Voss, Anthony, '*From Man to Man*: Heroic Fragment', in *The Flawed Diamond: Essays on Olive Schreiner*, ed. Itala Vivan (Sydney: Dangaroo Press, 1991), 135–45.

GENERAL STUDIES (BOOKS AND ESSAYS) REFERRING TO SCHREINER

Beeton, Ridley, *Facets of Olive Schreiner: A Manuscript Source Book* (Craighall, Johannesburg: Ad Donker, 1987).

Burdett, Carolyn, 'A Difficult Vindication: Olive Schreiner's Wollstonecraft Introduction', *History Workshop Journal* 37/ (1994), 177–87.

Bristow, Joseph, 'Introduction' to *The Story of an African Farm*, Oxford World's Classics series (Oxford: Oxford University Press, 1992), vii–xxxii.

Chetty, Rajendra, and Matthew Curr, 'Deaf to Women: Rhodes's refusal to hear women or his own feminine voice within—a reading of Schreiner's *Trooper Peter Halket of Mashonaland*', *International Journal of African Renaissance*, 11/1 (2016), 5–21.

Chrisman, Laura, 'Allegory, Feminist Thought and the *Dreams* of Olive Schreiner', in *Edward Carpenter and Late Victorian Radicalism*, ed. Tony Brown (London: Frank Cass, 1990), 126–50.

Chrisman, Laura, 'Colonialism and Feminism in Olive Schreiner's 1890s Fiction', *English in Africa* 20/1 (1993), 25–38.

Chrisman, Laura, *Rereading The Imperial Romance: British Imperialism and South African Resistance in Haggard, Schreiner, and Plaatje* (Oxford: Clarendon, 2000).

Clayton, Cherry, '"A Case for the Indigenous": Olive Schreiner in South Africa', *South African Historical Journal*, 22/1 (1990), 184–91.

Clayton, Cherry (ed.), *Olive Schreiner*, South African Literature Series no. 4 (Johannesburg: McGraw-Hill, 1983).

Clayton, Cherry, 'Olive Schreiner in Johannesburg', *English Academy Review*, 1/1 (1983): 65–82.

Clayton, Cherry, 'Olive Schreiner: Paradoxical Pioneer', *Women and Writing in South Africa: A Critical Anthology*, ed. Cherry Clayton (Johannesburg: Heinemann Southern Africa, 1989), 41–59.

Coetzee, J. M., *White Writing: On the Culture of Letters in South Africa* (New Haven: Yale University Press, 1988).

Colby, Vineta, *The Singular Anomaly: Women Novelists of the Nineteenth Century* (New York: New York University Press, 1970) ch. 2 (47–110) 'The Imperative Impulse: Olive Schreiner'.

Davenport, Rodney, 'Olive Schreiner and South African Politics', in *Olive Schreiner and After: Essays on Southern African Literature in Honour of Guy Butler*, ed. Malvern van Wyk Smith and Don Maclennan (Cape Town: David Philip, 1983), 93–107.

DuPlessis, Rachel Blau, *Writing beyond the Ending: Narrative Strategies of Twentieth-Century Women Writers* (Bloomington: Indiana University Press, 1985), ch. 2 (20–30) 'The Rupture of Story and *The Story of an African Farm*' *et passim*.

Flint, Kate. *The Woman Reader, 1837–1914* (Oxford: Oxford University Press, 1993).

Fradkin, Betty, 'Olive Schreiner and Karl Pearson', *Quarterly Bulletin of the South African Library*, 31/4 (June 1977), 83–93.

Friedlander, Zelder, *Until the Heart Changes: A Garland for Olive Schreiner* (Cape Town: Tafelberg, 1967).

Gilbert, Sandra M., and Gubar, Susan, *No Man's Land: The Place of the Woman Writer in the Twentieth Century, Vol. 2: Sexchanges* (New Haven: Yale University Press, 1988).

Gill, Clare, 'Olive Schreiner, Marie Corelli and the Anxieties of Female Authorship', *Journal of Victorian Culture*, 24/4 (2020), 574–92.

Gill, Clare, 'Reading the "Religion of Socialism": Olive Schreiner, the Labour Church and the Construction of Left-Wing Reading Communities in the 1890s', in *The History of Reading, Volume 2: Evidence from the British Isles*, ed. Katie Halsey and W. R. Owens (Basingstoke: Palgrave, 2011), 48–64.

Gordimer, Nadine, 'The Prison-House of Colonialism' [review of First and Scott, *Olive Schreiner*], rpt. in Barash, 221–27, *supra*; and in Van Wyk Smith and Maclennan, 14–9, *infra*.

Graham, Lucy, *State of Peril: Race and Rape in South African Literature* (Oxford: Oxford University Press, 2012).

Graham, Lucy Valerie, '"Utterly Divided?" The Feminist Perspectives of Lauretta Ngcobo and Olive Schreiner', *Scrutiny 2*, 22/1 (2017), 86–94.

Gray, Stephen, *Southern African Literature: An Introduction* (Claremont, Cape Town: David Philip, 1979), ch. 6 (133–59) 'Schreiner and the Novel Tradition'.

Green, Louise, 'Olive Schreiner and the Labour of Writing', *English Academy Review: Southern African Journal of English Studies*, 20/1 (2003), 54–68.

Heywood, Christopher, *A History of South African Literature* (Cambridge: Cambridge University Press, 2004), ch. 4 (87–110) 'Prose Classics: Schreiner to Mofolo'.

Johnson, David, *Dreaming of Freedom in South Africa: Literature Between Critique and Utopia* (Edinburgh: Edinburgh University Press, 2019).

Krebs, Paula, *Gender, Race and the Writing of Empire: Public Discourse and the Boer War* (Cambridge: Cambridge University Press, 1999).

Kuchich, John, 'Psychoanalytic Historicism: Shadow Discourse and the Gender Politics of Masochism in Ellis, Schreiner, and Haggard', *PMLA*, 126/1 (2011), 88–106.

Kuchich, John, 'Olive Schreiner's Preoedipal Dreams: Feminism, Class, and the South African War', *Imperial Masochism: British Fiction, Fantasy and Social Class* (Princeton and Oxford: Princeton University Press, 2009), 86–135.

Ledger, Sally, *The New Woman: Fiction and Feminism at the Fin de Siècle* (Manchester: Manchester University Press, 1997).

Lessing, Doris, 'Olive Schreiner', *Time Bites: Views and Reviews* (London: HarperCollins, 2004), 195–200.

Lewis, Simon, 'Reading Olive Schreiner Reading W. E. B. Du Bois', *Research in African Literatures*, 45/2 (2014), 150–67.

Lewis, Simon, 'The Transnational Circulation of Dissent: Olive Schreiner and the Colonial Counter-Flows of Unitarian Freethinking', *Safundi: The Journal of South African and American Studies*, 14/1 (2013), 1–15.

Lewis, Simon, *White Women Writers and Their African Invention* (Gainesville: University Press of Florida, 2003).

Livesey, Ruth, *Socialism, Sex, and the Culture of Aestheticism in Britain, 1880–1914* (Oxford: Oxford University Press, 2007).

Murphy, Patricia, *Time is of the Essence: Temporality, Gender, and the New Woman* (Albany, N.Y.: State University of New York Press, 2001).

Monsman, Gerald, 'Writing the Self on the Imperial Frontier: Olive Schreiner and the Stories of Africa', *The Bucknell Review*, 37/1 (1993), 134–55.

Munslow Ong, Jade, 'Dream Time and Anti-Imperialism in the Writings of Olive Schreiner', *Journal of Postcolonial Writing* 50/6 (2014), 704–16.

Pechey, Graham, '*The Story of an African Farm*: Colonial History and the Discontinuous Text', *Critical Arts*, 3/1 (1983), 65–78.

Samuelson, Meg, 'Writing Women', in *Cambridge History of South African Literature*, ed. David Atwell and Derek Attridge (Cambridge: Cambridge University Press, 2012), 757–78.

Sanders, Mark, *Complicities: The Intellectual and Apartheid* (Durham: Duke University Press, 2002).

Showalter, Elaine, *A Literature of Their Own: British Women Novelists from Bronte to Lessing* (Princeton, N.J.: Princeton University Press, 1977), ch. VIII (182–215) 'The Feminist Novelists' *et passim*; see also Showalter's 'Twenty Years On: A Literature of Their Own Revisited,' *Novel: A Forum on Fiction*, 31/3 (1998), 399–413.

Stanley, Liz, 'The Reader, the Text and the Editor', *English in Africa* 42/1 (2015), 59–76.

Stanley, Liz, 'Shadows Lying Across Her Pages: Epistolary Aspects of Reading "The Eventful I" in Olive Schreiner's Letters', *Journal of European Studies*, 32/125–6 (2002), 251–66.

Stanley, Liz, 'Turning Points: Olive Schreiner Changing Her Mind About Race Matters', in *Olive Schreiner: Writing Networks and Global Contexts*, ed. Jade Munslow Ong and Andrew van der Vlies (Edinburgh: University of Edinburgh Press, 2024), 99–114.

Stanley, Liz and Dampier, Helen, '"Men selling their souls & the future – and fate watching them": Olive Schreiner on Union', *Quarterly Bulletin of the National Library of South Africa*, 64/3 (2010), 121–36.

Van der Vlies, Andrew, *South African Textual Cultures: White, Black, Read all Over* (Manchester: Manchester University Press, 2007), ch. 2 (20–45) 'Farming Stories (I): Olive Schreiner's Fates'.

Van der Vlies, Andrew, and Jade Munslow Ong (eds.), *Olive Schreiner: Writing Networks Global Contexts* (Edinburgh: Edinburgh University Press, 2024).

Van Wyk Smith, Malvern, and Don Maclennan (eds.), *Olive Schreiner and After: Essays on Southern African Literature in Honour of Guy Butler* (Cape Town: David Philip, 1983).

Vivan, Itala (ed.), *The Flawed Diamond: Essays on Olive Schreiner* (Sydney: Dangaroo Press, 1991).

LITERARY, POLITICAL AND HISTORICAL CONTEXT

Becker, Heike, 'The Least Sexist Society? Perspectives on Gender, Change and Violence among Southern African San', *Journal of Southern African Studies* 29/1 (2003), 5–23.

Bland, Lucy, *Banishing the Beast: Sexuality and the Early Feminists* (New York: The New Press, 1995).

Chapman, Michael, *Southern African Literatures* (London and New York: Longman, 1996).

Ellis, Havelock, *My Life* (London: Heinemann, 1940).

Foster, Jeremy, *Washed with Sun: Landscape and the Making of White South Africa* (Pittsburgh: University of Pittsburgh Press, 2008).

Gray, Stephen, 'The Koodoo on Our Kar(r)oo: Reclaiming and Editing Our Literary Heritage', *Journal of Literary Studies*, 26/2 (2010), 5–1.

Gray, Stephen, 'Two Dissident Dream-Walkers: The Hardly Explored Reformist Alliance between Olive Schreiner and Edward Carpenter', *English Academy Review*, 30/2 (2013), 53–66.

Grosskurth, Phyllis, *Havelock Ellis* (London: Allen Lane, 1980).

Heywood, Christopher, 'Olive Schreiner's Influence on George Moore and D. H. Lawrence', in *Aspects of South African Literature*, ed. Christopher Heywood (London: Heinemann Educational, 1976), 42–53.

Hilton, John, 'Gandhi, Carpenter, Schreiner and the Crisis of Modern Civilization at the Turn of the Century', *African Studies*, 74/2 (2015), 157–74.

Hirson, Baruch, *The Cape Town Intellectuals: Ruth Schechter and her Circle, 1907–1934* (Cape Town: Merlin Press, 2001).

Jacobs, Aletta, *Memories: My Life as an International Leader in Health, Suffrage and Peace*, ed. Harriet Feinberg, trans. Annie Wright (New York: The Feminist Press at the City University of New York, 1996).

Johnson, David, *Imagining the Cape Colony: History, Literature, and the South African Nation* (Edinburgh: Edinburgh University Press, 2012).

Kapp, Yvonne, *Eleanor Marx: A Biography. Vol. 2: The Crowded Years, 1884–1898* (London: Lawrence & Wishart, 1976).

Keegan, Timothy, 'Gender, Degeneration and Sexual Danger: Imagining Race and Class in South Africa, ca. 1912', *Journal of Southern African Studies*, 27/3 (2001), 459–477.

Klopper, Dirk, 'Dry Bones: The Story of Paleoanthropology in South Africa', *Safundi*, 20/1 (2019), 33–57.

Lenta, Margaret, 'Literary Language in the Postcolony: Focus on Southern Africa', *English in Africa*, 39/2 (2012), 155–74.

Magubane, Zine, *Bringing the Empire Home: Race, Class, and Gender in Britain and Colonial South Africa* (Chicago and London: University of Chicago Press, 2004).

Masilela, Ntongela, 'New African Modernity and the New African Movement', in *Cambridge History of South African Literature,* ed. David Atwell and Derek Attridge (Cambridge: Cambridge University Press, 2012), 325–338.

Munslow Ong, Jade, '"Too Uncompromising a Figure to be so Disposed of": Virginia Woolf and / on Olive Schreiner', *English Studies in Africa*, 65/1 (2022), 31–45.

Ngcobo, Lauretta, 'A Black South African Writing Long After Schreiner', in *The Flawed Diamond: Essays on Olive Schreiner*, ed. Itala Vivan (Sydney: Dangaroo Press, 1991), 189–99.

Porter, Theodore M., *Karl Pearson: The Scientific Life in a Statistical Age* (Princeton, N.J.: Princeton University Press, 2004).

Renier, Olive, *Before the Bonfire* (Shipton-on-Stour, Warwickshire: P. Drinkwater, 1984).

Richardson, Angelique, *Love and Eugenics in the Late Nineteenth Century: Rational Reproduction and the New Woman* (Oxford: Oxford University Press, 2003).

Ross, Robert, *A Concise History of South Africa* (Cambridge: Cambridge University Press, 1999).

Rowbotham, Sheila, *Women, Resistance and Revolution* (London: Allen Lane, Penguin, 1972), chs. 1, 2, 3 and 4 (15–98), 'Impudent Lasses', 'Utopian Proposals', 'Dialectical Disturbances', and 'Dreams and Dilemmas'.

Rowbotham, Sheila, and Jeffrey Weeks, *Socialism and the New Life: The Personal and Sexual Politics of Edward Carpenter and Havelock Ellis* (London: Pluto Press, 1977).

Van Wyk Smith, Malvern, *Grounds of Contest: A Survey of South African English Literature* (Kenwyn, Cape Town: Juta, 1990), ch. 1 (1–32) 'Origins and Frontiers'.

Walker, Cherryl, *Women and Resistance in South Africa*, 2nd edn. (New York: Monthly Review Press, 1991).

Walkowitz, Judith, *City of Dreadful Delight: Narratives of Sexual Danger in Late Victorian London* (London: Virago, 1992).

Walkowitz, Judith, 'Science, Feminism, and Romance: The Men and Women's Club 1885–1889', *History Workshop Journal*, 21/1 (1986), 37–59.

Walters, Paul, and Jeremy Fogg, ' "This morning a year ago . . . ": Annotated Extracts from Samuel Cronwright's Diaries (September 1921-November 1923), *English in Africa* 42/1 (2015), 103–29.

Willan, Brian, *Sol Plaatje: A Life of Solomon Tshekisho Plaatje, 1876–1932* (Auckland Park, Johannesburg: Jacana, 2018).

Winkler, Barbara Scott, 'Victorian Daughters: The Lives and Feminism of Charlotte Perkins Gilman and Olive Schreiner', in *Critical Essays on Charlotte Perkins Gilman*, ed. Joanne B. Karpinski (New York: G. K. Hall, 1992), 173–83.

FURTHER READING IN OXFORD WORLD'S CLASSICS

Haggard, H. Rider, *King Solomon's Mines*, ed. Roger Luckhurst.

Haggard, H. Rider, *She*, ed. Daniel Karlin.

Moore, George, *Esther Waters*, ed. Stephen Regan.

Schreiner, Olive, *The Story of an African Farm*, ed. Joseph Bristow.

A CHRONOLOGY OF OLIVE SCHREINER

1855 (24 March) Olive Schreiner (OS) born at Wittebergen Mission Station in the Herschel district of the north-east region of the British Cape Colony, close to the border of the Orange Free State (a Boer Republic under British suzerainty) and just over the border of Basutoland (soon to be a British Protectorate; now Lesotho), to Gottlob and Rebecca (née Lyndall) Schreiner, from east Germany and London respectively; Gottlob was employed by first the London Missionary Society and then the Wesleyan Missionary Society. Christened Olive Emilie (birth certificate has Emily) Albertina, and called Em, names drawn from her deceased male siblings Oliver, Emile, and Albert. The older children are Catherine (Kate), Frederick (Fred), Theophilis (Theo), Alice, and Henrietta (Ettie); Fred has already left for schooling in England.

1856 In British Caffraria, established after the Xhosa defeat in the Seventh Frontier War (1846–7), a young Xhosa woman named Nonqawuse prophesies the return of the ancestors and the flight of the British if the people's cattle are sacrificed. The consequence is widespread famine.

1857 William (Will) Philip Schreiner born.

1858 (March) War breaks out between the Orange Free State and the Basotho (continues to 1868): Basotho refugees flock to the Wittebergen area. Brother Theo leaves for schooling in England.

1860 Sister Kate marries.

1861 Family moves to Healdtown, father as head of Wesleyan Missionary Native Training (Industrial) Institution.

1863 Brother Theo returns from England; sister Alice marries.

1865 (August) Death of youngest Schreiner child, Helen (Ellie), b. 1864, to whom *From Man to Man* will be partially dedicated. Gottlob is dismissed from the Wesleyan Mission Society and the Training Institute for small-time trading; near year-end, family moves to Balfour, Eastern Cape; Gottlob becomes a travelling trader.

1866 Gottlob declared insolvent. Theo takes up teaching position in Grahamstown (now Makhanda), Eastern Cape.

1867 OS (still under the name Emily) and Will join Theo and Ettie in Cradock, over the next years partly attending the school Theo now headmasters, partly staying with various family members and friends.

1870 Stays with Orpen family (cousins) at Avoca, near Barkly East, Eastern Cape, in her first informal position as household help/childminder/governess.

1871 Stays in Hermon, Basutoland, with her mother's half-sister Elizabeth Rolland at the Paris Evangelical Mission. Here she meets the freethinking Willie Bertram; reads his copy of Herbert Spencer's *First Principles* whose articulation of the unity of life squares with her own early childhood experience. Changes her name to Olive. Works as childminder for the Robinson family in Dordrecht, Eastern Cape, and meets Julius Gau and his sister. Her asthma attacks begin at around this time.

1872 Stays in Dordrecht with the Gau family; travels with Julius, a representative of a Swiss insurance company, to her parents' home in Hertzog; (August) they become briefly engaged to be married but the relationship ends. OS writes 'The Lost Joy'. (December) Joins Theo and Ettie at the New Rush diamond fields (later known as Kimberley). Teaches school; helps work the family claim.

1873 Completes 'Diamond Fields'; starts writing *Undine*, *The Story of an African Farm*, and *From Man to Man* (under different titles). Visits sister Alice in Fraserburg, Northern Cape, where she meets Mary Brown née Solomon and her husband Dr John Brown, who encourage her writing and projected medical training.

1874 (*c.*April–May) OS takes up first extended post as a governess, at the Weakleys in Colesburg, Eastern Cape. Purchases Ralph Waldo Emerson's *Essays*. Works on *Undine*.

1875 Works as governess at the Fouchés at Klein Ganna Hoek farm near Cradock; makes friends with the Cawoods on the neighbouring farm, Ganna Hoek. Reads John Stuart Mill's *Logic*.

1876 Completes *Undine*. Works as governess at the Martins at Ratel Hoek near Tarkastad until early 1879. Reads Goethe and Montaigne. (August) Father dies. (December) Visits her mother, who has become a Catholic convert, in Seymour, Eastern Cape; these visits will continue over the next few years. Invited to open a school in Tarkastad but declines, though strongly tempted, for fear of drawing pupils away from an existing school run by some 'poor girls', and of curtailing her own writing time. This year also sees the start of the last of the Cape Frontier Wars, a series of nine wars between the Xhosa and the European settlers, which began in 1779.

1877 (April) Britain annexes the South African Republic (Transvaal); the Afrikaner Bond is later (1879–81) established in protest. OS completes *Saints and Sinners* (early version of *From Man to Man*). Brother Fred establishes New College, a private boys' school in Eastbourne, Sussex.

1878 The Ninth Frontier War spills over into the Cape Colony, OS writing to her sister Katie that all the men in the district of Seymour are armed but 'I don't think we are in any real danger yet'.

1879 OS moves from the Martins to the Cawoods at Ganna Hoek, who are shocked at reading an early version of *African Farm*; Erilda Cawood breaks off friendship (this will be restored by 1881). (July) OS moves as governess to the Fouchés at Lelie (Lily) Kloof (Afk. Leliekloof), Eastern Cape. Reads W. H. Lecky's controversial *History of European Morals*, which raises questions about prostitution and the relation between 'reason' and 'appetite'. Formal end of the Cape Frontier Wars, with Xhosa defeat.

1880 From Lelie Kloof OS sends manuscript of *African Farm* to the Browns' relatives in England. Over next two years, works on revisions. First Anglo-Boer War breaks out between the Transvaal and the British; the latter defeated within four months (March 1881). OS writes 'Dream Life and Real Life'. Applies for training in nursing at Edinburgh Royal Infirmary.

1881 The Transvaal (South African Republic) regains independence from Britain. (March) OS travels to Britain, stays first with brother Fred in Eastbourne. His school publication, *New College Magazine*, accepts four allegorical stories, including 'Dream Life and Real Life'. Under pseudonym Ralph Iron, OS submits *Saints and Sinners* to Chapman and Hall publishers but it is rejected. Starts revising it and continues through much of 1880s, renaming it *From Man to Man*. Changes to midwifery training at Endell Street Hospital, London; curtailed by illness. Befriends Eleanor Marx, Karl Marx's daughter, writer and labour organizer, the friendship continuing until Eleanor's death. (December) Starts sending *African Farm* to publishers under pseudonym Ralph Iron.

1883 *African Farm* published (first under pseudonym Ralph Iron; reprint same year bears her own name). With Eleanor Marx, attends the foundational meeting of the Social Democratic Federation's women's branch.

1883–4 Writes the start of a family history, 'Reminiscences' (*c.*3,000 words).

1884 Meets medical student and budding sexologist Havelock Ellis; forms long-lasting close friendship and intellectual partnership with him. Asthma attacks and chest infections have now brought an end to medical training. Attends meetings of the Progressive Association (which Ellis founded) and the Fellowship of the New Life.

1885 Joins the radical Men and Women's Club newly convened by sociologist Karl Pearson; they develop an intellectual bond and friendship. OS drafts club's appreciation of W. T. Stead's explosive exposé of child prostitution (both published in *Pall Mall Gazette*). Through the Fellowship of the New Life, meets and forms lifelong friendship with radical socialist and gay rights crusader Edward Carpenter, author of *Towards Democracy*. Declines marriage proposal from George Moore, Irish novelist. Spends bulk of time in informal social work among London prostitutes and advising female friends and acquaintances.

1886 Commissioned to write introduction to Mary Wollstonecraft's *A Vindication of the Rights of Women*; drafts some pages but produces numerous allegories instead; starts work on her 'sex book'; this will later become *Woman and Labour*. Declines marriage proposal from Bryan Donkin, physician to many radical intellectuals. Relations with Pearson break down. Leaves for Europe; stays mainly in Alassio, Italy; wards off mental and physical collapse.

1886–7 Works passionately on *From Man to Man*, exploring disagreement with Pearson's Social Darwinism, the relation between marriage and prostitution, and questions of gender, labour, and sexual desire.

1888 Moves between Alassio, Menton (France), and England. 'The Lost' ('The Lost Joy') published in *Woman's World* (editor Oscar Wilde). Considers continuing with midwifery training, but decides on South African sociological/anthropogical research instead. Eleanor Marx publishes 'The Woman Question' with her partner, Edward Aveling.

1889 OS publishes two more allegories in *Woman's World*. In England, meets Arthur Symons, decadent and symbolist poet and critic. (October) Returns to South Africa; visits mother in Roman Catholic convent in Grahamstown. Cecil John Rhodes's newly formed British South African Company is granted a Royal Charter to colonize occupied land north of the Limpopo in search for minerals.

1890 OS settles in Matjesfontein, Western Cape, finding relief from asthma. Revises allegories; begins series of essays on South Africa for projected collection, 'Stray Thoughts on South Africa'; these will appear in periodicals in her lifetime, but will be published only posthumously as *Thoughts on South Africa*. Starts loving correspondence with Mary

Sauer (wife of a prominent Liberal Cape politician) whom she met at the end of 1889. Meets Rhodes in Cape Town; rumours fly about a love affair. (July) Rhodes is elected prime minister, with Afrikaner Bond support. His annexation of Mashonaland is underway, meeting armed resistance from the Shona and Ndebele. *Dreams* published by T. Fisher Unwin (London) to high acclaim; dedicated to Karl Pearson's stepdaughter after his marriage: 'A small girl-child, who may live to grasp somewhat of that which for us in yet sight, not touch'.

1891 OS starts lifelong friendship with Elizabeth (Betty) Molteno and her partner Alice Greene, both anti-imperialist, anti-racist, and socialist. Publishes 'A Woman's Rose' in *New Review* (London); 'South Africa, its Natural Features' in *Fortnightly Review* (London), *Cape Times* (Cape Town), *Living Age* (Boston), and *Review of Reviews* (London); and 'Our Waste Land in Mashonaland' (*Cape Times*). Disgusted by Rhodes's 'Strop Bill' (permitting flogging of black servants).

1892 Still in Matjesfontein, ends association with Rhodes. Visits the Cawoods at Ganna Hoek; meets Samuel 'Cron' Cronwright, ostrich farmer at Krantz Plaats, near Cradock. Works on allegories, including 'The Buddhist Priest's Wife'. Publishes 'The Policy in Favour of Protection in the Australian Colonies' in *Harper's Weekly: A Journal of Civilization* (New York). *African Farm* appears in Russian, Dutch, and German translations.

1893 In England for six months; publishes *Dream Life and Real Life* with Unwin, and sees increasing international interest in *African Farm* and *Dreams*, with translations in Russian and several other European languages. Rhodes's British South African Company meets Lobengula's resistance in Matabeleland with brutal slaughter (the Shona and Matabele now fully dispossessed, their land renamed Rhodesia). Some Cape Liberals turn away from Rhodes, who forms new ministry without them, but OS's brother Will becomes attorney-general, though resigns later in year. OS embarks on long-term correspondence with local parliamentarians in effort to encourage racial and socialist awareness. At year-end returns to Cape Colony; lives in Middelburg, Eastern Cape.

1894 Marries Cronwright in a civil ceremony in Middelburg; he adopts her name, becoming Samuel Cron Cronwright-Schreiner (SCCS). Asthma attacks compel move from Krantz Plaats to Kimberley, Northern Cape; promises to complete *From Man to Man* and another novel within two years. Rhodes passes the Glen Gray Act to introduce individual rather than communal land tenure for Africans. In opposition, SCCS tries to transform the local farmers' associations into a political party; OS prefers him to campaign as an independent. *Dreams* appears in German and French translation, and *Dream Life and Real Life* in Dutch.

1895 (April) Daughter born; dies within sixteen hours; *From Man to Man* will be part dedicated to her. Several miscarriages over next few years. (August) Co-writes *The Political Situation* with SCCS (attack on Rhodes and British imperialism).

1896 (Early January) Failure of Rhodes's Jameson Raid plot to take over Transvaal Republic; he resigns as prime minister, concentrating instead on 'pacifying' Rhodesia. OS now completely distanced from him; divergent attitudes to the raid and to Rhodes split the Schreiner family. Publishes *The Political Situation* (Unwin), later critiqued in *Cape Times* for not recognizing benefits of individualism and capitalism. Publishes 'The Wanderings of the Boer' in *Fortnightly Review*, and extracts from 'The Boer' in *Cape Times*, *Daily News* (London), and *Fortnightly Review*. Dutch periodical serializes several essays. Travels to England (with Betty Molteno, Alice Greene, and SCCS) to publish *Trooper Peter Halket of Mashonaland*, a fictional attack in allegory form on Rhodes and the Chartered Company, for rape, massacre, and other atrocities; it fails to change British minds.

1897 Still in England, OS's warnings of impending war between the British colony and the Transvaal republic go unheeded. *Trooper Peter Halket* published in Dutch translation.

1898 Eleanor Marx's suicide; Aveling destroys her correspondence with OS. OS rejects offer of annuity from Transvaal government, but rumours fly that she was paid to produce *Peter Halket*. Publication of German translation of *Peter Halket* (shortened for schools). *Cosmopolitan* (New York) publishes 'The Boer Woman and the Nineteenth Century Woman'. Will Schreiner becomes prime minister of the Cape Colony. Towards year end, asthma worsening, OS moves to Johannesburg's higher altitude.

1899 French translation of *Peter Halket*. Hodder & Stoughton (London) publishes *An English South African's View of the Situation*, sections of which appear in periodicals—*South African News*, *The Standard and Digger's News*, *Review of Reviews*—and in book form as *The South African Question* by Charles H. Sergel Company (Chicago). OS suffers severe asthma attack. Interview with J. A. Hobson, special correspondent for the *Manchester Guardian*, about impending war. (October/November) start of Second Anglo-Boer War; a.k.a.

South African War. OS declines invitation from *New York Journal* to be war correspondent (anxious about her heart). Her politics continue to offend brother Will, but she stays with him in Cape Town.

1900 (January–June) OS delivers anti-war, pro-Boer speeches at public meetings in Graaff-Reinet and Cape Town. (May) British annexation of Orange Free State, and (September) of South African Republic (Transvaal). (July–December) OS sends protest letters to be read out at women's conventions in Paarl and Somerset East. SCCS tours England delivering anti-war speeches. Publishes 'The Boer' (as 'The African Boer') in *Cosmopolitan* (New York). Hobson includes her 1899 interview in *The War in South Africa*; the Dutch publish translation of *Thoughts on South Africa*. OS hears about looting of their Johannesburg dwelling, her box of manuscripts likely destroyed.

1901 Living in Hanover, Cape, under martial law; denied access to books, newspapers, and magazines. Works with Betty Molteno, Alice Greene, and others, including Emily Hobhouse, to help those affected by martial law. Writes short story, 'Eighteen-Ninety-Nine'. SCCS starts typing the Prelude and subsequent six chapters of *From Man to Man*. French translation of *African Farm*.

1902 Peace treaty signed between Britain and Boer Republics. OS visits Johannesburg and confirms loss of manuscript of *Woman and Labour* and other material. Starts rewriting the former, works on *From Man to Man*, and produces several stories. Will stay in Hanover for several years, making annual trips to Cape Town, and spending time in Matjesfontein too. Her asthma is relieved, but heart pains disturb her.

1903 Mother dies. Emmeline Pethwick-Lawrence, a leading suffragist, brings her a copy of W. E. B. Du Bois, *The Souls of Black Folk*. *African Farm* published in Czech translation.

1905 OS supports newly founded Social Democratic Federation. Publishes letter supporting demonstration by the Johannesburg Shop Assistants' Union, and another on 'the Taal' (Afrikaans language). Continues through these years writing politically strategic letters to wide variety of politicians and (sometimes) their wives, urging more careful thought about questions of labour in relation to race and gender.

1906 'Letter on the Jew' is read out at a Cape Town meeting in protest at Russian pogroms; points to Karl Marx as exemplary figure in social and political reform; published first in *Cape Times* and then as booklet.

1907 OS helps found Women's Enfranchisement League, sharing vice-presidency with Mary Brown. Ukrainian translation of *Dreams*. Joins SCCS in De Aar when he transfers his office from Hanover.

1908 OS moves between De Aar, Matjesfontein, and Cape Town, such movements continue till 1913. Befriends Mohandas Gandhi, the Indian political leader, on his release from jail for supporting Indian anti-pass campaign. Delegates from the four colonies meet in National Convention, and the *Transvaal Leader* invites her to discuss way forward. OS resigns (as vice-president and member) from the Women's Enfranchisement League because majority supports franchise for white women only.

1909 With sister Ettie, stages a public meeting with Gandhi on Cape Town docks. Publishes *Closer Union* (reprint of the *Transvaal Leader* article) with the Constitutional Reform Association (Cape Town). 'Our Waste Land in Mashonaland' is reprinted in F. R. N. Findlay's *Big Game Shooting and Travel in South-East Africa*. The Cape Women's Enfranchisement League publishes *Olive Schreiner's Thoughts about Women* (extracts from *African Farm* and *Dreams*).

1910 The Union of South Africa formally established as a self-governing British dominion; the Act of Union limits the franchise to whites only, throughout the four provinces, to OS's disgust.

1911 OS visits Victoria Falls in Rhodesia (now Zimbabwe). Has revised draft of the Prelude and following six chapters of *From Man to Man* retyped (titled 'The Camel Thorn' manually amended to 'Perhaps Only—). *Woman and Labour* published by Unwin; hailed as 'Bible' of the Women's Movement.

1912 South African Native National Congress founded (later renamed as African National Congress). OS's heart problems worsening. Sister Ettie dies.

1913 The Natives Land Act is passed, reserving only 13 per cent of country for African use and occupation. OS sails for England at year-end.

1914 Travelling in Italy and Germany seeking remedies for heart problems; visits Aletta Jacobs in Holland. Outbreak of First World War compels return to London, where OS remains until 1918. Distressed at Gandhi's unexpected expression of support for British troops. Over the next years engages in pacifist activities.

1916 Publishes pacifist text in *Labour Leader*, a British socialist newspaper. Plaatje's *Native Life in South Africa* is published in London, exposing damage wrought by the 1913 Land Act. OS refuses to support his petition for assistance from the British government since he offers black South African military help in return.

1917 Works on MS entitled 'The Dawn of Civilisation: Stray thoughts on Peace and War. The Homely Personal Confessions of a Believer in Human Unity', of which only fragments remain.

1919 (June) Brother Will dies. OS in deep depression; her heart condition worsening.

1920 Death of Alice Greene; death of brother Theo (the last of her siblings). OS meets SCCS in London after separation of five years. (August) Returns alone to South Africa. In Bloemfontein Charlotte Maxeke organizes women in a protest against passes (many women are jailed) and in Port Elizabeth (now Gqeberha) the Native Labour Union organizes a dock workers' strike; OS helps collect funds for the defence of its organizer, Samuel Masabala. (Night of 10–11 December) She dies peacefully of heart failure in a boarding house in Wynberg, Cape Town.

1921 'The Dawn' (draft introduction to 'The Dawn of Civilisation') published in *The Nation and Athenaeum* (London). SCCS fulfils OS's request to be buried (reinterred) on Buffelskop near Cradock, overlooking Klein Ganna Hoek; their day-old baby daughter is similarly reinterred.

1923 SCCS embarks on his Schreiner project, publishing *Dreams*, *Thoughts on South Africa*, and *Stories, Dreams and Allegories* with Unwin, and the last-mentioned with Stokes (New York) as well.

1924 SCCS publishes *The Life of Olive Schreiner* and *The Letters of Olive Schreiner 1870–1920* with Unwin, as well as a reprint of *African Farm*, and an expanded edition of *Stories, Dreams and Allegories*, now containing 'The Dawn of Civilisation (Stray thoughts on peace and war. The homely personal confession of a believer in human unity)'.

1926 SCCS publishes *From Man to Man or Perhaps Only* . . . with Unwin (London). Two US editions appear the following year: Harper & Brothers and Grosset & Dunlap (both in New York).

1928 SCCS publishes *Undine* with Harper & Brothers, and, in London, with Ernest Benn (which took over Unwin) the following year.

FROM MAN TO MAN OR PERHAPS ONLY—

DEDICATED

TO

MY SISTER LITTLE ELLIE*

WHO DIED, EIGHTEEN MONTHS, WHEN I WAS NINE YEARS OLD

"Nor knowest though what argument
Thy life to thy neighbour's creed hath lent"

ALSO

TO

MY ONLY DAUGHTER*

BORN ON THE 30TH OF APRIL, AND DIED ON THE 1ST OF MAY [1895]

CONTENTS

I

PRELUDE: THE CHILD'S DAY

THE little mother* lay in the agony of childbirth. Outside all was still but the buzzing of the bees, some of which now and then found their way into the half-darkened room. The scent of the orange trees and of the flowers from the garden beyond came in through the partly opened window, with the rich, dry odour of a warm, African summer morning. The little mother groaned in her anguish.

Old Ayah,* the Hottentot* woman, stood at the bedside with her hands folded and her long fingers crooked, the veins on the back standing out like cords. She said, 'O ja, God! Wat zal ons nou zeg?'* and re-adjusted the little shawl upon her shoulders. The window was open three inches, and the blind was drawn below it to keep out the heat. The mother groaned.

At the end of the passage in the dining room the father sat with his elbows on the deal table and his head in his hands, reading Swedenborg;* but the words had no clear meaning for him. Every now and then he looked up at the clock over the fireplace. It was a quarter before ten; and the house was very quiet.

At the back of the house, on the kitchen doorstep, stood Rebekah, the little five years old daughter. She looked up into the intensely blue sky, and then down to the ducks who were waddling before the lowest step, picking up the crusts she had thrown to them. She wore a short pink cotton dress with little white knickerbockers buttoned below the knees and a white kappie* with a large curtain that came almost to her waist. She took the kappie off and looked up again into the sky. There was something almost oppressive in the quiet. The Kaffir* maids had been sent home to their huts, except one who was heating water in the kitchen, and the little Kaffirs were playing away beyond the kraals* on the old kraal heap.* It was like Sunday. She drew a slight sigh, and looked up again into the sapphire-blue sky: it was going to be very hot. The farmhouse stood on the spur of a mountain, and the thorn trees* in the flat* below were already shimmering in the sunlight. After a while she put on her kappie and walked slowly down the steps and across the bare space which served for a farmyard. Beyond it she passed into the low bushes. She soon came to a spot just behind the kraal where the ground was flat and bare; the surface soil had been washed off, and a circular floor of smooth and unbroken stone was exposed, like the smooth floor of a great round room. The bushes about were just high enough to hide her from the farmhouse, though it was only fifty yards off. She stepped onto the stone slowly, on tiptoe. She was building a house here. It stood in the centre of the stone floor; it was a foot and a half high and about a foot across, and was built of little flat stones placed very carefully on one another; and it was round like a tower. The lower storey opened onto the ground by a little doorway two inches high; in the upper storey there was a small door in the wall; and a ladder made of sticks, with smaller sticks fastened across, led up to it. She stepped up to the house very softly. She was building it for mice. Once a Kaffir boy told her he had built a house of stones, and as he passed the next day a mouse ran out at the front door. She had thought a great deal of it; always, she seemed to see the mouse living in the house and going in and out at the front door; and at last she built this one. She had built it in two storeys, so that the family could live on the lower floor and keep their grain on the top. She had put a great flat stone to roof the lower storey, and another flat stone for the roof on the very top; and she had put a moss carpet in the lower floor for them to sleep on, and corn, ready for them to use, above. She stepped very softly up to the house and peeped in at the little door; there was nothing there but the brown moss. She sat down flat on the stone before it, and peered in. Half, she expected the mice to come; and half, she knew they never would!

Presently she took a few little polished flat stones out of her pocket and began to place them carefully round the top to form a turret; then she straightened the ladder a little. Then she sat, watching the house. It was too hot to go and look for more stones. After a while she stretched out her right hand, and drew its sides together, and made the fingers look as it were* a little mouse; and moved it softly along the stone, creeping, creeping up to the door; she let it go in. Then after a minute she drew it slowly back and sat up. It was becoming intensely hot now; the sun beating down on the stone drew little beads of perspiration on her forehead.

How still it was! She listened to hear whether anyone from the house would call her. It was long past ten o'clock and she was never allowed to be out in the sun so late. She sat listening: then she got a curious feeling that something was happening at the house; and stood up quickly and walked away towards it.

As she passed the dining-room window, whose lower edge was on a level with her chin, she looked in. Her father was gone; but his glasses and his open book still lay on the table. Rebekah walked round to the kitchen door. Even the ducks were gone; no one was in the kitchen, only the flames were leaping up and crackling in the open fireplace, and the water was spluttering out of the mouth of the big black kettle. She stood for a moment to watch it. Then a sound struck her ear. She walked with quick sharp steps into the dining room, and threw her kappie on the table, and stood listening. Again the sound came, faint, and strange. She walked out into the long passage into which all the bedrooms opened. Suddenly the sound became loud and clear from her mother's bedroom. Rebekah walked quickly up the coconut-matted passage, and knocked at her mother's door, three short, sharp knocks with her knuckle. There was a noise of moving and talking inside; then the door opened a little.

'I want to come in!—Please, what is the matter?'

Someone said, 'Shall she come in?' and then a faint voice answered, 'Yes, let her come.'

Rebekah walked in; there was but a little light* coming in under the blind through the slightly opened window. Her mother was lying in the large bed and her father standing at the bedside. A strange woman from the next farm, whom she had never seen before, sat in the elbow chair in the corner beyond the bed, with something on her lap; old Ayah stood near the drawers, folding some linen cloths.

Rebekah stood for a moment, motionless and hesitating, on the ox skin in the middle of the floor; then she walked straight up to the strange woman in the corner.

'Ask her to show you what she has got, Rebekah,' said her father.

The woman unfolded a large brown shawl, inside of which there was a white one. Even in the dim light in the corner you could see a little red face, with two hands doubled up on the chest, peeping out from it.

Rebekah looked.

'Was it *this* that made that noise?' she asked.

The woman smiled and nodded.

Her father came up.

'Kiss it, Rebekah; it is your little sister.'

Rebekah looked quietly at it.

'No—I won't—I don't like it,' she said slowly.

But her father had already moved across the room to speak to old Ayah.

Rebekah turned sharply on her heel and walked to the large bed. Her mother lay on it with her eyes shut. Rebekah stood at the foot, her eyes on a level with the white coverlet, looking at her mother.

As she stood there she heard old Ayah whisper to the father, and they both went out to the spare bedroom opposite. The strange woman came and bent over the mother, and said something to her: she nodded her head without opening her eyes. The woman made a space at her side, and laid the white bundle down in it; she put the baby's head on the mother's arm. The mother opened her eyes then, and looked down at it with a half smile; and drew the quilt up a little higher to shield it. Rebekah watched them; then she walked softly to the door.

'Please open it for me,' she said. The handle was too high for her.

The woman let her out.

For a moment she stood outside the closed door looking at it, her tiny features curiously set almost with the firmness of a woman's; then she turned and walked down the passage. She saw her father and old Ayah come out of the spare room. Old Ayah locked the door and put the key into her pocket, and they went back to her mother's bedroom.

Rebekah picked up her kappie from the dining-room table, put it on, and went out again onto the steps at the kitchen door. The sun was blazing in the yard now, the very stones seemed to throw up a red reflection. Standing on the top step in the shade, Rebekah shivered with heat.

Then she wandered slowly down the steps and across the yard. She could feel the ground burn under her feet, through the soles of her little shoes. She walked to her flat stone. The mouse house stood baking in the sun with all the little crystals in the rock glittering. She sat down before the house, drawing her skirts carefully under her, the rock burned so. She drew her knees up to her chin, and folded her arms about them, and sat looking at the mouse house. She knew she ought not to be there in the hot sun; she knew it was wicked; but she liked the heat to burn her that morning.

After a while the little drops of perspiration began to gather under her eyes and on her upper lip; she would not wipe them off. Her face began to get very red, and her temples to throb; the heat was fierce. She looked out at the mouse house from under her white kappie with blinking red eyes. She could feel the heat scorching her arms through her little cotton dress, and she liked it.

By half past eleven the heat was so intense she could not bear it, and there began to be a sound like a little cicada singing in her ears:

so she got up, and walked slowly towards the house; but did not go in at the kitchen door.

She went to the back, where the wall of the house made a deep shadow, and went to the window of the spare room. It was her favourite place, to which she went whenever she wanted to be quite safe and alone. No one ever went there. The beds were generally left unmade till visitors came, with only the mattresses and pillows on them, and under one bed she kept her box of specially prized playthings. She unclosed the outer shutters. The window was so low that she could easily raise the sash and climb in from the ground. She pushed it up, and stepped into the room. It was beautifully cool there and almost dark: she drew up the blind a very little to let in some light. She was walking towards the bed under which her box was, when something struck her eye. On the large table in the middle of the room there was a something with a white sheet spread over it. Rebekah walked up to it: this was something quite new.

She drew a chair to the side of the table and climbed up. She lifted the top of the sheet. Under it there was another sheet and a pillow; and, with its head on the pillow, dressed in pure white, was a little baby. Rebekah stood upright on the chair, holding the sheet in her hand.

After a while she let it down carefully, but so turning it back that the baby's face and hand were exposed. How fast it was sleeping!

She bent down and peered into its face. There was a curious resemblance between her own small, sharply marked features and those of the baby. She put out her forefinger gently and touched one of its hands. They were very cool. She watched it for some time; then she climbed down and went to the wardrobe where the best going-to-town clothes were kept hanging. With some difficulty she unhooked a little fur-trimmed red cape of her own; with this she climbed back onto the chair and laid it across the baby's feet. It was evidently not warm enough, though the day was hot.

She bent down over it again. On the top of its head was a little mass of soft, down-like curly black hair; she put her face down softly and touched the hair with her cheek and kissed it. She dared not kiss its face for fear of waking it. She sat down beside it, motionless, for a long time, on the edge of the table. Seeing it did not stir, after a time she climbed down, and taking off her shoes and leaving them at the foot of the table, went on tiptoe to the bed, and drew from under it her box.

It was a large soap box with an odd collection of things in it. On the top was a dried monkey's skin and a large alphabet book with coloured pictures; below were different little boxes and bags; some held stones; one was full of brightly coloured beetles and grasshoppers she had picked up dead; in one, all by itself, was a very large bright crystal, carefully wrapped in cottonwool and tied with a string. Below was an oblong-shaped, common brown stone about eighteen inches in length; it was dressed in doll's clothes and it had a shawl wrapped round it. Beside it was a small shop doll with pink cheeks and flaxen hair, which she had got on her last birthday; but it had no shawl and its face was turned to the wood. The stone she had had two years, and she loved it; the shop doll was only interesting. Besides these there was a round Bushman* stone with a hole in the middle, which she had picked up behind the kraal, and a flat, slate-coloured stone with the impression of a fossilised leaf,* which she found on the path going up to the mountain; and, at the very bottom in the corner, was a work-box, with a silver thimble and needles and cottons inside, which she thought very grand; and two little brightly coloured boxes with chocolates and peppermints with holes through them like whistles, which she had got on Christmas Day, but thought too pretty to eat; and there was also a head of Queen Victoria, cut out of the tinsel label of a sardine tin, and which she kept wrapped up in white paper.

She took all the things out of the box and handled them carefully, deliberating for a while. At last she selected the alphabet book, the Bushman stone, the silver thimble and a paper of needles, Queen Victoria's head, and a stick of chocolate. When she had packed the other things back, she went with them to the table. She climbed up on the chair. She laid the thimble and paper of needles on the cushion on the left of the baby's head, and the Bushman stone and the tinsel Queen Victoria head on the right. Very gently and slowly she slipped the alphabet book under the baby's doubled-up arm; and then, turning back the silver paper at one end of the chocolate stick, she forced the other end very gently into its closed fist, leaving the uncovered end near to its mouth. Then she stood upright on the chair with her hands folded before her, looking down at them all, with a curious contentment about her mouth.

After a little time she got down and went to her box at the foot of the bed, and sat down upon it; to wait till the baby woke.

Her face was seamed under the eyes with lines hot perspiration and dust had left, and she was very tired. She leaned her arm on the bed and rested her head on it.

At half past one it was dinner time, and old Ayah could not find her. She often crept in the heat of the day behind the piano or into the wagon loft, and fell asleep there where no one could discover her. So old Ayah put some dinner for her in a tin plate in the oven to keep warm.

Then everyone went to lie down; the shutters of all the doors and windows were closed, and there was not a sound in all the house but the buzzing of the flies in the darkened rooms.

Only old Ayah did not sleep today, and was sewing a piece of white calico into a long, narrow, white robe with a stiff frill down the front for a tiny baby. She sat working in the dining room with the shutters very slightly apart to let in enough light.

When she had done it she went down the passage to the door of the spare room and unlocked it.

The first thing she noticed was that the outer shutters she had left carefully closed were partly open, that the window had been raised, and the blind was an inch or two drawn up. She walked to the table. The baby lay with the sheet removed from its face, and the Bushman stone, and thimble, and needles, and picture, on its pillow, and the alphabet book under its arm, and the chocolate stick in its hand. She glanced round. Rebekah was still sitting on her box at the foot of the bed with her stockinged feet crossed and her head resting on her arm on the mattress, fast asleep, her shoes standing side by side at the foot of the table.

Old Ayah walked up to her and shook her by the shoulder. Rebekah opened her eyes slowly and looked at her dreamily, without raising her head.

'What are you doing in here? Couldn't you see, if the door was locked, that you weren't meant to get in here?' she said in the Cape Dutch she always spoke.

Rebekah sat up, still looking round vacantly; then in an instant all came back to her, and she stood up.

'Aren't you a wicked, naughty child, letting all the flies and the sun come in! What have you been doing?'

'Oh, please don't talk so loud,' whispered Rebekah, quickly, bending forward and stretching out her hand; 'please, you'll wake it!'

'O Lord!'* said old Ayah, looking at her, 'what would your mother say if she knew you'd been in here playing with that blessed baby! You naughty child, how dared you touch it!'

'It's mine: *I* found it!' said Rebekah, walking softly up to the foot of the table.

Old Ayah came up too.

'Oh, please,' said Rebekah, putting out her hand again. '*Don't* touch it. Don't touch it! I *don't* want it waked!'

She looked up at old Ayah with full lustrous eyes, as a bitch looks when you handle her pups.

'O my God!'* said old Ayah, 'the child is mad! How can it be yours? It's your mother's.'

'It is mine,' said Rebekah slowly; 'I found it. Mietje found hers in the hut, and Katje* found hers behind the kraal. My mother found hers that cries so, in the bedroom. *This one*, is mine!'

'O Lord, Lord!' cried old Ayah. 'I tell you this is your mother's baby; she had two, and this one is dead. I put it here myself.'

Rebekah looked at her.

'This one is dead: it'll never open its eyes again; it can't breathe.'

The old Hottentot woman began taking the alphabet book from under its arm and the stick from its hand, and took the things from the pillow.

Rebekah did not look at her; her gaze was fixed on the baby's face.

'Here, take these things!'

But Rebekah raised her hand, and touched the baby's feet; a coldness went up her arm, even through the sheet. She dropped her hand.

'Child, what is it? —Here!—Take your shoes!'

She thrust the shoes into her hand. Rebekah held them, but let them slide between her fingers onto the floor; she was still staring at the table.

Old Ayah gathered up the child's apron and put into it the things she had taken from the baby, and forced the shoes back into her other hand.

'Here, take them, I say; and go away! And get your face washed and your hair done; and tell Mietje to put you on a clean dress* and white pinafore. What would your mother say to see you looking such an ugly, dirty little fright!'

Rebekah turned away slowly, with the gathered apron in one hand and the shoes in the other, and walked to the door; when she got there she turned and looked dreamily back; then she went out into the passage.

After she had had her face washed and her hair brushed, and had got on a clean starched pink dress and a white overall pinafore, she went to the dining room. Old Ayah had put her plate of warmed dinner on the table ready for her, and she sat down on the bench to eat it. She felt better now she was washed and had a clean starched dress on.

The heat outside was still very oppressive, and only a little light came in through the cracks in the shutter; and the blue flies* were buzzing round everywhere in the dark. She did not feel very hungry, and played with her dinner; but she drank all the water in her mug. Then she pushed her plate from her, found her kappie and went out into the great front room. All was quiet there also, and almost quite dark. She took a large worn picture book from the side table, and opened the double door and went out onto the front stoep.* The vine leaves on the front wall hung dry and stiff, and even the orange leaves on the great orange trees before the door hung curled and flaccid.

It was nearly three o'clock, and the heat was hardly less intense than at midday, though there was already shade on that side of the house. The hollyhocks and dahlias in the flower garden beyond the orange trees were hanging their heads, and the four-o'clocks* were curled up tight, though the trees sheltered them.

She walked down through the flower garden, on, into the orchard beyond.

All was very still and brown there also. The little peach trees that stood in rows were shedding their half-ripe fruit, which fell into the long yellow grass beneath them, and the fig trees along the wall had curled up the edges of their leaves. Rebekah followed a little winding footpath among the grass to the middle of the orchard, where a large pear tree stood, with a gnarled and knotted stem. There was a bench under the tree, and the grass grew very long all about it. She looked around to find a spot where the tree cast a deeper shade than elsewhere. Here she walked round and round on the grass, like a dog, and then lay down on her back in the place she had made. It was like a nest, with the grass standing several inches high all round.

She drew up her legs, cocking one knee over the other, so that one foot waved in the air.

It was very nice. She lay for a while with her hands clasped across the top of her head, from which she had thrown her white kappie. The pear leaves were so thick overhead you could hardly see any sky through them. She yawned luxuriously. Beyond the edges of the pear branches, here and there as you looked through half-closed eyes, were strips of blue sky, and some great white masses of thundercloud were showing in them, like ships sailing in the blue. She watched them for a while with her eyes half shut; then she took up the book that lay on the grass at her side, stood it open on her chest against her knee, and gently waved the foot that was cocked up in the air.

The book opened of itself about the middle at a certain page. On it was a picture: Peter, a great boy with a red face looking out through the top of the letter P, and at his feet was a little pig with a curled tail. Besides this there were in the picture, in the distance, fields and a stile, and a winding path leading far away over the hills: and in the foreground was a milestone with weeds growing around it: below was written, '**P** stands for Peter and Pig.'

She had had the book ever since she could remember; she had kept it very clean, there was no torn place or mark in it; but the page of *Peter and his Pig** was brown and worn round the edges. It was her favourite picture. Whenever she looked at it she wanted to make up stories. She had made one long story about it: how people were not kind to Peter and he had no one to love him but his pig, and how they both ran away together by that far-off road that went over the hill, and saw all the beautiful things on the other side. She liked this book better than her new books. She stood it up on her chest and looked into the picture. But today it had no meaning; it suggested nothing. Then she looked away again beyond the edges of the pear branches, where two great masses of white cloud were floating in the blue; they dazzled her eyes so she closed them.

Presently she made a story that one of those clouds was a ship and she was sailing in it (she had never seen the sea or a ship but she was always making stories about them); and as she sailed, she came at last to an island. The ship stopped there. And on the edge of the shore was a lady standing, dressed in beautiful clothes, all gold and silver. When she stepped onto the shore, the lady came up to her, and bowed to her, and said, 'I am Queen Victoria;* who are you?'

And Rebekah answered her, 'I am the little Queen Victoria of South Africa.'*

And they bowed to each other.

(The child under the tree moved her head very slightly, without opening her eyes.)

The Queen asked her where she came from. She said, 'From a country far away from here; not such a *very* nice country! Things are not always nice there—only sometimes they are.'

The Queen said, 'I have many islands that belong to me: but this island belongs to no one; why don't you come and live here? No one will ever scold you here, and you can do just what you like.'

Rebekah said, 'I should like it very much; but I must first go and fetch my books out of the ship.' And when she had brought her books, she said to the Queen, 'Here is a little box of presents I have got for all the people who live on the farm where I used to live: for my father and my mother and the servants and the little Kaffirs—and even old Ayah.* Would you please give it to them as you go past?' And the Queen said she would; and she said, 'Goodbye, Little Queen Victoria!' And Rebekah said, 'Goodbye, Big Queen Victoria!' and they bowed to each other; and the old Queen went away in the ship in which she had come.

Then she was all alone on her island. (She had never seen an island except a lump of ground in the furrow, with some thyme and forget-me-nots growing on it; but when she grew up she found she had pictured that island just as a real island might have been!) The island had many large trees and bushes, and the grass and thyme and forget-me-nots grew down to the water's edge. She walked a little way, and she came to a river with trees on each side, and on it were two swans swimming, with their long white necks bent. She had had a book with the picture of a swan swimming in a lake, and she had always thought she must die of joy if she should see a real swan swimming up and down; and here were two!

A little further, on the bank of the river, there was a little house standing. It was as high in proportion to her as grown-up people's houses are in proportion to them. The doors were just high enough for her to go in and out at, and all things fitted her. One room was covered with books from the floor to the ceiling, with a little empty shelf for her own books, and there was a microscope on the table like her father's; which she was never allowed to touch; but this one was hers!

Outside, in the garden, there were little rakes and spades that came as high as her shoulder. (Rebekah had always had to dig with a man's spade that made her arms ache.) At the side of the house there were all the things lying one uses for building houses; and a pile of bricks; and a bit of bare ground where you could make as much mud as you liked and make more bricks. But she hadn't time to stay and make bricks then. She went on further.

Presently she came to a place where the trees hung very low down over the water, and the grass was very thick; and there, from a large white bush, hanging right over, and nearly touching the water, she saw a snow-white pod, nearly as long as her arm. It was like a pea pod, but it was covered all over with a white, frosted silver. She reached down over the edge and tried to pick it. It was very heavy; at last she broke it off, and carried it away in her pinafore, and she sat on a bank with it on her lap. She pressed with her finger all up and down the joint, and slowly the pod cracked and cracked, and opened from one end to the other, like a mimosa pod* does.

And there, lying inside it, like the seeds lie inside the pod of a mimosa tree—was a little baby! It was quite pink and naked. It was as long in proportion to her, as a Kaffir woman's new baby is in proportion to a Kaffir woman, when she first finds it. She tried to lift it out: but it was tied to the pod like the mimosa seeds are, with a little curled-up string. She broke the string and lifted it out. Then she wrapped it up in her pinafore and skirt and put its head on her arm and carried it home.

(The book which was still standing up against her knee, here fell over softly into the breast of the child under the pear tree.)

When she got home she fed it with milk from a tiny bottle as one feeds a hand-lamb,* and she wrapped it up in a soft white shawl, and put it on her bed and lay down beside it. She held it close against her with one arm, and stroked its hair softly with the other hand.

'Go to sleep, my baby,' she said, 'you must be very tired this first day. The world is so large. Tomorrow you can see all the things, and I'll tell you about them.

'If you should wake in the night, my baby,' she said presently, 'and hear anything, don't be afraid: just call to me. I'll be close by. And, if you hear the clock ticking, *don't* think it means any of those dreadful things—it doesn't! I'll stop it if it makes you sad. And, if you want to see the angels, then just shut your eyes and press on them *hard* with your two fingers, like this—' (the child under the tree moved her hand as though to raise it to her eyes, but did not). 'Those black things with the light all round which you see going round and round when you press your eyes, are the angels' heads; just like it says in the hymn:

"And through the hours of darkness keep
Their watch around my bed."*

They are good angels, though they are black in the middle. I always used to see them when I was a little girl and I pressed my eyes. I'll put a chocolate stick under your pillow, that you can find it and suck it if you feel lonely. *Don't* be sorry you are come into the world, my baby. *I* will take care of you!'

She was going to rise from the bed, then she remembered other things that had to be said, and lay down again.

'When you are grown older, I'll teach you the multiplication table and spelling, because you can't grow up if you don't know these things. I know how bad it is to learn them; I had to when I was little, and so at last I grew up.

'Kaffirs grow up without learning tables or spelling; that's why it would be nice to be a Kaffir. If you've something hard to learn, pray God to help you: sometimes he does and sometimes he doesn't. If he doesn't, it's because you've prayed wrong; but it's no use praying again on that same day, especially if it's hot—wait till the next.'

Again there was a long pause.

'My baby, I shall *never* call *you* "a strange child"! You can climb trees and tear your clothes; but, if you find any birds' nests, you mustn't take the eggs; you can just put your hand in and feel; and if it's a very little nest you must only put one finger in. Especially cock-o-veet's* eggs you must *not* take! Kaffir boys take birds' eggs.'

Again there was a pause.

'My baby, shall I tell you a little story? It's one I made myself, and a rather nice little story:

'Once there was a little girl, and she went for a walk in the bush. And when she had gone a little way, a cock-o-veet came flying up to her and took hold of her pinafore by the corner with its beak. And the little girl said, "Cock-o-veet, dear, what is it?"

'And the cock-o-veet said, "Make your hand like a little round nest."

'So she made it so—so!'* (The child as she lay under the tree with her closed eyes drew the fingers of her right hand together and made a hollow.)

'And the cock-o-veet sat down in her hand; and when it got up, there—was—a little—real—blue—egg—lying there!

'And the little girl said, "O cock-o-veet!"*

'And the cock-o-veet said, "Put the egg in my nest, and I will sit on it and make a little bird come out, for you!" And the cock-o-veet showed the little girl where her nest was; and she put the egg in; and the cock-o-veet sat down on it, and said, "Goodbye; I'll call you when it comes out."

'And when she had gone further, she saw some monkeys sitting in the high trees, little long-tail monkeys;* and they put their hands out to her. And she looked up and said, "O little monkeys, what do you want?"

'And they said, "Come up in the trees and have tea with us."

'And she said, "What kind of tea do you have, O monkeys?"

'And they said, "Nam-nams* and Kaffir plums."*

'So she climbed up and sat with them on a branch, and they gave her of* their nam-nams and Kaffir plums with their little black hands, and she gave them some cakes out of a little bag she had with her.

'And when they had finished the monkeys kissed her, and she kissed them, and she climbed down and went on.

'And presently she came to a place where some very large rocks were lying deep in the bush, and the trees were hanging over them, and it was dark under the rock. And the little girl thought it looked rather like a tiger's* sleeping place!

'And when she looked under the rock, there *was* a great tiger lying! And she said, "O tiger!"

'And the tiger winked with his eyes*—so!

'And she said, "I'm rather frightened of you, Mr Tiger!"

'But the tiger said, "Come here!"

'So she came.

'And the tiger said, "You can just play being my cub if you like!"

'So she lay down by the tiger, and the tiger rolled her over and made believe to bite her.

'And the tiger said, "Cubbie, would you like to sleep a little? You look rather tired." And he made a place for her between his front legs, where she could lie down with her head on his side, and it was nice and soft.

'And the tiger said, "If the flies trouble you, I'll just switch them away with my tail!"

'And the little girl said, "I'll just leave my little bag of cakes open so that if you like you can help yourself while I'm asleep."

'And she went to sleep on the tiger. And when she woke the tiger licked all over her face and said, "Goodbye"; and she went on.

'And by and by, as she was going up a very steep road right up on the mountain, there was a lion standing right before her.

'And the little girl said, "O Mr Lion!"

'And he said, "Come up to me!"

'So she came up; and he rubbed his head against her pinafore and she rubbed her head in his stiff curls.

'And the lion said, "Aren't you afraid to come walking in the bush alone?"

'And she said, "Oh no!"

'And he yawned.

'And she said, "Don't you open your mouth so *very* wide, please! It's so *very* big!"

'And he said, "I'm only yawning a little; it's nothing."

'And the little girl gave him some of her cakes. She said, "I've made them myself."

'He licked his mouth and said they were nice cakes; and he said he would walk home with her. She said there was no need, because perhaps the people at the farmhouse mightn't quite like it; but that if ever he had a thorn in his foot he must just let her know and she'd take it out. He said he hadn't a thorn just then, but he'd let her know when he had. So they rubbed their heads against each other, and she went away.'

(The mouth of the child under the tree was drawn in at the corners as if half smiling, a quiet smile.)

'Then the little girl went down the mountain and into her father's garden. And, just as she was going in at the gate under the dam wall, she heard something go puff—puff—puff! And she looked round, and, there, just by her,* was a great puff-adder sitting up! And she said, "O Puff-puffie!"

'And the puff-adder said, "Come with me, my dear!"

'And the little girl said, "But Puff-puffie, I'm rather afraid!"

'And the puff-adder said, "Don't be, my dear; *I* never bite little girls!" And she took the little girl to a hole in the wall, where all her little puff-adders were. And she said, "You can put your hand in and take a few out. They've all got little poison bags, but they don't use them. They only eat grass and sand; and they like a little drop of milk now and then when they can get it."

'And the little girl put her hand in and took out the little puff-adders, till her pinafore was full.

'And she said, "I shall not forget to bring them a little drop of milk when I have any!" And she put them back in the hole, and she wished good afternoon to the puff-adder, and the puff-adder wished her good afternoon and went to sleep under a stone.

'And then the little girl went down further in the garden; and she hadn't gone very far when she saw a great cobra lying on the grass, with his bright eyes looking at her.

'And she said, "O Mr Cobra!"

'And he said, "Good afternoon, my dear. Won't you take me on your lap and warm me a little? I'm so cold today!"

'So she held out her pinafore and the cobra climbed in: he made her pinafore quite full. And she walked to the sod wall with him and sat down on the top, where the sun could shine on him, and she sang to the cobra; and he went to sleep in her lap. And that's the end of the story.'

(The child under the tree seemed to be dropping asleep also; her lips had ceased to move, and her breath came evenly, but her mind went on.)

'You know that's only a story, my baby. You can't really go into the bush and do so with all the animals. They don't understand—yet. Perhaps, if you could talk to them—from a long way off—so that they knew what you meant?—My father brought a tiger down from the bush once, that they caught with* a trap. I was sorry for him because he was shut up in a cage, and looked so sad. So I saved my meat for him at dinner, and I took it out to him when the others were asleep; his eyes were quite nearly shut and his head was on his feet. But just when I put my hand in with the meat he jumped up; he tried to bite me. I didn't tell anyone.

'Only dogs understand. If a great dog comes at you, my baby, don't you run away. Just say, "Sibby! Sibby! Sibby!" and make—so*—with your fingers; say, "P-o-o-r dog, *p-o-o-r*, P-O-O-R little Sibby!" Even if he's big, you can say "little"; dogs always like to be called "little". Even if he's got his mouth on a side—so—and you can see his one tooth, don't be afraid: just stand and talk to him. He'll understand. But other things don't. The best thing is to feed them.

'My baby, was it a nice little story I've told you? If I tell you a secret, you mustn't tell anyone else! I'm a person that makes stories! I write *books*! When I was little I used to scribble them in a copybook with a stick, when I didn't know how to write. But when I grew up I learnt to write—I wrote real books, a whole room full! I've written a book about birds, and about animals, and about the world; and one day I'm going to write a book something like the Bible. If you like to make up stories, I shall never let anyone laugh at *you*, when you walk up and down and talk to yourself. I know you *must*.

'There are some stories I didn't make that I like too. There's one I like best of all. Shall I tell it you?'

(The child under the tree moved her arms a little as if drawing something closer to her.)

'It's rather a hard story because it's a grown-up people's story; I heard it one Sunday afternoon; my father read it to my mother. They thought I couldn't understand, but I did. I don't know if I tell it right, because I only heard it once, but I often looked at the picture. I'll make it as easy as I can.

'You see, it's called *What Hester Durham Lived For*.* Hester Durham was a woman, and she sat by the table talking; and the Minister came and talked with her. And she said, "Oh, I wish I was dead! My husband isn't very kind to me, and my boy, whom I loved so much, is dead; and now I wish I was dead too."

'And the Clergyman (that is a Minister) said to her, "Oh, you mustn't say that; perhaps one day you'll have something to do for someone."

'And so, the lady went away to India—that's a land far away where black people live—and the black soldiers (they call them Sepoys*) wanted to kill them. They came all round the house, calling and yelling, with swords and sticks. They were only women and children there; and all of them were very frightened; even the old black Ayah. But Hester Durham was not afraid. In the picture* they are all standing round her and some of them have caught hold of her dress, and some are lying on the ground close to her; and you can see the men's faces outside, with their eyes very big, wanting to come in and kill them all, and their mouths open, screaming! Then it says in the book: "*Alone, like a rock in a raging sea, Hester Durham stood there.*"* They hadn't been *so* afraid, because she was there to comfort them. And at last the Sepoys did come in, and killed them all; but—"*to comfort* *those frail women and children in their last hour of despair, that was what Hester Durham lived for*"—those are the words I heard my father read.It's rather a difficult story; but you'll know what it means when you're grown up, when you are five years old—I did—though it is difficult.

'I can teach you many things, my baby; poems; there's a nice one:

"The Assyrian came down—"*

'And another:

"Like mist on the mountains,
Like ships on the sea—"*

'But the nicest of all is about a woman. The Romans came and they took away her country and they beat her till the blood ran off her back onto the ground, and they were cruel to her daughters. The Romans were people who took other people's countries; and she got into a chariot and her two daughters and her long hair flying in the wind; and under the tree sat an old man with a long white beard; and he said:

"Rome shall perish; write that word
In the blood that she hath spilt—" '*

(The child under the pear tree with her eyes still fast closed raised her right hand, and her lips moved making a low sound.)

' "Rome, for Empire far renown
Tramps on a thousand States;
Soon her pride shall kiss the ground:
Hark!—The Gaul is at her gates!" '*

(The child under the tree lifted her hand higher and waved it dramatically with her eyes still closed.)

'And the Gauls did come; and they knocked at the gates, and they burned it down. "Hark!—The Gaul is at her gates!"—I'm glad they burned it, aren't you?'

(The child's hand dropped.)

'It's a long poem. I'll teach it you. I could understand it all, except "For-Empire" and "far-renown"—I don't know what "far-renown" is—or "for-Empire—" '

(The child under the tree knit her forehead a little.)

'Grown-up people's things are nicer than children's. I didn't like Jane Taylor's *Hymns for Infant Minds.** You'll never have to learn them. The Bible is nice, especially about Elijah,* and some texts; one beautiful one: "And instead of the thorn tree shall come up the fir tree; and instead of the briar shall come up the myrtle tree."* It's just like water going—so—! But Miss Plumtree's Bible stories* are horrid! My mother used to read them to me.'

(The child under the tree turned her head a little to one side and bent it, as though bringing it nearer to something that lay on her arm.)

'My baby, do you know who Charles is?—He's the boy who always plays with me. You won't mind if I love him more than you, because I've known him so very long. He always tells me stories, and I tell him stories, and we walk up and down together. He's a little older than me. He's not a *real* boy, you know! I made him up. He is the Prince Consort of South Africa, and I am the Queen.

'I don't like *real* boys. We had two came to visit us once:* they were my cousins: Frank was the biggest. Before they came I meant to play with them and show them all my things; but afterwards I didn't: I wouldn't even show them my flat stone. Frank laughed at me and called me "Goody-no-shoes."* Well, I didn't mind that so much, it's not so bad as to be called a "Tom-boy,"* or "a strange child!"—but he was so unkind to the cat! He held her up by her tail. I don't like cats, they eat birds; but you can't do *that* to them! He used to come after me when I wanted to be alone, and say, "Ha, ha, Miss! I've found you!" and he said I'd have to marry him when I grew up—but I said I never would.'

She paused for a long while.

'I liked him better than John-Ferdinand—that was his brother. One day John-Ferdinand saw the little Kaffir maid break the churn stick, and he went and told old Ayah; and old Ayah beat her. Frank and I saw it too, but we didn't say anything. Frank said I ought to say to him:

"You tell tale tit,
Your tongue shall be slit,
And every dog in the town
Shall have a little bit!"*

'It wasn't such a very nice little poem; my mother said I mustn't say it up.* I just tell you what Frank said. He knew many other little poems:

"Four and twenty tailors
Went to catch a snail"*

'and

"Boobee-Boobee! Black-face!"

'They are not such very nice poems; but rather funny; and you can say them up if you like, I won't mind. He could make wagons—but I was glad when they went away. I don't like live boys: they are something like Kaffirs. Jan married Mietje our Kaffir maid, and he used to beat her. I'm glad I'm not a Kaffir man's wife.

'My baby, I'm so glad you are a little girl. I'll make you a pair of thick trousers to climb trees in; these white ones tear so when you slide down, and then the people call you "Tom-boy".

'Now put your arms tight round Mother's neck, and hold Mother tight.'

(The child under the tree turned yet slightly more onto her side and moved her left arm as though she were drawing something nearer to her.)

'Mother will tell you just one little story before you go to sleep, a very easy one.

'Once there was a little blue egg in a nest, and the mother bird sat on it. And one day out came a bird; it had no feathers and its eyes were shut, and the mother bird sat on it. By and by the feathers began to come and the eyes opened. And one night, when the mother bird was fast asleep in the nest and the little bird was under her, it put out its head from under the mother's wing and looked. And what do you think it saw?—It saw all the stars shining!—And it sat up and looked at them!

'That's the end of the story.' She paused for a while.

(The child under the tree knit her brows a little, and her hand moved softly up and down on her bosom.)

'My baby, I'm so sorry I have to give you food out of a bottle—Kaffir women have milk for their babies—and cows and sheep too—but I am like the birds.'

(She moved her hand over her little flat breast.)

'I'm so sorry. Now go to sleep, my baby.* Put your arms round Mother's neck. You must always try to be a good little girl: I always did when I was little—at least—I didn't always—but you must, please. Now go to sleep. Mother will sing you a little song.'

(The child under the tree made a queer piping little sound in her throat, and half-formed words came from her lips.)

'London's burning!
London's burning!
Fire! Fire!
Bring some water! Bring some water!
London's burning!
London's burning!'*

(The song died away, and the child under the tree lay quite motionless; but her dream still went on.)

She thought when the baby had gone to sleep that she got softly off the bed and went out. The evening air was blowing over the island, and it was near sunset. She went to the side of the house where the building materials lay. She was going to build a playroom for the baby. She rolled up her sleeves and dug a foundation and filled it with stones. (She had seen the workmen build the wagon house.) Then she mixed mud, and took off her shoes and socks, and danced in it. (She had seen the Kaffirs treading the mud to build the wagon house, but she had never been allowed to help.) Then she began to build. She took the bricks in one hand and the trowel in the other; she threw the bricks round in one hand and cut off the rough points with the trowel, as the workmen did. Then she placed each brick carefully on the layer of mortar, and tap-tapped them with the end of the handle of the trowel to see if they were quite straight.

When the little wall was two layers high, she looked round. The sun was setting on the island, and over the trees a strange soft evening light shone. There was a pink glow in the sky, and it reflected itself on everything. She stood perfectly still, holding the trowel in her hand, and looked at it. The swans were swimming up and down in the quiet water, far away, with their necks bent; they left a long snow-white mark in the water, like the swans in the picture.

'The swan swam in a silvery lake.
Well swam the swan!'*

A spasm of delight thrilled up the spine of the child under the pear tree. When a full-grown woman, long years afterwards, she could always recall that island, the little house, the bricks, the wonderful light over earth and sky and the swans swimming on the still water.*

After a time she half opened her eyes and looked up. Above her was the pear tree, with its stiff branches and dull green leaves. Slowly she raised herself into a sitting posture and looked round.

All about lay the parched yellow grass, and the little dried peach trees, with their shrivelled leaves and drooping yellow peaches. Everything was brown and dry; she stretched herself and yawned.

Then she stood up. Suddenly she saw a herd of little pigs a short way off, feeding under the peach trees. They had got in through a hole in the wall and were eating the fallen fruit among the grass. They would soon make their way up to the flower garden.

With a shout and whoop she rushed off after them, waving her kappie at them by one string. The little pigs squeaked and grunted and scattered in all directions. She chased them till she had got them in a herd all together, and drove them out through one of the gaps in the sod wall. Then she stood on the wall and shouted frantically after them, still waving her kappie, though they were all running as fast as they could, with their little curled-up tails. She stood on the wall and waved till they disappeared behind the kraals.

The severest heat of the afternoon was now past, and there was a certain mellow haziness beginning to creep into the afternoon air. She shaded her eyes with her hand and looked away over the flat below the homestead, where the thorn trees grew. There seemed a kind of soft, yellow, transparent veil over it all; and there were little gnats in the air. Presently, as she stood dreamily gazing, she saw some figures moving far away in the flat below the house, near the great dam with the willow trees. The foremost figure carried something on its shoulders; it looked like Long Jan* the Kaffir: then came her father, and then two Kaffir boys with something over their shoulders that looked like spades. She could not see well; they were so far away and the soft yellow haze made things dreamy. They passed through the new lands;* and then they went out of sight, behind the great willow trees round the dam.

She stood still, looking out at them very drowsily; thinking of nothing in particular, and hardly noting them.

Suddenly a small shrill voice called from the back steps of the house, 'Get down from that wall, child, will you! Standing there with nothing on your head! You'll be burned as black as a Kaffir* before your mother gets up. Put your kappie on!'

It was old Ayah, who had come to the back door to throw water into the pigs' wash.

Rebekah climbed from the wall on the garden side, and walked away; but she did not put her kappie on: she tied it round her waist by its long strings, and walked back to the pear tree. Everything seemed a little bald and empty; she had no wish to make more stories, and there was nothing to do. It seemed to her all at once that it was a very long afternoon. Then there came back to her the picture of her mother lying in the bed with the baby's head on her arm, which she had been trying to put from her all day. She saw the embroidered wrist of her mother's nightdress; and she saw her mother drawing up the cover to shield the baby's head. She tried to think of something else.

There was a strange little blind footpath among the grass under the pear tree on the left side. It was a few feet long, trodden hard and flat, and led to nothing. She had made it by walking up and down there when she and Charles made stories and talked.

She began to walk up and down on it now, rather dragging her feet. By and by she and Charles began to talk; she talked in a quite audible voice, now for Charles, and then for herself. They told each other no stories, but they began to discuss a little about the house of stramonium* stalks they were going to build; he said what he thought was the best way of making the roof would be with stramonium branches,* she said she thought peach branches would be stronger and better. But neither had much of interest to say that afternoon.

It began to get cooler now. The large white butterflies that had sat with folded wings during the great heat were beginning to hover over the brown grass; and there was a faint movement in the air, which showed that the evening cool was going to begin.

Then, as she walked, her eye caught sight of a white ball sticking on the bark of the pear tree. She walked round to the stem to look at it, and broke a bit of dry bark off to get it out. It was a soft fluffy ball. She put it on the ground, and opened it carefully with two sticks, bending over it, her knees drawn up almost to her chest, and all her little white knickerbockers showing. Inside of it were little grey things that looked like tiny spiders' eggs. She examined it carefully and long, sticking her under lip out over the upper. It was very curious. She was going to examine it more closely, when she caught sight of a row of black ants walking across her own footpath, like a file of little soldiers, one after the other; each one had a pink egg in its mandibles: a few inches further was another line of little black ants returning across the footpath, probably to fetch more of the eggs which were in some nest hidden in the grass. She wheeled round, still on her heels, with a hand on each knee to balance herself, and watched them closely. Presently a huge ant, like those running up and down the stem of the pear tree, dashed into the path from the grass and seized one of the tiny ants that were carrying the eggs. The ant dropped the egg. The large ant held it exactly in the middle with its large nippers. In an instant she started up, drew her lips tighter, and seized a stick of straw, and tried to divide them; but the large one held so tightly she found she would crush both. She took two withered leaves and softly tried to separate them. The large one caught the leaf with its nippers and the small one got free; it ran away to look for its dropped egg. The large one was clinging angrily to the leaf, and trying to bite it. She bent intently over it, watching it.

Suddenly she looked up: she had a curious feeling that someone was looking at her! She looked round and up into the pear tree, still balancing herself carefully in her half-sitting position; there was nothing there but the green dried leaves, and all about nothing but the long brown grass, in some places partly trodden down, in others still standing upright.

She looked back at the ants. Then she glanced round again inquiringly. Two feet from the round spot in the grass which she had trodden down to lie in, was the head of a large yellow cobra. Most of its body was hidden in the grass; but its head was out: and it was watching her. It was the colour of the grass, pale yellow with brown marks. Had it been there all the afternoon? She stood softly upright and stared at it. It looked at her with its glittering unblinking eyes. Then it began to move. Krinkle! krinkle! krinkle!* It drew its long body out over the grass, with a sound like a lady walking in a stiff starched print dress. She gazed at it in fixed horror, motionless.

She was not afraid of snakes. When she was three years old she had carried one home in her pinafore, as a great treasure, and been punished for doing so. Since she understood what they were, she was not afraid of them, but they had become a nightmare to her. They spoiled her world. Krinkle, krinkle, krinkle!—it moved away over the grass towards a hole in the sod wall, winding its long six feet of body after it.

She seized her book and ran up the path through the orchard. According to rule, she should have gone to the house and called people* to look for it and kill it. But she ran quickly through the flower garden and up the steps onto the front stoep; then she stood still. Her heart was beating so she could hear it;* she had a sense of an abandoned wickedness somewhere—it was almost as if *she herself* were a snake, and had gone krinkle! krinkle! krinkle! over the grass. She had a sense of all the world being abandonedly wicked; and a pain in her left side. When her heart had stopped throbbing quite so loud, she opened the door slowly and went into the large front room.

No one had remembered to open the shutters that afternoon though it was almost sunset; it was dusky in the room even with the door open. On the wall hung two great framed pictures of Queen Victoria and the Prince Consort,* in regal dress. She always played the Queen was herself, and the Prince, Charles; and once, when no one was about, she had put a chair on the side table and climbed up onto it, and kissed her own hand, and put it high up where she could touch Charles' face with it.

But tonight she did not look at them. The chair in which her mother always sat stood empty beside the little work table, and the footstool before it was covered with dust. She opened the drawer of the table and took out a calico duster, and carefully dusted the chair and stool. When she had put the duster back, she opened another drawer and took out a spelling book. She drew her own little square wooden footstool between her mother's chair and the open door and sat down on it, with her spelling book in her hand. She began to learn a short column of spelling which she should have learnt in the morning. She held up the book before her so that the light from the door might fall on the page, and spelt out—

'T-h-e-i-r—their.'

She repeated it a few score of times; then she went on to—

'T-h-o-s-e—those'

—and then turned to her multiplication table. It was printed on the cover of the book. She was learning six-times. She repeated slowly over and over to herself:

'Six times six is—thirty-six,
And six times six is—thirty-six.'

The soft, fading evening light was creeping over the orange trees outside the door.

She drawled slower:

'And, six times six is—thirty-six,
And, six times six is—thirty-six,
And, six times six is—thirty-six,
And, six times six—is—thirty-seven,
And, six times six—is—thirty-seven.'

She repeated it slowly about a hundred times, sometimes right, and sometimes wrong, looking out dreamily all the while over the book, through the open door, her mind almost a complete blank; then she paused. In a moment, something had flashed on her! She knew now what those figures had meant which she had seen walking down in the flat in the afternoon when she stood on the sod wall. She knew now what it was Long Jan was carrying; she knew why her father walked behind him, and the two Kaffir boys had spades over their shoulders. In an instant, she knew well, and with an absolute certainty, that if she went down to the great dam behind the willow trees beyond the new lands, she would find there a little mound of earth, and that the baby from the spare room would be under it. All day she had not let herself think of that baby since old Ayah had driven her out of the room. She knew, also, something else; she knew at that moment—vaguely, but quite certainly—something of what birth and death mean, which she had not known before. She would never again look for a new little baby, or expect to find it anywhere; vaguely but quite certainly something of its genesis had flashed on her.

She stood up in the quickly darkening room; put her multiplication book back into the drawer, and walked straight to the door that opened into the dining room, and closed it behind her.

In the dining room also it was getting dark now, though it looked towards the west and the window was open, and here also [it] was very quiet. This was generally the noisy time of the day, when there was a stir and a bustle everywhere: her mother was generally giving out rations, and the herds and maids who had come from the huts to fetch their food stood about the storehouse door outside laughing and talking. The Kaffir maids who worked in the house were generally chatting loudly in the kitchen; and the little Kaffirs, who might not approach at any other time, often stood about the kitchen steps waiting for their mothers; and from the milking kraal you could hear the men shouting to the cows and calves, and calling to one another; and the dogs felt the excitement and barked; and above everything could always be heard old Ayah's voice, in a shrill, small key, giving orders everywhere, which no one ever obeyed. But tonight it was all quiet: you could only hear the lowing of the cows and the bleating of the sheep. The men hardly shouted. The rations had been given out early in the morning, and the little Kaffirs had been told not to come about the back door.

Through the great square window the twilight was beginning to come in. She would not go to her mother's room, and she had nowhere else to go. She sat down on a deal bench without a back, that stood against the wall. No one came to light the candles; and you could see the dim outlines of the tall clock in the corner, and the wooden chairs and tables standing out as shadows from the whitewashed walls. Presently, as it grew quite darker, a bat came in at the window and flapped about from side to side, and went out again. Then the room grew pitch dark. Rebekah drew her legs up under her onto the form, and leaned her head back against the whitewashed wall.

By and by the two Kaffir maids came in from the milk house,* each carrying a bucket of milk. They had a lighted candle. They went through the dining room into the pantry; they were laughing and talking softly; the light from the open pantry door came back into the dining room.

Presently old Ayah came in from the mother's bedroom. 'What are you sitting here all alone in the dark for, child?' she said.

She went into the pantry, and came out with a large basin of bread and milk sop, and a little pannikin of pure milk. She set them down on the side of the table next to the bench with a tallow candle beside them, in a low candlestick.

'Why didn't you eat your dinner, little white face?'

Rebekah sat upright; old Ayah pushed the table a little nearer to her, and she began to eat. She had not known before that she was hungry. Now she ate ravenously and drank at the milk out of her pannikin.

Old Ayah went back into the pantry and scolded the maids in Dutch because the wooden milk pail was leaking. Very soon the maids and old Ayah came back to the dining room, and rested the pail on the end of the dining table to examine what was gone wrong. One of the maids held the lighted candle, while the other was chewing tallow to put in the cracks.

'What's the baby like, old Ayah?' asked the maid holding the light, as old Ayah examined the leak.

'A fine child,' said old Ayah, without looking up. 'She'd make four of *that* child when she was born. Its hands are nearly as large as hers now.'

The maid who was chewing the tallow pressed some down on the open seam. 'Where has *she* been all day?' she asked, nicking her head at Rebekah.

'Oh, God knows!' said old Ayah; 'I've hardly seen her. You might as well try to keep your eye on a meerkat* among its holes as on *that* child.'

They talked of her to her face as if she were a stone wall.

Rebekah kept on eating her supper, gazing straight into her basin, and taking large mouthfuls.

'Look at her now!' said the first Kaffir maid. 'How she eats! She's trying to swallow the spoon!'

'*Zij's een snaakse kind!*'* said old Ayah. ('She's a strange child!')

Rebekah kept on eating steadily and looking into the basin. It hurt her so that they talked of her.

When they had done stopping the hand-pail, the two maids went to the kitchen, and old Ayah went back to the mother's room. Immediately they were gone Rebekah pushed her basin with what was left in it from her, and leaned back on the bench. She drew up one leg, leaned her elbow on the bench and rested her head against the whitewashed wall. She was very tired. She watched the tallow candle fixedly; it was burning up red, and flickering a little, as the moths and night flies that came in through the open window fluttered round it. It seemed so long since she had got up in the morning. It was her bedtime, but no one came to tell her to go to bed.

Then she began to watch the wick of the tallow candle more fixedly as it burned larger and redder. She pressed two of her fingers on her eyes, half closing them; then she saw two candles; she took them away, and there was only one. She wondered how that was, and tried it again. When she moved one finger a little, the one light went up slowly and stood over the other; she moved the other finger and they came so close, they were almost one. She took her hand away and looked at the candle, half closing her eyes; she did not see two candles now, but only four long rays of red light, the two higher ones darker and the two lower lighter. She was slowly getting very interested in it.

She held up her hand and let the light shine through her fingers; the hand made a long dark shadow on the wall to the left of the room.

Why was the shadow so much longer than the hand, she wondered, and why did it fall just where it did? She moved her hand and watched the shadow move. If only one were grown up, one would know all about these things! She dropped her hand on her side. Perhaps, even grown-up people didn't know all. Perhaps only God knew what lights and shadows were!*

She lay still, watching the candle. The wick had burned so long it was beginning to droop and turn over a little on one side. The next morning she would get up early before anyone was up, and begin learning her multiplication table and spelling: perhaps she would know it before evening. She would not play once the whole day, or make up stories. She would learn the whole day. It would all help to make you grow up quickly, and know everything!

It was half past eight now. Her eyelids began to droop; she only kept them open with a strong effort: she could not bear to go to sleep; but her head bowed, nodding even though she leaned it against the wall.

Suddenly she sat bolt upright; her eyes opened widely. They seemed to grow larger and larger at each instant. She listened intently. From her mother's bedroom there came a sound, a loud, wailing cry. Rebekah got off the bench and stood rigid and upright. Her small sharp-cut face, pale before, became now a deathly white. There was silence for a moment; then another cry, then another, and another, each louder and longer than before. Her hands doubled into fists; she turned a bright pink. The crying went on. She raised her chin; her throat swelled till it looked like the full throat of a tiny woman; the veins stood out like little whipcords. She drew in the corners of her mouth. Again there was a cry, but this time, fainter. A dark purple flush came up over her forehead; her eyelids drooped. She rushed out at the door, striking herself against it. She flew up the dark passage to the door of her mother's room. She tried to reach the handle, but it was too high. With hands and feet she struck the panels of the door till they rebounded.

'Let me in! Let me in! I say, let me in! I will—I—will*—I say—I will come in!'

The baby inside had left off crying.

Rebekah heard nothing but the surging of the blood in her own ears. Old Ayah opened the door.

'Let me in! Let me in!—I will come in!'

Old Ayah tried to put her back with her hand.

'Leave me alone!—Leave me alone!' she cried; 'You are killing it like the other one! Leave me alone, I say! Leave me alone!'

Old Ayah tried to hold her fast, but she caught the Hottentot woman's skirts and twisted them round with her arms and legs.

The little mother from the bed asked in a sleepy voice what was the matter.

'Don't ask me what is the matter!' cried old Ayah indignantly, in Cape Dutch. 'Ask the Father of all Evil! This child is mad!'

She wrenched her skirts free from Rebekah's grasp, and thrust her into the room. Rebekah stood on the ox skin in the centre of the floor, vibrating from the soles of her feet to her head.

The candle was on a stand beside her mother's bed, and threw its light full onto her, as she lay with the baby's head on her arm, and onto her hand with the white frill thrown across it.* On the right side of the great four-poster bed they had pinned up a red cotton quilt, with great lions and palm trees printed on it, to keep off the draught from the open window; and the quilt reflected a soft red light over the mother and child. In the far right-hand corner of the room was Rebekah's own little cot, where she had slept ever since she was born.

'God only does know what possesses this child!' said old Ayah, fixing her twinkling black eyes on Rebekah and talking at her. 'If she were my child, I wouldn't let her come into the house at all, where respectable people live who like to be indoors. I'd just tie her fast with a chain to a monkey post outside, and let her go round and round there. Then she could eat Kaffir beans* like a baboon, and climb and scream as much as she liked!'

'What did you make such a noise for, Rebekah?' the little mother said gently. 'Did you think they were hurting the baby?'

Rebekah said nothing; the blood was leaving her head and running into her heart, and she felt faint.

'Twisting a person's clothes almost off their backs! Can't one even wash and dress a child without this little wild thing coming howling, and dancing round one!' Old Ayah smoothed out her crumpled skirt.

'Do you want to see the baby, Rebekah?' asked her mother.

Rebekah walked unsteadily to the foot of the bed and stood beside the great wooden bedpost.

Old Ayah took up the baby's bath and walked out of the room with it, muttering that some children ought to live with the baboons.

'If you would like to come and see the baby, you can climb up,' said her mother drowsily, with half-closed eyes.

Rebekah waited a moment; then she clambered softly up onto the bed, and sat down at the foot, half kneeling, with her back against the post. Her mother, who was very tired, had re-closed her eyes. The baby's red face pressed against the mother's white breast. The light shone on them both.

Rebekah drew up her knees and clasped her arms round them, and sat watching.

'It's drinking, isn't it, eh,* Mother?' she said at last, very softly.

'Yes,' said her mother, without opening her eyes.

'It's *your* little baby? Eh, Mother?' she whispered again softly, after a long pause.

Her mother nodded dreamily.

Rebekah stroked her little skirts down over her knees.

'It *must* drink!' she said after a time. 'It *must* have milk, eh, Mother?—It's your little baby, eh, Mother?'—she added after a long pause.

But the little mother made no answer; she had dropped away into sleep.

Rebekah sat watching them.

By and by the baby moved its hand, which stuck out from the white flannel wrapper about it: it opened its fingers slowly; it stretched them out one after the other and closed them up again into a fist. Rebekah watched it intently.

Presently she leaned forward, resting one elbow on the bed, and slowly stretched out her other hand, and with one forefinger touched the hand of the baby. Her mouth quivered; she sat up quickly, and watched them again. She leaned her head back against the post at the foot of the bed and sat gazing at them, her eyes never moving.

At half past nine old Ayah came in again, bringing in the hot water bottle and an etna* to warm the gruel during the night.

'My fatherland's force!* You not in bed yet! Are you going to sit up till morning?'

The mother woke up. 'Have you been sitting here all this while, Rebekah?' she asked gently.

Old Ayah put the warm water bottle at the mother's feet.

'She'd never go to bed if she could help it!' old Ayah muttered. 'It's my belief, if you came in at three o'clock in the morning, you'd find her sitting up in her bed, talking to the spiders in the dark. She'd talk to the stars if she hadn't anything else to talk to, just not to go to sleep like other children!'

'Mother,' said Rebekah in a very slow, clear voice, stroking down her knees, 'Mother, will you let me have *your* baby to sleep by me for a little while?'

She spoke each word slowly and distinctly, as one who repeats what they have carefully prepared.

'No, dear,' said the mother; 'it's too small; you can't have it to sleep with you yet.'

'Have it to sleep with you!' said old Ayah. 'I should think not! Why, you'd kill it!'

'I should take great care of it,' said Rebekah, very slowly, still stroking her knees, her eyes very wide open and fixed steadily on her mother; 'I wouldn't lie on it, nor let it fall. I only want to take care of it, and teach it.'

'Teach it!—Teach it, indeed!' said old Ayah, tucking in the mother's feet. 'You just want to teach her to be a naughty Tom-boy like you. We'll take care she doesn't play with you, and learn all your wild ways.'

Rebekah stroked her knees more heavily. 'I didn't mean to teach her anything wrong,' she said slowly; 'I wasn't even going to teach her to hate *you*.'

'Hate me!—Rather!—I should think not! What next! Why should you teach her to hate me?'

Rebekah turned her eyes onto old Ayah and gazed at her. 'Because *I* hate you so!' she said.

'Don't quarrel with her any more, Ayah,' said the mother; 'the child really doesn't know what she is talking about; she's half asleep already. Come, get off the bed, Rebekah, and go and undress. You can't have the baby.'

But Rebekah sat motionless. Slowly the tears gathered under her eyelids. She closed them, and the tears lay in large heavy drops under the lashes without falling.

She raised her face with its closed eyes to the canopy of the bed.

'Oh, I can't bear it!—I can't bear it!' she said slowly. 'What shall I do?—What shall I do?—Oh, what shall I do?' She moved her upturned face with its closed eyes slowly from side to side. 'I meant to love it so!—Oh, I meant—all my things—my Peter book—all my stones—Oh, if you would have let me love it!' The bed shook, but no tears fell from the closed eyes. She stroked her knees with both hands. 'It's not any use!—you see—it's not any use!—I have tried!—I have tried!—Oh, I wish I was dead—I wish I was dead—I wish I was dead!'

Even old Ayah looked at her in silence.

'The child is really three parts asleep,' said the mother. 'It's been a long trying day for her, running about with no one to look after her. She is but a baby, though she is so old-fashioned.* Get off the bed, Rebekah, and old Ayah will undress you.'

But Rebekah felt her way to the foot of the bed and slid down: 'I can undress myself,' she heaved.

She stood on the floor in the middle of the room with her eyes still closed, the lids swollen and fastened together, and unbuttoned her things one by one, letting them drop on the floor, until she stood there in her little white shift; her small naked shoulders still vibrating. Old Ayah brought her her nightdress.

'*Das een snaakse kind!*'* she muttered. (''Tis a strange child!')

Rebekah slipped it over her own head, and then, with her hand stretched out, she felt her way to the bed in the corner. She climbed up over the side of the cot and lay down. The long vibrating movement still went on; it was almost as if a man were crying.

'I can't have that,' said the little mother. 'She'll go on with it half the night in her sleep. I know the child. I think she dreams of things. Take the baby and lay it by her just for a little while. It's been a long day, and she's very tired.'

Old Ayah shook her head forebodingly; but she took up the baby, wrapped it in its shawl, and carried it across the room. She turned back the cover and made a place for it beside Rebekah. The child stretched out her arm for its head; the Hottentot woman laid it down on it, and drew the cover up over both. Then she turned and went out, to fetch the gruel and the night light.

The elder sister slipped her hand under the shawl till she found the baby's hand; she clasped her fingers softly into its tiny fingers, and held them. With the other hand she tried to draw its body up close against her.

Presently there was a queer quavering little sound, as though someone were trying to sing; but nothing came of it; then all was quiet.

When old Ayah came back in fifteen minutes everyone in the room was quiet and asleep.

She put the gruel and night light down on the drawers, and came to the bedside to remove the baby. But when she turned down the cover she found the hands of the sisters so interlocked, and the arm of the elder sister so closely round the younger, that she could not remove it without awaking both.

Old Ayah shook her head, and drew the cover up softly. She blew out the candle, and put the night light down on the floor beyond the bed, and walked softly towards the door of the room, with her naked yellow feet, her figure casting a long dark shadow on the wall. When she got to the door as she passed out she turned and looked back. Along the floor the night light shone, casting deep shadows into far corners, especially that in which the two children lay!

But they were all sleeping well.*

II

THE BOOK: THE WOMAN'S DAY

CHAPTER I

SHOWING WHAT BABY-BERTIE THOUGHT OF HER NEW TUTOR; AND HOW REBEKAH GOT MARRIED

TUCKED away among the ribs of a mountain in the Eastern Province of the Cape of Good Hope is a quiet, tree-covered farm. The owner of this farm twenty-five years ago was an Englishman, a gentleman in a rough and unveneered fashion; a man fond of his books, of his trees, of his land: little given to speaking, much given to thinking, and seldom going further than his own beacons.* In truth, there was little to tempt anyone further; the neighbours were unlettered, velskoen-wearing* Dutchmen, or equally unlettered English settlers, and they did not often trouble their neighbours with a visit: a fact which no one regretted except the little mother, who was of a lively and sociable turn, and who rejoiced greatly over even the arrival of an old Boer Tante.* It was a quiet, monotonous life; the farmer himself, the little mother, their children, with a score of Hottentot and Kaffir servants, completed the catalogue of the farm's inhabitants: the human inhabitants, for of wild animal life there was no want. In the bush that covered the mountainsides were leopards, who came down at night and carried off lambs from the kraals; in the tall trees in the bush were little grey long-tailed monkeys, and wood doves, and cock-o-veets, who cried and called all day; in the rocks that crowned the mountain, troops of baboons climbed and fought; and down in the valley among the thorn trees were meerkats and great tortoises, and hares who paid visits to the lands. Almost all day from the open windows of the house you might see at intervals the sheep among the long grass on the mountainside or down in the flat; or catch sight of, far off, moving specks, which were the goats moving in and out among the thorn trees. All day long the great glass doors and windows stood open; through them came the scent of orange blossoms from the orangery before the door, and from the garden beyond where the hollyhocks and dahlias and marigolds and four-o'clocks made a bed of colour. In spring times there was the sweet scent of the blossoms from the long orchard beyond the flower garden; and in the summer, at Christmas time, the flat was a sea of gold with the yellow flowers of the thorn trees, and the honey scent came up to the house; and in autumn there was the faint, acid smell from the falling figs and peaches which lay on the ground in the brown trampled grass, and which the little Kaffirs and pigs came over the gaps in the wall to revel among.

Over the nek* came the road from the town. It wound in and out, in and out, a line of white among the thorn trees. It disappeared altogether on the flat, till it came out near the mielie* lands and by the great dam with the willow trees. In that dam on hot summer nights the frogs loved to croak. Baby-Bertie, the farmer's youngest daughter, said she loved to hear them as she lay in her bed at night; but Rebekah, her elder sister, said it was a sad sound and made one think of when one was a child, long ago. But Bertie, Baby-Bertie, as they called her, was only fifteen and two months, and she had not a very long, long ago to think of. Rebekah, her sister, was twenty, and had once been on a visit to Cape Town, and knew a great deal, and had read a great deal, and that might make it seem a long time since she was a child; but to Bertie, it was only yesterday, though she could already touch the oranges no other woman on the farm could reach, and her chin was higher than her father's shoulder. So, to her, the croaking of the frogs at night was as pleasant as the lowing of the cows when they came down the mountainside in the evening.

On one afternoon, Baby-Bertie stood at the window of the spare room, putting dahlias and lilies into a slender green glass; Rebekah, her sister, knelt in the room behind her, pinning a white valance around the bed. Outside, all the flat was full of yellow blossoms, for the thorn trees were in flower. Once or twice Bertie put her head far out of the window, and looked across the flat, and drew it back again.

She was a velvety creature, with long eyelashes turned back till they almost touched her straight eyebrows. Her forehead was low and very broad, the hair hanging over it in brown curls, up each one of which you might have slipped a finger; but what one looked at most were the large round brown eyes and the velvety cheeks. Rebekah, her sister, was a small woman, with dark, fine hair, wavy and parted down the middle; she had a very white face, except when she flushed, and then it seemed as if the blood might burn through the skin. You could always see the veins in her temples. When she was a child she used to run behind the bed and kneel down and repeat Bonar's hymn—

'Calm me, my God, and keep me calm!
Let Thine outstretched wing
Be as the shade of Elim's palm'*

—because her heart beat so fast sometimes she thought it was going to burst. Now she seldom needed to pray that; she was always busy with her books and her microscope and collections of insects, and stones, when she was not busy working in the kitchen or milk room, or helping her father with his farming.

And now she was to be married the next day to her cousin Frank, who had come from Cape Town to fetch her. He was tall and large, and fair and full, with blue eyes, and a light moustache; he smoked cigars and wore very spotless shirts and collars, whether they were white or striped and coloured.

He had always wanted to have her for his wife since as a boy of eleven he came with his parents from England to visit their relatives in South Africa. He had gone back to England, but ten years later he had come out again and settled in Cape Town to manage a branch of his father's business, and he had visited the farm once a year for four years; and had always asked Rebekah to marry him when he came, but she had always said she could not. Now everyone was surprised: she had suddenly written to him that she would; and she was to be married the next day; and the wedding breakfast was already laid out in the back dining room, with a white cloth pinned over it to keep the dust off. She was to be married in a lilac silk in the large front room; and her father and mother and Bertie and the servants would be there; and Queen Victoria and the Prince Consort would look down from the picture frames upon the wall.

Rebekah had wished there should be no feast and to be married in her little blue gardening dress, but her mother and Bertie said a wedding was no wedding without these things; and even the bridegroom laughed at the idea.

The magistrate was coming from the town to marry them; because Rebekah wanted no church service. Frank was willing; he said it did not matter in the country, where no one knew what you did; though [he] would not have liked it done in the town where everyone would have noticed it.

He was the only man who had ever asked Rebekah to marry him, except his brother, John-Ferdinand, whom she had met when she went to Cape Town two years before, and who had asked her, but she had refused him. Except for that visit to Cape Town, and a visit to the seaside once with her mother when she was a child, she had never left the farm, except to drive into the next up-country village for the day's shopping. There the shop clerks and young businessmen seemed people so far out of her world that she hardly knew who they were. Once the young bank clerk invited himself out to the farm and spent a day and night there, but she only spoke to him when she poured out the tea to know if he would have more, and spent the afternoon by herself in the kloof.* His account of his visit did not encourage other young men to come; and only the little mother suspected what he had been there for. Rebekah had never been to a ball or a theatre or paid a formal call, and her world was a very little world except in the direction of books.

Now she and Bertie were getting the spare room ready, because Bertie's tutor was coming, who was to teach her, when Rebekah was gone. Bertie herself had no greater appetite for books and learning than her hand-lamb for carrots, which he ate as it were under compulsion, if you offered them to him, for fear of paining you, but under no other conditions whatever. But Rebekah and her father both said she ought to learn more.

This tutor was a delicate young man from England, who had advertised for a situation on a farm where he might, in return for teaching three hours a day, receive his board.

No one had seen him, but he had good credentials, and Rebekah said men were generally better teachers than women; and everyone followed Rebekah's advice on the farm.

Bertie put her head out of the window again; but there was nothing to be seen except the flat shimmering in the afternoon sunshine, and the white road over the nek.

'Perhaps Jan has got drunk and turned the cart over; or perhaps it has broken down,' she said, straining her head further.

'It is not four yet,' her sister said.

Bertie drew her head in and took the glass with the dahlias and white lilies to the mantelpiece. She stood looking at them.

'Do you think he will like them, Rebekah?'

At this moment three little Kaffirs whom Bertie had set to watch on the top step of the loft ladder set up a series of frantic yells. Bertie put down the loose flowers she had just begun to collect and rushed from the room. Rebekah pinned on. She never seemed very much excited now, even when she found a new germ under her microscope, or when one of her grafts budded, or a new book came from Town; and those were the things she seemed to care for most. Soon after Bertie put her face in at the door again.

'Rebekah, do come and see him! He's just come! He is so lovely and small! He's hardly a bit bigger than you!—I thought I should be afraid of him, but I'm not a bit!—He's smaller than I am—he keeps on smiling—he's got coal-black hair—he's got a little curl, just like a drake's tail right above his ear! Do come and see him!'

Rebekah was pinning the last fold.

'Oh, come, Rebekah; he's shaking hands with Father and Mother and coming up the steps already!' She rushed out again. Rebekah rose from her knees slowly, and then stooped to gather the flowers Bertie had thrown away in her haste; she looked round once to see that the room was all in readiness. Then she went into the front room. A little man was sitting at the end of the sofa, who certainly looked not more than twenty-five years old, though he had given his age as thirty-five in his credentials. He was sitting with his hands between his knees; but he smiled, and rose as she came in, with his face slightly turned down. His forehead was rounded and protruding, and had a gleam upon it as though oiled; his nose was small, and was rounded except at the point, where it seemed to have been sliced off, leaving a small square tip.* Rebekah shook hands with him; but his restless, beadlike small eyes looked away at the piano. When she had gone out, he sat down again and talked to the little mother, who sat at her work table, while Bertie, too excited, or not venturing to come in, peeped through the dining-room door as she passed.

That afternoon they had their tea at four o'clock in the little front workroom, because the wedding breakfast was laid out in the dining room. The room opened with a large window onto the front stoep. All the family collected there except Frank, Rebekah's cousin, who lay out under the orange trees before the door on his back on a reed mat, smoking, and whose tea had been carried out to him by Bertie. He looked very cool in a spotless grey suit, with a white shirt and no waistcoat. He was reading a yellow-backed book,* and his pointer, whom he had brought with him in case there was any shooting, lay near his feet, with her head upon her paws.

Presently he lifted his hand as he read and drew her nearer by the ears; she winced a little, but crept up and put her nose against his arm. By and by, when he had emptied his cup, he raised his large not ungraceful body and sauntered to the house with the cup.

In the small sitting room the others had finished their tea and had all left, except Rebekah, who sat dreamily in her place near the window, cutting stars out of the orange peel on her plate. She had been up since five that morning, busy with housework, and preparations for the next day, and was tired.

Presently there came the scent of a whiff from a cigar through the open window, and then her cousin Frank put his handsome face and shoulders in.

'All alone?' he said.

He stretched out his hand and set the empty cup down on the table. 'Come out and sit under the orange trees? It's splendidly cool there.'

'I can't; I've so many little things to do yet if we are to start tomorrow at eleven.'

He folded his arms on the window ledge, and drew softly from his cigar.

'How nice you look in that dress,' he said slowly. She was dressed in white muslin, with a little blue sleeveless jacket cut away from the waist. 'I like that jacket; it shows your little waist. What a little ting-ting-kie* it is!' He put out his large, soft, well-shaped hand, and let it rest gently on her waist for a moment. Then he drew it back and refolded his arms on the window, and smoked. He blew a long whiff of smoke softly at her; he knew she liked it.

She began collecting the empty teacups onto the tray. There was a quiet contentment in his eye as he watched her.

'What do you think of the new arrival?' he said, taking his cigar from his mouth and holding it between his two first fingers.

'I dislike him.'

Frank laughed. 'He's not attractive. I'm sure he uses coconut oil for his hair. One can forgive a man a great many sins, but not that.' He put his cigar between his lips again and drew a long whiff. 'Don't you think it's a little dangerous too?'

'What?' Rebekah looked up at him quickly.

'Oh, settling him and Bertie down every day for three hours with nothing but the table to divide them and French verbs to unite them! It's a dangerous thing for any young man or old either to have a head of curls like Bertie's dancing within three feet of him!'

Rebekah stood up quickly again. 'I think—' she said.

He blew a whiff of smoke softly towards her across the table, which did not reach her, and laughed. 'Oh, I know just what you are going to say—men should teach women and women should teach men, what difference does it make?—But it's not the Garden of Eden yet! Bertie'll be the finest looking woman in Africa in a few years. Have you noticed how she's developed since I was here six months ago?'

Before Rebekah could answer, Bertie thrust her head in at the door to say old Ayah wanted her to come and see if the cakes were done; and dashed away again; and Rebekah took up the tray to carry it out with her.

'Then you won't come out under the trees with me?—I must go and be lazy alone!—What a busy little ting-ting-kie!—Well, tomorrow!—' He kissed the fingers of his left hand towards her and turned away from the window, his dog following close at his heels. As he walked along the stoep he hummed in a soft, sweet tenor:

'Ten little nigger boys fuddling over wine,
One got so jolly drunk, then there were nine!'*

He went back and lay down on his mat under the orange trees; and Rebekah went to see if the cakes were burning.

At nine o'clock that evening Rebekah sat out on the stoep. It was a dark night; the beetles buzzed about among the vine leaves on the wall and about her head. She was sitting on the step opposite the front door with her back turned to it; a square of light fell from the open door across the stoep beside her, and more dimly lighted up the stems of the orange trees beyond. She rested her elbows on her knees and sat looking out into the dark. After a while she glanced back through the open door. In the room behind her she could see the little mother sitting in the rocking chair in the far corner beside the work table, rocking herself and smiling, and nodding her head, keeping time at the wrong places; and Percy Lawrie, the new tutor, sitting at the piano, playing; and Bertie standing with her elbow on the top of the piano, with her eyes fixed on his face, so that at a movement of his head, she might turn the page for him. She could see her lover lying on the sofa with his large arm thrown across his forehead, listening to the music, which was good; and in the room beyond she could catch sight of her father sitting at the bare deal table reading, with his grizzled beard pressed against his breast. She looked in for a moment, and then she looked away again.

What was she leaving it for, that quiet, peaceful life? She folded her arms on her knees. What was she leaving it for? The light that streamed out from the door lay in a square about her, and the little night flies gathered thicker above her head. Tonight, almost too late, she took up the old balances and began to weigh again, as she had done before. What was she leaving it for, that quiet, peaceful life—a life in which the right was pleasantest and easiest to do, and lay right ahead; in which there was no being torn asunder living between 'I would' and 'I must'; a life in which there was just as much to be done for others as might yield a grateful sense of satisfaction, yet leaving space for the individual life undisturbed; a placid, peaceful life, into which the noisy, babbling, worried, worrying world crept only once a week through the postbag of the boy who brought the letters and newspapers from the town; a life in which news from the outer world came to one with a freshness it could never bear for those living in the hurry and turmoil of the great streams of life; a studious life, in which one might grow wise exceedingly over plants, and suck whatever joy there was in insects and stones; a thoughtful life, in which one might read and creep into the hearts of books, as they can only be crept into when the wheels of the daily life are grinding soft and low; a life in which suffering was small, and pleasure, if grey-tinted, calm and constant? What was she leaving it for? She looked back again into the room, and then out into the dark. That scale looked heavy.

On the other hand, there was—well—a vague insatiable hunger. Books, black-beetles, well-performed duties—she had tried them all, and she was dying of hunger. Was it for that, that of which the far-off blue and purple mountains whisper, when they say, 'Come! Come! Come! We have that to give you know not of! Come! Come! Come to us!'?* Or, was it a voice from that primal depth of nature which, before man was man, called beast to beast and kind to kind? Which through all the ages has summoned the human woman, in spite of the great Chaldean curse, 'I will greatly multiply thy sorrow and thy conception,'* along one path? An ox at the roadside, when it is dying of hunger and thirst, does not lie down; it walks up and down, up and down, seeking it knows not what—but it does not lie down.

She looked back into the sitting room, where her cousin Frank still lay, with his large, rounded arm in its grey coat sleepily thrown across his forehead, his full, well-shaped lips almost smiling.

For four years, when he had placed the question before her, she had always decided she could not go with him; why was it that, six months before, his face had become always present to her; and at night even, she saw his hands, and heard his soft sweet voice? She looked out again into the dark; and she knew as she sat there in the dark with her elbows on her knees, that, if she had been wholly free that night, and had to decide over again, she would yet have decided exactly as she had done.

She folded her arms closer on her knees, and looked out at the dark stems of the orange trees, while the little night beetles fluttered thicker and almost rested on her dark head.

After a while, everyone went to the back dining room to drink coffee, and they took the lamps with them; Rebekah still sat on alone in the dark, only a faint streak of light coming from the door of the dining room beyond the passage.

Then Bertie came out with a cup for her, feeling her way along the uneven stoep with her feet.

'I can hardly see you, the light has dazzled my eyes so.' She sat down beside her sister on the step, close to her, holding the coffee cup for her.

'I hope the little Kaffirs will come and call me very early in the morning, before it's light: will you wake me if they don't? I want to go up in the bush and fetch more creepers and berries.' She slid her hand through her sister's arm and let it rest in her lap; she still held the saucer of the cup. 'If I tell you something, you mustn't tell anyone, Rebekah! But we've made an arch up in the bush, and just before you are married we are going to bring it down, the little niggers* and I, and fasten it over the front door; and you and Frank will have to go out under it! Don't tell anyone: it'll be such a surprise! And we're going to fasten a paper bag of rice in the top, and just as you go out, one of the little niggers is going to poke it with a long stick, and all the rice'll come down on you. All Frank's collar and shirt will be full, and your dress, but you won't mind, eh?'

She took the empty coffee cup from Rebekah and put it down, and then slipped her hand into hers, so that their palms lay against each other.

'Do you know that something happened this evening, Rebekah?' She bent her head closer. 'Frank gave me your wedding ring to try on. I went into the kitchen to show old Ayah, and when I was taking it off it fell under the wood pile, and we had such a trouble to find it. We had to pack all the wood out. Old Ayah was angry with me; she said it was unlucky to try on other people's wedding rings. She said if you did, you never married, and that the most dreadful thing in the world happened to you. She wouldn't tell me what. It's only a "geloofje,"* isn't it, eh, Rebekah?—Rebekah, what *is* the most dreadful thing that *could* happen to anyone?'

'It would depend on who the person was,' Rebekah said, still dreaming her own thoughts; but she drew her sister's head closer into hers.

'It must be so nice to get married,' Bertie said. 'But when I get married I shan't like to go so far from the farm. I should like to be married to someone with a farm near here, and then you could come and visit me every year, and I could come and visit you. It must be so nice to be married. But I should like to have a pure white dress to be married in, not a mauve one like yours.' Bertie laid her head on her sister's shoulder. 'I suppose I shall be married some day; only I don't know who I shall find to marry here. Perhaps someone will come like Frank did—from far away. Rebekah, can I come and visit you some day soon?'

'Yes, dear, as soon as you've learnt a little more, you shall come to me for a long time, a year or six months if you like.' Bertie sat silent with her cheek resting softly on her sister's shoulder, and the crown of her head pressed against her sister's cheek.

Sometimes I think, if one should live to be ninety, and all the sights and sounds of the world about become dim to one, that then, as one sits alone in the firelight dreaming, or out in the sunshine, the child sister who was young with us will come back and sit with us there. No one will see her; and we two will sit there alone, she with her long, flowing hair; and we will look out at life together with our young eager eyes that have known no mighty sorrow. I think it is, perhaps, that she may sit there with us, that we treasure her memory so all life through. We two will be always young when we are together.

After Bertie had gone back into the house through the dark front room, Rebekah's lover came through it, feeling his way; he came out onto the stoep.

'Where is my little Goody-two-shoes?* All alone in the dark, as usual?' He felt for her with his hands, and raised her up. 'What an unsociable little mortal it is! Come and walk with me.'

He put her hand through his arm and drew the little blue shawl she had across her arm about her. He lit his cigar, and they paced up and down on the long stoep. Her head hardly reached his shoulder. 'Chilly tonight,' he said.

By and by the little mother came into the front room and, when she had bid them both goodnight, left the lamp on the table; and they paced on together.

'I must go to bed now,' Rebekah said, after a few minutes. 'I have to be up so early tomorrow.'

'Don't make yourself too tired; we have a long day's journey before us.'

He drew her close up to him, and before him. They were standing in front of the door where the lamplight fell full on them. He raised her hands in his and put them alternately softly to his lips. He put down his head and whispered something very softly. Her cheeks turned the colour of the pale carnation she had fastened in his buttonhole before supper.

'Goodnight, my little one! My queen! My love!'

Suddenly, with a little curious caressing movement, she raised herself and put her face against the side of his as he bent.

'What is it? Do you want to say something?'

She said nothing; but he thought he felt the soft touch of her lips against his neck; then she glided quickly from him.

He stretched out his arms towards her, for her to come back to him; but she shook her head softly and called out goodnight; and the little figure in blue and white fluttered away through the front room.

He turned round slowly to pace up and down to finish his cigar before he took up the lamp and retired.

When Rebekah left him she went out into the long passage. She called out a second goodnight at the door of her mother's room as she passed, and both her parents answered it; then she went to her own room at the end of the passage.

She lit a candle, and set it on the table, and then sat down on the side of her small bed. The window was standing open and the pitch darkness seemed to come in through it from outside; it looked out towards the kloof on the mountain, and the bush came down close to it. That little room had been hers for fifteen years, ever since she had given up to the new baby the cot in her mother's room.

It was bare and dismantled now. In one corner were two boxes, packed and corded, which contained her luggage ready for tomorrow's journey. Above the little table were marks on the wall where a bookshelf had been taken down. When her father first put it up for her, it was one little shelf containing a few children's books; but it had slowly mounted upward till there were shelves holding fifty or sixty volumes.* A tall rough glass cabinet that had stood in the corner, in which she had kept her fossils and insects and her microscope, was packed up too; and above her bed, at the head, was a square mark on the wall and the holes of four tacks. When she was a child of six she had found in an old copy of the *Illustrated London News** a rough print of Raphael's Madonna della Sedia,* and she had cut it out and fastened it there. No one told her it was a great picture, but when she looked at the little John, and the baby with its hand inside its mother's breast glancing round, and the mother with her striped shawl looking down at it, a thrill of quiet joy ran through her, that no other picture made her feel. She called it '*My* picture.' Now it was taken down and folded away with her other things to go to her new home.

She sat on the side of her bed and looked out of the window. A curious weight and heaviness seemed suddenly to rest on her. The wick of the candle which stood on the table began to burn long and red and bend over a little as the soft night breeze blew it. She snuffed it and then took up the light, and walked to the door at the end of her room which led into Bertie's.

Baby-Bertie lay on her bed with her arms thrown back on the pillow above her head. The sleeve of her nightdress had fallen back and showed her round arm, so small at the wrist, so large above the elbow; and one button at the neck had become unfastened and showed her small white throat: her face was flushed, though the window stood wide open and night air came in over the bed. The pillow was covered with a tangle of her brown curls.

Almost every night when, as a very small child, she had been moved into that room, Rebekah had lain by her to sing her to sleep; and when she grew older Rebekah had still crept in to lie beside her to talk and caress her before she slept. Tonight Rebekah put the light down on the floor, and knelt beside the bed. She put her head down upon Bertie's breast, under Bertie's arm, and pressed it there. It was as though, tonight, it was she who wanted to be caressed. But Bertie slept on, a deep, calm sleep. Presently Rebekah rose, and partly closed the window that the air might not blow so fully on her. On a chair near the bed Bertie had laid out the lilac silk wedding dress Rebekah was to wear the next day; and the white tulle veil lay over it; the orange blossoms Bertie would gather early in the morning. Beside it on another chair hung the muslin gown Bertie herself was to wear.

Rebekah did not glance at them; she took up the light and went back to her room. Through the open window you could hear the baboons shouting and calling to one another high up on the mountainside.

She undressed slowly. When she stood ready at the bedside in her nightdress, she took from under the pillow an envelope, and sat down again on the side of her bed and opened it. It was brown and worn, but you could still see the address. It held the first letter her cousin Frank had written to her, after his visit six months before, when she had written to him telling him she had changed her mind and would marry him. She read it again—'My one love! My own love! My only love!' She had slept with it under her pillow ever since. In the envelope were parts of other letters. She took them out; and looked at them. She did not need to read them: she knew them by heart. She kissed them one by one and then put them back in the envelope and the envelope under her pillow. When she had got into bed she put out the light, but two hours later, she still lay awake. She* could hear the baboons outside in the dark, shouting and fighting among the rocks on the mountainside.

The next day Rebekah got married.

CHAPTER II

A WILD-FLOWER GARDEN IN THE BUSH

FOR a while after Rebekah went things seemed askew and out of tune at the old farm; but they soon made grooves for themselves and ran on smoothly enough.

In the bush the wood doves cooed to one another, and the cock-o-veets called; the little, grey, long-tailed monkeys climbed the trees and slid down by the monkey ropes:* the hares and porcupines visited the lands at night by the great dam; and the leopard sometimes came down on very dark nights to prowl about the kraals; and snakes made their nests and reared their young in the garden and under the dam walls. The great flat stone still lay baking in the sun on hot days; and the trapdoor spiders made lids to their nests and lined them with white silk, and opened and shut them, though no little child with passionately interested eyes sat patiently waiting to see them open or shut; and at evening, the avondbloem* in the grass on the mountain opened their drab-tinted flowers and sent their rich sweet scent far and wide—though the small personage that had moved among them for twenty years, as a child and woman, was gone.

If the father missed his wise little daughter when he went down to the lands to see how a new variety of wheat was doing, and had no one to advise with* over his grafts and flutes,* or to discuss with him new remedies for cattle disease, he said nothing, but buried himself deeper than ever in the pages of his Swedenborg. And the little mother, if she missed her eldest daughter on baking days, and in the vegetable garden, and every day when rations were given out, yet found great consolation in the fact that she had now a new subject to lament over.

Old Ayah said that everything had gone wrong since Miss Rebekah went, and that there was no one to keep order, or who knew how things ought to be done; but she cooked the food and scolded the little Kaffirs, just as of old; and shook her head continually over the tergiversations of mankind in general.

Baby-Bertie missed her. She cried herself to sleep for several nights after she went; but even for her time brought compensations. After a while there were long weekly letters from Rebekah and great excitement when the boy came with the postbag over the nek. She told about her little house, and its furniture, and the garden; and now and then there were little parcels with bits of muslin or silk to be made up into kappies or aprons for Bertie or the little mother, and odds and ends for old Ayah and the servants: and all these brought a new element of excitement into life, and were something to look forward to.

And there was the new tutor. Everyone liked him at the farm, except perhaps the father; and he only showed dislike if he felt it, by speaking even less than usual if he was by.*

The little mother liked him. He would sit listening to her for hours while she lamented over the hardships of her life and described her home in England, which she had left as a girl twenty-five years before. It had been a simple country parsonage, but, seen through the refracting mist of twenty-five years of African life, it had slowly assumed always increasing proportions of luxury and beauty. The schoolmaster could paint beautiful illumined mottoes, with borders copied from the flowers which Bertie brought him. He painted one to hang in the mother's bedroom, for her birthday, with a border of roses and lilies, and on it the motto, 'Blessed are the pure in heart.'*

Bertie liked him. He did not trouble himself as to whether she remembered what he taught her; and he could play beautiful, dreamy music, especially on Sunday afternoons, when Bertie, whom nothing else could keep long quiet, would crouch in the corner with her cat in her lap, and cry softly, she did not know why.

When her three hours of school was over, he often helped her to work in the flower garden, which she had taken care of since Rebekah left, because Rebekah liked it so. Up in the bush he helped her to make a little garden for wild flowers; which he said would do better up there in their natural soil than down in the old soil of the farmhouse garden. She and he went often to see how the things were growing; and that was something new to Bertie, who had not been fond of the bush as Rebekah was, and had hardly ever gone there.

Then the autumn came. The gentians and everlasting flowers* had died in the grass on the mountainside; and the thorn trees in the flat were covered with long seed pods, and their thorns became a more shiny white. Nothing important had happened at the farm since Rebekah left; except that one old batch of Kaffir servants had left and another had come; and the turkeys and goslings and chickens had bred out well and the yard was full; and the little mother had made two fine boilings of soap.

Then the winter passed, and the spring came. It was ten months since Rebekah had gone. And then came the news she had a baby. The little mother cried. Old Ayah cried also, and said she felt sure the Cape Town servants would mismanage all the house while Rebekah was ill. And the father said, 'Rebekah? Rebekah? Can it be?' and walked out to the far lands. And Baby-Bertie first laughed and then cried, and then ran away to tell her tutor the news—and then things settled down again.

One afternoon, when everyone had risen from the afternoon nap, the little mother sat sewing at her work table in the corner of the front room. The door onto the stoep was open, and through it she could see Percy Lawrie, the tutor, sitting on a chair on the stoep, reading. By and by Bertie came round to the front of the house from the yard, and sat down on the edge of the stoep, just before him.

She threw off her kappie and fanned herself with it; and then looked up towards the chair where her tutor sat.

'You aren't angry with me, are you, Mr Lawrie?'

The tutor glanced down from his book at her, and then with one restless little black eye glanced in the direction of the open door where from his position he could see the mother sitting.

'No, Miss Bertie, oh no, of course not.'

'Because you said—'

He made a quick movement as if to drive away one of the bees that was coming towards him: 'Miss Bertie, there it is close to your forehead!'

She shook her head: 'I don't mind.' Then stretching out one hand towards him with a deprecatory little gesture: 'I couldn't bear you to be angry with me! I don't like anyone to be angry with me—not even the servants! You *do* love me, don't you?'

She looked up at him with the expression a puppy dog might have had, looking up into the face of a master he half feared he might have offended.

'Certainly I am not angry with you, Miss Bertie. I have no reason to be. You do your lessons very well.'

'Baby-Bertie!' called the little mother from the sitting room, 'go to the yard and see if the hen is letting the goslings she brought out get to the little dam. Don't let her drive them back to the fowl house: make haste.'

Bertie rose slowly and went round the house again to the yard.

A little later the mother went to the kitchen door herself and found Bertie sitting on the lowest step with her white apron full of goslings which she had been feeding, and which she was going to carry down to the dam, as the hen refused to lead them. The black hen moved round her feet restlessly, anxious as to what was to become of her brood.

The mother stood on the top step.

'Baby-Bertie,' she said a little uncertainly, 'I want to speak to you.'

Bertie lifted her head and half turned it to her.

The little mother hesitated. 'Just now, when you were round on the front stoep, I was sitting in the front room and heard you speaking to your tutor. I didn't quite like the way in which you spoke to him, dear.'

Bertie turned her head more fully and looked up into her mother's face. 'Well, I didn't mean to be rude to him,' she said; 'but, after dinner, when you all went to lie down, he asked me to go up with him to see our plants in the kloof, and I didn't want to go because I wanted to sleep. He seemed cross about it, but I didn't mean to be rude to him.'

'Oh, you weren't rude to him, dear,' said the little mother nervously; 'it's not that.' The brown eyes that looked up into hers abashed her. 'You were quite polite to him; but you know, Bertie, girls and women don't ask grown-up men if they love them.* You are not a real baby, Bertie, although we call you so. But it's all right, my dear,' she added, quickly, seeing the surprise in Bertie's face, 'only don't ask any man that again, dear. Take the goslings to the dam.'

The little mother turned and hurried quickly into the house; Bertie rose slowly with the goslings in her apron and walked away towards the small dam beyond the wagon house, with the black hen anxiously following her.

It was about ten days after that the little mother fell ill. She had one of her bad sick headaches which sometimes kept her in bed for several days. All the house was kept perfectly still for her, and even the cocks were driven away from the back door because their crowing disturbed her. Bertie gave up all her lessons and waited on her, bringing in little basins of soup or of gruel she had made; and driving away the little Kaffirs if they came to play too near the farmhouse; and keeping everything in order like an old, experienced housewife. Even old Ayah allowed she was turning into a wonderful housewife since Rebekah left, though she would never allow she was as good. The little mother almost liked to lie in bed and see her trip softly in and out of her room, with her gruel, and soup, and fresh flowers, in her white muslin dress.

On the morning of the fourth day the little mother was better and fell early into a heavy sleep. About half past eleven she woke, and lay expecting Bertie to come in: but all the house was still; Bertie had put no new flowers in the vase beside her, nor brought in her lemon and water. For more than half an hour the little mother lay there waiting and wondering. Then the quiet grew oppressive; she rose, and partly dressed herself, and went out into the passage. There was not a soul stirring in the house nor a sound to be heard but the far-off voices of the men as they called to their oxen ploughing in the mielie lands. She went to the kitchen and found old Ayah standing before the fire shredding 'snysels'* into the soup pot; she said she had not seen Bertie since just after breakfast; the father was gone to the far mielie lands and the Kaffir maids to wash the churns at the fountain.* The little mother went back to her own room, but, feeling restless, she went out again to the room that used to be Rebekah's and was now Bertie's, and opened the door. Bertie was sitting there with her arms folded on the low dressing table before the window, and her head resting on them. The little mother stepped gently up to her, thinking she was asleep. She laid her hand softly on her shoulder. Bertie raised her head slowly and looked into her mother's face. 'Are you ill, my Baby?' she asked, bending down. Bertie said nothing. There was in the large eyes the look that an animal has when it is in pain; the mute fear of a creature that cannot understand its own hurt.

She dropped her head upon her arm again.

The little mother saw nothing in it but the look of one who has a violent sick headache.

'You are ill, my Baby, you are very ill! Lie down on the bed and let me cover your feet with the rug.' She took Bertie's arm and walked beside her to the bedside. Bertie moved heavily. 'You have done too much these last few days—you have taken too much care of me—do not let your feet hang down so, dear—so—that is better! You take after me with these terrible headaches. I always had them when I was young.'

The little mother drew down the window blind. 'Lie still; I'll go and tell old Ayah to bring you hot water for your feet. We'll get

Mr Percy Lawrie to ride over to Mrs de Wet's and bring some blue-gum leaves; they are wonderful things for these sick headaches.'

She trotted out of the room, forgetting wholly in her anxiety that she herself had been ill. At the kitchen door she met old Ayah, and told her what ailed Bertie, and discussed the blue-gum leaves. Old Ayah said they would have to send one of the Kaffir boys on foot for them, as, about half past ten that morning, Mr Percy Lawrie had come down from the bush, and had said he must ride into the town for the post at once, himself; and had gone on the only horse in the stable.

When the Kaffir boy had been found and sent off, old Ayah made up the fire to get some warm water, and the little mother went back to Bertie with a glass of lemon; but she was lying with her face close to the wall, as though she were asleep, and did not stir when spoken to; and the little mother stepped softly out again.

That evening at eight o'clock the horse came back from the town; but there was a strange boy riding it whom Mr Lawrie had hired in the town. And there was a letter from him among the other post, in which he said that when he got to town he found a letter from his English relations awaiting him; which told him that his mother was dangerously ill and very anxious to see him before she died; it was therefore necessary for him to take the first postcart and go on to the Bay* at once, if he wished to catch the next mail steamer for England; so he regretted he could not return to the farm to say goodbye. They need not concern themselves about any clothes, music, or books that he had left, but might give them away: neither need they trouble about his last half-quarter's salary, as he was leaving without notice. He thanked them for all their kindness. He did not send any special message to Bertie, but wished to be kindly remembered to all.

As soon as she had read the letter, the little mother hurried away to Bertie's room to tell her the news. She had refused to take any supper; but she had undressed herself and was still lying on the bed with her face to the wall. The little mother sat in the rocking chair by the bed-side and rocked herself, and cried intermittently. She said, it was always so, troubles never come singly; first she had been ill, then Bertie, and now the dear, good, schoolmaster had gone away, in such trouble! But Bertie said nothing. The little mother asked her if she had pain; she said, no, only her head ached; and turned her face deeper into the pillow.

In the middle of the night the mother got up and came and stood at the door of Bertie's room, then opened it, and went in softly. She thought she had heard someone crying bitterly; but when she got to the bedside Bertie was lying motionless and seemed to be asleep, with her face turned towards the dark: and the little mother went away, thinking it must have been the owl hooting, who came every night to see if any stray chickens were left out.

But the next morning very early before anyone was up Bertie got up and dressed herself, and went for a walk up into the kloof. When she came back she went straight to her own room and lay down; and took nothing all day, but a little tea.

In the evening a little Kaffir herd, who had been up in the bush to look for some goats, came back with the news that Bertie's little wild-flower garden was destroyed; that all the plants had been pulled up by the roots, and the ground trampled flat; but when the little mother went to tell Bertie about it she took no notice; and lay with her eyes half shut.

The next day she got up at the usual time, and said she was well, that her head did not ache; but she ate hardly anything, and was white-faced, with rings under her eyes; and old Ayah and the little mother agreed that she had been very seriously unwell.

As the days passed, she went as usual about what household duties she had, but remained white and silent; seldom speaking to anyone; and taking no interest in anything. As soon as her work was ended she went back to her own room, and closed the door, and lay on the bed. The little mother thought she had been studying too hard; but old Ayah said it was a sickness which young girls often suffered from when they were about sixteen, and advised saffron root* boiled in milk. Once or twice again at night the little mother thought she heard the sound of low crying, but when she went to Bertie's room all was silent, and she felt sure it must be owls on the roof.

Twice Bertie began a letter to Rebekah; but both times she tore the letter up, and it was never sent.

Of the little schoolmaster Bertie never spoke, though the little mother was always talking of him, speculating as to why he did not write again before he left Port Elizabeth, or as to whether his mother would be alive when he got to England. All the bits of music which he had left behind with his name written on them, disappeared, one by one; and from the walls the mottoes he had painted with frames of everlasting flowers about them, which he had helped Bertie to make, vanished. Only in the little mother's bedroom her motto with the painted border of lilies and roses still hung; otherwise there was nothing to recall him in the house.

One Sunday afternoon, two months after he went away, it had been a strangely sultry day: and since dinner Bertie had been lying down in her own room. About half past four the storm burst; the lightning flashed incessantly, the thunder crashing close over the roof, while the rain fell in torrents till you could not see the wagon house: the tiny stream that came down from the kloof was a roaring, foaming river; and all the little footpaths were rushing streams.

Just before sunset, when it was all over, Bertie came out of her room and went to the back of the house which faced the sunset, and sat down on the rough stone step at the door of the milk room.

All the earth had been washed clean and fresh. The little streams in the footpaths had ceased to run, but in all the hollows in the hard ground were pools of water; and you could hear the stream still rushing in the bed of the mountain torrent.

Baby-Bertie leaned her head back against the door; a rich, fragrant odour rose from the fresh earth; she drew the white shawl she had thrown over her head closer round her face, and sat watching the wet world. The sun was setting at the end of the great valley below the farmhouse; all the west was a bloody pall of crimson, all the east a faint reflection of its redness. On the water of the great dam by the willows, in the windows of the farmhouse, in the puddles in the roadway, on the wet leaves of the thorn trees, even there it was reflected; and the little flat and the lower hills on the other side of the valley and the tall mountains were all touched with its redness. A curious feeling came over her as she sat there watching it; it was as though a strong great hand were put out and took fast hold of her heart that trembled and was so heavy, and held it fast. A curious quiet came over her. Was there not something that might make the past as if it never had been, and the 'I have done it' as meaningless as 'I have dreamed it'?

She sat gazing at that drenched world. It seemed as though the great hand stretched itself out and stroked her.

Slowly the crimson vanished and a faint glow lingered only at the far end of the valley.*

Her father as he passed her on his way back from the sheep kraals laid his hand upon her shoulder: 'It grows late and cold,' he muttered;* and she stood up and followed him into the house.

When Bertie went to her bedroom that night and closed the door, she felt no terror of the room, as she had done lately, even though* it was better to be there alone than anywhere else. After she had got into bed it seemed as though a great hand made an arch over her, and she crept in under it, and was safe. She drew the cover up high about her and clasped her arms about a pillow as if it were a person, and drew it close to her. Even the croaking of the frogs filled her with no horror: and when she fell asleep, she slept till morning without awaking.

CHAPTER III

THE DAM WALL

THORN KLOOF was expecting visitors, and the life-blood stirred in its sluggish old veins. From the superannuated chairs and churns in the loft, to the china in the front-room cupboard, everything was turned upside down and inside out and washed and scrubbed and renovated. Even the pigsty was whitewashed and had a new trough, and the kraal walls were built up higher with thorn branches.

For the visitors were many and important whom Thorn Kloof was expecting, and it behoved it to put on its best face. Even the little Kaffirs who danced about naked all day on the old kraal heaps knew that something unusual was about to happen; and came to the house to beg for cast-off clothing, paper collars, or old shoes, in which to bedeck their small naked bodies; and they danced about in the sunshine more contentedly than ever, with a collar, or a boot, or a torn waistcoat. All day the Kaffir maids were busy scrubbing and cleaning, laughing and chattering; and all day the little mother trotted about giving orders, and old Ayah clucked and scolded; and Griet, the little Bushman girl, whom Bertie had got from her drunken mother a little while before for a pair of old shoes and a bottle of wine,* rushed about hither and thither, doing nothing; but flaunting her little yellow petticoats in everybody's face, and chattering at the top of her voice, and tormenting the Kaffir maids. Bertie herself got up before sunrise every morning to gather oranges and figs for preserves, and was busy all day making jams and almond cakes.

It was just four full years since Rebekah married, and now she was coming to visit them for the first time, bringing with her her three small children, the eldest of whom was three years and three months old, and the youngest a new-born baby of eight weeks. She had almost died when it was born, and was coming home to rest for a while. Of late years she had often not written long letters though she wrote every week; she seemed always to be having a baby or nursing it, or to be otherwise engaged. Her husband was not coming with her, she wrote, as his business kept him in Cape Town, and later he was going for a six weeks' hunting trip into the western Karroo.* But her husband's brother, John-Ferdinand, was coming; he had come out again from England for his health; and was going to buy a farm in South Africa and settle there. He was coming to ask his uncle's advice as to the choice of a place.

A few weeks later, there was coming also another visitor, a lady from England, who was delicate and recommended to their care by their English relatives; but no one knew much of her, or could tell what she would be like.

The excitement at the old farm was intense; everything was in motion.

One Saturday afternoon the wagon they had sent to the coast to fetch Rebekah came over the nek. The little mother began to cry as soon as they told her it was coming; and then everyone gathered at the back door to wait for it. Bertie would have liked to put on her kappie and run through the thorn trees to meet it, but she thought her mother would rather they all met Rebekah together.

At last the wagon drew up at the kitchen door, and Rebekah herself got out first. She looked smaller and more like a child than ever, with her little white face and her large eight-weeks' baby on her arm. While the little mother was kissing her and crying, the driver handed down to the father a stout, fair boy of two, and then lifted down a shy boy of three, who looked like Rebekah, and hid his face in his mother's skirt as soon as he got to the ground. They all gathered close round Rebekah. Bertie caught up the boy of two and covered him with kisses, and ran towards the house with him; the little mother took the baby from Rebekah and began to cry afresh; old Ayah caught hold of its long white skirt and began to cry also; and Griet did all she could to coax the shy boy to take his face from his mother's gown and let her carry him; but he kept his face carefully turned away as they walked towards the house.

They were so absorbed in Rebekah and her children they did not notice John-Ferdinand, her cousin, who had been walking some way behind the wagon, and who had now come up. He was a tall, slender man, with a very small, delicate head and face, and black hair, curling close to his head, and eyes of such an exceedingly dark blue they seemed black, except in certain lights. His fingers were very long and tapered, and his hands transparently white.

Only the father saw him, and went up to shake hands with him, and said he was glad to see him. When he went away to give orders about the oxen, John-Ferdinand stood alone by the great whitewashed brick oven that jutted out from the side of the kitchen.

He was dressed in dark clothes and wore a soft, black felt hat; he leaned his elbow almost gracefully on the oven and stood watching the unpacking of the wagon. The Kaffir maids had come up from the huts now, and were dragging mattresses, pillows, boxes, canisters and bundles out of the wagon, and throwing them down in heaps, or carrying them into the house, all laughing, running, and talking. Over all Griet, with her small, yellow-brown Bushman face, with its touch of Hottentot,* was giving pretended orders to the Kaffir maids, and screaming in a shrill voice; tumbling in and out of the wagon over the heads of the others, doing nothing; and glorying in the confusion.

Presently Bertie came to the back door to see how they were getting on. Then she noticed John-Ferdinand standing alone by the oven. It seemed to her he must feel lonely and neglected standing leaning there, no one speaking to him, and she ran down the steps towards him. He reminded her of the picture of Charles the First the night before his execution in her old school history, with his deep blue eyes looking out so gravely. When she came near him she suddenly felt shy, and almost turned away; but he came slowly forward to meet her.

'You are my cousin, Baby-Bertie, are you not? I think you were not born when I was here twenty-one years ago.'

He spoke gravely and held out his white hand. Bertie took it shyly.

'I have heard much of you from my brother and his wife; I think I should have known you anywhere had I met you.'

Bertie said nothing, and hesitated; then, seeing a large canister standing on the front box of the wagon ready to be carried into the house, she turned towards it and seized it. Her cousin came forward.

'That is too heavy for you.' He took it from her very gently and gravely. When their hands were near each other on the canister, she noticed how brown, and even rough, her hands were compared to his. She wrapped her right hand up quickly in her little silk apron as she walked behind him to the house. He put the canister down solemnly on the kitchen table; she thanked him quickly, and he went slowly out again.

That night when Rebekah lay on the bed in the spare room hushing her babies to sleep, Baby-Bertie came in. She had changed since the old days when Rebekah married and Percy Lawrie was her tutor. The exuberant brown curls were gathered into a knot at the back of her head, which showed better the beautiful outline of her small round neck and broad shoulders, and the small round head. She had grown, as Frank prophesied, into a magnificent woman; but she had become quiet; the noisy gaiety of her early girlhood had passed, and she spoke and moved almost heavily. She would have been almost majestic if it had not been for the infant-like expression of the face, and something uncertain and almost wavering in her walk, rising from the fact that her feet were almost too small for her body.* Her rich colouring was more perfect than ever; but in her round brown eyes there was a slight wistfulness, almost as though asking a perpetual question; and the corners of her small, full-lipped mouth were more drawn in than they had been, as though always wearing a placid half smile.

She stood at the foot of Rebekah's bed, dressed in a white muslin gown with blue bows down the front. Rebekah's eldest son lay at her back, with his arms twisted round her neck, and her baby lay at her breast; but the little fat blue-eyed boy had already gone to sleep in his cot in the corner.

She crept onto the bed, and laid her head softly on her sister's knee. 'It is so nice to have you here, eh, Rebekah,' she said slowly. 'It seems like long ago.' She uncovered the baby's feet and looked at them: 'Aren't they beautiful?' She held them in her hand:* 'So soft and warm!' She held her cheek against them for a moment, and then laid her head back again on Rebekah's knee.

Rebekah smoothed her hair with her free hand. 'Aren't you very lonely here sometimes, Baby-Bertie?' she asked after a time.

Bertie smiled, the soft dreamy smile that was seldom wholly absent from her face. 'No,' she said. 'Sometimes I feel as if I should like to go to Cape Town and be with you and the children; and sometimes I feel as if I would like to go somewhere and see people and things and be where other people are.' She rubbed her cheek softly against Rebekah's knee. 'And then again I feel, no, it's better to be here shut in safety, by the old mountains.' A slightly troubled look crept into her face; then she said, 'You know it isn't because I don't want to be with you, Rebekah; I am always wanting you; like when I was little.' They were silent for a time, as the little boy with his arms round his mother's neck was just dropping asleep. 'Rebekah,' Bertie whispered, as he seemed to have gone off, 'does cousin John-Ferdinand always look so grave?'

'Yes, he does not often smile; I never heard him laugh.'

Bertie lay still: 'Keep on stroking my hair, Rebekah; I like it so. Don't you like people to touch you; I mean, if you like them?' After a while she added, 'He's very clever, isn't he?'

'He took his degree well at the university.'

Bertie caressed the baby's feet softly with her hand. 'Don't you think he's very beautiful, Rebekah?'

At first Rebekah thought she meant the baby, then she understood. 'Yes, in a way. Most people think so. His beauty doesn't touch me.'

'I feel so afraid of him, Rebekah. He's not merry like Frank who used always to be laughing and joking. Do you feel afraid of him, Rebekah?'

'No.'

'Oh!' said Bertie, and lay still.

Presently Griet came in to tell Bertie the milk was come and it was time to get supper ready. Soon after the little mother came in and sat in the rocking chair at the bedside and told Rebekah how much greater her troubles were than they used to be: the maids did less work than ever, and the father was more silent and said 'Um! Um!' in answer, when you tried to talk with him. She said Bertie was a dear, good, beautiful child, but she spoiled Griet and was like her father in not caring to talk much. She said how happy Rebekah must be with a husband always ready to chat and laugh, and how nice it must be to live in a town where you could get your bread ready baked, and all kinds of things you couldn't get on a farm; and she lamented on till Bertie came to call them to supper.

A few nights after, when the father and little mother lay in bed, the father reading with his book open on his breast, and the candle on the stand near his head, the little mother said, 'Rebekah *is* changed, you know.'

The father made a sound which might mean attention or not, from under his thick, iron-grey moustache.

'It's always when you talk to her as if she were thinking of something else; as if she didn't quite see you. She's different, she's quite different from what she used to be!'

'The cares of life,' muttered the father, still looking at his book, and growing sleepy.

'What cares has she?' said the little mother. 'She hasn't quite such an easy life as she would have had if she'd married John-Ferdinand. I've sometimes wondered why she didn't marry him, with the twelve thousand pounds of his own his aunt left him, when Frank had only his business. But, after all, I should have chosen Frank! He's so big and strong, and he's doing well, she says. Of course she has a great many children and only one servant and an outside boy, and no nurse—but she *will* look after the children herself—Rebekah always did work harder than anyone else! She never complains, but it's as if she was thinking of something else. Even when she—'

But the father's book had dropped over onto his chest and he was breathing heavily; and the little mother put the light out.

During the days that followed Rebekah's arrival the womenfolk at the house did not see much of John-Ferdinand. Sometimes he was out riding with the father, to look at the farms in the country round, to see if any suited him; and when he was at home he took his book after breakfast and roamed away with his rug into the bush and did not come back till dinner. After the afternoon sleep and tea he generally went for a walk again. At meal times he sometimes talked a little to the father and Rebekah about books. He was annotating a copy of Tennyson's *Idylls of the King*,* and generally had it with his pencil in his pocket. The little mother feared he must feel lonely, and offered him the gun to go out shooting; but he said he never hunted; and she felt ashamed, as if she had offered him something wrong.

Yet, after the first ten or twelve days had gone, he began to stay more in and about the farmhouse. Sometimes, when in the morning Rebekah lay under the orange trees with her boys creeping about her, catching at the orange blossoms as they fell and stuffing them down her neck or making little heaps of them on the reed mat and the baby lay on her arm, and Bertie was sitting at her feet shelling peas or peeling fruit, and chatting away softly about the wild cat that had stolen all her last brood of turkeys, or the man on the next farm who would quarrel about the beacons or the sheep that had strayed in her father's veld,* it would happen that Bertie would look up suddenly and see John-Ferdinand standing close behind them with his hands resting on the head of his cane, looking down at them; and she would at once become still and shell her peas or peel her fruit in silence, while John-Ferdinand said a few words to Rebekah, or walked on into the garden. He began also to sit a good deal too in the back dining room, reading at table, where Bertie passed and re-passed as she went about her work between the pantry and kitchen.

One morning, when Rebekah had been there more than three weeks, Baby-Bertie was kneeling in the pantry, making Boer biscuits.* She had the dough in a large wooden trough on a low bench, and the black pans she had to fill placed across and across on the end. She was kneeling on a footstool because she was too tall when she stood. She had finished kneading and was just going to begin making up, when she looked round and saw John-Ferdinand standing in the pantry door, watching her with his grave eyes, and his delicate head a little on one side.

'Rebekah isn't here,' she said quickly and shyly; 'she's gone down to the garden, and Mother is in the ration room.'*

'I am not looking for either of them, thank you.'

He stood still, and then came a step nearer.

'May I come in and watch you?'

He seated himself on the wooden churn that was turned upside down in the corner between the bench and the dresser. He leaned forward slightly and watched her. A lock of her brown hair had escaped and hung in one little ringed curl over her low, broad forehead; her sleeves were turned up far above her elbows, and she had on a great snow-white coarse apron covering her dress.

She put the making-up board across the trough and broke off a lump of dough and began to make it up. She turned it this way and that, her downy cheeks growing pinker and pinker. First she tried to make snake curls, but they often broke in two as she was twisting them; then she made up double balls, and the one would hardly stick onto the other; she tried quickly three or four different patterns. She knew John-Ferdinand must think her so stupid, not even to be able to make up biscuits well. She would not have minded so much if the curl had not been hanging over her forehead, and she could not lift it off because her hands were doughy.

At last the six pans were full, and she stood up with a flushed face.

John-Ferdinand had not spoken once all the time.

He rose also.

'I am going for a walk in the bush up in the kloof,' he said, 'will you come with me?'

'I—Oh—I don't know—my hands are full of dough.'

'But you can wash them,' he said gravely, almost smiling.

Baby-Bertie called to the girl to take the pans away, and went to her own room. She put on her best white dress and a large, white kappie with embroidery round it. Then she came out without saying a word to anyone; and John-Ferdinand and she walked round the back of the house, and up towards the kloof.

First they went through the belt of small thorn trees, with seed pods just forming and the soft green this-year's-thorns turning white and hard, and with little honey creepers* hanging from them here and there; and on, past the great round kunee trees,* in whose depths you could hear the little birds hopping though you could not see them; and on, into the real bush, where the tall forest trees grew straight and high over the bed of the mountain torrent, and made a great stillness in which the woodpeckers worked and there was always shade. Here the monkey ropes hung down from the trees, and the Kaffir-bean trees shed their great seeds, till the ground was brown with them; and here and there out of the banks hung the great roots that the Kaffirs use to make medicine of.* They crossed the bed of the mountain torrent, where the little stream of water, not thicker now in the dry weather than two fingers, was running among the great rocks, making clear pools here and there. On the other side of the torrent the path grew quickly steeper, and the mountainside rose abruptly. She took the narrow upward footpath made by the Kaffir maids when they went to fetch wood; the nam-nams and jasmine shrubs* made a thick wall on either side, and the wild asparagus hung out long waving arms. By and by they came to a patch where olive-wood trees grew thick among fragments of fallen rocks covered with long dry moss. Just here, suddenly, they came to a small open space; two mighty rocks that must have fallen from their home in the crags on the mountain tops centuries before lay there, covered with long dry moss and red lichens. In the crack in one, tall slender young trees were growing and the space between the rocks was bare, covered only by a smooth carpet of moss and sorrel, with little fern leaves intermingled here and there; and the small, sweet-scented mountain geranium with its tiny pale blossom was growing close to the foot of the rocks. A bush of the tall scarlet geranium, with its brilliant blossoms, grew up against one rock. On the other side the bush rose like a solid wall, nam-nams and sweet-henries* mingling with the larger trees. The bare space between the rocks and the bush was just like a little almost square room, with a rich soft carpet.

John-Ferdinand broke away a branch of scarlet geranium, which left clear a little mound covered with fern and moss, close to the foot of one rock.

'Sit there,' he said. 'This is my little parlour; I come here often.'

She sat down on the mound, and he stretched himself at her feet on the carpet of moss and sorrel.

'It is very nice here,' she said.

'Yes,' he answered.

She took her great muslin kappie off and laid it across her knee. 'It's quite cool,' she said.

'Yes,' he said.

Then they were quiet for a long time. At last he stretched out his hand, and from the branch of scarlet geranium he had broken he began plucking the brightest blossoms and mixing them with the small fern leaves in the carpet. When he had gathered a tiny bunch, he laid it upon her knee.

'They are very beautiful,' he said.

'Yes,' she answered—then he stretched out his hand and scattered them again over the moss and sorrel.

'Oh—I liked them!'

'They do not belong to you. I should not have given them you,' he said slowly. 'This is yours.'

He rose and from the wall of bush he plucked a small spray of the plumbago* that hung out everywhere.

'This is the sweetest flower of South Africa,' he said. He placed it on her knee close to her hand, and lay down again on the carpet at her feet. 'Those others are not for you,' he said, looking up at her. 'They are for women in crowded ballrooms and theatres. They can live there, in the hot, stifling air—these are yours—they would fade there in a moment.'

Bertie touched softly with her finger the delicate blue leaves and the spirally curled buds.

He turned round onto his face again; the crushed leaves of the tiny mountain geraniums sent up a sweet, aromatic odour as he moved.

'Would you mind my reading?' he asked.

'Oh, no.'

He took out his book and laid it open before him on the turf, and leaned on his folded arms, reading at her feet.

Baby-Bertie fastened the sweet-henry spray he had given her with a pin to the front of her white dress; then she sat still. She could hear the wood doves cooing and the cock-o-veets calling in the cool morning air.

There was much wondering at the farmhouse and no little searching when dinner time came near and Baby-Bertie was not to be found. It was an unheard-of thing that she should wander further than the kraals, or the milk house, or at most the end of the orchard. Griet, Bertie's little Bushman maid, who had been sent to look for her, and who had searched for her even in the oven at last, now sat down on the step of the loft ladder and howled, covering her face with her pinafore, and knocking her heels against the lower rung; but partly peering out from the side of her pinafore now and then to see what effect her grief had on the group of little Kaffirs gathered below to watch her. She declared that the great spook with red eyes, whom she had seen at the fountain the evening before when she went to fetch water, had certainly carried off Miss Bertie and eaten her. The little Kaffirs looked up at her with wonder and awe. They regarded her as a person highly favoured and much gifted.

Presently she saw Bertie coming down the kloof road in the hot sun, for the day had now grown warm, with John-Ferdinand following her; and the sweet-henry on her breast, curled up but still fastened there.

Then Griet got down quickly and stood with her face buried in the wall of the gable, sobbing bitterly. (She had seen Bertie go up the kloof road, and knew where she was all the time.) She thought Bertie would stop as she passed her to find out the cause of her grief and when she did would pat her on the head, and perhaps promise to give her the point of the sheep's tail,* to console her.

But Bertie walked by her without seeing her.

'Daddy-long-legs!* Why didn't he stay in his own country!'—Griet whirled round from the gable wall, making her little skirts stand out all stiffly. 'Daddy-long-legs! Why did he ever come here! Taking our Miss Bertie away from us, to walk with him! Let him stay in his own country!' She whirled till there was only a cloud of yellow petticoats, and the little naked Kaffirs looked on.

After that day everyone knew where Bertie was when she was not to be found in the milk room or the kitchen or the garden.

She and John-Ferdinand often went for walks. Sometimes they went in the early morning when the dew was on the grass, and you were afraid to set your foot down because you broke the spangles, and when the calves were putting their faces through the wet bars of their kraals and the cows were lowing for them, and the sheep had their backs dark with the dew, as they streamed out of their kraals, with the herd boy with his two sticks in his hand behind them: and when, as you walked through the mimosa trees and touched a branch, the dew rained down on you, and the long beams of the early sun made it sparkle like a shower of diamonds.

Sometimes they went in the evening up the steep bare spur of the mountainside that lay to the left of the farmhouse, where the long waving grass grew; and they passed the herd boy coming down with his flock of curly Angora goats,* a great Boer goat* leading them with a bell round his neck, and the Angoras running hither and thither on every side to have a last nibble at the few thorn trees among the long grass. Then they sat high up on the ridge and saw the sun set at the end of the valley, and the farmhouse on the other spur of the mountain below them looked like a white speck among the dark orange trees; and they watched the long curls of blue smoke rising in the still air from the Kaffir huts, where the maids were lighting the evening fires with mielie cobs: and they saw the line of dust which hung over the road by which the sheep were going to the kraal; and in the dry grass about them the avondbloem were coming out, and the air was full of the sweet night scent. Then they would walk down the steep stony footpath together, and say nothing; except John-Ferdinand asked her which was the best footpath to take, or she told him the name of one of some little night insects which began to buzz by them. They were very silent.

But especially in the middle of the day, when it was too hot to walk anywhere else, they went up to the little parlour in the bush. John-Ferdinand lay on the ground and read, and Baby-Bertie took out sewing she had brought with her and sat at the foot of the rock; and they stayed there long hours, often without speaking.

The little mother was glad she went out with him; it was a change for Bertie, and it was bad to have a visitor one did not know how to entertain. No one thought it strange she should like to walk out with her cousin. Only Griet resented it. She turned up the little flattened ball in the centre of her face which was her nose, whenever she mentioned him.

When Bertie was at home she was unusually silent, and went about her work more quietly than ever; only the placid half smile that was always upon her face was deepened into something softer.

Rebekah was quiet too. When she was not actively attending to her babies she was always reading. She read when she woke in the morning; in the grey dawn she drew back the curtain and lay on the side of the bed with her book stretched out that the early light might fall on it, while the baby lay drinking at her breast. She read at night; when supper was over and she could go to her own room and shut her door and lie reading without interruption, sometimes till the old cock at the wagon house began to crow; and often when she blew the light out she found the square of the window was already becoming dimly visible. She read in the afternoon, for a large part of the time when everyone else slept. Even when she was taking care of her children under the orange trees or in the orchard, she had always a book in her hand; and if one came near to interrupt her, she looked up with an eager, sharp look—the look of a hungry dog eating a bone, when someone comes near him. She seemed like a creature returning to its old habitat and resuming its old instincts and habits; but never, even when she was a child and first learnt to read, had she read with such a concentration of almost fierce avidity. It was as though she hardly saw the world about her; even Bertie and her parents and the old farm she saw as through a mist, and only the world of her thought was real to her.

But one evening, when Baby-Bertie was in the milk room skimming the pans, Rebekah came with a mug to fetch fresh cream for her children. It was quite dark in the milk room already, and Bertie bent over the table holding a lighted tallow candle in one hand, and the saucer in the other, with which she went over the pans, putting the cream into the little wooden cream vat at her side.

Rebekah stood still for a moment just inside the doorway. The light of the candle her sister held shed its yellow light full upon her, on her plain white dress, and lovely downturned face, and made her stand out from the dark shadows which filled the rest of the low room, almost illuminated. Rebekah stood looking at her for some seconds; then she came in and put her mug on the end of the long table. Bertie filled it. Still Rebekah waited, watching her work.

Suddenly Bertie said, 'Rebekah, I wish I was different and not like I am! I wish I was clever. I am so big and heavy! I am so stupid!—I wish I were like you!' She looked up, and under her curled lashes the candlelight showed a tear had gathered.

'I can understand about work and such things,' she said slowly, looking back at her work, 'but I can't talk about books and all the clever things other people talk of. Sometimes when Father and you and Cousin John-Ferdinand are talking together at meal times—sometimes I wish I was dead. I want so to be different!' She bent down over her work. 'Rebekah, do you think anyone could ever love me who was very clever and not stupid like I am?'

Rebekah stood looking at the lovely face, half turned from her as it bent over its work. She almost laughed softly: 'You need not fear people will not love you, darling, you will be loved wherever you go; I am only afraid you will be loved too much.'

'Rebekah, I like so to be loved!'

Rebekah made a little caressing movement as though she would have put out her hand and touched the hand nearest her in which Bertie held the candle; then she heard the baby crying through the spare-room window and hurried away with her mug. Before Bertie had finished the milk, the quiet dreamy smile had settled down on her face again.

The next morning, as Rebekah lay under the orange trees, with her book in her hand and her baby asleep on her arm, her boys playing beside her, John-Ferdinand came out of the house and appeared to be looking for someone and then turned to pass on to the orchard. Rebekah put down her book, and told him she wished to go for a walk with him.

'I am sorry I cannot,' he said. 'I have asked Bertie to go with me as soon as her work is done.'

'That does not matter. I shall not keep you long.'

She rose and, calling Griet to watch the children, led the way round the corner of the house and past the kraals; she took the short cut through the mimosa trees towards the great dam in the flat. John-Ferdinand followed her with the copy of Milton* he had been reading showing from his breast pocket. The path among the trees was so narrow that the thorns in the mimosa trees pecked at them as they passed.

When they got to the dam, Rebekah led the way along the narrow footpath that ran on to the broad top of the earthen wall that formed the dam. The path was almost overgrown with love-grass* and chickweed* and widows;* and the great willow trees which grew at intervals hung over the path and dipped their branches into the water beyond. Rebekah and John-Ferdinand stood knee deep among the weeds under the willows. They had not spoken all the way down, and they still stood silent for a few minutes.

On the other side of the dam where the water was shallower the lilies and water plants floated; and the goslings swam in and out among them, and disappeared and reappeared among the chickweed and wild mustard* that grew rank to the water's edge. Beyond them was a little mound where Bertie's twin sister, who had died when she was born, had been buried. Bertie often came down to weed about it and keep it clear; but during the last weeks she had forgotten it, and the weeds had almost overgrown it.

Rebekah took off her kappie and held it in her hand.

'John-Ferdinand,' she said, 'I wish to speak to you about Bertie.'

John-Ferdinand bowed his head gravely, to show he was attending, and looked down at her.

'She has led a lonely life here. A woman who grows up alone on a solitary farm in South Africa is not quite in the position of most other women. A child of ten who has lived in a village or town, and has gone to a school, and grown up among other children, has more knowledge of the world in a thousand ways than she can have, even at fifteen or twenty. She may know much of books, and be skilled in domestic labour or—she may even be exceptionally advanced intellectually in many ways; she is still a child in the knowledge of men and life. Bertie does not know even the world of books.'

John-Ferdinand bowed again, and looked down at her with his dark head delicately poised a little on one side.

'You have seen a great deal of her since you came here; I do not blame you; it was natural you should. She is the only interesting thing here; and she is very beautiful. But I am afraid she may possibly grow to care a little for you, John-Ferdinand, seeing no one else.'

John-Ferdinand moved as if he were about to speak, but she raised her hand and stopped him.

'She has said nothing of her feeling towards you to me; I am acting entirely on my own judgment. But she has seen no men in her life, but a few shop clerks and farmers' sons who may have come here on business, or have served her in a shop when she was in town: you are the first man of mental and physical attractions with whom she has been thrown into close contact. It has been almost inevitable that she should be attracted to you; and it has been almost as inevitable that you should feel attracted towards her. And yet, when you marry, you will probably require in your wife certain qualities which Baby-Bertie has not: more intellect, and more calm strength of character. Now, if this is the case, John-Ferdinand,'—she looked up at him—'and you feel that, in spite of her great beauty, she is not the type of woman you can make your wife, then I think you ought to go away from the farm and not seek to meet her again. It is an absorbing love she would love you with, John-Ferdinand; a love you probably cannot understand. You might become all the world to her. Some women with complex, many-sided natures, if love fails them and one half of their nature dies, can still draw a kind of broken life through the other. The world of the impersonal is left them: they can still turn fiercely to it, and through the intellect draw in a kind of life—a poor, broken, half-asphyxiated life, not what it might have been; like the life of a man with one lung eaten out by disease, who has to live through the other alone—but still life. But Bertie and such as Bertie have only one life possible, the life of personal relations; if that fails them all fails. If you chop down the stem of a mimosa tree, years after you may come and find from the bottom of the old dead stem sprouts have sprung, which will even bear flowers, though there will never be the glory of the central stem; but an aloe has one flower, once; if you cut that down, nothing more comes.* If the life of personal relations fails Bertie, all will have failed her; I want to save her from this. You are a man of principle, John-Ferdinand; I know you are a man who always does what he believes to be his duty. I think you will feel it your duty to go, if you know you cannot care for her.'

'Rebekah,' he said softly, still looking at her, 'I love your little sister. She is the one absolutely pure and beautiful thing life has ever yet shown me. From all the world of men and women I turn to her to find in her the one absolutely spotless, Christ-like thing I have known. I am a nobler and a better man when I am in her presence. No other woman ever could be, or ever will be to me, what she is. When as a youth I asked you to marry me I was drawn to you by your intellect, your strange intensity, and delicate physical refinement and beauty, and your devotion to your duties. My feeling for her is wholly different. For the first time I understand now how men have made a god of woman—the eternal virgin mother!—If I am all the world to her, Rebekah, she is more than all the world to me.'

Rebekah looked up at him, and then away across the water. There was no mistaking the ring of sincerity in the man's voice; his dark blue eyes were moist with unshed tears. They stood quiet for a moment. The willow trees sifted down the last of the spring's little dried catkins on Rebekah's brown hair and John-Ferdinand's black felt hat.

'If I have not yet spoken to her of my love, Rebekah, it has been because she has seemed to me almost too pure and sacred a thing for me to approach. Can you understand? Have you never felt on a solitary mountainside that some delicate flower you have found growing there was too beautiful to be plucked? That it was too pure for your finger to touch it?—When your father has helped me to secure a farm in this neighbourhood, so that I shall not need to take her far from her parents and her old home, I shall lay my love before her. I hope it will not be long before I take her to myself forever.'

Rebekah looked away from him to where the little goslings swam in and out among the water lilies.

'If that is so,' she said slowly, 'I have no right to say more, and perhaps I should not have said what I have.' She gathered together her little skirts, and turned to lead the way along the little footpath. Then suddenly she turned. 'If I knew,' she said, 'that you would ever fail her, I, I, with my own hand would rather take her life, and see her lying buried there, beside her little sister.' The crimson flush had risen suddenly over her face, darkening even her forehead; it died away in an instant, and left the face paler than before. She walked on before him, the black widows, shaken from bushes as they passed, sticking fast to her skirts and to his black trousers. When they got off the dam wall, she took the path among the thorn trees, and walked so fast John-Ferdinand could hardly keep up with her. When they had climbed almost to the top of the long rise on which the house stood, she stood still for an instant and took out her penknife, and cut a large, many-horned gall growth from one of the mimosa branches. 'I am collecting these,' she said, half turning to him, 'to see whether the galls on the different species of mimosa are all quite alike, or whether they are different on different species of the tree.' Then she walked on quickly.

When they came out of the thorn trees at the kraals, they saw the white tent of a cart, which stood outspanned near the back door.

'The woman from England must have come,' she said. 'They were expecting her today.'

As they came nearer the house they saw Bertie standing on the top kitchen doorstep, and beside her a tall woman with square shoulders, dressed in a starched mauve cotton dress, with white collar and cuffs.

Bertie, in her white muslin and blue ribbons, was motioning with her right hand, evidently pointing out to the stranger the interesting points in the landscape, from the wagon house and pig sty, to the great dam, and the road over the nek, which could all be seen to advantage from the top of the steps. As they approached the steps, Bertie and the newcomer came down to meet them. She had light hair of an almost drab shade touched with yellow, and parted down the centre. It was brushed smoothly down on each side, showing strikingly the large, flat-topped, broad shape of the head. Her forehead was high and arched in the middle; and her large eyebrows were even more arched, so that between them and the pale blue eyes below, over which the eyelids habitually drooped, almost the whole bulb of the eyeball showed under its eyelid. Her eyelashes were thick and almost white, and drooped over her cheeks readily as she looked down. She walked towards them with a long, even stride that contrasted with Bertie's wavering, uneven little footsteps.

She held out a large, flat, cool hand to Rebekah and John-Ferdinand, when Bertie introduced her.

It was not easy to say what her age was; it might have been anything between twenty-eight and thirty-eight; the perfect placidity of her face might make her appear older than she was; or being old might make her appear younger.

'You must have had a warm drive from the town,' John-Ferdinand said.

'No, it was very pleasant,' she said slowly; 'the view was very interesting.'

Then they all turned and went into the house.

CHAPTER IV

SHOWING HOW BABY-BERTIE HEARD THE CICADA'S CRY

'WHEREIN lies this woman's charm?'

This question Rebekah had asked herself more than once before Veronica Grey had been at the farm three weeks.

She looked at the angular high shoulders, at the rather large mouth, somewhat drawn down at the corners, as in a fixed half smile; at the thickened fingertips on the large, flat, snow-white hands; and at the white eyelashes—and found no immediate answer.

Everyone at the farm seemed to like her except Griet.*

The father liked her. He seldom went to his mielie lands to examine the new varieties of grain he was experimenting with, or to the orchard to look at his grafts, but he took her with him. Her past life in a villa in the south of London could hardly have yielded her an extensive knowledge of African field growths, and she did not know a mielie land from a wheat field, or a bed of sweet potatoes from one of pumpkins;* but she always said, 'Ah, yes,' when the father discussed the varying growth in his beds and their manures; and when she looked at the grafts she said, 'How *very* interesting!' or 'How *wonderfully* they are growing!' and the father liked her company.

The little mother liked her. On days when she had a headache and went to lie down, Veronica came and sat in the rocking chair beside her bed, knitting, and saying nothing; and when the little mother was better and able to talk, she sat rocking and listened to all her complaints, and never tried to put a good complexion onto her troubles; she only said, 'How strange!' or 'That is just what my mother often said!' and the little mother liked her.

Bertie liked her; she was something new to take care of. When the hand-lambs and all the poultry had been fed, and there were no sick Kaffirs to attend to, and Rebekah's children needed nothing, there was always still Veronica. She used to bring a glass of milk to her bed at six in the morning, when the cows were first milked, and little cups of broth or beaten-up egg and wine between breakfast and dinner; and she insisted on her sleeping in the room next to her own, which used to be Rebekah's, so that if she woke in the night and needed anything she might knock on the wall and not feel lonely—as Bertie herself still often felt she did when she woke in the night, and had to clasp a pillow to her and hold it tight in her arms to make herself feel as if there were someone sleeping by her and caring for her.* She ironed Veronica's white dresses herself; because the maids could not make them smooth and stiff enough.

John-Ferdinand liked her. When Bertie was busy with her housework, he used to read aloud to her from *Idylls of the King* or *Paradise Lost*, and she would sit knitting and listening; and often she would drop the work into her lap, and sit with her hands across upon it, and her blue eyes fixed on the cover of the book he was reading from; for half an hour she would sit motionless, listening; and sometimes she asked him to read a long passage over again; and that he liked most of all.

Old Ayah liked her; she said she gave no trouble; and kept her room beautifully neat; there was never a thread or a scrap of paper on her carpet; and her large, flat-soled, thick English boots stood exactly side by side under the dressing table, toe to toe; and her gloves lay ready on the dressing table in case she should be going out, finger to finger and thumb to thumb; and she gave old Ayah, who did her room, a shawl she had knitted.*

As for Rebekah, she was so busy attending to her children, and reading, that she seldom spoke to anyone; and no one noticed that she never addressed a remark to Veronica, and generally left the room or the stoep when Veronica came there.

But Griet showed her dislike actively. One evening when she went to the fountain to fetch water for the baths, she found a fine, large toad under a stone, with great warts on his back. Carefully catching it with two sticks, she put it into the pail, which she carried home on her head and emptied into Veronica's bath. She hoped that when Veronica got up the next morning and stepped into the bath, she might not notice it till she was in the bath. About the time Veronica usually got up, Griet stood outside her bedroom door, first on one leg and then on the other, rolling her eyes and holding her breath, momentarily expecting to hear a step into the bath and then a wild cry* and a flight across the floor. But instead a calm voice called to her from the bedroom, 'Griet, I think there is something moving in my bath; come in and see what it is and take it out!' and Griet, bursting with rage, had to come in and recapture her toad. 'How did that "thin-eyes" know that I was there!' she cried indignantly when rehearsing the story to herself as she emptied the bath;* and her defeat increased her antipathy; but she contented herself with setting Veronica the cracked plate at tea time, and the bluntest knife at dinner; and occasionally putting a small drop of aloes* into the coffee she took to her room in the morning, in which case Veronica always left it undrunk.

One Saturday night, when Veronica Grey had been just eight weeks at the farm, the father and John-Ferdinand came home to supper. They said they had signed an agreement with the owner of the next farm, the tops of the tall blue-gum trees about whose homestead were just visible over the nek* when you climbed the mountainside, to sell his farm to John-Ferdinand for five thousand pounds, and to give him possession at once.

There was much talking about it at the supper that evening. Veronica Grey said she had often wondered what that farm was like, and John-Ferdinand said they should all go and see it the next week. Only Rebekah could not go, as her visit had come to its close; and she was leaving at daybreak on Monday morning in the ox-wagon to begin her journey to Algoa Bay,* from which she would go by sea to Cape Town.

After supper, the mother, who had a headache, went early to bed, and Rebekah went to her own room; the father sat with his books in the dining room; Bertie, who was finishing a dress for Griet to wear the next day, sat by the lamp at the centre table in the front room sewing, and John-Ferdinand sat beside her reading, but now and again he looked away from his book, and watched her fingers as they sewed. Veronica sat in an armchair in the far corner of the room knitting; as she knitted from time to time her eyes from under their long white lashes rested on the two who sat together at the table. At last she rose and gathered her work into its bag; and went to the little mother's bedroom.

'Would not you like me to come and sit by you a little?' she asked; and she seated herself on the rocking chair beside the bed. For a long time there was nothing to be heard but the tick, tick of her needles. By and by, however, her hands dropped into her lap and she sat looking at the painted motto that hung on the wall opposite the bed with its border of lilies and roses.

Then the little mother, who had been half dozing, woke up feeling much better; and showed an inclination to talk.

Veronica said that was a very pretty motto on the wall. The mother lay on her side and told her all the story of Percy Lawrie, how he had stayed on the farm and taught Bertie, and how nicely he could paint; how he had had bad news from England and had gone away suddenly and they had never heard any news of him again. Veronica listened, and knitted, and rocked herself. Then the little mother gradually got drowsy again and went off to sleep.

When she was sleeping soundly, Veronica rose and rolled up her work and put it into the little bag upon her arm, and went out of the room, closing the door behind her. In the passage all was quiet, but you could hear Bertie at the piano singing sacred music, and John-Ferdinand's voice singing the bass, through the closed door of the front room. The long passage itself was dark; but through the half-open door of John-Ferdinand's bedroom at the far end shone a light. He had evidently not put his candle out when he went to supper. As she went towards her own room she passed John-Ferdinand's door. She looked round quickly; every other door into the passage was closed, and John-Ferdinand's and Bertie's voices could still be heard singing.

With a long, light, smooth step she passed into John-Ferdinand's room. The candle stood on the dressing table. She looked round the room. It was the first time she had ever stood alone in a man's bedroom. Her father had died in her early childhood and her brother had been grown up and gone to China before she could well remember, and in the quiet home in the south of London, where her widowed mother and four unmarried sisters lived, no men visitors had ever come. She stood just inside the door and looked round. On a rack against the wall behind the door hung a row of articles of man's clothing—coats and jackets and waistcoats and trousers; under the dressing table was a row of boots, and a pair of man's slippers stood beside the bed. She walked up to the clothes behind the door and passed her hand softly over them; she took down a greatcoat and felt the velvet collar and the buttons; she rubbed her cheek gently against the shoulder of the coat. So a man's shoulder felt when you put your face against it. She took down a pair of trousers, stroked them, and hung them up again; she felt the buckles at the back of a waistcoat; then she walked to the washing stand. There was nothing there but the ordinary soap and sponge and toothbrush that any woman might have used, as John-Ferdinand did not shave but clipped his soft beard; but she touched the soap and toothbrush with her finger. She went to the bedside; there was a large braided bag before the pillows; she turned back the flap; there was a man's thick linen garment inside; she did not take it out, but stood listening to hear if anyone were coming. But Bertie and John-Ferdinand were still singing in the front room, and there was no other sound. She turned to the dressing table; there were his brushes and combs and a large bottle of lavender water. On each side of the glass was a small pile of books. She ran her fingers quickly over them. From under the looking glass protruded the end of a closed, old-fashioned portrait case. She drew it out and tried to open it; she moved the little hook that fastened it. Inside the case was an old daguerreotype portrait. It was the portrait of a little child of four with a mass of brown curls about its head; the face was smiling; there were dimples in the cheek and in the chin; the child seemed bursting with life and joy, and in its hand it held a bunch of flowers. The old tinted daguerreotype had the colour of life, the cheeks and lips were red. She held it sloping towards the candle, at such an angle that she could see it truly through the glass. There was no mistaking whom it represented. It was Bertie as a child, and the only photograph of her in existence. John-Ferdinand had begged the loan of it from the mother, that he might send it to Cape Town with Rebekah to have a life-sized enlargement taken from it.

Veronica looked down closely into the face, and her eyes contracted slowly at the inner corners. Quickly she put the case down open on the table, and placing her large flat thumb on the face, she pressed; in a moment the photograph had cracked into a hundred fine little splinters of glass radiating from the face, which was indistinguishable. With smooth quickness she closed the case and slipped it under the looking glass, without one bit of glass falling from its place. She stood listening to hear whether anyone was coming. There was no one; and with one or two long, even steps she glided out of the room; with three or four more she had reached her own, and closed the door.

The next day the morning broke, peaceful and windless, but it promised to be unusually hot later. A deep Sunday stillness reigned about the farmhouse after breakfast; the Kaffir servants were gone to their huts to have their Sunday rest; old Ayah sat at the kitchen door slicing salad and keeping an eye on the pots inside with the Sunday dinner. Griet had gone off to the far lands to pick some green mielies; swearing vengeance upon all the world because she had been accused by old Ayah of breaking Bertie's photograph when she dusted John-Ferdinand's room, and had narrowly escaped the force of old Ayah's hand by Bertie's intervention. The father in his Sunday best was reading Swedenborg* in the front room, with his hair very much brushed. The little mother was busy in her bedroom, and Rebekah with her boys was, as always, out under the orange trees upon the mats.

John-Ferdinand came out at the front door, looking for Bertie to go for a walk with him. Rebekah did not glance up from her book as he passed, and he walked on through the flower garden and down into the orchard beyond.

Of late, without actually shunning him, Bertie had seemed to elude him; it seemed almost as though she feared to be alone with him; yet when he spoke to her there was a wavering in her colour, and a soft brightening about her face she could not hide.

He wandered into the orchard. The long dry grass was brown under the trees, the young unripe peaches had fallen by hundreds into it, and the leaves of the peach trees were beginning to grow yellow for want of rain. At the great pear tree in the middle of the orchard, on the bench which Rebekah had had put up* around the stem when she was sixteen, he saw someone sitting. At first he thought it might be Bertie, but when he came closer he saw it was Veronica Grey.

She was dressed in one of her spotless, stiff, cotton dresses, with broad, stiff, white linen collar and cuffs; a great straw hat with only a simple band of ribbon tied about the crown lay on the bench beside her, and a book of Sunday sermons lay open beside it. The little sunbeams came through the pear branches and played on her smoothly brushed yellow and drab hair; but her eyes were fixed on the row of peach trees before her, and her long white fingers were clasped together upon her knee.

John-Ferdinand stood still at a little distance and watched her. It was a curious picture of placid calm, not a line in figure or dress moving as she sat under the soft playing shadows and lights. He stepped closer to her and asked her if she had seen Bertie. Without unclasping her hands she turned her face towards him and said slowly, 'No,' and then looked back again at the trees.

John-Ferdinand turned away; yet as he wandered up through the orchard the placid picture under the tree was with him. He walked through the flower garden and out at the gate at the north gable of the house, and took the little footpath among the mimosa trees that led up into the kloof.

Now he was thinking only of Bertie. He pictured the farmhouse among the blue-gum trees as it would be when he and Bertie lived there; Bertie, with her beautiful face and queenly figure lighting up the world about her, till lambs and servants and everyday work reflected that beauty, that had made the old farm so lovely to him. He saw her as she had looked that morning at breakfast, when someone had told her that the old Kaffir man she was nursing* was worse, and she had left her breakfast and gone out with a jug of hot milk in one hand, and the bottle of medicine in the other, to go to the huts, and see if she could do anything for him; as deeply concerned, as if it mattered to anyone but herself, whether there was one old woolly head in the world more or less. A creature so full of loveliness, and love for every living thing, was she not satisfying to the whole soul and body of a man? As he followed the little footpath among the trees, his mind ran on to the long years that were to come; he saw children with their mother's fawnlike eyes looking up at him and calling him father, and the thing he loved lying always in his bosom to comfort and complete his life: it was as though he looked up a long valley where ridge succeeds ridge in new colours, till the far end was reddened with sunset glory.

So far had his thoughts led him, that he had crossed the almost dry bed of the mountain torrent and had reached their little room, and almost trodden on a little ungloved hand, before he saw that Baby-Bertie was before him, sitting at the foot of their rocks, with one hand resting on the moss beside her.

'Why did you come without me?' he said, as he lay down on the turf beside her, so close that his folded arms rested on the edge of her white dress. He had never before done so. 'I thought I should find you here.'

She was dressed in her best white Sunday dress, with bows all down the front, and a blue ribbon round her neck.

'Do you know what I was thinking of as I came up?' he said after a while; 'I seemed to be looking into the future; and it seemed to me,' he added softly, 'that I was looking down a long sunlit path that passed over ridge after ridge, each one more beautiful than the last, till the end, far beyond human sight, lay hidden in glory.'

Bertie sat quiet; she was thinking of no beauty in the future, only of a hand very near to her that she would have liked to bow down to and kiss humbly.

John-Ferdinand spoke in a yet lower voice: 'Nothing can ever alter, nothing can ever change, our happiness, that springs from such deep love. Death itself will be but going home to the Father's house to be made perfect there in that which made us loved and loving here.' He looked up at her. 'For those who love as we love, there is no parting, and no death, only eternal union.'

She listened, and the sound of his voice was music to her; but of the meaning she took in little.

'I do not like to think of what will come,' she said, bending her head; 'I like all things to be just as they are, now; never, never to change! I wish they would always be just so!'

He too at that moment seemed content with an unchanged present. He lay still watching the little hand that rested on the sorrel close to his; and once he looked up at the opening overhead, across which at intervals small thunderclouds were already beginning to move quickly against the hot blue sky. Why did it seem so hard to take that woman to his arms, and tell her how he loved her? Why did she seem, without repulsing him, to move away from his hands when he meant to put them out and hold her?

It was already nearly midday and a sultry stillness was beginning to settle down over the bush. Nothing broke it but the shrill cry of some cicadas hidden in the thickets, and in the stems of the trees.

Then he rose from the ground, and leaned his elbow against the rock, and bent down over her.

'Bertie, my darling,' he said softly, 'you must not miss me too much if I go away next week. I shall only be gone for a few days, that I may get all that will be necessary for our new home. And then I will come back to you, and you will come to me and we will be together forever; never, never to part while life is left us. You are my wife now, already, my darling; are you not?'

He bent down and wound his left arm round her, half drawing her up to him. For a moment it seemed as though she would have leaped up and nestled close to him; then she loosened herself from his arm and sat down again on the bank.* 'You must not touch me, you must not kiss me—you must stand still, just where you are—against the rock—I want to say something to you—I want to tell you something.'

For a moment he tried to draw her to him again; then silently, wondering, he obeyed her. She sat on the mound at his feet. There was that in her voice that compelled him to listen, and the dimpled hand that had rested on the turf was on her knee now and quivering; her face he could not see; he looked down at her waving hair that hung in little curls about her forehead.

For a moment she was quiet. He waited; but still she said nothing.

'My little Baby, what is it you want to say to me? I only have not long ago told you how I love you, only because I thought you knew, as I knew, how you loved me.'*

He bent over her again, with his face above her head.

'I do not know what to say—stand back as you were before—with your arm against the rock.'

He obeyed her, and waited.

'Long ago I had a schoolmaster; his name was Percy Lawrie—I—I—liked him—I liked him very much. He was very kind to me. I liked him at first, then afterwards I hated him.' The hands she had now folded together in her lap were covered in the palms with a cold perspiration. 'I did not know—he said he would be angry with me—I did not want him to be angry with me—I didn't want to—I didn't know, you see!—Oh, what shall I do!—What shall I do!' She half started up, and then sank down on the mound again.

John-Ferdinand looked down at her, white, motionless.

'He went away that day—I never saw him any more!'

John-Ferdinand leaned heavily on his arm on the rock above her, his face an ashen white. The scent of the crushed geraniums on which he stood seemed to rise up overpoweringly strong: and the only sound was the crying out of the cicadas: they seemed glorying in the hot stillness of the bush.

John-Ferdinand took his elbow from the rock.

For a moment Bertie made a movement as though she would have moved up close to him; then she sat down motionless.

'Bertie, do you mean that you gave yourself to him?'

She nodded.

He waited in silence. 'My poor cousin!' he said slowly.

There was a cicada in the bush, just to the left, that cried louder and louder; its cry seemed to ring through her brain; she wondered when it would leave off.

'Let us go home, Bertie,' he said slowly.

She stood up from the mound. The bush had become very hot and deadly still; only the cicadas cry* seemed ringing everywhere. She began to walk down the little path; John-Ferdinand followed her. The leaves of the plumbago bushes on either side hung flaccid and curled, and even the asparagus branches drooped, waiting for the storm that must come later. They crossed the bed of the mountain stream and climbed the bank on the other side where the great roots hung out, and the ground was covered with the fallen Kaffir beans; the leaves and dried sticks cracked under their feet as they walked.* Just here, where the trees were tallest and met overhead and the monkey ropes hung down, and where there was deep shade and stillness, they met Veronica Grey coming up from the farmhouse into the bush, holding her stiff white skirt about her with one hand and in the other, which drooped in front of her, her half-open book, with her finger between the leaves. She smiled tranquilly as she passed them.

'What a peaceful Sabbath stillness reigns up here!' she said; and she walked on higher into the bush, as John-Ferdinand and Bertie went down.

When they had got beyond the belt of tall trees where the small mimosa trees and scattered kunee trees grew, she turned suddenly and looked up at him. 'I hurt you so! I hurt you so!' she said.

He looked down at her. 'It is not pain that matters, Bertie; it is sin,' he said slowly.

She looked up into his white, drawn face with its compressed nostrils. Then she gathered her skirts tight about her and fled down the winding footpath. An outstretched branch of mimosa caught in her skirt and tore it from top to bottom; but she did not pause. In an instant she was out of sight. There was nothing, when John-Ferdinand passed the next winding, but the tiny rag of white muslin with its blue bow hanging from a thorn to show she had been there.

That night, at ten o'clock, all the boxes and bedding had already been packed into the ox-wagon, which was drawn out before the back door, prepared for Rebekah's start the next morning before dawn. The yokes were laid out in order before the wagon, and the riems* hung over the side ready to inspan* in the dark; and the oxen were sleeping in the kraal. The household had retired early, as they had to rise so soon; only Rebekah was still busy in her room arranging the clothes which the children would require to put on in the morning, and tying up the last parcels.

When she had finished, she went to Bertie's room. Bertie had been there since before dinner, complaining of feeling unwell; and even the great thunderstorm which had burst in the afternoon had not revived her.

Rebekah opened the door very gently, fearing to awake her if she had dropped asleep. But Bertie was kneeling on the floor in the middle of the room, a large box open before her, and a candle balanced on one corner; while Griet, with much alacrity, was adding the contents of the lowest drawer in the chest to the pile of clothes that lay on the floor at Bertie's side. Bertie was putting the articles one by one into the box.

Rebekah set down her candle on the dressing table, and walked up to her, looking down with astonishment. Bertie did not look up, but went on mechanically fitting the articles in.

'Bertie, what is this?' Rebekah asked.

She did not look up: 'I am going with you,' she said shortly, in a voice almost low and gruff; and went on packing. Her face was turned downwards; her lips looked heavy and protruding; but there was no sign of her having wept.

Rebekah put her hand on Bertie's arm: 'How is this, Bertie?* What is it?'

'I am going with you.' There was a dull, dogged persistency in the tone.

'But does Mother know of this?'

'I am going with you.'

Griet, who had just added the very last article of the drawer to the heap on the floor, stood with her eyes rolling and glittering, delighted with the general confusion and the excitement of something unusual happening, though she did not understand what.* Rebekah sent her out to go to her bed. When the door was closed, she knelt down beside Bertie.

'What is the matter, my dear one? You have always said you would not leave the farm or go with me, when I have asked you. Has anything happened?'

Bertie said nothing; her heavy face was still turned down. There flashed on Rebekah the remembrance of John-Ferdinand's white, stiff face all that day.

'My darling, is there anything I can do to help you? Anything I can say?'

'Go and tell Mother I am going with you,' she said slowly. 'Make her understand I am going. I will go.'*

Rebekah stood up, but bent down again, putting one hand on her shoulder: 'There is nothing I might say to John-Ferdinand, which could be of any use to you, is there?'

In an instant Bertie had leaped to her feet and caught both Rebekah's hands in hers. 'Oh, no, no!—Rebekah, promise me—you will never—never speak to him of me—never ask him about me—never ask him anything! Promise me, Rebekah!—Promise me!'

For the only time in her life Rebekah saw Bertie transfixed with passion.

'I will do whatever you ask of me, dear one.'

Bertie sank back again on her knees before the box, and Rebekah went out to see the father and the little mother in their bedroom; and tell them of Bertie's resolve. The little mother, who had been half asleep, woke up, and began to whine that it was all so sudden; that she could not bear sudden things; that Bertie had no clothes; that she ought to have told them before; that it was unlike Bertie to take people so by surprise. But when Rebekah had explained that the new clothes could be better got in Cape Town; that the little mother had always wished her to go with her for a visit; that Bertie needed change and ought to see something of life after twenty years on the farm; and, when the father had expressed his full approval of her going, the little mother, still whimpering, insisted on getting up and going to see Bertie; but gave her consent. Bertie gave her as little explanation as she had given Rebekah. She only said stolidly she was going. And the little mother was at last persuaded by Rebekah to go back to her bedroom, still whimpering that she couldn't bear surprises; that she wouldn't have wondered if it had been Rebekah, but that Bertie took after her and never took anyone by surprise; that perhaps after all Bertie took after her father also; and she had no child who really resembled her! But she had no valid objection to make; when Rebekah had bid her goodnight and she found the father was asleep and she had no one to hear her, she got quietly into bed and was soon asleep.

When Rebekah had helped Bertie to pack all her things and they had strapped the last box, it was nearly twelve o'clock. They had spoken only of the work they were busied with. When all was done, Rebekah put her arm softly about Bertie and drew her head onto her breast.

'There is nothing you would like to tell me, Bertie?'

'No, nothing.' She almost drew herself from her sister; who, when she had helped her to undress, went to her own room for a few hours' rest, before the early start.

At half past three the next morning the driver came and knocked at all doors and bedroom windows to rouse them, and everyone lit candles and got up.

It was still absolutely dark outside. The men were at the kraal, sorting out the oxen, and old Ayah stood before the kitchen fire, drawing her little yellow kerchief* tighter about her shoulders, and watching the flame and smoke go up about the kettle, and saying, 'O, ja, Heere!'* partly because she wanted to persuade herself she was quite wide awake, and partly because it was so chilly. Under the dining-room table Griet, who had just been awakened, was sitting upright on the skin on which she slept, and rubbing her eyes and blubbering, partly with cold and sleepiness, and partly because old Ayah had told her that Bertie was going away for six months.

When old Ayah had made the coffee and put it on the dining-room table, they began to file in one by one, and stood round the table drinking it and making believe to eat dried biscuit: the father in his great overcoat with the collar turned up; the little mother in her dressing gown with a shawl over her head; Rebekah in her travelling dress with a large white kappie; while Griet on the bench in the corner sat holding Rebekah's baby, the two boys having been already carried out fast asleep to their bed in the wagon. Then Veronica came in, fully dressed in her starched gown, with collar and cuffs, her hair smooth, and the braids coiled carefully at the back, and a pale blue scarf over her shoulders pinned up neatly at one side. They stood round the table drinking the coffee and eating the biscuit, almost in silence. Only Baby-Bertie and John-Ferdinand were not yet there.

As Bertie came out of her bedroom into the long passage, she saw John-Ferdinand come out of his room. It was almost dark at her end of the passage, and she stood still, thinking he would pass on to the dining room without noticing her. But he saw her and came up the passage towards her. She drew herself close to the wall as if to let him pass, but he stopped when he reached her.

'Bertie,' he said, standing near her, and speaking in a slow, even voice, 'I fear you may think I dealt very hardly with you yesterday. If you feel, that by my expressing my love for you, and showing it as

I have done, I have at all committed myself to you, I am still willing to marry you, if you feel that I should do so! My poor cousin!'

'Oh, no!' she said, in a quick, thick voice. 'No! no! no!' Holding her skirt that it might not touch him, she ran down the passage to the dining room, and John-Ferdinand passed slowly out through the dark front room and round to the back of the house where the wagon was standing.

A little later they were all gathered about the kitchen doorsteps to say goodbye. The light streamed in a great square from the door. Rebekah said goodbye and climbed into the wagon to take her baby. The father folded Bertie in his great arms and kissed her eyes and her mouth. The little mother cried, and reminded her of some of the clothing she ought to buy for herself as soon as she got to Cape Town. Old Ayah and Griet caught hold of her at the same time, both crying; then Veronica, standing in the middle of the doorway, held both Bertie's hands fast in hers and looked full into her face: 'I hope,' she said, 'you will have a happy, a very happy, time in Cape Town. I shall do all I can to fill your place to your dear father and mother. Come back soon!'

Bertie drew her hands from her and went down the steps.

John-Ferdinand stood in the dark beside the oven. Bertie would have walked quickly by him and got into the wagon, but he stepped forward and put into her hand a hand as cold as hers. Then the father helped her to climb in, and the driver clapped his whip and called aloud to the oxen, and slowly the great wagon began to roll away in the dark. Bertie flung herself down on the bed beside the children and buried her face in a pillow; but Rebekah moved to the back of the wagon and sat leaning against the back plank. As the wagon rounded the kraal, she could still see in the bright square of light at the kitchen doorway her father and mother, and Griet and old Ayah standing at the foot of the steps and Veronica standing full in the door,* and John-Ferdinand slowly mounting the steps to go in. Then the house passed out of sight. Half an hour later, as the wagon was climbing the nek,* Rebekah, who still sat looking out at the back, could see in the first grey breaks of dawn the farmhouse glimmering as a white speck among the peaceful orange trees. But Bertie still lay with her face buried in the pillow, as though she were sleeping heavily.

CHAPTER V

JOHN-FERDINAND SHOWS HIS NEW HOUSE*

THE old farm was curiously quiet after Bertie and Rebekah went.

Veronica tried to fill Bertie's place: she poured out the tea and coffee at table, and got the mother to show her how to make bread, and even went to the milk room at night to skim the milk; but she was so curiously still in all her movements that the house seemed quiet and empty.

Griet resented bitterly her attempts to fill Bertie's place. Why should she sit in Miss Bertie's chair, attend to Miss Bertie's flowers, and even move into Miss Bertie's bedroom? And Griet, as far as she was able, took care it did not go well with the bread making; and flower gardening did not prosper as in Baby-Bertie's time.

In the afternoon, when she was sent out by Veronica to water the flowers, after working for a little while she would carefully peer through the stems of the orange trees and look up and down towards the orchard: and if she saw no one coming, she would kneel down quickly and, producing from her little yellow print sleeve a sharp table knife, would slip it under the sod at the root of some balsam or larkspur or brilliantly coloured four-o'clock and cut the stem off two inches below the surface. The next day when Veronica came to inspect the garden she found it drooping; and the day or two after Griet was ordered to pull it up and throw it away. When Veronica asked her what she thought was the cause of the flowers withering, she always fixed her twinkling black eyes on Veronica's face and said, 'Worms, worms!'—a reply which satisfied Veronica, who in her ignorance of gardening did not note it as remarkable that only the annuals died, while the perennials, which would still be there when Bertie returned in six months, were left untouched. Also, why Veronica's bread never rose, and why it sometimes had a strong taste of garlic, and she had at last to leave it for old Ayah to make, was a mystery Veronica never fathomed.

John-Ferdinand had left the farm the day after Bertie and Rebekah went, to go to the next little up-country town to get workmen and material for enlarging and repairing the house on his farm, and also to buy some furniture for it. If he now regretted purchasing it, there was now no way left of getting rid of his bargain.

At the end of ten days he returned to his farm; but to everyone's surprise, though it was only a half-hour's ride on horseback from the old farm, he never came over. It was as though he had no wish to see the place. When he wanted the father's advice on any matter, he sent over a boy with a letter; or he asked him to come over and see him.

At last one afternoon, when he had been on his new farm over five weeks, John-Ferdinand drove over to ask the father's advice about using the dredger to enlarge his dam.

His aunt insisted on his staying to supper, and when it was over, as it was already late and there was no moon, he slept the night there.

The little mother, who was much concerned at his loneliness at his new farm, and the fact that he had only a Kaffir cook,* begged him to come over often. And after that night his visits were not infrequent. He generally drove over in the evening when his day's work of superintendence was ended, and had supper with them. After supper the father went to his books, and then to bed; and as the little mother often could not sit out on the stoep on account of her neuralgic headaches, and as the evenings were now too hot to sit indoors, John-Ferdinand and Veronica often sat on the stoep alone.

Sometimes they talked of England and the places they had both been to; oftener, as they sat in the half darkness, he recited passages from Young's *Night Thoughts** or Keble's hymns,* which Veronica said she admired much; and sometimes they sat quiet and rested.

After a time it became almost a rule that he should drive over in the evenings and sleep at the old farm, returning to his own early in the morning; and on Sunday he always came and spent the whole day. In that way, as the little mother said, he got at least one good meal a day, and it was a break in the solitary monotony of his life; she told him to bring over all his darning and mending; and, as she was generally busy, Veronica did it for him.

One night, about three months after Bertie had gone, he asked the mother if she would drive over with him to his farm the next morning and help him hang his curtains, and give him advice about arranging the china and linen, which had just arrived from England, and which he had ordered before he bought the farm, in view of his marriage with Bertie.

The little mother said she could not go, as it was baking day, but that, if Veronica would go, she would send over two of the best of the

Kaffir maids to help her in arranging the things; and the next morning Veronica drove over with John-Ferdinand.

They came back in the evening just as it was getting dark, and for three days running Veronica went to help him.

The next time the little mother wrote the weekly letter to Rebekah, she said:

'There is generally no news to give you from this dull place, but tonight there is great news, that will very much surprise you.

'Veronica Grey went over with John-Ferdinand to help him to arrange his house for several days, and when they came back last night, after supper he told me and your father he wished to speak with us, and he told us he had asked Veronica to marry him, and that they were engaged and would be married in a few weeks. I was surprised, though your father did not seem to be; I think nothing surprises him. I am very glad about it. It was lonely for him there; and it will be very nice to have relations there. Veronica has been very good trying to help me since Bertie left, and I feel almost as if she were my daughter! Tell Bertie. I know she will be glad.

'John-Ferdinand has seemed ill and depressed during the last months. It's living alone there, and not getting proper food. It will be so good for him to have her to take care of him. Her health is much better now; her cough is almost gone: you would hardly know her, she looks so bright. She is not much of a housekeeper; her bread always turns out bad, and the flower garden hasn't done well since she looked after it; but she is well off and they will always be able to have good servants and need not trouble much about the farming. They seem made for each other.

'It will be very nice for Bertie, when she comes home, to have them so near for company. Tell her her hand-lamb of last year, which has been running with the sheep, has got two lambs. I hope the air is suiting her better than you said it did at first. I will write to her next week. I will make you the biltong* as soon as it gets cooler. I feel so excited still about the engagement I can hardly write.'

Six weeks afterwards Veronica Grey and John-Ferdinand were married. Veronica said there was no need to wait for letters from England, as she knew her mother would be delighted to hear of her marriage; and if she were married at once she could help John-Ferdinand to get the house and farm quite straight. The clergyman came from the town and they were quietly married at the old farm, and Veronica promised the little mother when she said goodbye that they would come over every Sunday and spend the day with her. As the cart drove away with them to their farm, the little mother cried, she hardly knew why; but Griet shouted hurrah and tossed up her little skirts, and then turned round and round like a dervish,* till you could see nothing but a whirl of yellow skirts and two little spindle legs; and the little mother left off crying and told her not to make such a spectacle of herself.

CHAPTER VI

HOW BABY-BERTIE WENT A-DANCING

TUCKED away among the great oak avenues in the suburbs of Cape Town was Rebekah's home. You might ride mile after mile on a hot summer's day and never feel the sunshine on you, so* the great oak trees met over your head; and here and there to the right and left were houses buried behind hedges, with trees touching the roofs, and verandas, and flower gardens.

Everywhere was the scent of fir trees; and pine plantations stretched away up the mountainsides;* and now and then there were vineyards stretching acre on acre, with the sunlight shimmering through their leaves, and with white and purple grapes kissing the ground. Behind all rose the mountain's side, sloping away towards the Devil's Peak.* On sunny days, as you looked up at it, it seemed as though that side of the mountain were a giant,* tranquilly leaning backwards and watching with great, godlike, placid eye* the pine woods and the dwellings of men curled about his feet.

It was very peaceful in the great avenues. Sometimes carts drove along and foot passengers walked there; in summer the acorns fell, and in winter the leaves strewed the sidewalks, and the beautiful tracery of the bare oak branches showed against the clear blue sky, and the lovely green of the pines and of the flower gardens seemed the brighter because the oak trees were bare.

In the houses at night you always heard the trees everywhere rustling with a sound like the distant moaning of a sea. Yet, if you entered a train at one of the little stations,* in half an hour or a little more you might be on the other side of the mountain and in the old seaport town itself, with its long streets, principally of single-storeyed houses but also here and there of double, with small-paned windows much as the old Dutch loved to build a hundred years ago. In the streets were Malays;* and fish carts blowing their horns; and Dutchmen, and Englishmen, and men of all nations and colours and mixtures; and in the side streets were little Malay and coloured* children playing happily in the gutters before their doors, or sitting on the stoep steps with a bunch of grapes in the one hand and a lump of bread in the other; and everywhere the peaceful, sleepy life of the old South African town crept on slowly; with its open drains, and its old families, and its old, quiet methods of business, still prevailing. And above it all towered the stupendous front of Table Mountain, its beetling crags seeming to look down always with a stern, calm contempt on the little seething world of men below.

Round the Peninsula* swept the Southern Sea, pale blue and deep green in fair weather, and black in storms; but always, whether in storm or in fair weather, restless and passionate as no other sea on earth is—the Cape of Storms.*

Rebekah's house was divided from the Avenue* by a tall hedge of blue plumbago, so high you saw no one that was passing in the avenue beyond, except it might be their heads, if they were very tall.

It was a small house, two great oak trees that grew in the back yard overhanging its roof; and before it was a little flower garden always brilliant with flowers in both summer and winter; and there was a small veranda between two jutting-out wing rooms. Under the windows ran a little rockery; and on the left side of the garden was a little rose hedge, of monthly roses almost always in bloom, which Rebekah had planted when she first came to live there.

Across the rose hedge was a large house with a rough grass lawn and some oak trees growing around it; and in the rose hedge was a small gate which Frank had had put there a year after they were married, as people they knew lived next door, and he wanted a passage between the houses.

It was to this little house among the trees that Rebekah brought Baby-Bertie; and gave her as bedroom the left-wing room, with a green wallpaper, which looked out into the flower garden.

But for a long time after she came Bertie seemed to take no interest in anything. She had no wish to see the people and the sights of the town; and for most part of the day she sat in the iron rocking chair on the veranda, watching the flower garden indifferently; she did not even notice the parrot swinging himself, above her, and calling to her, from the cage over her head; and the needlework she had brought out lay often untouched in her lap all the morning.

When Frank came home at evening with his laughter and talk, it did not rouse her. Sometimes he brought men in for a game of billiards in the billiard room at the back of the house. Sometimes they had supper at eleven, and came out afterwards to sit on the veranda and smoke; but Bertie generally slipped away to bed, and seemed to feel no interest in them. She, who had always been fastidious about her clothes, and as a little child had loved bright ribbons and shoes, now often wore one white dress till it was frowsy and tumbled. Rebekah had never asked her for an explanation of her sudden desire to leave the farm and come with her, nor had she ever offered one: and the name of John-Ferdinand was never mentioned between them. In her heart Rebekah did not grieve if any misunderstanding had separated her cousin from her sister.*

Rebekah, who had only one little coloured maid to help her, was generally too busy with her household work and children to have much time to spend with her; but she brought her cups of soup and plates of fruit; and she bought her material to make new dresses, but Bertie put them away in a drawer without troubling to make them. Now and then a neighbour who had rooms in the large house across the little rose hedge came over through the little gate and brought her fancy work, and sat on the veranda with Bertie, and talked to her. She was a Mrs Drummond, a little, slight woman, with so long a neck and waist that when she sat, or until she stood beside another woman, she looked almost tall. She was always beautifully dressed; whatever she wore was graceful and was perfectly thought out. If she changed her scarf or waistcoat, she changed also her breast pin and earrings to match them; she was as thoughtfully dressed in the morning in a cotton wrap with little moonstones set in dull silver in her ears, as in the afternoon when she wore Indian muslin and lace, or in the evening, when she wore delicate Chinese silks and little diamond stars for earrings. Even her little drawing room was softly draped in Indian silks or oriental tapestries in a way other people's were not; there was not a hard outline or bare corner. The curtains at the window were tied back with gold filigree work that matched the brown and gold wallpaper; and her little real china teacups matched her own slippers, and both harmonised with the Indian footstool on which she rested her feet. If you picked up in the Avenue a bow she had dropped from her dress, you might have guessed it must be hers from its graceful, limp fall. Other women tried to imitate her dresses and the draperies of her little drawing room, but they never made their things look quite as hers did.

She was not pretty, but she was too graceful to be plain; her hair was neither dark nor light; and she had large white teeth which some people said were false, and some real, and which she always showed when she smiled, as she did continually, with a sudden, short movement of her upper lip, which moved alone, while the rest of the face was at rest as though it were mechanically drawn up, and then suddenly let down again. Her face was oblong, and was long, like her neck and her body; and she generally preferred to sit instead of standing and walking, when it was possible, because her long neck and waist made her look more tall and graceful, when the shortness of her legs was hidden. She often sat leaning a little forward, with her hands drooping over the edge of her lap, and with her head very slightly on one side, as that showed the outline of her chin, which she knew was the best point about her.

She had come to the Cape from England two years before Rebekah was married, with her husband; but he had gone to travel in the interior of Africa, while she had remained in Cape Town; he had gone on from Central Africa to India and Burma and the Far East, and had never come back during the seven years.

When Mrs Drummond first came, men had been very attentive to her, and women had imitated her dress and manners much. Now, the men who knew her began often to discuss her at their club, and in their smoking rooms; she had said she was twenty-eight years old when she came, and she was twenty-eight still; and they sometimes speculated as to when she would have another birthday, and as to whether the huge coil of hair at the back of her head were real or artificial; and they mimicked her little mannerisms; but the women still copied her dresses, though not quite so much as at first; and both men and women came to the croquet parties she gave on the lawn of the large house, part of which she had hired. She went to dances and receptions, and at dances still got partners; though not so many as at first; and young girls and older women still thought that if Mrs Drummond wore or did anything, it must be 'the right style'. Sometimes the men made jokes about her husband's long absence ribaldly; and the women now and then discussed it seriously; but on the whole it attracted little attention; it had come about so gradually. She had always said he was coming back in six months, or in eight, or next year (she said so still), and she showed handsome silks and embroideries which she said he sent her from the East; and she told the women he wrote to her every week, and was always longing to come back to her: so people never found the matter of great interest.

She had known Rebekah's husband before he married; she and her husband had come out in the same steamer, when he was returning from a visit to Europe; and it was she who had chosen the little house next door for him, when he determined to marry, and had helped him to furnish it. They were both musical, and sang in the same glee club* and had belonged to the same church choir; but at the time Bertie came they did not see much of each other. He had left the choir, and he laughed as other men did about the twenty-eight years, and the large unchanging coil of fair hair at the back of her head; and the little gate that he had had put in the rose hedge, that he might go over more easily to practise his music with her, was now almost unused, and the grass grew in the path.

But as soon as Bertie came she called, and offered to come and sit with her as she so seldom went out; and almost every afternoon she tripped over with the little silk bag over her arm, the bag varied to match each costume, and in which she carried the fancy work she was always doing for church bazaars. Sometimes she chatted to Bertie about her work, and told her about the bazaars; and sometimes she told her of her friends in England, her father a retired army officer, and their little place in the country; and sometimes she talked of the presents her husband sent her from the Far East, and what a clever man he was. She said he had a whole box full of manuscripts that he wouldn't print just because he didn't care to, or he might have made a heap of money; but generally she talked of dresses, and the prices of things in the shops in Cape Town; and now and then she told some gossip about people Bertie had never seen, why some lady was never called on, or how a certain young girl was getting herself talked about. But generally she talked of more trivial matters. Rebekah never came out and sat with them while she was there, but sent them out tea and cake.* And Bertie would sit still listening to her. Often Mrs Drummond stayed so late that when Frank came home in the evening she was still sitting there.

One afternoon, when she had just left, and Bertie sat with her hands crossed on her work, and one little foot with its slipper half off dragging under the rocking chair, her brother-in-law opened the garden gate and came up towards the steps. Rebekah had heard him and had come to the front door to meet him. She had always met him there in the first days of their marriage, when he had called out from the gate, 'Where is Goody-two-shoes?' and whistled for her; and now, when he did not call or whistle, she still met him there every day when she heard the click of the gate and the step on the gravel. As he gave her his bag in the doorway he said, 'Great news! What do you think—the immaculate John-Ferdinand writes he is to be married to a Miss Veronica Grey, a lady who was staying at the farm for her health. He says you know her. John married!' he laughed.

As Rebekah took his bag from him, she glanced round at Bertie: she was sitting bolt upright, and looking out over the flower garden. Rebekah drew him in; but Bertie heard him laughing from the dining room, 'I wonder whether he proposed to her, or she to him!—the saintly John!'*

When Rebekah went onto the veranda again she found Bertie gone, and only her slipper lying under the rocking chair.

When supper time came Bertie did not appear, having gone to her room feeling unwell, she said, and the next day was so unwell that Rebekah sent for a doctor, who said she was suffering from anaemia and must take rest and a tonic; and for some weeks she lay about eating little, seldom even sitting on the veranda to be talked to by Mrs Drummond, but lying on a sofa Rebekah had placed there for her, often seeming half asleep. She even discontinued the short weekly notes she had been in the habit of writing home. Rebekah took care that John-Ferdinand's engagement was never mentioned before her, and she wished she could have prevented her receiving the little mother's letters, which were always full of news of preparations for the marriage.

Then came the news of John-Ferdinand's wedding. The little mother's letters were full of it: and Rebekah watched Bertie anxiously. But a strange change came over her. She lolled about no more. She seemed suddenly to wake up from a sleep. She was suddenly always active and restless. She laughed, and talked, and romped wildly with the children, whom she had hardly noticed before. She began making the dresses, the material for which Rebekah had bought her when she first came. Sometimes she suddenly insisted on turning out a whole room, and shaking the carpets, and washing the windows herself; and then she would rush over to Mrs Drummond's to get advice about trimming a new hat. When she came back she would begin weeding a flowerbed, or go into the kitchen to make a cake. She seemed able to do anything but to rest quietly, or be alone. When her dresses were made, Mrs Drummond insisted on her coming to her croquet parties, and introduced her to people. Soon invitations came to her for dinner parties and dances, and as Rebekah did not go out, she went under Mrs Drummond's care or with Frank; and Mrs Drummond taught her to dance. After a time the invitations became so numerous that she was always busy getting a new dress ready, or repairing an old one; and seemed to live in a low fever of excitement. Frank took her to concerts and entertainments, and was proud of the attention his pretty sister-in-law awakened everywhere.

One evening, a little more than two months after the marriage, Bertie, who was going to a whist party with Mrs Drummond, knelt partly undressed on the floor before her sister with her back turned to her, that Rebekah might arrange her hair for her. All the while she talked restlessly about the dress Mrs Drummond was going to wear that night; and about the way she was going to change the old wedding dress which Rebekah had given her into a dancing skirt for herself. Suddenly in the midst of her talk she glanced round; 'Rebekah, aren't you laughing at me?—you think me so foolish!'—She turned herself round, and clasped her large, beautifully shaped white arms round Rebekah's little body. 'I talk of nothing but dressing and dancing! You must think me so foolish!—But, Rebekah, when you want to forget anything, you can read and think: you are so clever—and you have your children—I—I am so stupid—I can't help it!' She laid her head against Rebekah's breast and nestled to her like a little child. Rebekah pressed her lips on the bare white shoulder. 'Rebekah, you will not let me go back to the farm?—You will keep me here?' she said quickly. 'I can never go back; I won't go back!—Never! Never!—Promise me!—Promise me!' Then, giving Rebekah no time to reply, she sprang up and ran away to her own room to finish dressing.

That was the first and last time at which, either then or ever afterwards, to any human being, Bertie ever referred directly or indirectly to John-Ferdinand's relation with herself.

When three months more had passed, Bertie had had three proposals of marriage. One was from a very wealthy young man, whose estate adjoined a tiny fruit farm Rebekah had bought, a few miles out in the country, and who had seen Bertie walking in the vineyard there with Rebekah's children, and who had found out where she lived, and got an introduction to her. Another was from an English officer whom she had met at Mrs Drummond's, who was spending two months at the Cape on his way to India, and who asked her to marry him the fourth time he saw her; and one was from a young beardless, penniless civil servant, whom she had danced with once or twice. Bertie refused them all. Frank and Mrs Drummond both thought her very foolish to refuse the English officer, who had appealed to both to further his suit; and who was a man with a large private income, and of an aristocratic family, and a first-rate fellow. But the only suitor who seemed to concern Bertie at all was the young civil servant. She cried when she told Rebekah how miserable he looked when she refused him; and said she would not go to dances any more, if dancing with people made them miserable; but her restlessness and dislike of being quiet or alone soon made her go again.

At this time there came a letter from John-Ferdinand saying he and his wife were coming for a short visit to Cape Town, as they had taken no honeymoon when they were married, and asking Rebekah to take rooms for them in the large house next door, in which Mrs Drummond also had her rooms, and where John-Ferdinand had himself stayed when in Cape Town before.

Rebekah took the rooms; but when John-Ferdinand and his wife came, she and Bertie with the children had gone to her little fruit and vine farm, and only the servants were in the house, as Frank also was away up-country on a shooting trip.

This little farm Rebekah had bought two years after her marriage, partly with the money her father had given her as her wedding gift; and partly she had paid for it by placing a bond on it. Her husband had laughed loudly at first at the idea of her buying and farming it, but as they were married by ante-nuptial contract* and he was not responsible for her debts, and as he was never much interested in any matter which did not immediately concern himself, he did not interfere.

Now he rather approved of it as it saved the expense of taking the children to the seaside when they needed change, and supplied the household with fruit and vegetables free of charge. Rebekah kept an old German and his wife there to look after it with the help of a coloured boy, and drove out herself when she had half a day to spare; and when her husband went away, as he often did, for hunting or fishing expeditions, she took the children and stayed there till he came back. She herself had helped to mend the roof of the old cottage and to plaster and whitewash the walls, and with her own hands had planted and grafted trees and vines. She liked the labour* in the open air, and she was studying books on winemaking so that if in time she were able to buy two vineyards adjoining she could make wine.

During the first days Veronica and John-Ferdinand spent much of their time sightseeing, as she had never visited Cape Town before; but he introduced her to Mrs Drummond, and in the mornings, which he generally spent walking in the pine woods with his book, after the first days Veronica was invited by Mrs Drummond to sit in her private drawing room with her and work and drink coffee at eleven. They were unlike physically and mentally, but they had tastes which harmonised. While Veronica sat upright on a high-backed chair knitting heavy squares for a bed quilt, Mrs Drummond on a low settee, with her head a little on one side, chose carefully the shades of silk for an altar cloth which she was making. They discussed their work, and the prices of things in Cape Town shops; and Mrs Drummond chirped continually the news of the place, especially of the house over the way, and Veronica listened. She said that when Rebekah was married she went out at first a great deal with her husband to dances and entertainments and dinners; but after about a year and a half gave it all up, and never went out visiting any more. She said she never entertained now except little men's suppers, which she cooked herself for the men who came sometimes to play billiards with her husband in the evenings, and to which she never asked women or sat down herself. She said it was so strange, she thought, that they should have a billiard table, when they had such a small house otherwise and kept only one servant and a stable boy. She believed Rebekah had paid for the building of the billiard room herself. She had had it done while her husband had been away on a long business trip—the contractor who had built it had re-papered her bedroom and had himself told her that Rebekah had paid for the room as a surprise for* her husband. Mrs Drummond supposed it was to keep him at home she built it. She said women didn't seem to care for Rebekah—she didn't think a woman had called there for over a year; she thought many of them didn't even know she existed, as she never went to church. She said she thought men cared for her as little as women: she had never seen a man call there, except when her husband was at home. It seemed so strange to her that Rebekah should have gone away to the farm with Bertie and the children just when she knew Veronica was coming, and looked inquiringly over her silks at Veronica.

Veronica said Rebekah was always strange.

Mrs Drummond said, Yes, she was; she used to dig in her garden with a big spade, where people could see her quite well over the gate; and she had heard someone say that, when she was out at her farm, they had seen her climb up a ladder right onto the roof, mending a smoky chimney.

Veronica said, Some people were born with those mannish ways. It was not Rebekah's mother's fault as she was quite a sweet womanly woman.

Mrs Drummond also had much to tell of Bertie; of how dull she had seemed when she first came; and how she had improved. She told of her dancing, and her dresses, and about the English officer (Bertie had not told her of her two other suitors) and she said she liked Bertie better than Rebekah.

Veronica said she thought she liked Rebekah the better of the two, though she was so strange, and not always very nice and womanly in her ways. She said it seemed to her that Bertie always cared too much to attract men's attention.

Mrs Drummond drew her upper lip up sharply and held her head a little more on a side; she said some people couldn't help attracting men's attention; and she looked very sideways with her eyes at Veronica's square shoulders and the flat foot showing below her plain skirt. She said one wondered how some women ever got married at all: but Veronica was looking down at her own square of bed quilt.

Mrs Drummond said she thought a woman ought to take care of her appearance: that Rebekah had worn the same old brown silk dress for three years whenever she went out shopping to Town, only altering it a little every year as the fashions changed, that it might not look too striking. She said a woman who could afford to build a billiard room ought to dress better. They spent all the mornings together.*

Sometimes in the afternoon they went into Town shopping together also; and when they did not, they all three* had tea under the oak trees on the lawn out of Mrs Drummond's delicate little china cups, unless it was her croquet afternoon.

At last the last day came of their visit to Cape Town. Then Veronica proposed to her husband that they should go and look at Rebekah's house and garden. She said the little mother would be so disappointed if they came back and could tell her nothing about it. John-Ferdinand felt sure his brother and sister-in-law would not object, and they walked over. They paced about Rebekah's little garden; the front door was not locked and they went in. John-Ferdinand sat down in the drawing room at the table to look at some books, and Veronica went to inspect the house. The stable boy was away exercising the horses, and the servant girl resting in her room across the yard, and Veronica passed alone from room to room. In the dining room she noted the things on the mantelpiece and the sideboard, and Rebekah's work basket and sewing machine on the table in the corner: she examined Rebekah's bedroom and the things on the dressing table and washing stand and Frank's little dressing room that opened from it, with its large dressing table and new carpet and comfortable easy chair: she went through to the children's bedroom opening out of Rebekah's, and tried the handle of Rebekah's little study which led out of the children's room, but that was the only place in the house which was locked. She examined the kitchen and outer pantry and examined the things on the shelves, and passed down the passage to the billiard room which was built out at the left side. She examined the cues which she had never seen before and lifted the holland cover* to look at the green cloth on the table; and went to the spare room which was now Bertie's bedroom, and looked at all her dresses hanging in the wardrobe and the whole row of boots and shoes under the dressing table, and unlocked and examined the large new dressing case upon it with brushes and scent bottles heavily mounted in real silver, which Bertie had received through the post from some unknown admirer, on her last birthday. She even went into the yard and lifted the lids of the tanks that held the water for the bathroom. When she had seen everything she went back to the little drawing room.

John-Ferdinand was still sitting at the table with his elbows resting on it; his head was supported by his hands; he was looking down so intently that he did not notice Veronica's soft entrance, till she had stepped up behind him, and put her large cool hands over both his eyes. 'Who is it?' she said with grave playfulness. He did not speak, but taking each of her hands in one of his took them down from his eyes and resting them on his shoulders held them fast there, while he looked back up into her face.

'What are you studying so deeply?'

'Only this,' he said, glancing down.

It was not a book that was open before him, but an album of photographs. On the page before him was a picture of Bertie which had just been taken at the request of the father and mother. Mrs Drummond, who had gone with Bertie to have it taken, had insisted it should be in full evening dress, that her beautiful arms and shoulders might show. The photographer also had tried to make what he believed to be an effective picture. He had turned her head a little over her shoulder and raised her chin, so that the lovely lines of the neck and upturned chin were not lost. He had put in her left hand a bunch of artificial flowers which she held against her breast, and he had required her to draw her lips into a smile. The picture resembled an imaginary type of beauty in a book of engravings rather than Bertie. The simplicity and directness of pose and manner, amounting almost to awkwardness, which was the character of her beauty, was lost.

Veronica looked down at the book over his shoulder. 'It is very finely taken; is it not?' she said. 'How well they take portraits here!'

He looked down at the face too. 'It's very handsome, and just like her!'

He loosened one of her hands, and with his right drew her to his side and made her kneel down beside him. He turned to her and took her face softly between both his hands and looked down into it—

' "And learn how pure,
How sweet can be,
My own wife's face!" '—*

he said softly.

A faint flush rose into Veronica's cheeks as he looked down into her face. He put one arm round her shoulders and drew her nearer to him.

'My wife,' he said, 'I want to confess something to you.'

But then he was silent. She crossed her hands upon his knees and looked up at him: 'What is it, my husband?'

His hand rested again on the side of the album; he was looking down at it.

'I told you once,' he said, 'on that day on the farm when we became engaged, that I had once been much attracted by my young cousin, but that we had had a difference, and I felt I could not marry her. But one thing I never told you—that after she left the farm, she was always with me. Wherever I went I seemed to see her. I dared not come to the old place because it reminded me of her. At last I wrote a letter telling her I could not live without her, and asking her to come back and marry me. That evening, when I rode over to her father's farm, for the first time after she had left, I came over partly that I might give it to the boy who was going to the town the next morning, to post. But you were so kind to me that evening—do you remember?—we sat out on the stoep, and I repeated that passage of Tennyson's to you that you liked so? It seemed to rest me to be with you, as if I got rid of her face as I saw it last look at me. And somehow, I did not post the letter that night, though it was in my pocket. Looking back now, though I didn't realise it at the time, I am sure it was your influence upon me that kept me from sending it.'

'Yes, dear!' she said.

'But, do you know, I did not destroy that letter? For weeks still I kept it in my pocket, and at any moment it might have been sent. Then came that day when you came over to my farm to help me put things right in my house. Even then I still always had the feeling that perhaps I was getting that house ready for her. But, darling, you know what happened that afternoon when we stood together on the back veranda? I never can quite understand it. It seemed as though some power stronger than myself were drawing me to you—and my arms were about you, and your head was on my breast, and you were to be my wife, before I knew! That night, when I went to my bedroom, I burned the letter. But, Veronica, my wife, do you know, that even since that time, that face has come in between you and me?' He raised the palm of his hand from Bertie's portrait. 'At night I have dreamed of it; the scent of geraniums and the sight of plumbago flowers have brought it back to me, even the darkness of the night has brought it to me. It has been a white face with great innocent eyes—a child's face, that I have always seen. It has mingled with all our life together at the farm. When I saw the sheep come out of the kraal in the morning with the dew on their backs—when I saw the thorn trees, or smelled an evening-flower, a kind of sudden trembling has come over me. Even when you first proposed we should come here for our holiday, you know how I resisted you? And still more when you proposed we should stay here in this house near to them—I felt I could not see her—could not be near her—and yet deep in my heart I knew it was best; that I must see her again, or the spell would never be broken.' He looked down at the portrait, half of which his hand covered. 'Even since I have been here and I have heard from you how she has devoted herself to pleasure, even when you told me of her flirtation with that

English military man for whom she yet cared nothing—it made no difference to me. But now—when I look at that—all is gone!' He raised his hand and dropped it again on the face of the picture. 'When I see *that*, I know it has all been an idle dream! She could never really have been mine—never been anything to me. Never have been what you are—

'"What have I done
That God should choose a wife for me?"'*

He bent down over her. 'My darling wife! Look up at me!' Veronica raised her eyes to his, and pressed her head close to his breast.

'Do you forgive me, my darling?'

She drew his head down with her hand so that his cheek rested on her hair: and then they heard the maidservant coming into the passage, and Veronica rose to her feet to explain to her how it was they were there.

Late that night when Veronica and John-Ferdinand lay in bed in the large room in the boarding house, the wind was blowing through the pine trees, and among the oak trees in the Avenue, making them crack their great branches, and tap the roofs of the houses. It was just a quarter to one when John-Ferdinand woke, and lay listening to the wind; then on the other side of the large bed he heard Veronica move.

'Are you awake?' he asked.

'I have not yet been asleep,' she said.

He stretched out his arm, and drew her a little nearer to him. 'You are not troubling about anything I told you this afternoon, beloved? You know it is all past?'

'Oh, yes!' she said.

He drew her closer to him, her head resting on his shoulder, his arm passing under her neck. 'You trust me utterly?'

'Oh, yes, my dear one!' They both lay looking upwards in the dark, and heard the wind tearing at the branches of the trees.

'There is *nothing* troubling you, my dear one?' He turned his face more towards her.

'No, nothing, dear—at least,' she hesitated, 'there is perhaps one very little thing—such a very little thing, that you will think me foolish! You must tell me if I'm wrong. You always know so much better what is right and wise, than I.'

'What is it, my dear one?' He put out his right hand and took her left that lay on the white coverlet.

She spoke slowly, lisping a little as a child might, talking to its mother, 'It's such a little thing—such a small thing—but, you know, ever since we were married, it has sometimes made me a little sad, I've felt as if you didn't *quite* trust me!'

'What is it?—There is nothing I know, or feel, or think I would not share with you!'

'Oh, it's only a little thing!—I've wondered sometimes,' she murmured softly, 'why you didn't tell me what you and Bertie quarrelled about! You told me you had a difference; but you never said what it was. You didn't even tell me today.'

He was quiet for a moment; then he said, 'I did not tell you because it was a matter more hers than mine. She did not ask me to make any promise not to repeat it—she asked nothing—but I took it that she was speaking to me in confidence. I could never have told anyone but you—but you are not someone else. You are me, myself! When I speak to you I speak within my own soul.'

'But you must not tell me anything, dear, that you would rather not. I always know that what you wish to do is right! You know better than I!'

'But I want to tell you! There shall be nothing that divides between us.' He turned on his side and drew her nearer to him, so that from shoulders to feet their long straight figures lay side by side.

'The reason why I could not marry my cousin,' he said, 'was this'—and then he told her the story of the parlour in the bush, and what Baby-Bertie told him.

Half an hour later the wind was still blowing as wildly as ever; but they lay asleep with their hands interclasped and his breath on her face.

The next day when all their trunks were strapped for starting, John-Ferdinand went to the station to call a cab. He returned sooner than he had expected as he had met one in the Avenue. As he came back into the bedroom Veronica was sitting with her travelling cloak on, and her hat on the table beside her, bending over the dressing table, writing. She thought it was the maid come to begin carrying things down, till he stood almost at her shoulders. She started lightly, and spread her broad hand over the page on which she was writing.

'What is it?' he asked, bending over her.

A faint tint of roses rushed into her white cheeks. 'A little surprise for you. A secret. Something you mustn't know about.'

He stooped and pressed his cheek against her smooth head; and turned to help the maid carry down the packages.*

An hour later they were driving through Cape Town on their way to the docks.

'I wish to stop at the post office,' she said. 'I have a letter to post about something I forgot to order at a shop, and which I want sent on to me.'

When they got to the post office he offered to get out and post it for her; but she said she was tired of sitting and would rather get out herself, and before he could speak, had jumped out and put it in the box. The letter was addressed to Mrs Drummond, but in a large round hand, quite unlike her own angular small one. When she had put it in the box, they drove down to the docks, and in two hours they had sailed away to their home in the Eastern Province.

CHAPTER VII

RAINDROPS IN THE AVENUE

When Bertie and Rebekah came back from the fruit farm, Rebekah was busy putting her house right, and no one noticed that, on the first morning she went to see Mrs Drummond, Bertie did not stay so long as usual, nor was there anyone to note that, neither on that day nor the next, nor the day after, did Mrs Drummond come to see her.

But on the day after that, as Bertie sat sewing on the veranda, Mrs Drummond came with her work bag on her arm and sat in the low cane chair opposite her; and Bertie thought it must have been her own fancy which had made it seem that Mrs Drummond had not been so glad to see her when she returned from the farm.

Mrs Drummond said it was a fine afternoon, and made a remark about the new pattern she was tatting;* and Bertie answered her; then they sat silent for a while, with the rich warm scent from Rebekah's flower garden coming up to them.

Then Mrs Drummond said, without raising her head, that her cousin John-Ferdinand's wife seemed a very nice woman; Bertie said yes, and asked Mrs Drummond if she thought it would not look better if she feather-stitched the sleeve of the baby's dress she was making. Mrs Drummond said she thought so: and then there was quiet again with only the sound of Bertie's needle and Mrs Drummond's shuttle and of their sleeves rustling against their sides as they worked. The parrot, who had been to sleep, woke suddenly and began throwing down grains of mielies on Bertie's head. Then Mrs Drummond drooped her head on the opposite side from the one on which it had been drooping before and said, 'Did you never go to school when you were a girl?'

'No,' said Bertie, without looking up, 'my sister taught me out of her old books; and my mother taught me to sew.'

Mrs Drummond drooped her head lower than before, looking at her work. 'So you never had any real teacher to teach you?' she said.

'No,' Bertie said. 'At least,' she added, hurriedly, 'once—for a few months—I had a teacher.'

Mrs Drummond drooped her head yet lower.

'I suppose,' she said, half glancing up, 'it was a lady whom you had to teach you?'

Bertie said quickly, 'No—it was a man—he did not stay long. Don't you think that the oranges I sent you yesterday were just right for marmalade?' she added quickly.

'Yes-s,' said Mrs Drummond slowly; then she looked up fully into Bertie's face.

For a little while Bertie heard only the click of the tatting shuttle, as it turned to let the thread out, and the tick of her own needle; the scent from the flower garden seemed to come up almost overpoweringly.

'Yes, the peels of the oranges were very fine and thick,' Mrs Drummond said slowly.

'I will go and fetch you some tea,' Bertie said quickly, rising; 'Rebekah will have made it by this time.'

'Oh, no thank you,' Mrs Drummond said, 'I have some people coming to have tea with me, and must go at once or they will find me out.'

'Oh, please do not trouble!' she said, as Bertie darted to pick up her ball of tatting cotton which had dropped from her lap as she rose. Bertie caught it and handed it to her, and she put it in her bag. 'How very nice your sister's flower garden looks this afternoon—she always seems to have more flowers and sweeter smelling than anyone else! Good afternoon!'

Then the little figure in its large-figured Japanese silk dress fluttered across the garden and out through the gate in the rose hedge and across the lawn to the house beyond.

When Mrs Drummond was gone Bertie sat in the rocking chair, sewing; there was a stain of red on each cheek deeper than the red of the damask rose in Rebekah's garden; gradually it turned to pale pink and then white.

The next afternoon Mrs Drummond had her weekly croquet party, but she did not send over to ask if Bertie was coming, and Bertie helped Rebekah to preserve the oranges they had brought, and did not go, but in the evening she went to explain why she had not been.

She found Mrs Drummond in her bedroom before the chest of drawers, putting them neat. Mrs Drummond did not pause in her work and hardly looked up; and when Bertie had stood beside her chatting for a little while she went away. Mrs Drummond seemed preoccupied. For two weeks after that she did not meet her again;

then she overtook her in the Avenue. Mrs Drummond talked of some purchases she had made in Town and said goodbye at the gate. Then for a week she did not see her again. Twice Bertie had gone as far as the rose hedge, meaning to ask her whether she had done anything to pain her; but both times she had turned back when her hand was on the gate.

Then came a Wednesday evening when Bertie was going to an evening party at a house two avenues off. It was to be a young people's dance in honour of the fifteenth birthday of the daughter of the house, and, as most of the dancers would be under thirty, she needed no older woman to go with her; and Frank was going, who, as he grew older, preferred going to the dances and picnics where very young girls were rather than to those where there were women nearer his own age.

As the house was close at hand they were to walk, and Rebekah had brought Bertie to her own room to dress her, because of the large glass there.

'Don't you think it looks nice?' Rebekah asked.

Bertie was standing before the wardrobe door; she looked like a head of a large white hydrangea in the gauze dress Rebekah had helped her to make: 'Oh, I think it looks lovely!'

Rebekah, standing behind her, looked at the dress critically. Her own small, delicate face was drawn and white, as though needing rest: 'Your hair is not high enough if you are to wear the flowers under it,' she said.

She mounted a footstool and stood behind Bertie and unwound the coils of back hair to pin them higher.

Then Bertie said in her low, soft drawl, 'Rebekah, haven't *you* ever wanted to go to dances? Don't you want to dance?'

'Yes,' Rebekah said, 'when I was a child I liked to dance. I used to go up into the kloof under the Kaffir-bean trees and dance and sing and throw up my arms till I got drunk and had to lie down on my face.'

'Oh, I don't mean that kind of dancing,' Bertie drawled slowly, 'alone, in the kloof, by yourself! I mean with pretty dresses and other people to ask you to dance. I don't like you to stay alone here when I go,' she said in a yet softer drawl; 'you'd look so pretty if you were dressed in pretty dresses like me—you'd look like a fairy. Don't you think it would be nice to dance with other people, eh, Rebekah?'

'Perhaps,' Rebekah said, 'if you had someone you liked very much, and you two were quite alone—and you could go on dancing on and on forever with no one there, it might be better than dancing alone—perhaps better than almost anything. That will do, I think.' She got off the stool.

Bertie still stood impassively with her arms hanging on either side. 'Yes,' she said dreamily, 'it would be nice to dance with someone you liked very much; I never have. But, Rebekah, you know, I don't care very much whom I dance with now. It's the light and the noise and the going round and round I like. All the men are so kind to me, too,' she added slowly, 'and all the girls also; they don't mind that I dance so much all the evening. Isn't it nice of them, Rebekah?'

'Very.' Rebekah was now fastening a white, half-blown rose on her breast.

'You know, I like it so when you go into a room, and they all look at you, and something so nice runs all up your body when they all look at you and think you look nice. I like it,' she said slowly. 'Have you ever been to a real ball, Rebekah?'

'When I was first married. Frank went; and I wanted to go with him.'

She turned to a wardrobe behind the door and took from it a dress of black diaphanous silky material speckled all over with tiny silver spangles, each carefully cut out and sewn on separately. She held it up by the shoulders.

'How beautiful!' exclaimed Bertie, crossing her hands. 'I never saw such a dress. Whose is it?'

'I made it for myself,' said Rebekah. Bertie came nearer to touch it. 'Mrs Drummond had one from Paris, like this, only white. Frank said it was the most beautiful dress he had ever seen. When she did not want it any more I bought it from her as a pattern.' She looked down at the dress. 'I cut out each little spangle separately and sewed it on. It took me three weeks to make it.' She turned the dress over. 'This was the wreath to wear with it,' she said, holding up a wreath of frosted leaves.

'You must have looked beautiful,' Bertie said. 'Your teeth, your dark hair—and the spangles—just like the night! Did Frank like it?'

'He said it was not bad.'

'Do you never wear it now?'

'No, I keep it.'

As she was hanging the dress up, Bertie said suddenly, 'Rebekah, do you think, if Mrs Drummond was your friend, that she—that she—would really care for you—that she—that she wouldn't—take part with anyone against you?'

'I don't know, dear. I know very little of her. We have nothing in common. I don't understand her.'

At that moment Frank's voice sounded from the hall, calling out that Bertie must hurry or it would rain before they started; and Rebekah wrapped her sister up in the large, red silk opera cloak she had made for herself when she had first married and folded Bertie's white satin dancing shoes in silver paper, that she might carry them.

'Don't mend the stockings,' Bertie whispered as she turned to go, half bending over her; 'I'll darn them all tomorrow.'

They went into the hall where Frank was waiting, and Rebekah saw to it that they had their umbrellas and waterproofs with them. The night was of inky blackness; it seemed it might rain at any moment, and Rebekah stood in the doorway holding the candle high to light them down the veranda steps and along the path to the gate. When the two figures had gone out at it, she closed the door and turned back into the house.

In the dining room she took from the work table a large basket with the week's mending in it, and, placing the lighted candle on the top, went through the room into the one where her children slept. She paused at each bed to see that the child in it was covered; and then, still carrying the lighted candle on the basket, she opened a door at the end of the room and went into the next.

The room was a small one, made by cutting off the end of the children's bedroom with a partition. She had had it before as a study for herself where she could always hear the children call if they needed her at night. It was hardly larger than a closet, but there was a window in it and a small outer door, and both looked out onto the rockery and the plumbago hedge but on nothing else, and there was a small door close beside the window, which she had had put in that at any time she might run out and work a little in the garden. The walls were covered with a red-brown paper, and in the centre stood a large oblong desk with drawers; before it stood an old armchair with a deep dent where a head had often rested. A waste-paper basket stood beside it. In the corner stood the tall wooden cabinet she had had when she was a girl to hold her fossils and insects, and which she had brought with her when she married; on a ledge in front her microscope stood. There was no other furniture on the floor, but on the walls hung three small bookshelves. One was behind the armchair, between the window and door; and in the corner beside it, on a little wooden bracket, was a tiny statue of Hercules* a few inches high in old discoloured marble. This she had got from Mrs Drummond when she first married, in exchange for a length of green silk which she had had as a wedding present. Mrs Drummond told her her husband had bought it when he was travelling in Italy, but had left it behind with many other things he did not want when he set out on his travels in the Far East.

On another hanging bookshelf to the right of the desk were books of poetry, science, history, and travel; all of them much-worn cheap editions except one handsome new copy of Darwin's *Variation of Plants and Animals under Domestication** bound in calf, which also she had got from Mrs Drummond two years before, in exchange for some pots of roses, to stand in her drawing room. It had been sent from England addressed to her husband, but as he was now in the mountains of Japan, and had said she need send nothing on to him, she was glad to let Rebekah have it.

On the wall to the left of the desk were three very small shelves, and on them were science primers and schoolbooks from which Rebekah had taught herself and most of which she had bought with the money her mother gave her for herself for drying peaches when she was a child. They were all now very old. What she felt for them was what no one feels for the books out of which they have been taught by another—it was what a full-grown doe might feel for a little mountain stream, which it had found for itself when it was a very young fawn wandering quite alone and parched with thirst, and from which it had drunk. It might have tasted of many finer clearer streams since then, but in none of them all would the water be to it like that in the little stream it found all for itself when it was a small thing, quite alone, and dying of thirst.

There was a *Cornwallis Grammar** with the back worn off with which she had followed her father about over the ploughed lands one day, trying to get him to explain to her what a preposition really was, and, when he answered her absently in the cut dried words of the book, she had gone away behind the hedge and lain with the book open before her, and prayed that she might really understand. There was a Smith's *Latin Principia*,* the gilt letters worn off its side and black back; she bought it when she was nine years old with three-and-sixpence which her father gave her when he went into the town to sell his wool and she went with him. She had bought it at a shop where they had books in the window, and had carried it home pressed against her chest all the way in the cart. She knew they would laugh at her if they knew she meant to learn Latin; but at night she sat up in her own room, writing the exercises by the light of a tallow candle she had begged from old Ayah, happy, thinking she would at last know all the Romans knew—what, she did not quite know.

On the shelf below were a number of cheap translations of Greek and Latin authors, which she had bought when she had found out she would never know Greek or Latin enough to read in the originals.

On the lowest shelf were five or six thin science primers in brown covers. She had seen them advertised in one of her father's newspapers, and she had sent money for them to a bookseller's in Cape Town who advertised them; when the parcel came by post she had opened it on her bed, and she had lain down by the books and felt nearly faint with gladness. The Botany she liked because it taught her how to examine the parts of flowers and helped to take away that almost painful longing she had felt when she looked at them to understand a little why they were as they were. The Geology she liked much; but it had distressed her because, like the botany book, it was written for people in England, and the plants and rocks and fossils mentioned she could not find in Africa. Her father had some shelves of old brown books: she had read nearly all of them; but, except the histories, none interested her much: they did not explain to her the world about her, what it was. He had one book called *Pre-Adamite Earth*,* which she read and agonised and prayed over, trying to understand it; only after she had grown up did she realise it was a book no human being could understand, least of all the man who wrote it. But he had a large old atlas which he gave her, which lay now on the top of her wooden cabinet. She used to lie on her back for hours, with the atlas open on her chest leaning against her drawn-up knees and with the Geography at her side for reference, and look at the different countries and seas, and picture them, and fancy she was there, especially China and Japan and Greenland and South America; till her heart got large with joy, the feeling that she was all over the world. On the shelf below were books of children's poetry, and the one or two storybooks she had as a child; but the books on the shelf above them were much more poetry to her. She felt so for them, that, if she had lived to be a woman of eighty and someone had suddenly come into the room where she was with one of those old worn books in his hand, her heart would have throbbed, and the memory of the hunger of the fierce young soul for knowledge, as it first looks out on life, would all have come back to her.

Over the door leading to the children's bedroom was tacked the picture of the Madonna from the *Illustrated London News* which she had had pasted over the head of her bed when she was a child. It was the only ornament the room held except the little statue of Hercules in the corner.

Often at night, as she sat alone in that room, she had pictured to herself what great works of art must be like, or great orchestral music; she had seen or heard neither, but she dreamed of them—as she dreamed of what it must be to be one of a company of men and women in a room together, all sharing somewhat the same outlook on life and therefore thinking somewhat the same thought, and able to understand one another without explanation—a thing she knew was possible somewhere in time and space—which actually did exist—though she might never know it.

On the brown carpet on the floor was a mark like a footpath where the nap had been worn off, running right round the desk.* This was where she walked round and round, because the room was not large enough to allow of her walking up and down, as she used to under the trees in the kloof.

For days often, and sometimes for weeks, she did not come into this room; but she knew it was there; and there was always a quiet spot in her mind answering to it.

Tonight she set the basket of darning down on the floor beside the desk and lit the reading lamp, and, when she had put the candle out, sat down in the armchair, leaning her head against its dented back.

It had been a long time since she got up before sunrise that morning to warm the baby's milk, and she was tired. She was to have another child in seven months, and her legs and the lower part of her body ached; but it was never the same to her if she sat to rest in that room as any other. From her shelves, the bindings of her books looked down at her, each one a little brown face that seemed to love her. Behind each was hidden the mind of some human creature which at some time had touched her own; they were all the intellectual intercourse she had ever known. Not one was there because it was a rare or old copy, or had an expensive binding; each one was there because at some time she had lived close to it and it had penetrated her.

After a time she drew the basket nearer her and began to work. For nearly an hour she sewed on buttons and darned little worn places in little garments, till there was nothing left in the basket but a few pairs of socks and stockings; she took up one and began to darn it, but soon put it with the mended things in the basket with the unmended at the top, and then leaned back again on her chair, resting.

Outside, the rain had begun to fall; it was dropping on the thatched roof with a soft soo-o-shing sound. She lay in the chair and listened to it.

After a time she drew her chair closer to the desk, and from one of the top drawers took a book. It was an exercise book in a black cover. She laid it open on the desk.

In the drawer below were six or seven such books; some filled with the sharply pointed writing of a very small child who tries to write a flowing hand. In these were verses and short stories and little allegories told in rhyme—one very long allegory in blank verse, which was never quite finished—and one book held a story as long as a novel, and quite finished—and there were a few prose passages copied from books, which had struck the child as beautiful.

Some others were filled with the larger, more rounded handwriting of a young girl from twelve to twenty. They also held stories, but few had verses; and there were discussions on abstract questions. One book was a diary full of small daily entries, a book read, a visit found,* seeds planted, but once or twice working out great plans for the life that was to be lived—countries to be visited—books to be written—scientific knowledge to be gained—all written with absolute confidence. Now and then there were passionate personal entries, almost incoherent little calls for love and friendship; but they came not often, and some had been scratched out.

There were a couple of books filled after marriage; but the entries dwindled. Months passed in which nothing was written. After a child had been born and it had been necessary to lie still for weeks, there were dissertations on some abstract matter, or an allegory; but generally there were only short scraps: outlines of stories never to be filled in, and short diary notes of a very practical nature: on such a date the baby was weaned, or a new servant was hired, or she had planted a seed in her garden and set down the date to mark how long it took to come up. And sometimes (generally after a long interval in which nothing had been written) there were short notices, so written that no one into whose hand the book should fall could have understood them; in which dashes and letters took the place of words; such as 'Came into the billiard room unexpectedly. J. D.—Under the table. Ran out. Well, it doesn't matter, it doesn't matter. J. F.' or 'Again—again—again—today!'

Tonight she drew the book towards her. It was four months since she had opened it; she had had no time since she returned from the Eastern Province. When last she wrote she had been sitting up for a night, to make poultices for her boy, who had bad earache, and, between whiles as he slept, she had written.

She had been carrying on a long discussion with herself as to what was the real cause of that curious hunger for an exact knowledge of things as they are, of naked truth about all things small or great, material and also psychic, which seems to haunt so many of us, and which seems so little to have affected the thought and life of Europe through so many ages. She had advanced the view that, to find any true likeness to the modern feeling, we had to go back to the life and thought of classical days, especially to the life and thought in Greece in the fourth century before Christ.

Here she had had to go and make a poultice, and she had branched off on a side line when she came back, to question if it were not just the resemblance on this point—this common desire for an exact knowledge of reality, of things exactly as they were, first and before all things—which gives us that strange sense of nearness to ancient classical thought and art. Was it not this deep reverence for reality, even in material things, which made us feel so curiously akin to, say, a little Greek statue, in which every muscle and organ has been carved with solemn care to follow life—sex organ and knee as devoutly as eye and forehead? Was it not this common hunger after a knowledge of reality as an end in itself which, in spite of the difference in our technical knowledge and outlook in many respects, yet makes us feel, when we read the page of a translation of some book two thousand years old, as if it might have been composed this morning by someone walking up and down in the pine woods behind the house, as well as by a peripatetic pacing the paths of a garden at Athens two thousand years ago?—Which makes us feel that if, in the sunshine on the gravelled path in our own garden today, a certain old man with flattened nose and rough cloak were found lying, we should be able to throw ourselves down beside him with our elbows on the earth and listen to his talk and share in his outlook, almost as we might have done two thousand years ago? Is it not this which, though we know thousands of things they never knew, yet, when we read them, makes us feel—'My own! My own!'?

Is it not perhaps just the absence of this passionate desire to penetrate into the nature of all things and know them exactly as they are, which, in spite of their much nearer relation to us in order of time and by ties of blood and descent, makes us feel so infinitely more removed from the worthy Christian fathers and the sometimes gifted writers and thinkers of the Middle Ages (save a few heretics), and even from the mass of men of our own time—perhaps the very parents who bore us or begot us—persons who, living in the present, belong yet to that past which, accepting all things, found virtue in faith and not in a keen, unending questioning of the facts of life; so that when we, who today share the new spirit, strive to come near them, we seem to be looking at them across an impassable mental chasm and through the haze of an almost infinite moral distance?

Here she had been interrupted again. When she came back she had gone on to seek more narrowly after the cause of the new spirit. Was it because we were more virtuous, that for us a knowledge of all reality—whether it concerned the shading of the down on a butterfly's wing, the exact nature of a handful of earth, the antennae of a beetle, the movements of a planet, the how of sexual emotions or of social organisation—was to us a matter of primary importance, all wilful shutting of our eyes to it a crime, and all wilful misleading of our fellows with regard to it a social wrong?—while to men of the past, or men of the present holding the attitude of the past, such knowledge was only desirable and to be sought after if direct personal advantage to individuals could be seen to flow from it, while the wilful shutting of one's eyes to it, or the misleading of one's fellows with regard to it, might even be most virtuous actions if personal good seemed to flow from it?

She had held that it was not because we were more virtuous, but that the difference between the two attitudes took its rise entirely from two opposing intellectual conceptions of the nature of the universe.*

According to the old Christian conception, the universe was a thing of shreds and patches and unconnected parts. Outside all we see and touch was the great individual Will, which had called into being wind and water, man, planet, star, stone, beast and plant, by the arbitrary action of its power, and which at any moment might return it all to nothingness, even the life that moves in animals having no permanence, and only that life in man which they called the soul having any future, though it had no past, and rose into being at an arbitrary fiat, like a stone and plant.

For the man intellectually holding this view to be true, the universe could resemble only the heap of toys which a child gathers about it on the floor: doll, bugle, brick, book, having no subtle, living connection with one another, being there together only because the will of the child has brought them there.

Solemnly to study each toy because, when you understood its structure, it might throw light on that of all the others, and closely to study their relation to one another—this doll lies at such an angle to that bugle—would be the work of a fool, when any moment a kick of the child might disturb all their relations.

For the man sincerely holding the old view, truth, the thing to be loved and sought after more than life, can be only a knowledge of the will of the arbitrary ruling individual, and the only thing of real importance in life must be the relation between that one indestructible element in man and the ruling individuality. Truth, as it regards the shading of a feather on a bird's wing, the movement of a planet, the order of social growth, the structure of a human body, can be of no value; it may even be a positive duty to misrepresent or repress the knowledge of facts, if they bear on, or seem to have a bearing injurious to, the relations of the individual man and the all-powerful individual.

For the man holding this view of the structure of the universe, 'truth,' in the sense in which it is a thing of value, cannot be simply the knowledge of all facts and all relations, as nearly as he can attain to it; it can be only the knowledge of certain facts for a definite purpose. The suppression of Galileo's discovery that the world moved—the habitual suppressing in art of certain aspects of life—the habit of continual questioning within oneself, not 'Is this thing true?' but 'What will be the effect of such knowledge or such a statement?'—is not, in the man holding this old view of the universe, a sign of low morality and antisocial feeling; it is simply the logical outcome of his view of the universe. For him to take any other course would not be rational, would not be virtuous, would not even be sane.

For us all this has changed.

Slowly advancing knowledge has forced on us an entirely new view of the universe. Step by step we have been brought almost to the standpoint from which many an old Greek looked out on life.

For us once again the universe has become one, a whole, and it lives in all its parts. Step by step advancing knowledge has shown us the internetting lines of action and reaction which bind together all that we see and are conscious of.

Between the furthest star and the planet earth we live on, between the most distant planet and the ground we tread on, between man, plant, bird, beast and clod of earth, everywhere the close internetted lines of interaction stretch; nowhere are we able to draw a sharp dividing line, nowhere find an isolated existence. The prism I hold in my hand, rightly understood, may throw light on the structure of the furthest sun; the fossil I dug out on the mountainside this morning, rightly studied, may throw light on the structure and meaning of the hand that unearths it; between the life that moved in the creature that ploughed in the mud of the lake shores three million years ago and the life which beats in my brain and moves in my eyes here in the sunshine today, I can see long, unbroken lines of connection. Between spirit that beats within me and body through which it acts, between mind and matter, between man and beast, between beast and plant and plant and earth, between the life that has been and the life that is, I am able to see nowhere a sharp line of severance, but a great, pulsating, always interacting whole. So that at last it comes to be, that, when I hear my own heart beat, I actually hear in it nothing but one throb in that life which has been and is—in which we live and move and have our being and are continually sustained.

Having this view of the nature of the universe forced on us, is it possible that our view of the nature and value of truth should not be changed?

The physiologist, when he seeks to study an organism, puts beneath his microscope an almost invisible spot of blood or shred of animal tissue, and devotes days or months to its study, not because he believes the individual shred or speck to be of any peculiar value, but because he knows that once rightly understood it may explain to him the nature of the entire organism of which it is a part. So we, who are dominated by this new conception of existence, are compelled to look upon the exact knowledge of even the smallest and most insignificant fact as sacred, never knowing when it may turn into the key which may unlock for us the meaning of part of that great universal life of which it is an integral fragment.

Holding this view of the universe, we are compelled to walk almost awe-filled among even the small things of life; and, as the old Christian father, after much contemplation, was compelled at last to cry, 'There *is* no small sin—all violation of the will of God is great,'* so we also are almost compelled to cry, 'There is no small truth—all truth is great!'

Holding the old conception of existence, it was quite possible to believe that, between God and man, mind and matter, soul and body, there were many chinks and crannies where a lie might creep in and hide itself and be quite innoxious.* For us there is no faith in such possibility; we can no more nurse a false conception without it causing injury than a foreign substance can be intruded into a highly organised body without causing disorganisation and disease. Whether the truth concerns the feathers on a pigeon's wing or the constitution of a lump of earth or a psychological fact, we know that it is vital.*

Here she had had to leave off the first night. When she began the next night she went on to discuss how this new intellectual conception of the nature of the universe necessarily influenced our spiritual and moral outlook: how, for the man dominated by it, the existence of an extraneous will dealing arbitrarily with the things of existence was inconceivable, and the true revelation of the unseen and unknown beyond was to be found in the study of the seen and knowable about us; how, for us, the true act of religious worship was the search after a knowledge of all reality; how, for us, not less devout and religious than the old monk, who spent his life in copying and embroidering his missal or studying his gospel, is the man who today humbly devotes his life to the study of a spider's eye or the nature of a mineral, not knowing or seeking any direct benefit to flow to himself from the knowledge, but dominated by the profound conviction that the true comprehension of the smallest existence about us brings us nearer to the comprehension of the whole.

Then she went on to argue to herself that, for us, the true atheist was of necessity no longer the man who denies a knowledge of an unknown and unseen personality, but rather the man who believes that by juggling with facts he can outwit the universe and make that which he knows is not as if it were; and that the greatest wrong a man can commit towards his fellow is the wilful misleading of him as to any reality; and the sin against the Holy Ghost—the sin which hath no forgiveness—is the conscious, wilful blinding of our own eyes to any form of reality.

So far she had scribbled four weeks before, when she was sitting up to make the poultices. Since then she had not thought of her discussion. But that morning, when she took the children to walk in the woods, she walked up and down under a pine tree, as they picked flowers, talking it over to herself. Tonight she opened her exercise book on the desk, climbed up in the chair and drew her feet back under her, partly because it was cold and she kept them warm so, and partly because the desk was a little high. She knelt up, bending low over the book, and began to write. She wrote quickly in a large, sprawling hand, because she had much to say.

She went on to illustrate how our new attitude towards truth influenced all our personal relations in practical life. She illustrated it first by the feeling of the mother who looks down at the head of her little newborn baby sleeping at her breast. The old mother, if she were religious, looked down at it and prayed for it that it might cling to the dogmas which she would teach it, and, allowing nothing to turn its faith from them, at last attain everlasting joy. The new mother, when she looks down at the little head upon her breast, whispers in her heart, 'Oh, may you seek after truth. If anything I teach you be false, may you throw it from you, and pass on to higher and deeper knowledge than I ever had. If you are an artist, may no love of wealth or fame or admiration and no fear of blame or misunderstanding make you ever paint, with pen or brush, an ideal or a picture of external life otherwise than as you see it; if you become a politician, may no success for your party or yourself or the seeming good of even your nation ever lead you to tamper with reality and play a diplomatic part. In all the difficulties which will arise in life, fling yourself down on the truth and cling to that as a drowning man in a stormy sea flings himself onto a plank and clings to it, knowing that, whether he sink or swim with it, it is the best he has. If you become a man of thought and learning, oh, never with your left hand be afraid to pull down what your right has painfully built up through the years of thought and study, if you see it at last not to be founded on that which is; die poor, unloved, unknown, a failure—but shut your eyes to nothing that seems to them the reality.'

Then she scribbled on to show how the new attitude influenced the emotional relations between man and woman.

All women of the past and in the present find woman's heaven when their head rests on the shoulder of the man they love and his strong arm is about them; and as dear to the women of today as to the women of the remotest past is the love and tenderness of the man she is bound to. But yet the cry of our hearts is not the same. Beyond the cry for passionate tenderness there is another—'Give us truth! Not jewels, not ease—nor even caresses, precious as they are to us—are the first thing we seek: give us truth. We are weary with seeking for truth and being baffled everywhere by subterfuge and seeming; in your eyes, beloved, let us never have to seek it, let it come out to meet us. The love which is not planted on a naked sincerity, which needs subterfuge and self-deception and the deception of another for its life, is a plucked flower stuck into the sand; what matter how soon it dies—it has no real life. Our love will more easily survive the most awful knowledge you can give us than the realisation that you have once willingly misled us. Should you lay your head upon our knees and tell us your heart had gone forever to another, it would be easier for us to bear than that you had fed us with one subterfuge to shield us from knowledge. The highest sacrament of love we thirst for between our two souls is an almighty sincerity; if there is not this, then for us love's holy of holies is defamed.'

She bent lower over her writing, scribbling quicker and quicker.

Then she painted the effect of our new feeling for reality upon the moral judgments we pass upon ourselves and others.

When we lie awake in the dark of night thinking, what causes us to start and our cheek to burn? That which makes us shift restlessly from side to side, as if we were trying to shake off something, is often not the remembrance of what men and women of the past would have regarded as our greatest crime; it may be no infringement of any decalogue that ever yet was written; it may be just some written or spoken word or some act, perhaps seeming to us, even at the moment it was written or spoken or done, to be right and even magnanimous, but which falsified our relation with another or that other's relation to someone else. We remember it with a pain which manifest wrongdoings, recognised by the world, have not left; it is, when we remember it, as if a little knife cut into our heart, and we know till death comes it will always be sticking there.

She scribbled on to show how it altered our moral judgment of others; how, for us, the great criminal was not necessarily the murderer, the ruffian, the drunkard, the prostitute, or even the frank, direct, and open liar; but, may be, a spirit encased in a fair and gentle body, rich in many graces of character and manner, openly breaking no social law and with no need to lie directly to others, because it lies always and so successfully to itself and within itself and acts persistently in harmony with that lie: a rotten apple with dead seeds and a worm at its core, and a shining surface. The old view was that the great sin lay in not speaking truth to your fellow when thereby you caused him practical loss; for us there is one infinitely greater—the sin of the soul that refuses to see the naked truth within itself and therefore can never show it. The man who lies to his fellow poisons an external relation—but the soul which lies in itself to itself, acting always a part before itself, becomes a poison, a deadly fungus that scatters its poisonous seeds unconsciously whenever it is touched.

The rain was now falling in torrents, running off the thatched roof and streaming down the rockery and along the garden path; but she scribbled on without hearing it.

She was trying now to show the effect of the new attitude with regard to truth on our feeling for art. For the man or woman holding the old view, the story, the picture, the statue in which certain artistically necessary aspects of life are intentionally suppressed or misrepresented for certain practical ends, the human nature falsely painted because it seemed undesirable to paint it as it is, the fig leaf tied across the loin of the noblest statue, gives no pain and is still art; while, for those of us who have long set an intellectual value on sincerity, a mental habit has been formed which makes the perception of the wilful suppression of truth emotionally painful and so destroys our sense of perfection in the object in which it appears. The true reproduction of a sunrise, or a narrative that shows the working of a lofty spirit, may be more delightful art for us than the art which reproduces the texture of a lady's dress or paints the picture of a small soul; but the representation of the smallest or slightest aspect of life, if we are conscious of truth in it, satisfies an emotional need in us and becomes for us, so far at least, an object of satisfaction; while no art can be art for us, however lofty its claims, which does not satisfy what has slowly become a master need of our natures. A work of art may have many other elements of beauty for us; but it must be a revelation of truth for us, or it means nothing. Better the true picture of a beggar in his rags than the wilfully false picture of a saint.

So she scribbled on, hearing nothing of the rain outside, bending low over her paper with her chin pressed down on her breast. But presently she began to write slower and slower, and presently raised herself and sat watching the lamp. Then she sank half back in the chair, still on her knees and, after a time, began slowly drawing with her outstretched hand the pictures of faces down one edge of the page she had written on. They came out slowly, one below the other, some with sharp features, some with dark beards and curls, some with blunt features, some grotesque and some beautiful; she did not seem to be looking at them as she drew them. When she got to the bottom of the page she dipped the pen into the ink again and sat turning it round and round in her fingers and dipped it again. She was questioning in how far she had been right in her conclusions, and arguing the other side. Then she jumped suddenly from the chair and began to pace the room in the footpath round the desk. She clasped her hands behind her with the pen still between her fingers, and it made a large ink spot at the back of her little blue print skirt.

What after all did she know of art, except the art in literature? The book of photographs of great statuary, which she had bought at great expense, had so disgusted her with the modern fig leaves tied on with wire that she had never brought it into her study but had thrown it into a corner of the drawing room. What would she really feel if she could study plastic art in all its forms, not only Greek, Assyrian, Egyptian, Indian, not through books at second hand, but through them all actually living, in climates that produced them. She shot out her left hand greedily as if grasping them.

After she had walked for a time, she stopped suddenly at the door of the children's room, and, half opening it, stood listening to hear if they were still quiet and asleep; then she closed it softly and walked on with her hands behind her. Her thoughts had wandered far now, though the new chain of thought was bound link by link to the old. From thinking of Greek art and literature, her thought wandered on to the old, old problem which had held so great a fascination for her, even when she was a child and read, in her father's old brown leather-covered *History of the Ancient World*,* its stiff, long-worded accounts of the Assyrian and Egyptian and Roman and other early empires, and had traced with a dry pen on the mildewed map in the front of the book the path over the mountains which the Goths and the Vandals and the Huns took when they came to overrun Italy and destroy Rome, till the map had worn quite thin there. It was the old, old problem that had always fascinated her: why, when a nation or a race or a dominant class has reached a certain point of culture and material advance, has it always seemed to fall back from it, and the nation or race or class to be swept away? Always the march of human progress has died out there, to be taken up again by some other race or class in some distant part of the globe or after the lapse of centuries—to die out there also after a time, never proceeding persistently in a straight line. Was there an immutable law, based on an organic and inherent quality in human nature, which caused this arrest? Was it futile for us to hope that human advance might ever proceed persistently and unbroken in one direction? Was that which governed its arrest an organic law, like that which ordains the length of a man's beard, which, however long the individual may live, when it has once reached a certain length will always stop growing? Is it absolutely futile to hope that humanity can ever advance as the fern palm grows, beautiful frond beyond beautiful frond opening one out of the other as it mounts up higher and higher?—or has the arrest and decay, so invariable in the past, been merely dependent on external and fortuitous conditions, having no one organic root in the human nature itself and therefore being possible to avoid?

That morning, when she had taken the children for their walk in the pine woods, she had been pacing up and down under a tree while the children picked the bluebells among the grass, and had been arguing over the matter, almost as she used to argue with Charles under the pear tree. She had taken first the standpoint that it was organic and inevitable. Tonight, as she walked round the desk, she took the other view (which was really her own) and tried to defend the position that there was no sufficient evidence that this arrest and decay was really organic and therefore inevitable. One thing alone would be enough to account for it—the fact that a high advance in intellectual culture and social organisation has never yet been attained by any but a minute section of the human race as a whole, and always by merely a small section of the inhabitants of any single territory. That such a minute section of humanity has never been able to maintain its advance proves nothing except that in humanity, being intimately in its nature a solidarity and a whole with all its parts reacting on one another, one minute fragment can never move very far ahead of the mass without ultimately being drawn back, either by internal disintegration, brought about through that body in the society itself which has not been included in the advance, or through external and violent contact with other parts of the race which have not shared its advance.

That all so-called advanced societies have, in the past, always disintegrated and fallen back does not prove that a hard rim-line exists which humanity can never surpass, and cannot prove this while we are in possession of a fact which adequately accounts for this retrogression without any such supposition.

She paced up and down quickly and more quickly with her hands behind her, still holding the pen, and went on in her thought to illustrate her view.

What was that high point of advance, intellectual and moral, which we speak of Greece having attained in the fourth century before Christ, and from which she receded so quickly and completely—was it indeed Greece which ever reached that point? What was that much vaunted culture, that high creative energy, that passionate thirst after intellectual insight, that demand for personal freedom, that search after physical beauty, but the possession of a few males who constituted the dominant class in a few cities of Greece? What was that much vaunted culture but a delicate iridescent film overlying the seething mass of servile agricultural and domestic slaves and of women, nominally of the dominant class, but hardly less servile and perhaps ignorant, who constituted the bulk of its inhabitants? As little could it be said to have been the property of the inhabitants of the land of Greece as the phosphorescent light on the surface of the ocean is the property of the fathoms of water stretching below it whose surface it illuminates. It would be as rational to expect that such a form of culture, brought into existence for a moment by a combination of happy conditions, could hand itself down from generation to generation, expanding and strengthening as it grew, as to expect a spray of shrub, plucked and placed in a vase of water in a hothouse, though it might bloom profusely for a few days, should permanently propagate itself and persistently grow when it was without ground and had no root.

But even had things been otherwise in Greece—had its women, they who alone have the power of transmitting the culture and outlook of one generation safely to the next, been sharers in the culture and freedom and labours of its males, not merely partially in the person of a few of its *hetairai*,* but in that of the bulk of its childbearing women—had every hand that laboured in the fields or the cities been that of a freeman, sharing to the full the civic rights of his State, possessing a stake in its material welfare and a culture that enabled him to rejoice in its art and share in its thought—had that happened, which never yet has happened in any land—had Greece been filled with a population homogeneous in their culture and freedom—had no untaught servile woman existed to suckle any Greek child—had no slave formed a rotten foundation stone in the social structure—had culture, freedom, and civic rights been the common property of every human who breathed on the soil of Greece—had the social superstructure been sound and homogeneous from foundation to coping stone—even then, though the vantage gained, instead of passing away in a couple of generations, might have remained for a few hundred years and there might have been more persistent progress; yet, could it have been even tolerably permanent?

For what was the whole of Greece itself but a mere spot on the earth's surface? What were its people but a drop in the ocean of humanity? Unless she could have walled herself in, shutting off all possibility of interaction with all the races beyond herself, sooner or later she must have been so interacted upon by the mass of humanity beyond, that change and disintegration, moral and intellectual, must have set in, and she must slowly have fallen back to the common level.

As she walked she had paused before the little statue of Hercules, and, taking it automatically from the bracket, stood holding it in one hand and softly stroking it down with the finger of the other as though she were feeling its outline: yet her eyes appeared not to see it. After a while she put it back on the stand and began pacing again.

All the civilisations of the past, in Egypt, in Assyria, in Persia, in India, what had they been but the blossoming of a minute, abnormally situated, abnormally nourished class, unsupported by any vital connection with the classes beneath them or the nations around? What had they resembled but the long, thin, tender, feathery green shoots which our small rose trees sometimes send out in spring, rising far into the air, but which we know long before the summer is over will have broken and fallen; not because they have grown to a height which no rose tree can ever attain, for ultimately the whole rose tree may be much higher than the shoot, but because they have shot out too far before their fellow branches to make permanence possible; having no support, wind and weather will sooner or later do their work and snap them off or wither them. Next year a dozen rich young shoots may sprout from the snapped stem and survive; it may not have shot upwards and been broken off without helping in the growth of the whole tree—but it, itself, perishes.

If the whole of our vaunted modern advance, our science, our art, our social ideals, our material refinement, were to pass away tomorrow, swept away by the barbarians we nurse within the hearts of our societies or which exist beyond: would it for a moment prove that humanity had reached its possible limit of growth, and not rather that a sectional growth is no permanent growth?—that, where the mass remain behind, the few are ultimately drawn back? (As the head of a tortoise, let it stretch it out as it will within certain limits, can never continue to advance while its hind legs are sticking in the mud; would it move, it must pull its hind legs forward.) Would it prove that our loftiest ideals of human progress were futile?—man moving ever in a little ring, advancing and forever falling backward as soon as the edge is reached—and not merely that the true cry of permanent human advance must always be 'Bring up your rears! Bring up your rears!'? Head and heart can ultimately move no further than the feet can carry them. Permanent human advance must be united advance!

Then she thought suddenly she heard the baby stir. She threw her pen down on the table and took up the lamp, went into the next room and bent over his cot. But he had only turned in his sleep and was resting quietly. She bent down and turned him onto his side and put the nipple of his feeding bottle into his fist and close to his lips that he might find it if he woke. She had had to wean him because of the new baby that was coming. Then she tucked the cover in at the back of his neck and went back, closed the door softly behind her and began to walk up and down.

If the advance of a nation or a race must always ultimately be stayed, partly because of the internal action of the undeveloped mass within itself which must in time disintegrate it, and partly because the interaction with humanity beyond itself must ultimately draw it down and back, how much more must it be the case that a solitary individual city can never reach its full development in a society far behind itself?

That the highest and most harmonious development of the individual which we dream of is never reached, and that the attempt to attain it seems always to lead to intense personal suffering or absolute social destruction for the individual striving, in no way proves that the ideal is ultimately beyond reach—an *ignis fatuus** which the human hand will never grasp. As the nation or the class which should first have developed so far that it turned all its energies entirely away from the creation and wielding of the arts of destruction and self-defence, and turned them entirely to the creation of the beautiful and useful arts which benefit all mankind, would, ultimately and probably very soon, be swept away, as long as anywhere on the earth's surface there were still races so retrograde that they devoted all their energies to the arts of destruction; and as the nation, which should have attained the moral standpoint at which it became no longer possible for the stronger to absorb all the good of life and in which therefore poverty and need become extinct, would inevitably be overcome by the wanting and miserable products in other societies where a lower moral standard prevailed, if any such society existed anywhere on the earth—so more surely the individual, who should arrive at a higher moral point of development and strive to realise his ideals in actual life, must inevitably suffer or be absolutely annihilated in a society which had not reached his standpoint; and this not because his ideal was inherently unattainable and might not be the ultimate goal of the race, but simply because, for its realisation harmoniously and successfully, it wanted more than the solitary unit, it wanted the interaction of the whole society. A wolf who should suddenly be smitten by the idea that, instead of tearing his fellows to pieces, it would be better if they made a league of co-operation and fellowship, and for that purpose filed down his canines, would quickly become a prey to his fellows, not because his ideal was incompatible with successful animal life, for other forms have attained to it, but because its attainment by one was impossible.

So the individual primitive man in a cannibal tribe who had become possessed with the idea that the eating of human flesh was undesirable, and who had refused to capture and feed, would have become an object of scorn and probably of hatred to his tribe and might probably have died of hunger in some time of pressure, not because his ideal was ultimately unattainable, for practically today the whole of humanity has reached it, but because change in the idea of his fellows and the common carrying out of agricultural and pastoral labours were necessary to its successful attainment.

The man who dreams today that the seeking of material good for himself alone is an evil, who persistently shares all he has with his fellows, is not necessarily a fool dreaming of that which never has been or will be; he is simply dreaming of that which will be perfectly attainable when the dream dominates his fellows and all give and share. Working it alone, it fails, because the individual is part of an organism which cannot reach its full unfolding quite alone.

The man who should have reached a point of development at which sex in all its manifestations, whether physical or mental, has become a matter for reverence and who should find his ideal reached only by a perfectly free and even comradeship between men and women at large in human society, and the personal ideal reached only in a relationship in which the mind fully shared with the body and in which the best in each half united into the perfect human creature called forth, who would desire that all that was most self-forgetful and heroic in his nature should be brought into play in the relation, as men desire to hang only the fairest wreaths before the shrine of the chief god in their temple—could such a man ever fully realise his ideal, or even attempt to realise it, without acute suffering and many-sided failure, in a society in which the brothel reigns and the ideals which the brothel presupposes, in which sex relationships are viewed by the mass of his fellows from the two standpoints of crude and selfish physical enjoyment or of gross material benefit? Might not his very attempts to bring men and women into freer and more equal fellowship in themselves seem to produce more evil than they remedied, simply because they were not ready for it? Would he himself not be almost certainly misunderstood and his personal relations end in irrevocable failure? What would this prove but that each man is but a cell in the human organism and that what his full development might be we shall never know till others share it with him?

The man whose ideal it is that, by the non-requital of injuries and the large expansion of sympathy even toward those who inflict suffering on himself, is human good and justice finally served—does his failure to evoke any response, and his final crushing beneath the hands he refused to strike, prove anything but the solidarity of humanity and that the foremost branch which grows too far beyond its fellows must ultimately be snapped off?* That no individual ever yet realised in life the highest development which the mind has dreamed of proves not that perfect truth and fellowship are not attainable to humanity, but that the one alone cannot compass them.

Is it not a paradox covering a mighty truth that not one slave toils under the lash on an Indian plantation but the freedom of every other man on earth is limited by it? That not one laugh of lust rings but each man's sexual life is less fair for it? That the full, all-rounded human life is impossible to any individual while one man lives who does not share it? 'Bring up your rears! Bring up your rears!'

She walked, whispering softly to herself. Outside, the rain had left off falling; only the drops fell from the branches of the trees over the roof as the wind moved them, and the great drops fell slowly from the thatched eaves; but she did not hear them, she was so happy talking to herself.

Now her thought shifted its standpoint. She imagined the mind she argued with to take a new view and to say, 'Granting you are right and that the fully developed individual and the race must be hampered and limited by that of the less developed, is it not practically our duty and for the benefit of humanity that we should forcibly suppress, cut off and destroy the less developed individuals and races, leaving only the highly developed to survive?' She imagined it to produce all the arguments for the destruction of inferior races and individuals, stating them as fairly as she could. Then she turned to the other side and stated the view which was really her own.

She walked quicker now, but with her head still down, striking the palm of one hand now and then with the doubled-up fist of the other.

Firstly, where is any body of humans to be found impartial enough, and untouched by the warping of personal and racial prejudices, to be able to determine for the race at large just what qualities are desirable and should be preserved and which should render their possessors liable to destruction? Would not each individual composing it be warped, not merely by a weakness for his own personal qualities, mental and physical, but would not racial prejudice make impartial judgment for humanity at large impossible?—the Chinaman judging from the Chinaman's standpoint; the Hindu from the Hindu's; the Englishman from the Englishman's? Could any but a race of crowned, immortal gods, untouched by human self-love with its bias, form any conclave which should dare determine, not merely what were the ideal qualities after which they individually should strive and which they should impress on the race by preaching and example, but which would justify them in physically destroying those unendowed with them?

But, granting that it were possible to find such a body of humans on the globe (which it is not and cannot be), who would draw up an infallible code of all the qualities desirable and to be sought after by expanding humanity and of all those to be crushed as undesirable to the race, two difficulties that could not be surmounted would yet remain. Firstly that, given this almost divine conclave had succeeded in drawing up a list of all the qualities which are desirable in advancing humanity—the physical qualities of muscular strength, organic soundness, physical beauty (the idea of which differs so much from race to race and even from person to person that no representative body of humans ever could agree in what it consisted)—that general vitality and harmony of parts and forces which makes physical life a joy—the mental qualities of reason, imagination and keen and quick perception—the social qualities of sympathy, kindliness, rectitude, and all other qualities desired by humans in their fellows—and should exactly define what was meant by each quality and by its reverse: would they be much nearer the solution of the question what individuals and what races should be destroyed as a weight and drawback on the development of the race, and which saved and sacrificed for as the highest development? For no extended list of desirable or undesirable human qualities could be drawn up, all of which could be found wholly incarnate in any race or individual.

You say, and rightly, physical health and strength are among the prime necessities of the fully developed human creature. The Kaffir and the South Sea Islander have often these in their very highest perfection: are these, therefore, the races to be preserved and which others are to be sacrificed for? You say a powerful reason is essential to the advance of the race: you find your man with the powerful reason, but diseased, antisocial, using his powerful intellect only as a means of preying on his fellow, often the great criminal. You say, at least let us kill out the hopelessly unfit, the invalid and the sickly and the consumptive: under this law you may ordain to destruction the bright, the lovely and most beneficent of the race. Has my view not as much to be said for it as yours that, if any on earth should be wilfully destroyed as the down-drawers of the race, it is not a Shelley or a Keats,* who have enriched and beautified existence on earth beyond fifty thousand whole men; but that it is the man of perfect physical health, with far less intelligence, and organically incapable of living for anything but his own wellbeing, finding no joy in any kind of sacrifice for his fellows and transmitting his qualities as surely as the consumptive or the weak, who is really the disease point in humanity, the creature who prevents the noblest social institutions and personal relations from coming into existence, because his egoisms can always be calculated to make them unworkable? You say that keen perceptions and the power of dominating are characteristics of the to-be-preserved races: but what if to me the little Bushman woman, who cannot count up to five and who, sitting alone and hidden on a koppie, sees danger approaching and stands up, raising a wild cry to warn her fellows in the plain below that the enemy are coming, though she knows she will fall dead, struck by poisonous arrows,* shows a quality higher and of more importance to the race than those of any Bismarck? What if I see in that little untaught savage the root out of which ultimately the noblest blossom of the human tree shall draw its strength? Who shall contend I am not right?

You say, 'Let it be granted that social qualities are to count as high as or higher than intellectual or physical, then at least it will be justified that all avowedly criminal individuals and classes should be destroyed.' But who are the criminals? You say the prostitute, the murderer, the robber, the gambler. But who are these? The judge who sits in his elbow chair sentencing the man who plays pitch and toss in the street and himself sits up till two o'clock over his cards—the king and the prince who, while every avenue of pleasure and good is open to them, hang round the tables of Monte Carlo—the poor man who opens his back cellar for gaming to make a wretched living—who is the gambler? Who is the prostitute—the wretched woman whom the policeman drags along the street, or the man, often of wealth and learning and power, whose selfish lust and gold alone keep alive the institution whose bitter fruit she is? When you have crushed and destroyed the woman prostitute, what have you done more than cut out the tiny rotten place on the surface of an apple, while you leave gnawing away in the dark at the core the worm that produced it? Who is the robber and murderer we have most to fear—the pirate who on the high seas grasps men and goods, the highwayman and the housebreaker, or the man who, shielding himself always carefully behind a law he sees works in his favour or knows how to evade, makes his wealth from the ill-paid labour of those in mines and factories working at the cost of life, and ornaments his wife and his daughters as much in bloodstained jewellery and garments as the robber who returning home puts on his wife's finger a ring cut from the hand of a living woman, or throws on his daughter's shoulders a garment spotted with a traveller's blood? Who is the man who robs his fellows of life and the fruit of their labour, that we may be sure he shall not slip through our fingers, leaving the wrong man there? Who is the gambler, prostitute, robber, murderer? Is he king, prince, judge, as well as beggar and tramp? How shall we make sure he gets judgment in exact proportion to his offence? And further, is there any definite action or state which, judging for the world as a whole, can be set down as marking out the criminal? Has not the buccaneer, the polygamist, the polyandrist been the hero and the virtuous man or woman of his community? Will any action more certainly bring down the judgment and social punishment of his society in some countries than refusing to bow the head to a passing wafer of flour, in others the eating of pork, or the refusal to take his dead brother's wife, or give his daughter to the chief harem? Have not robber chiefs been regarded as quite as respectable and unliable to punishment in their society as the wealthy wage robber and the prostitute king* and the hangman who are with us? What definite action will you set down as marking the criminal?

You say that of course no definite concrete action can be set down as marking out the criminal, that it is one in one society and another in another, but that he is yet easily marked off: he is the man who in any society refuses to submit to the laws which its dominating power has instituted and who persists in facing the punishments and penalties it ordains; and that, if he were in all societies destroyed and prevented from perpetuating himself, his type might become absolutely extinct and the qualities he possesses die out from the human race.

Perhaps this would be so; but are you sure you know what you are doing? For on that broad road of opposition to law and authority, along which stream the millions of humanity too low to grasp even the value of laws and institutions about them, resisting them from an ignorant and blind selfishness which makes them believe they are improving their own condition by violating them, there are found walking men of a totally different order—white-robed sons of the gods with the light on their foreheads, who have left the narrow paths walled in by laws and conventions, not because they were too weak to walk in them, or because the goals toward which they led were too high, but because infinitely higher goals and straighter paths were calling to them—the new pathfinders of the race! These men, who rise as high above the laws and conventions of their social world as the mass who violate them fall below, are yet inextricably blended with them in the stream of souls who walk in the path of resistance to law. From the monk Telemachus, who, springing into the Roman arena to stop the gladiatorial conflict,* fell, violating the laws and conventions of his society—a criminal, but almost a god—up and down all the ages man has been on earth there have been found these social resisters and violators of the accepted order, the saviours and leaders of men on the path to higher forms of life.

It is true that if, persistently and with a rigour from which none escaped alive, you could in every land exterminate the resisters of social law, you might at last produce a race on earth in which even the wish or the power to resist social institutions will have died out; your prisons might be empty, your hangmen and judges without occupation. But what would you have done? Seeking to cut out humanity's corns, to remove its cataract, to amputate its diseased limbs, you would have put out its eyes, cut off its tongue, maimed its legs; unable to see or move or express, its heart would beat slower and slower and death would come.

There is no net which can be shaped to capture the self-seeking, ignorant violator of law which shall not also capture in its meshes the hero, the prophet, the thinker, the leader—the life of the world!

As the oak tree cannot grow unless, with each new ring it adds, its old bark cracks and splits, so humanity cannot develop without the rupture of its old institutions and laws; and it has been exactly because the bulk of humanity have never of necessity been able to distinguish between this healthful disruptive process and unhealthful decay, and have sought to crush and annihilate the particles causing it, that the growth of humanity has been as slow as it has. To suggest the more rigorous extermination of all non-law-submitting humans is simply to suggest a slow suicide as far as human development is concerned. In all ages the multitude has looked upon Barabbas* as a less violent and dangerous disrupter of social laws than the Christ—not this man but Barabbas!

But you may say the criminal is, of course, not to be marked off in all societies merely as the breaker of any of its laws, for then, of course, the man who strives after better ideals would be included with the man who strives after lower; you say the true criminal is that man who, whether within or without the law, is willing to inflict suffering and loss on others for his own gain; and undoubtedly this is the true criminal. But how is he to be found, since it is not by the committal of any definite, marked-off act, or by the violation of public enactments, but by the nature of his motive, that he becomes a criminal? It is certainly not a Lucrezia Borgia, adulteress and murderer, who of necessity, judged by the standard of motive and the amount of suffering caused to others, will always come out the great criminal. The fair gentlewoman, never transgressing any enacted law, always seeking for love and sympathy and determined to gain it at all cost to others and all sacrifice of direct sincerity, may inflict in the course of her life an amount of suffering and wrong before which a few direct murders count as nothing; not merely by the love she takes from others or the friends she divides, but by the much more terrible distrust of human nature she awakens; by showing that, below so much gentleness and virtue, self-seeking and rottenness may lie, she strikes at our faith in our fellows, than which no more terrible wrong can be done. Yet under what code or before which tribunal could she be condemned to death? She is the snake in the Garden of Eden; yet who can swear she has poison as she glides noiselessly by?* When we all lie silent in our last sleep with our feet turned upwards, if a god of life, knowing all things, should pass us, meting out judgment according as we had caused suffering in the search after our own good, would he of necessity pause over the worn-out drunkard and the street-treading outcast? Might it not also be over the woman of virtue and philanthropy or the man, hail-fellow-well-met with all men, who paid his debts of honour and owed no man anything—saying, 'There lies the great criminal!'?

But, you may say, granting that we cannot determine who the criminals are who should be destroyed for the benefit of the race, or the kind or degree of ill health which should be followed by instant destruction, yet surely such an ideal body of humans should find no difficulty in desiring the annihilation of all dark and primitive races who are manifestly a down-draught on humanity.

But are they so?

Is there really any superiority at all implied in degrees of pigmentation, and are the European races, except in their egoistic distortion of imagination, more desirable or highly developed than the Asiatic? Are we not in our vanity like the parvenu* who, having wrung wealth out of the labour of others and surrounded himself with the results of all human toil and knowledge, stands in his gorgeous room filled with the works of art and use of all nations and, with his hands in his pockets and his full belly, looks round with infinite satisfaction at what he has accumulated about him, and says, 'All these are mine,' believing really that their existence and creation has something to do with himself? Are we modern Europeans not the parvenus among the human race? From the ancient civilisations of Asia and Africa, ancient and complete, when we were merely savage, have we not got all the foundation and much of the superstructure* of what we possess? Art, science, letters, all are their original creation, merely taken over by us; even our very religion, such as it is, we could not invent for ourselves but had to take it over from a hook-nosed, swarthy, Semitic people. And, if the learning and art and industry of Asia and Africa, passing into the hands of that marvellous bloom of humanity the Greek race, in its little span improved and enlarged what it took, it yet has been no work of ours, the Northern barbarians; we were running naked and staining ourselves with woad in our woods, when the looms of India and China were producing the delicate fabrics we seek now to imitate, when Asiatics ate from golden-flowered and delicate china, when temples and statues were raised that are our wonder and admiration, when philosophers taught and thought, and books were written and great legal systems enacted, while we sat round our fires on the dung and gambled with knucklebones or danced war dances to the shouts of our fellows. It ill becomes us, who are but the tamed children of yesterday, to talk of primitive savages. Even today, when we have inherited all, is it so certain that our vaunted civilisation is so much statelier and on all sides wider and with nobler elements of truth lying at its foundation than the older civilisations of the yellow and brown races? Is it so sure we are the people, and wisdom will die with us? Is it not possible, for instance, that there is something of deep wisdom in the Chinese ideal which gives so much of the beauty of life to the end, which gives even the woman when she is old, the mother and grandmother, so honoured and tender a place in society? Is it quite wise to sacrifice all to youth, so that every man and woman fears old age and would sacrifice all to avoid it? Must not the whole of life be more beautiful when men wait for good at the end, the joy of the sunset? Is not the religion which permeates Asia, and which came to life while our fathers still dreamed of heaven as a hall where men drank wine from the skulls of their enemies, more in harmony with the teaching of modern knowledge, which is reshaping us, than even that other Asiatic religion which we have adopted? Did not the deep-seeing eye of the Buddha, hundreds of years before the Jewish teacher walked in Syria, perceive clearly beneath all the complexities of form and individuality the unity in life upon the earth? He did not get at it as the modern man of reason, slowly, by measurement and calculation; by deep perception he knew that our little brothers look out at us from the eyes of animals, that the life of no beast and bird or insect is alien and unconnected with ours, that life flows on earth as one large stream with many divided branches, and under his mystical doctrine of the transmigration of souls he covered the same radical truth which 'evolution' expresses in other but perhaps more absolutely accurate terms. We Northern fair-skins have had great men; our glimpses of new truths, new masteries over matter, have added our grain to humanity's sum of riches even in the direction of creative art; but, when we look around us on what we call our civilisation, how little is really ours alone and not drawn from the great stream of human labours and creation so largely non-European? We scorn the Chinaman because his women compress their feet, not perceiving how infinitely more deadly and grotesque is the compression of our bodies; we ridicule, in certain Asiatic races, the pigtail of the Chinaman or the darkened tooth of the Japanese, blinded by egoism to the infinite degradation of the Northern races in their passionate strife to imitate ever-changing costumes and modes, alike so far removed from nature and beauty that even we, when a few years are past, perceive their grotesqueness and vulgarity, the slavish imitation of fashions which, by their unending change, feed on the vitals of the race through their ignoble demand on the brain of its womanhood, absorbing energy, reason, imagination, and setting, so long as their diseased reign lasts, a limit to the progress and expansion of woman and, with her, of the race. We accuse of immorality the Asiatics who consume the opium we forced upon them at the point of the sword; but we fair Northerns deserve today, as fully as when the Roman spoke it two thousand years ago, the judgment that as a people our chief pleasures were drinking and gambling; our race courses and card tables are as essential to our happiness as the dice and knucklebones to our forebears. Is it not more than possible that, infinite as has been the debt of humanity to the ancient non-European peoples in the past, they have yet more to confer in the future?

You may answer (she walked quicker and quicker, looking down at the carpet) that no sane, informed mind could regard the old master races of the East, who have led in the path of civilisation, as consigned to destruction by their inferiority; that it is the dark and primitive races still leading a life of nature that it is so necessary should be removed and suppressed in the cause of humanity.

But not only does it ill become us, the latest tamed of all civilised races, to speak slightingly of any primitive barbarian; not only among ourselves is a race such as the Prussians,* who were civilised many centuries later than the men of France or Spain, in no way considered by us inferior to these, but we hold, and perhaps rightly, that by the engrafting of our savage forebears on the older civilisations of Europe, though we mercilessly destroyed them for the time being and plunged all Europe into barbarous chaos for over ten centuries, that we yet vivified human life and that our savage eruption was in the end a benefit. The older civilisations were too nearly extinct, we say, by excessive civilisation; a back-beat* to the unclothed men of the woods and nomads of tents was necessary to vivify them. But if this were so, may not the most primitive races have the same function to fulfil towards us? Is it not possible that man, a creature of the plains and hills, naked and always in unbroken activity in the free air, cannot survive beyond a certain time when he goes about loaded with materials from all the vegetable and animal and mineral kingdoms which he has gathered from all quarters of the globe—as a mantis collects mud and shells to make a case for himself, when he buries himself deep among his little erections of mud and stone, shutting off from body and brain light and air, when he has so constructed life that half of his body social is parasitic and enervated by want of labour, and the half it feeds with crushed under the superimposed weight—is it not possible that the primitive man, individually and structurally as well as socially, may, in some future aeon, have the same restorative function to fulfil towards ourselves as we imagine ourselves to have played towards older decadent civilisations?

You say that the primitive barbarian is ugly and repulsive to us: were not our forebears so to Greeks and Romans? Were not Attila and the Huns so horrible, physically and mentally, in their eyes that they were believed to be the offspring of witches and evil spirits, nothing wholly human being possibly so repulsive? Was it not death to the Roman woman who wedded a barbarian? To have eaten or drunk or slept with him was disgrace. He was supposed even to have an unendurable smell. Was the difference not at least as great between the lovely, cultured Greek and the trained, imperial Roman, between Pericles and Virgil, and the naked and spear-brandishing, long-haired savage, drinking blood from the skulls of his enemies, as between his modern descendant and any primitive savage on earth? Who shall say that, in destroying the child of nature with his perhaps simpler organisation and untried nerves, we are not destroying that of which humanity may yet in the aeons to come have need to keep the race upon the earth?

At the worst, which is fairer and more akin to the ideals towards which humanity seems to move?—the little Bushman in his open cave on the mountain brow, etching away into the rock with his little sharpened flint the picture of hunting or wild beast, and looking down in the glory of sunshine on the place below where the wild things graze, or a swell-chinned, ragged woman staggering out of a public house in one of our centres of civilisation, while the man who made the drink dwells in high places? Which is lovelier here, now, or in any place or time—the troop of men and women on a South Sea island, naked and gladly disporting themselves in the water or wandering together in the sunshine and sharing their love in the open light of day, or the scene that night by night our great cities witness? Which fills us with a sense of the greatness of the human spirit—the Kaffirs on their flat-topped mountain refusing to surrender month after month,* till the conquerors when they mount at last find only one or two hardly moving skeletons—men, women and children having died with hunger—or the civilised soldier who has sworn to die, but when a tenth part of his numbers have fallen puts up the white flag, willing to take life but not to lose it?

He needs be a brave man who would dare ordain destruction to all primitive and barbarous people, who could feel so sure humanity will have no need of them on her march through the future.

But letting all those difficulties pass (she stretched out one hand with the palm extended): supposing it were possible for us to find an individual, a class or a race, so constituted that it presented in itself all the conceivable disadvantages and deficiencies which can afflict human nature and none of the advantages; supposing it were possible—which it never would be—to find anywhere a body of humans as diseased, as devoid of physical health and the vital enjoyment of life as a worn-out man of fashion and debauch, as stupid and ill-shaped as a Bushman, as brutal as the savage, as false as the worst civilised man, as antisocial as the criminal, as hypocritical as the Pharisee,* physically deformed and mentally wanting, combining in itself all the drawbacks of each form and stage of human growth and none of the advantages—you may say: 'Here at least we have found at last the creature or class whom, to perfect its own growth, it is necessary society should slay and mercilessly destroy.' But is this so? If such individual or race were found, would it even then be proved that the highest use which society could make of them would be to destroy them? Does not the essential element, which it is most important to develop, if human life on earth is ever to attain to its full blossoming, lie in just that very sensitiveness towards the right of existence of all other human units, that deep-seated and at last organic desire not to benefit ourselves at the cost of others, which this course of action would tend to blunt and kill? In attempting to remove the undesirable and, to us, retrograde portions of human society, are we not blunting and striking at the very existence of the quality in ourselves which is above all essential to full human unfolding? Might not an immensely more productive use be made of such undesirable elements of life, by using them as objects for the development of those broad and generous human feelings which are the crowning beauty of life? In seeking to exterminate the undesirable of the race when we find him, may not society be striking at the very heart of its own progress, inflicting a mortal wound upon itself which exceeds in deadliness any which the undesirable individuals could have inflicted on it? Is it not an act of moral suicide?

And (she stretched out her hand softly again) if even this point also were waived, if it be allowed that it might be possible to find a body of humans so perfect and impartial that they are fit to legislate for the race, and that it might be possible for them to discover persons and races so hopelessly undesirable that for the benefit of the race's growth they must be destroyed, yet there remains the second great difficulty—who would bell the cat? Supposing this body of enlightened, impartial and thoughtful humans decided that tyrants, drunkards, gamblers, murderers, robbers, hypocrites and all inflicters of suffering on their kind, stupid and blindly narrow persons, were an evil to the race and should be destroyed—would this enlightened and philosophic body of persons be themselves able to carry out their edict of destruction and become captors and executioners? And, if they had to delegate it to others, would not the very persons to be destroyed be often the persons fit and able to carry it out? The debauched judge, the ignorant, stupid and narrow jailer, the brutal and stupid soldier, the bloodthirsty tyrant, the very individuals ordained to destruction, may be the most impossible to get at. You may condemn Nero* but you cannot compel him to destroy himself, and you may not be able to find anyone capable and willing to do so. The very conditions of lofty intelligence and wide, unbiassed sympathy, which would alone endow any human being with the gift necessary for impartially judging for the race, are the very qualities which might render him unfit and incapable as executioner.

But you may say that all this is merely irrelevant child's play; that no sane person supposes you could find a body of humans wise enough and impartial enough to determine for the whole race which are the retrograde elements which must be destroyed for its benefit or powerful enough to destroy them when it has so determined; that the same end is attained much more securely and quickly by simply allowing all the physically stronger elements in humanity everywhere to destroy the weaker; that, by the stronger everywhere destroying the physically weaker with a wonderful automatic action, all that is undesirable in humanity is killed out and all that is desirable remains. But is this so?

You say that, by this process through the ages of the past, all improvement and unfolding in life on the earth has taken place, and that nothing else is necessary to produce the fullest beauty, joy and strength for the race on earth.

But is this so? Has life on the globe or has mankind attained to its present position, low as that is in many ways, because the physically stronger has preyed on the physically, for the moment at least, weaker?

You say this is the great law of the survival of the fittest* which leads to all beauty, strength and unfolding in sentient life; that to interfere with it in any way is to interfere with nature's one plan for attaining perfection.

You shelter yourself under the name of science. Are you not, and one-eyedly, perverting the teaching of great minds, as the priestly in all ages pervert and make falsehood of the perception of the great prophets who preceded them?

(She was whispering so loudly to herself that, in the next room, you would have thought she was speaking to someone beside her.)

You say all evolution in life has been caused simply by this destruction of the weaker by the stronger.

From every cave and den and nest, from the depths of the sea, from air and earth, from the recesses of the human breast, rises but one great 'No!' that refutes you. Neither man nor bird nor beast, nor even insect, is what it is and has survived here today simply because the stronger has preyed on the weaker. The law of its life and its growth and survival has been far otherwise. From the time when, in a dimly living form, amoeba sought and touched amoeba, and, meeting, broke out into a larger form and divided into fresh forms, life has been governed, step by step, through the long march and advance in stages of life, by union; love and expansion of the ego to others has governed life. From the insect, following that unselfconscious reason we call instinct, who climbs to the top of the highest bough to fasten there her eggs where the tender shoots will first sprout to feed them, on to the bird who draws the soft down from her breast to warm the nest, who toils to feed and warm, and hovers about before the feet of the dangerous stranger that he may be drawn to attack her and not find her young, and who draws up the food from her own crop to feed them, till love becomes incarnate in the female mammal feeding her young from her breast—this is my blood which I give for the life of the world—through all nature, life and growth and evolution are possible only because of mother-love. Touch this, lay one cold finger on it and still it in the heart of the female, and, in fifty years, life in all its higher forms on the planet world would be extinct; man, bird and beast would have vanished and the cold, dim dawn of sentient existence would alone exist on a silent, empty earth. Everywhere mother-love and the tender nurturing of the weak underlie life, and the higher the creature the larger the part it plays. Man individually and as a race is possible on earth only because, not for weeks or months but for years, love and the guardianship of the strong over the weak have existed. You may almost estimate the height of development in the creature by the amount of mother-love and care he stands for.

You may say that mother-love forms an exception in the rule of nature, which, for perfecting life, demands the destruction of the weak by the strong. But what of the protective care of the male, not only of his own young and his related females, but of all the most helpless of his group? It is not only the sea lion who carries about his young in the bag on his own person;* but through all sea life runs the defence of the weak by the stronger. Could the ostrich breed out its eggs in the wastes, where long journeys for food are needed, if the male did not daily take his hours of brooding on the nest to keep the eggs warm and care for and watch over the young with a tenderness even greater than their mother's while she goes afar to seek for food? Could the female bird of many kinds rear and feed her young without the continual aid of the male? Nor is it only parental sympathy, but a much wider feeling for the weak, which makes possible much of the higher animal life about us. It is not only for the defence of his own young that the old stag stands ceaselessly watching for danger and raises his shrill cry when he sees it approaching, at the greatest risk to himself. I have seen upon a cliff a baboon stand defending the one defile where dogs could mount, hurling them down with his hands and glancing back every moment anxiously to see how the troop of males and females carrying their young were escaping, clinging to his post till he fell torn to fragments by the dogs, saving his race and his species, not by his vast power of destruction, but by his willingness to be destroyed that others might live. The survival of the meerkat, so small and defenceless on the barren plains where so many other creatures become extinct in the presence of danger and of enemies, is accountable only when you know that each meerkat acts for all; not for their own young only, but for one another, and, for the younger and more helpless, all labour and sacrifice themselves. When the hawk approaches, if the older males and females be gone out far to look for food, tiny creatures, themselves hardly weaned, will seize all the tinier ones half an inch shorter than themselves and in desperate anguish strive to carry them off to the hole, forgetting all fear for themselves in their passionate attempt to save those who may have no blood relationship with themselves, while the older males and females grow gaunt and thin in the breeding time, because almost all food they find is brought to lay at the feet of the young, while mothers go away to seek food which will supply the quite small with food. It is this passionate love for one another, this endless self-sacrifice of all, this devotion to the weaker by the stronger, which makes it possible for these little delicate furry creatures with their beautiful eyes and small powers of defence to survive in our terrible barren enemy-filled plains. The panther and the lion have vanished in the terrible presence of man, and many other forms of life grow very scarce, but these tiny creatures are still surviving, aided by their passionate devotion and self-sacrifice.

Then among men in their very struggles with one another, is it always the strongest fist and the fiercest heart which aids races or individuals to survive? Has not a great love lain behind those marvellous victories of which the world's history is full, where small and relatively weak nations and individuals have survived and driven back the large and powerful—a love for an idea, for a race, for a land, which, by blotting out personal considerations, has given weakness the power to protect itself and survive? The legend of the Swiss who gathered a score of spears into his breast, and so made room for his fellows to break the phalanx and win their nation's freedom,* is only emblematic of one of the deepest seated, transforming and preserving forces in human nature. The legend of the mother,* which in varying form almost every country possesses, who, to save her child from the bird of prey, climbed where the foot of the bravest and strongest could never tread, to recover it, is universal because it outlines the profound truth recognised everywhere: that an almighty affection and the instinct for even self-immolation in the serving of others is not merely one of the highest but one of the strongest forces modifying human life. Almost everywhere in the record of human life on earth are the traces of rapine and slaughter and the suppression or destruction of the weak form by the strong; and they have left their marks not only in the heavy and to us hideously protruding jaw and beetling eyebrows of the male gorilla, dividing him from the more human female and young, but giving him that strength of bony structure which is necessary to enable him to rend and destroy; not only in the structure of the scorpion, all sting and tail, so loathsome from the human standpoint that, were it not that it bears its young about upon its back, it would seem so unredeemably repulsive as to be none other than a nightmare; but it may have given the springbuck her long graceful legs to flee from the jaws of her enemies, and have brightened the eye of the gazelle to see in the far distance the destroyer and to aid in its escape. It may even have rendered more intense some of the most complex emotions in the higher animal, because the species in which individuals were most inclined to defend the weak at their own cost may have survived where more purely self-centred varieties fell. It has played its part, and a vast part, in the history of life on earth. But to regard this destructive element in existence as the key-note to life on earth is a strange inversion. When we look from a hill-top on a herd of wild antelope on the plain below us and two old males come into conflict and desperately wound and perhaps kill one the other, the very fact that we are so struck by the incident and absorbed in watching shows it is not the universal, the all-pervading element, of the life before us. The care of the young by the mother, the drawing of sex to sex, the feeding together in good-fellowship of hundreds of creatures—all this rouses no curious remark in us, because it is but of the universal substance of life that things should be so. To attempt to explain and sum up life by considering this element only is like the man who should attempt to represent a great musical symphony by playing its lower bass notes alone,* like a man who should try to reproduce a great composer's masterpiece by striking all the discords in it without any of the harmonies into which they resolve themselves and with reference to which alone they have any meaning. From the mysterious drawing together of amoeba to amoeba, their union and increase, on through all the forms of sentient life, and in the life of the very vegetable world, the moving original power is always this stretching-out, uniting, creative force; shaping itself in the union of male and female, of begetting with their begotten; drawing together creatures of like and unlike kinds, bringing into all the forms of friendship and union and love, it lies at the root of existence; it shapes the petals of flowers, not for death but to call the insects to suck their sweetness and carry fertilisings to one another; it sings in the song of all songbirds calling to their mates; it blossoms into human speech; to kill, man might have been silent; but to communicate with and bind himself to his fellow, child to mother, mother to child, the sexes to reach each other, man, to reach man belonging to his social organism, was obliged to blossom into speech. Everywhere this binding, moving, creative force moves at the very heart of things, growing more and more important and complex as the creatures mount in the scale of life, till it reaches its apotheosis in the artist, in whom the desire to create dominates all else, who, not from himself but by the necessity of some force within himself, is spent and must spend himself to produce that which gives infinite joy without ever being used up, over which there need be no struggle; for not-seeing the statue or not-hearing the story or not-singing the song makes others poorer. Men have so recognised that this creative (and not the destructive) power was the fount and core of life that in all ages they have tended to call the highest intelligence they could conceive of, and therefore their supreme God, 'the great Creator'; and their devils have been destroyers. It is false to say that the mighty jaw and the almighty claw,* and the stomach that is never filled and is always seeking to fill itself, are the fundamental moving power in life—

> ''Tis love that makes the world go round,
> The world go round, the world go round!'*

(She was speaking so animatedly now you could almost have heard what she said in the next room.)

But you may say that, granting love and self-obliteration in the cause of others plays a dominant part in the sentient life among kindred and groups, and that the mysterious instinct to create and continue to reproduce lies as the fundamental hidden power manifested in all we call life—granting all this, yet you must allow that, at least between species and species and distinct groups,* a terrible conflict has always gone on, that this victory of the strongest jaw and the longest claw and the biggest belly has resulted in the survival of the fittest, and that, in the world in which this strife has gone on, we have many beautiful things—singing birds, flowers, the wonderful intelligence of man and beast—this has grown up under the struggle!

Yes, the struggle has gone on and the fittest have survived. The fittest?—to survive; not of necessity the fittest in any other sense in which we humans use the word.

The fittest has survived! Under water, half buried in mud, only the outline of the jaw and two deep-slit eyes show where the alligator lies. Age after age he has lain in the mud and slime. The gazelle has come down to the water to drink and has been drawn in by the mighty jaw; the little monkey, delicate, quick, high-witted, swinging from branch to branch and stretching its hands out to dabble in the water, has come too near, and the brown stump has moved and snapped it up; the human child has come to play upon the bank and disappeared; the young girl has come to draw water and only her broken pitcher has been left on the mud to show where she was drawn under; all have gone to fill the almighty maw and been crushed by the mighty jaw; the creature survives. In the ages which have passed since it came into being, many fair and rare forms have existed and passed out of existence. The little winged creatures with large eyes and brains, reptile in order but fitted for flitting in the air and sunshine, whose images we find impressed on the rocks, have gone; they may have had rare and beautiful colours for anything we know and may have had notes of song, but they are gone; fishes and birds and beasts that have been, have passed forever; even in our own ages lofty forms of life have passed and are passing away; but the alligator survives. Not because it was more fair, more beautiful, more complex, more brave, than the creatures upon whom it lived or whose stay on earth it outstayed, but because its long jaw set with serrated teeth, its dead, solid hide, its absorption simply in seeking food for itself, its torpid, half-buried existence on mud banks and amid slime, fitted it to destroy the complex, pulsating animals and to outlive the beautiful aerial forms which had not its almighty jaw and its mighty stomach. It was fittest to survive. The boa constrictor wakes in the morning, and before night bird and beast have been crushed in its mighty folds; it lies stupefied and torpid with the creatures it has consumed in its expansive inside. It has survived them, not because it was fairer or higher in the scale of being than they, but because so greasily and silently it could creep on them. The cobra strikes dead man and beast, and survives, not because she is braver or higher or even stronger, but because beneath that tooth she carries that little poison bag and strikes so silently and, it may be, in the dark.

If a ship full of poets and philosophers and men of science, bound for some distant place of meeting, were wrecked on the shore of Africa and a cannibal tribe met them, they would be consumed. The savage would rub down and oil his sides with the fat of the poet; the brain of the philosopher would frizzle before the fire; the cannibal's belly would be full of man of science and artist; in a time of famine the cannibal might survive and beget his kind, when a neighbouring tribe died out from hunger for want of timely poet and thinker! Would the fact that he had eaten poet and philosopher prove he was higher than the men who filled his belly and gave strength to his muscles? The fittest to survive—but the fittest for what else? Even when nation sweeps out nation, what does it mean? Is it always the loftier, more desirable form that survives? When the barbarian swept Greece till

Athens was left like an empty and bleaching skull, is it certain that the savage was higher than the race which he supplanted? In nearly two thousand years in that land of blue seas and mountains, he and his descendants have produced nothing that the world prizes or desires. The fittest survived!—the fittest for what?

You say, at least it must be allowed that, along with this struggle among sentient beings and the survival of the strongest jaw and the longest claw and the biggest belly, rare and beautiful things have survived and are among us today?

Singing birds are with us, insects of beauty and colour, beasts of intelligence and heroic forms, and man, who, in spite of all, has instincts and powers latent within him of rare beauty, and strength, reason, imagination, sympathy and joy. Yes, this we have—but, oh, for the songs that will never be heard on earth now!—for the beauty we shall never see!—for the forms of light and glory which will never flit among earth's trees!—for the creatures of intelligence and complexity that will never tread earth's floor!—Oh, the might-have-been, which is forever impossible now! Much has escaped—but, oh, for that which in the long, long, ravening struggle of the ages, has not escaped from the strong jaw and the long claw and the poison bag! Oh, for the forms of life, perhaps higher than any we know or ever shall know, which in their very first incipience were cut away and made impossible forever! In this awful struggle (a struggle waged with no purpose of bringing the great and beautiful to life) what has been saved, we know; what has been lost, we shall never know. The gorilla and chimpanzee are with us; but what if, in some hidden forest, a yet more beneficent intelligent type arose, developing quite away from the predatory to a more social form, till, meeting with the stronger-armed, heavier-jawed gorilla, it was exterminated, and one line of beneficent growth shut off forever? It is difficult to understand how what we call man ever came into being—the manikin thing with such small physical powers of defence and attack, whose young for years, in spite of mother-love and male protection, could so easily fall a prey to any wild beast, and who at his best is physically small and powerless—unless he first, for long periods, developed in some sheltered situations where attacks from predatory saurians or more modern carnivora were rare; but what if somewhere, it might be among inaccessible mountain peaks and valleys in the dim times when man was shaping, a branch existed in whom in time, having to expend no great force in purely predatory or physically self-defensive directions, the germ of other faculties developed higher artistic and musical and reasoning powers, deeper and broader powers of originality, all that for the last many millenniums we have been slowly and with difficulty marching towards when the conditions of life have allowed; if this variety ever were thrown into contact with a more gorilla-like form intent on destruction, it must have been swept away; that one act of destruction would have delayed the march of humanity for ages—nay, prevented it forever perhaps from attaining certain noble and to us desirable shapes.

If it were possible for us to land upon a planet in most things like our own and launched on its course with ours, it is quite possible we should find upon it a being as much higher, and from our standpoint more desirable, than our highest ideals are higher than ourselves; our early stage of sentient growth might have been the same, and this difference, now so vast, might have arisen merely because, once or twice in the course of growth through the aeons, their highest intellectual and moral type might have escaped destruction by its lower. This is certain: that the lower and more brutal self which slumbers within each one of us today, with regard to which the chief difference between man and man is this, that one man's life is passed in submitting to it and another man's in struggling with and crushing it—this more brutal self, which the Christians have called inbred sin and all students of the human heart have under different names recognised—this body of qualities, which seems to some forever to limit human growth, so ineradicable and heavy in its weight it seems—has it not gained its strength and vitality, is it not still within us in such mighty force, because age after age not merely those races but those individuals in whom its existence was weakest have been killed off by the individuals most incarnate of the lower nature and not allowed by the latter to perpetuate themselves freely, either physically or spiritually? Lies are so easy to us because age after age the lying and subtle and insincere have conquered and crushed the individuals in whom sincerity and openness were budding. It is so difficult for us to consider others justly and impartially if they have terribly injured us, because age after age the individuals striking most mercilessly at whatever limited their pleasure, without consideration of justice or sympathy, have killed out and suppressed those in whom generosity and justice were beginning to dawn. Lust, divided from all love and inborn self-forgetfulness, is so dominant within thousands of us (making the world of sexual relations, which in our ideals are the highest, often the lowest, in life), because age after age the most brutally lustful has perpetuated himself, where the less lustful and brutal has failed to rape and force the woman or kill the opposing males. Because, age after age, the individual tendency to expend force in the direction of impersonal intellectual activity has again and again fallen victim to the individual more concentrated on personal aim, we today find the complex intellectual gift of the thinker and artistic creator so rare and so heavily conflicted with by the lower opponents. Because the stronger sex has so perpetually attempted to crush the physically smaller, the individuals who attempted to resist force by force being at once wiped out, sex has acquired almost as a secondary sexual characteristic a subtleness and power of finesse to which it now flies almost as instinctively as a crab to the water when it sees danger approaching, the struggles against which being the sternest that sex has to carry off within itself if it would attain moral emancipation. Because the larger male has so long and so mercilessly suppressed the weaker and exterminated those who refused to submit while the servile survived, we find perhaps that lowest of all human qualities, the material tendency to truckle before success and power, which in some humans seems instinctive and in them at least is ineradicable. For it is not alone through the physical destruction and annihilation of the weaker by the brutally stronger that we have suffered. What has humanity not lost by the suppression and subjection of the weaker sex by the muscularly stronger sex alone? We have a Shakespeare; but what of the possible Shakespeares we might have had,* who passed their life from youth upward brewing currant wine and making pastries for fat country squires to eat, with no glimpse of the freedom of life and action, necessary even to poach on deer in the green forests,* stifled out without one line written, simply because, being of the weaker sex, life gave no room for action and grasp on life? Here and there, where queens have been born as rulers, the vast powers for governance and the keen insight the sex possesses have been shown; but what of the millions of the race in all ages whose vast powers of intellect and insight and creation have been lost to us because they were physically the weaker sex, whose line of life was rigidly apportioned to them at the will of the stronger, which governed the structure of their societies? What statesmen, what rulers and leaders, what creative intelligences have been lost to humanity, because there has been no free trade in the powers and gifts of the muscularly smaller and weaker sex?

Therefore let no man lay the flattering unction to his soul that, by rushing out and destroying what is weaker than himself, or that, by using and bending to his own purposes all that live in the society in which he lives, he is thereby aiding nature in the great and lofty and perfect life on earth. The struggle between sentient creatures and the conquest by the most cunning, the most merciless, the most consuming, the muscularly or osseously* stronger, has had powerful effects on the shapes which life takes on; it may have added to the keenness of the eagle's eye, the length of the springbuck's graceful bound; it may even have added to that intensity of anguished love which makes one baby meerkat try to drag a smaller away to safety when it sees the hawk approaching, because the little people have learnt by a long racial experience what the claw and beak mean, and those who have loved and aided one another most have survived—the fittest to live, not the fittest to kill in that case!—it may have sharpened the wits of all creatures who had to escape, as the poison bag of the serpent teaches great caution in the country where it prevails (we always part the grass with our foot as we walk—though it might be just as well to walk without parting!); it has left many beautiful and curious forms of life, but has also destroyed many; it has nursed into being all the vices which lie deep buried in sentient life; it has age after age killed out among advancing human creatures the individuals who, to reason, love, or any of the impersonal ends of life, sacrificed the arts of destruction and self-defence; it has hanged its Christ and poisoned its Socrates; it has nurtured in every one of us the brute which we shrink from in another when he turns it to us; it has killed out the winged reptile and a thousand noble, complex and brilliant forms of life, and has saved the crocodile and the python. The only strength which it directly preserves is predatory strength; strength of reason, strength of self-government, strength of affection, all the forms of strength most prized by the human creature as it advances, are not preserved of any necessity by it. The struggle between the forms of sentient life and action within a species, and the survival of those most fit to destroy, have no more made existence what it is than the road on a mountainside makes a mountain. It has modified, in some directions powerfully modified, the external forms of life, but no more made it what it is than a hatchet used to chop trees in an orchard makes the trees; the hatchet, wisely used or by accident so used, in lopping off certain branches may make the trees bear larger or more fruit; but used otherwise it may entirely destroy the tree, and, used recklessly and by chance, might cut down the whole garden. The process of pruning itself, however wisely carried on to produce certain ends, is an entirely subsidiary process, whose end, in increasing the size or abundance of the fruit, may generally be equally attained by manuring and feeding the tree; but it fails utterly to account really for the tree, whose essential life and essence lie in its power of growth, in the mysterious power of absorbing and adding to its substance in certain directions and along certain lines and of reproducing itself. All the pruning and cutting off in the world can never account for the fundamental mystery of one bud becoming a flower, for one grain of matter in the soil or particle of gas in the air being transformed into bark, for the kernel and reality of life. Pruning is a process which creates and produces nothing new, but which, wisely used, may tend to accelerate vitality and desirable variation; which, applied haphazardly, may produce mixed desirable and undesirable results; and which, used unwisely, may mean absolute destruction. Therefore let no man lay the flattering unction to his soul that, by destroying all he can destroy, and using and consuming all he can use or consume, he is aiding nature in the only way possible in perfecting the human race on earth. Let him not imagine when he prates of the survival of the fittest that he is enshrouding himself and his desires in impenetrable armour; he is only an ass masquerading in the scientific lion's skin put on hind side before!

You say that, with your guns shooting so many shots a minute, you can destroy any race of men armed only with spears; but how does that prove your superiority, except as the superiority of the crocodile is proved when it eats a human baby, because it has long teeth and baby has none? You say the fact that you can command the labour of so many of your fellow men and gratify your desires proves that you are higher than they; it proves that your belly is large and your power of filling it great; but what, in these matters, are even you compared to the old saurians with their vast claws and paws and rough tongues, who could have licked you off the face of the earth in a moment? The theory that humanity can be perfected on earth only by the stronger jawed, longer clawed, biggest bellied preying on the smaller is a devil's doctrine bred in the head of a fool.

But you may say: If the perfecting of humanity is not to be accomplished by this destruction of one part by the other, how then is it to be accomplished?

(She was walking very slowly now, and looking before her and saying nothing.)

Is it not possible only in two ways? Is there any hope of our in any way raising and hastening the rate of human advance if we cannot do it by the killing out and suppressing of individuals?

Surely there are ways. Has not the human only now, at last, command of two vast means for the modifying of life and the conscious perfecting of humanity? In that strange and lovely power which enables us to see and picture that which we have not in all parts ever fully seen, in the ideals which are clear before the human spirit, have we not the goal to be moved towards? And in our powers of reason the means to find, step by step, the paths that lead to them, have we not now reached a plane of life in which the struggle for existence that is to perfect human life need not in any sense be one between individual lives but between qualities within the individual—a struggle within each man to be fought mainly here (she raised her little doubled-up fist and laid it softly on her breast)—here, where alone each man rules omnipotently and where alone the kingdom of heaven on earth he dreams of can be brought to pass—here, where the ideal must be formed and realised, or nowhere? Has not the time come when the slow perfecting of humanity can find no aid from the destruction of the weak by the stronger, but by the continual bending down of the stronger to the weaker to share with them their ideals and aid them in the struggle with their qualities? Is it not by the passionate persistent determination to realise within ourselves our highest ideal, and then, by that strange power which makes every man's life unconsciously a voice calling to his fellows to follow, to be able to call on those who have not yet seen so far? Is it not so, and not in any other way, that the real blossoming time of man on earth will ever come? And no man liveth to himself and no man dieth to himself.* It is not by destroying and crushing.

She was walking very slowly now, with her eyes wide open, but seeing nothing—then a picture leaped out before her mind that seemed to have no direct connection with the thoughts passing there.

She saw a great plain, and on it a woman standing, large and beautiful; a loose garment draped the lower part, but the great arms and shoulders were bare, and the long hair, turned back from the beautiful face, flowed over the shoulders; but the beautiful eyes were filled with tears and the forehead bent with pain. Beside it there was a great rush of wings and then another figure stood there, heroically large, half poised on one foot, as though just descended, and with wings half open as if ready for flight again.

She stood still.... After a minute she turned to her desk and, leaning across it from the side, drew her book towards her and, opening it at the end, began to write quickly on the inside of the cover, the writing running diagonally across it:

'When the Spirit of the Ages,* whose moments are millenniums, whose minutes are aeons, and whose hours are a human eternity, passed amongst the worlds of space seeing how it fared there, he chanced on a planet. A wide plain stretched there, no trace of plant or shrub was on it anywhere, and burning sands stretched everywhere; but far away in the distance rose mountains; on their sides one could see that streams flowed and that the earth was green and trees waved. Alone in the centre of the plain stood a woman's figure, bare and beautiful from the waist upwards, but clothed below in a coarse garment. Her eyes were fixed on the distant mountains; again and again as she looked she wrung her hands and tears streamed from the beautiful eyes. And the Spirit paused in his flight and alit* on the earth beside her, and he cried, "Beautiful one, why do you stand here weeping alone in this desolate spot, where no fair thing is, and the snake has left its track in the sand at your feet and the only footprint is the mark of the wild beast's claw? On the mountains there is verdure; surely birds are singing among the trees and the grass is heavy with flowers; why linger here in this desolate spot?"* But she wrung her hands and cried, "I cannot move; always and always I look out for one to come and deliver me and take me with him to the mountains, but he never comes." And he said, "Beautiful one, your forehead is high, your bosom is full, your arms are strong, your hands well knit; why cannot you move forward?" And she wept and raised the robe that was about her, and the Spirit saw that, while from the waist upwards she was fair and powerful, from the waist downward she was ill nourished and loathsome. About her feet were iron fetters, upon the limbs were marks of unhealed stripes, old gangrenous wounds festered there, and the flesh was shrunken from the bones and the feet deep sunken in the sand. And she cried, "My head is clear, my heart is sound, my arms are strong, but my feet, my feet, they bind me here! I wound and strike them, but they will not move; I bind them with chains in my anger. It is they, it is they, who keep me here!" And again she wept. Then the Spirit dropped his wing and drew nearer to her and whispered, "Despairing one, no deliverer will ever come. You, you yourself must save yourself. From those weak limbs strike off the fetters; with your strong hands bend down and heal the wounds your hands have made; remove the sand about the heavily sunken feet. When they are healed and free and strong, they, they and not another, will bear you to the mountains where you would be." And he asked her, "What is your name?" And she answered, "My name is Humanity." And he said, "When the years have flown I shall return again and see how it fares with you." And he smote his wings together and rose upwards: and Humanity was alone upon the plain.'

She wrote quickly across the inside of the cover; when that was full she went on to the flyleaf opposite; then she paused a moment; at the head of what she had written she put as a title, 'The Spirit of the Ages.' Then she drew her pen through the words as if not satisfied. Then she threw her pen down on the table. She looked round. All the room seemed strange; the old brown walls, the little bookshelves, the lamp throwing down its light on the worn leather cover of the desk, the old exercise book she had been writing in—they looked like things look when you come back from a long visit, when all about the house is strangely familiar and yet new.

She closed the exercise book and put it in the drawer. Perhaps some day the little allegory would enlarge itself and she would write it in fit words to make others see the picture. Probably she would never touch it again because it takes time to write things for other people. But the little picture she would never forget, because the pictures one sees are actual and one never forgets them. She walked to her armchair and sat down. She knew suddenly that she was very tired; she had been walking nearly three hours; but it was a delicious kind of tiredness, like one feels when one comes home from a long walk in the open air: as if something was resting by being used. She leaned back her head into the little dent. The rain was falling now in torrents. She leaned back listening to it. It was a delicious sound. It made her feel as though great strong arms were folding themselves about her, and a great strong hand were stroking her down softly. She lay still; but after some time she drew herself up and curled her legs under her, and turning sideways half buried her face in the dent in the chair's back. She tucked one hand under her cheek and after a while closed her eyes. Her thoughts ran around in a dreamy way now. How nice it would be to be a man. She fancied she was one till she felt her very body grow strong and hard and shaped like a man's.* She felt the great freedom opened to her, no place shut off from her, the long chain broken, all work possible for her, no law to say this and this is for woman, you are woman; she drew a long breath and smiled an expansive smile. Oh, how beautiful to be a man and be able to take care of and defend all the creatures weaker and smaller than you are. Then she dreamed away and half asleep made one of those little stories, 'self-to-self' stories, that she made as she was going to sleep, not for other people, too sweet and close, just for herself. She was a man, she thought, and she lived in a cottage about which there was bush and high forest, as at the old farm. It was night, and she thought she was lying there and outside the trees were rustling as the wind moved them. It seemed she was lying on the earth, on mats in the hut, and beside her lay the woman she loved, fast asleep. She felt the little head on her shoulder, the soft hair against her cheek, and the little body within her arm; then she heard the wind blowing and the tree branches touching the roof as the wind grew strong. The little one beside her moved uneasily, and as it lay so close she felt the little body throb and knew it was the life within it that he had wakened. (She was him now, not herself any more.) And such a great tenderness came over him, and he drew her close and bound his limbs about her so that she was quite wrapped about, but the little wife upon his arms slept on, not knowing how she was loved. And then it was another day, and the little child was born so small and soft, and he held it in his arms and put his lips to its soft, tiny lips (she felt the lips touch hers), and then he took it in both his hands and put it close into the little mother's arms against her breast and bent down over them—and then it all shimmered away and she, Rebekah, was asleep.

She had slept peacefully in the chair for perhaps half an hour; the oil in the great transparent glass bowl of the lamp was burnt down three quarters of the way when suddenly she woke with a start and leaped to her feet. It seemed to her she had heard the front door close with a great bang. Perhaps it was her husband and Bertie come home; she stood to listen, but there was no sound of their voices. She was taking up the lamp to go and see, when she remembered it was the stable boy's evening out, and that when he came back late he often came in at the front door instead of going round the back way to the yard where the servants had their rooms if he saw lights in the house. Still, she took up the lamp; in the children's room they were all sleeping quietly, and when she went through her bedroom and the dining room into the passage she found no sign of anyone having been there, and went back to the study.

Her sleep had refreshed her, but left her stupid and dull. The rain had left off and there was only the sound of a few large drops falling softly from the trees over the house as the wind shook them. She yawned and stretched herself and sat down in the armchair again. She drew her work basket to the side and put the lamp on the edge of the desk and went on darning the stockings that were left. She darned on mechanically, thinking of nothing much, but she remembered she must count the wash-clothes the next morning and ask the washerwoman about the three pairs of socks that were missing. And then she wondered whether she should mix on* the sour dough now or leave it till the morning, and she decided to leave it. She watched the needle move in and out among the blue threads in the stocking, almost without seeing them, and was growing very sleepy again, when, just as she was darning the last pair, she heard a click at the gate and a step on the garden path that she knew was her husband's. She lit the fat-candle quickly and went to the hall to meet him. He was hanging up his cap but had still his greatcoat on.

'Where is Bertie?' she asked.

'That is what I wanted to ask you. Hasn't she come home?'

'No, I've not seen her.'

'I suppose she has. I went to have a round with some of the young ones in the back room; and a quarter of an hour ago, when I wanted to leave, I went to look for her and couldn't find her. The curious thing is she left her walking shoes and cloak and all behind her. But no doubt she's here all right.'

Rebekah turned down the side passage from which Bertie's room opened, and her husband, still in his greatcoat, followed her.

She opened the door and looked in. 'She's here,' she said. She walked in, shading the light with her hand. On the large, old-fashioned four-poster bed which stretched right across the end of the room, so that there was just space for a person to stand at the foot, Bertie lay asleep. She was still in her ball dress, lying on her back in the centre of the bed, with no pillow under her head and with one arm thrown across her forehead. The train of the white skirt hung wet and draggled with mud against the white quilt. Rebekah stepped to the bedside, shading the light with her hand that it might not fall on Bertie's eyes. Frank stood beside her.

'What on earth made her run off like that? She was dancing hard when I left the ballroom.'

Rebekah gave him the candle to hold and stooped down to put a pillow softly under her head.

'What a magnificent creature she is,' he said. Her right arm was stretched at her side, and the great white rose, partly faded, was fastened at her breast. 'There's not another woman like her in the Peninsula, not in South Africa! And so unconscious! That's what men like. Young Smith came twice to talk about her to me this week. Did I think she'd ever change her mind and have him!'

He expanded his chest, his white shirt-front showing between the parted edges of his overcoat. Rebekah was smoothing the pillow.

'Women think,' he said importantly, 'that men don't see through them when they ogle and flirt and try to captivate every fellow they meet; but we do! That style of woman's all very well to dance and flirt with, but when he really wants a wife and means to settle down he looks for something different!'

Rebekah had gone round to the foot of the bed and was kneeling down, taking off the little drenched white satin slippers. 'What can have made her run home in these things?'

'Now I knew what I was about when I looked out a certain little woman!' he said, still holding the candle and smiling down. 'There were half a dozen damsels in the Peninsula thought they were quite sure of me, but I knew where on a certain farm in the Karroo a little woman was to be found who wouldn't always be running away to balls and croquet parties to flirt with other men and forgetting all about her husband and house—and a nice pretty little woman too.'

Rebekah had risen to put down the damp shoes and stockings she had drawn from Bertie's feet; he chucked her softly under the chin with his two forefingers as she passed him; 'Wouldn't take "No" for an answer either! Smart fellow, eh? Knows what he wants when he sees it!'

Rebekah knelt down to cut off with the scissors from her chatelaine* the wet draggled end of Bertie's train; if that were taken off she would be dry enough to sleep on till morning without harm, and the dress would never be any good again.

Frank had had three glasses of champagne and was in a good humour, exceedingly pleased with himself. He was an abstemious man; he took care never to allow himself more than was good for himself in the matter of drink or any other personal indulgence. Only twice in all their married life had Rebekah really seen him the worse for drink: once when he returned home at four in the morning and said he had been kept sitting up at his office to make up his books, and once on another occasion. He could drink several glasses without feeling them, but champagne always had an expansive effect on his nature, making him more sunny and talkative.

'I knew very well whom I was going to have,' he said, looking down appreciatingly at the bed where Bertie was lying and Rebekah was kneeling, cutting off the train; 'ever since that day on Table Mountain when the rain came on and a certain little woman covered the lunch basket with her own waterproof and saved us from going home hungry, while all the other girls came running up to the rocks for us to help them up into shelter, timorous little darlings. I held a sunshade open over the head of one and gave her my hand, but all the while I was looking at a certain little woman down below tucking the covers in, with all the rain streaming off her. Oh, men aren't such fools as they seem.' He laughed. 'I'd always had a fancy for her since she was five and used to fight like a tiger-cat if I wanted to kiss her—"I don't love you! You're ugly! Go away! Don't come near me! You horrid, ugly, cruel boy!"' He imitated the shrill, agonised voice of a child, and laughed. 'But that day decided me.' He was holding the candle a little crooked.

Rebekah had heard that story often before; it was one of those he often told in expansive moods. She had even heard him tell it to the men in the billiard room when they were praising her milk punch.

'She looks pale,' said Rebekah, rising. 'I hope she wasn't ill.'

'Ill—you should have seen her dancing! A freak, I suppose, to come home like this in the wet. You can't account for a woman, my dear. I've found that out long ago. Haven't I been married seven years!' He would have touched her under the chin again but she had turned to the wardrobe to get a shawl to put across Bertie's feet. 'Is supper ready? They had good wine there, but really nothing fit to eat.'

'Yes, I got it ready before you left. You'll find the matches and lamp on the sideboard as you go in.'

He put the candle down on the dressing table and went out, whistling one of the tunes they had danced to.

When he was gone Rebekah bent down to cover Bertie's feet. She stroked them softly with her hand. They were pink and dimpled as a baby's, such tiny feet for such a big woman. Then she covered them up carefully with the shawl, turning up the damp edge of the dress that it might not touch them. She put a candle and matches on a chair at the bedside, that Bertie might find them when she woke, and then she took up the light and went to the dining room.

Her husband had taken off his greatcoat, and sat at the head of the table, in his white shirt-front and beamingly contented face above it.

'Won't you sit down and take some too? This bobotie* is excellent. No, you won't? You've been off your feed the last day or two. Oh!'—he looked up and laughed—'I'd quite forgotten what you told me this morning! I'm to be the patriarch Jacob, eh? "Now Jacob had twelve sons and twelve daughters"—or was it Job?'* He laughed again. 'Take a little soda water? That's more in your line at such times, I think. Who'd be a woman! You're always a bit off colour the first month or two.'

Rebekah sat down at the side of the table before the glass of soda he had poured out for her.

'This cold bobotie is really excellent.' He helped himself again. 'Had some at Brownlee's* the other night, such stuff! This just wants the very *smallest* touch of cayenne, though! Is there any on the sideboard?' She rose to fetch it him. 'Just bring me the brandy too while you are up—no—on second thoughts I won't; I've had enough. I'll have milk with my soda. Did the boy clean my fishing boots?'

'Yes, but he hadn't time to polish the billiard-room floor. He'll do that tomorrow before you come back.' She sat down again at the side of the table and leaned her elbows on it. 'I don't know what's the matter with the girl. She leaves all her work for him and me. And she was so good when she first came. I liked her better than I ever liked any servant before. She is so strange now; she knocks against me in the passage though there's plenty of room to pass. She is so rude to me, as if she hated me. I can't understand it. If I—'

He interrupted her quickly; 'I'll change my mind and have a little brandy if you'll bring it me; just a tiny drop. Pour it out for me, one dessertspoonful—so! Pure soda isn't good to go to sleep on, except for a little woman in a certain blissful condition.' He laughed more boisterously than there seemed need. 'Isn't that the baby crying?' he said.

She listened; 'I can't hear it!' But she rose and took the candle and went to see if it were all right.

He finished his supper in silence; then he rose and paced the room twice; then he stopped at the window that looked out into the back yard, and drew the blind a little aside, and looked out; but there was nothing to be seen except the dark. Then he turned down the lamp and went to his dressing room.

Now, what really happened to Baby-Bertie was this.

When she and Frank got to the house where the party was to be held they found it brilliantly lighted up, the garden and veranda full of Japanese lanterns,* and light streaming from doors and windows, through which came the sound of music, for dancing had already begun.

A little sitting room on the right of the entrance had been turned into a dressing room, with a large mirror and dressing table, and Bertie went in to take off her wrappers. Behind the dressing room was a small bedroom, where the maid put away slippers and cloaks of the guests as she took them. Bertie could hardly wait to take hers off when she heard the music, and as there was someone using the glass she did not even look at herself before she hurried across the hall to the dancing room. Most of the dancers were youths and girls under twenty-one, with a few of older growth. Near the window to the right as she went in stood the daughter of the house whose birthday it was, with two other young girls and a young man. As Bertie walked up to them the two young girls turned away, but the daughter of the house accepted her congratulations, and the young man spoke to Bertie. Then two men, who had seen her coming in, came towards her from opposite sides of the room; the one who reached her first asked her to dance with him, and soon she forgot everything but the light and the music and the delicious whirl as she danced. As soon as one dance was over someone asked her for the next. Sometimes one of her partners suggested that they should go and sit on one of the closed-in verandas and talk and rest, but she always said she would rather dance. She had one dance with Frank, about eleven o'clock. He liked to dance with her, partly because he liked her and partly because he knew they looked well dancing together and men envied him his pretty sister-in-law.

After that, he had gone to the back veranda to have a smoke and to chat and romp with the younger girls from twelve to sixteen, who had gone there to play round games because there was no room for them in the dancing room.

And Bertie danced on.

Once in a dance, as Bertie passed a girl she knew, she smiled and nodded to her; but the girl seemed to be looking the other way and did not notice her. The rain poured, and left off, and poured again; but she heard nothing of it as she danced.

By and by, as the band was playing a very fast waltz and she was whirling round and round with it, someone trod on her dress. The white gauze which covered the silk skirt tore from the waist to the bottom* and the long gossamer flounce made a streamer behind her. She caught it with one hand and, holding it together, laughed and nodded to her partner, and ran away to the dressing room.

There was no one there now. She stood before the mirror to examine the torn skirt; then she began taking pins from the plate on the dressing table to pin it with. She began at the waist and pinned downwards.

The throb of the dance was still in her feet.

The rain had left off, only the sound of the great drops falling from the eaves and the branches of the trees outside interfered with the sound of the music which came loud through the two closed doors:

'Oh the torture and the anguish
That cannot follow thee,'*

the band was playing. She hurried to get back. She had to bend down very low at one side to pin on the flounce, so that her head was halfway to the floor; then, amid the music she heard the sound of voices talking in the little bedroom at the back where the cloaks were stored. She paid no attention to them but hurried on, her face pink with bending so low in a sideward position. Suddenly a name struck her—it was Rebekah's. Two old ladies who had brought three young daughters had gone to the little back room to be out of the way of the noise and dancing and were talking together. The noise of the drops falling from the eaves and the music and dancing prevented her hearing all that was said, but she heard part. 'It seems strange she should have been asked,' one said. 'Yes, but the invitation three weeks ago'—and then the music broke in with a particularly loud burst—'to bring her here among our innocent young girls!'

Bertie kept on pinning; she heard 'she' and 'she says' and 'to her'. Then she heard Rebekah's name again; and then—'but perhaps her sister did not know.'

Bertie was motionless with a pin in one hand, her figure still half bent down over her dress, but her head raised to listen.

She heard Mrs Drummond's name, and then—'it was her schoolmaster.'

Quickly and noiselessly she raised herself; she dropped the pin softly onto the floor; she looked round the room with her deathly white face.

If she went out by the door that led into the hall, someone would be nearly sure to meet her. Again she looked round the room. There was a large French window at the side of the room which opened in the gable into the flower garden and shrubbery. It was low, and was hooked open two inches to let in the air. Softly she unhooked it and turned it back. It made no sound; she stepped out through it. Below was a bed of rose bushes; as she stepped into the bed of rich, soft mould her feet sank almost ankle deep into it. She turned and closed the window softly, and with difficulty drew her feet out of the wet earth. She stepped into the gravel path. All the Chinese lanterns had long gone out with the rain, and the shrubbery was quite dark; she walked through the bushes, keeping away from the house and near the wall till she came to the gate. She opened it noiselessly and shut it again. She was now in the great avenue. She caught her skirt and threw it over her left arm, and began to walk quickly. The drops from the trees as the wind shook the branches fell on her naked arms and shoulders and ran down her back. She began to run; the skirt slipped from her arm and the train, bellying out behind her, whipped through the puddles of mud and water, drawing up the sticks and dead leaves. Faster and faster she ran. She turned into the next avenue. At last she was at Rebekah's gate.* She opened it softly and crept up the little gravelled path to the steps. She could see there was still a light in Rebekah's study; it was shining through the window on the plumbago hedge at the end of the house. She stole up the steps and across the veranda and turned the handle of the front door without a sound; but, as she turned to shut it from the inside, it slipped from her wet fingers and closed with a loud noise. She stood still, listening to hear if Rebekah was coming, but there was no sound, and she turned down the side passage and went into her own room and closed the door behind her.

She knew there was a candle and matches on the dressing table, but she did not light it. The large four-poster bed stood across the end of the little room with the window opening over it at the side; at the foot of the bed there was just room for a person to get in between the bed and the wall. She crept in and knelt up, pressing her face against the wallpaper. The old, old, terrible feeling had come back, the feeling she had lost for so many years; it was here again. Something following her, following her, following her! She pressed her face closer against the wall and folded her arms over her head. She felt as if everything in her were pressing down, down, down. It was so nice to press in there between the wall and the bed, it seemed to hold one up. If only one did not feel so cold. The cold seemed to break out from her heart over her whole body. She did not think of anything particular; she only felt so cold.

After a time she began feeling faint kneeling up there; she crept into the bed. She threw herself down on her back in the middle of the bed. After a time the faintness seemed to get better and she fell into a heavy sleep. It was so that Rebekah and Frank found her when they came into the room.

After Rebekah had covered her and left her, she slept on for a long while, a heavy, motionless sleep. Then, suddenly, she began to move restlessly and to moan. She was having a dream. She thought she was in a great round theatre like a circus; it was filled from floor to ceiling with seats which rose tier above tier over each other, and all were crowded with people. She was sitting halfway down on one side. In the circle in the centre of the theatre there was white sand scattered, and women in white dresses were dancing there, and all the crowd were looking down at them, and she looked down too. Then suddenly she noticed that the people were not looking at the women any more, they were all looking round the theatre as though they were seeking for someone; and she looked about too, to see what it was they were looking for. Then she noticed a man on the other side of the theatre just opposite her, with a great red fat face, who rose from his seat. She felt a kind of horror when she looked at him. He rose from his seat, and pointed with his great red fat finger, and cried, 'That is she!' And all the people from the floor to the ceiling rose to their feet; and still the man pointed with his forefinger and cried, 'That is she!' Then she looked round also to see who it was they were looking at—and then, suddenly, she knew it was herself they were looking at! Tier above tier, all round that vast place, the faces looked at her, and the man pointed with his red forefinger, and cried, 'That is she!' A cold sweat broke out on her (in truth it broke out on her as she lay on the bed); she tried to slip down between her seat and the one before it and hide, but she could not move. She seized the back of the seat before her with both hands and tried to force herself down, but she could not stir; she was as if fastened to the seat. And from floor to ceiling the faces looked down at her; she saw her father and her mother there and the old farm servants: old Ayah and a little yellow shawl over her shoulders, and Griet looking from under her arm; there were all the men she had danced with: high up near the roof she saw John-Ferdinand looking down at her and Veronica standing just behind him, and low down she saw Mrs Drummond with a lace handkerchief at her lips, looking at her. Everyone she had ever known was there. Then suddenly it seemed as if the white dress of one of the dancers in the circle below got torn; a long white trail hung down from it, and as the dancer swept round and round it grew longer and longer. It skirled as she whirled, it bellied out and out at the back and grew fuller and fuller; it frilled into soft billowy waves and passed over the heads of the dancers, filling all the circle below with a sea of misty white; it rose higher and higher, unrolling and unrolling; it came to the place where she sat; it passed her and rose to the ceiling and they were all suffocating. With a wild cry Bertie sprang up, struggling; before she knew where she was, she was standing on the floor with the cold perspiration streaming down her, and the four-poster iron bedstead still rattling. At first she tried to remember how she came to be standing there in her clothes on the floor in the dark, and could not: then slowly she remembered everything.

Without lighting the candle she undressed, dropping her clothes on the floor where she stood. She felt for her nightdress and crept into bed; she drew the cover up high over her head. Yes, the old, old feeling she used to have at the farm had come back to her; something following her, following her, following her, and everything in her sinking down, down, down! She drew one of the pillows from under her head and laid it against her, and folded both her arms round it and pressed it to her as if it had been a person. It comforted her a little to hold it so close; it seemed to prevent that sinking feeling. She tucked the cover in tighter over her head. If she could only keep everything out.

When she woke the next morning it was already late; she could see by the lines of light through the venetian blind at her bedside that the sun was shining, though the room was still darkened with the drawn blind. Rebekah had evidently been in early, for a tray with biscuits and coffee, which was now cold, could dimly be seen on the chair at the bedside. Bertie lay still. It pained her to see the light coming in under the bars of the blind. If it could only always be night and one would never need to see anyone.

Then she heard the sound of steps coming up the gravelled path; she half sat up and raised slightly the corner of the blind; but it was only the butcher's boy coming for orders, whistling. She let it drop again. She could not bear people to come up the path.

After a time she got up and sat down in her nightgown on the floor at the side of the bed and began in the semi-darkness to put on the stockings Rebekah had put ready for her beside her boots. Slowly she drew one on; then, before she had gartered it, she drew up her knees and folded her arms about them and leaned her forehead on her arms. She sat so motionless she might have gone to sleep again.

Then suddenly she sat up and began to pull on the other stocking.

'I will go to Aunt Mary-Anna,' she said. 'I will go to my Aunt Mary-Anna!' She began putting on her boots and lacing them up in the darkness. Her lips were puffed and her face a little swollen. There was a dull, obstinate resolution in it; the only form of strength her face ever wore.

This Aunt Mary-Anna was a sister of her mother's and of Frank and John-Ferdinand's father. Many years before she had come out to visit her sister, and at the old farm had met a young man from the next town whom she had married. Later they had moved to a small town further up-country, where her husband was a general agent, and where two daughters had been born to her, who were several years younger than Bertie. They had been sent to England now for some years to finish their education, and she had written many times to ask Bertie, who was her godchild, to come up and stay with her while they were away. But Bertie had never wished to leave the old farm till she had left so suddenly with Rebekah. Now it came to her suddenly that she might go to her aunt's; it was so far away from everywhere. She pictured to herself the long miles of rolling karroo, the rocks and koppies and sand and whole mountain range that lay between it and anywhere. She would go first by train and then by postcart—on, and on, and on; she would have to go for days to get there.

'I must go! I will go!' she muttered, as she laced her boots in the half dark, with her lips heavy set.

When she told Rebekah of her plan, Rebekah was not surprised. The little mother was always writing to ask when she was coming home, and it would seem a step on her way if she went to her aunt's, which was somewhat nearer the old farm than Cape Town. So Rebekah helped her to pack her things. She could not leave the next day as she wished, because she had to catch the postcart, which only travelled once a week; but three days after she left.

As she was so busy packing, Rebekah did not wonder she went to say goodbye to no one. There would not be room in the postcart for all her things; so Rebekah hung her evening dress and smart gowns in the wardrobe in Bertie's room, where she would find them when she came next year to visit her again. But Bertie knew she never would.

CHAPTER VIII

YOU CANNOT CAPTURE THE IDEAL BY A COUP D'ÉTAT

It was four months now since Bertie had left. Spring had come; the oak trees had broken into their delicate spring green; the arms of the dark fir trees were sending out pale shoots at the tips, and near the old summer house in the pine woods, where Rebekah loved to walk with the children, the ground between the pines was carpeted with bluebells, and under the pines themselves the smell of the needles was sweet.

In two months her child would be born, and she was busy making clothes for the other children to wear in the months when she could not do much more than look after the baby. She never went out anywhere except to the pine woods; and if people said anything she never heard them. Bertie wrote to say she was happy at her aunt's, and her mother had written to say she might stay there till her cousins returned from their school in England.

And Rebekah was happy. It was one of those peaceful, halcyon times that come in life, when the absence of new daily recurring matter of pain makes possible that upspringing of joy which only that which morning by morning tramples it down can permanently keep out of life.

She was happy when she kneaded her bread or mixed the salads in the pantry, and when she sat at work at the children's clothes; it gave her exquisite pleasure to see the great streaks of yellow afternoon sunshine lie on the carpet, and at night it was a pleasure to lie awake and hear the branches of the trees move against the roof.

Her husband was more at home than he had been since they were first married; he stayed at home, not only when it was necessary to eat and sleep, or when men came to play billiards, but often without need he came home an hour earlier than usual from office and when she came back from the pine woods with the children she found him in the rocking chair on the veranda with a magazine or paper in his hands, smoking and smiling contentedly. And on Sunday he would stay at home the whole morning, looking at the roses in the front garden or the fernery on the back stoep, or going round to the stables to look at his horses, or would sit in the shade on the back veranda, reading.

Perhaps life would always be so peaceful and beautiful now; perhaps all the struggle and anguish were passed; all things have to come to an end, and why not sorrow too? If one walked on silently, would not everything come right at last? She sometimes even wondered if she had not fancied that life was so hard as it had been in the past, and whether she could not have made things clearer. She was like a donkey who, having drawn a load to the top of a hill, when it goes down the other side for a little way thinks it must have been all a dream that there ever was a hillside. She was quite contented; she wanted nothing more. Even the coloured servant girl was not quite so rude now, though she was dull and silent and would do little work. Rebekah had hired her for a year from her mother, a respectable woman on a mission station, and it was as though she feared being sent home to her and forbore to press things too far. And the black boy* whom they had had since they were first married, and whose only regular work was to attend to the stables and yard and to his master's boots and fishing tackle and guns, showed a particular kindness and would, when in the kitchen, help her lift a heavy pot, clean the kitchen window and weed her garden without being asked. Sometimes she fancied she caught him looking at her almost with a pitying, questioning look, which she fancied must be because he realised that physical work was unusually hard for her.

In the branches of the oak tree that grew in the yard and overhung the house, two small birds had made their nest. She had watched them carry on the first sticks and straws for the nest; now the little hen was beginning to sit for a great part of the day and her mate carried scraps of food he found about the yard and garden to her. In less than a month the little ones would be out. When she woke in the early morning as she lay in her bed and the sun had just risen, she could see clearly printed against the window blind the shadow of their two little figures as they walked up and down on the top crossbar of the veranda or sat close together on it. In after years she knew how closely she had watched those little birds, because the memory of that time never came back to her without those two little shadows on the window blind.

She had no time to write in her diaries because when her work was done she had to lie down and rest; but, lying on her back under the pine trees or at night when she could not sleep, she read a great deal.

She had got a book about lichens and moss, and she had collected some from the roots of the fir trees and the thatch of the roof and from under the rose trees in the garden, and found them all beautifully different; she had examined them under her microscope, which she had not touched for years. All the little things of life were of much interest to her again, almost as they had been when she was a little child.

One Saturday evening Frank came home earlier than usual; before ten o'clock he said he would go to bed as he was starting at sunrise for a fishing expedition to a place beyond Simon's Town.* Rebekah had packed his lunch basket, it stood ready in the hall beside his rods and tackle, so she said goodnight and went to her own room. She slept in the children's room now on a little bed between the eldest boy's and the baby's, because, now the new child was coming, she slept badly and moved from side to side when she was asleep and Frank said it disturbed him to have her in the same room. So she slept in the bed of her second little boy who now slept in the bed in the corner of his father's room.

After she had lain in bed for some time reading, she put out the light and tried to go to sleep; her husband had already put out his; she could see there was no light from the crack under the door between the two rooms. At first she felt very sleepy, but the sense of weight and physical discomfort would not let her sleep; she moved from side to side. At last she piled the pillows up under her head and lay in a half-sitting position with her arms crossed over her head. She was more comfortable so. Her thoughts did not run in that clear ordered fashion in which they follow one another when one lies awake, simply because the brain is too busily secreting to rest, but in the disconnected way in which pictures and sounds succeed each other automatically when one is really very sleepy. She thought of little household things; she saw pictures of them, saw the kitchen shelf with the row of tins on it and the dust she must dust off tomorrow, saw the large bag of wash clothes she must count; then she saw the little cups of moss she had been looking at under her microscope that day, so delicate and so minute the naked eye could not see them; then she saw a place in the kloof on the old farm deep up in the bush where some trees were growing which were covered with long hoary moss hanging down like rough hair; there were two kinds; she wondered if they were male and female of the same species, or distinct species growing side by side, because the conditions suited them both; she wondered why she had never examined them and thought she would if she ever went out to the old farm again. Then she saw the place nearby, in the bed of the mountain stream, where the great rocks were piled up and the Kaffir-bean trees hung over, and where Frank had lifted her down once; she seemed to feel his strong firmly fleshed hands holding her as he lifted her down and his eyes with a beautiful intense light fixed on hers. It made her heart, the heart of the little tired pregnant woman lying there, beat when she remembered it, as the heart of the young girl had beaten. Then her thoughts went to the man in the next room lying there on his side, with his soft light hair pressed to the pillow and his strong shoulder showing above the cover. A great tenderness swept over her as when one thinks of one's little child, as if all the heart were being drawn out of her to him. The beautiful boy, the father of all her children! It rose and surged through her, the old wave that so often, through years since their marriage when he was away from home, had made her rise suddenly at night and fetch his overcoat and lie sleeping with it in her arms, with her face pressed to the collar where his neck had been, which came to her often in the night while she lay awake beside him and which, as she listened to his even breathing, made it seem to her the most precious thing in life—a wave that swelled and swelled till it filled her with a confident hope, and she knew when he woke there would be a new heaven and a new earth for them both. Tonight she only felt a great wish to be near him, to slip her arm under his and wind it softly round his waist—just to feel him and hear him breathe. She lay still for a while, then she got up softly; she could go in softly without making any noise and creep into bed and lie down behind him and put her arms around him without waking him, and, when she felt she was getting sleepy, she would creep back to her own bed. She had done it more than once already without waking him. She opened the door of the next room and closed it softly and slipped across the room with her bare feet; she had no slippers on, for fear of making a noise. The room was quite dark. It was a large room, looking out into the back yard, and in the far corner stood the large four-poster bedstead; near the window, close to the door by which she had entered, stood the little bed in which her second boy was sleeping.

She knew the room so well she felt her way without any difficulty to the side of the bed in the far corner; she put out her hand softly and touched the quilt at the foot; she felt upwards; it seemed to be thrown back; she felt higher; the bed seemed to be thrown open and no one there. She took a match from the box on the stand at the bedside and struck it; the bed was open; there was a dent in the pillow where the head had been, and when she put her hand down on the sheet it was warm. The match had burned out, and she dropped the end on the floor. No doubt he was gone to the stables; he told her that, on several nights lately, he had to get up because he heard the new stallion fighting with the other horses in the stable; and the coloured boy, though his room opened out of the stable, slept so soundly that he heard nothing. Rebekah hesitated; she thought she would climb up on the bed and wait till he came, but he was always angry when he had to get up at night, and it might displease him more if he had to talk to anyone. She turned to go back to her room. As she passed the bed of her little son her feet caught in his down quilt which had fallen on the floor; then she stooped to pick it up and pushed it in round his shoulders; then, as she was tucking it round his feet, she paused a moment and lifted the corner of the blind to see if she could see her husband. It was a dazzling moonlight night; all the veranda that ran along the back of the house and the half of the yard covered by the oak tree was in deep shadow, but over the rest of the yard the moonlight fell in a sheet of white light from the moon almost overhead. The stones in the gravel of the yard glittered; on the opposite side of the yard the roughcast whitewashed walls of the servants' rooms and the side of the stables seemed to radiate light; even the green window shutter and the door of the servant girl's room seemed almost black in the intense light. The outline of the oak leaves at the tips of the branches was printed in shadow on the gravel almost as sharply and exactly as at midday. Not a breath was stirring. Everything seemed to glint. Then she saw in the door of the kitchen, which formed a wing at the end of the veranda, her husband standing. In the shadow of the veranda she could see him in his grey dressing gown near the stand of ferns. Then, instead of walking across the left of the yard towards the little side passage into which the stables opened, he came straight along the veranda. Just as he came opposite the window at which she was standing he stooped and took off his slippers; he carried them hanging from the first two fingers of his right hand; he moved in past the window of the children's bedroom, and then at the end of the veranda turned up, keeping near the wall in the shadow of the oak tree; then he turned again and came out into the full moonlight, just beyond the oak tree's shadow, and stopped opposite her, before the little green-shuttered window of the servant girl's room. He glanced back at the house quickly; then softly, with the tips of the two forefingers of his left hand, struck two short blows on the wood of the shutter which covered the glass of the closed window; light as the taps were, Rebekah heard them; she saw his white naked feet on the gravel and the moonlight on his fair hair. Then the door opened; and she saw him bend his broad shoulders and bow his head a little as he stepped down through the low door. Then it closed. She looked at the gravel glinting in the moonlight and the whitewashed wall that seemed almost to throw out light at her. Whether she stood there for fifteen minutes or for twenty or for half an hour, she could not tell; a cold blast was blowing on her and froze her; then the door opened and her husband came out. The moonlight fell full on his face. He glanced at the house, then walked quickly straight across the yard to the kitchen door. Rebekah loosened her fingers from the blind, went slowly into the next room, the door closing itself behind her, and dropped on the little bed.

At half past four all was quiet in the house; the dawn had not yet begun to make the darkness paler along the horizon.

Rebekah sat in her nightdress in her study with her head resting on the edge of her desk. In the transparent glass bowl of her lamp the oil was almost exhausted, as though it had burned all night. On the floor beside her the waste-paper basket held pages of paper, wholly or partially covered with writing and then torn up. At her elbow lay an envelope addressed to her husband. She sat as if asleep, but the slight irregularity of her breathing told it was not so.

When the first grey dawn was beginning to make a clearer line along the Flats* and even there among the trees to make the darkness less intense, she rose and took up the letter and the lamp and went into the children's room. Her teeth were chattering slightly with the chill of the morning. She opened the door in the left-hand corner of the room which led into her husband's dressing room. It was in a way the pleasantest room in the house; a large double bow window looked out into the front garden; before it stood a dressing table with a large mirror and her husband's shaving materials and silver-backed brushes arranged upon it; before the dressing table on a chair hung the clothes she had put out the night before for the day's excursion. At the back of the room was a door that opened into their bedroom, his and hers, where he lay sleeping. She put the lamp down on the table and stood for a moment with the letter in her hand. At first she laid it down among the shaving things upon the table; then she took it up and fastened it with a breast pin from the cushion onto the breast of the coat that hung over the chair. Then she took up the lamp and went back to the children's room. She was shivering violently now. She put on her little blue dressing gown and her red slippers and lay down on the stretcher between the two children's beds. The lamp, which was exhausted, flickered and she turned it out. She lay listening but her teeth chattered. After it might be fifty minutes she heard the door from the bedroom into the dressing room open and shut. She hardly breathed; then she got softly up from the bed. She walked up and down the room. Her steps were noiseless but her breathing short and quick; it might have been heard in the next room. Suddenly she stood still before the door; there was a sound of water running loud in her ears. Then she opened it and went in.

Her husband was standing before the dressing table in his trousers and shirt. He had just blown out the two candles by whose light he had been shaving. The blinds were drawn up to the very top; enough dawn light came in to make everything clear. He was running a red necktie under the soft collar of his flannel shirt. He raised his chin to run the knot of the tie up. Beside the shaving case on the table lay the letter with his address upon it.

She stood by, breathing heavily. She moved her hand towards it.

'You've seen it, haven't you?' she said almost thickly.

'That!—oh yes!—certainly,' he said slowly, 'but you don't suppose I'm going to get up at five o'clock in the morning* to read letters?' He raised his chin higher and looked into the glass. 'Horrid little spot this—just in the very turn—always seems to catch the razor!' He dipped his finger into a silver-topped salve pot that stood open and put a small touch on the spot.

'I knew you wouldn't read it now,' she said hurriedly and softly. 'I wrote on the outside you must take it with you and read it today on the beach when you have time—between the fishing.'

He turned his face partly away from her, still appearing to look at the spot with an absorbed interest. 'Really, Rebekah,' he said quietly, 'I thought you'd become more sensible! What on earth should I read letters for from a person who is living in the same house with me and whom I can see every day! There are going to be a lot of people there and it would be very nice for me to be sitting there all day reading a letter from my wife!' He put on the lid of the salve pot with an exaggerated slowness.

Rebekah stepped forward suddenly, her hands knit in each other.

'Oh, please read it! Please, my husband! Please! I've sat up all night to write it. I had to write it!—Oh, please—please! I haven't meant to hurt you; I've tried to be gentle—Oh, please, please! It's something I know!—Oh, please, please read it!'

With his face still partly turned away from her as if he were looking for something on the table, he said, 'Now really, Rebekah, this is too bad! You've been so decent and sensible the last few years, I'd thought you'd given up this kind of thing: you, the mother of three children and on the point of having another, to go on in this nonsensical way!' He sat down on the chair and began to tuck the bottom of his trousers into his boots. 'No, I'll *not* read the letter; and I shall *not* take it with me!'

'Oh, please read it! Please read it!' She looked at him with distraught eyes; then she knelt down between his knees and looked up at him.

'Oh, please, please, my husband! I sat up all night to write it!—I will go mad if you don't!—I can't bear it any more!—I can't—I can't—I can't!' She beat with her hands softly, softly, up and down on the grey trousers that covered closely his powerful legs on either side of her; they moved up and down so fast they seemed at last like butterfly wings fluttering; you could hardly see them. 'Oh, please, my dear husband, please!' Her eyes, as she looked up at him, seemed not to see him.

He looked down at her, doubtful just what line to pursue.

Then he shook himself roughly free from her and stood up. 'Really, Rebekah, you shouldn't make such a damned jackass-fool* of yourself!—It's Mrs Drummond, I suppose, you are jealous about again—what with her false hair and false teeth and eyebrows getting darker every day as she grows older! It's ridiculous! It's ridiculous!' He knew he had hardly spoken to Mrs Drummond for three months, and was glad to turn matters in that direction. 'I simply won't come home at all if I'm to be met in this way.' He turned and seized his Norfolk jacket* from the chair. 'You've seemed so awfully sensible the last years! I thought you had got over this idiotic tomfoolery.' He spoke a little more gently.

She had risen and stood looking at him with her arms crossed above her head.

'Please read it!—Please read it!' she spoke in a low almost inaudible whisper; 'I sat up all night to write it!—I haven't slept—oh please—please help me!—I can't—I can't—.' She beat her head softly with her two hands.

'Then why the dickens don't you sleep! If you choose to sit up all night making an ass of yourself, is that any reason you should come here howling to me? "You know, you know,"—some nonsense you've trumped up. If you don't care anything for me or yourself, you might at least think of your duty towards the child. It can't be very good for you to be going on this way.'

'The child—oh, the child—my duty towards the child!—I—don't—do—my—duty—towards—the—child!' She raised a long low cry, like a stricken dog. She turned away from him.

He seized her arm. 'Look here, Rebekah, be silent at once! How dare you make such a noise in this house!' His anger was not assumed now, it was real. 'Do you want to wake the children, and have them running in to see what's the matter? If you've no sense of right, or shame, or decency left in you, please remember I have. You are not fit to be allowed to have children at all if you conduct yourself in this manner!'

He took up his thick gloves and the little case with extra fishhooks and thrust them into his coat pocket.

She stood looking at him silently with her arms still folded over her head.

'I hope you'll be a little more sensible when I come back; you're acting like a mad woman now!'

He turned to the door at the back of the room, banging it to behind him so that the wall seemed to shake. She heard him shut the bedroom door in the same way; then for a little while he was in the front hall taking up his fishing rods and the luncheon basket; then she heard him going down the garden path, the footsteps she knew from all others in the world, that she had spent so many scores of hours in her life in waiting for. The gate closed. Then in the Avenue, just outside the gate, on the other side of the tall plumbago hedge before the window, someone met him.

'Where are you off to so early?' The voices raised in the still damp morning air came clearly into the room.

'Going fishing. And you?'

'Off for a tramp; getting too stout. Were you at the club last night?'

'No; I came home early. Had business.'

'You didn't hear the latest then?' The man's voice sank; then she could hear, as she stood there, only a scattered word here and there as they spoke. It was evidently some club story. Then a thick, jovial guffaw of laughter burst from her husband.

'Well, see you tomorrow.' She heard him laugh again as he walked one way and the man the other.

She stood still. The dawn light was coming full into the room now; soon the sun would rise. She looked at her letter lying on the table; she took it up and twisted it slowly with both hands till it was a stiff twisted roll. She walked into the children's room. The back veranda and the oak tree made it still almost as dark as night there. She walked to the stretcher and lay down on it on her back, the letter still clasped tight in her hand. It was so early that not even the bread and milk carts had begun to go up and down in the Avenue. There was dead silence. Presently the birds began to twitter in the oak tree outside. She lay with wide-open eyes looking up as the dark shadows of the rafters in the ceiling became slowly visible. The letter was pressed by her hand against her body.

After a while the youngest baby woke. He raised his head and called imperiously to be taken into her bed to play, as was the custom. Finding no one took any notice of him, he laid it down again, and lifting his small legs into the air began to play with his toes.

What the letter, which Rebekah held twisted in her hand, contained, was this:

'MY HUSBAND,

'You must read this letter. I am writing it in the night. I know what has happened tonight. I know where you have been. Do not think that it is because of this that I write.

'We have lived together for years now, and we have never spoken the truth to each other, nor opened our hearts; yet we are bound together; and all we do or think reacts upon the other. You know that when I have tried to speak to you of our relationship you have silenced me. And when I have written you have not read or have not answered what I wrote.

'But tonight I *must* write; and you *must* read what I write.

'I love you, my husband. Oh! I have loved you so, you—' (this sentence she had scratched out so that it was not legible, and went on:)

'In the years before we were married, when you were asking me to marry you, and after we were engaged, I never doubted your love for me. My fear was always that I could not love you with a love as great and intense as yours. If there was any absence of truth and openness between us, I thought it would rise from my nature. Your frank, careless nature seemed to me of necessity more truthful and beautiful than mine, which was more reserved and perhaps complex. Those letters you wrote from England and after your return from the last voyage seemed to wrap me round with a flame of love.

'Even now I wake in the night sometimes and the cry from them seems to come back to me, "My one love, my own love, my only love—come to me!" and sometimes I seem holding your letter in my hand in the garden under the pear tree, and reading, "My queen, my queen, I need you! I need nothing but you, my love!"—and, when you have wondered why I have suddenly put my arms about you in the dark and crept close to you, it has been that cry I have heard call me. It has been possible for me to go on living during these last years, because I have heard it. When I have felt my self-respect dying, and a leaden humiliation of despair creeping over me, that has saved me. I want you to know that, whatever has happened in the years since we were together, or whatever may happen in the years to come, I never have doubted, and never shall doubt, the truth of your love for me then.

'When we had been married two days, I knew I had been mistaken in thinking my love for you was not great enough; it rose in me as a wave that swept all, even my old self, away before it. When we had been married six months, to cook your food and listen for your step coming up the gravel path, to watch you sitting in the armchair to smoke, made the world quite beautiful to me. I had only one regret, that I had not accepted you when you first asked me, so that we might have had the years together which I wasted away from you.

'When you went to dinners or dances I wanted to go too, because it was beautiful to see you walking about and talking to the other people, and at night the happiest time of all was when I lay awake and heard you breathe close to me.

'After we were married you began to express your love less to me in words and caresses; but that seemed to me so right. When you are seeking to make your love known you must speak of it even in crude language; but when union is complete then the silence of fellowship and trust expresses it. When I felt the need of laying my face against your knee if I were sitting near you, or something compelled me to stand behind your chair and touch the little curls at the back of your neck, and you were seldom impelled towards me in the same way as you were before we married, I thought it was because your deeper man's nature had not need for these small forms of expression when the central union was there.

'Even afterwards, when you went for a day's fishing or to a dance or dinner and suggested it might be better for me not to go too because I had a baby coming, or afterwards had it to nurse, I never thought you did not want me; I thought you were afraid I might get tired. And even once or twice when you had decided to go to a place and I said afterwards I would go with you, I thought it was because you felt I was going for your sake.

'Never, for one moment, in all that first year and a half, did it ever once come within the range of possible thought to me that you did not love me just as you had. It would have been as mentally, I might almost say as physically, impossible for me to have doubted your loyalty or dreamed that you had put another woman in my place, even in your thoughts, without telling me of it, as it would be for me now, if one of my little children climbed up in the chair behind me, to dream that it had a knife in its hand and was going to run it in under my shoulder blade and stab me to the heart.

'There are things one cannot think.

'If you had been surrounded by all the most beautiful, all the most talented, all the most brilliant women in the world, it would never have struck me to fear them. What could they all be to you compared to me; I was your nearest, I was your dearest—I was your wife!

'As I have never suspected that my feet were trying to fling down my body, so I had never suspected any hidden thought or act of yours.

'You may ask, did I not know that sometimes after men and women had married they might find they had made a mistake, that, however loyal and true was the love they had given, they might find some human creature who might have been more to them than the one they married?

'And I answer, yes, I had thought of this; it had seemed to me the great attendant tragedy that waits on human marriage. It was because of this fear that, passionately as you drew me, I waited two years before I gave myself to you. For I said always, "Can I give him that love which is forever till death without possibility that another shadow may fall on it and darken it?" And it was only when the greatness of your love and your need of me had burned away all doubt of myself that I gave myself to you. Even if the thought of that shadow had come to me after we were married, which it never did, I should not have feared you, for I should have known that, if either of us saw such a shadow approaching, we would have gone straight to the other and laid all before them for advice and help; and I had never doubted that two souls true to each other would have found a way to the light. But after we were married no such thoughts ever came to me.

'But, you may say, did I not know there were men and women to whom marriage was only a form, who freely entered on a lifelong union meaning some day to violate it, and who took the soul and body of a creature into their hand meaning to betray it?

'And I answer, yes, I knew that there were such things, as I knew there were thugs and assassins and slow poisoners and professional murderers—but that such things would ever enter into my personal life and play a part there I had never dreamed.

'I have always known there were octopuses in the sea with tentacles twenty feet long which, if they caught you, would drag you down and absorb you;* I have always known that there were somewhere in the world basins of boiling mud into which if a man slipped suddenly he would be swallowed up, and that sometimes there were rifts in the earth in which whole villages and cities disappeared; but I had never thought, when I was walking alone on the sea shore, that a tentacle might stretch out and drag me down, or when I was walking among the karroo bushes that a basin of boiling mud might appear before my feet and I slip into it or the earth rend open and swallow me.

'These things I knew existed somewhere in time and space—but what were they to me?

'I knew of them as I knew that there were women in the streets of great cities willing to sell their bodies, and men prostitutes who fell so low that they bought them (I had even shuddered walking down a street thinking I might without knowing it have passed such a one!); I knew of them as I knew there were shipwrecks in northern seas, where men and women with frozen hands clung to spars and masts till slowly the frozen fingers relaxed their grasp and they fell back with a thud into the sea; I knew of these things, but that they could ever enter my life, or had anything personally to do with me, I had never for one moment supposed. For me, personally, they had no existence.

'I knew you were friendly with many men and women; and I liked to see you with them; you always looked to me like a great blaze of sunshine among dull uncoloured masses; when I saw you dance or talk with other women, how happy they must think me to be part of you.

'When you introduced me to Mrs Drummond I rather shrank from her because she seemed to me cold and narrow, but I knew she had come out in the same steamer with you and had been very kind in helping you to buy the furniture and get the house ready for me, and I tried to be polite to her as I was to all your friends. I was glad she could play your accompaniments and when you practised your parts in the choir; and as you both sang and went to the same church it seemed most natural and right you should walk home with her; and I was glad you had her croquet parties to go to next door, just as I was glad to economise that we might have money to build the billiard room, because both made life pleasanter for you. I knew you admired her dress; I who hardly ever notice dress admired it too, but I did not think you liked her even as well as most of the women we met, for you often said small slighting things of her that you never said of them. If anyone had said to me that you loved Mrs Drummond as well as half the tip of my little finger, I should have laughed, because you and I were one in a living circle; outside was all the world we loved and liked and helped wherever we could—but it wasn't us.

'You must please forgive me for taking so long to tell you this, but we are talking now for all the rest of our lives and we must understand each other. You can't if you don't know how happy I was then.

'Oh, please give up just one morning to reading this; it's for all our lives.

'Do you remember that night you went out to the whist party? I was going, but you said it was damp and might rain and I must run no risks while I nursed, so I stayed at home. I sat sewing in the dining room till half past ten; then, though I knew it was early, I went and sat in the rocking chair on the veranda that I might hear your steps when you came. I had not sat there ten minutes when I thought I heard your steps coming down the Avenue. No one else could have heard them, but I always did even from the corner. It seemed to me your steps stopped at the gate next door, and that I heard it open and shut; it was such a still dark night one heard everything very clearly. I thought you were taking the short cut and coming across the lawn and through the rose-hedge gate, and I went down to meet you at the gate, but as I walked I fancied I saw the figure turn up and go towards the other side of the great house. It was so dark one could only see very dimly, and there was no sound on the grass. I thought you were going to the door on the other side of the house, and no doubt were going to fetch the music you had lent Mrs Drummond to copy two days before. I was standing at the gate, when I saw against the yellow silk blind of Mrs Drummond's little drawing room the shadow of your shoulders and head. You were taking off your coat. Then I knew you must be going to practise the music with her and could not be back directly. At first I felt inclined to run over and sit there while you sang, but I never liked going to Mrs Drummond's; and it was drizzling, so I went back to my needlework in the dining room.

'It was a little after half past eleven when I heard the front gate in the Avenue open and your steps coming quickly up the path. I ran to the front hall. You were just going to take off your coat. You kissed me, and said you were rather late, but you had tied, so you had to stay and play a deciding rubber. Your face was flushed as if you had been walking fast. I was helping you to take your coat off, and I said, "Wasn't it strange? I thought I saw you going up to Mrs Drummond's more than an hour ago." You pulled your coat out of my hand and turned round on me and said, "So, you go peeping, watching me in the dark!" And I laughed; I thought you were playing with me, as you often did then. I caught your arm to lead you in to supper, and said, "See what I've got for you." You threw my hand off so that I almost stumbled against the other side of the passage. I still thought you were playing, and I tried to catch you again, laughing.

'Then you said, "I suppose you fancy I am always running after other women; and you do nothing but pry, and try to find out!—I haven't seen Mrs Drummond since the day before yesterday when she came to fetch the music!" I looked up at you and saw then you weren't playing. You said, "That's what comes of being eaten up with jealousy! You are making an idiotic fool of yourself!" and you walked towards the dining room; and then I knew you meant what you said. Frank, I walked after you, but I didn't know what I was doing. It was as if each word you said was the blow of a great iron bar falling on my head. All the words you said to me that night start out at me even now sometimes in the middle of the night when I wake suddenly; and sometimes when I am busy with my housework I suddenly hear them ringing in my ears. I ran into the dining room after you and tried to put my hands on your shoulders and ask you what it was, but you shook me off you. You said many things. You said I thought you went to service only to walk home with Mrs Drummond; you said I followed you everywhere; you said I even asked the servants about you! Oh, Frank, Frank! I couldn't say anything, I could only look at you. You said you wouldn't have any supper and you went into the bedroom and banged the door. I ran to the door to go in after you, and then I couldn't, and I ran out into the front garden and walked up and down in the drizzle. I didn't know what it was, or what I should do. Afterwards I saw you through the window come out of your bedroom and sit down to eat your supper. I wanted to run in and beg you to tell me that you had never said those words—that it was a horrible dream, but I couldn't. Afterwards you went back to the bedroom, but I still walked for a long time. Afterwards I went into the house, and then I wrote a letter to you. You see, what had stunned me was that you had thought it possible for me to doubt you. I told you I couldn't, I didn't. I told you how I had trusted your love, and I begged you to forgive me if I had ever done or said anything that made you feel I doubted it. Of course, when you said you had been kept playing, I knew I had been mistaken and that it must be another man. I told you that, wherever you went or whatever you did, I could never doubt you, that I knew your nature was much nobler and simpler than mine. I begged you to forgive me for anything I had unconsciously done.

'When I knew you would be fast asleep I went into the bedroom and put the letter on the stand beside you. I thought how you would open it in the morning and read it and turn and take me in your arms and lay my head upon your shoulder and tell me you would never think I doubted you again, and explain to me how it all happened. I lay awake at your back all night waiting for the morning, but just when the dawn was coming I fell asleep. When I woke it was not late, but you were gone and the letter was gone too. I got up quickly and put on my dressing gown, and went into the dining room. You were just finishing your breakfast. You got up and kissed me and said you had something to eat as you had to catch the early train, and began to take up your things. I put my hand on your arm to say something, but you said you had to go at once, and you kissed me quickly and went. When you were gone I saw my letter, torn very, very small, in the waste-paper basket by the fireplace. I couldn't understand it that you had not spoken to me of it. I thought perhaps your heart was still too sore; and yet you did not seem bitter, you looked just as always. Though you had kissed me so quickly, you had been kind to me, even more kindly than sometimes. Then I remembered I had heard older women say that no woman understands what a man is till she has been married for some years; that unmarried women never understand men. I thought that perhaps, though you had forgiven me, the pain your man's nature had felt as though I had mistrusted you was so deep you could not speak of it as a woman would have done. I thought of my father; but he was always silent and reserved, and you spoke always to everyone you met about everything. I thought of the silent agony you must have felt all those days when something I had done had made you think I doubted you, showing no sign at all, and I felt I must learn to understand you. The only thing I could think of that might have made you think I mistrusted you was that I always stood waiting at the door for your steps when it was time for you to come home. You had liked it when we were first married; you called me your little watching bird. I thought that, when we were both in bed that night, I would creep very close to you and ask you in a whisper to explain to me what I had done. That couldn't hurt you. I walked up and down a long time thinking; then I stood at the table, breaking some biscuit into a basin for the baby's breakfast before I went to dress, when the servant opened the door; she said the servant girl from next door wanted to see me. I told her to bring her in. She came and held out her hand with a little twisted bit of white paper in it; she gave it me. She said she had picked up what it held when she was sweeping the floor of her mistress's rooms just now and thought it belonged to you. I opened the paper; inside was one of the gold sleeve links I gave you on your last birthday with your initials and mine on it. The night before I had put them into your white shirt ready for you before you went out to play whist. I gave her some money, and then I mixed the baby's food and gave it to the girl to give him; and then I walked up and down with the sleeve link in my hand, and then I went to your dressing room. Over the chair was the shirt; there was a link in one sleeve and none in the other.

'Perhaps you will find it hard to believe me (I can hardly believe it now), but in the white daze that came to me when all the world seemed to have worn away from me, though I knew you had lied to me, the only feeling I had was that in some way I must so terribly have made you misunderstand me that you could not pursue a simple, kindly human relation without having to lie to me about it. In my darkness all I could think was that you had noticed my cold shrinking from Mrs Drummond, from the first day I met her, that you had attributed it to resentment on my part regarding your politeness to her, and that you had in consequence felt you could not go to see her openly but had to hide it from me. I can't understand it now, but that was how I felt. I resolved that, by great kindness and politeness to her, I would show you that I have never misunderstood your friendship for her. I remembered that, though you had often spoken slightingly of her, you had always wished me to go to see her and invite her to our house. At once I sat down and wrote to her. I told her I was going to shop in Town that afternoon and asked her if she would come with her work and spend the afternoon at my house so that my baby would not be alone with the servant. It was the first favour I had ever asked of her, and I thought she would understand what it meant; and I resolved to stay away till long after your time for returning. I sent the note over with the largest bunch of roses I had ever cut from my garden, and when her answer came I spent the morning making tea cakes for her and you while I was away. It seemed to smooth my brain.

'I went in the afternoon and I did not come back till long after I knew you would be home, so that you might have a long time with her. When I came home she had gone, but you had brought two men for dinner with you. You seemed in very good spirits; after dinner you sang comic songs in the drawing room, before you went to the billiard room. It was nearly twelve when they went. I thought you would say something to me; but you said you were dead tired, and you got into bed at once when you came from your dressing room, and lay on your shoulder and closed your eyes, and I could say nothing.

'The next morning when I kissed you in the passage before you went out, I asked you if you had read the letter. You laughed and chucked me under the chin, and said, "Don't be a silly little woman, don't be a little fool," and hurried out. And I saw you did not mean to speak of it, and I could not.

'I noticed that you did not go over to Mrs Drummond as you usually did; and she did not come to our house; but I sent her cakes and flowers; and I knew one day you would take me to you and say, "I know you have always trusted me, little woman," and then my heart would rest. But while you held me from you I could not speak.

'One day I sent over some flowers to Mrs Drummond, and the servant said she had gone to Somerset Strand* for a holiday and would be gone some time.

'I think she'd been gone about two weeks when the postboy brought the letters to the door. We were at breakfast, and I went to fetch them; I saw the top one was addressed in Mrs Drummond's handwriting to you at your office, and had come by mistake to the house. I passed it to you across the table. I didn't wonder she wrote to you; I knew you did all her business for her; and there were many things she might write about. You glanced at the first sheet and said she wanted you to pay some accounts for her; and you put it in your pocket. Then you took up a half sheet that had been enclosed. You began to read it; then you said, "Oh, this is some woman's business for you," and you passed it on to me. It was marked P.S., and began, "Please tell your wife there is a woman here who makes very good *ingelegte-vis* (pickled fish) if she wants any;" and then she went on to give the price and to say how she packed it in stone jars which had to be returned to her when they were empty; and then without any break went on, "Tomorrow will be the 27th of January, that never-to-be-forgotten and best and dearest of all days of my life which first brought you to me. Do you remember?"— Then I read no more. I handed the sheet back to you. You took it, almost without looking at it or me, and tore it up and threw it into the waste-paper basket behind you. Then you stood up and gathered the rest of your papers together. You didn't notice me. Then you went out; I didn't go with you to say goodbye at the door. I only sat. Then I heard your feet go down the path. And then an impulse came on me to stoop down and gather together the bits of paper in the basket and piece them together and read them. I knew if I waited an instant I should do it. I grasped them up in my two hands and ran to the kitchen fire and dropped them in. I didn't want to know what more she had written; I wanted to forget what I had read. I held my brain stiff that I might not realise it. Only I knew that, from the moment I read the letter, there has always been a burning pain at my heart that has never quite gone and a weight that never was there before. All the day I worked and cooked to keep myself from thinking. It was only late in the afternoon that I was forced to see what the letter meant. I did not think for a moment you loved her or could have been physically unfaithful to me by so much as the pressure of a hand, but I knew there was a friendship between you greater than you let be seen, that perhaps she loved you, and that it was your consciousness of this had made you fancy I mistrusted you. Further I would not look; I let down an iron door without a crack between that part of my brain which knew about it and the rest of my mind; and I worked without stopping. But I was conscious there was a deadened part of my brain lying behind that iron door all the while, waiting to come to life. I had talked so much to myself always about the duty of not shutting one's eyes to anything and facing all facts; and now I was trying to keep my eyes shut.

'It was two days after that you said you had to go up to Robertson and Worcester* on business and you would be gone five days.

'For the first two days after you left I was busy; I turned the whole house out and had the yard and outbuildings cleaned. On the third day I got a letter dated "Worcester" saying you would be back in three days.

'The next day I was sitting sewing in the front room about ten o'clock, when a curious thing happened to me. I had had a restless feeling that I could not understand ever since I got up. But I sat sewing quietly. Suddenly a feeling came to me that I must go to Muizenberg.* I had never been since just after we were married when you took me to spend a day there. I had never since thought of going there. Now, as I was glancing up from my work at the bees humming above among the flowers, it came to me, not as a desire, but as a pressing necessity, that I must go. I don't think I even questioned myself as to why I should go; it only seemed to me an imperative command: I must go. I had never taken a holiday by myself since I was married, nor ever left the house while you were away. I went to the back yard and told the boy to inspan the buggy and the girl to dress that she might hold the baby while I drove. I felt a kind of wild exhilaration and excitement upon me. It was only after we had started and driven some distance that it struck me how very strange it was we should be going. I thought the kind of excitement, almost fever, that was upon me must be a reaction from the many days I had been holding myself down so. Everything looked so beautiful—the green trees, the bushes with the sun shining on them. When we got to Muizenberg it was midday, there was a light southeaster blowing, the blue water was sparkling in the sun. At Farmer Peck's* I told them to take the horses to the stable and feed them. They said their early dinner was over. I said I should go down to the beach for an hour and then return to have coffee and bread. But I asked them to show me a bedroom to lay the baby down in, as he had dropped asleep. They showed me into a little room, and I told the girl to sit by him till he woke and then bring him to the beach to me. Just as I was going out through the front room I saw hanging over a wooden chair near the door a cloak. It was of soft maroon colour and lined with silk and edged with fur. It struck me as familiar; then I recognised it was Mrs Drummond's. No one else in Cape Town had a cloak like that. A feeling of heaviness came over me; I did not want to see her on the beach where I had come to be glad. It seemed strange she should have come there from Somerset Strand. Then I saw, partly hidden by her cloak, on the same chair was a man's overcoat. I was going out when something struck my eye. Out of the pocket of the coat was hanging part of a blue silk muffler with white squares upon it. I stood looking at it. I gave you such a muffler at Xmas. In the corner I had worked initials in white silk. They were there. At first I seemed dulled. I couldn't touch them, I only stood looking at them. I only felt I wanted to creep away and hide. If the girl had not been there I think I should have crept into the bedroom and hidden beside the bed. It was only for a moment, and then the feeling came over me I must run out and look for something, I didn't say to myself what. I rushed out; I did not keep to the road; I almost leaped over the bushes and stones on the way to the beach, and all the time I was crying out aloud with my teeth tight, "It's a lie! It's a lie! It's a lie! It isn't he! It isn't he!"

'When I got to the sandy beach it was lying there all so calm and beautiful. Not the mark of a human foot was upon it, and only the great white seagulls* were flying over the sea. I stood suddenly still as though a great hand were laid on my forehead. Had I been mad? It was all a dream!

'I stood and looked at the sea and sand and the great white birds for quite a long time, and then I began to walk slowly to the part where the rocks lay. The tide was high and running softly in and out among them. I got to a little rise where the stones lay just below me. There was not a sign of a human creature anywhere.

'Then quite close to me, just below, I heard voices. There was a large flat rock with the water washing round its base; on it lay a smaller rock and over the top of it I saw two heads of people who were sitting on the large rock and leaning back against the smaller. Of the head of one only a little black bonnet with an aigrette* standing up could be seen, but I saw the felt hat and the row of tiny curls and the broad thick neck of the other. I could not doubt any more. She said something and then you answered her and bent your head a little and laughed, and then she laughed, that little snipped-off laugh I knew. I couldn't doubt any more. You could have heard me breathing where I stood, only the water ran in and out among the rocks, gurgling. If you had turned and seen me, perhaps all our lives would have been different, because I had lost all control of myself that day. I knew if I heard your voice again (my voice!—my voice!), I should shriek and rush down to you. So I turned and ran. I felt the one thing was I must escape. I gave the boy ten shillings to inspan quickly and I got the girl and baby. I saw the woman of the place standing in the door looking at me as if she thought I was mad. And then we started. We had the wind in our faces. It was the feet of the horses that saved me. They got wilder and wilder; they kicked up the mud and stones into the air. Sometimes as I looked from their heads I caught sight of their feet. I held hard; I didn't touch them, but they knew they had to go. When we had gone some way, some coloured men working in a field ran out and tried to stop them; they thought they were trying to run away; but I shouted to them to let us go. When I got near to the suburbs a policeman came up and stopped me; he said I could not drive so fast among the houses. So I took the road down into the Flats, and we drove round miles, but we got home at last. It was because they helped me that day that when last year you wanted to sell one of them who had broken his knees, I bought him from you and put him on my farm to do nothing.

'It was three days more before you came home: I had had a miscarriage during that time. The doctor said I was very ill, and when you came you only kissed me and went away, because the fever was high. They thought it was my body caused it, but it was my brain. I was in hell. Night and day I heard Mrs Drummond's laugh, and I heard your voice, that low voice I know, speak to her. It seemed as if I was gnawing my own soul. They said if I got out of bed and walked about I should bleed to death, and I sometimes felt I must get up and end it all. The third night after you came back I slept heavily, and when I woke in the dawn such a curious calm had come to me. You were sleeping in the spare room, and the nurse was lying in the bed in the corner. I began to think I could see things quite calmly and clearly, as though they did not concern me.

'What if you loved Mrs Drummond? What if after you married me you found I was not what you thought, and she was the woman who could satisfy you? What if you had deceived me about her and your feeling for her, because your love for her was so infinite that you could not risk my knowing of your friendship?

'If I had had a son and he had loved another woman not his wife, and he had come and laid his head on my breast and told me about it, would I not have sympathised with him and tried to help him to find a way that was truthful and open? And should I sympathise with you less and help you less, who were more to me than all the sons I would ever bear? I thought it all out in the dawn, and during the day I got a pencil and wrote to you. Oh, I know it was tender, because I felt to you then as I can't even now; I only wanted to help you and give myself up for you. I told you I knew you cared for Mrs Drummond, but I didn't tell you how I knew or what I [had seen] because I wanted *you* to tell *me* everything. I only told you that I knew you cared for her more than you allowed to me and that I did not blame you if, after you married me, I had disappointed you and you felt you needed her friendship. I told you that if you wanted to see more of her than you could as things were, I would go for a long visit to my mother with the children, and I would ask her to come and keep house for you while I was away. I should tell everyone before I went that I had asked her, so there would be no scandal; and if, when you had been with her two or three months, you wished then I would stay away forever, you could sue me to return, and, when I did not return, you could get a divorce, and no one would blame you. And then if you and she wished to marry I would write to her husband, and I would beg him to act as I had done, and make it possible for you to be happy together. I told you how much I loved you, but that the joy of helping you to what was best for you would cover my pain and heal it at last. Oh, I know I wrote tenderly, because I never felt so tender to my little baby when it lay sucking at my breast as I felt to you that day. Even to Mrs Drummond I felt no bitterness; if you loved her, why should I judge her! For three days I kept the letter in my breast, because

I didn't think it fair to give it you while I was lying in bed, because you could not have spoken as you would. Even after I got up I kept it for three days. I always seemed to feel a hot place where it lay in my heart; I thought you would understand all when you read it.

'I could not give it you myself, because my breath got so short when I came near you; so I gave it the servant to give you on Sunday morning while I was still in bed. After breakfast when I got up I went to the billiard room where you were practising with the balls.

'I waited a little, and then I asked you if she had given you my letter. You said yes, and kept on playing the balls as though you had hardly heard me. I asked you if you had read it, and you said yes, and went on playing. And then I asked you if, when I went to visit my mother, you would like me to ask Mrs Drummond to come and keep house for you. And you burst out laughing; you said I must be very hipped* to think of such a thing; that Mrs Drummond would run up enough bills in a month to run our house for a year; you said I must be completely hipped to write such nonsense. You kept looking at the balls as if all your thoughts were with them. You said I seemed to have Mrs Drummond on the brain; that the only excuse for me was that I was ill. You said that if there was only one woman in the world, and that woman Mrs Drummond, you wouldn't marry her. That any man who had the settling of her business for her, and the sending to England of cheques for her dresses, would have only one feeling about her and that was pity for her husband; and then you laughed again. You asked me why I wasted my time writing such nonsense, and you went on playing. And then it was suddenly as if something broke in me, and I lost my self-restraint. I cried out I knew you loved her, I knew everything; and I begged you to tell me the truth; and I threw myself down at your feet and I clasped them and I told you I was quite willing you should get a divorce from me, and I would go away and take care of the child and would love you all my life just the same, and I kissed your feet and cried out to you, "Please tell me the truth," and told you I loved you. I begged you only to speak the truth to me, nothing else. And then you pushed me from you and swore; you said I must be mad to talk such nonsense about a divorce and leaving you. You said even my illness did not make any excuse for my making such a miserable exhibition of myself, and then you went away.

'You may say, why didn't I tell you exactly what I had seen and knew. Oh, didn't you see I couldn't? It was you who had to tell me!

I would have taken your last chance from you! Would you have been any greater, would you have been any better, because I had forced your hand? Then I saw what you wanted was not truth between us, but just to be left alone to lead your own life.

'I was ill and had to go to bed again; and you never referred to what had happened; and I never did. But you knew that, if you wished it, you could be free and that I would not keep you.

'It was about two weeks after that that something else happened. I was about again, but hadn't done any work in my garden. I hadn't seemed to care what happened to it. But one morning the sun was shining and I had a feeling I wanted to put it neat. I took my mat and sat on the ground picking up the weeds and rubbish that had blown in. I was tired, and was just going back to the house, when I saw a quantity of dried leaves and bits of paper gathered among the forked roots of my large rose tree, and I sat down on my mat by it to clean it out. I was scratching the rubbish out with my fingers and the trowel when I pulled out half a sheet of notepaper yellow with the mud and rain and a little bit scorched at the bottom as if it had been thrown into the fire. I threw it down with the other leaves and rubbish before me, and then I saw my name on it. It was written in a clear round hand that I knew was Mrs Drummond's. It was a letter dated three months before, therefore before I saw you go to Mrs Drummond's that night. It began, "My Friend"—but from what came next I saw it was to you. You and she had evidently been discussing me. She spoke of marriage generally, and then quoted with inverted commas what you had said about our relation to each other, even our physical relation. She began to comment on what you had said, then came the bottom with the last line burnt off. I did not turn it over to read what was on the other side. For a little time I sat as if I was dead. Then I took my trowel and cut at it. I chopped and chopped it till it was the finest fragments; I chopped at it till it disappeared into the ground and there was not a sign of it left.

'I had believed, older women had told me, that a man never talked of his wife to other women, that he might be unfaithful to her, that he might humiliate her into the dust at his own feet, but that, as long as she was his wife, he never allowed any other woman to speak of her; as long as she was a part of himself he put his hand out over her and covered her as a man covers the nakedness of his own body. I had never doubted it. I think it is because many women believe this that they stay on with men when their hearts are breaking: they say, "*Am I not still his wife?*"

'Afterwards, Mrs Drummond came back and you never went to her croquet parties and seldom saw her. I knew it wasn't only when I was by you avoided her, because she often came over when she expected you would be home and seemed always restlessly looking for you. But oh, I didn't care; nothing mattered. When she looked at me there were little contractions in the inner corner of her eye that come to some women when they look at another whom they hate; but nothing mattered to me. I knew I would have given you up to her if you had really loved her.

'One night I was putting the children to bed and you were smoking on the veranda with some men. I came to your dressing room to put your clothes ready for the next morning, and I could hear what was said. They were discussing Mrs Drummond. One man laughed and said she was ten years older than she professed to be. The other talked of her husband, and laughed about the way she always professed he was longing to come back to her, but he never returned. And you laughed and said you had heard she was bald at the top of her head and had two wigs, one to wear by day and the other at night, so that if she were taken ill suddenly no one might find out. And then you all laughed. Oh, don't think it comforted me to hear you laugh at her. The only thing that could have saved me would have been to believe you loved her with such a mighty passion that it swept all before it, even me! It made me see the thing I was trying to press from me with both hands that I might not see it. The less your love for her, the lower I fell, and you. Was it for this you had put me from you!

'After that, when I was expecting Frank, I became very weak; the doctor said my heart was going, that I was bearing too quickly and working too much. Oh, it wasn't the childbearing or the work or the miscarriages; a woman can bear all and do all if the arms of a man are tight about her. I had loved so to bear for you and to work for you. Now nothing mattered; I couldn't read, I couldn't think! Oh, it isn't only the body of a woman that a man touches when he takes her in his hands; it's her brain, it's her intellect, it's her whole life! He puts his hand in among the finest cords of her being and rends and tears them if he will, so that they never produce anything more but discord and disharmony, or he puts his hand on them gently, and draws out all the music and makes them strong. Oh, it isn't only her body a woman gives a man—' (this paragraph Rebekah had not finished and had scratched out).

'Some time after that, but just after Frank was born, you said you must go into Town by the early train; you had always gone by the late one because you said you hated the crush of the business people and the children going to school; but you said you had more business. You always seemed angry and irritable if you thought breakfast would be late; I thought your work was troubling you. You seldom noticed me or the children, and seemed always absorbed. One night the girl was out, and I brought the tray with refreshments to the billiard room myself. One of the men was hanging up the rest as I came in, and his back was to the door; he was laughing, and he said something about "that young inamorata of yours who is so faithful to you in the train." He turned and saw me and took up his cue and began to play. I took no notice of what he said; I did not even know to which of the men in the room he was speaking. I took it as some man's joke; but afterwards I remembered.

'One evening you decided suddenly to go the next day to Simon's Town, and you had some papers at the house you said it was necessary should be in your office the first thing in the morning. I said I would take them in for you, and you gave me them before you started in the morning in the leathern handbag you always carried with your initials on it. I thought I would make sure you were in time, and I hurried to catch the early train. I had just taken my seat in the carriage when a girl put her head in as if she were seeking for someone and went on. In a few moments she came past again, still looking in at the windows. She was just going by, and then it seemed she caught sight of something. She looked up at me and stared, and then, just as the train was moving, jumped in. She was a stout girl of about fourteen or fifteen, but wearing very short dresses and with a satchel of school books on her arm. She sat down opposite me, and as she stuck her feet out across the carriage you could see the great thickness of her legs. She had a great head of short curly black hair, very tousled and standing out at the sides, with a red jellybag* stuck on the top. She had large, round, dark eyes, and beautiful white teeth; and, though her mouth was very large, she would have been good looking if her round face had not been covered with pimples with little blackheads. As she sat opposite me she stared at the bag on my lap and then up at me; and then she tossed the end of the jellybag from one side of her head to the other and stared again. I felt she was coarse and unpleasant, but I soon forgot about her. When the train got to Cape Town she jumped out and ran up the platform at once; when I came to the gate she was standing there watching the men from the smoking carriages as they came up. I passed her and went out of the station. When I was crossing over to the other side of the road I happened to look back and saw her standing before the station, staring after me. I hurried on to the office and forgot all about her. I gave the bag in at the office and went to Adderley Street* to do some shopping. I had finished and was going slowly down the street to the station, when suddenly something struck my brain; it seemed as though a cold hand had grasped my heart, crushing the life out; in a moment I knew everything just as I know it now. I knew what the man meant in the billiard room; I knew why you went to Town by the early train; I knew why the girl stared at your bag and at me. I had no ground for knowing it; one moment before I knew nothing, I was thinking of my purchases. It flashed out on me as a moving picture in a street flashes on your eye; you see all parts of it almost in a second. It was like when one makes a story; one does not think, all the characters flash out before you in a moment, speaking and acting—you *see* them!

'When you came back that night you were as usual, and the next morning you went to Town by the early train. I tried all day to put the thing that had flashed on me away from me; I tried to say it was a fancy; but deep in my heart I *knew* it wasn't. You came back at mid-day for dinner because it was Saturday; at dinner you said I was looking very pale, and you said I ought to take the children and the servant and go into the pine woods for the afternoon; you said you were going to the Flats to see a friend, so you would not be at home. I thought it kind of you to think of how I looked; almost gladness came to me. At three o'clock I took the children and the servant and went; you were still reading the papers on the front stoep; you said as soon as you had finished you were going and would lock the front doors; the stable boy was at the back and could look after the yard entrance. When we got up to the old summerhouse and had been there for some time the girl found she had forgotten the basket with the baby's feeding bottle, and I said I would go back and fetch it. When I got there the stable boy was sitting before the back gate cleaning harness, and when I went into the house all the front doors and windows were locked, and I thought you had gone out. I had got the bottle and was just going out of the dining room into the passage that leads to the kitchen and billiard room, when I heard a noise of laughing and shouting. I went into the passage; at the far end the door of the billiard room was open and I saw two figures chasing each other round the table; the one seemed to me to be you, and the other the girl I had seen in the train. I walked straight down the passage to the door of the billiard room. You had caught her by that time; she was lying on the floor on her back; her legs were under the billiard table but her head out, and you were kneeling on the floor at her head bending over and tickling her. Your back was to the door. She was gasping with laughter and kicking with her feet against the underside of the table and crying between the gasps, "You horrid man—I'll pull your moustache again—like I did the day before yesterday!" And you said, "Will you! Will you! Will you!" and kept on tickling her. The soles of your feet were turned to me as you knelt, and I saw your beautiful broad shoulders and the curls above your thick neck as you bent over her. You said something in your soft thick way between your half-closed lips; only she could hear it, and she laughed louder. Then I turned and ran; I ran as I have never run in my life. I threw down the basket in the kitchen and my cloak caught the door and closed it loud behind me; I ran across the yard and up the side passage by the stable boy and up through the woods and up the mountain. I climbed and climbed; when I got to the blockhouse* I dropped on my face, but as soon as I had breath I got up and I climbed till I climbed so high there were only the crags of the mountain above me where the gorge comes down to the silver trees.* Then I lay on the ground. I was deaf and blind. I heard nothing of the outer world; only inside my brain I heard always—"The father of your children!—the lord of your body!—the owner of your life!" When I called your name aloud, "Frank!—Frank!"—that was the answer that came back to me. All the time I ran up the mountain and all the time I lay there, the only thing I saw was your broad back and the curls about your neck and the girl's legs with the rim of the red flannel petticoat that showed as she kicked and laughed.

'When it was dark I felt my way down the mountain back to our house. It was half past eight when I got there, but you had not come back. I went to bath the children. Afterwards you came in; you were very friendly and in high good spirits. You came into the bedroom and stood by the bath, and said how nice and fat the baby was growing, and squirted him with water; you didn't notice that I said nothing.

But afterwards, when we were at supper, sometimes as you ate you glanced up at me from under your eyebrows; as if you had heard the door slam or the stable boy had told you I'd been home. You didn't say anything, but, just as you got up from the table, you half turned and said quickly, "Oh, by the way, there was a girl here this afternoon, the stationmaster's cousin or niece or something of the kind. She had some lace her aunt had made to sell, and she wanted to see if you would buy it. I told her you were out and she must come again when you were here; it wasn't in my line!" and then you laughed your little laugh and went out of the room.

'Perhaps you'll say again, why didn't I speak to you directly and tell you what I had seen? Oh, I couldn't, don't you see I couldn't! If you had sworn at me, and spoken as you spoke before, I would have died, and my baby was six weeks old.

'The next day was Sunday and you stayed at home, and you played with the children. But I was in hell, wandering in the dark.

'On Monday morning you went to catch the early train as usual. I was washing the baby; and suddenly the feeling swept over me that I *must* follow, that I *must* see you meet her. I hadn't a definite plan of saying or doing anything, just the feeling I must go. I laid the baby down on the bed and put on my hat and without dressing I ran down the Avenue after you, till I got to the place where the second avenue turns to the station; then I stopped. An awful wave of humiliation swept over me, and I turned and came home again.

'All the week you were the same as usual, only in better spirits; you sang and whistled more. Late the next Sunday afternoon you said you were going to visit a man and would go straight from his house to church and I need not expect you back till nine o'clock for supper. About an hour after you left someone came to say the old Malay cook we had when we were first married was very ill and wanted to see me. I went and stayed with her nearly an hour. When I came out it was beginning to get dark; so I didn't take the short cut through the woods; I went the long road past the station. When I got near the station it was almost dark; I saw, without noticing, a man's figure standing near a gate in a hedge in the road. It had never struck me it was you, as you had gone in the opposite direction. As I got nearer I saw in the dusk a woman standing inside the gate, leaning over it and evidently talking with the man. As I was almost opposite the gate on the other side of the side road under the fir trees, I saw suddenly that it was you and the girl I met in the train. You were saying goodbye to her, and you had her hand; you were holding it between both yours, and you drew yours slowly and softly away till her hand fell, as you used to say goodbye to me at the farm. You turned away and walked slowly up the road in the other direction, and I took the turn towards our house. That night, when you had gone to sleep, I lay awake behind you, thinking and thinking.

'It seemed to me I might have been unjust in the bitterness of those last days. I had understood that you should love Mrs Drummond with her refined face and her graceful figure and her beautiful dresses and her many tastes in common with yours and her years almost the same. It had seemed quite possible to me you loved her with great love; I had been able to make so many justifications for you in my own mind—this had been so different. I had envied Mrs Drummond when you sat on the rocks with her and called her "my friend". *This* had only filled me with a creepy horror, that had passed from her to you. Now, when I remember how you stood at the gate drawing her hand through yours, the thought came to me that perhaps I had been unjust. What if it were that very sensitiveness and refinement, which Mrs Drummond and I had each in our own way, which ultimately repelled you from us when you came close to us and made you feel you could not permanently love us? What if your nature required just that animal element, without thought and without self-restraint, to draw out its depth of loyalty and love. What if the round pimpled face, and the loud laugh, and her stare which filled me with horror were the things your nature needed to draw you permanently? Was there not a whole side in your laughter-loving, sport-loving nature which was nearer her than to me or Mrs Drummond? Was there not even a likeness between your rounded face and figure and hers? Might not she much more easily be mistaken for your child or your sister than I? And must not like seek like? Had I any right to think there could be nothing beautiful and tender in your feeling for her because I could not have loved her? I even said to myself that perhaps I had been wholly unjust to you. What if after all there was nothing of sex in your feeling for her, if you simply longed for young light-hearted society and romped with her as you might with your own boys, when they were older. What if you concealed it from me simply because you thought I could not sympathise with or understand your feeling? Was not what I had thought the terrible sex-desire of a man, who had already brought a child into life, for a child less than half his age, merely a paternal joy in young life? Was it not the same desire to gambol with a young creature which made you squirt the water in the baby's face where I only wanted to kiss it and sing to it? Was it not the same feeling that made you care only for awkward gambolling young puppies, while I cared for older more matured animals? Was it not perhaps I, who had thought myself large and able to sympathise with others, who was really small and narrow, measuring you by my own little standard? I thought so long lying there behind you, that at last I had persuaded myself it was I who was wrong in not giving you a larger generous sympathy. Oh, can't you see I had to! If a woman loses her feeling of honour for the man she has given herself to, then she'd better be dead! Her love for him is like a little lamp that she carries in her breast, that she must shield with both hands from every wind that blows, because if it goes out it means death to her.

'The next day I sent the servant to the stationmaster's wife with a letter to say I had been out when her niece called with the lace, but if she would come again that afternoon at five I would be glad to see it.

'At five o'clock I had spread the table in the veranda with cakes and preserves, and soon after five the girl came. She looked hard at me as she was walking up the path; she handed me a bit of paper with a small bit of crochet lace in it. I asked her to sit down at the table and I made her tea. I offered her six shillings for the lace; I knew it was only worth one, but I wanted to show her I felt friendly. I tried to talk to her about flowers and fancywork, but she hardly answered me. She sat eating cake, picking the plums out with her fingers, and looking every now and then at the gate. At last she asked what time you generally came home. I told her you would be home soon. A curious half smile came over her mouth; it was as though she thought I knew nothing of your friendship with her and I was unconsciously playing into her hand. It was a look—a little of triumph, almost of scorn.

'When she saw you come in at the gate she drew herself up and all her face changed. She looked full at you and smiled, all her white teeth showing when you said good day to her. I showed you the lace and told you what I gave for it, and went away at once to make you fresh tea. I was gone a quarter of an hour; when I came back with the tea she was sitting alone eating dates; she said you said you had to go out again at once. I picked her a large bunch of roses because she said she had none in their garden, and I asked her whenever she wanted some more to come any afternoon and fetch them.

'When you came home to dinner you did not mention her, but when you were undressing in the evening you said, "What on earth made you give six shillings for that bit of lace? It wasn't worth one; but it's your own money if you like to squander it." You didn't say anything more about her.

'Twice the next week she came, about five, to fetch roses. I always gave her tea and cake, and never mentioned your name to her. The first time when you came home you stopped and said a few words to her, and then walked on into the billiard room; the second time you hardly spoke to her, and went straight in. She waited very long, but you did not come back. Then just as she was going down the path to the gate you came to the dining-room window and looked out. She was just shutting the gate. You said, "What monstrous legs that girl has! She'll be a tower of fat and deformity before she's twenty-five." As I was putting the tea things together you said, "What on earth do you have that great lolloping larrikin of a girl here for? If you want to have her, I wish you'd take her into the drawing room and keep her out of my way."

'The next day you said you wanted breakfast at the old time, as there was no need for you to go in by the early train. For nearly two weeks after that the girl never came again. Then one afternoon I saw her coming up the path: she looked very heavy and sullen. I went in and got her tea. She did not keep on eating cake as she generally did; she crumbled it up in her lap and kept her eyes fixed on the ground or looked up staring at me. She said not a word, only moved her head sullenly in answer to my remarks; and I felt as if she had some purpose in coming. I cut a large bunch of roses for her; she seized them and, hardly saying goodbye, turned to go. When she got to the gate she turned and flung the roses all over the path. "We've got flowers of our own," she said; "we don't want yours!" Then when she had got outside the gate and had shut it she turned and leaned her folded arms on the top. I was standing before the veranda on the path. She looked full at me with her eyes very wide open, then she burst into a loud artificial laugh with all her white teeth showing. "You think you've got him all to yourself, do you! You think because you've taken him away from me you've got him! He doesn't care two straws for you! He'll go after another girl; I expect he's got one already!" She opened her mouth wide and laughed, and then she went away.

'Then I knew you had deserted her, and there was no use my trying to do anything. I have never tried again to have anything to do with a woman who was your friend.

'And after that the dark closed in about me. It wasn't faith in your love I had lost—it was all faith in life. I didn't care for anything any more—not for the children, not for the house, not for books, not for nature; I only wanted to die. I did my work because I must; but the only time I felt glad was when I thought of death; it seemed that then there was a faint stirring at my heart like hope. And sometimes in the morning, just when I woke, there used to come a feeling to me that somewhere, somehow, sometime, something would come to help me, some person, some man, some woman, some book. Sometimes in my dazed state I have even gone out and looked up and down the front avenue as if I thought some visible human being was coming to help me. Nothing goes on always in this world; it seemed I couldn't be left always in my despair. Life can't go on forever letting a human creature seem alive, who really is dead.

'And at last help did come, but not from a man, or a woman, or a book. You had gone away for three weeks to the Eastern Province by sea, and it was the day after you left. I was sitting in the rocking chair on the stoep with a newspaper on my lap, open, but I was not reading. As I looked mechanically at it my eye caught certain words. It was a small wine garden to sell just beyond the suburbs. It gave the price and the agent's name. I read it once or twice mechanically. Then suddenly I grasped it and began to think. I got up and began walking up and down with the paper in my hand. I had thought that, if once I could find some man or woman to whom I could tell everything and who would hold my hand tight and let me creep close to them I should be saved. But this did it. I had the money my father gave me when I was married; it would almost pay for the ground, and I could raise a mortgage for the rest of the money to work the farm with.

'I thought all the morning, and in the afternoon I went to see the agent and the farm.

'He would not give me the title deeds till he had seen you and you had given your consent, because I was a woman.* But I paid him the money and he gave me possession at once. I put my old Malay cook and her husband and son there, and for three weeks I and the children lived there. They played in the sun on the grass, and I worked. I climbed onto the roof and pulled out the old thatch and helped the man to re-thatch the shanty. We cleaned and planted; before you came back it was almost in order. The seeds I had planted were coming up, and the vineyard was clean. I could not study, and I dared not feel; but I could still [work]; it was my hold on freedom and life and it has been so to me ever since.

'Frank, you must forgive me that I write to you in detail; I know it will tire you. But it is for all our lives. You must understand where I stand, and how I stand there, because now the silence between us must end.

'I need not write fully about the things that have happened later; they have always kept on happening, and I think you have suspected that I suspected them. Sometimes for a little time nothing happened, and then a hope rose in me that things had changed; but they always did happen at last, and I have realised what we have to deal with is not an isolated event but a permanent condition. Such little things—but they always keep on happening.

'Do you remember two Xmases ago when we were walking down Adderley Street to buy the children presents? I was walking just a little in front of you looking in at the windows when I heard a rustle of silk skirts and someone running down the pavement behind us. I glanced back and there was a woman with a red dress and black bonnet with red roses in it; she had just caught hold of your arm from behind and called out "Hello!" You turned quickly towards her; I heard you say three words in a low voice: I could not fully catch them, though I think I know what they were, and you glanced at me. In an instant she let your arm go, and stood looking at me with her head a little on one side with that half-curious, half-contemptuous smile I saw first on the stationmaster's niece's face, but which I have seen since so often. Then she laughed softly and drew her skirt up tight about her and crossed to the other side of the street, and you came quickly to my side. I think you must have noticed that I saw her catch your arm, for presently you said, "I wonder who that woman can have been that came up to me just now? Seems she mistook me for someone else!"

'I said, "Have you not seen her before?"

'You said, "Oh, I may have. Rather expect she's one of the actresses that came over on the steamer with me last time I came from Port

Elizabeth!" And then you began talking about the toys in the window. All these years they've kept on happening. Once you sent me a note from the office to say you had to make up the quarter's books, and you wouldn't be home till very late; I mustn't sit up for you. At four o'clock you came home in a cab. Your face was swollen with tiredness and you dropped on the bed and went to sleep at once. I kept the house very quiet the next morning because I thought after your hard work you needed sleep. At nine o'clock your clerk came and said he wanted the key of the safe to get out a document. I said I didn't like to wake you because you had sat working so late making up the books. He looked at me surprised and said, "But we made up all the books last week!"

'Another time, perhaps you remember it, I went into Town to buy new oilcloth for the billiard room. I thought I would ask you to come with me to choose it. When I got to the office it was closed up. The caretaker said you had given the clerks a holiday to go to the races, and had closed at eleven o'clock. I bought the oilcloth and went home. In the evening you were an hour late for dinner. I went to the door to meet you. I was just going to say that I wished I had known you were going to the races, because I had never seen any and would have gone too, when you said you were afraid you had kept dinner waiting but there had been such a succession of people in the office all day you'd had no breathing time. You said your head ached and you did not want dinner, only a cup of coffee on the veranda. I could not understand why it was you should wish to hide from me you had gone, but the next day a woman came (it was Mrs Drummond, but Rebekah did not say so) and asked me if I had been to the races. I said I had never been to races. She said she thought I must have been, as someone had said they had seen my husband driving in a carriage with the girl who kept his books and two others, but that she had felt sure it must be me and some of my friends; and she looked at me to see how I felt it. A few days after I met a man in the Avenue who stopped to say good day to me. He asked if I had been at the races the week before: I said I had not. He laughed and said, "You should look after your husband a little; you shouldn't let him be so gay!" And he looked at me with a curious inquiring smile. One of the strangest things to me has been how not only women, but men, men who call themselves men, come close to you and prod their fingers into your wound to see how much you feel; it is like when wild animals gather round the wounded one of the herd and prod it with their horns when it falls wounded. It came to this at last, that I felt as if nothing mattered to me if people didn't come and talk to me of you and show me that they knew.* There was a cow at the farm one day whose side was torn open by a barbed-wire fence, so that her entrails hung out; she tried always to turn that side away from the other animals, and they seemed always trying to come round to it, till we shot her.

'Perhaps you will say if life has been so to me, why haven't I left you and gone home to my father? Oh, you know I asked you to divorce me or send me away if you wished, and you said nothing. I have often asked myself why I didn't get up and go. Is it perhaps the spirit of those old ancestresses of mine who for millions of years have followed the man over steppes and through deserts and across mountains, with stripes* and burdens, always following, following, following—which today cries out in us, "Follow—follow—till he sets you free!" I do not know how it is that I, who would bear binding to no other human creature, feel an iron chain about my heart binding me to you. Often I have said, "Why do I not get up and go!"—and then something cries out in me, "If he should need me!—If he should want me!—If I am good for him!" When I have thought of leaving you against your will, it has been as if I left my little child while it cried for me; something begins to bleed inside of me.

'When I went last year to visit my mother at the farm even my brain seemed rigid. But when I saw the places where I had been when I was a little child, when I saw the long moss still hanging from the tree in the kloof and picked up the Kaffir beans that had fallen from the trees and saw the old great pear tree under which I used to play, I walked about alone and cried for joy, and my heart came back again to me soft, like before I married. I felt as if something went out from me and clasped itself about everything. I wanted to read and to think again; and when I had been there a month such a strange tenderness to you sprang up in my heart. It seemed all my fault that I had not wound my arms about you and made you talk about things to me, and so we should have got to understand each other. At last I had only one desire, a hunger to see your face and to hear your voice. And when you wrote a letter in which you said you missed me and the children and would never let us go so far away again, I packed up my things and came home a month sooner than I had meant. I thought when I came back the past was going to be past, that what I had wanted for so long was going to happen, because deep hidden in my heart there had always been a hope; I see it now.

'And when we came back all did seem better; you spoke kindly to me almost as you spoke to other women, and never spoke roughly to me before the children and servant; but you wouldn't let me come near enough to you to speak of anything. I was glad you had Bertie to go out with, and when I knew this child was coming I was glad, almost as when the first was coming; the other two had been so terrible.

'After Bertie was gone things seemed just as bright; you still cared to stay at home and seemed happy here with us. I thought I was making you happy; I didn't want anything more; it seemed I could let an iron curtain down between me and the past; I could be quite satisfied just to live peacefully and attend to you and the children and feel you near me, and nothing ever happening. Oh! I asked so little, so little!

'Now tonight what has happened has made me feel we must speak the truth to each other. I have been afraid of you all these years; I have been afraid if I wrote or spoke to you and you answered me as you did years ago, something would break in me. But tonight I am not afraid.

'Do not think that, because what happened in the yard tonight would give me the legal right to freedom in any court, therefore I write to you, who have been silent so long. In the eyes of the world it might seem a grosser and more brutal thing—but not in mine. When I saw you and Mrs Drummond on the rocks at Muizenberg, and when I picked up the letter beginning "My Friend", in which you discussed marriage and me, my youth died in me, and it will never come back; this is not so great. When I saw you in the billiard room that day you did not inflict such anguish on me as when in the last years you have often sat talking with women in the same room with me, bending perhaps over a young girl, plain it might be, with the same passionate light in your eyes begging for a return of sexual feeling, which you once turned on me; not caring that I was present to see, or the glances other women directed to me; and when, just because it meant nothing permanent and she might pass out of your life in a few days, it has inflicted deeper humiliation on you and me and the bond that bound us. It is the lightness of the attraction which could come between your manhood and my womanhood that is the measure of our degradation.

'I do not know whether other women feel so, but I can understand, I can almost sympathise with, a wave of black, primitive bestial desire surging up at some moment in life in a nature otherwise pure and lofty. I can imagine it for an instant sweeping all before it, so that the creature itself cried out in the pain of a grasp it cannot comprehend, which drives it forward to action it abhors—the resurrection of that long-buried animal past, when man on earth knew not of love and loyalty; and I can understand that the creature, man or woman, should shrink with horror from the force within them while they fell before it. There are lands where, in the course of centuries or scores or decades of years, the earth rends and opens and sulphurous fumes desolate it and darkness covers it; and yet men live in it and love it and it is still a fair land, except at that rare and terrible moment when the convulsion falls on it; but a land that always trembled, that was never still, when from every smallest crack the foetid fume rose, and a fine, almost imperceptible, fall of ashes covered it: the very dogs would leave it—no man would live there!

'Do not think that I am taking a mean advantage because tonight you have weakly committed yourself into my hand; it is not what you have done that makes me speak; it is because something has happened in me that never happened before. I feel that tonight the end has come, and you and I must speak openly and sincerely to each other. I am not afraid of you. I am not a woman speaking to the man who owns her, before whom she trembles; we are two free souls looking at each other. If you will not read this letter, then you shall hear me speak. But that long life of silence and repression and deception ends here. You must hear me.

'It seems to me that there are just three possible courses open to us.

'The first is, that you should get a divorce from me. As I told you years ago, when I thought you loved Mrs Drummond, if you wish for one I shall do all I can to make it easy for you. I will go to my parents; you can demand my return, and, when I refuse, divorce me. Then all blame will rest upon me. I have my farm and I can work. I will support the children, but for your sake, for yourself, I think you ought to. This seems to me the best plan; then we shall both be free to lead our lives—such as they can be now.

'The second is, if you do not want the disgrace of a divorce (I know you will fear it; I do not fear it; it will not touch me), that we should separate. I can go on my little wine farm; it will not attract much attention; you can come sometimes, if you will, to see the children.

We can each lead our own lives; but it will not be so right as if the tie were utterly severed and openly.

'Then there is a third. If, if it so happens that you still think you love me and do not wish me to go from you, then there is yet one course open for us. You must meet me, fairly and straightly, as one man meets another, and speak to me as one speaks to one's own soul. You must tell me what you feel, what you desire and wherein you think I have failed, as I have told you in this letter. There must be no subterfuge or concealment between us. Then, if you still wish to possess me, I will live with you; as long as you are loyal to me I will be loyal to you; I will bear children for you. I will forget the past; never by a word or a sign shall I recall it.

'Oh, Frank, Frank, I have loved you! Oh, even now I love you, as you have not known, as you never will know! Only once in all the years we have been together has it ever seemed for a moment to have gone out. We were sitting at dinner at the time you were still friendly with the stationmaster's niece. You were eating with your eyes fixed intently on your plate, but evidently not thinking of what you were eating. As I looked up at you, as I looked at your mouth and your jaw, a wave of horror swept over me. It was not as if you were the man who was myself, but any other man whom one might see at a restaurant for the first time. The horror and shrinking swept over me so I rose and left the table. If I had continued to feel so, then I must have left you at once. But it passed almost immediately and remained only as a terrible memory. It may have been some thought that was in your mind, written on your face for the moment, which affected me so, but, except then, never in the darkest moment has my love died. You have never been to me as another man.

'Frank, I have tried to blame myself; I have sought, as a rat in a trap seeks a way of escape, to find out I was wrong and you were right. I have tried to understand you. I do even now see there may be elements in your nature forcing you almost irresistibly to certain courses of action that I cannot rightly understand, because those forces are not in me. I see that I must be unjust to you if I measure you by my standard. Can love and marriage and the relationship of human to human have the same meaning to you and to me, when in everything else we differ? Sometimes I have lain awake whole nights thinking over it.

'You care for wild animals. You will spend days in the blazing sun or the cutting winds, you will creep on hands and knees over rough koppies or through the mud of vleis* to stalk a buck or a bird you have fixed on. When you get near it you shoot it; when you get to it, you pick it up and turn it over in your hand, or you kick it over with your foot. That is the end; you have got it. You sometimes care so little for a buck you have spent half the day in stalking that, rather than carry it back on your shoulder to the cart, you will give it to the man that is with you. Only if one who is shooting with you should say his gun brought it down, then it becomes of importance to you, and, rather than let him have it, you would battle over it.

'I have cared for wild animals too. I had a wood dove that the Kaffir boys had caught and crushed in their stone trap; I bought it from them with the only sixpence I had, and I nursed it and cured it. It made a nest in the garden, and sometimes when I woke in the morning it was fluttering round my bed or sitting on the rail at the bottom singing and waiting for me to wake. I had a raven they shot in the land and broke its wing and leg. I tied splints to it, and, though it could never fly, it lived; and when I went out in the morning into the yard a thrill of joy used to come over me when I saw it hop out of the wagon house with its one stiff leg and its head on one side coming to peck at my skirt that I might pick it up and let it ride on my shoulder. I also had a passion for wild animals; but it has been to possess them and know they knew me and wanted me.

'If you have a spare day, you go fishing, and you stand on the rocks from the morning to the evening, sometimes soaked with spray to bring a few fishes to land. I have seen your eye gleaming and your whole being intent as you have seen your float move or have reeled one to the shore. And yet, when you had them, when you had put your fingers through their gills, your interest in them was ended. You threw them into the basket with the others. Only if it were a very large one, and you wanted to take it home and weigh it and tell your friends its size, would you often care to take it home. I have known you give a whole basketful to the coloured boys on the beach because they were not worth carrying. I would not. I would not endure the labour you go through in catching them for anything but to save my children or someone dependent on me from absolute hunger. Yes, if I were standing in the water and a fish should creep up to me and glide between my feet and over them, not fearing me, I should stand still shivering with delight every time its beautiful body touched me. I have always dreamed of having a tame fish, one that would come to me when

I called and lie with its slow palpitating beautiful belly on my hand in the water and let me feel it.

'Only once I tried to capture a thing, when I was six years old, and I saw for the first time one of those great purple butterflies with the golden eyes on their wings. It seemed so beautiful, I desired it so passionately, I think I would have committed a crime to have it. I ran after it all the way to the great dam and through the mielie lands, though I knew I should not go so far, and when it sat on a karroo bush I fell down on it and caught it. When I stood up and looked it was crushed, and the fine fluff was clinging to my hand. I lay down on the ground and cried beside it. You see, what I had really wanted was not to catch it, but to have it, and I thought I could if I caught it. I don't think since then I have ever wanted to catch anything that has tried to escape from me, an animal or a human creature. I have understood that what I wanted from living things was what they could *give* me, not what I could take from them. The supreme moment to me is not when I kill or conquer a living thing, but that moment its eye and mine meet and a line of connection is formed between me and the life that is in it. It knows and understands me and we are united by something within us. Then it is mine; and I want it.

'There is the same difference between us in everything. If I have a few hours to spare on an afternoon, I like to go to the blockhouse on the mountain and lie down and see the town below me and the bay and the mountains and the bush. I lie and look at it till I feel it all belongs to me. And my little life, which sometimes seems so small when I am shut up in the house alone, grows great and beautiful. And I have my half holiday.

'And if you have a free afternoon, if you have no animal to pursue, you go to the cricket ground or play croquet; you strike or chase the balls; even if they are not alive, you have the pleasure of trying to do it better than another man; and, if you cannot play yourself, you watch others do it; you are pleased so long as there is winning, conquering, taking—sport!

'If you have a dog, you like it because it is thoroughbred and wins prizes at shows or hunts well, and you flog it when it makes mistakes. The dog I have loved best was a terrier of no full breed.* For six years he slept at the foot of my bed; and even now, when I wake in the night, something in me cries out to feel him creep softly up in the dark and lie between my arm and my side with his little head on my shoulder and his little heart beating against my side; and if there were another world where we could see again the things we have loved here, one of the first things I should ask to see would be those eyes which when I woke I used to find watching me, when he lay with his two paws on my chest waiting for me to wake.

'And, sometimes, I have asked myself, if we feel so differently with regard to everything in life, is it not also inevitable we should feel differently about love? What if for you a woman is only "sport"? What if there is something irresistible in your nature which compels you to feel that the woman who has once wholly given herself to you is a dead bird, a fish, through whose gills you have put your fingers?*

'Long ago you met Mrs Drummond secretly and got letters from her; you were careful I should not see and seemed to care much for her, but as soon as I said that I would go away that you might have her for six months in the house with you, and that if you wished it you could divorce me and marry her—then you cared nothing more for her; when she waited at the gate for you, you tried to avoid her; when she asked you to her parties, you never went; when she waited about for you and sent you presents and you knew you could absolutely possess her, she had no more value for you. Only two years ago, when the old Major was so attentive to her and was always coming to see her, you too went to see her and took her out till he left off coming, and then you left off going to her too, till last year, when there was gossip about the young bank clerk who came so often to see her; then you went to church with her and brought her home and went to her croquet till she left off having anything to do with him; and then you left her too. You liked to meet the stationmaster's niece and go to Town with her while it was secretly done, but when I asked her here and you could have seen her every day in your own house, then you avoided her and you got to dislike her following you and waiting for you. Hasn't it always been so, you haven't cared for any woman for long?

'I have sometimes thought that perhaps if I had been another kind of woman—not if I had taken more care of your house and the children, not if I had been more eager to satisfy the wants of your nature, not if your touch had been more precious to me—but if, when you came home, you were never quite sure who you would find had been taking tea with me; if, when I went for a walk in the woods, you never were quite sure that it was alone; if, instead of showing all my letters and telegrams to you, you had noticed that I tried to prevent any falling into your hands; if I had carried on a long correspondence with a married man, whose letters you never saw or mine to him, and met him when you were from home; if, at balls and assemblies, you had seen me sit with men of my own age and men much younger bending over me, and you had seen my cheeks burn and my eyes grow bright with a colour they never wore for you—then perhaps you would have been able to keep on loving me! I have thought that perhaps the only woman you could have kept on loving all your life would have been a woman of whom you were never quite sure, that there must be at least a flutter in the bird's wings, a possibility of its again taking flight, to make it of value to you!

'If I am mistaken in this, tell me so. But if I am not, if you know it to be true, why should we not both face the fact plainly? If it is not possible for your nature to keep on caring for a thing that absolutely belongs to you and yields no excitement of chase, is it not as unjust to demand it of you as it would be to demand of me with my nature that I should desire to kill things simply because they were alive and I saw them move?

'I sometimes think that why you were attracted to me, when I was a little girl and you first saw me, was simply because I always ran away from you to hide in the bush; if I had hung about you and wanted to play with you, you would have driven me away; but when I climbed into the top of the willow tree and you set the dogs to find me and stood at the bottom of the tree declaring you would stay the whole day if I did not come down and play, and I refused, then you liked me. I believe that afterwards it was the fact that I noticed no man, that I had accepted none of the proposals made me that drew you to me. You loved me then. When you lifted me off the rocks, when I hurried in late to breakfast and you rose and drew out the old wooden chair for me, as you looked down at me, the light upon your face seemed to me God's light shining out upon my life; when I think of it even now, I want to push everything from me and run to you and creep close to you—even now. After we were married I never saw it again on your face for me—my light; but I saw it shine on your face for others. In a ballroom I have seen you stoop to pick up a fan dropped by a young girl you did not know and who did not know you; as you have handed it her, her face has burned softly crimson and then white and she has gone away fingering the fan softly, and I know at night she has dreamed of the face with the light upon it.

'I have seen it play on your face as you helped a woman much older than yourself into a carriage; I have seen it come for a girl you were saying an ordinary goodbye to at a railway station, and my heart has beaten with the feeling that when you turned to me it would shine on me also, but it has been dead when you turned and said, "Are you ready, Rebekah?" I have seen you on a sofa beside a girl not young, not beautiful, bending over her, with the light upon your face so clearly that every person in the room has noted it and in a way quietly smiled, and the woman has thought she had won you wholly and looked up at me with the scorn of the victor; but the next week or the next month it has been just so for another woman. What is it but the old, old lure light, the decoy light, that through the ages has led woman on, crying to her, "Here is light! Here is warmth!" and when she has followed it up hills and down valleys and, reaching it, stretches out her hands to warm them, she finds a few white ashes.

'If the fish could see it, is it not the same light that burns with deep intensity in the eye that watches him rise slowly to take the bait? What is it but the *ignis fatuus* which leads woman on to surrender and toil and bear for man, the very memory of which, even when it has gone, binds her to him so that she cannot break the tie? Oh, now, even now, when I know what it means, something in me cries out to see it once again, my light, for me, just once before I die!' (She scratched out this last sentence.)

'Sometimes, in hours of great darkness, it has come to me that perhaps there is nothing strange in our fate; that perhaps in all these houses with their tender gardens and their little front gates, and between all these men and women whom one sees walking smoothly to church together and going out to dinner and sitting on the stoep, there lies the same ghastly reality that the strange joy which fills the heart of the man and the woman we see walking alone together as they plan their future home and life, from whom we turn away when we meet them in the pine woods lest we should trespass on the beautiful solitude—that perhaps in the end it all comes to this—that the love and fellowship which we are taught to look to as our end in life, which compensates us for all that larger world of duties and actions, which we dream of from our earliest girlhood as that which is to consecrate our lives, means in the end only this—an hour's light, and then a long darkness; the higher the flame has leaped, the colder and deader the ashes.

'If I believed this always, if it came to me otherwise than as a nightmare, I would not live; because human life would be false at its core. Even the animals know what love is; the eagle mates once and never again, they say, if its mate dies; the singing birds mate with a companion whom they tend and follow; even those beasts whose union is a moment of sensuous life have no deception; the moment after, both are free; the wide world is before them; the very polygamous beasts do not win their partners by protestations of eternal love; each is free to form another union when it will. Is man the creature whose love is a falsehood by nature; who has one decoy song, crying, "My love is eternal," which in the anguish of childbearing and the years without freedom she is to hear no more? For in spring the bird may call to a new mate and she to whom he cried last year answers to a new call; is woman the only creature for whom there is no spring, and no fresh call when the old song is dead? Is the passion cry with which the man follows one woman for weeks or months or years, chanting that his love ends only with death, with no refrain to say that its death hour is possession and that its life is long because it passes on endlessly to others—is this always a conscious or unconscious lie?

'Sometimes I have believed this—but it is only in a nightmare. When I wake from it I know that the loveliest thing that has blossomed on the earth is the binding of man and woman in one body, one fellowship, and I know that all the failures are only the broken steps which Humanity builds in stairs she is shaping for herself to climb by, which she will have to rebuild better in the future. All man's love cry is not delusion, and the dreams we have dreamed in our girlhood will have their realisation though it may never be by us.

'And, when I see this, the feeling comes over me that, oh, somewhere, the woman must exist whom you could love; perhaps some young girl or some older riper woman, who, if you could meet, would draw out all the tenderness and beauty and self-devotion of your nature which I have never been able to touch, whom you would be loyal to, not for her sake but for your own, because she was yourself. And sometimes it has even come to me that perhaps, at a future day, I might be that woman, that perhaps we may yet meet each other and understand each other, and all the past—'

She had scratched out the whole of this unfinished paragraph. When she wrote next it was with another pen and more hurried and illegible.

'Oh, can't we speak the truth to each other just like two men? Can't we tell each other just what we think and feel? If you can't love me, tell me so; do not be afraid of hurting me. If you feel you cannot love one woman long and that only a succession of women can make you happy, I will try to understand. I will try to be a man with you. Oh, nothing can be so terrible as this awful silence that has been between us through these long years. It is that that has crushed me, always to hold myself down with an iron hand. I do not ask you to love me, only to speak the truth to me, as you would if I were another man.

'Oh Frank, my love, my husband, I have loved you, I have loved you! You will never know how I have loved you! If there were any woman you loved more than all the world, I would do everything in my power to bring her to you. If you had a little child that was yours and not mine, I would take it to my heart and love it as if it were my own. If you, if you don't love me, but you want me still to live with you, I will do all you ask of me; but, oh, we must speak the truth to each other, we must speak the truth. It is this life of lies and subterfuges which we have been living which is dragging down both our souls to hell.'

Here she seemed to have paused a long time and paced the room, for the handwriting when she went on was suddenly quite changed and almost illegible.

'Oh Frank, my love, my husband, please help me! I want to do what is right and I cannot see the way! I am like a little child that has lost itself in the wood and it is dark everywhere. Oh, please take my hand and help me. You are much **stronger than I**; you are the only human being who can help me. Take my hand in yours and let us find the path.'

Here it ended suddenly.

This was the letter held twisted in a roll in her hand as she lay looking at the shadows among the rafters. The baby had grown tired of playing with his toes and had dropped asleep again, and there was no sound in the room but the even breathing of the still sleeping children.

Then Rebekah stood up and went out onto the back veranda. Dressed still in her blue dressing gown, with only the little blue slippers on her bare feet, she walked up the side passage of the yard, past the closed stable door, and out at the back gate.

There the early morning sunlight was shooting down a clear light through the young green oak leaves and playing delicately on the ground; below and beyond, where the pine trees began, single shafts of light fell through the tall branches across their stems and onto the moss and pine needles, wet with the early morning dew. Rebekah stood with her back to the outer wall of the stable gazing into the woods, but her eyes were sightless. Then she began slowly walking up and down close to the wall. Her feet made a little pathway among the weeds and the bits of dry straw that had blown there from the yard gate. Presently she leaned the crown of her head against the roughcast whitewashed wall and looked downwards. She watched the little weeds at her feet and the bits of straw against the wall. Then something rose and surged through her; from her feet it seemed to mount till it reached to her brain and swept all before it. She would go into the house and gather them all in her arms, those children born of lust and falsehood, and they and she and the unborn would pass away together! For an instant the impulse seemed to gain upon her with fearful force. Then slowly her will took command again and she annihilated it. But in years that came, when in some chance newspaper she had read of a woman in despair who had taken her children out of life with her, to her it was no impossible nightmare; she knew the steps by which a woman's soul may pass, till it stands looking down into that awful abysm.

She stood motionless, but with her head pressed to the wall, so that tiny fragments of the rough plaster clung to her soft brown hair. She tried to think; but, like a mockery, from a voice outside herself, broke in the old proverb she had read first in the little brown history,* 'You cannot make a silk purse out of a sow's ear!' She began to walk up and down again. 'You—cannot—make—a silk purse—out—of—a sow's—ear!' And still she paced up and down trying to think.

A coloured man, passing through the woods early to look for his master's cow, paused for a moment in the distance to look at the little figure in its blue dressing gown with bare slippered feet pacing up and down, with its low bent head—and then wondering passed on.

At last, as she walked, that quiet onlooking self, which, except in moments of rare anguish of body and soul, can always regain the mastery, woke in her. She walked along slowly. The question came, 'Why are you agonising here? Are *you* the only creature in the world who has suffered wrong? If life has no value to you, are there not others weaker than yourself to whom you can make it of value? Because in your anguish you are alone and no hand comes to help you, can you put out your hand to none? Are you the only woman in the world who has suffered?'

She raised her head; as she looked up she saw for the first time the green and golden glory of the light through the young oak leaves and the bright shafts shooting through the dark branches of the pine wood and the soft moist earth below. She raised herself and stood looking at it; it seemed as if a soft dew were falling on her mind.

'When all hope is dead in your own life, is there yet nothing left to live for? Are there not others?' She stood looking at the morning world, like a soul come back from a long journey; then she walked in at the little gate. The door of the stable was open now and the stable boy had evidently taken the horses out to exercise. At the end of the passage way she turned into the yard. The milkman had evidently been, for the milk can stood in the stand at the kitchen door, but there was no sign of any other creature moving except two sparrows walking in the sunshine on the gravel of the yard. The green wooden shutter of the servant girl's bedroom was thrown open; but the door was still shut. Rebekah passed across the yard to it, then she stood for a moment and glanced back at the sparrows and the sunshine; and then she knocked at the door. At first there was no answer, and she knocked again. Then a voice called out in Cape Dutch, 'Who is there?' And Rebekah said softly, 'It is I,' and opened the door. She stood for a moment before she stepped down the one step that led into the room.

Before the window on the side of her single bed the servant girl was sitting. She was half dressed: her short black wool, with difficulty parted, was combed out to stand in two solid masses on each side of her head; her small dark face, with its puckered forehead even a little blacker than the rest, was raised as Rebekah opened the door. She had on a red striped flannel petticoat and a pair of crimson satin corsets, embroidered with white flowers; above the corsets, from a mass of frilled white lace, showed her puny black arms and bare shoulders; on the bed beside her lay a white nightdress heavy with bows; on the other side lay the serge dress she was just going to put on. The girl placed a closed fist on each of her hips, and raising her chin in the air looked at Rebekah through her half-closed twinkling eyes.

'*Wat wil jij hê*?'* she said, throwing her chin yet higher.

Rebekah stood silent; all she had determined to say passed from her. The girl threw back her head yet further and burst into a laugh, intended to be defiant but with an undertone of fear, all her white teeth showing between her thick dark lips, as she sat with her fists on her hips.

Then, as Rebekah looked at her, Rebekah knew that it was with that girl even as it was with herself that day.

Softly she turned and went out; she closed the door behind her. Almost on tiptoe, softly and quickly, she ran across the yard, like one who fears something that is following them and tries to escape.

She disappeared through the back door.

It was late that night when Frank returned. He had had a successful day's fishing. The friend with whom he had driven had put him down at the gate. As he walked up the path he saw the front door open and the lamp burning on the stand, but Rebekah was not there to meet him and take his bag.

He set down his things on the hall table and went into the dining room. The lamp was lit, his supper was laid ready, his soda water was cooling in the window, but no one was there. He passed into their bedroom; it was dark; but in his dressing room a light was burning and his change of clothes hung ready for him over the chair, but there was no sign of anyone stirring in the house though it was not yet eleven. The servants were, of course, in bed, but it was the first time in all his married life, except when Rebekah was in childbed or suffering from a miscarriage, that he had come home at such an hour and found no one to attend to him.

He washed and changed his fishing clothes for the light grey lounging suit; then he opened the door into the children's bedroom. That room also was dark, but from the crack under the door he saw there was light in Rebekah's study. He felt no particular wish to call her just then, so he went to the dining room and sat down to his supper. He enjoyed the chicken and bobotie and even took three glasses of wine; but as he finished a sense of the strangeness of things came over him that he did not like. He took a cigar and lit it and went on the front veranda to smoke. After a while he sat down in the rocking chair, but he felt restless. When his cigar was half done he threw it away and lit another. Perhaps after all it would be better to go and see Rebekah now and have it over; it was most unlikely she would speak about anything that had happened in the morning; she never did if you gave her time—she was an awfully sensible woman if only you gave her time—gave her time! He took his new cigar between his first and second fingers and lounged away to the study door in an almost exaggeratedly easy style, as though he were preparing himself for a certain attitude of mind.

He opened the door without knocking and walked in easily.

'Hello, old girl!' he said, and seated himself on the edge of her desk with one knee thrown over the corner and the hand with the lighted cigar resting on it.

'Had a good day!' he said, 'the best I've had this season!—Thought everyone was dead in the house when I came home, it's so quiet.' He raised his cigar to his lips. 'Hope Wilson came and fetched those two cues to mend. Don't like giving the other fellows my favourite cues!' He looked at the smoke from his mouth rather than at her. 'Think I shall go to bed soon, I'm awfully tired!' He expanded his chest and raised his shoulders as people do who yawn, but no yawn came. He knocked some imperceptible ashes off the tip of his cigar with his little finger.

Rebekah, who had been sitting in her chair when he came, still sat there leaning back, with her head a little raised. Now she leaned forward a little and laid her hand on a large sheet of open blue foolscap paper on the desk on which there were some lines written in large clear characters.

'You must take this,' she said slowly, 'whether you wish to or not'—she was looking full up at him—'and tomorrow I want your answer.'

He put his cigar back into his mouth and looked at her. He had an unpleasant sensation that she was looking at him as if she were looking at a tree or a wall—or any other man—not at *him*. The little sensitive almost imperceptible contraction about her mouth and eye, that he was always accustomed to see when she looked at him and spoke, seemed not there.

'Last night,' she continued, 'when I wrote that letter that you called a book and would not take, I said there were three lines of action on which I was willing our future relationship to each other should be based—now there are only two!'

He took the cigar from his mouth as if to speak, but something stopped him.

'They are there,' she said, moving the paper towards him. 'They are short, and will not take you more than sixty seconds to read.' She rested her fingers on the paper as she spoke. He had an unpleasant sensation as he looked at her that she was growing physically taller and larger by the moment.

'Either,' she said, looking at him, 'you must procure a legal divorce from me; in which case, both you and I will be free and may marry again, or not, as we wish. I would take the children to my farm or to my parents; if you wish it, I will support them; if, as I hope you do, you feel it is your duty, you can assist in their support. Under any conditions, we shall be free, and I think this is the best course; it is the one I prefer.' She let her fingers drop on the paper. 'If, on the other hand, you do not like these conditions, if you are afraid of what the world will say, then there is another course.' She looked at him, but, as though absorbed in her own thought, she hardly seemed to see him: 'I will, if you wish, continue to live in this house. I will look after your children and I will attend to your material wants; I will provide for my personal needs as I have already done for some years; but you will understand that, from tonight, you and I will never be anything more to each other than any man or woman who pass one another in the street for the first time. You will be free to lead your own life, to think your own thoughts, to form your own friendships; but you will understand that I also am equally free. Last night I gave you the choice of a third course; tonight there are only these two. You can let me know your decision tomorrow before twelve o'clock.' She pointed to the paper on the table.

He looked down at her; for a moment he thought of bursting into a fit of rage such as had always silenced her; he would say he was shamefully treated, swear at her, and violently close the door; but that intuitive perception, which in him took the place of reason and was almost preternaturally keen where his own interests were concerned, told him it would be useless now.

He looked down at her curiously. 'Oh, it's all too ridiculous, Rebekah; what do you mean? You are tired, little woman'—he spoke gently—'your condition makes you take these silly little fancies into your head! You need a good night's rest. How you live, with so little sleep as you take, I don't know! I'd be a washed-out rag!—I'm jolly tired too tonight,' he said slowly, rising from the desk and drawing back his shoulders; 'I've had a long, tiring day of it. I can hardly keep my eyes open.'

She rose too. 'Take that paper,' she said quietly; 'I have put it down in writing to avoid any mistake. I have kept a copy.' She folded it up and held it out to him.

He was going to speak; he looked into her face, and a sense of something that seemed almost preternatural and inverted came over him. It was as if a man called to his own dog, who had followed him for years, and it walked by with its head down, no quiver even in its tail, and turned a dead eye on him. He took the paper from her, holding it a little in one hand, while in the other he held the lighted cigar. He moved almost awkwardly from one leg to the other.

'Well, I'll take it, of course, as you want me to,' he said; 'but you know, of course, it's absolutely ridiculous! You're tired tonight, that's what it is!' He tried to smile, but it died away at the corners of his mouth in a kind of twitch. 'Of course, you must know it's all nonsense. I'm just taking it not to upset you tonight.' He put it in his pocket. 'I'm really awfully tired! I think I'll turn in. I suppose you're going to sit up a bit?'

He turned towards the door; when he had opened it and was going out, he began to recover himself; he turned and looked back at her with the door in his hand.

'Oh, this is all very well, you know,' he laughed, but with his mouth a little on one side; 'we know what'll happen before tomorrow morning! It won't be dawn, a fellow'll just be having his first sleep and he'll feel a tickling at the back of his neck; some small individual shedding tears upon it and combing out little curls with her fingers—kissing them too!—Eh?' He laughed again. 'Happened before—hasn't it?'

Rebekah was still standing by the desk, staring at him.

'It'll be all right in the morning!—Eh?—Goodnight!' He shut the door behind him. When he was on the other side, the smile died out. Deep in his heart he knew it would not be all right in the morning. He had seen that look on the face of women before, and he knew what it meant. Without the shadow of a doubt he knew that the quicklime had ceased to act, that the net was broken, that the bird was out! He walked through the dark bedrooms into the dining room and took the paper from his pocket and read it under the hanging lamp. There were only twenty lines in a neat round hand, stating two alternatives. He walked up and down the room once or twice with it in his hand; then he put it in his pocket and walked to the window, lifting the corner of the blind a little. The window of the dining room looked out into the back yard as the window of the bedroom did. The white moonlight was flooding the yard; when he looked across it to the servant's room it seemed to him that both door and window stood wide open. He put his face close to the pane. The door of the servant's room was exactly opposite the dining-room window, and as the moonlight fell in at the open door it seemed to him that the green box which had always stood just inside the door was not there.

He drew a soft, almost noiseless, indrawn whistle, and let the blind fall. He paced the room twice; then, glancing round to see that the door into the bedroom was closed, and listening to hear if there was any sound, he went out into the back yard. At first he walked as if to go to the stable passage; then, glancing once back at the house, he walked to the door of the servant's room and looked in. It was empty. A great splash of whitewash lay on the earthen floor where the patch of moonlight fell in through the door; the room held nothing but a bare iron bedstead standing in the centre, and there was a strong smell of fresh whitewash. So that was it!

A flush of anger rose to his face as he turned quickly and walked to the house. Was it that devil of a stable boy? He had given him ten shillings twice, just to keep quiet in case he had noticed anything. Was it the girl herself who had talked?—you never could trust a nigger, do what you would for them!—had Rebekah noticed anything for herself?—He walked into the dining room and took another cigar from the mantelshelf and bit off the end, throwing it into the waste-paper basket, but he did not light it. It had all come of being too soft-hearted! He ought to have sent her away two months ago, when she first told him, instead of listening to all her nonsense. If her mother did cut up rough about it he could easily have settled it with money. It was all nonsense about her coming to talk to Rebekah about it—she would have had nothing to gain! And now Rebekah knew! He had been an absolute fool—that was what he had been!

He bit the end of his cigar again, forgetting what he had done, and began to pace the room once more with the unlighted cigar between his first and second fingers. After a while he lit the cigar and began to smoke, blowing clouds of smoke, and his brain began to work smoothly and quietly. He faced the entire position now that there was no escape. Whatever the girl might do and wherever she might go, it really did not matter, now Rebekah knew! At the worst, if she did turn up again, it would only be a matter of a few shillings a week—a dirty, beastly, little nigger!—but perhaps it would never be born? There flashed through his mind the rate of infant mortality among the coloured population which he had seen in some paper: at the worst that could be all set right with money; there was no need to think of it.

Then he walked, smoking more slowly and looking down. After a time he went and stood still before the mantelpiece, deep in thought.

Then he sat down at the little desk in the corner where Rebekah wrote her orders and kept her accounts. He took a sheet of paper and wrote:

'DEAREST WIFE,

'A certain little person was so cut-uppie tonight that I quite forgot to tell her I have to start for Caledon* before five o'clock tomorrow. I have to go and see about some farms; the man will be waiting for me at the hotel with his cart. I shall be gone from a week to ten days. I won't wake you and the children, as no doubt you will be asleep when I start. I'll write if there's any chance, but it's not very likely, as it's an out-of-the-way part. Expect me when you see me. Take care of yourself and the children.

'Your loving husband,

'Frank.'

He put it in an envelope and closed it and put it in his breast pocket. Then he turned out the lamp and went to his dressing room. He put the few clothes he would need into a small portmanteau and stood it out of sight behind the door; then he undressed. He listened for a moment near the door of the children's room, but there was no sound, so no doubt she was still in her study. He took up the lamp and went to the bedroom, set it down on the stand at the bedside, and then, before he took off his dressing gown and opened the bed, he sat on the bedside with his legs stretched out and folded across each other; and for a long time he sat looking down at his bare feet. Then he took Rebekah's paper out of the pocket of his dressing gown and read it again. An angry flush rose to his face and dyed it red at the top of his forehead. 'And in that case, both you and I would be free to marry again.' How could Rebekah write a thing like that! She, whom he had always looked upon as the type of all that was pure and womanly, to talk of giving herself to another man! He crumpled the paper in his hand. NO, there would be no divorce. It was impure, it was unclean for her even to talk of such a thing. It was enough to kill all a man's faith in women! He rose as if to pace the room, then he sat down again. But of course there was no need to consider that—the scandal—the gossip—and, what would be gained by it? He fell to considering the other proposition. After all it was not so bad! If she said she would do a thing, she would go through with it. She would be always there to look after the house and children; no one would know anything; if there was one thing you could depend on Rebekah for, it was to hold her tongue. A more placid look came over his face and all signs of anger died. Even if she carried out what she said she would, it would not be bad. When a woman has borne four children and had several miscarriages, she's not just what she was when you married her, and after seven years of marriage it would be nonsense to pretend there was very much romance: a slight placid expansion, almost like a smile, spread over his lips and drew back the corners of his mouth; it was the look of deep, inward contentment with himself and the world that made people call him the best-tempered jolliest man in his club. She was not the only woman in the world! A dreamy smile played over his face, as if he were recalling past events. If only he got away for ten days, and avoided discussing matters while they were hot; that was the great thing. At the end of that time when he came back—well, if it had to be discussed—his forehead contracted a little at the thought—it would be quite a different matter from discussing it now. Give her time, give her time! Rebekah was a sensible woman if you gave her time and didn't take her on the hop while she was warm. He sat looking down at his feet. Who could tell but that, after a time, she—then he stopped, and knit his forehead; he knew that, as between him and her, things were at an end forever. He got up and threw his dressing gown over a chair. It was all a damned nuisance! But it was no use worrying about it any more. He got into bed. At the head of the bed a little silk satchel hung in which Rebekah always put the daily papers for him to read after he got into bed. He took out the evening's sheet and began to read the account of the last cricket match at Sea Point.* He ran his eyes carefully down the row of figures, noting who had done well and who had not, but his thoughts wandered, and when he had gone twice over the figures he stuck the paper back in the holder; he turned the lamp out and drew the cover up over his shoulder and turned his face on one side. After all, the great thing was just to give her time! Things would all settle themselves somehow! In ten minutes he had gone to sleep.

When her husband had closed the door of her study, Rebekah stood silent for a moment looking at it. Then she sat down in her armchair and leaned her head back against it. She folded her hands over her head and looked up at the dark little ceiling. She drew a long breath; but it was not the ceiling of the little room she saw as she sat there staring upwards. It was as though a vast dome were reared over her, as though a dark pall, which for years had been stretched out just above her, were folded up and removed and she looked up into almost infinite space. So wide, so still, so peaceful—and she was alone there!

After half an hour she stood up; as she turned out the lamp and lit the candle to take to the room, a curious sensation came to her, as if she were a little child again. Even the candle she had lighted and held in her hand seemed like candles used to, long ago. At the door of the room she turned and looked back; she seemed to have come from a long journey and to be seeing it all again—the little statue of Hercules in the corner which she had bought when she first married, her shelves with the books, the cabinet with the fossils in it that she had loved so; she saw them all as she used to see them. It seemed as if some great crease of anguish which had lain in her brain for years had smoothed itself out.

She closed the door and went to her little stretcher between the boys' beds. She had not slept for thirty-six hours. She undressed and put out her light, and in a few minutes was in a deep unbroken sleep.

When the stable boy brought the coffee to her door early the next morning, he told her that his master had called him before daylight to make coffee and to drive him to Town, and he gave her a letter his master had left for her. She opened it before the window and read it. A relaxation passed over her lips as she finished it: it was not bitterness, it was not disappointment; it was a placid recognition of the inevitable which always repeats itself.

He did not return till the eighth day. A nurse met him at the front door. She said Rebekah had been confined four days before of a seven months' child. She had had a bad time, and, until the day before, her life had been despaired of. The child, she said, was very puny, but it was alive. She had driven out to her farm twice, once the day before he left and again the next day, and the jolting might have been too much for her, otherwise there was no explanation of her illness. He could not see her, the nurse said, but he might see the child. She took him into his own bedroom. Rebekah lay in the children's room, where she had been taken ill; she had refused to be removed into the large room. From the small bed in the corner the nurse took up a pillow and uncovered on it a tiny morsel of flesh, eyebrowless, hairless, with a small, wizened face. He had been proud of his other children; they had all weighed ten or twelve pounds, and people had called them prize babies; he'd even boasted of them to men at his club. For this sorrowful, tiny thing he had a feeling of horror, almost of loathing; he turned away from it quickly. He told the nurse as Rebekah was so ill he would go to an hotel in Town, to save giving trouble in the house; but he asked her to let him know at once if she were worse or there was anything she needed, and he would himself try to come out in the evening to hear how she was.

He went to his dressing room and filled his portmanteau with the things he would need in Town, then carrying it in his hand he walked through the dining room. The room looked dusty and unused. On the table in the corner stood her work basket, on the top of which lay one of his white shirts onto which she had been sewing a new wristband; the needle was stuck upright into the work with the thimble balanced on the top, as she had left it the last day when she was taken ill. As he looked at it, a sensation of what was perhaps the sharpest pain he ever felt in the course of his life over anything that did not touch him personally ran through him. He passed on quickly to the front veranda and down the garden path. All her lilies and roses were in bloom, and as the sun shone on them the mignonette and verbena sent up a strong scent; the trowel she had been weeding with lay in the soft mould near the garden gate. He hurried out quickly and shut the gate and walked down the Avenue.

After all, it was not his fault if she chose to go driving out two days running in a jolting cart. She had said she was not going to the farm again till after the baby was born—and she might yet get well again! As he passed the little suburban chemist's shop at the corner, he went in and bought two bottles of scent of a kind he knew she liked when she was ill, and ordered the chemist to send it up at once to the house with a cut-glass spray. After he got into the train he resolved to go and buy three books he had heard her say she would like and a little ring they had seen in the window of a jeweller's shop in Adderley Street the last time they were out together, which she had admired. She so seldom noticed jewellery or anything of that kind; and he had never given her anything since they were married. When he got out he went to the bookseller's and ordered the books to be sent out at once; then he walked up the street to the jeweller's; just as he was going in he stopped; after all, the ring would cost seven or eight pounds, and she might not really care for it; anyhow, he could get it later. Then he walked on to his office. It was too late to settle down to work before lunch, so he soon went out. On the way to the club he met a friend who condoled with him on his wife's serious illness and they went in and had a drink together—a thing he seldom did—and they had a short game of billiards together before lunch. After lunch he felt better and went back to his office.

When the office closed he went out to the suburbs to hear how his wife was. The nurse met him at the door; she said Rebekah had been sleeping quietly the greater part of the day, that the fever had quite left her and the doctors thought the danger was passed. She had asked to see the baby—a thing she had not done yet. He said he would not come in, and walked down the Avenue again. After all, she was *not* going to die; she would have had to be ill and have the baby some time; perhaps it was just as well it came when it did! It would be a week certainly before he could see her, and then probably a fortnight before they could discuss things. It would be very different from discussing everything while it was still fresh! After all, how much better it was to let things slide! Men made half their own troubles by walking up to things and grasping hold of them. Perhaps it was just as well everything was as it was!

A little lower down the Avenue he met an old friend, who asked how his wife was and condoled with him and asked him to come in to dinner. All the family were very kind and sympathetic and after dinner the two eldest daughters played and sang for him.

CHAPTER IX

CART TRACKS IN THE SAND

UP-COUNTRY, in the red karroo,* was the town where Aunt Mary-Anna lived,* red karroo to right of it, red karroo to left. A river bed* ran below the town, in winter full of dried mud banks and reaches of gravel and bare stone, but, in the summer rains, coming down red and full, the dark, sand-laden water lying level with the banks and bearing on its waves trees and stumps, the carcasses of drowned animals, and even sometimes at long intervals a human corpse.*

All round the plain were flat-topped mountains, some broken into jagged points, but still bearing the marks, in their flat structure, of what had been the shores of seas and lakes, the remains of whose mammoth amphibious beasts lay still within the stratified shale, turned in the course of the ages to stone themselves.

There were three churches in the town and a great square full of sand with shops and houses round it, where, in the early morning, buck-wagons* drawn by long teams of oxen rolled slowly in, laden with produce from the country, skins and pumpkins and firewood, bags of meal or mielies and sometimes butter and garden growths; and the little market master held the morning market. There the townsmen gathered to hear the latest news and send round the latest gossip, till by eight o'clock they had all gone home to their breakfasts, the wagons had rolled out and the square was left empty and silent enough all day, crossed occasionally by customers making their way to the different shops or businessmen going home to their meals, and, at eleven o'clock, by streams of men coming to the hotel at the corner* where they went to have their morning drink of soda and brandy and to smoke and chat for a while on the hotel stoep.

Three times a week the postcart with its dusty wheels and horses came in, blowing its bugle and bringing its news from the outer world, and everyone hurried to the post office to get their letters. And twice a week came Cobb and Co.'s* great coaches, swinging on their great leather straps; and their teams of six horses, bearing passengers to and from the Diamond Fields,* drew up before the hotel door, when for two hours the town was alive and excited with the new arrivals;

then the horses would be put in again and pass away in a cloud of dust and the town would be left to its silent monotony.

There were two croquet clubs in the place frequented by the members of two churches which formed the two great cliques; there was a courthouse where occasionally the members of one church gave a dance which the other church thought wicked and never went to, and once or twice a year some travelling showman would arrive and give an entertainment there. Every year the members of each church had a large Sunday-school picnic to which all the members of that congregation went; and sometimes a lady would give a high tea and invite a few friends, for no one dined late there.

In the upper part of the town there were rows of little flat houses, generally kept shut up and empty, where the Dutch farmers stayed when they came in once in three months to the Lord's Supper ('Nagmaal'*) and now and then to the Sunday services in the weeks between. But on Monday they all went out again, and the houses were left empty, and the town to its English inhabitants.

During nine months of the year, while the winds blew, clouds of dust whirled along the streets before thunderstorms; when the gusts came, great clouds of sand rose from the market square and met the still mightier clouds raised from the wide sandy plain; and the town was shrouded in sand.

It was a dull narrow little life enough, lived there among the flat-roofed houses, far removed from the currents of life and thought of the great world beyond.

Yet, if some summer morning you rose at half past four and went out to the koppie at the end of the town and climbed its round black ironstones,* and stood looking down at the little town with its long rows of houses and the little brown huts of the Kaffir Location* sleeping at your feet in the still blue morning air, while the damp of the night yet rested on everything and nothing moved or stirred, except where here and there a Kaffir servant might be seen hurrying from the Location to the town, her shawl drawn tight about her to shut out the chill morning air; till by and by, from some of the chimneys in the town, long blue curls of smoke began to rise, standing upright and almost motionless in the still air; then suddenly the bleak moist stone on which you stood turned golden at your feet; a shaft of light had shot across the plain and struck it; another came, and the little ice-plant in the crevice of the rock at your feet glittered in every crystal drop; then another, and the whole plain was golden and the roofs of the little flat houses glinted—then the town was beautiful.

Bertie's aunt and uncle lived in a street leading out of the square, so close to it that from the front windows you could see half across it. It was an old dingy house, a foot lower than the street and the water furrow above, with a little strip of flower garden six feet wide and a low paling before it.

Her uncle's business place was on another plot across the square. He was a general agent; he held auction sales, conducted cases in the little magistrate's court, drew up wills and managed estates, and speculated on his own account. He was thin, silent, and rather hatchet-faced: he was regarded by his fellow townsmen as a clever businessman, though he was said to have lately burnt his fingers in some speculation and to have lost on a company he had fitted out and sent up to the Diamond Fields; he was hard in business matters and said to love money; but he was a leading man in the church of which he was a member and was regarded as one of the principal men in the town. More than twenty years before he had married Bertie's aunt, whom he had met when she was on a visit from England to her sister, the little mother at the old farm; and had brought her to his little up-country town, where they had lived in the same house ever since, with the same furniture and the same strip of flower garden, and where their two daughters, now in England, had been born. Her aunt was not unlike the little mother in feature, but tall and thin and much less pretty, and with a cold measured manner. Her head, like Bertie's, was small compared to the size of her body, and three rows of short faded white curls hung on each side of her head. In the chapel she was the leader at prayer meetings and all religious gatherings and was one of the most esteemed women of the town.

Besides her uncle and aunt, there was no one in the house but Dorcas,* the tall, heavy-faced Kaffir servant, who always wore a red kerchief* bound across her head and helped in the kitchen.

Once Bertie might have found the dingy, flat little house with its three inhabitants lonely. Now she loved it.

On the first day when Bertie was unpacking her clothes her aunt admired her mantle, and Bertie had begged her aunt for her old silk shawl and out of it by the next Sunday had made a mantle exactly like her own, and had re-made her aunt's bonnet and re-trimmed it with lace from one of her own ball dresses; so that when Aunt Mary-Anna appeared in chapel everyone thought it was a new mantle and bonnet. Some said that if the general agent were really in business difficulties she should not purchase such expensive things, others that perhaps they were presents from a rich niece in Cape Town, but everyone admired them.

The next week Bertie got from her uncle a large roll of flower-covered chintz that had been lying in his sale room for months and with it made covers for every chair and sofa, till all the old dingy furniture blossomed out in pink roses. And the next week, when her aunt went to a farm for three days, she bought with her own money some cheap wallpaper and, with Dorcas to help her, re-papered the passage and the front parlour, she standing at the top of the ladder and Dorcas at the bottom; and she took up the carpet in the parlour that had lain there for twenty-four years and cut it down the middle and re-sewed it so that the worn centre came to the sides, when, by placing furniture over the worn patches, it looked like a new carpet; so that when Aunt Mary-Anna returned she was filled with surprise and delight; and the house looked as if the general agent were re-furnishing.

Early in the morning Bertie was up making curry and hot rolls for breakfast; for dinner and supper she made sosatie* and bobotie and pumpkin fritters and puffs and grilled chops, as she had learnt from old Ayah; and the hatchet face of the general agent, who for twenty-four years had suffered from bad cooking, seemed to be perceptibly filling out. When she had no cooking to do, she rummaged her aunt's old wardrobe and boxes and, from ends of lace and bits of old material, shaped little caps and aprons, and, by unpicking and cleaning and re-shaping old dresses, made her aunt's wardrobe full of wearable dresses.

'I really don't know how we ever got on without you,' her aunt used to say. 'You must never leave us, or, if you do, you must promise to remain for eight months after the girls come home, so that they may learn from you.'

Even her silent uncle praised her food, and, as he passed through the kitchen where she was stooping over a pot, stirring its contents, would say, 'Our little cook must not burn her face too much, though I know it's something good she's going to turn out';* and Bertie's cheeks would flush a deeper red, more with pride and happiness than from the heat of the fire.

Even Dorcas liked her; she coaxed her so gently, and, when Bertie had given her a white silk kerchief to tie in with her red one on Sundays and had shown her how to arrange it round her head and had made her a cotton blouse with red butterflies on it, Dorcas would do anything for her.

'I am very very happy here,' she wrote to Rebekah; 'I should never like to go away. Everyone loves me.'

After the first Sunday when Bertie appeared in church, the ladies of the town had called to see her, and her aunt said it was necessary she should return their calls with her; but after that she refused to go out. She accepted no invitations to picnics or parties and declined to join the croquet club. At first her aunt tried to persuade her to go out; but when she found she really did not wish to go and that Bertie's staying at home gave her more time to attend prayer meetings and classes and to fulfil her duties as leading woman in the church, she gave way; and the only times when Bertie was ever seen out were when she went twice to church every Sunday and once on a week night, and when she now and then went out shopping for her aunt. The mothers of the place all praised her and held her up to their daughters as an example of devotion to hard work and duty.

When she first came the young girls of the place felt to her much as the ducks in a farmyard might to one that had wandered in from the open. They all said she was not nearly so pretty as the men said, that she looked proud and her curls were not natural. But when, after some weeks, they found she never crossed their paths, when she had lent them the patterns of her dresses and had helped two of the prettiest girls in the place to make bonnets for themselves exactly like her own, they all said she was nice and much the prettiest girl that had ever come to the town, that her curly hair was beautiful, and that they thought her aunt unkind to keep her so much at home.

The young men had not many opportunities of seeing her except in church; two, who had always gone to the other church, began to attend there, and two who had sat in the centre moved into a wing so that they sat opposite the general agent's pew. On Sunday and week nights such as knew the general agent and his wife hurried to the church door and tried to walk home with them. But Bertie seemed always to manage to walk between her uncle and aunt; and if they spoke across to her as they walked she said 'yes' or 'no' and seemed not to see them. And if she went to a shop to buy anything, and the young shopman spoke to her of the weather or the dust or of anything but business, she answered him quickly and softly and went out.

Even the magistrate's clerk, who wore a black coat and carried a little walking stick, and said there was no one in the town he could associate with, and never took notice of any girl, called three times formally at the general agent's after Bertie came; but as she did not appear, he had to content himself with sitting opposite the general agent's pew.

Bertie was very happy all day. If ever, as she worked, a thought came to her she did not like, she put it from her quickly, saying within herself, 'They all love me here! I will never go away! They will always let me stay.'

Only at night when she had gone to bed and put out the light and was just dropping off to sleep, suddenly the old dream which she used to have on the farm when she was a little child used to come back to her—she was running down the road in the dark and on, behind her, came something with heavy breath; she knew its tongue lolled out and she heard its steps, and as she ran it came nearer and nearer!—till she woke shrieking; and Rebekah used to hear her and come from her bed and lie beside her and sing 'London's Burning! Fire! Fire!'* till she went to sleep.

Now it often came back to her; she would wake with the bed trembling beneath her and would sit up wringing her hands, before she remembered where she was. Then she would lie down quickly and pull the cover close over her head and take a pillow and hold it longways against her and clasp it tight, with both arms around it, so that it seemed like something living she was clinging to.

One day at breakfast her uncle brought the post in and gave her a letter. She read it, sitting behind the coffee urn at the head of the table.

'I hope you have no bad news, my dear,' Aunt Mary-Anna said.

'Oh no,' Bertie said, 'it's from Mother.' But when breakfast was over she hurried to her own room and knelt down beside the bed and laid the letter open before her and read it through. As she read her cheeks darkened slowly to a red as deep as the darkest of Rebekah's roses in the garden at Cape Town. She buried her burning face in the letter and knelt motionless. What the letter said was this:

'MY DEAR BABY-BERTIE,

'I am glad you are so happy at your aunt's, but I wish you could come home by Xmas time. John-Ferdinand and Veronica come over and spend every Sunday with us and generally drive over once a week, so I'm not so lonely. But Veronica is going to have a baby at Xmas time and I shall have to go and stay with her for some weeks. Of course, old Ayah can stay and look after the house and your father, but come if you can, unless your aunt very much wants you and you want to stay.'

Then came much farm news that she read without noting; then came the P.S.

'Veronica is looking so well. . . . She has a lovely colour and her face is getting quite round. . . . You would hardly know her.'

After a time Bertie lifted her face from the letter; it was growing slowly white; she put it in her breast and went to knead the bread in the kitchen.

After dinner, when her aunt was asleep and her uncle had gone to his business, she slipped out and went to a shop across the square. There she bought the finest muslin and lace and embroidery the town held and needles and thread even finer than those she generally used; then she slipped back to her own room and all the afternoon sat cutting out and sewing. She got up early the next morning as soon as the sun rose and went back to her work, and at night she sat sewing at her bedside till one or two o'clock. Her aunt noticed that now, as soon as her work was done, she went to her own room, but thought she was doing sewing for herself.

Slowly the scores of little tucks and the fine embroidery shaped themselves. At the end of a week there were two tiny armholes. Again and again she would stop in her work to put her fingers into them and fill them out. At the end of a fortnight the long white robe with its delicate invisible stitching was almost complete. At night, before she put it away, she would lay it out on the bed, putting a pillow at the top and filling it out so that it almost seemed there was something inside it; and she would stand across the room looking at it. One day it was finished. She packed it in white tissue paper with a few little bits of fresh lavender put in it. She tied it with pink ribbons and packed it into a handkerchief box with red rosebuds on the lid; then she carefully folded brown paper round it and tied it with string across and across. When her aunt went to sleep after dinner, again she stole out and went to the post office and stamped it and sent it off. After it was gone she was always picturing how it travelled: it would take seven days to reach the farm; it might have to wait two days at the post office in the village if no special messenger came to fetch it; then on Sunday morning it would get to the farm; someone would open it. She never would let herself think any further; she began picturing the journey over again.

The poet, when his heart is weighted, writes a sonnet, and the painter paints a picture, and the thinker throws himself into the world of thought, and the publican and the man of business may throw themselves into the world of action; but the woman who is only a woman, what has she but her needle? In that torn bit of brown leather brace* worked through and through with yellow silk, in that bit of white rag with invisible stitching, lying among the fallen leaves and rubbish that the wind has blown into the gutter or the street corner, lies all the passion of some woman's soul finding voiceless expression. Has the pen or the pencil dipped so deep in the blood of the human race as the needle?

After that the summer began to grow hotter, every afternoon clouds of dust wheeled along the streets and over the plains; and now and then a thunderstorm broke at four o'clock and laid the dust for that day.

The week before Christmas the post brought no letter for Bertie, but her aunt came into the kitchen where she was shelling peas and said she had had a few lines from the little mother, who could not write to Bertie because at six o'clock on the day she wrote Veronica had had a fine little boy. Mother and child were doing well. Bertie went on shelling the peas and got dinner ready; after dinner she went to bed with a sick headache and did not come to supper, but early the next morning she was up kneading the bread and said she was quite well. Some days after that came the news that Rebekah also had a little son, born prematurely, and that she was very ill; then news that she was better. Then a long time passed when nothing happened.

Slowly the summer heat began to die and the nights to become cool, sometimes almost sharp. All the housewives were busy plucking fruit and drying and preserving. Bertie had made rows and rows of bottles of peach and quince jam which lined the shelves of her aunt's pantry; and now she was making watermelon preserve. Her aunt's daughters would be out in five months, and everything was being got ready for the teas and suppers when they came.

Then a curious experience began to come to Bertie. It was as though a weight seemed always resting on her; it might be the change to the autumn's coolness, but something heavy seemed always pressing on her. She tried to shake it off; but from being a vague feeling it grew till it almost took definite shape. Sometimes if she went out to a shop or to carry a message to her uncle's office, if girls she met passed her and she wished them good day they returned her greeting, but, if she did not, they seemed to pass without seeing her. When one of her aunt's women friends called and she went to open the door, they did not smile, but asked gravely if her aunt was in. It might have been her fancy, but it seemed to her that when her uncle and aunt spoke to her they did not look at her, and they spoke more seldom. A curious silence seemed to have settled down on the house. One morning, when her aunt was having her breakfast in bed and Bertie sat, as she always did, at the table behind the tray, she looked up suddenly and saw her uncle, who sat at the other end of the table, looking at her intently over the top of the newspaper he held. The moment he saw she had noticed him he dropped his eyes and raised the paper so that only the top of his head was visible over it; and several times, when she came into a room where her uncle and aunt were, they were talking together in a low tone, but stopped at once when she came in.

On Sundays after church there were still some young men about the door, but, if the general agent did not speak to them, they did not force their company as they used to, and the three walked home alone together. One Sunday the magistrate's clerk, who had never waited near the door like other young men, walked straight up to them and forced his way in between Bertie and her uncle and walked next to her, talking to her; but there seemed something strange in the way he walked and talked, looking round at all the people they passed, as if he were challenging them to see where he walked. That afternoon, when her uncle and aunt were sleeping, Bertie sat alone in her bedroom with her hands in her lap; it seemed to her all the while that a lump kept rising in her throat and she wanted to cry, though she could not tell why.

The autumn was closing in fast now, the leaves were falling from the trees in the street and filling the furrows and covering the side-walks in the lower part of the town. In the gardens everything but the winter crops was drying out.

One afternoon about five o'clock Bertie sat in the little parlour that looked out across the garden into the street; she sat sewing before the window on the little low chair on which she always sat, and her aunt sat opposite in a high-backed cane rocking chair, knitting. For nearly an hour they had sat there with no sound but the click of Aunt Mary-Anna's needles to break the silence. The sky was becoming slightly overcast as though it was going to rain, and the light was already beginning to grow duller in the little low room. Suddenly Bertie leaned forward and laid her hand, with the threaded needle in it, on her aunt's knee.

'Aunt Mary-Anna,' she said quickly, in a low, slightly thick voice, 'have I done anything to displease you? Are you angry with me?'

'No, Bertie, no,' she said, knitting quickly. She dropped three stitches but knitted on without noticing them.

'I was so afraid I had done something to displease you,' Bertie said, looking up at her.

'No—you have done nothing to me, Bertie.' She knitted on without looking at her. 'And yet,' she said, after a pause, 'it is perhaps quite as well you spoke, because I have been wishing to speak to you. Your uncle and I think'—she waited a little—'it is perhaps quite as well you went home. In fact, your uncle wrote yesterday to your father, and posted the letter today, to say you would be leaving us by next Thursday's postcart, and they must send to meet you at the town next week.'

Bertie sat upright in her chair, looking at her aunt with wide-open eyes.

'But I can't go home, I don't want to go,' she said, in a low thick voice. 'You said I could stay here with you. Oh, what have I done?'

For a moment Aunt Mary-Anna knitted on blunderingly, then she stopped and looked at Bertie. 'There is no need for us to discuss the matter, my dear. You have been very kind and of great use to me, and your uncle and I will always be grateful for the many ways in which you have helped us. But we both think it best you should go home now. You have been here nearly six months and your mother may be wanting you.'

'But you said I could stay! Oh, please let me stay! I don't want to go! I can't go back there!' She laid her hand again on Aunt Mary-Anna's knee and looked up at her with large wide-open eyes.

Aunt Mary-Anna hesitated. Then she drew herself up. 'Perhaps I had better tell you the truth, Bertie. It is as well you should know it. People here have been saying very strange things about you.' Bertie looked up into her face with eyes that seemed to grow wider. 'Your uncle heard something first in the town, and he told me; and afterwards the minister's wife called and told me the same thing. She said she felt it her duty to tell me what people were saying. It is the common talk of the town now. I don't believe a word of it, neither does your uncle; and I have told everyone so who has spoken to me. And after you have gone I shall deny it everywhere. But with my two girls coming home, you will understand, Bertie, that, as it is something regarding your conduct as a young girl, I could not have you staying on here with them. It may be all perfectly untrue, my dear'—there was something almost of kindliness in Aunt Mary-Anna's tone—'but a woman's character is like gossamer, when you've once dropped it in the mud and pulled it about it can never be put right again. With a man it's different; he can live down anything. People say, "Oh, he was young, he's changed"; they never say that of a woman; but the soap isn't invented that can wash a woman's character clean.'

Bertie leaned further forward, looking at her. Her aunt moved restlessly.

'Of course I don't believe a word of it; it's just silly talk of what happened when you were a schoolgirl of fifteen. I know there's no truth in it. But that doesn't make any practical difference. You are one of the best girls I ever knew.' Bertie leaned yet more forward and laid her hand on her aunt's knee.

'But if it is true?' she whispered.

Her aunt drew herself up suddenly and looked down at her wide eyes. Bertie stretched out both her hands; it seemed as if she would have caught hold of her aunt's hands. 'I'll tell you—I'll tell you everything!'

Aunt Mary-Anna rose quickly. 'Really, Bertie, I am astonished at you! I will beg of you to tell me nothing. If there is any truth in what they have been saying about you, the least you can do is to keep quiet about it. I have asked you no questions, and you should at least leave me the power of denying it. You have cost me trouble enough as it is. Your mother and Rebekah did very wrong in letting you come here, knowing I had young girls.'

'Oh, they don't know! No one knows! I have only told one person about it!' Bertie rose and stood before her. A blind look was in her eyes as though she saw nothing; she moved her hands aimlessly. 'I was so young,' she wailed suddenly. 'Oh!'—she moved her hands.

'Will you lower your voice, Bertie! Do you want Dorcas, who is in the kitchen, to hear everything you say! If you want to tell anyone about it, tell your mother and your sister.'

'Oh, I can't! They must never know! They think I'm a baby still!—Oh, I can't go home! I never can go home!'

'You must go home,' said her aunt quietly, 'and not later than by next Thursday's cart.'

At that moment there was a sound at the front door and of feet in the passage, and then the general agent flung open the door of the little parlour. Beside him shuffled a little figure. He ushered him in. Aunt Mary-Anna turned quickly to the door; but Bertie still stood motionless before the window, where the quickly fading light fell full on her. She had a little crimson rosebud fastened at the throat of her white dress, which made her face of a more deadly paleness under its cloud of brown curling hair, and the eyelashes of her drooping eyes seemed printed on her cheeks. Aunt Mary-Anna stepped forward to greet the visitor, whom she had evidently met before. She shook hands with him and asked him if he had arrived by that evening's coach from the Fields.*

He was a small man of about fifty, with slightly bent shoulders and thin, small limbs. His face was of a dull oriental pallor, and his piercing dark eyes and marked nose proclaimed him at once a Jew; above a high square forehead rose a tower of stiffly curling, grey, upright hair. He spoke with a strong foreign accent. The general agent introduced him to Bertie. She gave him a cold dead hand without looking at him and then turned slowly to the window and with her back to the room stood looking out, her hands hanging lifeless at either side. The Jew took his seat on a small chair in the dark corner between the sideboard and the wall, and twisted his feet into the legs of the chair. The general agent begged him to stay to supper; he assented shortly and sat looking keenly about the room, now at Bertie's figure as she stood before the window, and then at the furniture, at the hanging lamp and the old piano and whatnot* and then back at Bertie. Her aunt asked her to go and put supper ready, and she left the room without looking round. Presently her aunt came into the kitchen and asked her to prepare the best supper she could, as their visitor was a man with whom her uncle had business dealings and wished to entertain as well as possible. She carried a lighted lamp into the parlour, where the general agent was inquiring from his guest the state of affairs at the

Fields and the condition of the country through which he had passed, to all which inquiries the Jew answered shortly and looked keenly about him. He was a moneylender and diamond speculator whose home was in London but who had come to South Africa several times since the discovery of diamonds, and he had lent the general agent a large sum of money at a high rate of interest* with which the agent had financed the diamond-digging venture that had failed. He knew it was to attend to this matter that the Jew had broken his journey from the Fields to England at the little town, and that, if the Jew pressed for immediate payment, it meant his insolvency, and he talked with unusual fluency and suaveness; but the Jew did not trouble himself to make conversation, and when the general agent ceased to speak there were long pauses.

When Bertie had prepared the supper she went to her aunt's bedroom, where her aunt stood before the glass putting on her best cap and collar and arranging her curls. Bertie who stood in the doorway said that all was ready, but that her head ached and she would like to go to her room instead of going to supper. Her aunt ran her curls round her fingers and said without looking back, 'You will do nothing of the kind, my dear. The least you can do for the few days you are still here is to allow no one to see that anything unusual has happened. You will at least come to the table if you do not care to eat.' Then she added, as she patted her curls, 'You will also please note, Bertie, that you need not refer again to anything that passed between us this evening while you are here. Your uncle has taken your seat in the post-cart that leaves on Thursday. He has not mentioned to your parents why you are going; he simply said that as your mother seemed to need you we could not think of keeping you here longer. One thing I should like to say to you, Bertie: never attempt such confidences as you were desirous of making to me this evening. If a woman has made a mistake there is only one course for her—silence!' Her aunt still looked into the glass and Bertie withdrew softly from the door.

At the supper table Bertie sat in her usual place behind the tray at the head, with the great coffee urn before her. Her aunt sat on the right side of the table and the Jew on the left and her uncle at the other end.

The Jew ate hurriedly and absorbedly, as people do who have lived through much of their life alone: he bent low over his plate, shovelling in the frikkedel* and gravy with his knife and seldom looking up.

Once or twice as he ate his eye passed from his plate to the end of the table where Bertie sat silent, her cheeks so pale they were almost sallow and her eyelashes almost resting on them as she looked down at the plate on which she toyed with her food.

When the supper was almost done, in answer to some remark of the general agent's as to the colour of diamonds, the Jew took from an inner breast pocket a small parcel wrapped in oilskin and carefully tied. He removed the oilskin and took out a small brown paper parcel, from the inside of which he took a small round japanned box. He opened and poured carefully into a plate a little shower of white, yellow-tinted stones, which glittered softly in the lamplight. He put the plate between himself and the general agent and began touching the different stones with his bent forefinger, describing their various qualities and values. The general agent's wife leaned forward to see them. He passed the plate over for her to examine them more closely. When she had handed the plate back to him, the Jew looked up to the end of the table where Bertie sat. 'And ze young lady, vill she not see too?'* he asked.

Bertie lifted her eyes heavily. He passed the plate up towards her; she put it down at her side, looking at them with her indifferent drooping eyes. 'They are nice,' she said slowly, and was going to return the plate, when the Jew bent forward. 'Vitch zinks she is ze best now?' he said, with his head a little on one side.

Indifferently, with her finger Bertie touched a small perfect octahedron stone. 'This,' she said, and handed the plate back to the Jew.

'Ha-ha! Zat is very good! It is small, but it is ze best. Ze young lady has a good eye.'

He put the stones back into the little box and returned it to its wrappings and put it into his breast pocket. Then they rose. The general agent invited him to return to the parlour; but he said he must leave. He shook hands with Bertie and her aunt.

In the hall, when the general agent had helped him on with his coat, he turned to him for a moment and said, 'Ze young lady, does she live viz you?'

The general agent explained that she was his wife's niece and only on a visit, and was to leave in two days. The Jew made an appointment to meet him at his office the next morning to discuss business. The general agent opened the door for him and wished him goodnight; the Jew shuffled out into the street, and the door closed behind him.

It was a glorious night. Up above, ten thousand stars were throwing down their points of light brighter than any diamonds and making dimly visible even the outlines of the houses in the dark town. The Jew began to shuffle through the thick sand in the street and the yet thicker sand of the square. But he saw neither the bright lights above him nor the dark earth about him.

Far away, across the mist of fifty years, he saw again a little garret room under the eaves in a North German city, where a small dark-eyed boy and girl played together when their parents had gone out to their work and had locked them in. He saw again the little garret window, through which they crept out onto the roof where the tall chimneys rose. Again they played at being storks, and, with tiny fragments in their mouths of the brown bread their parents had left them to eat during their absence, pretended to feed tiny imaginary storklings in an imaginary nest between the chimneys; again he heard the little girl's cry of admiration at his courage and of terror lest he should fall when the boy walked to the extreme edge of the roof to peer down into the street below; again he held fast the skirts of the little girl as she crept back through the window lest they should sweep against the box of mignonettes their mother had planted there and break them. And then it was later, and a boy of seventeen and a girl of sixteen whose parents had died in Germany were living alone in London in an East End garret* whose roof sloped to the floor at one side. Again it was early morning and the boy with the black curls hanging into his neck and an old black bag over his shoulders paced the streets of Bloomsbury; again he felt the nip of the fog-laden London morning air in his nostrils, and again he felt the fresh young blood coursing through his veins as the boy raised his cry, 'Old clothes! Old clothes!'* and raised his eyes anxiously to the grim rows of houses to see if from door or window came an answering beck or nod. And then it was evening and the bag was full, and, up the flights of stairs in the East End lodging house, the boy was mounting three steps at a time. Then he saw the door open and the pile of clothes on the floor and the girl in the fading light at the little sloping window bending over her work, till she raised her dark soft eyes with their curled lashes to greet him, and they prepared their evening meal of fried fish on the little stove in the corner, and to save light and keep warm sat down on a heap of clothes before the stove and ate it together from one plate; and when it was ended sat talking of the prices she had got at the shops for the clothes she had repaired, and the things he had in the bag. When she grew tired, she laid her head on his knee, and, staring at the small bed of coals, he talked of the future, of the time when their savings would have mounted and they too would possess a tall house in Bloomsbury. He talked of the jewels he would buy her and the carriage they would keep, and she talked of the food she would see he had and the things they would do for their aunt and her children in Germany who were the only relations they had. And all the while, as he saw the pictures, he saw also dimly Bertie's face at the head of the table, with the thick curling hair above the low forehead and the large eyes with the curled lashes that had awoken the old pictures.

He struck his foot against the lowest step of the little hotel stoep and swore and shuffled up them. In the bar the men were gathered drinking and talking; he went in and sat for a while listening, now and then putting in a remark to see if no news as to the general agent's monetary position was to be gathered, and then he went upstairs. When he had undressed and put his oilcloth-wrapped parcel under his pillow, he got into bed and blew out the light. His long day's journey on the coach had tired him, but he could not sleep. First his thoughts travelled over the news he had heard of the general agent in the bar room: would it, or would it not, be best to push him? Then his thoughts travelled back to the Diamond Fields, to the man he had left at the River Diggings to buy claims for him, to New Rush* and his claims there. Then they led back to London, to the tall grim house in Bloomsbury, where hundreds of houses, equally yellow and dull and deadly in their exact likeness to one another from attic to basement, filled the long weary street in which he had lived alone for twenty years, with only Martha, his grimy broad-shouldered housekeeper, and later on her weak-eyed short-witted son, with a gait like his own,* to keep him company. He wondered irritably if the woman was not burning too many coals and using too much food during his absence and whether Isaac always remembered to lock the area gate; and then he saw Bertie sitting at the agent's table, with her large eyes and her drooping lashes and the curly hair that had brought back the past. He tossed wearily. He lit the candle and looked at his watch; it was half past eleven; then he blew the light out and tried to sleep again. But when the clock struck twelve he was still lying staring up into the dark.

Then the Jew rose; he lit the candle and took from under his pillow the parcel of stones. Carefully he opened it and, examining the stones, selected the one which Bertie had touched that evening. He held it in the palm of his hand, looking at it by the candlelight. Softly he touched it with the forefinger of the other hand, caressing its soft soapy surface as a mother might the hair of a child with which she was to part. He extended his arm, holding it close to the candle, and drew back his head that he might look at it from a distance; then he put it down on a fragment of the brown paper and wrapped it carefully in it; then he cut off a piece of the oilskin and folded it in that; then he tied the tiny parcel carefully and put it in his purse. He re-folded the large parcel and put it with his purse under the pillow. Then he got quickly into bed and was soon asleep.

The next morning the Jew visited the general agent's office; he discussed their business; he asked at what rate the general agent would be willing to pay if he left the money due now in a few weeks for another two years, and what securities he could give; but he gave the general agent no definite answer as to whether he would accept his terms or not, but said he should hear from him later in the day.

As he was turning to go the Jew took from his purse the small brown parcel and handed it to the general agent.

'Ze young lady, she liked zat stone. Vill you say I have ze honour to present it to her viz my compliments?' Then he went out at the door without waiting for thanks.

When the agent went home to dinner he gave Bertie the gift. She opened it with no sign of pleasure. At his request she wrote a note of three lines thanking the Jew. After dinner, when she had gone to her room to finish her packing, Aunt Mary-Anna turned to her husband.

'Why did he give it her?' she asked.

'How can I tell?' asked the general agent.

She looked at him. 'Is he married?'

'For all I can tell he may have a wife and half a dozen children in Hamburg or England or wherever his headquarters may be!' But he divined her meaning as the slowest people who have lived together for twenty years will do without words.

'The idea did just flit across my mind also,' said the general agent, answering her thought, 'but it's ridiculous. No doubt he admired her; she's the kind of woman every man finds attractive. But Jews don't marry Christians, even supposing him to be unmarried. A Jew will eat sucking pig, he will be a Christian in all his manners and customs, but when it comes to legal marriage, he's a Jew. It's a ridiculous idea, and he's leaving tomorrow.'

'It's very strange he should give away a valuable stone like that to a girl he has only exchanged three words with!'

'Not at all. You never can account for what a Jew will do. I've known a Jew give thirty pounds for a Sunday-school picnic for Christian children, when he would have wrung ten shillings out of a starving man who owed it him: a Jew has whims like a woman.' He went back to his office.

That evening Bertie had finished all her packing; her large box stood ready locked and tied to go by transport wagon, her small portmanteau and hat box were standing ready at the foot of her bed, to be put in the postcart the next morning. Her aunt had gone out to a mothers' prayer meeting, and at four o'clock Bertie took a ball of cotton and a crochet needle and went to the low rocking chair before the parlour window where she sat every afternoon. For a time she crocheted, then she rested her hands on the ball in her lap and looked out of the window across the four feet of garden, with its faded geraniums and pinks and across the little green paling into the street. After a time she leaned her forehead on the window ledge. The world was so large, so large, why was there no place for her? Her thoughts went back to Rebekah's house among the oak trees at Cape Town and the old farm with the blue gums, to John-Ferdinand's homestead almost showing over the nek; and she felt a hand laid on her heart. She thought of the whole world, of the Far East that Rebekah taught her of when she was a little girl, of India with its swarming millions and Juggernaut cars and palm trees, of China with its pagodas and little bells there, there, far away, if one could only get there, one would be lost among all those millions, there one would be free. Why, why was there no place for her in the world where she could go and no one ever find her! Slowly the tears gathered in her eyes and fell upon her lap. Only a few hours and she would be in the postcart, and then a few days more and she would be at the farm, and John-Ferdinand and Veronica would come over to see her. She moved her hands passionately in her lap. Then the front gate clicked. She sat up and dried her eyes. Dorcas had answered the knock and opened the parlour door and ushered in the Jew. Bertie rose to meet him; the tear stains were still upon her cheeks, but she held out her hand passively to him. He asked if her aunt were in, as he had come to say goodbye. Bertie said she was out but would be back in a very short time: she was expecting her every moment. The Jew sat down on a small stiff-legged chair to her left, and Bertie sat down passively in her low seat. She made no effort to speak, but turned her face towards the window, so that only her profile was visible to the Jew.

For a few moments he sat quiet, then he said, 'It looks it vill rain tonight! It grows dark.'

'Yes,' said Bertie slowly. And then there was a long silence. The Jew sat watching her with his keen eyes, his feet twisted round the two forelegs of the chair.

'You are not vell?' he asked at last, bending forward.

'Yes—yes—I am quite well, thank you.' She still looked out of the window. The Jew watched her.

'You vill go away tomorrow?' he said presently.

'Yes,' she said slowly.

'I go on viz ze postcart, you viz it too?'

'Yes,' she said, without looking at him.

Then there was a long silence and the Jew thought of something to say. 'You vill like zat you go to your home and your family again?'

Bertie turned her face slowly from the window. 'No,' she said slowly, and then turned it back again. The tear marks were clearly visible on her cheeks. The Jew felt curiously perturbed.

'Vat is it zat you cry?' he said suddenly, bending forward low; 'your uncle, your aunt, are zey not good to you?'

'Oh yes, yes, they are.'

The Jew waited a moment and looked at her motionless figure.

'Ven you shall vish to stay longer, shall I not speak viz your uncle zat he let you stay?'

'Oh no, no!' Bertie started and looked round at him. 'Don't, don't say anything to him!'

'Ven I speak to your uncle he shall let you stay. He shall hear vat I say!' A little gleam of conscious power crept into the Jew's eye.

Bertie had half started up, moving her hands quickly; the ball and crochet needle fell to the floor. 'I don't want to stay here,' she said. Then she sank back into the chair. Suddenly she bent forward to the Jew: 'I want to find work, some place where I can work. You—you have been all over the world; don't you know where I could get some work?' Her hands interclasped themselves in her lap. 'I can do nearly anything,' she said, with her eyes now wide open and fixed on him, 'that a woman does with her hands. I can cook and sew, and I can trim hats; I could take care of a baby or house. Wouldn't anyone at the Fields want me? I could do anything. I wouldn't mind working hard.' She looked full up into the Jew's face.

'Ze Fields is not ze place for you!' he said. His eyes swerved from her face and fixed themselves on the hands in her lap, rounded and dimpled and so small for her large body. 'You are for ze joy, ze life, ze beautiful clothes, ze beautiful zings: you are not for ze hard work!'

'Oh, I can work!' she said, bending closer to his knees. 'I could do anything. If your wife wanted someone to help her, I could do all she wanted. I wouldn't mind going to another land, I would like it. If I could only—' They saw the shadow of Aunt Mary-Anna's figure fall across the window as she passed it. The gate clicked and she opened the front door. Bertie drew back and sat upright in the shadow of the curtain. The Jew rose to his feet as she entered the parlour. He said he had done himself the honour to come and wish her goodbye and to thank her for the very good supper he had had the night before.

Aunt Mary-Anna thanked him properly for the diamond he had given Bertie and asked him to stay to supper again. But he declined, as he had business. He shook hands with Bertie without addressing her, and her aunt conducted him to the front door.

It was half past one that night. Bertie lay in the bed in the dark. She had slept for an hour after getting into bed, but since then had lain awake. Again and again she tried to draw the pillow to her and pull the cover over her head; but no sleep came. She lay now looking up into the dark. She heard the clock in the dining room strike the half hour. Every moment brought nearer the time of her going, and then the journey, and then the arrival at the farm. Again and again she went over the steps that always ended with the arrival of John-Ferdinand and Veronica from their farm. She listened to the deadly stillness in the house and felt the inevitableness that drew her on; she must start the next morning, she must arrive at the farm, she must see them all. She turned onto her side; the curls on her forehead were damp with a chilly sweat. The clock struck two. Then she threw back the cover and stepped out of bed. In her white nightgown she walked to the door and opened it and walked softly with her bare feet across the little passage and opened the kitchen door. From the large uncurtained window a great square of dazzling moonlight fell on the stone-paved floor, making every crack visible in the stones where it lay and lighting up dimly the whole kitchen, so that even the pots on the wall and the legs of the table and chairs were visible. On the floor before the fireplace, wrapped in her brown blanket, Dorcas the Kaffir girl lay, with only a fragment of her red kerchief showing at one end of the living brown roll. Bertie glided softly across the floor and knelt beside the roll with one knee on the floor and one raised.

'Dorcas! Dorcas!' she called softly. Dorcas did not stir.

'Dorcas, please wake!' She touched her softly. 'Oh, please wake, Dorcas!'

Dorcas gave a low guttural sound; her head protruded slightly from the blanket like a caddis-worm creeping out of its case;* but her eyes were fast closed.

'I'm so lonely, Dorcas! Oh, please let me hold your hand!'

Dorcas snored and turned slightly on her side. Bertie put down her hand under the blanket and took the thick coarse hand of the Kaffir woman and held it tight in her own. 'I'm so lonely, Dorcas!' But Dorcas moved heavily and then lay motionless. Bertie shivered; after a while she withdrew her hand and rose softly and glided with her naked feet back to her own room.

At half past four the postcart driver had inspanned his horses and had drawn up before the post office on the square and was blowing a great blast on his bugle, while the cold sleepy postmaster was dragging out the bags. Twenty minutes later he had drawn up before the general agent's door and blew another blast. Bertie, who had long been up and dressed, went to her aunt, who was still in bed, while the general agent, who had risen hastily and put on his slippers and dressing gown, carried her hat box and portmanteau to the front door. When Bertie got to the door the four grey horses were champing their bits and moving their heads in the sharp morning air; the coloured driver was fastening her hat box and portmanteau onto the back of the cart, while before the front seat the post bags were packed higher than the splashboard. On the back seat of the cart sat the little Jew wrapped in a fur-lined coat whose turned-up collar hid almost all but the sharp eyes and nose that looked out above them. The general agent stood shivering on the doorstep, with his hands in the pockets of his dressing gown, and was remarking to the Jew that it would be warmer as soon as the sun rose. All the square and the street had been drenched with a heavy night dew, and the moist trees and houses looked damp in the still morning air. The Jew moved his head in greeting to Bertie, who had a thick grey veil drawn over her face; and, when the man had fastened on her luggage at the back and had climbed into his place on the front seat with his legs hanging over the post bags and had gathered up the reins, the general agent turned to Bertie and helped her into the cart to her seat on the back bench beside the Jew. He passed her up her little handbag and asked the Jew to take care of her, as far as their path lay together, and asked her to write and tell of her arrival as soon as she got to the farm; he raised his arm to shake hands with the Jew over the side of the cart, and the Jew told him he would hear from him from the Bay in a few days' time.

The driver put the bugle to his lips and blew a loud call, then he drew the reins closer and the horses made a great turn and swept out of the street into the square. The general agent looked after them for a second and then went back into the house and closed the door. As they crossed the square and swept out at the upper end past the hotel, Bertie raised her veil a little and looked out over the back of the cart at the square with the sleeping houses and the church like a great damp white angel watching over it.

Then they passed out of sight and there was no trace of them but the deep tracks of cart wheels across the damp sand of the square.

CHAPTER X

HOW GRIET SAT ON THE STONE WALL AND WATCHED THE GNATS

It was a rich yellow afternoon. All the valley was filled with a haze, through which you saw the outline of the hills and the trees and the flats through a sheen of gold. The air was so thick it seemed you might have cut it with a knife, and yet so clear you could see the farthest object through it, and so warm and balmy you had only one wish, to sit still in it and breathe it.

On the kitchen doorstep old Ayah sat working, hemming a yellow handkerchief that was pinned to her knee. Every now and then she would rest her hands in her lap and look away up the valley, and then sigh deeply and take a pinch of snuff and say slowly, 'Ach!—ja, God!' and then take up her sewing, till her hands fell to rest again.

Away off, on the stone wall that ran from the wagon house, which broke off suddenly and left a large gateless opening for carts and wagons to come through and then was continued to the sod wall of the garden, Griet sat. She had a piece of blue sewing in her lap, but it was tucked in between her knees; her little bare heels tapped slowly against the wall as she swung them to and fro, but her head was thrown back as far as it would go, and she was looking up into the air where dozens of gnats were wheeling their flight above her; she turned her head slowly from this side to that, following them, and sometimes pretending to snap at them. Presently she glanced round to see if old Ayah was watching her, but the afternoon was too balmy and peaceful for old Ayah even to trouble herself with other folks' concerns. So Griet went on looking up.

Suddenly she closed her mouth with a snap and threw her chin down onto her breast. Her eye roved far off across the flats, not where the road came over the nek from the town, but round the hill from the next farm. She bent her head a little on one side to listen, as for all the long generations of the past her foremothers had listened on the great pathless plains for the coming step of the antelope that meant food, or of the enemy that meant war—death. Then she raised her head and looked. Yes, there, coming through, moving among the mimosa trees, whose branches seemed white with thorns everywhere now their leaves had fallen, was the yet whiter tent of a cart. Griet looked round; but old Ayah had observed nothing. She took up her sewing and bent devoutly over it. The cart went out of sight at the drift and then came out near the dam, clearly visible now. Griet looked at it, wrinkling her little flat nose scornfully, and then bent down over her work, sewing on diligently, and began humming the verse of a hymn to herself.

Then the cart came out at the kraal just below her. On the front seat sat John-Ferdinand; his broad felt hat covered the large dark eyes that looked out gravely above his close-curling pointed beard. Behind him on the back seat was Veronica in a light print dress, her face shaded by a large mushroom-shaped straw hat bound round with white muslin. On her arm lay the baby, wrapped in a white shawl. Griet did not raise her head but bent low over her work as the cart passed her into the yard. It came so quietly that old Ayah, who was growing a little deaf, did not notice it till it drew up a few feet from the kitchen door. 'Child of sin!' she cried to Griet, 'why did you not let me know people were coming, that I might have had coffee ready? Go pick up chips to make the kettle boil quickly; there are always eyes enough in your head when there is nothing to be seen but, when there is, you are as blind as an earth-snake!'*

Meanwhile John-Ferdinand had fastened the horses' heads to the horse post, showing he did not intend to stay long; and, when he had helped Veronica out with the baby, they walked into the house, Griet walking slowly to the wood pile beside the wagon house, where she carefully searched among the piles of mimosa cuttings for the very greenest and sap-oozing chips. With these drawn up in her print dress in front, she walked slowly to the house, flaunting her little short skirts superciliously with each step and wrinkling her nose slightly as she passed the cart.

In the little whitewashed dining room, when John-Ferdinand and Veronica entered it, the father was still sitting at the table in his shirt-sleeves with his spectacles on his nose, his volume of Swedenborg open before him; but he seemed to have been half asleep as he took his glasses quickly off his nose and wiped them before he rose to welcome his visitors. The little mother had heard the sound of their voices and ran in from the bedroom, where she had been lying down, her little pink print dress still crumpled as she had lain in it. 'Oh, I am so glad to see you,' she said; 'why didn't you let me know you were coming this morning when I sent the boy over for the sour dough? I should have had the cakes ready.'

'We did not know we were coming,' said Veronica.

The little mother tripped away into the kitchen to see if the kettle was on. Veronica had seated herself in the chair in the corner near the door; her face, which had been painfully long and straight, had filled out so that it was a long smooth oval; there was a warm rose colour in her cheeks, and her blue eyes, though still with deep-set orbits* under the high-arched brows, were fuller and had a light in their pale blueness they never wore in her maidenhood. She removed the shawl and hood from her child's head and laid it to her large white bosom, against which it pressed its little fingers and thumb, while she drew across it a small lace handkerchief, partly concealing it. John-Ferdinand stood somewhat awkwardly beside her, while the father, still rubbing his glasses, asked if he would not outspan.*

Before he had answered, the little mother had hurried back. 'The boy came again from the town this morning. It will be three weeks next Thursday since the day they wrote she was leaving. I can't understand why your uncle doesn't write; he must have got our letter asking why she didn't come! I haven't slept all this week. Your father says if she was ill they would have written, but I—' She looked suddenly from John-Ferdinand to Veronica: 'You haven't any news, have you?'

John-Ferdinand looked down at his wife. 'Yes, aunt; that is why we came over; we have a letter from uncle,' said Veronica.

'Oh, she's ill! She's dead!' cried the little mother, wringing her hands and dancing before Veronica like a little child.

'No, dear aunt; no, she's quite well. They are well.'

John-Ferdinand put into his wife's hand a letter and walked quickly past her into the front room and out onto the stoep. The father sat suddenly upright looking at her; and Veronica, with her right hand, took the letter from the envelope. The little mother stood before her motionless. 'It's from her uncle,' Veronica said slowly, unfolding the letter; 'he asked us to come over and see you about it.'

Then, partly reading and partly explaining, Veronica began to give the contents of the letter. The general agent wrote that she had left, as he said she would, by the Thursday's postcart, and he had not doubted she had arrived home safely till, on the day before he wrote, thirteen days after her leaving, he got letters from the farm saying she had not come; on the same day he had also received a letter from Bertie without any date or address saying she did not wish to return home, and that she had of her own free will and at her own request gone away with the Jew who had been her fellow passenger in the postcart. She said she did not wish anyone to follow her, but that she would write shortly to her mother and Rebekah when she had reached her journey's end. Where that would be she did not say.

'Has she married him—married him! A Jew—a man we know nothing of!' cried the little mother. 'Oh, if Rebekah were here!'

'I don't think she has married him, dear aunt,' Veronica said, holding down the letter; 'from what her uncle writes I should say she has gone to live with him but is not married.'

The little mother stood transfixed but the father rose and tore the letter from Veronica's hand to read it himself. With a faint helpless little cry the mother ran out of the room and to the stoep where John-Ferdinand stood looking into the dark green of an orange tree. She stood before him, stretching out her hands to him. 'Oh, please explain to me, please explain! I can't understand. Oh, it's so terrible! Tell me what it is!'

John-Ferdinand took her hands in his. 'My dear aunt, it is our Father's will. We cannot understand the strange and terrible dispensations that come to us in life. We can but submit.'

'But Bertie, my little Bertie!' she cried. Then she tore her hands from his and ran back into the dining room. 'Oh, where is she? Where is she?' The father stood with the letter in his hand, still reading it, unconscious of anyone's presence. 'You must go and fetch her back! John-Ferdinand must go, Rebekah must go!'

Veronica had taken her breast from the baby, who had now fallen asleep, and was drawing her dress back over it. 'My dear aunt, in the part of the letter he is reading now, Bertie's uncle says he has no idea where she and the man have gone; it may be to the Diamond Fields, to the Free State, to the Transvaal, to England, to South America, to Cape Town; and he says, very wisely, that we should make no fuss and not make public inquiries and let the thing get into the papers. He knows the man slightly, who, he says, is very wealthy and is sure to be kind to her; and there are other people to think of, his children and Rebekah's and mine. A thing like this, if it is once talked of, is never forgotten, never. For Bertie's sake, for all our sakes, it must be kept quiet.'

The father held the letter in his hand. The little mother looked, almost silenced by the whiteness of his face.

'You see,' said Veronica slowly, 'whatever has been done is done. For Bertie's own sake, for the sake of the innocent who would suffer with her, we must not act hastily. She is over twenty-one and of full age; she has a right to do as she wishes.'

'I will start tonight. I will go to her uncle and learn all he can tell me,' the father said; 'we must bring her home.' The mother flung herself upon his breast with her arms about his neck: 'Oh, she was my little baby—she was such a child!—she knows nothing!'

Twenty minutes later John-Ferdinand and Veronica, with the baby in her arms, walked through the kitchen. There was nothing they could do for the old people, and they felt it better to leave them. Old Ayah, who had just come back from the milk room with fresh cream and butter, apologised that there was no tea. Not only had the chips burned faintly under the kettle, but Griet had absent-mindedly put two beakers of fresh cold water into it before she slipped off to her old seat on the wall.

John-Ferdinand helped his wife and child into the cart, loosened the horses' heads from the stake and turned the cart round; then, mounting the front seat, drove slowly away. As the cart passed through the gap in the wall, Griet on her perch seemed deeply absorbed in her sewing and did not once raise her head to glance at it, but, as soon as it was once well through and passing down beside the kraal, she threw down her work and, extending her arms with the thumbs sticking outwards towards the back of the cart and the fingers pointing inwards towards herself, raised a low snort of scorn and disapproval. Then she sat still watching it as it passed slowly down the rise among the thorn trees.

In the house a strange stillness reigned. In the little whitewashed dining room, with the afternoon sunshine playing on the wall, the father sat with his shirtsleeved arms stretched out on the table and his head resting on them; his volume, which had fallen, was lying on the floor at his feet.

In the bedroom on the great bed on which her children had been born the little mother lay, with closed eyes, sobbing noiselessly, while old Ayah laid rags damped with vinegar and water on the forehead and wrists. As she bent she sighed deeply with sympathy; not that the little mother had yet told her what happened, but she felt that some bad news had come which had some connection with Bertie, and she had a vague feeling, for which she could give no reason, that the bearers of the news were somehow to blame for it.

Griet watched the cart till it had passed the great dam and the last glint of its white tent had been lost among the thorn trees beyond; then, seeing that no one called her and a dead stillness reigned everywhere, she fell to her old occupation and, with her head back as far as it would go, watched the gnats as they buzzed above her in the warm yellow air.

CHAPTER XI

HOW THE RAIN RAINS IN LONDON

THE Jew beat his feet on the pavement. It was eleven o'clock and a rainy night. Up and down the street the rain was falling; it made a wall so dense it almost shut out the light of the few gas lamps that glimmered through that long Bloomsbury street. The raindrops hung in beads round the hat of the cabman whom the lamps of his cab made dimly visible as he sat on the front seat.

The Jew went up the house steps and rang the bell loudly; then without waiting he rang again. There was a sound in the passage and then the door opened a few inches. The Jew kicked it wide. Inside, a figure could be seen holding a lighted candle.

'Vhy ze davil can you not come ven I ring? And vhy you not light ze hall lamp?'

Then he turned down the steps and opened the cab door, helping Bertie to alight. She was thickly veiled and wrapped from neck to feet in a fur cloak. The Jew led the way up the steps into the hall.

On the large, new, empty hatstand the candle was standing, and the woman who had held it stood on a chair lighting the hall lamp. There was an overpowering smell of paint and varnish and oilcloth everywhere. In the back of the passage behind the stairs a moving figure was dimly visible.

'Isaac! Isaac! Vhy you not come and bring ze zings in?'

From the back of the hall the figure shuffled forward slowly. It was a youth of about seventeen, with a high, narrow, sloping forehead, above which rose a tower of strongly curling hair like the Jew's but of a pale sandy colour, though further, except in the shuffling gait, there was nothing to recall the Jew.* He had a long straight nose slightly crooked, the tip of which was so sharply a four-sided square that it almost suggested that the point had been artificially cut off instead of being the work of nature.* He had weak, bleared, blue eyes, and walked with his shoulders bent and his head stretched forward as if trying to see. He shuffled past Bertie without seeing her.

The Jew nodded at the candle. 'You take ze lady upstairs to ze room,' he said to the woman; and he followed Isaac out to the cab.

The woman who had descended from the chair took up the candle. She was a woman of about forty; her grizzled dark hair, drawn into an untidy knot at the back of her head, hung over her forehead till it almost touched her heavy eyebrows. She began without a word to mount the stairs, and Bertie followed her. She was short and broad-shouldered, and Bertie noticed, as she followed her, that the wrist of the hand in which she held the candle was almost as thick and strong as a man's and a little hairy.* Her shabby black dress had a three-sided rent at the back and hung down, almost touching the stairs as she mounted. On the first landing she stopped and opened a door, and Bertie followed her into a large room. Here the smell of new paint and new furniture was even stronger than below. There was no light in the room, but the woman led the way with the candle. Bertie saw the glittering of a great cut-glass chandelier hanging from the ceiling in the centre of the room and of chairs and sofas and mirrors everywhere. The woman opened a small door in the folding door which cut off the room from the one behind it, and Bertie followed her in. Here a great coal fire was burning, the warm light making visible the great bed and large drawers and wardrobes with glass doors. On the dressing table the woman put down the light. Drawn up before the fire there was a sofa covered with purple velvet. Bertie sat down on it. For a second the woman glanced at her curiously, then went out and closed the door. Bertie took off her hat and laid it on the head of the sofa and unbuttoned her fur cloak, but did not take it off. In a few moments the Jew and Isaac came bringing up the luggage, which Isaac set down within the door and went. The Jew came up to her. 'You like ze fire?' he said, looking down at her. 'I vill tell ze woman zat she bring you some supper.' He took a little bunch of keys out of his pocket. 'All ze drawers, ze wardrobes are your zings in; ven you vant zomezing you vill open zem!' He put the keys on the mantelpiece. 'I vill go down now to my office—it below—and see some letters of business, and vill come up soon.' He stood looking at her anxiously, shifting from one leg to the other. 'Ven you vant anyzing you vill ring?—You are tired?' He looked down at her. 'I vill tell ze woman zat she bring your supper soon,' he said; then he went out and closed the door.

When he was gone she opened her cloak yet further and threw it partly back; once she glanced round the room and then she looked back at the fire. She was very tired. For two weeks the Jew had delayed their journey at Madeira that the repairs and furnishing might be completed before they came. She had only landed that day, and the journey in the damp chill air, to which she was unaccustomed, had made her very heavy. After a little she leaned back on the purple velvet pillows and drew up her feet, and lay with one arm over her head and the other hanging at her side, looking at the fire. How soft the velvet cushions were!

In about ten minutes there was a knock at the door and, no one answering, it was pushed open. The woman looked in; she was carrying a silver tray with the supper set on it; she put it down on the dressing table. She looked at Bertie; from her slow even breathing it was evident she was fast asleep. After a moment the woman walked toward the sofa from behind and, coming to the top, bent down over it. The firelight was shimmering on the silk linings of Bertie's open fur cloak and cast a ruddy soft light on her face; she bent over Bertie a little; like her son she was near-sighted and saw nothing clearly till she came close. She bent her face low over Bertie and noticed the roundness of her snowy throat and the fullness of the little rounded chin, and looked at the long curled lashes on the pink cheeks; she put out one thick, unwashed, grimy finger, almost as if she were going to feel the cheek to see if its soft curves were real; then she turned and went softly out of the room with a not unpleased smile about her mouth as she closed the door.

About half an hour later the Jew came up. When he left Bertie he had gone down to a room on the ground floor; originally it had been the back dining room of the house, but the Jew had bricked up the door between it and the front room, and for nearly twenty years it had been his home. Here he lived and ate and slept when at home, while the rest of the house, which Martha attended to, had been let to lodgers. There was a stretcher on one side with a folded grimy quilt; a little iron stove was in the corner with a black kettle on it, on which the Jew made himself hot water without the trouble of calling anyone. In the other corner was a large sofa; the table was covered with papers and documents; an old cracked lamp, blackened with age, hung over it, and the paper was a faded yellow, grimed with the smoke and wear of twenty years. When all the rest of the house had been renovated and refurnished, this room alone had been left untouched. Here for twenty years he had eaten, drunk, slept and sat up to work at night and the mustiness and the grime were home to him.

When he went into it that evening he took off his new black coat, hung it behind the door, put on a short black jacket, greasy and shiny, and sat down at the table to his papers. Most of them were bills for the decorating and furnishing of the home. There were long bills from silversmiths for cutlery and plate; there were yet longer bills from the Bond Street* dressmakers, to whom he had sent Bertie's measurements with orders to supply her with a complete lady's outfit with which to fill the drawers and wardrobes in her room; there was a lengthy bill from his agent, who had been obliged to compensate the lodgers turned out of the house without the full month's notice. He added up the costs and sat looking down at the large total they came to, with a certain gleam of satisfaction. Yes, it had cost well.

Then, before he went on to the other papers, the Jew rose. He put off the little jacket and put on the black coat, and for a moment looked into the little cracked, eight-inch looking glass that hung on the wall, to see that his front hair stood up straight; then he went up the stairs to Bertie's room. After knocking twice and getting no answer, he opened the door and saw her still asleep on the purple sofa. Very softly he closed the door and walked on tiptoe to the foot of the couch. She was still fast asleep with the firelight playing on her. Very gently, to make no sound, he knelt down on the floor, loosened the buttons of her little shoes, drew them off and placed them on the floor. He ran his hands very softly, so softly, along the curves of her feet, so tiny for the body. He looked at them for a moment, he put down his face as if he were going to press the soles against it, as women press the feet of little children. Then he rose and went to the bed and fetched a large down pillow. She was lying so low in the pillows that her feet almost hung over the end of the sofa; he slipped the cushion very carefully under them to raise and support them. Then he went to a wardrobe and discovered a large white fluffy shawl. He heaped it softly over her feet, tucking it in at the sides of the pillow. He blew out the candle, that its light might not add to the glare of the fire; then he stood looking at her for a few seconds with his hands curved before him; and then he went down to his room and his greasy coat to go on examining his letters.

When Bertie woke the next morning it was half past [?eight].* She raised herself on the sofa. Someone had been in and built the fire, for it was burning still. She stood up and threw from her the fur cloak in which her arms had been all night. A curious dull grey light came through the two windows at the other end of the room (it seemed hardly like daylight) and a far-off roaring sound, like a million sounds breaking into one. Bertie listened to it for a minute and then walked towards the windows. Her little stockinged feet sank noiselessly into the soft pile of the carpet as into moss by the rocks in the kloof. She drew up both blinds and stood before a window looking out. A grey damp was everywhere. It seemed to ooze out of the walls of the buildings opposite, to ascend from the ground as much as come down from the sky. Opposite were the backs of houses in the next street, all built of the same dead yellow-grey brick, and all oozing. There were rows of windows all alike. Out of two windows on a top floor a line was stretched and a shirt was hanging out on it, but it was not drying; the water dripped from its sleeves as they hung down. Up above, in what looked like a loft, a window was open and a boy's face looked out, then the window closed. Down below, between the tall houses, tiny back yards with high walls were crushed. She pressed her face against the window to look down into them. In one were a few broken flower pots lying in the wet, and a great grey cat was stealthily walking along the top of the wall, drenching wet but seemingly accustomed to it, for it did not try to climb down. There was a pungent curious smell that seemed to burn in her nostrils, something like when they burned harpuis bushes* on the lands at home. Bertie wondered what it was; she shivered; she looked out for a moment longer, and then turned back to the room. There all was beautiful. The soft double-piled carpet had pink roses in it; on the great brass bed was a blue embroidered satin quilt. There were two great mahogany wardrobes with two mirrors in each and two chests of drawers with brass fittings; the dressing table had another large mirror and there was another over the mantelpiece that reflected the whole room; besides the velvet sofa there were two armchairs and a table with a purple velvet cover. Bertie walked about softly, touching the things with her hands: how wonderful and beautiful it was; and it was hers, all hers. She ran her finger along the edge of the brass bed, of the tables and chairs; even the white marble of the fireplace seemed beautiful to her; she had never seen it before. She thought of the little stained deal wardrobe in the best bedroom at home, and the little deal dressing table with the muslin on it; and a curious kind of pain came to her. She took the keys from the mantelpiece and began to open the drawers and wardrobes. In the drawers were piles of linen so delicate she hardly liked to touch it roughly; she laid out on the bed a nightgown with so much of fine lace and soft ribbons falling about it that at first it seemed to her it must be an evening dress. In the wardrobes hung gowns in silk and muslin and velvet and lace. She took them down and looked at them in turn. Then she came to one: all her life she had dreamed of having a dress made of thick black silk, with large blue daisies with white centres embroidered in raised work all over it at intervals. Her mother had had such a bit of silk in a patchwork quilt she had brought from England with her. Once on board ship the Jew had asked her what sort of a dress she would like best, and she had described it made of such stuff, quite plainly and with a long train, and a fine lace scarf to throw over the shoulders and hang down in front. In the wardrobe were the dress and the scarf. She put the dress on and hung the scarf about the low body so that the long ends hung down, and then she walked up and down in it. There were three mirrors where she could see herself in the dress; it was as beautiful as she had thought. Then there was a knock at the door and the woman stood there with a tray of breakfast; on the tray was a note from the Jew saying he had had to go to his office in the City before she woke but he would be back for lunch at one. Bertie sat in one of the purple velvet chairs with her breakfast beside her on a little table, and ate it luxuriously. She was hungry; she had not eaten since early the afternoon before. Then she leaned back and fanned herself. There was a black fan with daisies on it that was attached by a silk cord to the side of the dress, and she fanned herself, not because it was hot but to use it. When she was tired of looking at the dresses she went into the next room. It was a large oblong room with two windows; the great cut-glass chandelier hung from the centre of the ceiling; on the mantelpiece and stands there were vases and candlesticks with cut-glass pendants that glittered; the couches and chairs were covered with crimson-coloured velvet, as rich as the purple in the bedroom; the carpet was as soft and deep; the velvet curtains at the window were lined with rich satin and had cords and ball fringe, as heavy as the curtains in the picture of Queen Victoria that hung in the front room at the farm. Bertie touched them and rubbed her cheek against them. How wonderful and soft they were! She walked about touching all the things. She rang for Isaac to make a fire in the room and then she went and stood at the window and looked out at the houses in the street; all the houses were the same, high and yellow and dark, and the rain dropped from them. Far down at the end of the street she could see a square opening; cabs drove up it, and a postman with the rain dripping from him walked quickly up the street knocking at all the houses. She shivered and turned away and went back to sit by the fire. At one she had put on a beautiful white woollen dress made like a Greek robe, and the Jew took her down to lunch in the great dining room below stairs; it had an immense sideboard and pictures of fruits and hunting, and the great mahogany chairs were so heavy she could hardly lift them. After lunch the Jew went away again and she looked at her dresses.

At four he came and told her to get ready and he would take her for a drive. The carriage came to the door; the coachman had a livery, but had an overcoat over it; Isaac had the same livery and overcoat and sat beside him. She and the Jew got in; it was still raining, but it was close and warm inside in her furs, and she looked out through the windows at the damp people hurrying by. The Jew took her to many shops. At the milliner's she asked the price of a hat. 'Zat is nozing! Zat is nozing! Take vot you vill'; and he made her buy three hats. At other shops she bought gloves, sweetmeats, flowers, lilies and orchids that cost sovereigns* a bunch, though she thought only a few pence. At one jeweller's the Jew bought her a diamond bracelet and emerald earrings. She bought ornaments and knick-knacks, all kinds of things she had never seen before. When they got into the carriage at last, the front seat was piled so high with parcels that they kept falling down. When they got home the Jew went to his room to work till dinner, and she unpacked and rearranged her things. She rang the bell and made Isaac go and call the Jew to see how she had arranged the flowers about the drawing room, and she pinned a buttonhole into the Jew's coat. At dinner she wore a low white dress with roses wreathing on the bodice. It seemed to her at first extravagance to wear such a dress for an ordinary dinner; but there were none commoner. The dinner was laid out with much silver and cut glass, and there were many courses and three kinds of wine. She had only seen things something like that when there was a grand dinner party at Cape Town. The Jew had ordered the best cook that money could buy through his agent. Bertie would not take wine, she wanted lemonade, and Isaac had to go out and get it for her; but she ate three helpings like a child of some wonderful cake with cream and almonds in the middle. She made the Jew pull crackers with her, and when a yellow crown came out of one she made him put it on, and she put on a bishop's mitre. When they went upstairs her train was so long she nearly fell over it, and she told the

Jew he would have to carry it for her. When the Jew had taken her up to the drawing room he soon went back to his little office, and she sat by the fire and looked at some of the purchases, and then listened to the roar of the city till she got tired and cold and went to bed. All the next morning she tried on her dresses and cloaks and hats. The Jew could not come back to lunch, and had ordered hers to be sent up to her; but he came at four o'clock to take her out in the carriage. She asked him to take her to a shop where they sold materials for fancy-work, and she bought work of every kind, and work boxes and a work table and a work basket, and all the evening while he wrote in his room she sat by the fire knitting him a silk purse. When he came up at eleven o'clock she was bending over her work with a flushed face, and asked him if he liked the pattern. He could hardly get her to go to bed she was so interested in her work.

The next day it rained too heavily to go out at all; she sat all day working, finishing the purse, and began a pair of slippers. The day after she was so busy working at the slippers she said she did not want to drive. But in the evening, when the Jew came from his office at bedtime, she was sitting before the fire with her work in her lap staring into the blaze.

Suddenly she looked up at him. 'Do you think by this time they have the letter I wrote?' she asked.

'Vhy, no,' the Jew said, looking down at her. 'It takes long.'

She sat still looking into the fire. 'But don't you think I ought to write and send them my address?' she said presently. 'I told them I was well, and you were kind to me, and I was happy; but perhaps they want to know just where I am.' She waited a moment. 'Perhaps they are anxious.'

The Jew looked down at her with his bright eyes.

'Vhy you vish to tell zem vere you are? I give zem ze address of my partner in Zous America, zat zey may sink ve are zare. Do you vish zat zey come here to fetch you?' He looked keenly at her.

'Oh no, no!' Bertie said, raising herself. 'Oh no, I never want to go back to Africa! I am so happy here with you; you are so kind to me. I—only—sometimes—I am afraid they are anxious. I—I am afraid of that.'

'Ven zey sink you go on to Zous America as soon as you come here it will be nine ten months before zey come to you here; do you vish zey come soon?'

'Oh no, no, I want to stay here. You won't let anyone take me back to Africa, will you?' She raised herself.

'No, no!' he said.

She took up her slipper and began working again; but soon the Jew said it was time to go to bed.

Every morning the Jew went to the city at eight and Bertie had her breakfast in bed, and in the morning she tried on her dresses and did fancy work, and at one Isaac brought her lunch up on a silver tray to the drawing room. The Jew had made her understand he did not wish her to go to the lower floor when he was not there, that her world was the first floor. After lunch she lay on the bed and tried to sleep, and then before the Jew came she dressed herself again, and if he was early enough and the weather not too bad they went for a drive in the closed carriage. When they came home she dressed again for dinner and did her hair and they went down to the dining room and had dinner, with the silver and glass and the massive furniture about them, and then the Jew went to work in his little office and she sat in the drawing room. Though it was summer, it was a wet summer, and however warm the day might be she kept large fires burning night and day in the drawing room and bedroom. The light of the fire was the only thing that gleamed.

One afternoon, when it was raining too heavily to go out, she asked the Jew what was in the floors above her, and, as she wished to see them, he took the keys and opened the door. There were three floors with the garret, but there was nothing in any of the rooms. They had been painted and papered and decorated, but they were quite empty. She said to the Jew it would be nice if they furnished them. The Jew asked what they should do with them. She looked round and said perhaps when he had visitors; but he said he never had visitors, and they locked them up and went back to the drawing room.

The next day when the Jew came home it was pouring with rain. Out in the street as he drove up he saw an organ grinder and with him a boy of eleven standing in the rain turning their barrel organ. When he went upstairs he found the front window of the drawing room wide open and Bertie standing before it, the rain beating in on her white dress as she threw out to the man and boy little balls of crystallised fruits and sweets wrapped in paper. She had just wrapped a box of chocolates in her lace pocket handkerchief and thrown it out to them when the Jew came up. 'Catch! Catch!' she called, flinging it. The Jew came up to her. 'Oh, look at that poor little boy! Do give me some money to give them! They've been playing so beautifully. It makes one's feet jump. I've been dancing all round the room by myself while they played. And I haven't anything to give them but sweets.'

'Look, look how wet you are!' the Jew cried, pulling down the window. He touched her dripping sleeves and bodice with his finger. 'You must not talk viz people in ze street. Bad people zat vill come and steal all ze zings!' The Jew turned quickly and went downstairs. He sent Isaac to tell them that if they ever came again he would send the police after them, and Isaac was to be always on the watch lest they or others should return. When he went upstairs again, he impressed on her that never again under any condition must she open a window and speak to anyone in the street; nor under any condition must she ever speak to anyone to whom he had not introduced her. In Africa you could do these things, but not in London. She listened to him quietly. 'You like ze music?' he asked. 'Oh yes,' she said, 'dance music I like. It makes me dance all over. I'm never tired when near dance music.'

The next day, when they returned from their drive and Bertie came back into the drawing room, there was a grand square piano, the most richly toned that money could buy, standing between the window and the door. With a little cry of joy she sprang towards it and flung her hat and gloves upon it and opened it. The Jew, who was following her closely, looked on with delight. She drew out the rich music stool and seated herself on it, still wearing her fur cloak. She began to play. 'I can't play very well, you know,' she said, half turning to the Jew, who stood beside her, 'not real grand music, but if I hear a thing I can always play it; and they always got me to play for them at dances because I kept the time so.'

She started a waltz, swaying her head gently from side to side.

'Oh how beautiful! It's a lovely piano! I never saw one like it.' Then she paused and began a reel. 'This is the "vastrap",'* she said, half turning her face to the Jew, who stood beside her, and nicking her head at the end of each part where the final step came. 'It's what the Hottentots dance; I learnt it from hearing them play it on the concertina. When Rebekah used to set me to practise my scales, I used to try to practise them, and then suddenly I used to find I was playing this!' She was smiling and nicking her head all the while she talked: 'You should see their old velskoens flying when they dance, all full of holes!'

She played louder and louder and with more emphasis. Then suddenly she put her arms down on the keys and rested her head on them. She was motionless. The Jew stepped closer and put his hand on her shoulder; it was quaking. 'Vat is it?' he asked. Her shoulders were slowly convulsed, and then wild suppressed sobs broke that seemed rending her shoulder.

The Jew moved from one foot to the other with his hands extended, as an old hen might shuffle whose chicken was in a convulsion she could not understand. 'Vat is it?—Vhy—' He bent over her. 'Are you not vell?'

She made no answer, the sobs growing wilder till her whole body seemed convulsed by them.

'You are tired? Ve have go to too many shops zis afternoon?' He put his hand on her, then he hurried downstairs to get her a glass of wine. When he came back she had left the piano and had thrown herself on her face on the sofa in front of the fire in her bedroom and had buried her face in the pillows. She was sobbing, but more slowly. He pressed her to take the wine; but she said she could not, her head ached and she would lie on the sofa and try to go to sleep. He covered her feet with a rug and built up the fire and stood looking at her as she lay extended, with questioning anxious eyes. She did not move again till just before dinner, when she dressed herself and came down and said her head was better.

After that she seldom played on the piano, and after a while not at all. As the summer passed it grew damper and duller, and she often declined to go out driving when the Jew came home. He never took her to the parks or places where she could see fashionable people walking about, but always offered to take her to the shops. Generally she said she needed nothing; but whenever she went out she still went to the flower shops and brought back the carriage filled with flowers, with which she decorated her drawing room and bedroom; and she went to the confectioner's after and brought back boxes of sweets, which she munched all day as she sat before the fire. She seldom did fancy work now; she had made all she could think of for the Jew, and the great sofa cover she began lay untouched day after day.

One evening the Jew came back later than usual and found the drawing-room door locked and the other door on the landing which led into her bedroom locked too. She came quickly to the door and opened it. He asked her why it was locked. She had a large fire burning and the room was bright with it. 'I don't know,' she said, resting her hand on his arm. 'I nearly always lock them now when you are away. I don't know what it is'—she drooped her head lower to his—'but I feel so lonely. I'm so afraid,' she said softly.

'Afraid? Afraid of vot?' the Jew asked her, looking up at her.

She still kept hold of his arm. 'I don't know,' she whispered softly, with the other hand shutting the door; 'but I always feel as if something was following me, as if something was coming upstairs after me. I can't go to sleep because I'm afraid it'll be just behind me when I wake, so I keep the doors locked. I'm so lonely,' she said, after a pause. She took her hand from the Jew's arm, and they walked to the fireplace.

'Ven you are alone,' said the Jew, 'vy do you not call Marzer zat she comes and sits viz you? I vill tell her.'

'Oh, no, no!' Bertie said hurriedly. 'I don't want her.' She stooped to the Jew and said, almost in his ear, 'It's *her* I'm afraid of! Her wrists are so large!'

'Did she ever zay zomezings to you zat you not like?' the Jew asked, his eyes flashing quickly.

'Oh no,' Bertie said, 'she's never spoken to me once; Isaac brings the things up. And when she does the bedroom I come in here. But I see her looking at me. Sometimes, when we come up from dinner, I see her looking up the stairs after me! But—but,' Bertie hesitated, 'it isn't her fault; it isn't really her I'm afraid of; it's—I sometimes feel as if something was just behind my left shoulder, and when I look back quickly it seems I'm just going to see it—but I never do! It's always my left shoulder.' She glanced round.

The Jew looked at her with a curious questioning face. He thought for a little and then he proposed that, whenever she felt lonely, she should ring for Isaac and let him come and sit on the chair just inside the door. She said she would feel safe then; she was not afraid of Isaac. After that day Isaac had orders to come and sit with her whenever she rang. But the Jew always impressed on him he was to answer no questions she asked, nor to carry out any letters to post for her, nor to give her any money.

The first day when Isaac came up she tried to talk with him once or twice. But the convulsions he had had as an infant, while they seemed to have left his brain more or less intact (for he could do his mother's shopping, making better bargains than she could, and showed an exceeding keenness where money matters were concerned), seemed to have broken the full relation between the brain and the organs of sense; he could not tie a shoe lace except very slowly and not exactly, and, when he spoke a word, it was only slowly and after much consideration that the brain carried the order to the tongue. Bertie found he did not easily answer her and after the first day made little effort to speak to him. Every day she rang he came and sat on the chair just inside the door in his green livery with silver facings and buttons, one hand spread open on each of the knees he kept close together before him, and with his head stretched a little forward, the blunted tip of his nose always turned to the fireplace at the far end, his faint blue eyes fixed and striving to see everything where Bertie sat before the fire—as a worshipper at the far end of a cathedral looks to the altar with its lights and incense and flowers and its slowly raised chalice which announces a sacred presence. He watched, breathing slowly while she dozed in her chair. His breath became a little quicker when she rose and moved or stirred the fire; his eyes were fixed on the bedroom door when she went in to change her dress, and when she came back he noted everything she had on—the little diamond earrings, the belt, the comb in her hair—and when sometimes she drew her chair, so that as she sat before the fire he saw nothing but the little crown of brown curls on top of her head, he watched that. He watched with an intensity of interest when she put a sweetmeat between her lips and sucked or broke it. She always shared her chocolates and crystallised fruits with him; but he never ate them while he sat there; and his mother could never get him to go and do her shopping; he was always waiting in the kitchen passage for Bertie's bell to ring.

When he had been three days she proposed that he should help her move the furniture. She put the tables where the sofa had been and the sofa where the chairs had been, and they moved the piano. When the Jew came back that afternoon Bertie showed him quite excitedly the changes she had made and asked him whether he did not think it nice. During the next few days they moved everything in the room; at the end of a week all the furniture and all the pictures had been turned round and everything had been in the place of everything else; then she began to get tired of moving them, and after a few days they remained where they were.

As the summer grew older it grew damper and more oppressive. She generally refused when the Jew offered to take her out in the carriage; she liked better to rest in her armchair close to the fire, eating sweets.

One afternoon he was driving her down towards the Strand* to a place where he had heard Persian sweets were kept. There was a block in the large street and they had to turn down Seven Dials.* So many vehicles had come that they had almost to stand for some moments; she rubbed the damp from the windowpane and looked out. There was a low dirty shop at her left, in the window of which were boxes with rabbits and kittens and some cages with birds. Next to the shop a door stood open that led directly up a flight of stairs; in the open doorway were five children in ragged clothes with matted hair and no shoes on their feet, the eldest holding an almost naked and very dirty baby of a few months old in her arms. The rain beat in through the open door upon them as they pressed on one another and looked out into the muddy street from which the pouring rain had driven them.

'Oh, do look at them,' she cried to the Jew, 'so dirty and so ragged, and no shoes on their feet! Oh, do give me something to give them.'

The only thing the Jew had never given her was money. He gave her two half crowns, and as the carriage moved on she opened the window and threw them in at the open door; but the carriage was already moving on, and the Jew said she must shut the window to keep the rain out.

That evening, when the Jew came up at half past nine, instead of finding her dozing in the armchair, she was sitting back in it with her eyes wide open staring interestedly into the fire, so absorbed that she did not turn, as she always did if she were awake, to nod or say some word to him when he came in. He sat down in the straight-backed chair near her; but she sat with her soft eyes unusually bright staring at the blaze.

Suddenly she asked him, but rather dreamily without looking at him, what the price of coconut matting was.

The Jew stared at her. 'Vhy,' he said, 'you vant zome?'

'No,' she said slowly, 'I don't want any; I'm only thinking.'

He told her the price. She was dressed in a red silk dress, and about her shoulders hung a cream lace scarf; she looked very beautiful leaning back there, and the Jew thought she had almost a smiling look about her face, which she seldom had now.

'And what is the price of whitewash?' she asked slowly, presently. 'At the farm we used to pay three-and-six for lime, but up at my uncle's it used to cost four shillings.'

The Jew gazed at her. 'But vot do you vant ze lime for?'

'Oh, you see,' she said slowly, her Cape drawl becoming intensified, as was always the case when she tried to make anything but a very short speech or to explain anything, 'I was just thinking, if someone gave me thirty pounds and said I could have that house and all those children that we saw in the door today and said I must put everything right, how I would do it: I don't know if I could do it with thirty pounds, but I think I could. You see,' she said, interfolding her hands in her lap, 'I would first get a big bath and wash them all and cut their hair quite short, and I'd buy that blue stuff for threepence a yard I saw the other day and make them all blouses or frocks, and I would make them warm petticoats. The boots and socks would be dear'—her voice got more dreamy—'but all the other things I would make myself. I'd put alum wash all over the floors and ceilings first, and then I'd whitewash. How many rooms are there, do you think, in a house like that? It's not high, like this.' She turned her head and looked at him. 'I should think there were four, eh?—I could do it for the thirty pounds, I'm sure, and buy new furniture, but it's the coconut matting I'm not sure of. For fifty I could do it! Coconut matting is such a help. It keeps a house clean. I could whitewash, myself,' she said, after a pause; 'the stairs one could have planed down; they are so very dirty. That second little girl would be very pretty if she was clean, and the boy too.'

She had looked away from the Jew back into the fire. He had never heard her talk so much before; he said not a word and sat staring at her, as he always did when they were together. Presently he asked if she was not sleepy, but she said it was early yet, and he went back to his office to work, and she sat looking at the fire. She had not untied the ribbon round the packet of sweets that lay in her lap and which she had brought with her after dinner to eat. The next day, when she drove out, she asked him to take her that way again; she leaned out when they came past the house, but the door was shut.

As the summer grew old it rained rather less, but the air grew heavier and more dull. Bertie now refused to drive out at all, and sat by the fire. She ate less and less but was growing very stout. At night, when the Jew woke, he somehow often felt the bed shaking, and when he looked at her she was crying. Sometimes she seemed to be crying in her sleep; but when he roused her and asked her what it was she said it was nothing, that her head ached. She began now seldom to ask Isaac to come and sit in the drawing room, and she cried nearly all the time. From the time the Jew left in the morning till he came back in the evening she sometimes cried. She shut the door so that no one could hear her, and walked about the rooms wringing her hands and crying. She did not know why she cried except that there was always a pressure on the top of her head and that everything was pain to her. She would be quite quiet and she would go and look out from the front window at the long row of yellowish drab houses opposite with their tiers of windows one above another, and she would fall at once into a passionate crying that nothing would stop for hours. If she was standing near the window and happened to stroke down the great soft velvet folds of the curtains, it would make her cry, or unfolding a dress, or opening a packet of sweets. Everything she saw or heard made her cry. When she woke in the morning and heard a voice outside say, 'Old clo'! Old clo'!' it made her draw the cover over her head. At dinner sometimes, just as she was going to eat, she used to burst out wildly crying and the Jew could do nothing to comfort her or stop the crying. She left off having Isaac to sit with her—she said she was not frightened—and passed most of her time lying on the sofa in the bedroom before the fireplace, with a white shawl over her head. The Jew bought her one day the most astonishing collection of things—jewellery, hats and knick-knacks—and sent them home all at once. When he came home in the evening she put her arm on his shoulder and thanked him, but the next morning he found them still all piled on the sofa in the drawing room, and some of the parcels were not even opened. When he asked her if she were ill, she said no, and when he asked if she wanted anything she said no. The only thing she ever complained of was a feeling of pressure on the top of her head. She wept so persistently that there were sometimes not six hours in the twenty-four when she was not weeping either waking or asleep. Sometimes the Jew lit the candle and, raising himself on his elbow, watched her weeping in her sleep till the pillow under her face was wet, the great tears bursting from under her eyelids. He had never dreamed that a living thing could weep so.

At last he sent for a doctor, an old Jew he had known for years. He examined Bertie carefully and said there was nothing organically wrong with her; she wanted change and excitement and above all exercise. He ordered she should live no more on milk and biscuits but should take a glass of wine with her meals and a glass of stout before she went to bed at night to make her sleep. He said she was right in not caring to drive in a closed carriage, that every day for at least an hour she must walk, and walk quickly. The Jew thought over it all and made plans. That evening when he came home he told her to dress in her best dress and jewels; he would take her to a theatre. She rose from the sofa and began at once to take her dresses from the wardrobe. She tried on ten before she decided on one to wear; it was a white heavy satin; with it she wore a small diamond and emerald necklace the Jew had given her, and a star in her hair above her forehead.

They had an early dinner, and she talked and laughed and drank the two glasses of champagne instead of the wine she always took with her meals. Afterwards when the carriage was waiting and he went to fetch her, he met her fully dressed on the landing outside the drawing room and was stricken dumb with her glittering beauty. Only the tiny feet, which hardly supported her large body, and gave her the slight uncertain swaying movement as she walked, took from her absolutely regal grandeur. He covered her with her cloak and took her to the carriage. She talked and laughed all the way. The Jew had taken a box. He placed her where she saw the stage well, just below her, but he drew the velvet curtain a little so that she was sheltered from the audience, and he sat between it and her and watched.

They were playing already, and for a little while she kept asking questions. In Cape Town there was no theatre, and she had only seen two domestic little plays very badly set.* In the first act there was a harvest scene. Men and women in country dresses appeared tossing hay and a wagon came on the scene, and behind a hayrick a young man declared his love to one of the pretty haymakers in a sunbonnet and asked her to marry him. Bertie was so deeply interested she leaned forward pressing before the Jew and resting her elbows on the edge of the box, looking down.

Then the curtain fell. When it rose the lights were turned down in the theatre, but on the stage it shone brilliantly; the crowd of women had returned who were haymakers in the last scene. Robbed of almost all their clothing, their lower limbs made more obtrusive with flesh-coloured tights, some wearing a few yards of spangled gilt about their waists, some only with bandages of silk drawing between their legs, the trousers cut away even from the hips, the women leaped and flung their limbs in smooth contortions. She sat gazing at them. Presently she put her head closer to the Jew's. 'Aren't they women?'* she asked, 'the same that were here a little while ago?'

'Yes,' the Jew said; 'now zey dance.'

Bertie's hand shaded her face away from him as she looked.

'Why do they do it?' she whispered.

'Zey get money, zey pay zem for ze dance!'

A moment after Bertie had drawn herself back in her seat into the shadow of the box. When the Jew looked round at her he thought he saw tears on her cheeks; when he went near her he found she was shaking convulsively. He asked her whether she felt ill. She only sobbed for answer; the tears were pouring down her cheeks. He asked her whether he should take her home. She nodded and sobbed, 'Yes, yes!' He wrapped her up and led her out. As she passed down the corridor she sobbed aloud, and the attendants looked curiously at her. When he got her into the carriage she sat back with her head in the corner, her white lace scarf wrapped completely over her face, sobbing heavily.

'Are you sick? Are you tired?' the Jew whispered.

'No, no!' she said, but sobbed louder, while he looked at her anxiously. His attempt at amusement seemed to have failed utterly.

When they got home she went straight upstairs and into her bedroom and, dressed as she was, flung herself face downward on the sofa before the fire. In half an hour the Jew came up with the glass of wine* the doctor had said she must always have before she slept. The fire was burning low and she had not lit the lamp, but he could see her lying motionless and silent with the shawl still over her head. He touched her arm and asked her to sit up and take it. She raised herself, but, just as she was going to take it, threw herself on her face on the pillows, sobbing, 'Why don't their mothers fetch them home?'

'Vot?' said the Jew, bending over her with the glass in one hand.

'Why—don't—their—mothers fetch—them—home?' she cried, her face half choked in the pillow; 'they are women!—they are women!—and—the—the men—they—they—they—' She sobbed incoherently.

The Jew put his hand on her softly. It was the first time she had ever tried to explain to him what she was crying about; was it always something so unintelligible?

'Vitch men? Vot men?' he asked. The ballet dancers and the men in the front rows of the stalls had completely passed from his mind. She made no answer, but sobbed more quietly.

'Come, drink zis!' the Jew said coaxingly, as one speaks to a little child. 'It vill do you good. Ze doctor says you are very veek. Here—' He drew her with his hand. Slowly she sat up; he put the glass to her lips and she drank the contents; then she rose, a sudden dead quiet having come to her crying. She stood in the dull glowing light of the fire in her white satin dress, and she folded her arms on the mantelpiece and leaned her forehead on it.

'Do you feel better?' asked the Jew.

'Yes,' she said. Then in an instant the wild sobs convulsed her again. 'And—some of them—were—so young!—and—no—no—no one—'

The Jew bent close to her, but could not distinguish the word in her sobbing. 'You are very tired,' he said gently, 'shall I light ze lamp and you go to bed and rest?'

'No—no—I—like the dark!'

She still kept her forehead on the mantelpiece.

'Shall I not take off your shoes?' said the Jew; but she shook her head and sobbed a stifled 'Thank you.'

As she stood there quite quiet again and there seemed nothing for him to do, the Jew said he would go down and write for an hour and then come up again. And when he came up she was in bed and asleep.

The next morning, before he went to business, he told her that it was the doctor's order she should walk every day for an hour; that at eleven every day she must be ready and Isaac would walk out with her till twelve. He begged her to be careful never to speak to anyone; he impressed on her that London was not like South Africa, and that if one spoke or even looked at anyone terrible things might happen. He spoke long to Isaac, telling him exactly the path they were to go: down the street through the square into Oxford Street and along it, but never further than Oxford Circus; then to come back, to walk close behind his mistress, to speak to no one, and, if anyone came to speak to her or stared much at her, to stand close behind her, and to come and tell the Jew everything as soon as they returned. 'Ven one should look at her, Isaac, ven one should walk after her, you vill tell me, Isaac,' the Jew said, his keen eyes fixed on Isaac; and though Isaac only nodded and said nothing, the Jew knew it would be done.

At eleven Bertie dressed herself very carefully in her smartest walking boots and cloth dress and walking hat. It was the first time she had walked, and she was even excited when she and Isaac started, Isaac in his best livery with gilt buttons walking behind her, carrying the waterproof goloshes and umbrella the Jew said he must always carry.

She enjoyed the walk and when the Jew came home told him of much she had seen, and asked questions about the cabs and omnibuses. She dressed herself carefully for dinner that evening, ate well, and did not cry all the night; and the Jew thought her cure had been found.

For some weeks she went every day. The early autumn was coming in drier and warmer than the rainy summer. The air was sometimes hot and oppressive, but she went every day.

For some time she dressed herself very carefully when she went out, and noticed closely all she saw and looked in at the shop windows; but after a while she became careless and walked more slowly and looked more down on the pavement. There were four things she always noticed, one a large place with its windows full of books. Before Rebekah married she had once bought some secondhand books, on the outside of which a yellow card was pasted with the words 'Mudie's Select Library, New Oxford Street.'* The first day she looked in at the window and saw the books it came to her with a strange thrill how Rebekah had sat under the orange trees and in her bedroom reading from a book. Always, without missing, every day she stopped at that window. She read the names of the books over and over, without thinking what they meant, and went on.

Another thing was far down the great street; there was a dark house that stood far back from the pavement, and out of huge doors upstairs men were nearly always throwing into carts or wagons below brown stuff with a smell like malt. She never passed without looking at it. She disliked the strange dank smell. She never asked what it was, but all her life it came back to her with sickening remembrance of the long walks.

The other thing she always looked at was a shop window a little lower down. It was full of filters of all kinds, and there was a little fountain there that played with three small balls. The water came up like a tiny geyser and threw the balls in the air and always as they fell the water caught them again and threw them up. Every day she looked at them. The first day she had looked with interest; afterwards it became a terrible compulsion—she must look. She knew just how long it would be before they fell and how the water would catch them up again, but she had to look. She felt a kind of sick shrinking; yet she always had to watch them always do the same thing—they were always the same, like the curtains in the drawing room and the chair before the fire and the sofa in the bedroom, always the same. They all made the dull feeling in the top of her head worse.

At first she had looked at the streams as they passed her, men and women, old and young, all pressing onward somewhere, up and down—people in omnibuses, people driving, people walking; and a strange feeling always came to her that they were not really people, but like the people from the photographs which you look at through the two glasses, who move when you pull a string and shake their heads and jaws.* And sometimes the thought would come to her that they *were* people; that they were people living just as people lived in Africa, with their homes, and relations, and people they visited, who had children and felt and laughed; that each one was real and alive, just as much as the people she had known. And sometimes a strange feeling used to come to her that she must go up to someone and put her hand on their arm and say, 'Talk to me, please talk to me!'

But after a while she left off noticing the people. She took no care about her dress any more, put on anything that lay nearest and walked all the while looking down at the paving stones. She got to know them all; after the very large one came the small ones and then one cracked across. When she came home, often she remembered nothing and had seen nothing but the paving stones and the window with the balls and perhaps Mudie's and the malt place. Often, if it was at all damp or chill, she would not go at all though she knew the Jew wished it.

One day, a dull brown day with no rain, but the thick sky just above the roofs of the houses and damp autumn thickness everywhere, when Isaac came at eleven to tell her he was ready, she was lying dozing on the sofa in the bedroom in the pink silk dressing gown she had worn since she rose. She did not take it off, but pinned it carelessly round her waist with two pins to shorten it, but so that it showed here and there a glimpse of her white heavy-laced petticoat. Over it she put on the great fur coat she had thrown over a chair when she returned the day before and which reached almost to the bottom of her dress. She took from a wardrobe, almost without looking at it, a steel-blue French bonnet and without looking in the glass placed it on her roughened curls and tied it under her chin; she took up a pair of gloves, but, instead of putting them on, thrust them into her coat pocket. She did not trouble to put on her walking boots, but followed Isaac out into the street still wearing her little high-heeled patent leather shoes with paste buckles; she followed him heavily and when he dropped behind her she walked, looking down, hardly seeing the shop with the filters or noticing anything as she walked. When they got to the end of the walk they turned to come back down the same side of the street. For a moment or two she stood passive, looking into the great plate-glass window of a shop where tiers of new autumn hats and dresses were displayed. She looked vaguely at them for a moment, conscious only of the heavy grey sky above. Then she looked round and saw, standing close beside her also looking in at the window, two ladies. The elder one was about forty, older than Rebekah and rather taller, with her hair, which was already partly grey, turned back from her forehead instead of being worn turned down at the side as Rebekah wore it; her eyes were blue, but there was the same full high forehead, the same delicate sharp-marked nose dominating the face, a delicate strong rounded little chin and the sensitive strong mouth. She was dressed in a sealskin jacket with a little brown bonnet and skirt, just as Rebekah might have dressed. The girl beside her was about sixteen with very light hair and the exquisite pink and white skin which Northern women often have; her large blue eyes and her dreamy mouth were smiling as she looked in at the window.

Bertie looked at them, and an irresistible impulse came over her; she put out her hand and laid it softly on the sleeve of the sealskin jacket. The woman glanced down quickly, as everyone glances at being touched in London. For an instant she looked at Bertie and took it all in—the beautiful round white face with its fringed eyes, the little fifteen-guinea French bonnet tied a little askew on the natural curls, the ninety-guinea sealskin coat with the edge of pink silk showing below it, and the points of white petticoat with priceless lace that had tipped here and there in the mud; she looked at the little house shoe with the paste buckle and the ungloved hand with the rings. All her face hardened. If she had asked her why she touched her, Bertie would have spoken; but she turned and said to her daughter, 'Dear, we must go now.' The girl, who had noticed nothing, smiled and turned from the window. Bertie stood looking after them with her head on one side as they disappeared into the crowd. Then she turned and walked back. She walked so slowly that it sometimes seemed to Isaac she was going to stand still. When she got home she went upstairs to the bedroom and lay on the sofa before the fire.

From that time the Jew found it impossible to make her go out for a walk. She said she was tired or was cold. Some days she lay in bed till twelve o'clock and sometimes till five. If she got up earlier, she generally half dressed in a loose dressing gown and lay on the sofa in the bedroom or sat in the chair before the fire in the drawing room with a great shawl wrapped round her. She ate more than she had eaten, and she never cried now; she drank two or three glasses of wine for dinner and with her lunch, and the Jew brought her up something before she went to bed. But as the time passed the Jew grew anxious; he almost wished she would have the old wild fits of crying. Her face grew whiter and whiter and stouter, till under her little round chin a double chin was gathering. She never spoke unless he spoke to her, and, when he brought the carriage, only if he insisted on it would she put something on and drive out with him. She never complained of her head any more, and she never asked Isaac to come and sit with her; she said she was not afraid. Nine months before she had looked much younger. Then she was like a girl in her early teens, and now she looked ten years older than she was. Her face was still very beautiful, but it was the heavy pallid face of a woman who might be thirty or more. She never asked if there were letters from her friends or referred to the Cape.

Again the Jew called in the old doctor. He said again she ailed nothing organically; she needed change and fresh air, and advised the Jew at once to take her to the seaside. The Jew was obliged to start for Hamburg on business at the end of the week, but before he left he went to St Leonards-on-Sea* and took rooms for her, and the next day he took her and Isaac down.

The rooms he had taken for her were in a house facing the sea, kept by a widow woman who was a cousin of Martha's and whose husband had owed the Jew money. He had been kind to her and started her in this house. He had hired all the rooms from her for the time of Bertie's stay, stipulating that no other lodger should be taken; but the rooms really reserved for Bertie's use were the drawing room on the first floor and the bedroom opening from it, also a tiny closet on the first floor just outside her door where Isaac was to sleep. She had been almost excited when the Jew told her she was going to the sea; she had begun at once to pack her boxes, and had laughed several times.

They got there late in the evening when they could see nothing, and Bertie was still in bed when the Jew left the next morning. He gave many parting instructions to Isaac never to leave his mistress for a moment, and to tell him when he returned if anyone had spoken to her or come to sit by her on the beach.

When Bertie had had her breakfast and was dressed, she called Isaac and walked out onto the esplanade.* As far as the eye could reach, long rows of grey houses, three or four storeys high, rose on the right hand; almost as far as the eye could reach the solid stone pavement stretched; and to the left, under a grey sky, was the grey sea, breaking with a soft 'sushing' sound its dull water on the long beach of rounded boulders and grey pebbles. She stood looking at it for a little while, then she began to walk along the stone pavement with the tall grey houses to her right and the sea to her left, and Isaac followed her. Here and there were still a few bathing houses and a few people bathing in the grey water, as the air was still and warm though so dull. On the stone pavement here and there were Bath chairs* with invalids in them being pushed by men, sometimes with other persons walking beside them; and there were nurses wheeling babies in perambulators, or little groups of children down on the pebbles playing. In only one spot the long endless line of pavement was broken, where in the middle of the esplanade stood a little group of shops under one roof—a fish shop, a chemist's, a greengrocer's, a flower shop. She stood for a while looking in at the windows. She wanted nothing. Then she walked on for half a mile, then they turned and walked back again. After a time they came to where a great square of houses all exactly alike opened onto the esplanade; but here there were more people, and she turned back and walked up the pavement again to the point where they first turned.

After an hour and a half they went back into the house; she took off her walking things and walked about the great empty drawing room with the windows looking out on the esplanade and the sea. She looked at a glass bowl with some goldfishes on the side table and at two little Dresden figures* holding vases on the mantelpiece; and then she went into the bedroom and drew down the blind and lay covered on the bed till lunch time.

Every day she and Isaac walked out on the broad pavement, with the sea on the one hand and the rows of houses on the other; every day she stopped at the little building in the middle of the pavement with the little shops; she noticed how the fish was crimped* at the fishmonger's, and the large Persian cat at the greengrocer's; then she walked on another half mile and they turned. She began to know the stones as she had known them in Oxford Street, the large stone with the cracks and the place fifty yards on where there was the bluish stone. Sometimes she looked up at the houses, the tall stuccoed houses storeys high, and then would come the strange thought to her that they were real houses, houses where men and women lived like at the Cape. They were homes. Once she noticed specially a man with a tall silk hat run up the steps and open the door with a latchkey; he was going home to lunch just as Rebekah's husband might go home; once she saw three girls come out with tennis racquets, laughing and talking; they were going to play; and once she noticed a mother come back with some little parcels, and the children upstairs waved at her from the window till she went in and the door shut. They were real houses, with real people; it was not a nightmare; they were all real; it was she and Isaac walking up and down, up and down on the pavement, that were so strange.

One day the sky had changed from grey to a dark, heavy, leaden blue; it seemed to rest just on the roofs of the grey houses; and the sea was very dark when Isaac came at eleven to ask whether she would walk; he said he thought it would rain, but she walked to the front door and Isaac followed her, carrying her umbrella and cloak. They passed the shops and came to the place where she generally turned, but she walked on. They passed more and more houses, still in an unbroken row, with the stone pavement stretching on with the pebbles below and the grey muddy sea breaking softly on them. She walked on till there were no more people on the pavement and the row of houses to the right was growing smaller. The esplanade itself grew narrower. To Bertie it seemed they walked for miles; then both houses and esplanade ended. At the end of the esplanade some steps with iron handrails led down to a curved pebbly beach and the houses died away, leaving a bit of cliff-like rise with gorse bushes upon it. Away in the little bay there were stakes sticking in the water and what looked like wickerwork baskets showing in some places; there were no human creatures in sight except some men loading two carts with pebbles from the beach, and higher, near the houses, some men digging what seemed to be the foundation for a new house. She stood resting her hands on the top of the iron railing that ran along the end of the esplanade; her eyes looked far out across the dull grey waters, to where, some sixteen miles off, a small grey headland* jutted out into the sea, strangely clear in the humid blue water-laden air. Presently Isaac touched her on the sleeve: 'It is going to rain,' he said. She shook her head without moving her eyes from the distance. A few more large drops fell on her, and he opened the umbrella, but she put out her hand to keep him from holding it over her and went down the steps. She sat down on the pebbles with her back to the wall of the esplanade; she drew up her knees and folded her arms round them and sat looking out across the grey water of the little bay with its stakes and baskets, away to the grey headland dimly visible in the blue moist air. Isaac came down the steps too and stood on the pebbles a few yards from her. Quickly as the rain began to gather in about them, the few large drops became a thick haze, coming partly from the sea and partly from the land, that grew damper and damper. After a while the outlines of the distant headland vanished and from all sides the rain was creeping up. Slowly it blotted out the distant landscape, and then the posts standing out in the water in the little bays nearby and the baskets vanished. The men loading the pebbles from the beach had turned up the collars of their coats and driven away. The men digging the foundations had put their tools together in the trench and were walking away. Isaac moved from one foot to the other, looking at Bertie, the rain beginning to run down him. The water was beginning to gather round the brim of Bertie's fur hat in large drops and to run slowly down her fur cloak.

After a while the gloved hands she kept clasped round her knees were soaked, and the small streams ran down from her cloak and dress and made little puddles in the pebbles and earth about her. The wall of rain closed in, so that nothing further than a few feet away was at last visible. And the water streamed down the steps. Then she looked at Isaac and saw him shivering where he stood three feet away from her, holding her closed umbrella and waterproof as the rain ran off him.

She rose. 'Let us go home,' she said. She climbed the steps and they walked home along the dripping parade on which there was now no one, seeing nothing further than two feet before them for the blinding drizzle. When they got into the house she undressed and went to bed and had her meals brought to her room and did not get up again that day.

The next day she got up, but the rain was falling; she went to the drawing-room windows after breakfast, but the grey rain was falling on a grey sea, and the great stones of the parade lay wet. She shivered and shuddered and went to her bed and drew the down quilt over her head and slept all day.

The next day and the next it rained and she did not go out. But the next morning the rain had left off. It was grey but no rain was falling. Before eleven o'clock she rang the bell and Isaac came. 'Isaac,' she said, standing before him and looking into his face, 'is there any country here? I want to go into the country.' She spoke very slowly that he might catch each word.

'Country,' he repeated.

'Yes, country. I mean a place where there are no houses and people. In my country where I come from we call it veld.'

Isaac looked at her. 'No houses, no people—country,' he said slowly. He seemed to be considering, then he said slowly, 'Yes, I can show you. Come.' And Bertie went into the bedroom and got ready, and they went out together.

He led her in the opposite direction from the one they always walked in, past many shops and hotels and busy streets and a little fishing quarter where the fishermen's nets were out drying on the beach and little children played, then up a hill where there were little houses about and the town lay at your feet, and into a hollow where there were still more houses. Then they climbed another rise; the path went up among rough grass and some gorse bushes along the cliff. Isaac walked on before, Bertie climbing after him in her dark puce-coloured silk dress, holding it high above her laced white petticoat to keep it from the mud into which their feet sank as they climbed. Then the path ran along the top of a cliff. To the right was the grey sea, with many little fishing boats out on it; overhead was the drab sky; the footpath was full of white chalky mud which clung to their boots. Then they came to a broken fence partly of brambles. Isaac helped her to get through, and they walked on a little further. Here was another hollow leading down to the cliffs and the grey sea. There were a few bushes and small trees growing below. Nearby, a few yards from where they stood, was a great building which was closed and seemed unused; it had a red roof covered over with a fine yellow lichen that stained it everywhere. Far off there were more houses. Suddenly Isaac turned round and stood still; she also stood still.

'This—this,' said Isaac slowly, 'is country.'* She looked about her.

On the slope about them everywhere there were the marks of cows' feet, which had sunk deep into the soft soaked turf. Some of the footprints were full of clear water; in some, blue flowers had been growing which raised themselves stooping and half crushed. She looked round at the grey sky, at the damp bushes, at the barn a few hundred feet off with its red roof, damp with yellow lichens, and at the mud and grass at their feet. The high heels of her little shoes were sinking deep into the grass as the cows' hoofs had done. She drew her skirt tight about her and stood looking.

'Let us go back,' she said, and turned, Isaac following her.

She led the way through the hedge and along the path upon the edge of the cliff, Isaac patiently following her. They passed the fishermen's houses and the streets with shops and hotels and got back to their own quarters with its long hopeless row of grey tall houses and its long endless pavement and grey sea breaking on the round grey pebbles and shingles. Bertie went straight up to her bedroom, took off her little wet shoes, and curled herself under a great shawl on the bed, took only a glass of wine with a biscuit for her lunch and did not rise till late in the afternoon.

That evening the Jew came. He had only returned from Hamburg that day.

He asked her whether she would like to stay longer where she was, but she begged him to take her back with him the next morning; and the Jew chuckled much to himself as he lay in bed that night thinking her life with him could not be so unbearable if she were so glad to return to it.

When Bertie got back, for the first two or three days she ate more and was a little less pale, but then she sank back into her old life. It was duller and damper now, so she never went out. She kept the blinds nearly always drawn down, but great fires burning night and day and lamps lighted if the fog were a little dark. She wore always one dress, a crimson velvet gown, loose and long, which had cost forty guineas. She put it on in the morning and wore it till night, never changing it for dinner. When the point lace* about the neck and shoulders grew soiled she did not remove it, but threw a lace scarf over it.

All day she sat deep in the armchair before the fire or lay on her sofa in the bedroom. For lunch she took nothing but a glass of ale with biscuits and at dinner she ate little, though she took some glasses of wine; yet her face and figure grew quickly heavier.

She never referred to her friends in Africa or spoke of her letters to them; a complete silence seemed to have fallen on her, and, unless it was quite necessary to answer some question the Jew put to her, she never spoke.

One evening as the Jew sat in his room writing, he looked round to see Isaac standing behind him and asked what he wanted. For a moment Isaac paused, drawing his power of speech together. Then he said slowly, bending his face near to the Jew's, 'The—lady likes—cats!'

The Jew started up. 'Cats!' He looked at Isaac.

'Yes,' said Isaac slowly. Then knitting his hands together as if for a great effort, so that the knuckles cracked, he said, 'I was—cleaning—the window—she came—she saw a black cat on the wall—she said, "Catch it for me. I—like—cats!"'

The Jew stared at him; no one had ever before heard Isaac attempt a description. The Jew had a horror of all living creatures except storks, and cats he shrank from especially. 'Cats?' he said. 'Cats?'

Isaac nodded, 'She—likes—cats.'

The Jew looked at him doubtfully. 'Can you get her one?'

'Three,' said Isaac slowly, 'kittens.'

For a moment the Jew hesitated, then took from his pocket a ten-shilling bit and put it into Isaac's hand. 'You vill get zem, Isaac. Zey vill be small and not to make a noise!'

Isaac nodded.

The next morning while Bertie still lay in bed, eating her milk and biscuit, someone tapped at the door. In answer to her question, the door was slowly pushed open a little and a basket thrust in; then the door was closed.

A little wheezing sound from the basket made her leap out of bed and go to it.

Half an hour after, when the Jew, who had just finished his breakfast, went up to say goodbye to her, he was astonished to hear shouts of laughter through the closed door; not knowing Isaac had already brought the kittens, he was astonished at the door to see Bertie kneeling on all fours in her white nightdress; on the hearthrug before the fire, one kitten was lapping milk from a saucer before her, one was mounted already on her back, and one, as she knelt with her head down, was leaping up at the long loose braid of curly hair hanging over her shoulder and trying to hold it with his paws.

She looked up laughing, 'Oh, aren't they lovely! One's climbed right on my back—look how this one plays with my hair; it means to climb up by it!' She half raised herself, taking the one off her back. 'There are two black and white and one grey and white; look, its eyes are quite blue; the other two are browny!' She stood up, still holding one in her hand. 'Oh, did you get them for me? It was so kind of you—' She rested her hand on his shoulder; standing in her white nightdress she looked like a tall white angel beside his little dark figure; the top of his head barely touched her chin. Then she stooped to pick the others up and gathered them all three in her arms, pressing her face against each. She asked the Jew whether it would be possible for him to let her have the carriage in the morning, as she wanted at once to go and buy some things for them. The Jew was very busy, but he returned at eleven o'clock and took her out.

She bought three exquisite little china bowls, decorated, one with a rose, one with holly and one with larkspur. She bought three rolls of ribbon exactly to match the flowers on each bowl and three tiny real silver bells. When she got home she tied on each its bell with a ribbon to match its bowl and gave each one the name of the flower on its bowl, Holly, Larkspur and Rose.

When the Jew came home at night, she rushed to the door and brought him to see them all drinking milk in a row, each out of its own bowl with its own little ribbon and own little bell.

At night she put their basket close by her bed on a chair where she could put out her hand and feel them. But the next day she was not satisfied with the basket, and drove out with the Jew in the afternoon to order a cradle she had thought of. It was of white wood, in three little compartments, all joined together and on rockers, with three little hoods, one over each compartment. The next day the cradle came and she spent three days lining it; from early morning when she rose till near midnight she was lining and draping it; she made the kittens tiny down mattresses and down pillows and tiny blankets and sheets, each with the kitten's name embroidered in silk in the corner; she made three little satin quilts with the flower of each kitten embroidered on it in silks; she edged them all with real lace. When the Jew came up to bed she took him into the bedroom and showed him the three little kittens lying before the fire, each in its own division in the cradle with its head on its own little pillow and tucked in under its own little quilt.

'Isn't it lovely?' she said, peering down at them; 'just like little babies, eh?' She bent over them and smoothed their little sleeping heads softly with her hand.

The Jew looked down at her with astonishment.

'Do you like babies?' he said after a time.

'Yes—of—course,' she said slowly.

'You see'—she raised herself—'you can put your foot on the end of the rocker—like this—and rock them all at once if they want to wake.' And she stood rocking them softly with her foot. The next day she made three little silk bags and hung them in a row by the drawing-room fireplace, and in each was a tiny silk handkerchief, embroidered with a kitten's name, with which to wipe their mouths after they had drunk milk.

For two or three evenings after they came she dressed herself in white for dinner and carried all the kittens down in her arms. They walked about the table and had three little china plates set at the end into which she put titbits.

The Jew turned cold with horror when they walked to his end of the table and put their whiskers into his glass and even their paws on the end of his plate, though he said nothing. She fed them with tiny morsels of chicken held between her lips and gathered them all up into her breast to carry upstairs again.

For nine or ten days when the Jew came home she sat for half an hour telling him all they had been doing—one had climbed onto the piano and broken a glass vase and one had been found asleep in the folds of the window curtain. Sometimes she asked the Jew to drive her out in the carriage as she said change of air was good for them, and she held them to the closed window to let them see the fog and dark of the street; but after that the excitement began to die down. When she had had them three weeks she had dropped back into the old life; she still fed them three times a day, but generally she put the food all in one bowl; their ribbons were unchanged for three or four days; they slept in any compartment of the cradle, and she never took them down to dinner; they went if they chose. Sometimes she stroked them as they climbed about her, and she let them sleep in her lap; but she spent her day silently dozing before the fire or watching it with wide-open eyes.

One rainy evening, just before dinner, she sat dozing before the fire in her red velvet gown with the lace scarf twisted about her throat. The Jew was in his little office downstairs, working at his books; the French cook who came in every day to make the dinner was busy dishing up with Martha in the kitchen, and Isaac was in his little room in the basement, dressing to wait at table, carefully brushing his hair before the little glass upon the wall to see if it were perfectly straight—as he always did before he went into Bertie's presence. Then there was a knock at the front door. Isaac not being ready, his mother went. In the doorway stood a tall handsome man of about thirty, whom she knew well as the son of the Jew's only surviving cousin, with whom thirty years before the Jew had quarrelled hopelessly because she had insisted on marrying a wealthy Christian; but he had partly made up the difference with the son, whom he sometimes asked to his house and often gave money to. It was supposed by the few who knew the Jew's affairs that, in spite of his being a Christian, the Jew might yet make him his heir, as he had no other near kin living; and Martha had never regarded him with favour. He asked if his cousin were in, and stepped into the hall. He stared round in astonishment at the change which had passed over the place since he was there last, glanced at the double-piled carpet on the stairs and at the glass and silver on the lighted dining-room table visible through the open door. The Jew, hearing sounds in the passage, came out of his den as his young cousin was taking off his overcoat and hanging it in the hall.

The young man turned and shook hands with the Jew. He apologised that he had not been able to see him for so long but for the last year he had been travelling abroad. As he spoke he glanced round and in at the dining-room door; and at that moment Isaac passed them with two dishes for the dining room.

'You have made things very comfortable here, I see,' he said.

The Jew gave him no explanation and asked him into his den, but when half an hour had passed and the young man made no sign of going, he asked him whether he would not stay to dinner and went up to the drawing room to see Bertie. She was lying back in her armchair with one kitten asleep on her shoulder and two playing with a worsted ball* on the hearthrug.

'It is dinner time,' he said.

'Yes, I don't know why Isaac has not rung the bell,' she said slowly.

The Jew looked down at her. 'My cousin is here; he comes to dinner too.'

'Yes,' she said, slowly stretching herself and preparing to rise.

'You vill not dress you a little?'

'No,' she said heavily, 'this will do.' She put the kitten down on the floor and ran her fingers indifferently through the brown curls above her forehead, but without looking in the glass. Then she turned and walked slowly towards the door, the Jew following her. She went straight to the dining room and took her seat at the table, while the Jew went to his den to where his cousin waited.

Then he brought him into the dining room. 'This is my cousin,' he said, pointing his hand towards him, but he gave Bertie no name. Bertie half rose, and a look of surprise came over her face. She merely bowed her head slightly and sat down again. (She had expected to see a man of the Jew's age and type. But the visitor was quite six feet high and nothing suggested the Jew but the brilliancy of his dark almond-shaped eyes with long lashes like her own and a slight curve in his finely shaped nose. His forehead was broad and smooth, shaded by smooth wavy black hair; his jaw and chin were powerful and well shaped, and the voluptuous fullness of the much-arched lips did not take away from their strength; they also closed firmly.)

The Jew showed him to a seat on the right side of the table opposite to Bertie, where Isaac had set a place for him. Between him and Bertie, somewhat obscuring her, was a silver stand full of flowers; but across it he was able to note the full voluptuous beauty of her figure even in the loose velvet gown, the richness of the curly hair above the flower-like white face and the perfect shaping of her arms, which the wide drooping sleeves of the old dressing gown made visible almost to her elbows.

Isaac handed round the soup. The Jew began to discuss the Stock Exchange in Paris, where his cousin had been spending some months, and Bertie, with eyes fixed on her plate, ate silently. It was not till the third course had been reached that the Jew's cousin, leaning forward a little to the side to escape the vase, said to her, 'These flowers are very beautiful. One hardly expects to see such flowers at this time of the year.'

'Yes,' Bertie said slowly, without raising her eyes from her plate. Then the Jew asked him another question, and it was only when they were finishing dessert that the visitor once again addressed her; there were oranges on the table and he was explaining the signs by which he knew these came from the south of France, and he described the orchards there. 'Perhaps you know the south of Europe?' he said, leaning forward and speaking to Bertie again.

'No,' she said slowly, hardly raising her eyelids and head.

The Jew glanced sharply from one to the other, but Bertie had not raised her head or glanced at the visitor and was passively picking her walnut out of its shell.

The Jew's cousin at once reverted to a business topic. He saw at once Bertie had not been born in England, and it puzzled him to guess where she came from; he had thought his question might lead to an answer.

Soon Bertie rose; she bowed slightly towards them at the table without saying anything and slowly moved towards the door. Without seeming to do so the Jew's cousin noted everything—the queenly body, the small lovely round head and neck, the long trailing untidy velvet gown, the slight swaying motion in the walk, the little hand hanging at her side with three rings on it.

When she had gone out he glanced at the Jew for a second to see if he would refer to her, but the Jew passed the wine bottle to him and told him how much he had paid per dozen when he bought it. When they had emptied their glasses he took him to his den; the young man stayed three hours longer than he had ever done before, but the Jew made no offer to take him to the drawing room, nor did he in any way refer to Bertie or explain her presence.

When he had left, the Jew went upstairs. He found Bertie as always in the chair before the fire; the kittens had gone to bed and she was lying back holding a large fan to screen her face from the hot blaze. The Jew stood for nearly four minutes beside her on the hearthrug. Then he said, still looking into the blaze, 'Vell, vot zink you of my cousin?'

She laid the fan down and stared into the fire. 'He's not like you,' she said.

The Jew looked keenly at her. 'He is young,' he said. 'He is handsome?'

'Yes,' she said slowly, 'he is handsome—but,' she added yet more slowly, turning her head towards him, 'he's not so nice as you.'

The Jew waited a moment. 'Do you not like him?'

She waited; then she said, dreamily looking at the fire, 'On the farm where I lived once, they caught a tiger, one of the large leopards, and Rebekah went to the cage every day to feed it; she wanted to make it love her, but I was afraid of it—' She paused as though she had lost the thread of her thought, then she said, remembering, 'And one day after dinner, when she was going to feed it, it nearly caught her hand and bit it off; my father just caught it in time and after that he sent it away to be sold.'

'Vell?'

She looked up. 'Oh, I'm frightened of him, like I was of the tiger too. Rebekah, my sister, wasn't frightened. She never was frightened of anything.'

'Vhy are you frightened of him?' the Jew asked, looking down at her.

'I don't know,' she said slowly. 'I think it's his eyes—his teeth are so white when he eats.'

'He is no good,' the Jew said. 'I give him much money; I have sent him to ze university. He has always no money; it is ze pleasure, ze gamble, ze horse race, all ze bad zings he likes.'

Bertie looked passively at the fire. She seemed to have nothing more to say; and presently the Jew went down to finish his work and soon she went to bed.

During the next ten days the Jew's cousin called three times—once in the afternoon, when Isaac answered the door and told him the Jew was out; once in the evening just before dinner, when Martha opened the door for him and he exchanged a few words with her before she showed him into the Jew's room—the Jew did not ask him to stay and he soon went; the third time he came Bertie had been staying in bed all day, as she often did when the fog was bad. Martha and he had a long talk in the hall and he left a gold coin in her hand as he went out.

It was three days after that visit, on a heavy drizzly night, that he called again about nine o'clock. Bertie was sitting fast asleep before the fire upstairs; Isaac was in his little room; the Jew was in his den working; when there came the sound of a tap against the window in the area, and presently Martha, without a light, came out of the kitchen door, went up the area steps, unlocked the gate and led the Jew's cousin down into the kitchen where a candle was burning; she put her finger to her lips when he began to speak. 'The boy is in his room,' she said, 'but he may not yet be asleep; he is very sharp—be quiet!' She slipped off her own shoes: 'You had better take off yours.' He hesitated. 'You can get them again when you go.'

He sat down on the kitchen chair and removed them. 'There is no possibility of his returning tonight?'

'Not till tomorrow night.'

He rose and with his boots in one hand prepared to mount the carpeted stairs. Martha followed him. He looked back at her. 'You are sure she expects me?'

Martha nodded her head and pointed to the door under the stairs to signify Isaac was there; then she whispered to him, 'Remember, it's the door facing you on the first landing, the door at the side going into the bedroom.' As he passed the door of the Jew's room he glanced at it, but it was closed and the light from the hall lamp was too strong to allow any light to shine from beneath it. Martha, standing at the back of the hall behind the stairs, motioned with her hand for him to put his boots down by the hatstand, but he shook his head, hung his hat on it, and carrying the boots in his hand went softly up the thickly carpeted stairs. At the door of the drawing room he paused, drew on his boots, drew off his soiled gloves and removed his overcoat; then he knocked softly. Bertie, dozing before the fire with the kittens in her lap, was half roused by it and sleepily called an answer; she fancied it was the Jew bringing her wine and biscuits. He entered, hung his coat over a chair near the door, and walked with long light steps across the room to the fireplace. It was not till he stood beside her on the hearthrug that she turned her head and saw him. She started, partly raising herself. He held out his hand to her, but in her startled surprise she did not see it.

'I am afraid you will have thought me very late, but they wouldn't let me come before.' He bent a little towards her. 'It was very good of you to let me come.' She turned her head to see if the Jew were coming; she thought the Jew must have asked him to spend the evening with them. He noticed her glance at the door and said, 'I have shut it.' He turned and drew a chair onto the hearthrug, not two feet away from her, and sat down on it, carelessly leaning his elbow on his knee and bending a little towards her. She saw how spotless his black coat was and his white cuffs, and noticed his white hands with their long delicately rounded fingernails.

'I don't wonder you are very lonely here all by yourself,' he said softly. He put out his hand with its white fingers and nails and stroked the kittens sleeping in her lap. She was sitting upright with her right elbow resting on the arm of her chair; the wide sleeve of the crimson gown had fallen back; her left hand rested near the kittens; she moved it a little that his hand might not come near hers as he touched them.

'I suppose you are very fond of them,' he said, looking up into her face.

'Yes, I like them,' she said.

He thought his eyes had never been so near the face of a woman which had looked at him in a manner so absolutely passion-dead.

'It's a shame all your affections should be showered on them,' he said softly. 'One envies them their resting place.'

He looked up into her face, then he withdrew his hand and raised himself a little. He looked down at her. 'How beautiful!' he said. 'You know, that was the first thing I noticed about you!' In a moment he had placed his full-curved lips upon her arm halfway between her elbow and her wrist.

With a half-suppressed cry Bertie rose; the kittens fell at her feet. 'How dare you! How dare you!' she cried, standing at her full height before him.

He also rose. 'I hope I have not been too hasty,' he said; his mouth drew back a little. 'After the kind message you sent me, I think'—he put his hand out towards her—'that perhaps—' He smiled.

'Oh, I never sent a message to you; you are so terrible to me; I can't bear you! I can't bear you! Go, go, please go!'

He looked at her shrinking face with its wide-open eyes, and at that moment his quick ear caught the sound of steps on the stairs outside the door. In an instant the truth flashed on him. There was a sound at the door. In an instant his eye glanced round the room; then without a moment's hesitation he glided past her; the door that led into her bedroom stood open behind her; with two long steps he had entered it and closed it slowly behind him; as he did so the drawing room door burst open and the Jew with Martha behind him stood there.

The Jew glanced wildly round the room. 'Vere is he?' he cried to Bertie, who stood before the fire. Before anyone could reach him he turned on Martha: 'You vitch, zere is no von; vhy did you lie to me!' He turned to the fireplace where Bertie stood crying, 'Oh, I'm so glad you've come, I'm so glad you've come!' But Martha took the overcoat from the chair beside the door and, holding it up high to her shoulders, called the Jew; he turned and looked at her. For a moment he stood transfixed; then he stepped near her, looking at the coat. Bertie had run up to him: 'Oh, he is horrible! Why did you let him come! Why did you let him come!' She put her two hands passionately on the Jew's arm; he was still staring at the coat. At that moment the street door closed loudly; the Jew's cousin had evidently made his way through the bedroom door on the landing. 'Oh, you must never let him come again! Never—never—never!'

The Jew turned an ashen grey face slowly to her. 'No, he will not come here again,' he said. A few drops of sweat stood out on his forehead; his face was shrunken; it was the face of a man of eighty. He looked at her. 'Come,' he said. He grasped her wrists, one in each hand, and drew her towards the door. 'Come!'

'Oh, you are hurting me!' she cried; 'what is it! What is it! Why do you look at me so!'

He had drawn her out of the door onto the landing; the kittens, suddenly awakened from their sleep, ran after her, climbing onto her train. On the landing he turned her round so that she was below him and he above, and pushed her slowly backwards down the first stair. It seemed impossible that the iron force with which he held her wrists resided in his little shrunken body.

'Oh, let me go!' she cried; 'what is the matter? Oh, what is it—what is it?'

He pressed her down, step by step; the kittens, trying to hold to her dress, slipped down the stairs behind her. His eyes were fixed on hers. 'I—I—' he said from between his closed teeth—'I took you—you told me—you had no home—I—' He grasped her wrists as he pushed her down.

'Oh, you are going to kill me! Oh, Martha, Martha, ask him to let me go, ask him to explain to me! Help me, help me, Martha!' They were halfway down the stairs now. Martha stood close behind the Jew with the man's overcoat over her arm. 'Oh, you are going to kill me,' she whispered. 'What is it! What have I done!' Then understanding something, she cried, 'It was not my fault that he came. You asked him! Oh, I hated him, I hated him so!'

Then something in the Jew's face silenced her; the only wish she had was to escape from him. They had reached the hall now. He pushed her towards the door; she offered no resistance. He loosened one of her wrists and, with the hand that had held it, he pulled from her fingers the three rings she wore, so roughly that the flesh of her fingers was torn. Then he turned and took from Martha the coat. He raised it and put it over Bertie's head and shoulders; quietly, almost gently, he opened the door and, taking both her wrists, pushed her out backwards. She offered no resistance; she gazed at his face in a kind of frozen horror.

'Go,' he said, 'somevere he vaits for you.' He shut the door.

For a while Bertie stood stupefied, with her face to the door and the man's coat thrown over her head and shoulders, on which the rain fell heavily. Then she felt dizzy and sat down on the step and leaned her face on her hands. It had happened so quickly it seemed dreamlike; only the pain in her wrists and fingers told her it was real. At last she rose and turned to the door as if to knock at it. She heard the sound of voices and steps in the hall, and a terror seized her. If the Jew had been alone she would have knocked till he opened and thrown herself at his feet, and, if he kicked her, have cried till he listened; but she feared Martha's face behind him. She walked down the steps, looking back to see that no one was following her, and then a little way down the street till she came to a place a few doors off where a short street opened from the long one and led into a square. She walked down it. The rain was falling softly and steadily on her head. There were a few lamps almost deadened by the rain, and in the centre of the square one saw dimly the outline of high iron railings and trees. At the corner of the square she stood still. Just beside her, in the first large house looking into the square, one of the blinds had not been pulled quite down. She stood close to the area railing and looked; it was a large dining room or sitting room; there was a great table; at the other end, with his back turned to it, as though he was sitting before a fire, was the head of an elderly man; at the table, near him, bending over her work, was the head of a woman with greyish hair and a white cap; two young girls and a boy were reading at it. There were books lying on it. The light inside was so intense and bright, seen from the dark outside, that she could see the pattern of the paper on the wall with a large gilt figure and the bottoms of the picture frames. She pressed close to the railing, looking in. Then from the other side of the quiet square someone came walking with long loud steps. She did not know it was a policeman, but she felt as if he noticed her, though on the other side of the square. She walked away a little distance and stood beside the railings shutting in the trees and plants in the centre of the square. She moved her arm in and out of the tall railing and rested her head on it. A shrub hung over the railing above her, but it did not shelter her; the rain fell on her back.

Suddenly a hand touched the sleeve of the man's coat; she started and looked round; someone brought his face close to hers. It was Isaac.

'I saw—all,' he said. 'I was behind the stairs. They think—I sleep.'

'Oh, Isaac, what have I done? Why did he do so?'

Isaac waited. 'She,' he said slowly, 'let him in at the kitchen—I saw—she took him up. She told *him*'—he made the curious motion with his thumb with which he always signified the Jew—'he came with his latch key himself—she said he often came to see you.'

'Oh, but Isaac, it isn't true, it isn't true,' she said; 'if I go back and tell him all the truth won't he believe me, won't he let me in?'

Isaac shook his head strongly. 'He,' he said slowly, 'killed—all—the cats!'

Bertie shivered.

'It's—no—use,' he said slowly.

'But where can I go, Isaac?—I've no money.' She wound her arm about the railing again and rested her head on it.

'I know,' he said. He took a black bundle from under his arm.

'Put it on,' he said. It was a black lace shawl, which she had left hanging in the hall when last she went out driving, because it got wet.

'Put—it—on,' he said. He took the man's coat that covered her and held it for her to put her arms in and slowly buttoned it before; then he put the shawl over her head.

'Come!' he said. 'I know—a place. Come!'

He opened the umbrella he had brought and held it over her head. He paused to pick up the train of her dress, which was hanging in the mud, and helped her to put it up. She was so faint and cold she asked him nothing. She walked close beside him.

The rain was pouring down, heavier now. For a little while they walked through dimly lighted squares and streets; then they got to the fuller light of Oxford Street. The shawl covering her head and shoulders prevented the strangeness of her coat from being very apparent.

Isaac called the first cab he saw and put her in it and got in beside her. She sat very close to him, almost pressing to his side. She clung to him as a drowning man clings to a rope, frail and worn it may be, but which is all that holds him to life. She felt faint and almost dizzy. When they got to a railway station he helped her out. When he had taken tickets he took her across a platform and got with her into a third-class carriage. She sat in a corner with her head thrown back into it. Only once she bent forward and said to Isaac: 'Don't you think he would ever believe me, and let me go back?'

Isaac shook his head. 'No—no,' he said.

When the train stopped and they got out they were still in the suburbs of London, but the air felt fresher and lighter. A slight mizzle* was yet falling.

Isaac walked close beside her with the umbrella. They went down a long rise among houses and then up, still among small houses closely packed together.

'Where are we going?' she said at last.

'To a woman,' he answered; then added, 'She—lodged in our house—I know her.'

As they passed the houses Isaac went up to one or two and peered at the numbers, which were hardly visible to his shortsighted eyes in the dimly lighted road. At last he stopped at one. Two or three steps led up to a little porch. He left Bertie standing on the pavement and went up and knocked. When he had knocked twice and waited for some time the door opened. In a very narrow passage the light of a dim gas lamp showed a woman of thirty in a shabby black dress, with a small, much worn and pinched face.

She recognised Isaac and asked him what he had come for. He took her to the back part of the passage and talked in a low voice. The woman peered towards the figure of Bertie out in the street, and they had some discussion; he took out his little red purse and slipped two pounds into her hand, and then went down the steps and brought Bertie in.

The woman stared at the tall figure in its strangely cut overcoat, and the black shawl, so draped about the head and face that little was visible. Isaac pointed to the woman. 'She,' he said, 'will show you.' He put his head nearer to hers and whispered, 'I will come again—soon—when I can.' Then, without shaking hands or saying goodbye, he turned and shambled out at the front door, shutting it behind him.

The woman looked up at Bertie with her sharp pinched face. 'You've no luggage, I suppose?' Bertie shook her head.

The woman took up a bedroom candlestick from the little shabby hatstand, lighted it and began to climb the very narrow flight of stairs, motioning Bertie to follow her up. Once Bertie's foot caught in a hole in the stair carpet. On the landing the woman stopped, opened a small door on the right and went in. Bertie followed her. She set the candlestick down on a chest of drawers with a soiled white cover. There was a single bed in the room, also with a white cover, and some other articles of furniture. She looked at Bertie as if expecting her to remove the shawl; then she went to see if there were water and a towel on the small hand-washstand.

'You don't want anything to eat, do you?' Bertie thanked her and said she did not; and the woman turned to go out. 'You ring if you want anything,' she said, pointing to the bell, and went out.

When she had gone Bertie turned and, without removing any of her wraps, threw herself down on her face on the bed. After a little while she seemed to feel the wraps strike her damp, for she stood up and took off the overcoat and shawl and threw them over the foot of the bed; then she took off her small red satin shoes, soaked through with the rain, and threw herself down again with her arm over her head.

In twenty minutes the woman came again to the door and knocked and, getting no answer, opened it. She came in and stood at the bedside, but Bertie was fast asleep. She took up the light and looked down at her, afterwards not unkindly, but shook her head, and put the light down again on the drawers and laid near it an old calico nightdress she had brought to lend her.

Then she went out, but Bertie still slept on heavily without stirring. It was nine o'clock the next morning before she woke. For a little while she looked about her in surprise and then sat up on the bed. It was a small room, with a common wallpaper with a dull yellow-brown ground covered with diamonds of dull blue transverse lines. Besides the bed and drawers there was a small wooden washstand and a yet smaller chair; over the little unpolished fireplace was a yellow mantelshelf, and above it hung a picture in a yellow polished oak frame of Queen Victoria when she was a young girl. The paper on which it was engraved was yellow with age and under the glass were large swelled marks all over it as if at some time tears had fallen on it and blistered it; there was a little window with a green blind, and below it, through one round hole in it as big as a shilling, two streaks of sunshine came; both fell on the torn strip of carpet beside the bed and showed the dust and dirt which had almost caked it over and obliterated the faint pattern.

She sat for a moment, then she got slowly off the bed and went to the window. She raised the blind and looked out. It was a long, curved street running up the side of a hill with little grey stucco houses built exactly alike and touching each other all the way along; each house had a little portico with mock pillars before the door and two or three steps leading up to it, and each had a little bow window on the right side of the steps. Some had a few pots of geraniums in the window, and some had none; that was all the difference between them; and one house far down had one tiny tree growing in its little area. The air of the suburb was clearer than it had ever been in Bloomsbury. The late autumn sunshine was brighter than any she had seen since she came to England, though it was December. She let the blind drop and sat down on the side of the bed.

Presently the door opened and her landlady came in, carrying a small tray with some tea and bread and butter. 'I've been in twice already,' she said, 'but you were fast asleep.' She put the tray on the drawers.

'I haven't any money to pay you for it,' said Bertie slowly.

The woman looked at her. 'Oh, the young man who came with you gave me a couple of shillings' (she did not mention it was two sovereigns) 'and I said I'd do for you till he came again. You'd better drink your tea before it gets cold.' She glanced down at Bertie's hands. 'You seem to have hurt yourself,' she said. There were blue marks round her wrists and the skin was torn a little on two fingers where the Jew had torn the rings off.

Bertie said nothing, and the woman went out and closed the door. She had four children to support and four lodgers to attend to. When her husband lived they had hired the garret floor at the Jew's house in Bloomsbury, but he had died of drink a year before and left her with the children to support. Isaac had been sent with her when she moved into her new house, purely because she owed the Jew money and he wanted to know exactly where she was; and twice he had been sent again to collect the instalments, so he knew the place well. She had no time to think of other people's affairs, the pressure of life was too hard on her, but she fancied Bertie must have had a room in the Jew's house and been turned out because she had not paid rent, or perhaps some man had deserted her. Isaac had told her she had lived for six months in the house at Bloomsbury.

Bertie stood up and drank some of the tea, but the mouthful of bread she bit seemed to oppress her and she took no more; she sat down on the bed again with her arm across her eyes. She seemed to see the farm, the great dam on the flats by the willow trees, with the little ducks wading in and out among the weeds, and below, where it ran out, the Kaffir girls sitting in the sun and beating the clothes on the stones and laughing. She saw the orange trees before the door and the flower garden beyond and old Ayah working at the milk house and scolding the maids and Griet dancing about pretending to put the rooms neat. She saw all the thorn trees on the flats beginning to burst into their yellow blossoms ready for Christmas; she saw her father and her mother. Oh, she would go back to them, she would go back to them; it didn't matter what they said.

And then she saw, fleetingly, pressing it from her as quickly as she could, the little parlour in the bush, and John-Ferdinand's face with its great dark eyes, and Veronica's, and she saw the little face*—she could not go back! She could never go back! Then she heard the voices of the women talking in the little back room at the dance and she had the feeling of running home through the Avenue, and the suffocating tightness across her chest; and the people that looked at her as she came out of the church at her aunt's—no, no—she could never go back, never—never—never! Oh, what should she do! Where should she go!

She stood up and began pacing the room. Oh, if only the Jew had killed her, if she hadn't got away! 'If I were dead! If I were dead!' she cried, wringing her hands and pacing up and down. The wild uncontrollable weeping that had left her so long returned to her. 'If I were dead! If I were dead! Oh, God! If I were dead!' All thought went from her as she paced, wringing her hands. 'Where shall I go! What shall I do! If I were dead!' By and by the woman came up and listened at the door. She had heard the pacing from below and fancied she heard cries. It was no affair of hers, so she went away again, and the pacing and crying went on.

At last Bertie stood still suddenly before the mantelpiece and leaned her head against it. Where was she? What was she doing? Everything in her brain seemed to stand still and be a blank; she did not cry. She raised her head and looked about her; it seemed as if she suddenly saw again, after being quite blind, the little lodging-house bedroom with the streaks of sunlight coming in through the hole in the blind. It did not come from under the blind any more. She leaned her elbows on the fireplace and looked at Queen Victoria as a girl. She noticed all the flyblows on the frame and the large teardrops swelling on the yellow paper under the glass. Was it her wedding dress, or do queens wear those coronets and veils flung behind at any time? The 'Queen Victoria' and the date printed below were quite faded. It must be twenty-five years old. Then she suddenly began wringing her hands and crying again. She paced the room quickly. That little ray of sunshine shone right on a hole in the dirty little strip of carpet.

Then suddenly a barrel organ, which a man had drawn up before him, struck up *Polly is my sweetheart, Polly is my darling.** She stood quite still and listened to it. When it had finished it played *My Grandfather's Clock**—'And it stopped short—Never to go again—When the old man—died!' It ate into her brain and made the pain at the top of her head worse. After a while it went away and played lower down the street, and then again lower down. And then it went away out of all hearing.

She lifted the blind and looked out into the street; it was perfectly empty and silent—not a thing moved there. All the houses were alike, so exactly alike. A horror of pain came on her, just as when she looked at Queen Victoria's picture or at the ray of light. She pulled the blind down. She went to lie down on the bed with her shawl wrapped right round her head and was quite still.

At one o'clock the woman brought her up a plate with some meat and cabbage, and Bertie got off the bed when she had gone and ate it all, and then lay down again. About three the woman came to fetch the plate. Bertie got up.

'I want to ask you something,' she said.

The woman stood still with the plate in her hand at the door.

'Couldn't you help me to get any work to do?'

'What can you do?'

'I could cook or sew, I could be a servant.'

'Well, you couldn't get a situation unless you had some reference. I don't know what they do in your country—the boy told me you came from some place far over the sea—but here no one takes people without references. You've never been a servant before, have you?'

'Oh no,' Bertie said slowly.

The woman looked keenly at her. 'Well, you'd get nothing to do in *those* clothes; you'd have to get something quite different. Why don't you go home to your friends? It is much the best thing you can do.'

'I can't. I haven't any friends in this country.'

'Well, you know your own business best. I couldn't help you to work; I do all my own. The young man said he'd come again; and perhaps he'll help you.'

She looked at Bertie's curled hair, swollen baby-pretty face and the red satin slippers, still wet from last night's soaking, which stood at the foot of the bed, and went out; and Bertie lay down: there was nothing else to do.

Just before dark she drew up the window blind and looked out again. There were more people in the street now; every now and then men passed up, principally clerks; and other men who had come home from the city walked up to one house or the other. The sky was dull and clouded over again as if it were going to rain and a wind was whirling down the road in gusts.

Then down the street from the top of the hill came a curious figure, a man who looked like a Chinaman. He had a curious straw hat on his head with little bells all round tied onto it; on his head was a drum, which he hit with two sticks fastened to his shoulders; before his lips he had a curious wind instrument fastened, which he played with his lips by moving his head; in his hands he had bones and a pair of cymbals. He stopped before the window when he saw her standing there and played all his instruments together, making a kind of band. Seeing she had nothing to give him, he went on and the darkness gathered down.

Presently the woman brought her up a candle and some tea and bread and jam, but she said she wanted only the tea, and undressed and went to bed in the landlady's nightgown. But when the woman went upstairs to her bedroom at eleven o'clock, she heard the crying and sobbing going on in Bertie's room when she stood close to the door.

The next day it rained heavily and Bertie lay in bed all the morning; the woman brought her dinner up at one o'clock. 'You really must try to eat something,' she said; 'you've taken nothing since you came but that little bit of dinner yesterday.' She told Bertie she was going out on business in the afternoon, but that, if she rang the bell, her little daughter was at home and would bring her anything she wanted. Bertie took a few mouthfuls of the food and then turned on her shoulder again and slept till three o'clock. Then she was stiff with lying so long, and she got up and dressed, but soon lay down again. She had no wish to cry any more; she was in a torpid state.

About four o'clock the landlady's little girl knocked at the door and opened it; she said a man had called and had asked to see Bertie.

Bertie rose quickly. So Isaac had not forgotten her.

The little child said she had asked him into the front sitting room downstairs, and if Bertie went there she would find him. Without looking into the glass to arrange her tumbled hair, Bertie went down the stairs; to the right of the passage was a door opening into the little sitting room, which was unlet just then, as there was no lodger who could afford to take it. It was a very small room, with a few geranium pots in the window and a discoloured pair of lace curtains, keeping out the little light that came in from the dull rainy world outside. In one corner was a little whatnot with a few china pigs and other animals upon it. There was a low horsehair sofa; four horsehair chairs stood about the room and an armchair with a broken spring in the seat stood in the corner next the window. Over the mantelpiece was a mirror with a flyblown gilt frame and bits of green tissue paper pinned about it, and before it stood two vases with hanging cut-glass ornaments, several of which were missing; a small Japanese umbrella was opened in the fireplace and the room was almost filled by a small square table that stood in the centre, covered with a faded red tapestry cloth. At first when Bertie slipped in she saw no one; then a figure rose from the broken horsehair armchair in the corner. It was not Isaac: Bertie started and looked at it. It was the Jew's cousin, who rose lightly to his full height and stepped towards the table. He had another overcoat on, open in front, and she could see the points of his sharply curled moustache as he moved towards her and held out his hand. She stood silent on the other side of the table and did not take it.

'I am not surprised you are astonished to see me, and not at all surprised that you should be angry with me,' he said softly, still bending across the table, 'but I felt that I owed it to you as well as to myself to explain to you about all the terrible trouble I've got you into. I'm so very, very sorry.'

Bertie stood still, with her arms drooping impassively at her sides. 'Please go away,' she said.

'Oh, don't ask me to do that! Don't be so unkind!' he said gently; 'I've taken such trouble to find you! I feel I must do something to put things right. Please sit down.' He put a chair round the corner of the table for her. Still she stood. 'It's all that terrible old woman, and the damnable lies she told! You really must let me explain to you; it won't take long. Please sit down!'

Bertie drew the chair he had set for her further, so that not only the corner of the table but the whole width was between them. He sat down also and leaned his elbow on the table and looked at her. The rather dim light was behind him but it faced her.

'I always knew she had a spite against me, but that she would do such a thing as this I didn't dream. I used to lodge in the first-floor rooms you had and she used to carry to my cousin all sorts of tales about me—the hours I came home and the people I had; but I never dreamed she could do such a thing. One day, when I came to see my cousin, she met me in the hall and talked about you.' (He did not mention that he had called specially, knowing the Jew was out, to see the woman and find out who Bertie was and what her relation was to the Jew!)

'And she told me how lonely you were, no one coming to see you, and that you had come from another country. I told her how much I admired you, and she told me you had wished that my cousin should bring me upstairs, but he refused it. In fact'—he bent forward a little more—'she implied that you felt lonely and would be glad to meet me. I sent a message to you to tell you how delighted and honoured I should be if I could see you. The next time I saw her she told me you would send me word the first time my cousin was away on business. Of course I quite understood how lonely you must be shut up there with no one but that old man to speak to.'

'He was always very kind to me,' Bertie said slowly, drawing herself up a little.

'Oh, of course, of course! Who could have been otherwise!' He moved his head a little and looked at her; it was a little difficult to explain to a woman who spoke and showed herself so little. 'She came to my rooms and told me my cousin had gone to the country for twenty-four hours and you would be willing to receive me; naturally I came. She assured me he was away and would not be back till the next morning. Of course I never dreamed she was lying and that all the while he was sitting in his office downstairs. Shall I shut the door?' He half rose.

'No,' Bertie said, putting out her hand to keep it open behind her.

'You really must forgive me!' he said in a low voice. 'I have suffered just as much as you have in a way. I am his only living relative, and it has always been supposed that when he died I should be remembered. That was just what the woman didn't like; she thought if I were out of the way it would be better for her and that boy. I've no doubt she was afraid of you too in the same way!'

'If I went to him and told him all, do you think he would let me go back?' she said slowly.

'Oh no, it would be quite useless. I made inquiries and I find that yesterday every stick of furniture went out of the house back to the dealers, and he's sold the lease. The new people take possession on Monday. I inquired at his office, and I find he sails for South America tonight. The boy and the old harridan are to go to Hamburg in a few days. It would be no use your trying to communicate with him; he's not a man who forgives.'

Bertie stood up and turned to the door.

'Oh, don't go, please don't go yet! If you knew what trouble I had taken to find you.' He rose also. 'You didn't think I went off and left you without a thought that night! I waited about outside; I knew how violent he was. I saw you come out and go round into the square. I followed you, but you know I'd been so deceived—I didn't know what further plot there might be. I saw Isaac come to you, and I followed you all the way here. I could not lose sight of you.' He lowered his voice a little and bent his head towards her. 'You must let me help you a little; you must let me take care of you. She told me you had no friends in this country—you must—' He put out his hand a little, almost as if he would have stretched it and touched hers.

Bertie, who had half turned and stood looking at him, shrank and drew herself together, and went out at the door.

He looked after her; under the red gown the sinuous movements of her body were visible and he noticed how beautifully the little head was set on the little neck. She beckoned to the little girl, who was sitting at the head of the kitchen stairs, to follow her, and went up to her room.

For a moment the man stood doubtful; then he rang the bell.

The landlady, who had just returned, answered it. She was astonished to find the tall handsome man, from his dress and voice evidently a gentleman of a type her house seldom saw, standing in her little front parlour. He told her he had come to call on the lady who was staying there, who was a friend of his; he hoped she would pay her every attention. He took from his pocket a card with his name and address upon it; under it he had slipped a sovereign. He placed both in her hand. He would call again soon, he said, but if by any possibility the lady should leave she would kindly communicate with him at once. At that moment the little girl came down carrying over her arm an overcoat which she said Bertie had told her to give the gentleman. He said he could not take it then, and asked them to hang it on the stand in the passage; he would fetch it when he called again the next day. He gave the little girl half a crown, and asked the woman to order anything Bertie might need and charge it to him. Then he opened his umbrella and walked out. The woman stood on the step for a moment watching the fashionably dressed figure in its overcoat and silk hat, and then went to the kitchen to prepare a good supper for Bertie.

It was three days after that Isaac stood at the same doorstep and knocked. It was a Sunday afternoon, and a soft mizzly rain was falling. He stood on the doorstep in his overcoat. He had not been able to get away before. His mother had kept him constantly employed and near her while the furniture was moving. Now she had gone to make some arrangements for their leaving the next morning for the **continent**, and he was free. In the pocket of his greatcoat he carried a little square parcel; in it was a very tiny leather bag with gold coins, about which were wrapped a tiny roll of five-pound notes; all were carefully wrapped up in a bit of thick cloth and tied with string. He had kept his left hand in his pocket and on the parcel ever since he had left the house. He had been collecting the sum ever since he was a little boy of five and the Jew gave him halfpence when he swept his office or cleaned his boots. Gradually the pence had become shillings and the shillings pounds, and at night, when his door was locked, he got out his little hoard from behind the loose plank in the wainscoting, where it was kept in the inner of two little iron boxes. He liked the rustle of the bank notes even better than the gold. He was going to say goodbye to Bertie, and then, just as he was going, he would take out the parcel and put it in her hand. After he was gone she would see what was in it. His money had never seemed so valuable to him before.

After some moments the woman opened the door and looked at Isaac with the raindrops dripping from his hat.

'I want—to—see—the lady,' he said slowly.

'She's not here.'

He waited. 'Has—she—gone—for a walk?'

'No, she's gone. She went away this morning.'

Isaac looked speechlessly at her. 'Where to?' he said at last.

'A gentleman who's been here three times to see her came this morning. They went away in a hansom cab.'

'Where—to?' asked Isaac.

But the woman said she did not know.

CHAPTER XII

FIREFLIES IN THE DARK

It was a still, hot night. Outside among the roses and lilies of Rebekah's garden the fireflies glinted. In the large bed of carnations, where the white blooms shone out like dim stars in the half dark, they flitted everywhere.

There was little change about the house or garden since that time five years before, when her youngest boy was born.* Only the window of her study was now a door; its inner door, that led into the children's bedroom, was walled up, so that you could reach it only from the garden; and, between the billiard room and the little rose hedge, a new square block of buildings had been raised, not connected with the house. It contained two rooms; the large front room looked out into the garden through windows and a wide glass door; in two of its corners were little white beds in which the two youngest boys slept; by day all the children played in it and at night learnt their lessons there; in the room behind, Rebekah slept with Sartje—a little, yellow-brown, frizzly-haired girl she had adopted five years before as a little baby and treated in all ways as her own child, except that she* was taught to call her **Mistress**. The two elder boys slept in the main building in the room which had once been the nursery and which opened out of their father's bedroom.

Tonight the French windows and glass door of the large room stood open and the heavy scent from the flowers in the garden came in with almost cloying sweetness on the night air. In the centre of the room on a large square table a lamp burned; about it hovered a cloud of insects and little night flies and moths, and curious creatures with long hard wings, and little flying beetles. Some hung about the opal shade of the lamp, others had stuck fast to the transparent glass bowl, while others walked slowly about on the brown tablecloth.

At the further end of the table the children were gathered. The eldest, a tall fair-haired lad, with delicate features and eyes that would exactly have repeated his mother's had they not been so pale, was bending over a drawing pad on which he was working with coloured pencils. Also at the table was his brother, a year younger than himself, but already as tall and very powerfully built, his face and figure repeating, with a curious exactness, his father's. He rested his elbows on the table, with his chin on his hands, and looked down from under his fair almost white eyelashes at his brother's pencils as they moved. Close to the left elbow of the eldest boy stood the third—dark, round-headed, with straight, short-cropped hair and curiously alert, dark, very round eyes; he was standing on tiptoe trying, with his elbows on the table, to raise himself high to see well what his brother was doing. At the other elbow stood Sartje, the adopted child, whose small head of woolly hair and glittering narrow eyes hardly showed above the edge of the table, but who also was trying to get a glimpse of the work. Only Bertie, the youngest of the boys, lay already in his little white bed in the corner, his cluster of brown curls spread out on the pillow, his delicate rosebud mouth and tinted cheek and round eyes shaded by long lashes recalling the aunt who had never seen him and whose name he bore; but there was a still dreaminess in the eyes that hers had never known. Before him on the white quilt lay one of the lesson books of the older children in which he had been looking at pictures; but now his little elbows rested on the quilt, and his small hands were raised, the fingertips of one hand playing softly with the other's, and he was whispering as he looked at them, as though telling them a story. Between the face on the pillow and the little, dark, wizen* face of the girl, who stood trying to look at the picture, there was a likeness; her forehead was drawn up with wrinkles, like an old woman's, as if from some pre-natal and inherited anxiety, while his was smooth as a white tablet; but both had the same low, broad outline; in both the hair grew directly up from the forehead in a long, straight line; her lips were blue and pouting and her black eyes twinkled between narrow lids; but both had the same perfect oval outline of face and the same rounded chin indented by a dimple—the likeness between a figure carved delicately in alabaster and the same cast roughly in brown clay; but it was there.*

'I say, man,' said Frank, the second boy, looking down at his brother's work over his hand and filling out his chest as he spoke, 'it's just wonderful how you do it all out of your head! When I am a man and rich, and you are an artist, I'll buy your pictures to hang all round my room.' He took one hand from under his chin to flick away a moth. 'Get away, Sartje! Get away!—I say, get away!—You are not to come too close to me, touching my arm! Get round the corner!'

Sartje got back to her first position close to the eldest boy, and slipped her hand onto his knee.

'When you've done this,' said Frank, again resting his chin on his hand, looking down at the work, 'you must draw a picture with fellows playing cricket in a field, all the fellows we know. I want to show the boys that you make them out of your head. That Grey boy* says you take them out of your books; he can't say that if it's fellows he knows.'

'And you'll make me catching the ball, won't you, eh?' said Hughie, laying his hand eagerly on his brother's arm.

'*You* catching a ball!' said Frank, biting a thumb nail as he spoke and without looking down at the small child. 'Why, you can't catch anything! You just pick up a ball when it rolls to your feet—and then you fancy you are a big boy and can field! Why, you can't even talk plain! You lisp worse than Sartje or Bertie—just like a baby.'

Hughie's face flushed and his eyes flashed over the top of the table. 'I—I—' he cried; then, suddenly realising the undeniable truth of the accusation, he slunk down from his tiptoes and almost disappeared behind his side of the table. 'I thall be theven nexth birffday,' he said softly, after a moment's pause, but whether because he wished to change the subject or at least to prove that the charge of babyhood was unfounded, no one asked him.

'There won't be time to draw another picture tonight,' Charles said, moving his head back to look at the effect of his work; then he bent low over the pad to add the finishing touches. 'I want to write to Grandmother tonight and tell her that Mother thinks we shall be able to come and visit her at the farm the month after next,' he said, without raising his head.

'Oh Goy!* Won't that be fine!' Frank slapped his legs with his left hand. 'Just the time the fruit's all ripe!'

'And you'll tell her to make muth peath thjam, eh?' said Hughie.

'Pugh!—you can't tell people when you are going to visit them what they must make before you come,' cried Frank, blowing out his lips. 'She'll think you are an awfully greedy boy.'

Hughie slunk down again till his head almost disappeared behind the eldest brother's arm.

At that moment a firefly, which had flitted in through the open door, settled down on the drawing pad. With a shout of delight the two elder boys stretched out their hands and, interlacing their fingers, raised over the firefly a small dome with their hands, leaving only one tiny opening between the fingers at the top.

'A peep show! A peep show!' shouted Frank. 'Does anyone want to pay a penny for looking in, and see a live candle walking about?' He put his own eye to the opening. 'She's just walking over the tree you made; I can see it quite plainly by the light.'

The elder boy put down his own eye to examine also, and Sartje and Hughie were both allowed to climb onto the table and peep in.

At that moment the door of the room behind opened and Rebekah stood in the doorway. She had changed little in the five years; but the drawn lines that had gathered about the eyes and mouth had grown faint, and there was a repose about the face that was perhaps not rest but calm.

She was dressed in the black dress covered with little silver stars which years before she had made after the fashion of Mrs Drummond's because she thought her husband would like it and which had always hung in her wardrobe. During the last five years she had not gone out in the evening; but tonight there was a concert in Town given by artists said to be the best who had yet visited South Africa. As Frank had said he was going, she had taken a ticket for herself for the seat next his and was going with him.

Generally her hair was brushed down in smooth waves at each side of her forehead, but tonight she had fastened it back and bound it up high with a silver fillet, and she had a little silver belt about her waist. The children, who had never seen her in evening dress before, looked round at her as she came in.

'Oh, how beautiful! How beautiful!' Charles cried, raising himself slowly from his seat and standing before her; while Sartje and Hughie ran to her and began feeling with their hands the little silver stars upon her skirt; and Frank, climbing slowly down from the table, stood with his hands in his pockets looking approvingly at her: 'I say—but you *are* a swell!'

She laughed.

'You are like Titania, the Queen of the Fairies,'* said Charles softly, twirling his pencil between his fingers. 'Where did you get it from, Mother?'

'I made it when you were a baby,' she said, moving forward, while the two little ones clung about her.

He looked at her with his head a little on one side. 'I'd like to do you so—like that'; he moved his pencil round and round softly. 'Only, you know, I couldn't. Perhaps—'

'Let *me* see too!' piped a small voice from the bed in the corner. Rebekah turned and threw the red silk cloak she carried on her arm (the same Bertie had worn the night she went to the dance) over the foot of the bed, and walked to the bedside.

Bertie hardly looked at the dress, but wove his small arms round her waist and drew her down to him. 'Tell me a story!' he whispered, creeping close to her.

'Ah yes, finish the one you were telling last night,' said Frank.

'I'm afraid there is no time,' she said, drawing out her watch.

'Oh yes, there is. I heard Father just now calling for the hot water for his bath; he won't be ready soon.'

She sat down on the side of the bed.

'Tell,' said Bertie.

Rebekah raised her little black-slippered feet onto the bed and leaned her head against its iron fretwork, while Bertie crept closer under her arm. The two elder boys sat down on the floor between the table and the bed with their knees crossed; Hugh clambered onto the bed's foot, while Sartje sat flat on the floor close to the side of the bed where Rebekah's train hung down so that she might count the stars upon it softly as her hand passed over them.

'You were just where the Robber Baron had put the two pilgrims in a dungeon and the young girl was coming down the stairs in the dark,'* said Charles.

It did not take Rebekah very long to finish the story; to tell how the girl, finding her father was going to starve the prisoners to death, had taken his keys from him as he lay in a drunken sleep; and how, having opened the dungeon, she took the prisoners to a secret gate in the castle walls, gave them food for the journey and directed them to a path through the woods by which they might escape to freedom.

The children listened intently; there was a moment's silence when she had finished. Generally they asked questions and there was a free discussion of the story when it was done; but tonight Frank burst forth suddenly, 'Mother, I want to say something to you: I'm never going to walk with Sartje again; never, never! In the streets or anywhere!'

Rebekah glanced down at him without raising her head. 'Why?' she asked slowly.

He puffed out his full cheeks a little and pushed forward his red lips. 'Because, when we came back from singing lesson yesterday, the boys at the corner house came out and laughed at us. They said, "Walking with a nigger-girl!—Walking with a nigger-girl!—Walking with a black nigger!" I'll never walk with Sartje again; never, never, never!'

Rebekah lay quite silent for a moment; she seemed looking at the wall opposite; then she said, very slowly, 'It was very cruel and very evil to speak as they did, and it is also not true. Sartje is not a black nigger any more than she is a pure white child.'

'She *is* a nigger!' Frank burst forth, looking down glumly at his hands. 'Father calls her that. I heard him say it to a man the other day—a black nigger; and that she and Bertie have to have their meals here and only come to table when Father is away. I know it!'

Rebekah started as he began to speak, then she lay back motionless, with her eyes fixed on the opposite wall as though she saw nothing.

'She's a black nigger,' Frank repeated, half under his breath, 'and I'll never walk with her again!'

Sartje, not understanding what was said but feeling she was being discussed in some way not wholly to her advantage, sat pressing the back of her head into the folds of Rebekah's skirts as they hung down from the bed, and looked out at the boys with her thick lips a little pursed.

Rebekah, still leaning her head back against the ironwork of the bed, had half closed her eyes and thrown one arm across her forehead; while Bertie, with his head tucked under the other, was softly stroking it where it was bare from the elbow to the wrist.

'Do you know, boys,' she said suddenly, after a pause, 'sometimes I have had a dream. I have dreamed that as we are living here in this old world, just as we have always lived, suddenly there has arrived among us a strange, terrible, new race of people, coming from I know not where, perhaps from the nearest star.'

She waited.

'I have dreamed they were like us in body and mind, but with terrible white faces; our skins are tinted, but theirs were white as the driven snow, and their hair like thick threads of solid gold.

'They talked and laughed just as we. Mothers brought their little babies into the world and trained and cared for them, and men and women had friends and relations that they loved, and when they died as we die bitter tears were shed into the new graves. When they were struck their bodies felt pain, and when they were insulted they resented it; they lived, living and fearing and hating and hoping, and in the end their bodies turned to dust like ours. They were human;* but there was this difference between them and us—that, of many things, they knew what we did not, and they could do things we could not.

'We, here on earth, have been so proud of our little cities and our little inventions, our ships and our books and our telescopes and our laws and our manners, and we have thought we were so wise and knew right from wrong, but, suddenly, when these terrible white-faced strangers came among us, all changed. The cities we had taken ages to build they shovelled away in a few days, and in their places raised palaces so large that our cathedrals went into their cellars. They had learnt how to grasp the force of the tidal wave and of the very movements of the earth, and to use it as they would. Where we with difficulty dug holes a few hundred yards into the earth, they with their wonderful machines cut in miles, as though it had been cheese. They had machines that drew great currents of cold air down from the higher regions to cool the tropical plains, and they could send vast currents of warm air up to heat the mountain peaks. They sent currents of warmed air and water to the poles to make perpetual spring there, and cooled the equator with water from the poles. If they wished to speak to one a thousand miles off they spoke and were heard, how we could not tell; and when they wrote they did not use their hand, they set something against their brains and the thoughts registered themselves. To go to the other side of the earth they had no need to use our little trains and ships; they passed through the air, and the highest mountain peaks warmed by hot currents from the plains were their resting places. They had instruments so delicate you could see the blood beat in the leg of a gnat no bigger than a pin's point; and others so strong you could see a pebble no larger than a thimble lying on the moon's surface, just as we now with our telescopes see the extinct volcanoes. They laughed at our dirty habit of putting diseased matter into our veins to save us from disease and of pouring poisons into our stomachs to mend all parts of our bodies. They had found out what it means when you say a thing lives and grows; they knew what passed on in our bodies, and when anything went wrong they knew how to go back to the cause to put it right. They called us savages. In their laboratories they shaped the most rare and delicious foods from gases and primitive atoms—foods such as we can get only when they have been drawn from the earth and air and combined in the living laboratories of the plants and animals. In every mouthful of food they ate they knew just how much of each substance the body needs was in it, and what the effect would be; they did not eat in the dark whatever came, as we do. The bloody flesh of our fellow creatures which we feed on, the roots we dig out of the ground too, the milk drawn out of the bodies of other living beasts, they thought as horrible and unclean as we think the grubs and entrails on which the Bushmen feed. And our clothes—the skin of dead creatures which we fasten over our hands and feet, the jackals' and bears' and skunks' skins which we hang about our shoulders with the tails flying and think ourselves so grand in, the feathers of birds and the dead birds which we mix with grass straws and fasten on our heads, the shreds of hair and wool from animals' backs, the threads from the insides of little worms,* the torn decayed fibre of plants that we beat into clothes and are so proud to carry about everywhere on our bodies and think others savages if they have not got them—they thought disgusting.

'They were so civilised they knew the body of a human being was more wonderful and beautiful than any covering matter made out of dead animals or decayed plants, and when they wore any covering it was only for warmth or to fasten on their wings. What they wore were beautiful scale-like things, woven as we weave glass out of sand, but soft and of many colours, fitting each human being's body as perfectly as their own skins; so that, when a man or woman was fitted out for flight with their wings on, they looked as a dragonfly looks when it is hovering over a pool. They thought our clothes and the way we hid our bodies from light and air uncleanly; and they turned their heads from us, as we turn our heads from natives dressed in skins and rubbed with fats.'

The two elder boys were leaning forward with their arms upon their knees and their lips apart following each word, and Hughie had knelt straight up at the foot of the bed, his eyes fixed on his mother's lips as she still lay with her eyes shut and her arm across her forehead. Bertie had still one arm tightly about her waist; the hand of the other was softly stroking down her arm but moving more and more slowly; and Sartje on the floor had drawn the folds of the bead-net train about her shoulders and was holding it fast at her chin, pretending she was a lady sitting in church with a black lace shawl on. The children were all quite silent when Rebekah paused for a moment. Then she went on:

'But it was not only about such things as clothes and food and houses they knew more than we. They had beautiful and wonderful things we have not even dreamed of—musical instruments more wonderful and sweet than ours, as our organs and violins are better than the gorra-gorras* which the Bushmen and Hottentots play on. If you listened to their music, it was as if all the stars were singing together; it filled the earth and sky.

'Their pictures talked and moved.

'Also, because their knowledge was different from ours, their laws and their ways of life were different. Things we had thought right they called wrong. They laughed at the things we believed, and called us ignorant and superstitious savages. They jeered at us when we put water on the foreheads of little babies to save them, and laughed when some of us said bread and wine could be changed into blood and meat because a man spoke a few words over them, just as we laugh at the Kaffir witchdoctors who mumble over bones and make charms.* They didn't feel sorry for us because we were ignorant; they only laughed at our books and our pictures and all that we made and did. They thought our bodies uglier than theirs, though we thought we were just as beautiful. They would not ride in the same airships with us nor breathe the same currents of air; they called us "The Inferior Races."

'Perhaps we were. But, in the world that had been ours, in which we had tried to grow and learn and make things a little more beautiful, *they* said there was no place for us unless we could serve and be of use to them. They broke down our little countries and our little governments and our little laws; they took all the earth. They said, "Work for us; that is all you are good for; we will let you go on living if you are of use to us."

'Here and there one tried to teach us and help us to know what they knew; but while one tried others cried, "This is sentiment; you are taking them out of their place; they are an Inferior Race." They wondered why we lived in the world at all, or what we had been made for.'

'And we? What did we do then?' asked Charles, softly, leaning further forward as she lay still.

'We ought to have driven them right out into the sea! If I'd been there I'd have shown them!' said Frank. 'What business had they coming here when we were here first? It was our world!'

Rebekah lay still an instant. 'We could not really fight them,' she said slowly: 'we could die, but could not fight them. Sometimes thousands of us did gather together. We said, "It is better to die with arms in our hands than to lie here like dogs and be trodden into our graves." And we gathered together our little guns and our little cannons, the things we had once been so proud of, and we came on in thousands; but we could not really fight them.* From high above in the air they saw us and poured down blasts of poisoned air upon us so that we died by hundreds and by thousands, as locusts die when you spray poison on them, without knowing where we were struck from. Sometimes they shot streams of liquid metal at us, and we fell as corn falls in the harvest. We could not fight them—we could only die. And sometimes, if by a strange chance we managed to take the life of one or two of their men, they called us murderers—but our dead lay in heaps.

'Thousands of the bravest of us fell so; whole nations were swept away from the earth and were forgotten. We could only fight to die.

'But to some of us a much more terrible thing happened. We did not try to fight and were not killed suddenly; a more awful fate overtook us.

'Because they despised *us*, we began to despise *ourselves*!

'If you pull up a tree suddenly by the roots and throw it down on the ground with all its roots exposed (the root through which it has sucked its life for so many years), for a little while the leaves may keep green and the sap run up the stem; but by and by the leaves will wither, and the tree dies. Even if you try to transplant it and stick it up carelessly in a bit of ground, if you do not spread out the roots in the new earth and press down the ground carefully on them and give it much water for a time—it dies.

'So, when they took from us all our old laws and our old customs, when they told us all we had thought right was wrong and all we had known foolishness—and when they made us believe them; when they did nothing to teach us their wisdom and make us grasp their freedom—then we despised ourselves; and so we died.

'We did not die suddenly; we faded and faded, as the leaves fade on an uprooted tree and grow browner and browner till they drop off and are blown hither and thither by the wind, till you see them no more. So we died by millions. And the strange white people said, "See, they are an Inferior Race; they melt away before us!"'

'And we, did we all die so?' asked Charles, bending yet more forward, his eyes fixed on his mother's shaded face.

'Not all,' she said, after a little while. 'Some of us, perhaps not always the bravest or the most beautiful, but the wisest of us, said, "We will not fight their weapons, only to die! Neither will we fade away. This world also is our home. We also are men. We will not die. We will grasp the new life, and live!"

'And we did not despair; and we did not despise ourselves. We learnt all the terrible white-faced strangers had to teach, and we worked for them. We worked—and we worked—and we worked—and we waited—and we waited—and we waited—'

'And then, what then?' asked the boys together, seeing she said no more.

She lay quiet for a moment. 'I do not know,' she said. 'The dream ends there.'*

Then suddenly she moved her arm from her forehead and sat upright. Bertie, whose large eyes were slowly closing, drooped his head softly over into her lap.

'You see, boys,' she said quickly, glancing down at those on the floor, 'when we talk of the dark peoples and the inferior races, it has often seemed to me, it is as with those terrible white-faced strangers of my dream.

'But we have not the excuse they had when they scorned us and tried to set their heel upon us. They came from another planet, and might say, "Those earth men and women, what are they to us? Except that we are parts of the same Universe, what connects us with them?"

'But we cannot say so of any men or women living.*

'Once, on this old Mother World of ours, there were no creatures living such as we see today. I do not know, but I think there was a great silence. Then the time came when there were living things in the seas and in the air. Fishes began to swim and shellfish fastened on the rocks near the shores and tiny living creatures by myriads moved everywhere.

'And then there came a time when there were four-footed beasts and great birdlike creatures—the old monsters whose bones we find now everywhere turned to stone in the rocks, but who are nowhere with us on the earth today.

'And then there came a time when on the earth walked beasts and in the sea were fishes and in the air were birds and on the trees climbed four-handed animals, many of them such as we know today: but still, there was no man!

'And the ages passed. And then a strange little creature began to lift itself up and look round on the world. It tried hard to set the sole of its hind limb flat on the ground and to straighten out its hip, so that the forelimb might be free to carry the helpless young, and to pick the fruits and dig out roots. And then at last the time came when between its thumb and forefinger it could pick up even a very little stick; but yet there was no man!

'And then the ages passed. And there came a time when the creature's foot stood firm and flat on the earth, and he could grasp the very smallest particle between his forefinger and thumb and hold it tight. He had found that if you rub two sticks together sparks will fall. And at night, when he and his fellows sat together over their fires, they made many sounds which each one understood; they talked!—and then, there was MAN!

'Perhaps not just man as we know him: not man of the many thoughts and the many words and the much possessing; but still, man!—the man whose little arrowheads and tools of flint we still find everywhere from the north seas to the equator, whose bones lie mixed with the bones of the animals he killed and the shells of the fishes he ate in the caves where he took shelter—caves from which he went out with his little flint and stone tools to hunt and fish. And the woman, perhaps with just such ringed stones* as those I picked up and have now in my study, went out to dig for roots and insects, with the stones fastened onto the end of her stick, and to look for grass seeds and berries, with her baby tied upon her shoulders and with a skin. And at night, in the firelight, as she sat waiting in the cave for the footsteps of the man who was to bring game, while her baby lay on the floor beside her or still hung on her back, she crooned to it the first little human love-song; and perhaps, as she sat waiting, she took a bone from the heap from which they had eaten and, with a sharp stone, began to carve on it those pictures and patterns which we find on the bones today, pictures like those the Bushmen have left in their caves, and patterns like those the Kaffir women ornament their pots with. And when the man came in with the game and they had cooked it in the embers, they threw fragments to the lean long-legged creature who lay near the cave entrance. And when they had finished they lay down to sleep beside the blaze; and the creature kept watch at the cave door, ready to bark as no wild thing ever barked if the steps of animals or men came near: then there was man, and woman, and child, and dog—there was home. Nowhere on the earth was there the civilised man that we know—but there was *Man* and *Home*!'

The boys leaned forward watching her intently. She had again leaned back with her head against the iron fretwork, looking upwards, hardly seeming to think of them, but her hand was on Bertie's head.

'And then again, the ages passed; and here and there, in this old earth of ours, men learnt something more. Somewhere women found that, if you shaped vessels of clay and baked them in fire, they would stand great heat, and they learnt to work in them. Somewhere men found that, if you put some kinds of earth into a great heat, you could smelt it, and they made iron and no more used bones and stones for weapons. Somewhere men found, perhaps in many parts of the earth, that if you hollowed out trees and guided them with sticks you could move on water—and there were boats. Sometimes, when female creatures were killed and their young caught, the women brought them up, and in time these had young and there were flocks and herds; and the milk of asses or camels or cattle made it easy for men to live without that terrible search for food every day. And in time women learnt it was better to plant grasses and roots, and water and tend them, than to seek for them every day, and then there were gardens. And the men did not always hunt; they tended the tame beasts and defended them, and the women built houses and wove the threads of grasses and fibres of leaves into coarse cloths, and then there were rough clothes. And in time men found it was better to gather into large bodies and build their houses near together and have their gardens joining, so that they might defend them and tend them together, and then there were villages. And, when they found it was best that strong wise men should lead them all, they chose chiefs, and there were tribes and a government. And at last in many parts of the world there were half-civilised men and women such as the Kaffirs were when we found them, with flocks and herds, and houses and gardens and lawns—but still, not just the civilised men we know.

'And then, as the ages passed, in different parts of the earth men went further. Here and there on different parts of the earth men learnt to do better than hollow out trees for boats; they made large vessels with sails. Instead of mud and straw or skin houses, men learnt to build them of stone and baked bricks. Women learnt to weave many kinds of clothing. Then men learnt to set down their thoughts in writing, so that what one generation knew was passed on to another—and then there was civilised man!—man with his palaces and temples and laws and cities and books—books, sometimes written on stone tables, sometimes on mud tablets, sometimes on leaves or bark or skin, but still books where the thought and knowledge of mankind might be stored and each generation begin where the last left off—and there was civilisation.

'Now it has spread from country to country. There are civilised men all over the earth, and we are proud of belonging to them. We despise the men who have not the material things we have and who have not learnt to read and write, who have not the command of the stored-up knowledge of the ages; we despise them as the half-civilised Kaffir and Hottentot despised the Bushman.

'And yet—and yet—Englishman and Frenchman, Chinaman and Greek, Hindu and German, Zulu and Japanese, Roman and Hottentot—if we go far enough back we all have to come together and stand before that cave door. The lady in her white satin with her jewels and broidered handkerchief, the king with his crown, the judge in his ermine, the poet and the thinker, the millionaire and the beggar, the warrior and the slave—we all stand huddled there; and, as we peep over one another's shoulders and bend to look in, we have still to whisper to what we see there—"Father!—Mother!" '

Her voice sank almost to a whisper.

'Perhaps you will say, "Yes, we know we were savages once, but what we are so proud of is that we are not now. We are right to despise the people who do not possess the things we possess and have not the knowledge we have. We are right to despise them and call them Inferior Peoples and to treat them as it would be right they should treat us."*

'But have we really any right to fill out our chests so proudly? Is it really our civilization—yours and mine—made by us?'

She sat up. 'Look at this little book!' She took up from the quilt the little schoolbook which Bertie had dropped there and held it up half open with the leaves turned to them. ' "It is our book," you will say, "written and printed in English by Englishmen"; and perhaps you feel a little proud that even small English boys* of ten and eleven can read it and understand all that is in it when the great chiefs and leaders of many barbarous nations could not. But how much of it have we made? Look at these little black lines and dots!' She held the book more open towards them. 'You will say they are only the alphabet, something so simple that even babes like Bertie and Sartje can learn them. Yes, and any fool can learn a thing when once it has been invented and another teaches him how to use and understand it—but who made them?—not we!'

She dropped her hand with the book upon the bed. 'From the old cave days men made pictures of birds and beasts and men on cave walls and stones and trees and bones; and at last a time came when they found these pictures could be made to speak to others. Sometimes I think I see a man carving figures with a flint on the stem of a tree; the sunlight about him is the sunlight of a day scores of thousands of years ago. He is drawing the pictures there, so that the friends whom he has lost in the chase may know he has been there, and he is the first man writing. As the centuries passed some men went further; they learnt to give each picture a meaning: a raven meant death and a serpent meant life, and a circle meant time, for instance; and then they would write long sentences in pictures, saying what men feel and think as well as what they say. And then the time came when men found that, by turning the pictures into short signs, by leaving out many lines they could write quicker—and so men wrote thousands of years ago in Egypt and Assyria and China. Then a time came when somewhere men found out the greatest thing men had discovered since they found out how to make fire; some men found out that if you used the signs not to mean words but simply sounds and put them together you could express at once and easily everything the human brain could put into words and the human lips utter—then there was the alphabet as we know it. For thousands of years men in Asia and Africa and on the shores of the Mediterranean laboured; the Phoenicians passed it on to Greece and Rome; and so today we read and write with it. Look at these little lines!' She held the book up again, where in parallel columns were rows of Roman and Arabian numerals. 'You will say they are only figures that any simpleton can read and even calculate with. Yes, but each one of them has a history thousands of years old, since that time when our little first fathers and mothers first began to count upon their fingers and were proud when at last they could reach five. Countless millions of men have counted and thought and invented that these little simple signs might exist; and, if the Arabian figures had never come to us from Asia, some of the work we are most proud of doing could never have been done. Look at this!' She held open a page on which was a picture of the solar system. 'Perhaps you think it very clever that little lads like you can tell the names of all the planets and how far they are from the sun, and tell much about the movements of the stars; but thousands of years ago, on the great solitary plains in Asia, dark-faced men through long nights lay and watched the stars, and in solitary towers night after night they watched how the heavens shifted and what rose and what set, and how the seasons of the year were marked; and, but for the labour of these solitary watchers, whose names we shall never know and whose very nations have passed away, the telescopes and observatory and calculations of which we are so proud could never have come into existence; they laid the foundations down; we raise the walls! The very paper of which this book is made—you will say, "At least that is ours, made out of rags spun in English mills and beaten into paper in English factories." But, when I hold these paper leaves between my fingers, far off across the countless ages I hear the sound of women beating out the fibres of hemp and flax to shape the first garment, and, above the roar of the wheels and spinnies* in the factory, I hear the whirr of the world's first spinning wheel and the voice of the woman singing to herself as she sits beside it, and know that without the labour of those first women kneeling over the fibres and beating them swiftly out, and without the hum of those early spinning wheels, neither factory nor paper pulp would ever have come into existence. If I tear one sheet of paper out of this little book and there were some being wise enough to tell me its whole story, with all the lines and dots and marks upon it, and what they mean and how they came to be, and how the leaf itself came into being, the whole story of the human race on earth would have to be told me, from the time our little forefathers and mothers rubbed two sticks together and made light. This little book!—this little book!—it has got its roots down, down, deep in the life of man on earth; it grows from there. It is not your book, it is not my book, it is not the African's book, or the Asiatic's book, or the European's book; it is THE WORLD'S BOOK!'

She dropped it again softly onto the quilt and leaned forward with her elbows resting on her slightly raised knees, so that Bertie's head within her lap was entirely hidden.

'Do you know what a parvenu is, boys? He is a man who becomes suddenly very rich. Often he keeps horses and carriages and houses and lands, and he swells himself out, and tries to make people believe he has always had these things; he would like to make people believe that the grand old house he lives in was built by his own ancestors, that the pictures on the walls were of his relatives, and that the beautiful old library was collected by him. He is proud of the things with the existence of which he had nothing to do and which he only enjoys because a fortunate chance has given him money—and men call him "upstart"—and perhaps they are right, because the lowest and most foolish sort of creature is one who is proud of the things which reflect no sort of credit on himself.

'I sometimes think, boys, that we, people like you and me, have to be very careful, lest we also become parvenus.

'For this one thing we have always to remember, because the moment we forget it, and speak and act not remembering it, we shall act like fools. It is this: We must always remember that, only the other day, as we count days in the life of men on earth, not even so many centuries ago as a savage would count on the fingers of his two hands—so short a time ago that perhaps the lichens which are growing on the rocks that have fallen from Table Mountain were growing exactly as they are today—our forefathers, yours and mine, were savages wandering naked in their woods and on their steppes, staining their bodies with coloured juices, wearing as their only covering the skins of wild beasts, and building for themselves huts of mud and straw.

'There were civilised men on the earth then. The Hindu had already built his great palaces and written his great books; the Chinaman had long wrapped his body in soft silken robes, and in delicately furnished rooms was sipping his tea out of China cups so delicate we cannot even now imitate them. The Medes and the Persians and Egyptians and nations whose names we do not know had had their great empires and their civilisations and had passed away; but we all the while lived the life of naked savages.

'Even the Greeks had gathered their learning from Asia and Africa and had already written their great books and carved their great statues and reared their great temples, while our forefathers were dancing naked round their wood fires at night. The Romans had built roads and cities and made collections of laws; they looked upon our savage Northern forefathers as "something hardly human"; "more like beasts than men" one old writer* called them. And if a Roman woman had married one of your ancestors and mine, the time was when they would have buried her alive as one who had eternally disgraced her race and people. And if they captured one of our ancestors and took him to Rome to follow one of their triumphal cars, he stared about him in the streets with the same stupefied wonder at all he saw, as a Zulu from the heart of Zululand, if he had never left his kraal, would stare if you set him down in the streets of London or Paris. Perhaps they were wrong to despise us so; there are ways in which a Zulu chief may be higher than a learned professor—but we were savages!

'For you see, it was not only with regard to clothes and food and houses and the material things of life that we knew less than some civilised peoples. When our forefathers were still sacrificing human beings to their gods under the oak trees, and their priests, like the Kaffir witchdoctors today, were "smelling out"* the people who should be killed; and when our forefathers dreamed that heaven was a place where men forever drank mead out of the skulls of their enemies—already—long ages before—the great teacher of Asia had sat under his Bo tree,* and had sent out to the earth his message of love and peace. And when our poet sings today,

"He prayeth well, who loveth well
Both man and bird and beast.

He prayeth best, who loveth best
All things both great and small,"*

he is only seeing over again what the man in Asia saw thousands of years ago. And our great men today are only slowly finding out bit by bit, as they climb along that path which we call science, what men of Asia saw years ago when they cried, "All life is one!"'

Her voice sank into silence. She seemed dreaming to herself rather than talking. Then she said gently, 'You know there are people who, before they eat, bend their heads and say a thanks. But for me, when

I read a beautiful book or a great poem or see lovely pictures—and even when I have been very happy walking along and thinking—then it comes to me that I want to raise my hand to my forehead and salute, as the soldiers do when their officers go past. I want to say—"To all the great dead, to all the men and women who have been before me whose names will never now be known, without whom I could never know what I know, or understand as I understand or think as I think—Be Thanks!"*

'And sometimes even when I am walking in my garden and I see the peach tree covered with blossoms in the corner and the roses and lilies growing all round, and the grapes hanging from the gable, and all the small flowers sending out their scent, the feeling comes to me, and I want to say—"To all the gardeners that have been before me—to the little old first mother, who scratched earth and put in roots and grasses—to Chinaman and Persian and Egyptian and Babylonian and Indian, and men and women of races whose names I shall never know, without whom I should never have this beauty—Thanks!" And sometimes as I work there I feel as if they were working beside me and the garden belongs to them and me. And sometimes I think perhaps in years to come, when I have long ages been dust, some woman working in a garden more beautiful than any I can dream of now will stretch out her hand and say—"To all the gardeners that have been before me—" and I, so long dead in the dust, will live in her heart again.'

There was a moment's silence. You could hear Bertie's slow, even breathing from her lap.

'You know, up-country on the great plains, where the camel thorn trees* grow, there are ant heaps as high almost as a man. Millions of ants have worked at them for years, and slowly and slowly they have grown a little and a little higher. Sometimes I have fancied, if a little ant should come on the top of one of these heaps, and should rear himself on his hind legs and wave his little antennae in the air, and should look around and say, "My ant heap, that I have made! My ant heap, from which I see so far!—My plains—my sky—my thorn trees—my earth!" and should wave his little antennae and cry, "I am at the [?beginning]* of all"—and that then suddenly a gust of wind should come! The ant heap would still be there, the ant heap on the top of which he chanced to be born; there would still be the trees and the plain and the sky; but he would be gone forever.

'I have sometimes wondered: Isn't it a little bit so with us, when we walk about so proud on the top of our little heap of civilisation? Because the most that any man can hope for, and the most that any nation can hope for, is this: the man—that, in the one little hour of life that is given him, he may be able to add one tiny grain, so small perhaps that no eye will ever see it, to the heap of things good and beautiful which men have slowly been gathering together through the ages; the nation—that,* when its time to pass comes as it comes to all, it may have added to the things good and beautiful, which humanity lays up through the ages for the use of all, one layer, perhaps one thin layer, but that so well and truly laid that all coming after shall say—"It was nobly done!"'

'Mother, Mother,' whispered Hughie, 'why are your eyes so big?' He was kneeling forward with his knuckles on the bed, staring intently into her face; but she did not seem to see him.

'You will hear people talking often of Inferior Races and of how superior we are—the people who may be speaking; but for me I know this, that, if you took from me bit by bit all I have gained and learnt from other races and other peoples in whom my blood never flowed, I should go back and back, and you would find me at last only a little cave mother with her baby tied by a skin onto her back, peeping out at the door of the cave to see if the man with his bone hook or flint arrows was coming home with game, while a dog who was not yet quite able to bark howled at the door. And when I think of all I have and all I know, the only feeling I have is—"Pass it on! Pass it on!"'

She lapsed into silence and the boys sat watching her.

'When I was a little girl,' she said, stretching her arms out upon her knees, 'I could not bear black or brown people. I thought they were ugly and dirty and stupid; the little naked Kaffirs, with their dusty black skins, that played on the walls of the kraal, I hated. They seemed so different from me in my white pinafores and my little stiff starched pink skirts that rustled as I walked. I felt I was so clever and they so stupid; I could not bear them.

'I always played that I was Queen Victoria and that all Africa belonged to me, and I could do whatever I liked. It always puzzled me when I walked up and down thinking what I should do with the black people; I did not like to kill them, because I could not hurt anything, and yet I could not have them near me. At last I made a plan. I made believe I built a high wall right across Africa* and put all the black people on the other side, and I said, "Stay there, and, the day you put one foot over, your heads will be cut off."

'I was very pleased when I made this plan. I used to walk up and down and make believe there were no black people in South Africa; I had it all to myself.

'But one day—I must have been about seven years old then—there was a war going on against the Kaffirs near where we lived, and a white man who had just been to the Front* came to see us. He sat talking to my father and mother in the front room and drinking coffee, and I sat on my stool in the corner, by my mother's work table, and listened. He told how many black men had been killed and only two white men hurt, one by falling off his horse. I did not mind that so many black people had been killed—they were only Kaffirs! Then he told about a fight he had been in the day before. It was a big fight. The white men had their cannon and all their soldiers on the top of a hill, and the Kaffirs came out below from the bush; there were hundreds of them; they had hardly any clothes or guns, only assegais,* and they came on naked up the slope; but before them walked a young Kaffir woman. Her arms were full of assegais. As the men threw their assegais she gave them new ones; she called on them to come on and not to be afraid to die. She walked up and down before the front row, and called on them to come on. The guns fired and the dead lay in heaps. When she got close up to the mouth of the cannon she was blown away too with the others. He said hardly any escaped, only a few got away into the bush again.* But I felt I was suffocating. I ran out quickly to my pear tree in the garden and walked up and down. I couldn't bear any more. I saw the woman walking with her bare arms glistening in the sun and her red blanket tied across her as I had often seen Kaffir women, and, with the assegais in her arms, calling the men to come on and not to be afraid to die. I walked up and down; at last I lay down on the ground and cried. After that, often in the night when I lay awake I thought I was the young Kaffir woman, and I called the men to come on—and then the cannon fired.

'And once, when I was an older child, about nine, I was sitting at the kitchen door on the lowest step feeding my chickens, and my mother and old Ayah were standing at the top, talking. I don't think they noticed me: they were talking of a Kaffir woman who used to live on the farm before I was born. I didn't quite understand everything they said—you know, children often don't when grown-up people talk; and yet in a way I did understand everything. They were talking of a trouble which had come to her—I know now it was the greatest trouble that could come to any person—and they said, when she couldn't bear it any more, she took her two little children and climbed the mountain to the very top where the precipice stands so high. And when she came to the place where it curves out, she tied her two children under her arms and jumped down. They talked of how all the morning they looked for her and wondered she did not come to work, and then another Kaffir woman said she had told her what she was going to do. Your grandfather and all the men went up, and there they found her, just where the precipice curves out, with the two children tied to her, quite dead.

'They did not know I knew what they said; but the next Saturday, when I had no lessons, when breakfast was done I went up into the bush. I told no one I was going; and I climbed up past where the tiger traps were, and then on where there was no path. And when it was nearly midday I got to the foot of the precipice where it curved out. The trees were all about and at the foot of the precipice were rocks that had fallen down with lichens on them and black ground between. I sat down on one of the stones. I knew that was where she fell. I thought perhaps if she knew it she would have liked to think that, so many years after she was dead, a little white child came and sat there and felt sorry for her. I had made up a little poem about how beautiful the world was, and how sad she must have been when she went away from it. And I sang it when I sat there. It was all I could do. And twice after that I came there, and often when I saw a Kaffir woman walking past I used to wonder if perhaps her husband was going to bring home a new wife, and if she felt as sad as that other woman did; and once I ran far down the road after a travelling woman I saw going by with her baby on her back, and gave her my slice of bread and jam, because I didn't know what might happen to her some day.

'And so you see,' she said, 'as I grew older and older I got to see that it wasn't the colour or the shape of the jaw or the cleverness that mattered; that if men and women could love very much and feel such great pain that their hearts broke, and if when they thought they were wronged they were glad to die, and that for others they could face death without a fear, as that young Kaffir woman with the assegais did, then they were mine and I was theirs, and the wall I had built across Africa had slowly to fall down.

'It's natural,' Rebekah said, 'that we should love those who are like ourselves. A little child feels very lonely if it has not another child of its own age and size to play with. And perhaps the greatest longing a human being can have is to find another being who feels and thinks as they do; and when they meet they are like two drops of water that run into one as soon as they touch. But, even if people aren't like us at all, deep down there is something that joins us together; and if you shrink from them at first, if you are very kind to them and try to help them, it's wonderful how you get to love them.'

She had dropped her right arm at her side, and the fingers of the hand were moving softly among the frizzled curls of Sartje's head which she had pressed back deep into her mistress's skirts, her drowsy eyes already full of sleep and dreams.

'And so, when I hear people talking of superior races and inferior peoples, and of keeping other races and peoples down, I hardly understand. Because, if I find people who seem to know a little less or to see a little less than I do, I always feel I want to say to them, "Oh, little earth-brother and sister, climbing with me that long climb out of the dark, through the cave doors and on we do not know up where—if it should happen that I have climbed onto a step a little bit higher than the one you stand on and can see a little further—here is my hand—let me help you up." '

For a moment she sat silent, her eyes looking straight forward almost as full of dreams as Sartje's. 'Out there in my garden,' she said softly, 'there are flowers of all kinds growing—tall queen lilies and roses and pinks and violets and little brown ranunculuses—and I love them all. But if the tall queen lilies were to say, "We must reign here alone, all the others must die to give place to us," I do not know, but I think I might say, "Is it not perhaps then best *you* should go?"*

'And perhaps the next day there might come a blighting frost; the rose bushes would live on and the little violets hidden at their roots, and even the little brown ranunculuses sheltered by higher branches would be alive; but the lilies—the tall white queen lilies—would all be dead!

'I am glad there are all kinds of men and animals living on the earth where I live, that I and men like me are not the only creatures. If the time should come when there was only one kind of creature left, then the blooming time of the gods' garden would be done, and I would be glad to creep away under the dust and sleep.'

She put Bertie's head down softly on the pillow, and slipping down herself, stood on the floor beside the bed, rousing Sartje from her half-waking slumber and causing her to sit upright on the floor.

'One thing I tell you, lads,' she said quickly, in a changed voice, looking at the two boys who themselves were now rising from their curved-knee position on the floor: 'it is this—I hope, I believe, I know, the day will come when you will regret utterly every slighting, every unkind word or act, that you have ever given place to* towards Sartje, and when you will be deeply grateful for every kind or generous thing you have done towards her. Sartje is not a black child any more than she is pure white. It is not her fault that she is not white, any more than it is your virtue that you are not half black. Sartje is alone in the world. Her mother does not want her; her father does not know that he has even such a daughter in the world. She has no one but us to take care of her. I shall not ever ask one of you to walk with her again. She shall walk with me.'

'Mother, Mother,' said Hughie, sliding down from the bed and catching hold of her skirt, glad that the conversation had suddenly taken a turn in which he could find a part, '*I* will walk with Sartje! And,' he cried, filling out his little chest and striking his fist against it, '*I* will walk with her in the big street; and if the boys laugh at her, *I* fthrow them wifth stones!'*

Rebekah put her hand on his short, dark hair. 'No you wouldn't; you'd just be like Rover; when little dogs come out and bark he goes past, he doesn't see them. You'll be Mother's big Rover!'

For a moment his face fell; then he said approvingly, 'Yesth, yesth, I *am* big Yover!'

'Well, and I'm sure,' said Frank, pursing out his lips, and pressing his double chin against his white collar as he looked downward at his hands, '*I* don't mind walking with Sartje, if it's in the pine woods or somewhere where people can't see. But I'm not going to walk with her in the main road or on the road to the station.' He pursed out his lips yet further.

Sartje, now wide awake, was paying no attention to anything that was said, as she was busy spreading out Rebekah's train in a great wide [?circle] on the floor.

'You mustn't think I don't understand, laddie,' she said, putting her hand for an instant on his shoulder; 'I am your mother and three times older than you, and I ought to be much wiser; but when I go down the Government Avenue, and the coloured girls sitting there laugh because they see I don't wear stays as other women do, it's as if a knife ran into me under my ribs. I know I'm right; that in years to come people will wonder women could be so mad and foolish as to deform themselves. And yet, when these women laugh at me, I am so full of pain I can hardly walk down to the station; and when I come home I feel I want to creep onto the bed and cry. I've tried to like coloured women and do all I can to help them, and then they jeer at me! I don't want for days to go out again. If I, your mother, who should be so much stronger and wiser, feel these things so, what right have I to expect that little boys like you can bear them? You would be heroes if you could.'

Frank had raised his chin from his collar and both boys were looking her full in the face. She looked at them a little wistfully.

'You know, laddies,' she said softly, 'you are always talking of being *men*, and how fine it will be when you are grown up. It is a finer thing to be a "man" than either of you can know now.* But it's not being able to lift a great weight or strike a great blow or crush things beneath you that can ever make you that. The thing that really matters is this: that, when that day comes, as it must come to you at last, when your bodies lie still and dead, whether it be in a palace or a poor man's hut, on a solitary Karroo plain or in a crowded city, whether you have been rich and famous or poor and unknown—what matters is this, that, if one should stand beside you and look down at you knowing all the story of your life, they should be able to say, "This strong man's hand was always stretched out to cover those feebler; this great man's body never sought good or pleasure for itself at the price of something weaker." Then, though no eye could see it, you would lie there, crowned—the noblest thing on earth, the body of a dead man who had lived the life of a man! No strength and no size and no beauty of body can ever give you that.'

The two boys stood with their eyes fixed on her face; but Hughie, who stood close beside her, pulled down her arm and peered anxiously up into her face; but there were not tears there.

At that moment, through the window, came the sound of the opening of the front door of the large house and there was sound of a step on the gravel. Rebekah turned quickly and took from the foot of the bed the red silk cloak which Bertie had worn to the dance five years before. She put it on and drew the hood over her hair.

'Oh, little Yed Yiding Hood!* Little Yed Yiding Hood,' cried Hughie, clapping his hands. Then, throwing himself on all fours on the ground—'Now I'll be the wolf!—Boo-hue-hue!' He careered round her while Sartje, pretending to be greatly appalled, leaped on the bed and buried her face by Bertie's, who still slept on. Rebekah whisked her train out of his [?hands] in affected fear, and stooped to pin up the skirt under her cloak. There was the pleasant scent of a good cigar, and, in the open doorway, the children's father stood.

He wore a grey cap and his overcoat, hanging open, showed a large expanse of white shirt front. He had grown stouter in the last five years, his face somewhat redder and the flesh stiffer. One passing him now in the street would hardly have noted him as a handsome man, but he had still a fine fully developed presence. But the latent vigour, which had given him charm as a young man, was lapsing into a placid self-content which made almost an impression of sluggishness.

'Well, what's the row about?' he said good humouredly, taking the cigar from his lips as he looked down at Hughie, who was still on all fours. 'I'm afraid I've kept you waiting,' he said to Rebekah; 'but when I'd had my bath I found unless we hurried we'd miss that train; so I took things leisurely. We should have been half an hour early if we'd gone by that, and now we shall be three quarters of an hour late'—he took out his watch—'but it's such a long programme, it's rather an advantage.'

'I didn't at all mind being kept,' Rebekah said; 'I will be with you in a minute.'

He put the cigar back in his mouth and blew a long whiff of smoke. 'Well, I'll wait for you at the gate. We've still twenty minutes to get to the station.' He called goodnight to the children and went down the steps.

Rebekah turned to Sartje: 'There is a candle burning in my room; go in and go to bed at once. There are three peppermints on the mantelpiece which you can take to go to sleep with. And you two big boys, go and get your mattresses and bedding from your own room and spread them here on the floor, so that if the young ones wake and cry before I come back you can be here to hear them.'

'Oh, a bivouac! a bivouac!' shouted Frank. 'We'll be Red Indians sleeping in a wood.'

'We'll have a make-believe fire with twisted papers, and sit round it,' said Charles.

'Yes, and you can go and find the box of chocolates in my top drawer, and put them on the fire for chops,' said Rebekah; 'but mind you give the little ones some—Sartje too. You must all be in bed by nine o'clock. I'll kiss you and tuck you all in when I come back.'

Hughie ran to fetch the chocolates, and the two elder boys prepared to rush off to fetch the bedding. As Charles passed her he laid his hand softly on her arm. 'Mother,' he whispered quickly, 'you know I will never mind walking with Sartje?'

'Yes, I know, dear,' she said softly, 'but for her own sake I will not let her. Thank you.' They exchanged a swift glance; then he ran out and she turned to the bed. For an instant she put her lips on Bertie's forehead and spread his curls on the pillow; then she went out through the glass door.

She stood on the top step for a moment, drawing on her glove. The night was very dark now and absolutely still; the scent from the flowerbeds rose up almost overpoweringly, and the fireflies seemed to flit by in dozens among them as she walked slowly past the beds to the gate. In after years the sight of a firefly brought always back that night to her, with a sense of the coming dawn after the dark.

Frank stood outside the gate smoking. He pushed it open and closed it. He was always polite to her now, sometimes almost attentive. When they had walked a few steps they passed Mrs Drummond's gate.

'I met her today,' he said, inclining his head in the dark to the house, 'sailing out of the booking office, as I went in to get our tickets. Hadn't seen her for months. She says her husband's come. Goes away in a week on a long journey into the interior—rather a short visit after twelve years' absence!' He laughed. 'He must have found her much younger than he left her; the story goes now that she goes to bed three days in each month ostensibly for her health; really, to have her face enamelled.'*

'I think it is going to rain tonight,' Rebekah said quickly, looking up at the sky.

'Why didn't you say so sooner, and I could have told the boy to come with the trap and fetch us?'

'Oh, it may not,' she said, looking up again, 'but it's so still and there were so many insects out tonight.'

Here they turned out of the main avenue into the short cut through the woods. The footpath was narrow, and he walked before, she following, holding tight her skirts.

'By the way,' he said, 'you don't want to buy that grey horse of mine, do you? He's too broken-winded for hunting any more, but he'd do well to draw that milk cart, or fruit cart, or whatever it is, on that wonderful farm of yours.'*

'No,' she said, 'that old horse I bought from the Malay for ten shillings because he was going to shoot him has turned out wonderfully. We feed him on warm bran and meal and give him two raw eggs a day, which he can eat without teeth, and he's got as fat as a young horse and takes the cart to the station twice a day.'

'Philanthropy turned out well this time, eh? I really must go and see this wonderful farm of yours. Growing quite a millionaire, I suppose! Sixpence for cabbages, sixpence for grapes, mounts up!'

'Well, it pays all my expenses and Sartje's, and keeps the man and woman at the farm, and we owe nothing.'

'Oh, I'll give you credit for making it pay,' he laughed. 'By the way,' he said, when they had gone a few steps further, 'I think I shan't put off my trip to the Eastern Province till you and the children return. I've practically made up my mind to go tomorrow. I know the captain going with this boat and there are some people I know going, so I might as well go now and perhaps have a week's shooting when I've done my business; it'll be the close season* if I wait till you come back.'

Rebekah fell to no speculation as to why he had suddenly changed his plans since the morning; she had long ceased to look for the real reasons of his obviously superficial explanations or to have instinctive perceptions about anything that concerned him.

'Yes,' she said, 'and it will be cooler now than later. I suppose you will take the black trunk and your small portmanteau.'

'Yes,' he said, 'you might see about packing them tomorrow, as the boat will not leave later than four.'

The path here got so intricate and uneven, that they walked in silence till they got out into the road at the station. When they got to the hall in Town where the concert was given they found it far advanced. Their own seats were in the front row but one, and the place seemed crowded. No place seemed vacant but the chair on Rebekah's left.

Rebekah felt very tired. She had been up and at work since six that morning, and she almost wished she had not come. Then four men on four violins began to render a passage by Beethoven. In a few moments she was leaning forward breathless and motionless like a little child who goes to the pantomime for the first time. It was the first music belonging to her own world she had ever heard: she did not see the men or their instruments, but had the joy one feels as one rides alone across a solitary Karroo plain in the sun and hears nothing but the rhythmic beat of the horse's feet.

Then it ended; and a woman, the great singer of the troupe, in a tight white silk dress, wearing many bracelets, stood on the platform; she shook out her dress and bangles, and bowed to the audience, and unfolded her music and began to sing. A wild burst of applause shook the hall when she finished, and again she bowed and smirked towards the audience and sang. Rebekah leaned back wearily, speculating why it was that one woman, with her song and her tight silk dress, should at once be able to produce an atmosphere as trivial and suffocating as an afternoon tea where women are discussing their neighbours' dresses and concerns.

And she fell to planning a new kind of concert room—quite round, with seats rising tier above tier and the music coming from the centre or one end, but all so arranged you could not see the players or the audience, high partitions shutting you off from your neighbours, and each seat so long that it was a couch on which you could lie down and lose every consciousness but that of sound; a dim soft light coming from veiled lights in the roof. She was a little distressed as to arranging the lights for the performers, so that while the sound was not impeded the light was not visible, and she was lost in this when her husband touched her to say he was going out.

The interval had come; almost all the men streamed out to the refreshment bar and the hall was left almost entirely to women. As she glanced back to look at the clock her eye fell on a man who had not gone out and sat in the seat beyond the empty one next to her. But beyond the fact that he had a closed music book upon his knees from which he had evidently been following the music, and that he was a stranger and not South African, he left no mark upon her thought. She sat back still trying to arrange the lights in the concert hall. As she sat dreaming her eye fell unseeingly on the hand which rested on the music book on the man's knee beside her. She started and looked at it consciously. She knew it; it was strangely familiar. It called back sensations of her childhood and of her past life; she looked up curiously into his face to see who he might be. But he was a man she had never seen before. His skin was bronzed like that of one long habituated to the open air; his beard was dark and close-clipped; his dark hair curled close to his head and, though he did not seem more than thirty-five, was slightly tinged with grey. She knew no such man. She glanced back at the hand again, and the same strange sense of familiarity came back to her, only it seemed to have been a hand smaller and softer. Long afterwards she knew that the hand it reminded her of was her own.

She sat back in her seat again, looking at the empty stage and continuing her plan, till the people who had gone out for the interval came streaming back again. Frank, when he came back again, spent the rest of the interval in looking round and telling her who of their acquaintances were or were not there.

'So Mrs Drummond didn't come after all,' he said in a low voice, fixing himself back in his seat.

'Perhaps she is in the gallery,' Rebekah said indifferently.

'Hush—no! that empty chair next you is hers; that's her husband sitting beyond you.'

Rebekah looked round quickly. So, he was the man whose little statue had stood for ten years in the corner of her room, whose notes on the margin of the book she had read and re-read with the text, and whose comments she had herself put notes to—this was Mrs Drummond's husband!

The time was long past when any mention of Mrs Drummond affected her as rough matter touching a naked nerve point; she had no living interest in her. But no creature which has ever crept into the core of our life, and fed on the bleeding macerated tissue it has created there, ever becomes for us again a matter of complete indifference. Anything connected with them makes in us a faint adumbration of pain.

Then the music began again, and she forgot him or was only faintly conscious of his presence.

Just before the concert ended, as the woman in white satin was for the last time raising her voice on the stage, there came the sound of pouring rain on the roof. It fell in torrents that almost drowned the woman's voice. People looked round anxiously, those who had not ordered carriages questioning how they were to reach the station or their homes in Town. And before the last notes of the woman's song had died, everyone rose and crushed towards the doors, eager to capture any stray cabs that might be waiting outside. From their seats in the front row it was long before Rebekah and Frank reached the entrance hall. By that time many of the audience had left in some conveyance, or had walked away in the rain. But the hall was still crowded with people waiting for the chance of a returning cab or a diminution of the rain.

Rebekah made her way to the front door and looked out. The rain still fell in torrents, and, except a couple of private and pre-engaged carriages, whose owners, knowing they were secure, were leisurely making their way out, there were no conveyances in the street.

To the left of the hall, where a veranda jutted out, the motley crowd which gathers outside the doors of places of amusement when the hour of departure arrives—coloured men and boys, white loafers, coloured and white women in gaudy finery or squalor—had taken refuge from the rain and were standing under it, laughing or swearing as they tried to force their way to inside places for shelter. She turned back into the hall.

'I suppose,' said Frank, who stood buttoning his coat, 'we had better wait till the worst is over.'

'I can't,' she said; 'the children are alone, and I shall miss the last train. I will run down quickly to the station at once.'

'Well, I shall stay in Town tonight. I'll have plenty to do in the morning if I'm to be off at four. You'll probably find someone at the other end who's going the same way as you are.'

She was trying to twist her dress about her to start, when someone, who stood pressed close behind them, accosted Frank. The hall was dimly lighted by one small lamp; she could not see that when Frank, in replying, held out his hand, the speaker seemed not to notice it.

'Let me introduce you to my wife. This is Mrs Drummond's husband,' he said rather hurriedly.

The man who stood close beside her bowed, without holding out his hand. 'You will excuse the liberty I am taking,' he said, 'but in these close quarters I could not avoid hearing that you were not going out to the suburbs tonight. I have a closed carriage waiting here; if your wife would do me the honour, I should be glad to put her down at her door. I believe the house is next to the one in which I stay.'

Before Rebekah could speak Frank had accepted the offer; the man pushed his way out to call the carriage to the kerbstone, and Frank, seizing her by the arm, hurried her towards the door: 'Of course you must go. It's no favour—you'll get soaking wet before you get to the station.' He hurried her across the pavement.

The man stood holding the door of the carriage open; when she had taken her seat, he stepped in and took the seat opposite to her; Frank closed the door and was about to pull up the window, when from the crowd under the veranda there rang out a long, reckless, gurgling laugh. It was unmistakably a woman's. In an instant Rebekah sprang forward and stretched her arm through the window, trying to turn the handle of the door.

'Let me out!—Let me out!' she cried, shaking the door with her left hand as the handle refused to turn. Then the door burst open and she leaped out.

'Rebekah, what are you doing?' Frank stretched out his hand to detain her.

'It's Bertie!' she said hoarsely, evading his hand, and ran across the sidewalk, now deep in water, towards the veranda, her long train and cloak fluttering out behind her. The man inside looked out. Frank drew up the collar of his coat and drew the lappet* of his cap closer over his ears and leaned in at the door, gaining shelter from the rain.

'I must really ask you to excuse my wife,' he said. 'She's really a most sensible and practical person generally, but there's one thing about which she's unhinged—a sister of hers who cleared off to England some years ago with a Jew; she and her people spent a small fortune trying to find her. Sent someone all the way to South America to look for her—found she'd never been there, been in London—stayed with the Jew for some time, then gone off with another man. The last they heard of her she'd landed in a brothel in Soho—never been able to hear of her since. My wife's possessed with the idea she'll turn up here some day. It's insanity. I've known her leap up at three o'clock in the morning and rush out in the Avenue because she thought she heard her step. She's fancied she heard her laugh now in that crowd, and she's gone to see. Of course you won't mention what I've told you to anyone, but since you saw what passed I thought it was best to give you an explanation.'

The man pushed past him and got out. 'Are you going to help her look?' he asked shortly.

'Oh no, she'll find out her mistake in a few moments and be back.' They stood looking towards the dark little crowd under the veranda. 'It wasn't her, of course,' said Frank, 'though the laugh did sound a little like her. What I can't get my wife to see is how much better it is for everyone she shouldn't turn up!' He drew the collar of his coat yet higher, but did not like to shelter himself in the cab while the man was standing in the rain. 'I don't believe there's a disreputable place in Cape Town or Simon's Town where my wife hasn't had her looked for. She was a very pretty girl; the prettiest woman I've seen yet; but she wasn't much good, I'm afraid.' Frank stood with his back closer to the carriage. 'Won't you get in again? You're getting awfully wet.'

The man appeared not to hear him; his face was turned towards the veranda.

'Of course,' Frank said, moving a step nearer him, 'I need not ask you not to mention to anyone what has happened tonight, or repeat anything I have said; having seen so much, I thought it was better to be frank. People know, of course, that there was some sort of a scandal when she went away, but, as far as I know, nothing definite—and things get so soon forgotten, if they're not talked of.'

The man turned his shoulder towards him.

Then they saw Rebekah coming through the rain. She was walking slowly; her train dragged behind her in the mud, and the light from the carriage lamps made the water glisten on her red cloak and hood as she came near.

'I am too wet to get in,' she said slowly; 'I will walk down to the station.'

She turned to go.

'Don't be ridiculous, Rebekah!' said Frank. The water from his cap was running into his neck. 'If you walked you would probably miss the train and have to stay in Town all night.' He seized her arm and half lifted her towards the step; the man was holding the door open.

'Don't,' Frank whispered, 'don't let us make any further public exhibition of ourselves.' He raised her into the carriage, and she dropped onto the back seat. The man got in and Frank closed the door. He put his head in at the window, 'I shall likely not get out till half past two tomorrow; but if you have the black trunk and the portmanteau ready, I shall be in time to get on board by four—Goodnight!' He withdrew his head and told the driver to move on, and then turned to hail a cab which was fortunately passing at the moment.

Rebekah sat drawn into the corner of the carriage, her head leaning back. The man opposite her drew up the window and sat silent till they passed the station. Then he took off his coat and leaned forward towards her.

'Your cloak is very damp,' he said, 'will you not take it off and put my coat round you? It is hardly damp.'

She shook her head and declined almost inaudibly. The reaction from the few moments of intense excitement and the long tiring day had left her almost exhausted. She leaned her head further into the corner; she was not conscious of the pressure of her damp clothes or anything but the soothing motion of the carriage.

Presently, without speaking, he folded his coat and laid it down on the floor. 'Set your feet on it: put them into the folds,' he said shortly and quickly. He bent for an instant and moved the long wet train of her skirt further from her.

'I have always found,' he said in a short sharp business tone, as he raised himself, 'in twelve years of travel and roughing it, that the secret of health lies in always keeping damp material from the feet, and, where that cannot be, in covering them. When we are civilised we shall wear no covering for the feet in warm climates.' His tone was markedly short and businesslike, precluding an answer, and he turned his face to the window. Little could be seen through the rain-speckled glass, and, as they got out into the suburbs, lights were few and far, and the landscape was dark outside, but he still appeared absorbed in watching it. For nearly three quarters of an hour they drove on slowly, the carriage moving through the mud of the drenched roads. Rebekah sat motionless, as if she were asleep.

After a time they got more completely into the country, where the trees grew higher and thicker, and later turned into the avenue that led to Rebekah's house. Then, for the first time, he turned from the window and leaned back in his place. They were almost within a stone's throw of her gate when he leaned forward.

'You will forgive my intrusion,' he said slowly and distinctly, 'but, when you had left the carriage, your husband told me you had gone to look for a friend whom you had long lost and hoped to find.' He paused. 'I should be intruding unforgivably,' he said, bending a little more forward and speaking yet more slowly and distinctly, 'but, that once in my life I found that which to the world seemed lost and worthless, and which, to me, became the good of life. If'—he paused, and then spoke a little more dryly—'I could be of use to you in helping you to seek, I should feel it an honour. I have a week to spend here;

and I have nothing to do. Unfortunately, as the world is today, a man has facilities of search in some directions that a woman has not. If you could make use of me, I should be glad. There is no house, however bad, which I could not enter to seek.'

Then he drew himself up quickly and the carriage stopped at Rebekah's gate. Again he leaned forward slightly before opening the door and said in a short whisper, 'If, thinking the matter over, you come to the conclusion I can be of use, will you set down on paper details that may be a guide to me? Send me a photograph, anything that would help me to identify. What you enclose in an envelope and address to the house next door will find me.'

He opened the door quickly and got out. Then he turned to help her. It seemed to her afterwards he had almost lifted her out and stood her on the ground. Then he turned sharply and opened the gate. She passed through it: he closed it, said shortly, 'Goodnight' without extending his hand, and turned and got into the carriage. She walked slowly up the path, and, when she got to the top step before the door of the new rooms, turned round and stood still. Then it struck her she had not thanked him for his offer or for driving her home. She still stood on the step. She heard the carriage, which had stopped before the gate of the next house, drive away; and there were steps going up to the house.

Then she turned and went in. The two boys lay in their beds on the floor; a few moths were still hovering round the lamp or lying dead on the table, and on the two little beds in the corners the small boys slept. She walked past them to her own room. She took the lamp from the drawers and set it down on the dressing table; then she dropped her wet cloak and dress upon the floor. Without removing any other article of her damp clothing she sat down before the dressing table. Out of the drawer she took the notebook and pencil with which she kept her household accounts and opened it on the table. She leaned her naked elbows on the edge and rested her face in her hands, thinking for a little while; then she began to write. Slowly she put down the items, numbering each one—colour of hair, height, walk, size of hands and feet. Sometimes she paused to think: then she took from her neck the gold chain and locket. There was a picture of Bertie as she was just before she left. She closed it and folded it in paper, and tore out the leaf of the pocket book on which she had written and folded it and laid it beside it. Then she sat still, looking at them; after a time she folded her arms on the edge of the table and leaned her head on them. When she raised it she unfolded the locket and put it away in the drawer, and tore up the page she had written and left the fragments on the toilet cover. Then she got up almost stiffly and removed her damp clothing; and when she had her nightgown on went round to tuck in each of the sleeping children.

CHAPTER XIII

THE VERANDA

THE next day Frank left, and four days passed; on the fifth Rebekah went to the farm to work all day and took Sartje with her.

When she returned at five o'clock she expected to find the boys home from school, playing cricket in the yard; but it was empty. She walked round to the front garden. Then she heard the sound of voices and the high ring of Hughie's laugh. She walked to the rose hedge and looked across.

Croquet had gone out of fashion and what used to be Mrs Drummond's lawn was now a tangle of long grass, with here and there a yellow flower; the late afternoon sunshine shining across it made it an intense green, the oak trees casting flickering shadows in some parts. Under the largest of the oak trees was a collection of heads bending down over something among the grass. The children were forbidden to go in without invitation, but she recognised the heads. She walked quickly to the little gate. It moved stiffly on its hinges now; the little path that had once been so deeply worn was now almost imperceptible. Frank seldom used it, nor did anyone come from Mrs Drummond's but now and then a servant to borrow something.

Rebekah stepped over the knee-deep grass. Lying at full length on his back under the oak tree, with his hands clasped under his head, was Mrs Drummond's husband. Little Bertie in his white embroidered dress sat at his head bending over it, dividing with his tiny fingers the short stiff curls along the top and stroking them; Hughie knelt on the left, his fingers planted on the man's chest and his eyes fixed on his face; the elder boys sat close to him on the right with their backs turned to her. He was speaking, and all were so intently listening they did not hear her steps.

Hughie saw her first, just as her shadow fell across them.

'Mofther, Mofther, it's about a baby chimpanzee was sticking fast, and the man—'

'He asked us to come, Mother,' said Charles, standing up; 'our ball came over from the yard, and he said we could come and look for it.'

The man raised his head and rose quickly to his feet: 'I hope I have not tempted them to break bounds,' he said; 'they have been entertaining me so well.'

'Mofther,' cried Hughie, running close up to her and trying to touch her chin with his hand, 'justh when he was going to take the baby chimpanzee the big mother—'

'He's been in a real big island,' said Frank, 'for more than two years, with no white people, and he dressed just like a nigger with only a cotton cloth about him, and once he went down a river on a log—'

Rebekah loosened Hughie's fingers, that were still trying to attract her attention by holding her chin. 'I'm afraid if you once began telling them stories, you did not find them very easy to get rid of.'

'Oh, I haven't done all the entertaining. Charles here'—he rested his hand on the boy's shoulder—'has been telling me things that interested me more than my stories did him.'

A delicate pink flush came into Charles's face. 'I didn't think you'd mind, Mother,' he said quickly. 'I tried to tell him about the ant heap and the dark people. He's been in Central Africa himself, and seen the great ant heaps and the camel thorns.'

'Mother,' broke in Frank, 'he says we can come again tomorrow and he'll tell us a story about a war they had up in Africa, and how he found a little boy with three Bushmen arrows sticking in him!'

Only Bertie was silent. He had risen gently and had caught hold of the man's forefinger, which he stood holding tightly.

'My fear is Mr Drummond will feel as the Britons did when they invited the Picts and Scots to come over the wall and couldn't get free of them,' Rebekah said.

'Oh no, he won't,' said Frank. 'What time shall we come tomorrow?'

'I shall be here about four; then I shall whistle for you, if your mother will let you come.'

'Oh yes, like the Lap did for the reindeer you said; and we'll all come trooping like a lot of reindeer.'

'Do not let them trouble you, please,' she said; 'send them back when they tire you.'

'Children and animals do not easily do that,' he said.

Rebekah turned to the children. 'You must come home for your tea now.' She held out her hand to Bertie. He loosened his hold of the finger, but turned to the man and stood looking up at him.

'Don't you seeth, he wanth to kissth you?' said Hughie.

The man stooped and lifted the child up and pressed his moustached lips softly against his; when he set him down Bertie walked to Rebekah and took her hand, but looked back as he walked. All the children shouted, 'Goodbye.' The man replied, 'Till tomorrow!' Rebekah said, 'Good night,' and they walked away to the gate in the rose hedge, Bertie holding her hand and stumbling over the grass as he walked with his head half twisted round to look at the man who was standing under the tree and watching them.

When they had gone he lay down in the same position as before and was completely lost among the grasses.

At tea all the children talked at once. Hughie said when he was grown up he was going to travel all over the world with the man. Frank said he had promised to show him a real boomerang and explain how the savages used it. Charles said he had invited them to go to his room on the other side of the big house where all his things were, which he was packing away to send to the museum in Europe—fossils and dried plants and photographs and collections of insects and savages' implements. Sartje whispered to Rebekah to know if they went whether she might go too. Only Bertie sat silent in his high chair, eating his bread and milk with large intent eyes.

The next afternoon the children heard the whistle and went. In the evening they came back full of the stories they had heard and the things they had seen.

'And, Mother,' said Charles, twisting his arm about her, 'he makes up stories like you. He has a little white box all full of manuscripts, and he let me read a little bit of one. It was beautiful. I could quite understand it.' But she did not question him about it.

The next day the children waited in the front garden; but there was no whistle calling them, or the next day either. Rebekah thought, as the week was nearly ended, perhaps he had left. On the third day they had gone to school at their governess's down the Avenue, and Rebekah was at home alone with Sartje, who was dressing her dolls on the back stoep. Rebekah went into the pantry to put the shelves neat. She was dressed in a blue cotton dress with a dark blue cotton overall pinafore that she always wore at her work in the morning. She resolved to turn out the whole pantry. It was not really necessary; there was sewing that needed even more to be done; but she felt she did not wish to sit still. She stood on a chair before the dresser taking down piles of plates and dishes and dusting them one by one, before she put fresh paper on the shelves. It all looked so bald; the sunshine coming in through the pantry window and dancing on the yellow-washed walls and yellow-white shelves. She counted the plates in piles of eight and put them up again; was it worth doing, was anything worth doing? She began taking down the jugs from the next shelf.

Then there was the sound of a knock at the front door. Often the carts with ferns and greenery to sell came up the front avenue at that hour and knocked at the front door. She called to the girl in the kitchen to go and see who it was. The girl came back and said it was the gentleman she had sometimes seen next door, who had called and wished to see her mistress for a moment. The girl handed up his card. She said he had declined to come in and was standing on the veranda waiting. Rebekah stepped quickly down from the chair, waited a moment, then hurried out through the kitchen and went round to her bedroom in the new building. Quickly she tore off the dark blue pinafore, and before she took off the dress went to the wardrobe and took down the white embroidered gown she often wore in the afternoon. She turned to the glass; her hair, brushed down at either side of her head and coiled in braids at the back, was a little ruffled in front with her morning's work. She caught up the brush and began to smooth it, making the dark waves show undulating and glossy. Then she paused and laid down the brush. If it had been an ordinary tradesman who had called, she would have gone just as she was; if it had been a formal caller, she would have dressed carefully. She hesitated. Why should she try to show herself to this man looking better than she often looked? Why should he not see her at her worst? For anyone else she would have dressed, but not for him. She turned to the chair and put on the blue pinafore and walked slowly back by the way she had come. In the front passage the door stood open; the man was standing with his back to it, looking out across the garden from the top of the veranda steps. As she came out he turned and raised his hat; he looked down very fully at her as she stood beside him.

'I hope I have not disturbed you by calling so early?' he said. She answered quickly that he had not. He looked away again across the garden.

'What an astonishing blaze of colour!'

'There's a pleasure,' she said, 'if you have a very small space, in seeing how much will live in it.'

'Yes,' he said, looking somewhat abstractedly at the garden. 'I've sometimes thought that a life itself might be lived more satisfactorily a little hedged about with narrow conditions which compelled one to expand oneself in that circle—there's such a thing as being dissipated with too large an horizon and too much liberty to expand in it.'

'If the hedges are too close round, they may kill the plants,' she said quickly.

'Yes, that is so!—The reason why I called,' he said, glancing down at her again and then looking back across the garden, 'is that, though you did not write to me nor give me permission, I thought perhaps you would forgive me if I tried to go on with the search you made the first night we met. I got a photograph and the information I needed next door, without mentioning your name. I have been to all the places, places where I don't think you could easily have entered, where there seemed possibility of news. The last two days I have spent at Simon's Town. Once it seemed to me there I was upon a track; but it disappeared again.'

'Thank you,' she said; 'but I have no hope really.'

'Do not say that,' he said, glancing down at her and speaking as one would to a little child. 'When we fix all our desires in one direction, I think one is almost bound to find what one hungers for at last. I have always had that feeling. I will not detain you longer; if I hear anything I will let you know.'

He touched his hat and began to descend the steps. But she walked down with him. He stopped as they passed a tall pink rose bush.

'How strange that is,' he said; 'one quite white rose where all the rest are pink.'*

'That bush has always done so,' she said.

He bent down over it. 'That's rather strange. I thought it might be some injury or growth that caused it. May I take it home to examine it?' Rebekah cut it with her scissors that hung from her belt. He held it, examining the stem and the back of the flower. 'It's particularly healthy and perfect,' he said, as he walked to the gate, still looking down at it.

'You said you would be leaving in a week,' she said. 'Your stay is almost ended, is it not?'

'No,' he said, 'I shall be here for three weeks.' He opened the front gate and went out, hasping it on the inside.

'Thank you for what you have done,' she said.

'Oh, it's my concern now, as much as yours.' He bowed and turned down the Avenue.

Rebekah turned and walked up the garden path. The roses had never been so red before and the lilies and carnations so white. The sky above was a dazzling radiant blue, and the light poured down over the flowers and drew their scent. She stood by the pink rose tree; it had the most delicate scent. In the pantry she put the jugs and dishes quickly back on the shelves, then she went through the garden again to her study and sat down in the armchair.

After a while she laid her arm across her forehead and half closed her eyes. The arm slid lower till it quite covered them; her breathing became as soft and even as a little child's sleep. But she was not asleep.

She fancied one day she went into the garden and the man said quite frankly, 'I have come to see you.' And she went up to him just as one little child goes up to another who has come to play with it. She said, 'Come and I'll show you all my things!' And she took him into her study. She led him to the corner where her statue stood on the little bracket. She told him what she felt about it; and he told her about where he got it, and what exactly it was. Then she took him to the glass cupboard and showed him the fossils. They took out each one and she told him where she had found it and how. She told him especially all about the large dicynodont's* head she had dug out in the krans* in the river bed, how she had felt when, bathed in perspiration in the streaming sunshine one day, the last stone broke away and she held in her hand the old head that so many million years had lain under the sand, come out to see the sunshine it once loved, the same old sun shining, the same old life beating in her hand that had once beat in the old sightless head; she showed him the beautiful winged reptile fossil,* that had played so large a part in her system of thought for so many years, being the first thing that had forced on her the knowledge how much of beauty and good has been killed out forever on earth by the brute struggle of animal power to kill; she explained to him all she felt about that, and he argued it with her; and then they went to her bookshelf and he held in his hand the little handbook of physiology which she had bought with her hoarded pence when a little child, and he understood how she had loved it; and she showed him his own old copy of *Plants and Animals* and his own notes in it, and hers written against them; and they argued over many things she'd wanted to argue with him for years; and she showed him great piles of notes and writing on Woman;* and they sat discussing—when the girl from the kitchen came to the study to say the water was boiling and it was time to make the pudding.

Rebekah dropped her arm from her eyes and started up. The drawers of the desk were all shut, and no manuscripts were about and no voices sounded. She rose and followed the maid to make the pudding.

The next day and the next she heard no more of him. On the morning of the third day, just after the children had started for school, Hughie rushed back into the kitchen.

'Mofther, Mofther,' he cried, 'he sayth he wanth to thee you. I've tooked him to your sthudy!' And without waiting to explain he rushed off to join the other boys, who were already going down the Avenue.

In her study Rebekah found him standing before her glass case of fossils. He turned quickly.

'I hope the little son* has made no mistake in showing me in here!' He glanced round the room at the desk and single chair, showing it was not meant for reception. 'He led me in here when I asked for you and planted me before the case, I suppose because I told him I should like to see your stones. They told me you had some.'

'Oh, it's quite right,' Rebekah said quickly.

'I came,' he said, 'to ask a favour—whether you would allow your coloured boy to come over for a few minutes and help me to cord some of the heavier boxes I am packing to send to Europe.'

'I will send him at once,' Rebekah said, and made a movement as though she would have moved to the door.

But he had turned to the case. 'You seem to have some very interesting things here,' he said. 'That's a fine head. I got three of the same kind when I was in Africa before, but yours is larger and more perfect.'

She took the key down from the corner of the hanging bookshelf and unlocked the glass case quickly. He took down the head and asked where it was found. She said on a farm in the Midlands.*

'Mine came from that part. May I look at the rest?'

She opened the other door wide and he took them out one after the other: bits of great leg bone and huge claws and prints of footmarks. Then he took up the small square slate with her winged reptile upon it. 'This is very curious, very valuable,' he said. He turned, walked a step nearer the door to get more light on it. 'Where was it found?'

'About two hundred feet from the head in the same bed of a mountain stream.'

He looked at it closely.

'What is it?' she said.

'I don't know. I have never seen anything quite like it. Did you find it yourself?'

'Yes,' she said.

He walked another step towards the door to look at it, then turned to return it to the case.

'Won't you take it?' she said. 'I don't need it.'

'Oh, I could not. It's the crown of your collection,' he said quickly.

'I'd like you to,' she said.

He hesitated: 'I don't collect for myself, you know. I send all my collections to a friend of mine in Vienna, and he puts them in his private museum or distributes them in public collections where others can make use of them. They are a kind of blood money with me, you see. One must, I suppose, contribute something to the world's scot and lot.* So I do this and then I feel I'm free to do what I like with the rest of my life with a clear conscience.' He laughed, still holding the stone in his hand.

'It's better so,' she said. 'Someone might make use of it. I never will.'

He looked down at it, hesitating for a moment; then, 'Thank you, I will take it,' he said. 'Have you noticed how beautifully clear the veinings in the wings are?' He was moving towards the door. 'I will not interrupt you any more: I am sure you are busy. Any time today will do for the boy to come over.'

At the door he turned and wished her good morning and went down the steps with the stone in his hand. She stood before the case. She closed it and began to pace up and down. He had been there; she had shown him nothing. All the things she had to tell him she had not said! She walked to the corner and looked at the statue he had bought, and to the shelf, and looked at his Darwin with the notes in it.

That night at eight, when the smaller children had been put to bed and the two elder boys were amusing themselves in the large room, she sat on the veranda of the house. A tin lamp with a reflector was fastened on the wall behind her and threw its light down over her as she sat in the rocking chair under it, darning the week's stockings. A cloud of little night flies and moths fluttered round the lamp, so thick they seemed to make a halo about it.

Suddenly the front gate opened and Mrs Drummond's husband came up the path. He did not go to the steps, but stood below her at the side of the veranda.

'Good evening!' he said. 'I have not come on any business; I have merely come to see you. May I sit down?'

She half rose to draw a chair forward for him.

'No, I would rather sit here,' he said, seating himself on the side of the stoep, which rose about two feet from the ground. 'One likes all the air one can get tonight.'

She pushed a little mat towards him, saying that the stones were cool.

'Oh, I shall take no harm: I am an old traveller,' he said, but he drew it to him and reseated himself. He sat about five feet from her with his back against the veranda post. He looked out across the garden, the darkness of which was partly lit by the light from the lamp's reflector.

'Would you mind my smoking?' he said. 'I don't think the smoke would reach you from here.' When she assented he took out his pipe and slowly filled and lit it.

'You should learn to smoke,' he said after a pause, turning to her again; 'persons who lead a very intense life too quickly, at too great a tension, should smoke to slow down; lymphatic* people never should.' He put the pipe back to his lips and drew a few long whiffs; then he took it out....*

'Of course you will say, trivial and insignificant as it is, the man had no right to have even that little picture to himself. Instead of jumping up and lurching out of the wagon and making his coffee and going off to seek for fossils, he should at once have seized a writing pad and scribbled it down on it, and spent a day in writing it out in proper form and he should have sent it home to a publisher and said, "How much will you pay me, one pound or two pounds or three pounds a page, what is it worth to you?"—bargain and chaffer* over it, and in the end he loses and the publisher makes everything. A man might as well take a child and put her up to auction—Yes, she is very pretty but her nose is a little too long, her hair doesn't curl quite enough; her arms are nice and firm—he ought to have cut her hair shorter in front.' He drew some more short draughts at his pipe. 'Pugh! Their blame and their praise are alike an insult. Who thinks a man begets children for them? Of course, if he's starving, he may have to put her up, but it's rather like eating your own flesh!'

By this time he had discovered his pipe was dead, and knocked it out vigorously against the brickwork of the stoep and began refilling it.

'I did publish a thing once,' he said; 'it was many years ago when I was a student. That friend I told you of needed money; the doctor thought they could perform an operation and cure him of his deformity, and he hadn't funds. I gave him a thing I'd written, a little thing, but I cared for it; and I said he could publish it without my name and use what he got for it. I hadn't means at that time. He arranged with a publisher, but he didn't have the papers properly signed; they promised him so much a copy; in the end he got £50, and the publisher made hundreds. The publisher said he could give him one third of what he had arranged for. A lawyer friend said we had better go to law. That would have been the ultimate prostitution: you have got my daughter, you have used her, and now you don't pay me properly. I got hundreds of letters from people all over the world'; he laughed a little inward laugh. 'They thought it must have been written to do them good or give them pleasure! I wonder how often, when a man begets a boy, he is thinking of the various instructions of the race it may undertake. One woman wrote me a love letter and said she didn't know my name, but she was sure we were made for each other, and she had four thousand a year. One man, an American, sent me a printed copy which he had had gloriously printed on thick paper in vellum binding, and told me I was please to write my name and an inscription in it, and he could assure me it would be placed in his library in company with the best writers of the day, Tom and Jack and Harry! I threw it into the fire.' He put his pipe back in his mouth and pulled. 'They think you write it for them! I suppose they think Newton struck on his great thoughts to please humanity, and Milton wrote *Paradise Lost* for the sake of the ten pounds he got: and so, of course, the small ephemera must do the same! They can't understand that their praise is as insolent as their blame, that there's no virtue or vice about the whole thing! It is because it had to be!' He puffed away for a good time in silence, and Rebekah's face was still bent over her work.

Then suddenly he bent nearer her, taking his pipe from his lips.

'There is something I want to ask you,' he said. 'I wasn't quite sincere in saying I only wanted to come and see you. I've a little thing I wrote ten years ago; would you read it if I sent it over with my Chinaman* tomorrow? It took me two days copying it out; I've done it in my best round schoolboy hand twice, so it won't be difficult to read. I've had it ready for some days, but I haven't ventured to send it. You needn't say anything about it. I just want you to read it.'

'I shall,' she said. 'Is it a story?'

'Well, yes—and yet—no. Hardly quite that. There are characters, men and women, in it, but you'll see it's Africa.' He smoked a little.

'Ten years or so ago I travelled there for a year and a half all over the country in my wagon. I went on towards the Kalahari* and away to Lake Ngami.* I had gone through a time of some stress before, and somehow the country appealed to me greatly. It's strange that ever since, though I've lived longer in so many countries, yet when anything comes to me, it's nearly always Africa—Africa that sets it. I've a curious feeling for the country as if it had a personal connection with myself; perhaps because I travelled through it when I was particularly open to the influences of nature, as one is when one's mind has been perturbed. I've always thought I should rather like to be buried there at last. I never wrote about it while I was there; one doesn't about things that are present, you know. It was when I'd gone home to England for four months. I was in a little seaside lodging, busy arranging my specimens and cataloguing them to send to my friend before I started on my journey through Russia to the East. It was a drizzly rainy day and I was sitting at my desk writing out a description of Bushmen, and their habits as I'd seen them, to go with some curios; I was just setting down the exact measurement of some skulls* I'd taken and was feeling rather depressed and heavy, when suddenly, in a moment, the whole of this little thing flashed on me. You know those folded-up views of seaside places and cities that you buy in a sort of little book, and as you pull them open they flash out one after the other in a moment. Well, it was so; in an instant, all the pictures in the thing ran out before me with a flash one after the other.* I threw down my pen. It was exactly as though someone quite external to myself had shown them me suddenly. I wrote them all out that night, and the next day, when I came to read them, I saw it was Africa, the scenery—but you'll see, I put it away in a box with the other scribbles, and I haven't looked at it since; but I've always liked it best of all. It took me only one night to write the rough, but it's taken me three days and the best part of the night to revise and write fair. I hope you'll like it!' He leaned forward a little and glanced up gently at her, almost like a little child seeking sympathy. Then he drew himself up and relit his pipe and leaned back against the veranda post.

'I sometimes think,' she said, 'that that curious sense of weight and depression, often appearing quite causeless, which one feels before some sudden flash of perception, is because some part of one's brain we are not conscious of has been working intensely, so that the part we are conscious of is ill supplied with blood; then something bursts and it comes into consciousness. So it is with intuition; I think it's what Socrates felt when he talked of his Demon.* We feel so entirely as if it were a flash from something beyond ourselves. I noticed it when I was a little child.'*

'But is it the brain at all?' he said, leaning back against the post. 'I have a conviction, possibly quite wrong but from which I cannot shake myself, that it isn't the brain at all, or not nearly so much as people suppose, with which any kind of imaginary work is done or any unwilled mental process takes place, that it's far more spinal and visceral than people think and that results are simply flashed up to the brain—anyhow, if it is the brain, it's the back part above the spine and the whole body, especially the trunk, that is concerned; why else, if you've been making stories for six hours, should it never be the front of the brain that was weary, as if you'd been calculating miserable figures or learning lists of words, but always the small of one's back and one's body that is tired? I suppose science will work the matter out some day. Why, at first waking, do pictures and things, entirely uncalled for by the will, rush full fledged into the brain, which they tell us is so ill fed with blood during sleep? Why, when one lies half dozing on one's back, does one start up with such a rush of ideas that by no power of will could one have evoked?'

He smoked on for a while in silence.

'I suppose,' he said at last, 'it's the spontaneous nature of imaginative work that makes one so impervious to criticism? If a man tells you you pronounce a word wrong, or don't hold your fork right, you feel pained and try to reform yourself—as to the other things, they are as they are and be damned to him!'

'And yet one can, to a certain extent, determine their coming,' she said. 'One can put oneself into the condition in which they may come. When, as a little girl, I wanted to be happy, I used to go and lie under a pear tree in the garden or walk up and down, and they nearly always came.'

'Yes, that's just it,' he said. 'You may put yourself into the condition in which they *may* come, but you cannot determine they shall come, or what they shall be within certain limits! Suppose, in some city of Greece, say, a crown of wild olives or a prize of many talents had been offered for a Winged Victory* and there were three artists of power. The first might keep his mind and body, especially the body, so absorbed in gymnastics or business or politics, that no picture comes to him, and he has either not to compete or to make up something he never saw, copied from others, and a complete failure. The second turns all his mind towards it and meditates over an ideal of victory, but there come to him only lovely Venuses and ripe Cupids that he can wing and call Victories, though they are not so, because in his soft nature lies nothing Victory can shape itself from. But the third, deep in whose nature is something of hope, virility, strength—to him, when he turns his dreams towards it, a hundred Winged Victories leap out; he could not say just how they come, but he would recognise one as the best, and he would seize it, he would embody it in marble; and then, through the ages, without a head, without an arm, smitten and ill treated, it would still stand as the embodiment of Victory, calling men and women to struggle and conquer, though only through its broken fragment; it would do it because it was in the man, because nothing can come out of the man that was not first in him; he must have felt all the Victory speaks before he could make it; it is his soul.' He sat looking out at the garden with the pipe in his hand. 'All that a man has seen and known and felt, all that lies within him, is, so to speak, the substance out of which his imagination has to work, the bricks laid before it from which it can select for its work. The small man may be an artist; only the great man can be a great artist. A boy might write a song of yearning unrequited love, because youth knows vague yearnings of love at sixteen, but no boy of sixteen could have written *Paradise Lost* or the *Iliad*; the dream-power might be there, but the matter for it to work on could not be there. And yet, you know,' he said, 'that is not all! Why is art prophetic? Why does a man dream and hear and see things and faces which, as far as he can judge, are suggested to him by nothing he has seen or known?—and yet, long years afterwards, the faces and the people and the incidents, the very characters and actions, which seemed almost impossible and unlikely to him when he first saw them, come out and look at him from real life? Why is it that he can paint the actions and emotions of characters in complex conditions in which he never was and of which he knew nothing—and yet life as it passes verifies his work? I believe that a European man with imagination, lost among savages from his birth, would be haunted by an ideal of a living European face which he had never seen and perhaps never would see!'

'Is it not,' she said, 'because no individual is an isolated monad? He may be one minute growth of the life of his race, of humanity, of living things on earth. Is an artist not simply a man in whom some of the accumulated life of his race, of the millions of human creatures who have been his ancestors in the ages past, is stored? Is not much of his work, if it be true artistic work, like the work of the bee who makes her perfect polygonal cell in the first year of her life? Is not the curious confidence of the artist that he is right due to the fact that he is working by a curious inborn necessity? You argue with the bee in vain, a four-sided cell is better; she builds it six; and, if you ask her why, she says she must—it is so, that's all! Her whole cell is meaningless unless you realise the storing of the honey and the bees that have yet to be born whom she has never seen and who will feed on the honey—but she builds.'

'Yes,' he said, 'but it's more than mere hereditary racial instinct; an artist sees that which his race has never seen. Take the matter of wings. Age after age the artists of every race have seen them on their gods and great spiritual beings—on their Winged Victory, on their angels and devils, on their very bull gods: "And with twain they covered their face and with twain did fly."* It is useless for the superficial onlooker to say those wings wouldn't carry them, that their pectoral muscles are not strong enough to carry them. The artist says, "I see them." In after ages, men will have wings; how they will get the force to move them, or so to fasten them on that they will move freely, we cannot say. One day the man of science will realise the poet's dream, that dream—"So it is!"—which he would not and could not be shaken out of. The creative artist does not so much recall the life of the race; he paints its future, just as he often does his own. It can't be explained!'

'Yes,' she said, after a pause, 'but, isn't the answer something the same? The life and movement in a single finger is quite incomprehensible unless you know that it belongs to a hand and acts as part of it, and a whole hand with all its functions and movements is quite incomprehensible unless you know it as part of a complex body with a life bound to it. We know the man, and we know a little the race and the life on earth which that expresses; but the life of which it is only part—of that we know nothing; and that is the moving power.'

'Oh yes,' he said, 'the life of which we know nothing—that is it!'

'I wish they gave it a larger name,' she said.

'Yes,' he said, 'the name circumscribes it.'

She had left off working and was leaning forward with her elbows on her knees. The little moths, who hovered in a cloud about the tin lamp above her, made a little halo round her head, and sometimes settled on her brown hair with its smooth parting.

'I often think,' she said after a few seconds, 'that why men so misunderstand the nature of art is because there are three distinct processes to be gone through before it is given to the world; and men confuse them, though they are really wholly distinct. The first, the all-important element, without which there can be no art and no creation, is the sudden flash, or the slowly growing and intensified perception, over which, as you say, the man has and can have no control; it shapes itself in him; it is here as clearly and as actually as the outer world, though he knows it to have no connection with it. It can, as you say, be large only in an individual who is large; but it may be as complete, though smaller, in a smaller individuality. It is perfectly spontaneous, made of the man's substance, himself-of-himself; yet he feels in a way that it is something not himself but shown to him, while yet he feels also it belongs to him more than anything else in the world ever can. That is the first stage. When once he has perceived it clearly, it exists absolutely, perfectly and entirely—but within himself. He has no power to unmake it or to make it other than it is. It is this first stage, the really creative stage of the things, which I think people misunderstand so, because they confuse it with the second stage.

'In the second stage, of course, the artist's will does come into play, though only within certain limits. He must will, consciously or unconsciously, to create it as an external image, or it would remain forever only in his mind. He must seek for the knowledge and the materials and the leisure or other conditions without which it cannot be incarnated. If he is a sculptor, for instance, he must find the marble, the tools, the spot to work in, and the leisure to work. So far his will is acting, but, even in this stage, only within limits. He can determine whether he will work at all, or with what tool or what shade of marble; and he can determine the amount of sacrifice of other labours and interests and passions which he shall give up to his work; but what the work shall be, beyond a certain limit, he cannot determine without artistic adultery, which means the giving of a spurious art to the work. Always, as he works, he must be looking at the copy within,* which is his only guarantee of truth and right. He must not reason and question; he must look. He may change, alter, break and try again, but always in the manner of following his copy. Afterwards, when the work is done or when any part is done, he may question it as to meaning and turn a fierce, unblind criticism on it, sterner than that he would throw on the work of any other man; but, while he works actually, there must be only one thought—the vision and the attempts to incarnate it. If the vision fails, the work should cease. Not only is his will bound in this way, but, I think, even in the undertaking, if there is generally (and the truer the artist the more certainly) a sort of restless pressure which *forces* him, or appears to him to force him, to his work. Of course literally he could resist it: the desire for sensual or other pleasures, the desire for wealth and the attempt to gain it, a sense of duty to others whose immediate service he believes must come first—all these may make a man resist it; but I believe with all true artists the desire to incarnate is instinctive;* it may defy their reason; it is almost like the necessity of a woman to give birth to her child when the full time has come; she might kill it, as she might herself; but it is rather nature who compels her to give birth.

'Then comes the third stage. Now the work is completed as far as ever it can be. Seldom, probably never, has a great artist looked at any work that has proceeded from him with the infinite satisfaction and certitude of the dream-god of the Semitics,* when he looked at his work and saw that it was good and rested. Perhaps that which he alone knows of remains always to him of a completeness and beauty which nothing he can create in the poor medium of words or paint or marble can show; perhaps that is why, to the true artist, no criticism of outsiders makes any difference in *his* estimate of the work; if they blame it, he knows that they have not seen the original which came to him and was not wilfully made by him; if they praise it, he knows how much better the original was. But the time comes when, as far as he can or will, the work is done. It is now severed from him; the cord is cut; it has now its organic existence quite apart from himself. As time passes he can turn upon it exactly the same objective criticism which he would on another man's creation. The child is weaned. Then comes the question, what shall he do with it? Here, in this last stage, his will is supreme; the question is one entirely of motive. He can burn or destroy it, he can sell it or keep it, publish or exhibit it, save it to be given to the world after his death, show it to one human being or to the world, as he wishes. I think it is because it is this phase of the giving of art to the world, which alone the ignorant person sees clearly, that makes him think so strangely of it. He supposes that, because a man can decide whether he will publish the book or exhibit the picture, his will was equally independent in determining what it should be; even with the highest work of art, ignorant people are probably of opinion it came into existence only for them to see. That is perhaps why they are so generous with their advice—"You ought to have done so!" "Why didn't you make it so?"—not simply "I like it" or "I don't like it"—which would be quite justified, if their opinion were asked.'*

He was still leaning back with his arms folded against the veranda post; he glanced round at her and laughed: 'And the author says, "Damn you, take it or leave it, as you like!" '

'Yes,' she laughed, 'or something stronger if he knows it!' Then she leaned further forward: 'I think all kinds of motives may make him give his work to the world—the feeling that makes a little child, when it finds a pretty flower, always run to its nurse or its mother that they may see it too—perhaps in some cases the idea of helping or comforting others—perhaps in some cases the mere love of fame and notoriety, though I think the art given out for such a cause would have something fraudulent in its very nature and not be true art—very often there is absolute necessity, such that, if a man is to go on producing art, he must live by it, and cannot so live unless he gives it out.'

'Often not then! It's the middleman gets it, whether it's a picture or a cradle!' he interjected softly between his teeth, still looking out at the flowerbeds, which near the veranda were made visible amid the surrounding darkness by the light from the tin reflector of the lamp.

She paused to listen to him, and then said, 'I think, with the true artist, whatever other motive there may be, there must always be this, consciously or unconsciously—not to let the thing die!* As he has striven and laboured to give it a perfect concrete form, that it may exist outside of his own mind, so there is in him a longing that it should live on—completely reflected in another mind as once it lived in his: "Shall I call to the birth and not cause to bring forth? saith the Lord"*—I think it's something like that!'

'Yes,' he said, still leaning back and staring away at the flowerbeds.

'I have never seen any great sculptor's art,' she said; 'but in my study is a little statue nine inches high; it's a Hercules or a Bacchus (it doesn't matter what it's called) with some vine leaves about its forehead; the man's nude body, with all its gigantic power of muscle, holds in its arms an infant, and the bearded face smiles down at it.* I think it was once yours; I bought it for a silk dress. Perhaps you, who have seen so much great art, might think nothing of it; it may be only a copy of some great work. But to me the glory is that—after all these hundreds, perhaps almost thousands, of years it has lain buried, while the man, whose being it first lived in, has for ages been Italian dust or rooted trees and plants on a Greek island—it has sprung out into life again—here, on the opposite side of the earth, after all those ages; with the joy, the comprehension of it, that throbbed in his brain when he saw it, beating here again in mine—the same, alive; it is *not* dead. When I finger it and feel its beauty, the throb in him lives, across all the centuries, as an actual throb in me. It's something like the feeling when you break off the last flake of stone and out comes the head of the creature that was an actual living being, having his day, as you are having yours, and as real; and it comes out into the sunshine, the very sunshine it loved and lived in millions of years ago. You feel and touch it—your fellow life—from across all the countless ages; and all life seems to be knit together even across boundless time.' She was speaking quickly, but stopped suddenly.

Then as though her thoughts had been wandering, she said after a few moments, 'I can fancy that, if a man were shut for years in some lonely castle by a lake, with no human companion and no hope of escape, he yet might find life tolerable if he found in his prison an old block and carved it year after year; and that, when the time came for him to be led out to execution, rather than that his captor should see it, rather than that they should possess it who could not understand it, he might take out his knife and utterly destroy it; but I have fancied also how he would have clambered up and dropped it out of the small window into the lake below, in the hope, as they led him to death, that some day it might be found and might fall into the hands of one who would understand it, and that all the agony and all the hope and despair graven into the block in those long years would find an answer in another heart. They would never know who had carved it, but the thing would live in another soul; and so I have fancied death would be easier to him. I think no artist need fear to give his work to the world because there are none who can understand. No human soul is so lonely as it feels itself, because no man is merely an individual but is a part of the great body of life; the thoughts he thinks are part of humanity's thoughts, the visions he sees are part of humanity's visions; the artist is only an eye in the great human body, seeing for those who share his life: somewhere, some time, his own exist.'

She was softly rumpling a tiny rumple in her little black silk apron between her thumb and forefinger. 'I have sometimes thought,' she said, 'that ages ago in Ancient Chaldea* there might have been some thinker whose thought seemed to have no relation to the men about him, whose vision seemed for himself alone; yet, recorded on a mud tablet and preserved through the years and coming to the light today, it might be found most closely connected with our needs and new life, might find its own here today and live again, though the man who made it might be forgotten. I cannot feel there is anything ignoble in the wish that, when we pass, the thing we love should live on its own life.* Even a woman feels that when she gives birth to a child; though, if she has not loved the man she lived with, she has not conceived it for the good it might do or the beauty it might show—yet, even then, when she is in the agony of childbirth, the thought will flash in her with sudden joy, "Perhaps it will live on when I am gone and be the beautiful and the good to others"; and the thought gives her joy, though those who win good and beauty from the child may never know it had a mother or who she was. I think there is nothing ignoble in this wish—that the thing we have loved, that has been so beautiful to us, should live on a little in the love of other souls, though we gain nothing by it and our names are not even known.'

'Yes,' he said, 'that is true.' She had gathered up her darning again and was beginning to work. He laughed a little soft internal laugh, such as people do who live much alone, conversing only with themselves.

Then turning to her and looking up at her, he said, 'You know, turning from the worldwide discussion of art and creation to a very trivial and insignificant thing, if you will allow me—what you say is true. Even with my own insignificant little scribblings, which might never be of the slightest value to anyone but myself, I always have deep down a curious feeling that I don't want *them* to die. Somewhere deep down in my mind I've always had a feeling that, when I grow old and have lived enough and seen enough and am wearying, then will be the time to settle down peacefully somewhere and throw them into such form that they could live for others. Ever since I was a boy,' he said, bending towards her and leaning the palm of one hand on the floor of the veranda, 'I've had an old deal box with a slipping lid that came to me from Germany full of wooden bricks, and ever since all or nearly all I've written has gone in there. I believe why I haven't written so much lately is because it's nearly full,' he laughed; 'but some day, I'm always conscious deep down in my heart, I'm going to make it fair and square. They can publish them after I die; it won't hurt me.'

She had dropped her work again. 'But life is so short,' she said.

He moved quickly. 'Yes!' Then he laughed again and sat upright. 'I am forty; I have another forty years to live. I've had only one serious illness in my life, and then I was too small to remember it. I'm good for eighty! May I smoke again?' He took out his pipe.

She was passing the needle evenly in and out in her darning. 'I have sometimes thought,' she said, 'it would be a terrible thing if, when death came to a man or woman, there stood about his bed, reproaching him, not for his sins, not for his crimes of commission and omission toward his fellow men, but for the thoughts and the visions that had come to him, and which he, not for the sake of sensuous pleasure or gain, had thrust always into the background, saying, "Because of my art, my love and my relations to my fellow men shall never suffer; there shall be no loaf of bread less baked, no sick left untended, no present human creature's need of me left unsatisfied because of it." And then, when he is dying, they gather round him, the things he might have incarnated and given life to—and would not. All that might have lived, and now must never live forever, look at him with their large reproachful eyes—his own dead visions reproaching him; as the children a woman has aborted and refused to give life to might gather about her at last, saying, "We came to you; you, only you, could have given us life. Now we are dead forever. Was it worth it? All the sense of duty you satisfied, the sense of necessity you laboured under: should you not have violated it and given us birth?" It has come upon me so vividly sometimes,' she said, 'that I have almost leaped out of bed to gain air—that suffocating sense that all his life long a man or a woman might live striving to do their duty and then at the end find it all wrong.' She had stopped in her work again and was breathing quickly.

'Yes,' he said slowly, as he smoked with his face turned to the garden and almost his back towards her, 'but remember this—that no art, no creative thought can be greater all round than the creature from whom it takes its birth. If the man or the woman dwarf themselves for the sake of their art, in devotion to their thought, the art and the thought are both shorn. Is a lovely life also nothing? Is it not the highest ideal to realise it? Many a man has shorn his life of all devotion to any aims except his art and thought, and in the end they have died starved out and weaklings.'

She had taken up her work again.

'I see that,' she said; 'but life is so terribly difficult. Men say it is so hard to do the right. I have never found that. The moment one knows what is right, I do it; it is easy to do it; the difficulty is to find what *is* right! There are such absolutely conflicting ideals; the ideal of absolute submission and endurance of wrong towards oneself—the ideal of noble resistance to all injustice and wrong, even when done to oneself—the ideal of the absolute devotion to the smaller, always present, call of life—and the ideal of a devotion to the larger aims sweeping all before it—all are beautiful. The agony of life is not the choice between good and evil, but between two evils or two goods!'

'Why don't you follow your demon? I do,' he said.

'I used to,' she replied. 'Long ago I always knew with absolute certainty, not what was the right course for another man, but for me—and I took it. But life grows so terribly complex as you grow older; there comes always the thought, "If I should be choosing the wrong." '

'Life doesn't become more complex to me,' he said; 'it lies right ahead. I know which path you would always choose,' he added.

'Which?' she asked.

'Whichever gave you most pain or least pleasure. You would always think that was the right one.'

At that moment the great clock in the hall struck half past nine and the two elder boys, whose bedtime it was, came rushing out from the new room to their bedroom in the large house. As they saw Drummond they raised the war shout, which was their appointed mode of greeting him. They begged to be allowed to sit up just ten minutes more to sit and talk to him, and sat down beside him on the edge of the stoep, Charles on his right hand and Frank, who was generally demonstrative, on his left with his arm across his shoulder.

'Put your watch on your knee, so we can see exactly how the time's going.'

'I have been trying to paint reindeer like the one you told us the story of, standing by her young when it was wounded. I can manage the reindeer and the blue, but I can't make the snow glitter; does it—'

'Oh, don't talk about your old picture; let him tell us an adventure instead; the time's half gone already.'

They talked till the ten minutes were over and then trooped away to bed, and Rebekah rose to go to the rooms to see if the three young ones* were all right.

He rose. 'I also must go,' he said.

'It's very early,' she said. 'I shall be back again in an instant.'

'Then if you will allow me I will smoke this pipe out.' He relit it and sat down again.

When she returned he was still sitting absorbed in smoking and she took up her work, but neither spoke till the pipe was empty. Then as he took it from his lips and knocked it out carefully against the side of the veranda, he said, 'It was a nice old custom of the Indians for a man to hand his pipe to another in token of amity and union. We lose much in modern life by doing away with these old symbols of deeper things.' He put the pipe away in his breast pocket as he stood up. He stood below the veranda, looking at her as she darned. 'Should I be trespassing too much if I asked you to allow me to see your fossils again? I did not half examine them, and some, I think, will be quite new to me.'

'You can come and see them at any time you like,' Rebekah said; 'the door of the room is hardly ever shut; if it is, you will find the key on the ledge above the door; and the little key of the cabinet is in the top left-hand drawer of the desk. Please come at any time you like.'

'Thank you. Goodnight.'

Without offering his hand he turned down the path towards the front gate; when he had almost reached it he turned back and stood just within the circle of light the lamp shed.

'Wouldn't you care to come and see my fossils? I have not finished packing them yet. I could easily show them you.'

She hesitated a moment. 'No, thank you,' she said.

'They are in an outer room on the other side of the house; I have two rooms there; you would interfere with no one.'

'No, thank you,' she said.

'All right. Goodnight!' He turned and walked quickly down to the gate.

APPENDIX 1

S. C. CRONWRIGHT-SCHREINER, INTRODUCTION TO THE FIRST EDITION (1926)

On the first day of May 1873 Olive Schreiner, then just eighteen, was living in tents at New Rush, the two-year-old Diamond Diggings now known as Kimberley. On that day she entered in her journal that she had written out the first chapter of *Other Men's Sins*, a name that does not appear again; but, when she was governess at the farm Ratel Hoek, she entered in her journal on the 3rd of August 1876 that she had made up her mind 'to write *A Small Bit of Mimosa* and *Wrecked* in one'; on the 21st of the same month that she had 'Got some idea of *Saints and Sinners*'; and, on the 10th of September, '*Saints and Sinners* is growing clearer'. I am inclined to think that, when she decided to blend *A Small Bit of Mimosa* and *Wrecked* (both then mentioned for the first time), she incorporated *Other Men's Sins* into the same plan. At any rate, we now have this novel fairly started; for *Saints and Sinners* was 'the original germ', as she styled it, of *From Man to Man*. Not only did she tell Havelock Ellis this in 1884, but it is abundantly clear otherwise. For instance, in September 1883 she enters in her London journal that she is 'At the Jew and "Rain in London"', which is now Chapter XI of this novel; and she adds: 'Thought of a name, *From Man to Man*.' This title is taken from a sentence of John (later Lord) Morley's, which runs as follows, except that I have forgotten the adjective: 'From man to man nothing matters but... charity.' The missing word connotes 'boundless', 'all-embracing', or some such large and generous attitude of mind.

Olive sailed to England for the first time early in March 1881, taking with her *Saints and Sinners* (as far as it was completed), in addition to *The Story of an African Farm*. While governessing at Ratel Hoek and Lelie Kloof, she had apparently made considerable progress with *Saints and Sinners*. For instance, at Lelie Kloof, in October 1880, this entry occurs in her journal: 'Had an idea about Bertie this afternoon—suicide, quite *strong*'; Bertie being one of the two chief characters of the novel. Such a reference seems to indicate that she had already made considerable progress in the plan of the work, for Bertie's death is bound to come late in the book.

From May 1876 to November 1883 this novel is always referred to as *Saints and Sinners*; thereafter it is styled *From Man to Man*. I have no recollection that, after November 1883, she ever referred to it, in speech or in writing, by any other name than *From Man to Man*; though, while we were 'detained' by the British military at Hanover during the greater part of the Boer War, I typed 'The Prelude', the first six chapters and part of the seventh, as she revised them in 1901 and 1902.

When we lived at De Aar, from 1907 onwards, it was her custom (necessitated by ill-health) to leave home every year to escape the great summer heat of the upper Karoo. She often spent such large absences in Cape Town; she was there in 1911, and then had 'The Prelude' and the first six chapters retyped in triplicate and sent to me by the typist from Woodstock (a suburb of Cape Town). Knowing what the package contained, I do not think I opened it then; I have no recollection of having done so; nor do I remember having then seen the alterations she had made in the Dedication and the Title. I put the package carefully away, and, when I left De Aar in December 1919, stored it there with my other things. Olive, who had sailed to England early in December 1914,[1] was unable to return to South Africa; and so, being free on retiring from De Aar, I went to England in 1920. She returned to South Africa in August of that year, leaving me to follow after the winter, but she died in her sleep at Wynberg in December.

I returned to South Africa in February 1921, but was too much occupied to get my De Aar things down to Cape Town and go through the papers until the end of that year; then I opened the Woodstock package that had been posted to me in March 1911. At that time I knew the book as *From Man to Man*, and by no other title; and I was familiar with the dedication, which, before the death of our baby in 1895, ran, '*To My Little Sister, Ellie, who died, aged eighteen months*,' with the relative couplet that now appears in the present dedication. In the Hanover typing of 1901–1902, the title and dedication remain the same except for the following addition: '*Also to My daughter and only child, Born the 30th April 1895, and Died the 1st May, aged one day. She never lived to shed a woman's tears*.' In the Woodstock typing of 1911 the title appears as *The Camel Thorn*, but the pen has been run through it and a new title, *Perhaps Only*, substituted therefor. (The Camel-thorn, Afrikaans *Kameel-doring*, is *Acacia giraffæ*.) The new title is taken from a sentence uttered by the little child in 'The Prelude': '*Perhaps only God knew what the lights and shadows were*.' She wrote this sentence (which appears on p. 67 of 'The Prelude'[2]) beneath the typing of the Woodstock title-page. I give a facsimile of the sentence as she wrote it with the pen, and in the same relative position.

The Woodstock dedication, as then typed, reads thus:—

[1] In fact it was 1913 [Editor's note].

[2] p. 37 in this edition [Editor's note].

Dedicated
to
My Little Sister Ellie
Who died, aged eighteen months, when I was nine years old.
*
Also
to
My Only Daughter
Born on the 30th April, and died the 1st May.
*
She never lived to know she was a woman.

The last line, so typed, stands wholly excised by Olive with pen and ink. The couplet under the dedication to little Ellie, as it now appears in this book, indicates the astounding effect Olive claims the infant's brief life and early death had upon her own life.

Except that the title (*The Camel Thorn*) is crossed out and *Perhaps Only* is written above it in largish letters, the 'prelim.' page of the Woodstock typing is as follows:—

THE CAMEL THORN
Prelude
The Child's Day
*
The Book
The Woman's Day
*
Part 1
(List of six chapters as they now appear.)

The original plan, or one of the early plans of the novel was, as I understand it, that *The Child's Day* should be Part 1, *The Woman's Day* Part 2, and *Rebekah* Part 3. I give a copy of an old page, just as I found it in Olive's handwriting:—

Chapter 8. Bertie wants Dorcas to hold her hand.
Chapter 9. Showing how Veronica took hens to the old farm.
Chapter 10. Bertie ties ribbons round the kittens' necks.
Chapter 11. Bertie seeks for the country and cannot find [it].
Chapter 12. 'Sally is my Sweetheart
Sally is my darling.'
End of Part 2.
Rebekah.
*

Chapter 1. Great White Angels.
Chapter 2. Rebekah's Books are Dead
Chapter 3. The Waterfall.
Chapter 4. Muizenberg.
Chapter 5. Sartje.
Chapter 6. Koonap Heights.
Chapter 7. The Old Farm.
Chapter 8. Baby-Bertie.
Chapter 9. A Bit of Mimosa.
Chapter 10. How the Wax Flowers Smell.

I now give a list of the chapters of what the whole novel was at one time meant to be, just as I found it:—

Perhaps Only.

Prelude: The Child's Day.
The Book: The Woman's Day.

Part one of the Woman's Day.

Chapter 1. Showing what Baby-Bertie thought of her new tutor and how Rebekah got married.
Chapter 2. A Wild-Flower Garden in the Bush.
Chapter 3. The Dam Wall.
Chapter 4. Showing how Baby-Bertie heard the Cicadas cry.
Chapter 5. John-Ferdinand shows Veronica his new House.
Chapter 6. How Baby-Bertie went a-dancing.
Chapter 7. You cannot capture the Ideal by a Coup d'Etat.

Part 2 of the Woman's Day.

Chapter 1. Fireflies in the Dark.
Chapter 2. The Little Black Curl.
Chapter 3. The Rocks again.
Chapter 4. Koonap Heights.
Chapter 5. The Glittering of the Sand.
Chapter 6. Veronica.
Chapter 7. The Lure Light.
Chapter 8. A Bit of Mimosa.
Chapter 9. The Kopje.

The End.

The thirteen chapters, as presented in this book, are all in the order in which Olive meant them to be. Chapter 14, 'The Pine Woods', was begun; but as there are less than a thousand words, as they are of no importance to the narrative, are unrevised, and lead nowhere, I do not think it necessary to give them. After the opening lines, Rebekah and Drummond begin a conversation, which, as far as it goes, has no significance, except possibly for its last few lines:—

' "Have you ever hated anyone?" he asked.
'She sat upright: "No, not if hatred means the wish to injure. I have loathed people; I have tried to forget some people." '

There the manuscript ends. There is not another word of the novel or of anything in connection with it. It is as though nothing more had ever been written. It was a custom with her to retain not only her first rapid drafts, but also any manuscript she had gone over and revised. For instance, there were three drafts of *The Buddhist Priest's Wife*, each progressively shorter than the previous one and none of them quite complete; to get the final draft I had to sort out the last two drafts in several ways—by handwriting, by age of the paper, and so on—then get the (often wrongly-numbered) sheets into consecutive order respectively, then compare and adjust them. It was much the same with *On the Banks of a Full River*, and with several other of her writings.

And so it was with this uncompleted novel; there were a considerable number of drafts of parts; there were fragments, revisions, etc.; but none of these had any relation to the book after the thirteenth chapter, except the few words, already referred to, of the fourteenth. I feel certain that she had 'finished' the novel in her mind; I think she had not only thus 'finished' the plan of it, but she had done so in considerable detail in parts; nothing, however, short of clear proof, will convince me that she wrote down any more after the few words I possess of the fourteenth chapter. I am unable to think she destroyed any of the manuscript of the fourteenth chapter or of any later chapters. After all her assertions, verbal and written, it may seem difficult to believe that her actual writing ceased with the beginning of Chapter 14; and yet that seems to me by far the most likely explanation. (Readers are referred, for comparison, to the strange story, related in the *Life*, of the 'Big Sex Book'.) Considering that she kept so much of the rejected, revised and incomplete manuscripts of other books while she was working on them, that she actually did the same with this specially loved and valued novel, knowing well also the unreliability of her statements about her work, I am simply unable to believe she destroyed the balance of the manuscript of *From Man to Man*. I do not believe a balance existed.

Well, there is the fact, which, extraordinary as it is, yet cannot seem so extraordinary to me as it may to other people. I have been carefully through all her papers; the manuscript of the novel, in whatever confusion, was in one bundle (as was, I think, each of her other sets of manuscripts); and there is not a single scrap of paper after the few opening lines of the fourteenth chapter. It is my considered opinion that she wrote no further than where the manuscript now ends, but that later, at various times and irregular intervals (sometimes intervals of years), she went back to the beginning and to other early parts and set to work on revision. If she had quite abandoned all hope of further work on this beloved book, if she had decided on its destruction and had had sufficient strength to carry out such decision (which I doubt), she would, in my opinion, have destroyed the whole novel except 'The Prelude'; she would not have destroyed merely a portion of the unrevised manuscript and left the revised and unrevised remainder. But I do not believe she ever abandoned all hope of still doing some work on the novel, and I do not believe she had it in her heart to destroy this greatly loved offspring of her mature mind any more than it could be in her heart to destroy a child of her physical body.

At the end of Chapter XIII, I give a brief account of what she told me as to the ending of the book. It is remarkable and fortunate that the novel does not stop until the tale is told almost to completion, and that the short account I am able to add will satisfy a legitimate desire of those whose interest will lie mainly in the incidents of the narrative; though, to all who love her work and recognise her power, there must ever remain the deep regret that she was unable to wind up the tale herself.

As to the name of the book, I have decided after much thought not to use the title I prefer (and which indeed I wish the book could be known by), but to adopt the one already familiar from its frequent use in the *Life* and *Letters*—the only title I ever heard Olive use. It seems to me that some confusion would result from the exclusive use of *Perhaps Only*; I do not feel at all sure that she would have used it; I am inclined to think she would have retained the title *From Man to Man*. As far as I know, the titles *Camel Thorn* and *Perhaps Only* were never mentioned to any person. Yet, though I believe I have decided rightly, I deeply regret that *Perhaps Only*—(so she wrote it) cannot be used except as an alternative title. As apparently her last choice, one might well expect it to be the most suitable, expressing with rare art, by the use of those two words taken from the wondering and deep-piercing mind of the child, a kind of stunned reluctance to judge the meaning (if there be a meaning) and the incomprehensibility of the 'ethic' (if there be an ethic) in the awful and mysterious living cosmos.

For purposes of this Introduction I went carefully through both the *Life* and *Letters* and copied out practically every reference to the novel contained therein. When all the extracts were before me in chronological order, I decided to leave them to tell their own tale. And so there follow, as a kind of supplement to this Introduction and without comment, nearly all of such references, made by herself and in her own words.

In dealing with the unrevised original text of the novel all I could do legitimately was, as far as possible, to give it to the world in the form in which Olive left it. I have striven to present it exactly as she might have presented it, if she herself, without further re-writing, had reduced to its final word-form the unrevised manuscript that came into my hands.

Olive loved this book more than anything else she ever wrote, and, of the book, she loved 'The Prelude' best. I have therefore printed 'The Prelude' (*The Child's Day*) just as it stands in the Woodstock typing of 1911, and as revised by herself at the time.

It may interest readers to know that many references to 'the old farm' are applicable to Klein Ganna Hoek, the farm where she was governess in 1875 and 1876, and where she wrote nearly all of *Undine* and much of *The Story of an African Farm*. But some other farm or farms, which I cannot identify, though I suspect Ratel Hoek for one and possibly Lelie Kloof, must also have been in her mind. 'The Child's Day' is certainly almost wholly autobiographical: to take one small incident—she herself built the little mouse-house on the bare rock at Witteberg[3] and waited for the mouse and then fashioned her hand to imitate the mouse entering into it.

S. C. CRONWRIGHT-SCHREINER

CAPE TOWN, SOUTH AFRICA
March, 1926

[3] Wittenberg [Editor's note].

APPENDIX 2

THE GENESIS AND COMPOSITION OF THE NOVEL

Introduction

THE story told here begins in 1873, when Olive Schreiner first started writing the novel on which she would try out so many names: 'Other Men's Sins', 'Wrecked', 'A Small Bit of Mimosa', 'Sinners & Saints', 'Saints & Sinners', 'Thorn Kloof', 'From Man to Man', and, on her final typescript in 1911, 'The Camel Thorn' and 'Perhaps Only—'.[1] And the story ends, of course, with Schreiner's death in 1920. Drawing on her journals and letters, it tells of her long labour on the novel and her passionate engagement with some of the key ideas that fed into its composition. It also offers insight into some of the issues that led to the novel's many revisions and, ultimately, to its abandonment. Schreiner's anguished remarks on the ill health that made it impossible for her to finalize the text become increasingly poignant.

The selection that follows is based in small part on the 'Note on the Genesis of the Book' that Samuel Cron Cronwright-Schreiner (SCCS) compiled for the Unwin and Harper editions of the novel. This 'Note' was made up of excerpts from her journals and letters which he used initially for his *Life of Olive Schreiner* (1924) or his *Letters of Olive Schreiner* (1924). After inserting into these publications the quotations he required, he destroyed the letters he had saved or procured, along with the bulk of her journals (the latter act—he claimed—was intended to protect Schreiner from scandal).[2] He did, however, deposit a large number of his transcriptions of the letters into the National Library of South Africa in Cape Town (NLSA).

[1] For discussion about some of these early titles, as well as about the decision to combine 'Perhaps Only' with 'From Man to Man' for the novel's ultimate title, see SCCS's introduction to the first edition (in Appendix 1, pp. 377–8 and 382). For 'Thorn Kloof' as an early version of *From Man to Man* (contrary to what SCCS claimed), as well as for general discussion of OS's various titles for the novel, see Karel Schoeman, *Olive Schreiner: A Woman in South Africa*, 387–90, in Select Bibliography, *supra*. And for a discussion of 'Saints & Sinners', see C. P. Ravilious, '"Saints and Sinners": An Unidentified Olive Schreiner Manuscript', 1–11, in Select Bibliography, *supra*.

[2] SCCS to Havelock Ellis, 25 May 1921 (HRC): 'I have finished Olive's "Journals", made the necessary extracts and destroyed them—a necessary step. Some things are pretty well closed up, I think.' For the abbreviations of sources that follow references to Schreiner's letters, see the Archival Acknowledgements and Abbreviations of Sources that follows this introduction.

Fortunately, in numerous archives across the UK, the USA and South Africa some 5,000 Schreiner letters have been preserved, most of which Cronwright-Schreiner had no access to. Verbatim transcriptions of these, along with transcriptions of the fragments that Cronwright-Schreiner preserved, have been made publicly available through *Olive Schreiner Letters Online* (*OSLO*, www.oliveschreiner.org), a resource of the greatest value to Schreiner scholars generally, including to myself, not least since—as an open access service—it was granted archival permissions (see Archival Acknowledgements at the end of this Appendix).[3] For the most part, then, *OSLO* is the source for what follows, enabling the present 'Genesis and Composition' to be more informative, comprehensive and reliable than Cronwright-Schreiner's 'Note on the Genesis of the Novel'. For the epistolary entries, this 'Genesis' is entirely dependent on *OSLO* for the date and place that preface each entry (although it makes certain adaptations to the naming of places)[4] and it is largely dependent on *OSLO*, too, for the biographical notes on the recipients of Schreiner's letters (these are provided at the end of the Appendix). That each entry in this Appendix is headed by the date, place and name that heads each *OSLO* transcription means that readers can all the more easily access the letters in *OSLO* if they wish to read further than the excerpts selected here.

OSLO's careful transcriptions show up the flaws of both SCCS's and Richard Rive's editorial mode, and in many ways it offers a more comprehensive coverage than theirs (Rive's is limited to the years 1871–99), as well as than Yaffa Claire Draznin's edition of letters, which is limited to the correspondence between Schreiner and Havelock Ellis, and excludes the swathe of Schreiner letters that Ellis sent SCCS for his book publications, and that were thereafter destroyed: Draznin reproduces letters only when originals exist.[5]

[3] Praise is to be directed at *OSLO*'s line-by-line decipherment of Schreiner's notoriously difficult handwriting, its scrupulous dating of the letters, its provision of place-names from which the letters were sent, and its explanatory annotations to many of the letters. It also provides useful biographical information about Schreiner's correspondents and their relation to her, and it gives access to some of Schreiner's other archival material. One caveat should, however, be noted: its search mechanism is cumbersome, imperfect and lacks the capacity to cover the more recent acquisitions in its collection (these are in a separate 'New Letters' section).

[4] Where necessary, and on first reference only, I adjust or expand on the named place; I use the term London rather than the specific suburbs *OSLO* names; I also reduce St Leonards-on-Sea, Bexhill-on-Sea, and Southbourne-on-Sea to their shorter terms on second reference.

[5] For Rive's and Draznin's editions, see Select Bibliography, *supra*. Like Rive, *OSLO* reproduces those letters SCCS transcribed for which no originals are extant and does so 'for sake of completeness', while reminding readers to regard them 'with caution'; they are identifiable via *OSLO*'s reference to the archival source: NLSA.

Of these three published editions, only Draznin's competes with *OSLO* in scholarly precision. For an instructive comparison in this regard, it is useful to look at the different ways in which SCCS, Rive, Draznin and *OSLO* reproduce Schreiner's letter to Havelock Ellis, written from Alassio on 5 April 1890 (in Appendix 2). For *OSLO*, Schreiner writes: 'I think I shall stay here till the end of August, unless I find I the winter too cold.' For SCCS, she writes, nonsensically: 'I think I shall stay here till the end of August, unless I find I am getting on with my work slowly and steadily, but not brilliantly' (*Letters*, 181). For Rive, she writes, equally nonsensically: 'I *think* I shall stay here till the end of August, unless I find I restrain myself" (167). But for Draznin, she writes much as *OSLO* has it: 'I *think* I shall stay here till the end of August, unless I find / the winter *too* cold' (458). As readers will note, Draznin uses a virgule to mark the line division; *OSLO* instead numbers the lines. Moreover, italics mark Schreiner's emphases; *OSLO* instead retains Schreiner's underlining. Further, in the subordinate clause, Draznin silently omits Schreiner's second 'I', which *OSLO* retains; it reproduces in italics Schreiner's stressed word 'too', which *OSLO* misses, but would have underlined. Their dating differs as well: because Schreiner started composing the letter on a Friday and continued into a Saturday, Draznin—while reproducing the given date—notes the correct date in brackets, 4–5 April: 5 April 1890 was not a Friday, which *OSLO* fails to notice.

These observations serve to lead into the editorial method adopted in the present selection. Geared as it is to *OSLO*, and to comply with *OSLO*'s search mechanism for the ease of current readers, the present selection retains 5 April as this particular letter's date. Speaking generally now, it also follows some of Draznin's editorial procedures (favouring literal transcription, while eschewing near-facsimile reproduction), but in some cases it further pursues readability against the grain of punctilious editorial practice. Thus *OSLO*'s transcriptions have been lightly edited. Schreiner's emphatic and characteristic underlining is preserved rather than transformed into italics, but her strike-through deletions are omitted, unless they are of special interest (in which case *OSLO*'s struck-through words and its strikethrough line is retained). Also omitted are the carets *OSLO* deploys for Schreiner's insertions, as well as the false starts Schreiner made before settling on a word (the letter t, for instance, standing on its own); also her careless lexical repetitions ('the the' for example); and what can read only as slips of the pen ('it comes in my minds', for example, in her letter to Richard Garnett, 5 January 1889, *OSLO*/HRC, in this Appendix), which may even be due to the notorious illegibility of some of her handwriting. However, in order to preserve the sense of immediacy of *OSLO*'s verbatim transcriptions, Schreiner's often erratic and idiosyncratic punctuation and hyphenation are retained, and, where necessary for the sake of quick and easy readability, added to; these editorial emendations are marked by curly brackets {...}. To mark any divergence from standard spelling or grammar, I dispense with the indicator '[*sic*]' that Draznin uses, but add clarifications, again within curly brackets {i.e. . . . } even when, for grammatically trained readers, they may seem unnecessary. Curly brackets are also used to identify words that I add, editorially, when they appear to have been clearly intended. While most kinds of emendations are not, then, rendered silent, an exception is made as regards apostrophes: these are silently added in the present selection, whether relating to possessives (*ten years' work*, for example) or abbreviations (*don't*, *won't*, *it's* versus *its*, for example). Schreiner only intermittently neglects to add them. Silent additions are in such cases preferable; curly brackets would be overly intrusive. Occasional adjustments to paragraphing follow the demands of coherence and readability; these are also kept silent.[6]

As for the texts drawn from SCCS's publications, the excerpts included in his 'Note on the Genesis' have been checked against the quotations in his *Life* and *Letters*; these publications are duly recorded as the source. They have also been supplemented by other relevant quotations reproduced in the *Life* and *Letters*. Part of Schreiner's 'Rattel [i.e. Ratel] Hoek Journal' remains extant: checking SCCS's excerpts has allowed for some correction as well as some supplementation.[7] To avoid the repetition of place in the headings for each entry, and for the sake of consistency, since SCCS (like Schreiner) shifts erratically between the two terms, 'diary' and 'journal', I use only the general term 'Journal' to designate SCCS's source, whether her Kimberley Diary, her Ratel Hoek Journal, her Leliekloof Diary, her London Diary, her England Diary, her Alassio Diary, her Menton Diary, her Hanover or Matjesfontein Diary (he does not quote from her Gannahoek Journal).

In my transcriptions of excerpts from letters for which no original exists and which are drawn from SCCS's *Life* or *Letters*, I necessarily retain any silent editorial emendations he may have made, but (like *OSLO*) I underline rather than italicize the words and phrases that Schreiner stressed.

[6] Schreiner did not use indentation, instead starting a new line or leaving a gap within a line which *OSLO* registers as paragraph breaks, as it does when her writing spills over into the margins.

[7] Part of what remains of the 'Rattel [i.e. Ratel] Hoek Journal' is held at HRC (a transcription is available through the University of Cape Town Digital Collections: http://www.digitalcollections.lib.uct.ac.za/ratel-hoek-journal), and part is held at NLSA. In the entries in 'Genesis' for 25 July 1876 and 24 March 1887, SCCS misreads 'write' for 'finish', and either misreads or edits 'good' for 'going'. Also (as internal evidence shows), he wrongly dates as '1876' a journal entry that was made in 1877 (see '18 April 1876' in *Life*, 129).

Unlike *OSLO*, however, I retain SCCS's italicization of book titles, since it cannot be known whether Schreiner underlined or quoted the titles, or did not mark them at all. I retain SCCS's square brackets to indicate his annotations (when I keep them) as well as his ellipses. Curly brackets indicate my own.

Although I am deeply indebted to *OSLO* for the annotations and brief biographical notes identifying the recipients of Schreiner's letters provided at the end of this Appendix (and indeed the greater detail their website offers will be of further interest to readers), I sometimes adjust or add to the information their website provides, and in the biographical notes I adjust the recipient's given name (Adela Constance Smith, for example). In its provision of one of its archival sources, *OSLO* uses, variously, three different names for a single institution: National Archives Depot, National Archives Repository, and National Archives of South Africa). I use only the last mentioned name, which is in general use as the umbrella term. And, on a few occasions, by kind favour of Amazwi, the University of Cape Town Special Collections, and the Harry Ransom Centre, my own decipherment of Schreiner's difficult handwriting differs from *OSLO*'s letter transcriptions: the hash sign (#) is used to signal my corrections.

I trust that the editorial procedure adopted here keeps close enough to Schreiner's own mode of letter-writing to prompt devoted readers into conducting epistolary research via first-hand archival investigation—into the question, for instance, whether her control of spelling and grammar diverged in relation to particular correspondents or particular times of her life: did she, for instance, take greater care over her letters to Pearson than to some others? Finally, on the topic of editorial procedure, and as a mark of respect to Schreiner, it needs also to be added that the author wished her letters to be destroyed on her death, which was indeed her wish for all her unfinished writing. The letters were written for private use and were certainly not intended for publication. Some readers may therefore find dubious the ethics of reproducing them, especially in verbatim or unedited reproduction that shows up what Schreiner may not have wanted shown up: apparent failures to spell and punctuate in the 'standard manner'.

Archival Acknowledgements and Abbreviations of Sources

BL British Library, Department of Manuscripts, London (Mary Gladstone Papers)

CL Cory Library, Rhodes University, Grahamstown (Henderson Papers)

GFP Greene Family Papers (Private Collection)

Harper Harper 1927 edition of *From Man to Man*

HRC	Harry Ransom Center, University of Texas at Austin (a.k.a. Humanities Research Center) (Havelock Ellis Collection, Olive Schreiner Collection, and Richard Garnett Collection)
HT	Hobhouse Trust, Canada
Journal	Olive Schreiner's various diaries and journals
Letters	*The Letters of Olive Schreiner* (1924)
LFP	Lytton Family Papers, Knebworth House, Hertfordshire
Life	*The Life of Olive Schreiner* (1924)
NASA	National Archives of South Africa, Pretoria (J. C. Smuts Collection, W. T. Stead Collection)
NELM	National English Literary Museum, Grahamstown, now renamed Amazwi Museum of South African Literature, Makhanda (Olive Schreiner Collection)
NLSA	National Library of South Africa (Special Collections), Cape Town (Olive Schreiner Collection, Anna Purcell Collection, John X. Merriman Collection, W. P. Schreiner Collection)
OSLO	*Olive Schreiner Letters Online* (www.oliveschreiner.org)
RLSC	Ronald Levine Sauer Collection (Private Collection)
SCL	Sheffield City Library (Archives & Local Studies) (Edward Carpenter Collection)
UCL	University College London Library (Special Collections) (Karl Pearson Papers)
UCT	University of Cape Town Libraries (Special Collections) (Brown Family Papers, Molteno Collection, Olive Schreiner Collection, Schreiner-Hemming Family Papers)
UG	University of Glasgow (Special Collections) (Papers of Robert Franklin Muirhead)
Unwin	Unwin 1926 edition of *From Man to Man*
WL	Women's Library, London School of Economics, London (Autograph Letters Collection: Alys Pearsall Smith)

1873

7 April 1873, Kimberley, Karoo. *Journal*: {T}hought out and began to write *Other Men's Sins*.' (*Life*, 92)

1 May 1873, Kimberley. *Journal*: 'I have, since I last wrote, written out the first half of the first chapter of *Other Men's Sins*.' (*Life*, 92)

1875

19 February 1875, Colesberg, Karoo. To Katie Schreiner: 'I made up my mind when I was quite a little child that as soon as I was able I would support myself for I see no reason why a woman should be dependent on her friends any more than a man should & as long as I am well enough I shall.' (*OSLO*/NLSA)

19 August 1875, Klein Ganna Hoek, near Cradock, Karoo. *Journal*: 'I am now reading Mill's *Logic*.' (*Life*, 116; John Stuart Mill, *A System of Logic, Ratiocinative and Inductive*, 1843)

1876

26 January 1876, Klein Ganna Hoek. *Journal*: 'I am reading Huxley's *Lay Sermons* and Darwin's *Plants and Animals*.' (*Life*, 118; T. H. Huxley, *Lay Sermons,* Addresses *and Reviews*, 1874, and Charles Darwin, *The Variation of Animals and Plants under Domestication*, 1868)

24 March 1876, Klein Ganna Hoek. *Journal*: 'Got a book of botany from Cape Town last week and have begun to study it. I shall do well with it.' (*Life*, 118)

24 July 1876, Ratel Hoek, near Cradock. *Journal*: 'I have not yet made up my mind whether I shall first finish *Undine* or *Thorn Kloof* {...} I mean to think tonight. {...} I have made up my mind not to introduce old Willie into *Thorn Kloof*.' (*OSLO*/HRC)

25 July 1876, Ratel Hoek. *Journal*: 'I am going to leave *Undine* & write *Thorn Kloof*. {...} Tomorrow as soon as school goes out I am going to walk up & down and finish *Thorn Kloof*.' (*OSLO*/HRC)

3 August 1876, Ratel Hoek. *Journal*: 'I've made up my mind {...} to write *A Small Bit of Mimosa* & *Wrecked* in one. I think it will be good.' (*OSLO*/HRC)

21 August 1876, Ratel Hoek. *Journal*: 'I have got some idea of *Sinners & Saints* & this morning came the thought of—A strong quiet married love, the characters strongly drawn. It will be my next work.' (*OSLO*/HRC)

10 September 1876, Ratel Hoek. *Journal*: '*Saints & Sinners* is growing clearer. I am reading Goethe's *Faust* & feel as if I had written it. I have got Montaigne's *Essays*; I have not got the spirit yet.' (*OSLO*/HRC; Johann Wolfgang von Goethe, *Faust*, 1808 & 1832, and Michel de Montaigne, *Essays*, 1580 & 1588)

23 September 1876, Ratel Hoek. *Journal*: 'I think I shall finish & read over *Undine* tomorrow. Then, to the next work. I got some good thought this evening, but it will be years before it is finished. It will be much better than poor little *Undine*. I am anxious to know how' (*OSLO*/HRC)

1 October 1876, Ratel Hoek. *Journal*: 'Finished writing but not writing out the first chapter of *Saints and Sinners*.' (*Life*, 128)

3 October 1876, Ratel Hoek. *Journal*: 'I am reading Shakespeare with intense enjoyment. I have got at his beauty at last. I think he will do me

good.' (*Life*, 128; see her letter of 29 January 1911 to Will Schreiner (*OSLO*/UCT): 'I read right through all {William} Shakespeare's plays again. I've not done that since I was 19')

11 November 1876, Ratel Hoek. *Journal*: 'I feel so disgusted with myself and all I do. I am sure *Undine* is one tissue of faults and *Thorn Kloof* is bald; but I am going to get it out and set to when I've finished this.' (*Life*, 128)

8 December 1876, Ratel Hoek. *Journal*: 'I am making slow head or rather no head. I can't write except on Saturday. This week I have done nothing. I think the reason of this is that I doubt my self, my powers, a little, & when doubt comes all power flies.' (*OSLO*/NSLA)

1877

2 February 1877, Ratel Hoek. *Journal*: 'I returned on Saturday {...}. I was very ill all the while but am now much better. {...} I am going to begin writing this morning.' (*OSLO*/NSLA)

24 March 1877, Ratel Hoek. *Journal*: 'It is the morning of my birthday. I got up pretty early walked up & down otherside the fig trees. {...} I must today begin the chapter concerning the evening party {see Ch. VII}. It is not yet quite clear in my mind. The boys are good to be introduced as relief.' (*OSLO*/NSLA; this is a possible reference to Ch. VII of *From Man to Man*, though without the 'boys')

18 April 1877, Ratel Hoek. *Journal*: 'I am now going to write; it is now the evening party; I have been at it for three weeks and not written more than a few dozen lines.' (*Life*, 130)

5 May 1877, Ratel Hoek. *Journal*: 'I am writing today the scene on the beach. I am reading *Decline and Fall* with interest and much profit.' (*Life*, 130; Edward Gibbon's *History of the Decline and Fall of Rome*, the six volumes of which were published between 1776 and 1789; see Ch. VIII for the possible scene on the beach, and Ch. VII for Gibbon's influence)

13 May 1877, Ratel Hoek. *Journal*: 'I am going to begin writing this evening and to work hard for the next three weeks [in view of the fact that her mother might be visiting her]. But this school work saps all my strength. {...} My heart is sore sometimes but generally I forget everything. I live in the present and a world of visions.' (*Life*, 130)

12 June 1877, Ratel Hoek. *Journal*: 'I am reading Hallam's *History of Literature* with profit. I have the outlines (vague) of a song that was never sung. I wonder if there is a really soul friendship in the world increasingly.' (*Life*, 131; Henry Hallam, *Introduction to the Literature of Europe, in the Fifteenth, Sixteenth and Seventeenth Centuries*, 1837)

12 August 1877, Ratel Hoek. *Journal*: 'I finished last night [the word is scratched out so thickly as to be illegible] have now to read over and correct and write out. I hope to get it done by October. I shall sit up late every night when once the correcting and altering is done; the writing will not take me long. (*Life*, 131)

30 September 1877, Ratel Hoek. *Journal*. 'We have got a week's holiday. I am going to try and read through, fill in, all the MS of *Saints and Sinners*. I am just correcting the scene between Mr and Mrs Drummond'. (*Life*, 131; the scene is evidently edited out)

12 October 1877, Katkop, near Cradock. *Journal*: 'The war scare has driven us from Ratel Hoek. I sit this afternoon between the open window and door in my room. I have done absolutely nothing since the first war news reached us on Tuesday evening, twelve days ago. I feel disgusted.' (*Life*, 131; OS's reference is to the Ninth Frontier War, 1877–1879)

1878

17 January 1878, Seymour, Eastern Cape. *To Erilda Cawood*: 'As far as the mere teaching goes, I don't think you would be at all disappointed in me but I'm getting to live so much in my books and my scribbling, that I'm not a bit a bright, pleasant person to have in a house. I can't bear to think of your being disappointed in me in any way. Can you understand the feeling? It's just because I love you so much that I have it.' (*Letters*, 3)

1879

26 February 1879, Ratel Hoek. *To Erilda Cawood*: 'If I had my way of educating children they would have a great deal less to do with dead language and a great deal more to do with nature. How interesting and eager the little creatures are if you try to explain to them the structure and uses of the parts of a flower, but if you have to press an irregular verb into their heads what labour it is.' (*Letters*, 8)

1880

18 October 1880, Lelie Kloof. *Journal*: 'I'm reading Lecky's *European Morals*. {. . .} I'm sure my fossil is a head.' (*Life*, 138; W. E. H. *History of European Morals*, see Ch. XIII, pp. 359 & 360 for references to the fossil)

23 October 1880, Lelie Kloof. *Journal*: I am still reading Lecky. Had an idea about Bertie this afternoon—suicide, quite *strong*.' (*Life*, 139)

2 November 1880, Lelie Kloof. *Journal*: 'I was struck in reading *Wilhelm Meister* by the marvelous unity between all thinking minds of a certain order. I am determined to be fearless; let every man speak out from the

depths of his heart, and take the result, coolly.' (*Life*, 139; Goethe's *Wilhelm Meister's Apprenticeship* first published in English translation in 1874)

1881

3 January 1881, Lelie Kloof. *Journal*: 'This afternoon I helped the poor coloured woman in the road when her baby was born. Mrs Fouché {her employer} wouldn't even give bread and sugar. I sent her my shawl by Plaatje. I hope I cut the string quite right.' (*Life*, 142)

18 October 1881, London. *Journal*: 'I am going to try and write at my *Saints and Sinners* tomorrow, but I am so sick and weak. Where am I blowing to? Where am I going to?' (*Life*, 151–2)

1882

26 March 1882, London. *Journal*: 'I am going to revise my *Saints and Sinners*.' (*Life*, 153)

21 April 1882, ?London. *Journal*: 'Darwin is dead.' (*Life*, 153)

14 October 1882, St Leonards-on-Sea, East Sussex. *Journal*: 'I am going to go on with my hateful *New Rush* now; I want to get it off my hands, then my delightful *Saints and Sinners*.' (*Life*, 157; for *New Rush*, see 'Diamond Fields', ed. Richard Rive, *English in Africa* 1/1 (1974), 3–29.

1883

22 January 1883, London. *Journal*: 'I am going to begin at my *Saints and Sinners* in earnest tomorrow; have put the MS open and ready.' (*Life*, 157)

19 April 1883, St Leonards. *To Philip Kent*: 'Mr Chapman knows I am writing another book. He offered to buy the one I am writing now for a few pounds, without ever having seen it. But I thought better not.' (*OSLO*/HRC; Frederic Chapman, younger son of Edward Chapman, founder of Chapman and Hall Publishers, London)

3 July 1883, Barnes near London. *Journal:* 'Working at *Saints and Sinners* etc.' (*Life,* 158)

September 1883, ?Barnes. *Journal*: 'I am at the Jew and "Rain in London". Thought of a name, *From Man to Man*.' (*Life*, 158; see Ch. XI)

2 November 1883, Bexhill-on-Sea, Sussex. *To Philip Kent*: 'I am going to try & get Blackwood as a publisher for my new book. It is not likely he will care to publish it, but he may.' (*OSLO*/HRC; William Blackwood & Sons, Edinburgh, George Eliot's publisher)

20 November 1883, St Leonards. *Journal*: 'I am going to work at *Saints and Sinners*. When will it be revised?' (*Life*, 159)

1884

25 February 1884, St Leonards. *To Havelock Ellis*: 'I intend bringing out another book towards the close of the year.' (*OSLO*/HRC)

9 March 1884, London. *Journal*: 'I am where Bertie is at lodging house {see Ch. XI}. I have "Nora" by Ibsen.' (*Life*, 167; Henrik Ibsen, *Nora;* the first English translation in 1882 used the name of the central character as the book title but later translations were titled *A Doll's House*)

28 March 1884, St Leonards. *To Havelock Ellis*: 'I shall read "Far from the madding crowd" & then I shall better be able to make up my mind as to whether I like Hardy much or not. Now I hardly know—there seems to me a certain shallowness & un-real-ness about his work—no, that's putting it too strongly; it seems to me as though he was only fingering his characters with his hands, not pressing them up against him till he felt their hearts beat. {…} Have you read a little play called *Nora* by Ibsen {…}? It is a most wonderful little work. {…} It shows some sides of woman's nature that are not often spoken of, & that some people do not believe exist – but they do. {…}

'{PS} It is very funny that in the book that I am revising now there is one character who reminds me somewhat of Knight in his relation to Elfride. The likeness is not strong, still it is there. He is a man who when the woman he loves confesses to him turns away from her; but my woman tells him that which he could never have known if she had not told him & he yet turns away from her. (*OSLO*/HRC; Thomas Hardy, *Far From the Madding Crowd*, 1874; Elfride is in Hardy's *A Pair of Blue Eyes*, 1873.

8 April 1884, St Leonards. *To Havelock Ellis*: 'You ask me whether Spencer is to me what he was. If one has a broken leg & a doctor sets it; when once it is set one may be said to have no more need of the doctor, neverthe-less one always walks on his leg. I think that is how it is with regard to myself & Herbert Spencer. I have read all his works once, some three & four times, now I read him no more. He helped me to believe in a unity underlying all nature; that was a great thing, but he has nothing else to give me now. {…}

'With regard to Nora. I think Ibsen does see the other side of the question, but in a book which is a work of art & not a mere philosophical dissertation {i.e. dissertation} it is not always possible to show all the sides. I have a sense of something wanting in the book, but I do not see how he could have supplied it.

'In the ideal condition for which we look, men & women will walk close, hand in hand, but now the fight has oftenest to be fought out alone by both. I think men suffer as much as women from the falseness of the relations.

Helmer's life lost as much as Nora's did through the fact that they never lived really together.

'I have not got "Far from the madding crowd" yet; but I have been reading C. Brontë's *Villette*. I think it splendid.' (*OSLO*/HRC; Charlotte Brontë's *Villette* was first published in 3 volumes in 1853. Spencer published five titles, one of which—*A System of Synthetic Philosophy*—came out in ten volumes between 1862 and 1893; his *First Principles* was the first volume)

19 April 1884, St Leonards. *To Havelock Ellis*: 'Sometimes I get an almost despairing feeling, that woman will have to save woman alone—& yet I feel that to be impossible. Strength comes when I see one man's heart that has seen these things, & burnt over them. {...} The book I am revising now is the story of a woman, a simple, child-like woman, that goes down, down. I wish I wish I had more power; I would put it all into this book; I would write so that no one who read it should ever forget it. You will find many artistic faults, but I think you will sympathize with it. {...} Strauss's life of Jesus is very different from 's, I think better; though I like Renan. I shall be glad when his life of his sister is published. It will be the record of a true relation between a man & a woman.' (*OSLO*/HRC; David Strauss's *Life of Jesus* was translated by George Eliot in 1864, and Ernest Renan's *Life of Jesus* was published in both German and English in 1863. In *Recollections of My Youth*, 1883, Renan speaks of his sister Henriette as the 'greatest influence' on his life, and refers to the privately circulated pamphlet he wrote about her as a projected posthumous publication)

2 May 1884, St Leonards. *To Havelock Ellis*: 'Heine is not understood, & I almost doubt whether anything one could do would cause him to be better understood. He belongs to his own, like {Ralph Waldo} Emerson. One might cause him to be more read (& that would be something) but the real man, the infinitely tender, burning, passionate heart will be known only to a few—it must be heart to heart.

'I have been reading that little book you lent me all the afternoon {Edward Carpenter's *Towards Democracy*}. I like it, & I like it more the more I read it, & when I re-read a page or two I like it better than at first. It is true, & it expresses what is in our hearts, ours of today. I must get Whitman & read him. I have read nothing of his yet. {...} I have sent for him to-day. {...}

'My feeling about Socialism is exactly yours. I sympathize with it, but when I see the works & aims of the men who are working for it in London my heart sinks. What will it benefitt {i.e. benefit} us to seize away the money from the rich? At the same moment that the greedy hands are seizing it there will pass over with it the disease of which the rich are dying, the selfishness, the hardness of heart, the greed for the material good. What we want is more love & more sympathy{....} I haven't faith in anything that promises to raise us by purely material means.

'{...} I think you are wrong in saying that scientific reading is not of much use. It is. To touch & handle would be far better, but it is better than nothing. You don't know what a gap would be left in my life if all the good {...} I have had from scientific books were taken out of it (making the word scientific cover everything from Darwin & Carl Vogt, to little primers on Heat & Light). I think that even the mere reading helps one to the feeling that truth is before all things, & to have a kind of love for things in their naked simplicity; I think that the tendency of science is always to awaken these two feelings; don't you?

'{...} The question of woman's having the vote, & independences & education, is only part of the question, there lies something deeper. {...}

'{PS}I love what you say about feeling a woman's heart throbbing in you.' (*OSLO*/HRC; Heinrich Heine, *English Fragments*, 1880; Walt Whitman, *Leaves of Grass*, 1855, expanded ed. 1860–1; Vogt wrote numerous books on natural history)

22 May 1884, London. *To Henry Norman*: 'Thinking the matter over I fancy it would be better to have nothing said about my new book till it is out. That may be soon, but it may not be for months.' (*OSLO*/HRC)

3 July 1884, Apsley Guise. *Journal*: 'Chapman wants my novel {submitted as *Saints & Sinners*, now being renamed *From Man to Man*}.' (*Life*, 169)

11 July 1884, Bole Hill, Wirksworth, Derbyshire. *To Havelock Ellis*: 'Henry, I am so depressed thinking of my work. You see, dear one, I have so cut up & changed the thing that there is hardly anything left & I don't know how to put it together. This afternoon I nearly got off the sofa, & burnt the whole MS. I would give hundreds of pounds if I had never touched it, & published it just as it was {...}

'My heart is heavy over my work. It is heavy because I am in uncertainty, & nothing has the same evil effect on my nature as uncertainty. The question in my mind is this.—Is it best to set my teeth together & to bring *From Man to Man* up to my standard, or to leave it & throw myself onto new-work? The last would be easiest{.} I could do splendid new work, but something in me{,} a kind of love for my work that perhaps no one can understand{,} makes me feel that I must labour on at my work till I am satisfied. I think it was the devil made me unpick it. Ach, I will set my teeth, & work at it & make it something better than it was, eh Henry. I can't have Bertie & Rebekah die. They are as much to me as ever Waldo or Lyndall were {in *The Story of an African Farm*}. You don't know how real my people are to me.

'{...} You know Henry all these months when I have been in such suffering, & have had that yearing {i.e. yearning} to do something for others that I feel when I am in pain I have always built upon the fact, "From man to man" will help other people, it will help to make men more tender to women because they will understand them better; it will help to make some women more tender to others; it will comfort some women but {i.e. by} showing them that others have felt as they do {...}. Now if I were to tell {i.e. let} it fall to the ground I should feel that so much of my life had been wasted, gone for nothing. Do you <u>long</u> so too sometimes to lessen the pain & suffering in the world? Especially the greatest agony, despair. That feeling is always growing in me & sometimes it breaks over me in a wave of passion. It isn't for happiness or good to myself, or to make others merry, it is to lessen the suffering of others that I have to live. It is for this that I have led the life that I have, that now when the power of self-feeling is almost worn out in me, I should comfort others.' (*OSLO*/HRC)

16 July 1884, Bole Hill. *To Havelock Ellis*: 'Last night it suddenly flashed into me, the solution of all my difficulties with "From man to man". It has been brooding in the back ground of my mind these many days, & now it has suddenly come. I shall have no more difficulty with it, it is as clear as day light. I have got what I wanted. It is so splendid, I mean #the feeling is, I get so excited I don't know what to do.' (*OSLO*/NELM)

21 July 1884, Bole Hill. *To Havelock Ellis*: 'I have done a little good work today & yesterday. Worked with such intense enjoyment, & then I know my work is good {...} My work is getting on splendidly {...} You will think perhaps that I'm writing sheets & sheets, but I'm not. It's wonderful what a lot of thought & feeling goes just to make a few lines when they are written {...} This book is going to be awfully outspoken. *An African Farm* was nothing to it in #heat.' (*OSLO*/HRC; *OSLO* queries the word 'heat' but my transcription at HRC confirms it)

24 July 1884, Bole Hill. *To Havelock Ellis*: 'Henry, what a great & solemn thing love is. I want in my life's work, if I work much & live long, to show what a wonderful power love has over the physical & through it over the mental nature, over what we call the soul, the inner-self. In this book I have tried to show it, but you see when I wrote it I did not know what the last three years have taught. I can only now try to show it here & there.' (*OSLO*/HRC)

2 August 1884, Bole Hill. *To Havelock Ellis*: 'I have to stick to my book till the winter (& I don't know that I shall have it ready by November).' (*OSLO*/HRC)

8 August 1884, Buxton. *To Havelock Ellis*: 'I am changing a whole chapter of "From man to man" from what I call the plain into the "ribbed" style.

Sometimes the plain is right, sometimes the "ribbed". I think I generally write descriptions in the plain, & philosophize or paint thought in the "ribbed". (You know in knitting there are two stitches, one makes a plain surface & the other makes ribs; I think I got it from that. Ribbed knitting isn't smooth it goes up & down, up & down.)' (*OSLO*/HRC)

14 September 1884, London. *Journal*: 'I have got to {where} Rebekah got married. The first chapter! Oh!' (*Life*, 169)

12 October 1884, St Leonards. *To Havelock Ellis*: 'Chapman has written asking me to let him have my book & saying he will pay me very liberally for it. It hurts me so when people talk about my work.' (*OSLO*/HRC)

31 October 1884, St Leonards. *To Havelock Ellis*: 'It's good for me to think & study about the woman question, especially prostitution, while I'm working at my book. It's the only thing that doesn't take me always from my work or that I can really study at the same time. Of course the subject of my book is prostitution & marriage. It is the story of a prostitute & of a married woman who loves another man, & whose husband is sensual & unfaithful.' (*OSLO*/HRC)

n.d. Monday, November 1884, ?St Leonards. *Journal*: 'Been working like the devil to-day.' (*Life*, 169)

21 November 1884, St Leonards. *To Havelock Ellis*: 'I am not adding to {...} my book. I {i.e. It} grows smaller & smaller. I am sure that all I am doing is improvement. Condense, condense, condense. But it's the most mentally wearing work. To cut out these few parts has cost me mentally more than to write the whole. {...} I do not alter much. I generally write things off best at first; the passionate parts, & leading scenes I never need to touch but the little bits between where there is not such intense feeling to guide one have to be thought over.' (*OSLO*/HRC)

26 November 1884, St Leonards. *To Havelock Ellis*: 'Please find out for me whether the *picture* of the horned beetle is in Darwin's "Descent of Man" or in "Variations of Plants &c." I make Rebekah say in Descent of Man. I am working. I am a little better this evening.' (*OSLO*/HRC; *The Descent of Man, and Selection in Relation to Sex, 1871;* for Darwin's *Variation* see entry for 26 January 1876; no such statement by Rebekah occurs in OS's manuscripts or the final version)

4 December 1884, Hastings. *To Havelock Ellis*: 'I am writing such a funny that is to say singular scene, I don't know how it came into my head, where Veronica goes to look at John F a man's clothes. It is in the place of a whole condensed chapter.' (*OSLO*/HRC; the passing reference is to John-Ferdinand; see Ch. IV)

7 December 1884, Hastings. *To Havelock Ellis*: 'Yes, that's a funny bit about Veronica{.} I don't know if it's very bad or very good.' (*OSLO*/HRC)

8 December 1884, Hastings. *To Havelock Ellis*: 'But my story gets smaller, & smaller, & smaller. I can't help myself{.} I'm driven on to make it smaller. I could have written three new works in this time {...} The last part of the book doesn't need any condensing or much touching. It's that abominable Veronica & John Ferdinand give me all this work {...} I am feeling very dissatisfied with my work, but the last part is good I know. The question is whether any body ever gets through the first.' (*OSLO*/HRC)

10 December 1884, Hastings. *To Havelock Ellis*: 'I am working hard to-day. {Either this or another letter written on the same day includes a fragment of a conversation between Frank and Rebekah on the night before their wedding}:

'"Don't mind my having a cigar?—have to get accustomed to it, ah?" He pressed her little arm against his arm. "What have you been doing{...} Listening to {...} Orpheus?" {...} A sweet smell of havanah smoke went in among the orange trees.

'"No," she said, "I have been thinking—thinking"

'"Ordeal of tomorrow?"' (*OSLO*/HRC; this conversation appears in neither OS's manuscripts nor the published version; the reference is to the music of one of the following: Gluck's *Orpheus and Eurydice*, Monteverdi's *Orpheus*, or Offenbach's *Orpheus in the Underworld*, the last mentioned an example of comic or satirical *opera-bouffon*)

14 December 1884, Hastings. *To Havelock Ellis*: '{...} just now practically I do not exist; my book exists; that is all, as far as my daily life goes. Bertie sitting there that hot day in the bush, with John Ferdinand. That is why writing makes me happy because then my own miserable little life *is not*. {...} I don't know if I used to write you nicer letters than now. You were just nothing to me compared to what you are now. I was trying to fall in love with you at first, that I might "forget". Now I know I cannot fall in love. If I love now it must be the slow long growth of years.' (*OSLO*/HRC; for the scene with Bertie and John Ferdinand, see Ch. IV)

26 December 1884, Hastings. *To Havelock Ellis*: '{...} I seem to have been living in a kind of dark dream for months, from physical causes so clouded over. {...} My book is pressing fearfully on me.' (*OSLO*/HRC)

1885

n.d. January/February 1885, ?Hastings. *Journal*: 'Am going to work this morning. Baby Bertie goes a-dancing. Love my work so.' (*Life*, 170)

3 February 1885, St Leonards. *To Havelock Ellis*: 'I'm as lively as a young cricket this morning. I'm going to try and write.' (*Letters*, 59)

5 February 1885, St Leonards. *To Havelock Ellis*: 'I'm getting so much better that I really don't need to go to London. I wrote to-day a little. [...] Last night I cried for hours, I don't know why. It was like a mad agony come on me.' (*Letters*, 59)

23 February 1885, Hastings. *To Havelock Ellis*: 'I have worked twelve hours already to-day, and am going to work some more before I go to bed. I feel so well in spite of a little cold, have enjoyed my work so. Life would be too beautiful if one were always well. If I could keep on feeling like this my book would be done in four weeks.' (*Letters*, 60)

24 February 1885, Hastings. *To Havelock Ellis*: 'After my fifteen hours of work of course I lay awake all night. Up early this morning and for a walk. Now going to have lunch, then to work again. I am trying to break myself into the habit of going to sleep before twelve and waking very early. I wrote with such delight and enjoyment yesterday.' (*Letters*, 60)

25 February 1885, Hastings. *To Havelock Ellis*: 'I am writing, not walking and getting excited. The change my visit to London worked in me is wonderful. My being so strong I have the feeling that always goes with that state.' (*Letters*, 60)

26 February 1885, Hastings. *To Havelock Ellis:* 'I have not read at all to-day, or thought about anything, but Bertie and Rebekah. I have such a nasty bit to revise to-morrow. I don't think it's interesting because I didn't enjoy writing it. It's about two mean scandal-talking women, and I can't bear writing about mean people. I don't dislike writing about wicked ones, it doesn't pain me if they're large. I have done with Rebekah's diary. I get on slowly though I work so much. You see I have to copy the whole book as well as revise. [. . .]I don't seem to have any self, I am all lost in my work.' (*Letters*, 60; the reference is to Veronica and Mrs Drummond as, later, in Ch. VI, and to Rebekah's diary entries in Ch. 6 of the 1887–9 MS, which foreshadow her different and far more extensive writing in Ch. VII)

2 March 1885, Hastings. *Journal*: 'Am working with such delight and strength.' (*Life*, 170)

2 March 1885, Hastings. *To Havelock Ellis*: 'I have been looking at that life of Schopenhauer to-day. If I had ever read him, or even knew before I came to England that such a man existed, one would say I had copied whole ideas in the *African Farm* and *From Man to Man* from him. {...} There's something so beautiful in coming on one's own very most inmost thoughts in

another. In one way it's one of the greatest pleasures one has. That Life [of Schopenhauer] by Miss Zimmern is very well written.

'The women's rights women are going mad, it seems to me. The latest idea is to set up a women's parliament to legislate for women and children!' (*Letters*, 61; Helen Zimmern, *Arthur Schopenhauer: His Life and Philosophy*, 1876)

4 March 1885 (?first letter), Hastings. *To Havelock Ellis*: 'I am going to finish off my scandal-talking women to-day. Somehow I can't bear them. I wish there were only noble people in the world, intense if wicked. {...} I am getting more and more to hate the world, dress, and material cares and pleasures.' (*Letters*, 62)

4 March 1885 (?second letter), Hastings. *To Havelock Ellis*: 'I have not been able to work to-day, that is, I haven't got on. I haven't any physical trouble to-day, I suppose that's why. That passionate feeling & the creative are like the two sides of one substance.' (*OSLO*/HRC)

7 March 1885, Hastings. *To Havelock Ellis*: 'I have just finished a chapter. When I am in the middle of a chapter I don't care for going out, my mind is dwelling on it so. I shall have to sit hard and fast at my book if I am to have it ready by the time I leave. I feel that I must not expect much for it. It is too strong for that.' (*Letters*, 62)

12 March 1885, Hastings. *To Havelock Ellis*: 'Have been working today again.

'{PS} Read Montaigne's magnificent essay on repentance. It is one of myfavourites. (*OSLO*/HRC; dated 14 March in *Letters*, 64; Michel de Montaigne's essay is in Book III of his *Essays*, 1580; OS was probably reading William Hazlitt's edition, published in 1877)

16 March 1885, Hastings. *To Havelock Ellis*: 'I send you a little present{.} It's some flowers I got this morning, gorse, on the top of the hill at Ecclesbourne. It's the walk Bertie went with the Jew's servant, they went passed {i.e. past} there. Only it was misty, not beautiful & sunny like this morning.' (*OSLO*/HRC; see Ch. XI)

20 March 1885, Hastings. *To Havelock Ellis*: 'Can one talk of a "croning" laugh? I say "Rebekah laughed the small croning laugh she laughed only at Bertie." I always use the word.' (*Letters*, 64; the word 'croning', perhaps derived from 'crone', perhaps intended here to celebrate the elder sister's wisdom or insight, does not appear in the novel)

23 March 1885, Hastings. *To Havelock Ellis*: 'I begin to be afraid I shan't get so much for this book. It will be so very small{,} one small volume after all this work. If people only knew how easy it was to write three, how difficult to write one.

'You know, darling, when I say I am happy {...} {i}t means that I am for a time in a condition to master my own feelings & keep them from rending me.' (*OSLO*/HRC)

29 March 1885 (?first letter), Hastings. *To Havelock Ellis*: 'Oh Havelock, when I have even £200 of my own, so that once again I can have that feeling of perfect freedom and independence! If it were you or any other man it would be the same. I can't live on dependence. Ah, freedom, freedom, freedom, that is the first great want of humanity. That is why I sympathise so much more with the Herbert Spencer school than with the Socialists, so called. If I thought Socialism would bring the subjection of the individual to the whole I would fight to the death. But human nature will assert itself under Socialism as elsewhere. Better to die of cold or hunger or thirst than to be robbed of your freedom of action, of your feeling that you are an absolutely free and independent unit.' (*OSLO*/HRC)

29 March 1885 (?second letter), Hastings. *To Havelock Ellis*: 'Only about 130 pages revised, and four or five hundred more! When will it be done? Yet I can't quicken myself. My mind must work at its own pace. [...] To-day I thought of these things that always goad me up into life and work again: my want to be independent, the thought that I may die and leave my book unfinished. I shall perhaps send you a couple of pages, revised and unrevised, and not tell you which is which, and see which you like. Oh, I must work, I must work. Death'll come and I've done nothing, and I've so much I want to say and so much I want to paint. You know my mind is beginning to feel a little like when I wrote the *African Farm*, and at Ganna Hoek and Lelie Kloof and Ratel Hoek. My work and my people seem more real to me than I myself.' (*Letters*, 66–7)

2 April 1885, Hastings. *To Havelock Ellis*: 'I've never left off work since I got up early this morning. If it were something new I should get on quickly. {...} I have got a horrid bit of my book to revise now; then I have only one more horrid bit; all the rest is delightful to the end.' (*Letters*, 68)

4 April 1885, Hastings. *To Havelock Ellis*: 'I am better. I am going nearly mad with my work. I have written this half chapter out nine times. Now I'm going back to the first, only I've torn it up.' (*Letters*, 68)

5 April 1885, Hastings. *To Havelock Ellis*: 'With regard to my scribbling, I have gone back to the original thing. I think I get silly over my work, I want more than I can have at last. I am getting so disgusted with my work; it seems I don't show people at all what I mean. But I suppose the ideal perfection is no more attainable in one's work than elsewhere.' (*Letters*, 68)

9 April 1885, Hastings. *To Havelock Ellis*: 'I have been writing hour after hour, page after page. I could write till to-morrow morning. I don't know where all the ideas come from if they've not been forming slowly these last few days while my mind has felt so blank.' (*Letters*, 68)

11 April 1885, Hastings. *To Havelock Ellis*: 'Long ago I used to think that was quite a discovery of mine that there is as much structure in prose as in verse. {...} {P}rose which has an artistic structure {...} is sometimes next to impossible to discover the law according to which it has been constructed. {...} With regard to my own work, I feel what I must, and what I must not, do; I know perfectly when a line or a word or a sentence breaks the law, and it causes me agony to let it go. But what law it breaks I don't know. I suppose that I could find out if I gave enough time to analysis. But it wouldn't help one a bit in one's work; one must only follow one's feeling there.' (*Letters*, 69–70)

15 July 1885, London. *Journal:* 'Fred {her brother} has written to say he doesn't want me to go to Eastbourne, or have anything to do with him, my *African Farm* brings him into trouble. I couldn't bear it, only I make myself quite hard and callous. I tasted the bitterness of death long ago, and now nothing touches me more than physical pain touches a ghost. I died in those awful days at St Leonards; I didn't go mad, so I had to die. I can't ever die again.' (*Life*, 170–1)

19 July 1885, London. *To Karl Pearson:* 'When I came home I carried on our conversation for an hour or more walking up & down my room. Yes, I knew you felt these things, but perhaps not in the way a woman can feel them. Sometimes when I have been walking in Gray's Inn Rd & seen one of those terrible old women that are so common there, the sense of agonised oneness with her that I have felt, that she was myself only under different circumstances, has stricken me almost mad. {...} I do not know if you will at all sympathize with me, but my feeling is not one of hatred to the men who do these things. One is irresistibly driven back to look at the women who bore these men, & in whose hand they lay for the first twelve or fourteen years {of} their life. What have these women done for them; upon the most solemn, the most beautiful, the most important and the life & death giving side of their natures, how have they been instructed? Of course you may say that these women were themselves the slaves of men, where were they to gain the physical, the intellectual & the moral knowledge, which would enable them to teach their sons the beauty {&} importance of the sexual sides of their natures{?} This is quite true; & so we come back to the old point, that we cannot hate any one. Man injures woman & woman injures man. It is not a case for crying out against individuals or against sexes, but simply for changing a whole system. When we have pure

strong mothers able {to} see the beauty & importance of the sexual side of life, we will have pure strong men able to guide themselves nobly. Before that day comes women will have to have made themselves absolutely free of material dependence on man, their reasons & their wills will have had to be cultivated.' (*OSLO*/UCL)

1886

20 March 1886, n.p. *Journal*: 'This morning the man [landlord] stormed at me for walking up and down, and said I mightn't stay in the house an hour longer. I was to go at once.' (*Life*, 172; OS habitually walked up and down while composing her stories)

1 April 1886 (?first letter), Southbourne-on-Sea. *To Havelock Ellis*: 'I have worked today so delightfully, am going to sit up and work more. {...} Would you like to see the first half of my book when it is done or wait till it's finished? You are not to say one word about it to me if I show it you. I don't want to know what anyone says of it. Either now or ever.' (*Letters*, 96)

1 April 1886 (?second letter), Southbourne. *To Havelock Ellis*: 'I've been writing about a sister to-day, & crying so I'm tired. It always touches me to the quick because it reminds me of Ettie.' (*OSLO*/HRC; she means Ellie; the two names are sometimes confused in her letters)

4 April 1886, London. *To Karl Pearson*: 'Have you ever read Montaigne's essay on friendship? I sometimes feel that he is my favourite writer, & that that is my favourite of his essays. Yes, friendship between men & women is a possibility, & our only escape from the suffering which sexual relationships now inflict. I was going to say, it is a possible thing only when both man & woman have reached a certain height in intellectual development not reached yet by the many—but when I remember such beautiful things as my friendship now ten years old with my old diamond digger who can hardly write a decent letter, & reads nothing but his bible & paper, then I feel that even that is not true.

'But is there not always a possibility of the consciousness of sex difference & the desires which spring from it creeping in, & spoiling the beautiful free frank friendship?—No, not when the friendship is true. {...} The most ideally perfect friendship between a man & a woman that I know of is one where the man in addition to sympathy with the woman's whole intellectual nature, feels that she is to him also sexually perfect; without friendship such a feeling would disturb & bring intense bitterness & sorrow; with friendship the fact that such a feeling exists on one side only adds to the quiet beauty of the relationship. If I so loved a man that I felt he were the only human being it would have been possible for me to love wifehood under; yet it would never touch my friendship for him{,} I should never even feel a wish that he should know it. "And if I love thee, what is that to thee?" that is the passion that grows out of friendship; not the old cruel sensual, "You must be mine! I will win your love though you die for it. I will tear you to pieces but I must have you."

'This passion you may say is a new thing. Yes, & so are the electric telegraph & the steam-ship; but they are not less real for that. There is nothing in which the race develops so much as in its forms of affection. But is it not possible that though a feeling of sex-love may not interfere with the most perfect, cold & reasonable friendship when felt on only one side, that, if it were mutually felt it would grow so strong as to kill out the more complex intellectual passion?—I cannot say from experience, but I can see no argument in right reason why it should do so. That friendships are possible between men & women without the least sex feeling on either side I have proved over and over again—the only question I have ever asked myself has been does "sex attraction" kill friendship? I think not.' (*OSLO*/UCL)

8 April 1886, London. *To Havelock Ellis*: 'Am working well so don't want to know what you think of MS. sent. My God! couldn't I cut it up. "Dam'd fine horse" is nothing to it.

'{PS} I see before this book is done I put it into the fire {...} The only thing that comforts me is that one day just before I left, I sat with S.A.F. {*The Story of an African Farm*} by my stream at Lily Koof {i.e. Kloof} at the place where I dug out my diconodon, & such disgust came over me at the way in which I had expressed what was so clear to me that I nearly through {i.e. threw} it into the water & let it drown for ever. One day if I live I will do work that satisfies me but all I have done I hate. It is true but there is perfect beauty *&* truth.' (*OSLO*/HRC; see 18 October 1880, *Journal*, for an earlier reference to the dicynodont fossil)

12 April 1886, London. *To Havelock Ellis*: 'I told you we were not to say anything about {the} MS. What you say is quite true, I put that in the last day I was at Southbourne. I was thinking of my sister Ettie, & I knew it wasn't art, that I'd have to take it out. What I think you don't see is that just at that point a "buffer" is necessary (if you know what a "buffer" is) it's something that you put in to raise (or to lower) the tone to a certain level, or to break a monotony of feeling. All through the book I have buffers that are only just in provision. I am taking out one of three sheets because by raising the tone of the dialogue I can do without it. Sometimes a "buffer" comes in with grand effect {...} (like the knocking scene in Mackbeth {i.e. Shakespeare's *Macbeth*}). That buffer doesn't answer because it isn't related to the story{,} it's related to my sister Ettie. That I sent is full of heaps of verbal errors. I never read it over when I wrote it out at Southbourne.' (*OSLO*/HRC)

1 May 1886, London. *To Havelock Ellis*: 'I'm going to try & keep awake & write today but the asthma kept me up. {…} I like to write lovingly about every one. I don't like to write about people like Veronica.' (*OSLO*/HRC; see Chs. IV and VI))

13 May 1886, London. *To Karl Pearson*: 'I couldn't write on "man's prejudices" because I don't believe there are any prejudices peculiar to man. I don't think anything so complicated and intellectual runs with the sex difference. I stand open to correction, but the conclusion which up to the present I have been led to, is this, that the mental difference which is correlated with & answers to the physical sex difference, will be found to consist almost entirely in an emotional difference showing itself in the emotions connected with sex. The differences I mean are such as these—that there is in the human male a tendency to prize the female more before he possesses her, & in the female to prize the male more after she has been sexually possessed by him. Of course friendship & sympathy & many other things may enter to obscure this, but I think a subtle & wide analysis will show it is there, & other difference of the same kind. I, however, feel still too uncertain & see too much on the other side to write on the subject. Maybe I am all on the wrong tack. It seems to me that without direct scientific experiment–such as I once mentioned to you–no certain conclusion in the matter can be arrived at, only a somewhat strong probability.

'If I go out to the Cape I will send you a very interesting paper for the club, being the views of Hottentot, Kaffir, Bushman & Basuto men *& women*, taken from their mouths, & set down word by word in answer to my questions, of course giving my questions also. This would be of real value.

'I never thought of the cheap edition of Mary Wollstonecraft knocking ours on the head {OS had been commissioned to write the introduction to Wollstonecraft's *A Vindication of the Rights of Woman*}; but it doesn't matter, one only wants people to read it & this will be cheaper. I doubt whether I shall be able to write the preface. {Ernest} Rhys {Walter Scott publisher's editor} is broad minded enough himself but the book has to pay. What I have to say of Mary Wollstonecraft is not to excuse her & not even to *justify* her; but to show that her greatness lay in this, her view with regard to marriage; & her action with regard to it. That she is the greatest of English women because she saw a hundred years ago with regard to sex & sex relationships what a few see today, & what the world will see in three hundred years' time. This will not be what Rhys wants I think. {…}

'{PS} It is monstrous of the Hintonians to say that a woman's desire for children corresponds to a man's desire for sexual love. A woman's desire for children corresponds to a man's desire, is the same. (*OSLO*/UCL; for the terms 'Hottentot', 'Kaffir', 'Bushmen', also used in letter to Edward Carpenter, 20 July 1890, see Explanatory Notes: Hottentot: pp. 484, 485 and 494; Bushman/Bushmen: pp. 485 and 494; and Kaffir, 484; Hintonians were followers of the British surgeon, James Hinton, 1822-1875, whose advocacy of polygamy, i.e. polygyny, as a social solution to the 'Woman Question' was a topic of discussion at the Men and Women's Club)

21 May 1886, London. *To Karl Pearson*: {J}ust now my work is taking my very life's blood. I send you a little bit out of a woman's diary in the book on the sex question {i.e. in her 1887-9 MS}. It's really to exemplify her intellectual structure & the suffering she endures in her life as a wife; but that subject of the relation between the sexual & intellectual functions is a very interesting one to me. I can see it leading out & bearing on so many different questions.' (*OSLO*/UCL)

29 June 1886, London. *To Havelock Ellis*: 'I feel so sad tonight, that general kind of depression, it's partly my sad part of the book.' (*OSLO*/HRC)

3 July 1886, London. *To Karl Pearson*: 'You say the senses of taste & touch seem to have no intellectual side, & so you doubt whether they can ever become aesthetic. But have they not? & are they not even now largely used aesthetically? I think so. Touch (the sense of pressure) most present in the hands & lips &c {...}, is the root of almost all our intellectual knowledge! {...} What is grasping a human hand at parting, or putting your hand under your pillow at night to feel the book you love, but the aesthetic use of touch. {...} When I was a child I remember climbing up at the risk of my neck on chairs & hassocks to stroke the face of a picture I thought beautiful. {...} Now, if sexual feeling is largely built up of these different kinds of sensations, & if they as they develop tend always to become largely aesthetic in their use, does it not seem that the sexual function must tend to become so too? {...} The little wild rose has stamens & pistol {i.e. pistils} & bears seed; but the cultivated rose having no more need of seed, turns all its sexual organs into petals, & doubles & doubles; it becomes entirely aesthetic. It is only for beauty not at all for the continuance of the race: yet it came into existence as all flowers do—simply as a collection of sexual organs. If that state were reached by the human race, then the sexual systems might be used exclusively aesthetically for purposes of pleasure; for sympathy & union between humanbeings. But we have *not* reached that state.' (*OSLO*/UCL)

n.d. July 1886, London. *To Karl Pearson*: 'Do you know what I think you fail to see? In all creative or productive minds there are different phases & I believe they have to pass through these phases, exactly as certain insects {...} on their way to maturity, have to pass through their different stages. In my own small experience I have traced it clearly. There is the receptive state when like the caterpillar, we eat & eat & eat. Have you ever watched a caterpillar{,} how it eats leaves greater than itself with its great greedy mouth, eats till you think it must die, & it grows & grows till its skin cracks off & it gets another one & that cracks off. & then it begins to get uneasy & doesn't want to eat any more, tries to & can't, & then it curls up & becomes a chrysalis? It seems to be dead, it doesn't move, it doesn't grow, it takes nothing in from outside—& then at last out comes the butterfly. It's a strange thing that {...} when it ceases to grow & lies still{,} absorbing nothing{,} then internal evolution begins, & the whole creature gradually develops within itself & the butterfly is formed. Have you never noticed these stages in yourself? I have, & I have at last come to understand that at the times when I am growing very rapidly & absorbing I must not expect myself to do creative work, & that when my mind is working on itself I cannot absorb, largely. The two moods are in antithesis.' (*OSLO*/UCL)

7 July 1886, London. *To Karl Pearson*: 'I cannot enter into the whole question, only touch one point. If the course of action which living creatures assume to end pain, or discomfort or to avoid danger, & the feeling of satisfaction which results when this is successfully done be rightly defined by the word "Aesthetic" then you are quite right in saying that all the senses are as entirely aesthetic in their origin as in their final development. I do not know that I ever accurately defined the word aesthetic to myself, but I think I never use it but in one sense. If I have tooth-ache & have my tooth drawn the sense of pleasure which I should experience when it was over would be extreme; but I should not call the action of having the tooth drawn nor the pleasure which succeeded it aesthetic. If a hungry cat catches a mouse & eats it, its enjoyment is intense, but I do not call it aesthetic. If I see that swing hanging outside & stretch out my hand to catch it, to prevent it from hitting my eye, I am very glad I have caught it, but my action & feeling, according to my definition, are not aesthetic. If I put chloroform in my mouth for the sake purely of the pleasant sensation, if a well-fed cat catches a mouse <u>simply</u> for the pleasure of catching it, if I stretch out my hand & rock the swing slowly to & fro for the pleasure of the restful motion, <u>then</u> I call these actions aesthetic. If I write a book because I am starving & want money I may feel great pleasure in doing it to get the money, but my pleasure is not aesthetic; if I write it simply for the joy I have in writing & the joy it may give others, my work is aesthetic. Further, if a man strives to attain to intellectual truth or knowledge for the hope of any material gain to himself, or because he philanthropically wants to lessen the sufferings of mankind, then his work is not aesthetic: if he strives after truth or knowledge simply for the infinite joy of holding it or that others may have the joy of holding it (this is the rarest, most complex & most lately developed form of aestheticism, & one which is rarely or <u>never</u> found combined with strong development of the lower forms of aestheticism such as regard{s} taste,

smell, dress) then the strife is I think aesthetic. Shortly I would define the aesthetic to be that course of action which has for its aim simply joy, & not the removal or avoidance of pain. Am I justified in so using the word? (I put this as a real question?) Of course a large number of our actions are partly aesthetic, partly not.

'To me the word aesthetic never in itself implies either praise or blame. The most degraded type of the human creature I have known is also one of the most aesthetic. A man who will send a little child quivering & crying out of a room because she has on a dress whose colour does not please him, who will get up & leave a table because there is some dish that offends him; who holds it impossible that an ugly woman or a deformed man should ever beloved by a person of the opposite sex; such a man is so immersed in the lower forms of aesthetic feeling that one knows the higher must be forever shut off from him.

'With regard to the sexual sense. (Is one right in calling it a sense?) There is little doubt that among the lower forms of animal life sex union is undertaken simply as a means of relieving unpleasant sensations, analogous to those of hunger & thirst. {...} But it is among wild bird{s} that the sex feeling seems to become really aesthetic. I have watched cock-o-veets playing for hours together in the bush at the Cape, rubbing their beaks together, singing before each other showing their feathers to each other, dancing up to rub their heads against each other when there were no birds near to act as rivals. Any one who could watch them & fail to see that it was entirely aesthetic, done only for mutual pleasure, must be a singularly bad observer. There is a reason which I think accounts for carnivorous & hard driven animals being unaesthetic & birds being so.

'You touched rightly on the false & weak point in what I said. I seemed to imply, & did imply, that the desire to produce children was in antithesis to the aesthetic development. Of course that is nonsense. The desire to have offspring may or may not be aesthetic; it depends upon the cause of the desire. The aesthetic or unaesthetic nature of the sex relation depends on the fact whether happiness intellectual or physical is the moving motive; where simply the avoidance of evil or removal of pain be the cause, according to my definition, it cannot be. {...} I think in this relation as in art & all other things, the aesthetic without a firm basis laid on utility is of the nature of a disease & a decay; it is not an undeveloped, it is an effete condition—but I have not thought it out.

'Yes, I see often a danger to the race from the development of the aesthetic in sexual matters. I see it coming from two opposite sides. From the side which is represented by the prostitution of our large cities, the degradation of the sex functions from child producing to the moment's sensuous pleasure; also I see it coming from the intellectual side. As the intellect plays increasingly a larger & larger part in our existence, unless we can keep the reproductive nature in close connection with it{,} will we not less & less care to exercise it, will not vitality die away from it, do we not already find with our own natures that our sex feeling might be entirely satisfied without the use of it? {...} It was however thinking out the first of these possibilities, (the extinction of the race through aimless sexual indulgence), that the thought struck me, that, sex relationships without the distinct aim of reproduction, which seemed to me at the moment the one thing we had to fight against & dread{,} was, possibly, not as much a degeneration as the final evolution of a universal law working always in the evolution of the senses. {...}

'Some parts of your letter seem to me not with understanding of what I said. When I was talking of aesthetic development, & sex, I had no thought of individual natures, but, as I always do when I speak of sex, unless I define that I am speaking specially of the human race or of particular human individuals, I was looking at the whole series of sex developments from the first division of the reproductive organs into two in the lowest existences, right up to man. What I said had no bearing on my individual thought or feeling, or yours. {...} Living here in this empty room with its bare floor & walls, with the chunk of bread & butter & weak tea for breakfast and supper, & a scanty meal that a servant would despise in the middle of the day, one finds life beautiful & rich, not in spite of the senses being robbed, but because of it. Yet I never go out in the town without buying sweets or fruit for the nuns & children, it is right they should have the only pleasure that can reach them. So also with regard to the sexual pleasures, it may be right, it may be beautiful that other men & women should have them in their simply sensuous form; for me it would be death. What is all the joy that the touch of a man's hand or life would give, compared to the touch of brain on brain. What do all the libertines in London{,} what do all the good husbands & wives know of happiness compared with what I knew when I lay all night on the floor before the fire in Dordrecht & read First Principles, & for the first time the whole theory of evolution which I had been feeling after in the dark burst in upon my sight! If the physical relation cannot be made subservient & helpful to the mental life then by some of us it must be left for ever; it may be good for the majority of human beings but not for us. To me personally, it seems that the keenest sexual delight which a woman could know would be that perhaps the man would gain in physical strength, & through the body the mind gain a new power; that intellectual work before impossible might be done easily, that a man should say not "Now I love you so absorbingly, I have no other thought but you, I cannot leave you", but "Now for months I could shut myself up alone concentrated on my work—so strong I am".

'To me sexual union to which there is no child born is like a statue left unfinished. There is one form of sexual pleasure which a woman can have

& not a man—it no doubt seems a very morbid one to you but to me it seems a very important one. It is the pleasure she has when she feels that by her suffering she is bringing something into another's life that he could not have had without it; a larger experience of life, the relation of father to child, without which a man's life does not seem to me quite complete.
'{PS} I wish you would define what you mean by the intellectual & the emotional. It seems to me very hard to draw a scientific line of demarcation between them. There are intellectual emotions just as there are unintellectual. I can't see how you will do it. I have tried & failed. (*OSLO*/UCL)

10 July 1886, London. *To Karl Pearson*: 'I am writing to ask you a favour. When I have the first printed proof sheets of my book completed, if I send them to you would you look at them, &, if you do not find anything in the spirit of the book that you do not sympathize with; & if further you do not think there is anything in it, which for you, in your position, (I mean as a public teacher), it would not be well to be associated with, I would like so much to dedicate it to you giving as my ground your sympathy with woman, & your scientific interest in her condition & development. Your promise would be conditional upon your approval, & I would trust you to tell me exactly what you felt without any consideration for my feelings.'

{Later in the letter, having summarised the novel and projected ending (see Appendix 3, pp. 471–6), Schreiner imagines Pearson's response:}

'(K. P. "Dear me! dear me! This is very, very sad! Emotions, unmixed, unmitigated emotions! I must write to my respected friend O. S. at once. I, K. P., sworn enemy of the emotions, Professor of Applied Mathematics{,} to have my name appended to so emotional an effusion, no I must write at once. It's not the morals I object to, but it's the emotions!!!" Takes out a sheet of paper & sets down: "My dear O. S.")

'But I don't want to put your name. I would only say "To a Friend", & no one but you & I need ever know who it was unless we liked. In the last four years, I who used to be made up of ambition have lost all ambition. I feel like a watch with the spring broken, all the works entire but nothing to set me in motion. I will spend days in worrying out an idea to its hiding place, & I am never alone for five minutes but I have fantastic dreams, but I never feel any wish to give out to the world. Just I for myself alone, I want to know the truth & to see; but the old longing which leads to giving out work to the world is gone. The work I have before me with my book is dreary. The parts which touch Rebekah & her friend & all the parts which interest me most I hardly need to touch, but I, when I wrote the book, treated Drummond's wife, & all the good hands-folded-in-the-lap philistines{,} with sarcastic bitterness. Now I feel that isn't right. I see now always in the men & women about me, "Durch tiefes Verderben ein menschliches Herz" {"Through deep ruin a human heart"; from Goethe's poem 'Der Gott und die Bajader',

The god and the bayadère}. I can't treat them so, & it's dreary work eating one's own fire. One woman I have practically to suppress altogether, because if I don't treat her sarcastically she's no reason for being there at all. If I thought that perhaps I could inscribe the book to you, I think it would just give the spring I want. ~~It seems childish but you will understand~~ (K.P. "Watches that can't go by themselves had better stand still.")

'This note, & my last, require no answer but a brief *yes* or no to my request, & the address of your German village, & word when you are going there.

'{PS} The part of my book I like writing best is about Rebekah & her eldest boy; the relation between mother & son when it is mental as well as physical is the ideal type of relationship, nothing can come near to it.' (*OSLO*/UCL; the son is Charles; see Chs. XII and XIII)

13 July 1886, Harrow. *To Karl Pearson*: 'Thank you very much for saying that I may perhaps dedicate my little book to you. You have not taught me anything definitely, & perhaps we have not been near enough to become close friends; but the little book seems to belong to you. I don't think I should ever have had the courage to revise & finish it if I had not known you. I wrote it long ago when I was full of hope. Then all that died away. I was so tired, I could do nothing. Without faith & hope in human nature, no artistic work. You have brought back my old faith.

'{PS} I'm going to work so desperately hard at my book. You are not to say it's "fantastic dreams" when it's done—though there are two live grave-diggers, real ones, at the end!!' (*OSLO*/UCL)

7 August 1886, London. *To Karl Pearson*: 'My work seemed so beautiful to me when I did it years ago; now it is all so small, so contemptible.' (*OSLO*/UCL)

16 August 1886, London. *To Havelock Ellis*: ' "What did Goethe's Faust sell himself for?" What is the one thing which we, any of us, the peculiar children of this age, would be willing to sell ourselves for? [...] It is the glory of Goethe's *Faust* that it alone embodies the cry of its age, the cry which no other age has heard, yet which is the moving power in Whitman and in all the deepest inspiration of our age: "We will not only know all things, we will be all things" {an approximate quotation from Whitman's "Song of Myself"}.' (*Letters*, 103; SCCS's erroneous italicisation of 'Faust' in line 1 has been dropped)

10 September 1886, London. *To Karl Pearson*: 'We want to watch those wonderful as yet uncomprehended forces working on primitive sentient matter & slowly shaping it into the form of male & female, with their wonderful interactive power. We want to raise the question of sex to its true place as one of the deep, reaching problems of the Universe, regarded

scornfully only by those who look at its surface & never see its wonderful depth. {...} I like to get even the vaguest sense of having my whole subject in my hand before I go to the parts. I don't care how long I work at a part, but I must realize it's a part of a whole & know what part it is.' (*OSLO*/UCL; the reference is to their planned book, but may also be pertinent to *From Man to Man* and to her difficulty with completing it)

12 September 1886, London. *Journal*: 'Writing out little story, too much smashed to do big work.' (*Life*, 172)

19 September 1886, London. *To Karl Pearson:* 'I haven't done anything to my book, that's why I haven't told you anything about it. I worked the first fortnight after you went away the first time, since then I've not done anything. But I've made little stories of the kind you hate! One can't do big work unless one feels strong & "vital". I've put my ms away.' (*OSLO*/UCL; reference is likely but not definitely to *From Man to Man*)

11 October 1886, London. *To Karl Pearson*: 'If only I could rest emotionally I could work here so splendidly all this winter & get my book done. I'm afraid it will never be worth dedicating to you!' (*OSLO*/UCL)

1887

12 January 1887, Clarens, Montreux, Switzerland. *To Havelock Ellis*: 'Am thinking of having *From Man to Man* copied by typist when I have money.' (*Letters*, 108)

31 January 1887, Clarens. *To Havelock Ellis*: 'With regard to Karl my feeling is just one of sharp pain that he should have misunderstood me so {...} I thought he was the <u>one</u> man who would understand me, between whom & me there could be love & friendship without any sex element. All that my sexual nature had to give I gave years ago, & it is <u>agony</u> to me now when men call on me for what my nature has not to give {...} I've loved Karl better than anyone else in the world ever since I was at Portsea Place but it's just the absence of sex feeling in him that has drawn {me.} I can't bear sexual relationships any more {...} I have tried hard to feel sexual to you & Donkin & you know how it sometimes hurts me. You don't know how much I've had a kind of Hintonian feeling (not idea!), that I ought to sacrifice my self & my feelings in this way. {...} Now I've got away from an agonizing pressure, I feel like a thing that got out of a net that was just going to kill it. {...}

'{PS} You don't know Pearson{,} the kind of love he makes women feel for him is like that of Dante for Beatrice. (*OSLO*/HRC; Bryan Donkin, a suitor and OS's doctor; for Hinton, see letter to Karl Pearson, 13 May 1886)

2 February 1887, Clarens. *To Havelock Ellis*: 'If I had had the only kind {i.e. only the kind} of feeling you seem to understand as love, do you think that caring for him {i.e. Karl Pearson} as I have done for two years nearly {…} I would deliberately have gone away to Bournemouth & shut myself up in the convent, just because I felt close & more one with him when physically was furthest away from him? The feeling I have is like that I have for Heine & Emerson only stronger infinitely. Only for a great man of genius could such a feeling be felt & I think only for one who was physically very weak. {…} I cannot show you any of the real letters that have passed between Karl & myself. If I could you would perhaps understand. If I thought him capable of ever the same amount of animality that is beautiful in other men, some thing would be gone from my life that would never come back to it. If a sex relationship were useful for his health or happiness of course I should enter on it, but I should feel that a great beauty had gone from my life. {…} I got a letter from him the other day {…} he seems in great agony & depression, but he must work out life's problem for himself. I shall not help him. (*OSLO*/HRC)

27 March 1887, Alassio, Italy. *To Havelock Ellis*: 'I like this place. I like this room. I like this sea. I like this sky. I like these olive trees, they are like the "bush" at Ganna Hoek. It's like the Cape altogether. {…} But the colours are not nearly so brilliant, or the blue of the sky as intense as at the Cape, quite different, still it's good.' (*OSLO*/HRC)

30 March 1887, Alassio. *To Havelock Ellis*: 'There came to me yesterday such a beautiful new scene for my book. It helped me so; but I have no strength to write it. It's where Rebekah says: "Forgive us our sins as we forgive those that trespass against us." Oh, Harry, just for one year's health to work in!' {…} Do you know {Robert}Browning's poem "Old Pictures in Florence"? I like the 21st and 22nd verses so much, and the 17th. Browning is the only poet I seem to have any sympathy with now. He is so impersonal.' (*Letters*, 112; Rebekah's prayer was evidently edited out)

12 April 1887, Alassio. *To Edward Carpenter*: 'I'll send you my book when it's done—which will be never.' (*OSLO*/SCL)

23 April 1887, Alassio. *To Edward Carpenter*: The last days I've not been working. I've got into a wild restless state again, & must "move on". {…} My book's going to be lovely, only no publisher will take it, & the libraries won't circulate it.' (*OSLO*/SCL)

20 June 1887, London. *To Havelock Ellis*: 'Do you know, I'm going to finish my book. I'm getting jolly hard, like I used to be at the Cape. I can work now.' (*Letters*, 120)

n.d. August 1887, London. *To Isaline Philpot*: 'I am reading Jowett's *Plato*. God will have to give Jowett a front seat in the Kingdom of Heaven. {...} I can't believe anything could be better. I seem to have found a friend I've been seeking for all my life.' (*Letters*, 120; Benjamin Jowett's translation of *The Dialogues of Plato* was first published in 4 volumes in 1871)

29 August 1887, ?London. *To Edward Carpenter*: 'I am going to make my book splendid if I live.' (*OSLO*/SCL)

24 November 1887, Alassio. *To Havelock Ellis*: 'What work I do is splendid, but my heart is somewhat like stone. Perhaps it is when one is so altogether dead that one's work lives. [...] The great lesson I have had to learn in the last three years is that one must be true to oneself in the first place and think of your fellow men second. I had to learn the opposite lesson in the few years before. Perhaps now I shall keep the balance, at least as long as I don't see a human being.' (*Letters*, 256)

4–7 December 1887, Alassio. *Journal*: 'I {...} am now sitting down to write out the bit about Truth. {This probably relates to Ch. 6 in the 1887–9 MS or to the discussion of 'the nature and value of truth' in Ch. VII.}

'*Monday*.—{...} I am going to {...} think out my work. I am getting a wonderful grasp over it. {...}

'*Wednesday night*.—{...} I worked all day, up and down, planning. Didn't know before that Rebekah went to sea in a sailing ship and heard "From too much love of living" {from Algernon Charles Swinburne's "The Garden of Proserpine"}. Some woman whose heart is lonely will be comforted by what I write, as I have been by what others write.' (*Life*, 179; Rebekah's sea voyage, whether along the South African coast between Cape Town and Algoa Bay or across the Atlantic to England, does not appear in the extant manuscripts or in OS's final version)

10 December 1887, Alassio. *To Havelock Ellis*: 'I love my new book so, a hundred times better than I ever loved *An African Farm*.' (*Letters*, 124)

12 December. 1887, Alassio. *To Havelock Ellis*: 'I thought out that about Greece and Rome having fallen because of conditions of women by myself. What's the use of thinking! Someone else will do it, the same thoughts come to all.' (*Letters*, 125)

13 December 1887, Alassio. *To Havelock Ellis*: 'Isn't it wonderful, I feel inclined to write the first time for months? Have seen wonderful beautiful things I never saw before. Such an odd kind of peace and rest is with me ever since I made a scene to-day in which Rebekah talks to her little son. What a great beautiful thing life is in spite of all its suffering! It will take me about twelve months steady work to perfect what I see. You know I feel like

I used to at Lelie Kloof and Ratel Hoek.' (*Letters*, 124–5; the scene where Rebekah talks to her 'little son' is unlikely to refer to the conversation in Ch. XIII about Charles's relation with Sartje, since the latter's entry into the novel appears to be a later addition; see OS's letter to Will Schreiner, 4 June 1908)

18 December 1887, Alassio. *To Havelock Ellis*: 'Am working hard. Never come back to myself sometimes for a couple of days and that is the only way in which work can be done. *From Man to Man* will be quite different from any other book that ever was written, whether good or bad I can't say. I never think; the story leads me, not I it, and I guess it's more likely to make an end of me than I am ever to make an end of it!' (*Letters*, 125)

22 December 1887, Alassio. *To Havelock Ellis*: 'I cannot tell you what this air and blue sea and sky are to me now I love them. I am working. I seem at last to have conquered, I think for ever. It may be not. [...] It is unlikely I shall see any publisher in England but Vizetelly {& Company, est. 1838) to take this book. I am getting so hopeless on the question of earning money. The Devil comes to me sometimes for a moment and says: "Wouldn't it be better to sell your soul and work for money, and so be free and independent?" I shall work night and day for a year or two years more, and then what shall I get for it?" (*Letters*, 125)

25 December 1887, Alassio. *To Havelock Ellis*: 'I haven't done any work, quite well, but can't pull together. Perhaps by this time next year I shall pass whole hours without thinking of Mrs.—{likely, Mrs Cobb, who intruded poisonously into her friendship with Karl Pearson}. That would be heaven.' (*Letters*, 126)

1888

3 January 1888, Alassio. *To Havelock Ellis*: 'How beautiful is this novel of mine! I'm going to work now.' (*OSLO*/HRC)

6 January 1888, Alassio. *To Mary Drew*: 'I am writing a long novel now & I love the people in it even better than in an African Farm, but 1 don't know when it will be done.' (*OSLO*/BL)

8 January 1888, Alassio. *To Edward Carpenter*: 'I am getting on with my novel, but very slowly. My nervous system is shattered, so that when I put pressure on it, even under my own hand, it gives. It will be a good book if ever it is done—if ever.' (*OSLO*/SCL)

19 January 1888, Alassio. *To T. Fisher Unwin*: 'You shall hear from me as soon as my novel is done. I am quite lost in it at present, know nothing else in heaven & earth.' (*OSLO*/HRC)

25 January 1888, Alassio. *To Havelock Ellis*: 'I didn't want that bit of MS. back{.} I've got piles & pile{s} like that that I just threw into the fire. I could write a book like that in a week{.} Yes, it's part of Rebekah's diary. Rebekah is me{,} I don't know which is which any more; but Bertie is me, & Drummond is me, & all is me, only not Veronica & Mrs Drummond (except a little!). Sometimes I really don't know whether I am I; or I am one of the others.' (*OSLO*/HRC; the reference may be to part of her 1887–9 MS)

27 January 1888, Alassio. *Journal*: 'I am doing chapter with Veronica and Mrs Drummond. I am doing the outburst; that relieves me so.' (*Life*, 180; Ch. VI, the only chapter dealing with both Veronica Grey and Mrs Drummond, does not include an 'outburst')

27 January 1888, Alassio. *To Havelock Ellis*: 'I have been working in great mental agony to-day. Sometimes I get almost practically blind, I can't see before me when I am walking, and then small external things crush me. I am writing about those two terrible women, Veronica and Mrs. Drummond. It is so terrible to have to realise them and grapple with them. I bear all kinds of wickedness, but not meanness and smallness. I shall be so glad to get back to Bertie and Rebekah, my beloveds. If they are ever so real to anyone as to me, how real they will be! [...] You know, if I had been married when I was twenty three, ten years ago, my life would have been quite different and my strength much greater. This celibacy has not been good for me; but it would have been worse to marry any man I have ever seen; except *possibly* one. I mean that I am sure celibacy is not good for the brain of a continual [brain-worker]. Schopenhauer, Goethe, Shakespeare; no really great steady thinker has ever been celibate. You must marry some day.' (*Letters*, 130)

28 January 1888, Alassio. *Journal*: 'I am going to work now like six devils. If only anything could wake up in me a spark of ambition, if only I could care one straw of what people said of me. The one thing I long for is that they should say nothing. It is such agony to be touched. Some day some woman born and agonized will read what I write and be comforted by it before she has got to that stage when you must live quite alone, when other people can't reach you.' (*Life*, 180)

1 April 1888, Paris. *To Edward Carpenter*: 'Will you tell me what you think of my Prelude now, <u>if</u> it doesn't come in the way of your work to read it {...} You're a great fool if you don't see that it's nice.' (*OSLO*/SCL)

10 April 1888, Alassio. *To Havelock Ellis*: 'I've stuck fast in my work. I've been agonising over it but it won't come right. I've been praying over it; sometimes that helps. When I stand up from my knees things come clear.

I pray a great deal over this work. Unless the Lord should help me I'll never get it done. And it'll be a damned poor little when it is done. It's wonderful what makes one work, what impulse drives one on. It's a sort of instinct, like what makes the bird make their nests. I'm going to pray some more by the sofa now. What else can I do when I don't know what comes next? It's all about sex in the human race.' (*Letters*, 134)

6 May 1888, Riva, Garda. *To Havelock Ellis*: 'You mustn't come out till I've finished my book. I don't mean to be interrupted, and don't mean to stir from Riva till it's done.' (*Letters*, 135)

16 June 1888, Harpenden. *To Mary Drew*: 'I should like to show you some day a little bit out of a story I once made, about a little child who finds its mother's still-born baby in the room where they have laid it out. It's a little founded on something that once happened to me when I was a child {...}. I was always praying when I was a small child to find a white baby.' (*OSLO*/BL; see the Prelude)

2 July 1888, Harpenden. *To Alys Smith*: 'I've been writing about little children & they're so much nicer to write about than grown up people.' (*OSLO*/WL)

22 July 1888, Harpenden. *To Havelock Ellis*: 'Yes, I can write better now than ever, my imagination has never worked so easily. My reason has never been so strong, nor my grasp anything like so wide. What I have lost is wish to produce for others. I wish it with my reason. I think I ought to wish it but I don't care. It is a terrible thing to have become so indifferent. {...} Please send back Prelude. Some little bits are not in yet{,} in one where she apologises to the baby for not having any milk for it! Poor little thing! I do love her so. Perhaps I would care more about life & work more if I could have my food cooked for me & my clothes made like a man, or if I could have two hundred a year.' (*OSLO*/HRC)

n.d. August 1888, London. *To Isaline Philpot*: 'It will be many years before either of my books are ready, I think. My big scientific book will take me five or six years; my work widens and widens out before me, and it isn't the getting done that's beautiful, it's the working and the learning more.' (*Letters*, 140; the 'big scientific book' is *Woman and Labour*)

23 August 1888, Harpenden. *To Frank Harris*: 'I don't want the series of articles on Sex Growth I wrote to you about to appear till I have published my two novels as they treat the same subject from the artistic side.' (*OSLO*/HRC; the other novel referred to is perhaps *The Buddhist Priest's Wife*, mentioned in her letter to Will Schreiner, 13 September 1892, but published posthumously as a short story)

4 September 1888, Harpenden. *Journal*: 'I am writing splendidly. Just today my imagination is on fire.' (*Life*, 181)

November 1888, Alassio. *To Isaline Philpot*: 'When I've finished this book and the next, I'm going to sit on the seashore day after day and play with the sand and do nothing else.' (*Letters*, 147)

3 November 1888, Alassio. *To Havelock Ellis*: 'I'm not like old #Toilstoy!!! Everything he teaches according to PMG {*Preach My Gospel*) is what I believe. His falseness lies in this, instead of saying simply "I see these things as truth," he wants to force them into the world under the old name of Christ. If what Jesus saw was truth, & in so far as it was{,} every one who pierces as deeply into the laws of human nature & life as he did will find {it} again.

'Neither Christ #or Tolstoy nor any one of us now living has yet seen & preached that doctrine of love & forgiveness as it will be preached in ages to come.

'{PS} If there be one soul you cannot love then you are lost.

'Please buy & send me a bible, as like my old one in size & print as you can. It was one of those cheap bibles published by the British & Foreign Bible Society. Not with the very fine print. I am always quoting from the bible{,} sometimes for the devil's own purposes & I find as the years pass my memory sometimes wavers with regard to an exact wording of a passage.' (*OSLO*/NELM; *Preach My Gospel* was a Mormon missionary handbook; the reference to Leo Tolstoy is likely to his *What I Believe*, 1884, translated into English in 1885; OS gave her own bible, annotated, to Pearson, probably sent with her farewell letter to him, 16 October 1886)

18 December 1888, Menton, France. *Journal*: 'I have killed out everything now, I think, except the wish to have a child. That I shall never quite kill. I think it's bodily.' (*Life*, 182; OS uses the Italian version of the name, Mentone, as do both SCCS and *OSLO*)

1889

5 January 1889, Menton. *To Richard Garnett*: 'Thank you for what you said about my work. No, you are quite mistaken {,} I never or seldom re-touch anything. I write down at a dash a thing as it comes in my mind. If I don't find it perfect (to my ideas & according to my powers) I burn it. Sometimes I write a thing entirely over again. As a rule I don't even re-read any thing till I see it in proof. Then I make corrections. I think however a great deal before I write. Sometimes I carry a thing about with me for years, before I set a word down. For the last 8 years I have been doing scientific work almost exclusively. <u>But it will all come back to me in the shape of art at last.</u> I write all this because you have shown such a friendly sympathy in my work.' (*OSLO*/HRC)

28 January 1889, Menton. *To Edward Carpenter*: '{PS} Do you know that my novel ends by the mother telling her children they'll all go up country & dance naked on the rocks!!!' (*OSLO*/SLC)

31 January 1889, Menton. *To Edward Carpenter*: 'You are entirely wrong about me, how people have got the idea that I re-touch & overwork my work I can't make out! My great fault as writer is that I cannot bear to re-touch, even to reread anything when once I have written it. I have three novels, two other books, a whole box of dreams, all dashed off & then never looked at again. Take my novel From Man to Man; for 9 years I have not touched or not opened or looked at any, but the first chapters. My fault is that I shall go on producing producing producing, & finishing off nothing in such a shape that I can present it to the world. If my ambition could wake up again it would be different, but it's quite dead, it seems to me I can't rouse it. I write for myself & to myself. This is the secret of my work as an artist. The very thought that I shall have to publish seems to kill out my power of work. This is why Karl Pearson was so good for me. Just for a little time while I was near him, he woke up my ambition, that is, my wish to express myself to others. The only reason I go on writing out at all now is because I want to get a lot of money to help other people to do their work.' (*OSLO*/SLC)

1 February 1889, Menton. *To Havelock Ellis*: 'I suppose it's my work makes me so happy. You know there's one little line in my Prelude, not in what you saw, that I love so. When you read it you must guess which it is. If you don't find out I shan't ever love you because it is the most beautiful thing I ever saw. It surprised me so when I saw it. It's a tiny thing.' (*Letters*, 153)

2 February 1889, Menton. *Journal*: 'I am copying my Prelude. I see my way clear to the end now. {...} I'm so well.' (*Life*, 182; SCCS gives the date as 8 February, but later, in his 'Genesis', he corrects this to 2 February; see Unwin, 25, and Harper, xxiv)

2 February 1889, Menton. *To Havelock Ellis*: 'My prelude is too lovely for any words{.} {...} I had a lovely time this afternoon{.} I went onto the top of a hill near here, & laid & slept half in a sweet dream kind of way with joy that my prelude was done. I'm going on at my book & Mary W. {the commissioned introduction}—& every thing else can go to the D—{...} The worst of this book of mine is that it's so womanly. I think it's the most womanly book that ever was written, & God knows that I've willed it other wise!' (*OSLO*/HRC)

14 February 1889, Menton. *To Mary Brown* (postcard): 'I'm going to send you the Prelude to one of my stories to read soon, instead of a letter. I'm

well & working so much that sometimes I forget I'm Olive Schreiner at all & wish anyone would tell me which of the characters I am.' (*OSLO*/NLSA)

17 March 1889, Menton. *To Isaline Philpot*: 'Oh, I love the two women in my book so{.} I am getting to love women more and more. I love men too, so very much only they don't need me.' (*Letters*, 157)

6 April 1889, Paris. *To Havelock Ellis*: 'You quite intentionally misunderstand me in every thing, or, sometimes I think are we grown so wide apart that no understanding is possible between us. As the strongest personal feelings my nature has known are gloriously "funny" & "absurd" to you, & my ideas, which after all are my real life{,} dearer much to me than any person or than my self{,} simply bore you, so even such a common place remark as that in my letter to my brother you willfully misunderstand or can't understand. No human creature's feelings could possibly be further removed with #regard to my artistic work—not of course the scientific—than mine from George Elliot's. Her great desire was to teach, mine to express my self for my self & to my self alone{.} The thought that hundreds of thousands will read my work does offend me & hinder me, not because I wish to teach them, but because terrible as it is to show them my work at all, the thought of throwing it to them to be trodden under foot is double desecrating of it. I'm almost beginning to hate my Prelude now because three or four people have looked at it. & if many more do I shall throw it into the fire. If you sermonized me on the wickedness of not caring & sharing my work with other people, you would be much nearer the truth.

'The best stories & dreams I have had nothing would induce me to write at all because I couldn't bear one person to read them. As for it's being a new development it's a feeling that's rather growing weaker, because as a child if Will {her brother} or anyone got hold of a scrap I'd written I tore up the whole thing at once. It was like a knife in my heart to-day when I saw an African Farm stuck up in a window. I get to #lothe {i.e. loathe} it when I think of how many people have read it. Do you think I could write Bertie's death scene, do you think I could show all the inmost working of Rebekah's heart if, I realized that anyone would ever read it. (*OSLO*/NELM; see Ch. XIII; and see Letter to John X Merriman, 29 June 1896, for a reference to George Eliot)

11 April 1889, Paris. *To Havelock Ellis*: '{PS} I'll be so glad to get back to my novel. I love it more than I love anything in the world. More than any place or person. {...} I've never loved any work so, & I haven't cared for it all these years. I've only cared for people. {Regarding her tendency to write with a certain kind of lilt she identifies with verse and that she hears

entering her allegory 'The Sunlight Lay Across My Bed', she adds, with apparent reference to *From Man to Man*:} Damned if I shan't write plain prose now right on to the end & get the thing done. It's an awful temptation to go on with that kind of thing, because as long as you do there's such a delicious sensation going on all through your body as if the whole of it was keeping time.' (*OSLO*/HRC)

16 April 1889, London. *To W. T. Stead*: 'I feel less & less able to call that relation love, in which one draws the other from the higher for the sake of possessing them. You will understand what I mean when my book is published. I can't express myself satisfactorily didactically.' (*OSLO*/NASA)

20 May 1889, Knaphill, Surrey. *To Isaline Philpot*: 'When all my work is done I'll go into Society—in another world. You know I would like society if men would accept me as a man among men, but now I know they never will, and I'd rather just go on alone.' (*Letters*, 164)

24 July 1889, London. *To Mary Brown*: 'I'm so glad you like Prelude, please send it back. I want to show it to some one.

'{PS} 'It's only rough cast just dashed off & then type written & it has all to be corrected & some things added.' (*OSLO*/UCT)

1890

7 January 1890, Cape Town. *To Havelock Ellis*: 'I went down to the market this morning, and this afternoon by train to Newlands to a strawberry garden. Newlands is the next station to Rondebosch where Rebekah lived. I always think when I go near Rondebosch I fancy I shall meet Rebekah coming down one of the avenues. Not Lyndall, not even Waldo, have been quite so absolutely real to me as she and Bertie. I cannot believe that they never lived. I say I believe it, but I don't. You see they have lived with me fifteen years.' (*Letters*, 175)

21 January 1890, Cape Town. *To Havelock Ellis*: 'I am sending my Prelude to you by this post. Please give it to Eleanor Marx {Karl Marx's daughter} to typewrite, paying her the full rate.' (*Letters*, 176)

30 January 1890, Cape Town. *To Havelock Ellis*: 'I am working delightfully. Yesterday I climbed to the top of Signal Hill. It was glorious lying there among the bushes, with the sun above and the blue Atlantic on one side and Table Mountain on the other. I am going to climb Table Mountain itself soon. Cape Town is the loveliest place on the whole earth. My heart is set on going up into the interior and I think I shall manage it some day, but it wants money.' (*Letters*, 176)

6 February 1890, Cape Town. *To Havelock Ellis*: 'I am perhaps going up to a desolate place called Matjesfontein in the Karroo. I will work better there.

{…} I don't think nowadays. I note unconsciously everything, the lights on the mountains, the shapes of the trees, but I don't think. I have thought, thought, thought, night and day, for so many years, I can rest a little now and <u>see</u> the external world again after this nine years introspective trance of thought.' (*Letters*, 176; OS habitually used the variant spelling, Karroo)

19 March 1890, Cape Town. *To Havelock Ellis*: 'You have none of you known what my physical agony has been through all these years. I was very near to the end when I left England.

'{…} Next year I am going up in the interior {…}. I am slowly maturing my plans, getting letters of introduction to travellers{,} traider {i.e. traders} & others who may help me on my line of march. Money is all I need.{…} I am reading nothing just now but African travels.

'{…}{I}n a way I am more solitary in this country than you can conceive. More lonely even than when I was a girl. I feel as if there were some ages stretching between me & these people. It's been a strange experience, how the same circumstance{s} bring back the same conditions.' (*OSLO*/HRC; see *Letters*, 178-9, where the letter is dated 16 March)

25 March 1890, Matjesfontein. *To Havelock Ellis*: 'Over the way at the railway station the coloured boys are at work already, digging the new foundations{.} I might be at Rattle {i.e. Ratel} Hoek as far as the sounds go. Now I am going to put my hat on & go out for a walk over the Karroo{.} Such a sense of wild exhilaration & freedom comes to me when I walk over the Karroo.' (*OSLO*/HRC)

5 April 1890, Matjesfontein. *To Havelock Ellis*: I <u>think</u> I shall stay here till the end of August, unless I find the winter too cold. {…} I am getting on with my work slowly & steadily, but not brillantly {i.e. brilliantly}. {…} Do you know the effect of this scenery is to make one so silent & strong & self contained, & it is all so bare{,} the rocks & the bushes{,} each bush standing separate alone by itself.

'Saturday{…} It is my period but I am working right through, & feel bright & strong.

'{…}I went {on} a lovely walk this morning away out into the Karroo & found some nice, large bent out trees in the dry river course. I will make that my walking up and down place.' (*OSLO*/HRC)

15 April 1890, Matjesfontein. *To Havelock Ellis*: 'I have finished a chapter this evening, so my mind feels nice and free. {…} I think [if] I lived fifty years in Africa I should never make one friend. There is one man I've heard of, Cecil Rhodes, the head of the Chartered Company, whom I think I should like if I could meet him; he's very fond of *An African Farm*. I can understand how bitter I used to feel against human beings, and how I hated

them, and felt myself utterly alone among them, and only liked the Boers and Kaffirs. Fancy a whole nation of lower middle-class Philistines, without an aristocracy of blood or intellect or of muscular labourers to save them! In a few months I want to go up to the centre of Africa.' (*Letters*, 182-3; the 'whole nation' appears to refer to English-speaking South Africans in the Cape Colony)

13 May 1890, Matjesfontein. *To Havelock Ellis*: '{T}he only French writes {i.e. writers} I know for whom I feel sympathy are Renan & George Sand; the others I only admire, I don't like or enjoy.{...}

'{PS} The plants here are so beautiful to me{,} & the red sand. The plants seem to me like living things & I love them so, I like to touch them. When I wake up in the night I think I shall seen {i.e. see} them the next day. They are the only things I feel near to in Africa, & the sky & the stars & the mountains. I like the ants too. & the little mierkats{.} I could never love other nature in Europe as I love this. The only thing I ever loved there, was the Alps in winter, & the sea in the Riviera.' (*OSLO*/HRC; see *Letters*, 185-6 where the letter is dated 12 May; for Renan, see letter to Havelock Ellis, 19 April 1884)

23 May 1890, Matjesfontein. *To Havelock Ellis*: 'Why don't I get {on} faster with my work? Why must I write everything with my blood? Other people don't. And I could write in water, three novels a year! What is this terrible compulsion over one? There must be a God or what is it? I am very lonely. {...} I've no where to go if I leave Matjesfontein.' (*OSLO*/HRC)

12 June 1890, Matjesfontein. *To Havelock Ellis*: 'Such a funny thing happened to me the other afternoon. I was very happy and well and went out to walk in the veld, taking Ruskin with me. It was a glorious afternoon, everything was beautiful, the sun shining on the bushes. Suddenly I found I was crying; not quietly but in a wild convulsed agony, just as one cries if one has had some terrible and heart-breaking news. And yet I wasn't crying. I kept saying to myself; "What is the matter? What am I crying about? I am quite happy." It was as if some terrible things, quite beyond the range of my conscious consciousness, were affecting me. It was the strangest mental condition I have ever experienced. It was like the agony one starts up with sometimes in the night; but I had not been to sleep and my whole mind was busily engaged with the book, and if I was conscious of anything else it was the beautiful peaceful sunset scene about me. It is a new and strange evidence of that double consciousness which I am sure exists in the brain, at least in mine. I am sure that these marvellous flashes, as when in one instant the whole of my Prelude flashed on me as I was sitting and writing things about Bushmen's heads, are not really a flash of revelation, but the result of absolutely unconscious cerebration that had been going on

in my brain.' (*Letters*; 188-9; see Ch. XIII for a comparable allusion to 'Bushmen's heads'; for John Ruskin, the book she was reading has not been identified, but the author is an occasional reference in her letters)

12 July 1890, Matjesfontein. *To W.T. Stead*: 'I hope soon after Xmas to start on my journey to Lake N'garmi & the Zambesi, & am trying to get all my work done first. (*OSLO*/NASA; Lake Ngami, Bechuanaland Protectorate, now Botswana; the Zambesi River is in present-day Zimbabwe, forming the northern border of what used to be Mashonaland and Matabeleland until renamed Rhodesia after Cecil John Rhodes' take-over)

20 July 1890, Matjesfontein. *To Edward Carpenter*: 'No, I have no friends here, but I am very friendly with all the Bushmen{,} Hottentot{,} Kaffers{,} & am very well & very very happy.' (*OSLO*/SCL)

11 August 1890, Matjesfontein. *To Havelock Ellis*: 'If I go up into the interior, when I have finished my book, would you care to come with me? It would not be wasted time. That is the only thing I look forward to in my life now, that journey to the interior.' (*Letters*, 195)

6 November 1890, Matjesfontein. *To Havelock Ellis*: 'I'm doing such beautiful work. This life is so peaceful. I'm happy, like when I was living on those farms, writing *An African Farm*. I feel just the same. [. . .]You know I think in this book I will say what I want to say. I mean I've sometimes felt as if I couldn't make this book say everything I want to say as *An African Farm* said what I wanted to say then. But it will! All that is in that "Sunlight Lay" {her allegory in *Dreams*} is in it, only simply in an objective form—the first, second, and third heaven {. . .} I would like to show you Africa, my Africa. It's not a bit like Australia, so wonderful with its mixture of races and peoples, and its marvellous diversity of natural scenery. I'm glad I wasn't born in any other land on earth.' (*Letters*, 199)

11 November 1890, Matjesfontein. *To Karl Pearson*: 'I have a favour to ask you & your wife, my dear friend. Many years ago I asked you if I might dedicate a work of mine to you, & you said I might. I wrote it 12 years ago, & for the first time I am finding time to revise it now. I will be done soon. What I have to ask is will you & she let me dedicate it to you together? {. . .}

'Another thing: the middle of next year I shall be starting to spend some years in the interior of Africa. I am learning Kaffir which is the key-language, so that I shall be able to study the people. {. . .} No-where in the world as {i.e. are} such vestiges of the primitive human condition to be found as among them. It would take too long or I would tell you of the wonderful relics of what you would call "the mother age" which are to be found among them, in their ceremonies & customs. If you & your wife will read Wood's Natural History of Man, you will be surprised how quite unconsciously he gives much evidence of that. {…}

'Yes, my dear friend, I have no need of personal intercourse with you any more. Don't you see what the help was you used to be to me? When you first knew me, & for many years before, I had simply lived at the beck & call of every woman who chose to make a demand on me. I was simply bleeding to death. You stopped that. {…} You always seemed to me like a lump of ice put on a wound from which one was bleeding to death & freezing it up. You may be tender, sympathetic, human—if you are it matters nothing to me; you helped me through that which the world calls cold, narrow, selfish: it was your self-consciousness & self concentration that helped me. You saved my life. Now I do not need you any more. I have learnt the lesson that to recklessly give yourself to the service of every man or woman who makes a demand upon you is gross immorality: that when I sit here at night writing I serve the prostitute much more than when I took her in from the streets & laid her in my bed, & sat up all night watching her sunken face in terror & agony. She had to go the next morning, I could do nothing for her, what was the use? I help the respectable woman more now, than when I gave up afternoons & evenings, to letting her sit & talk, hour after hour, of her displeasure with life, & then when she went, throw myself in agony on the floor to cry, because of my wasted life, all given for what! for what! With no result! And then I would get up & write letters till two o'clock for fear I should pain some one.

'Mark you, Karl Pearson, I do not regret that life; I am grateful. Those women taught me what I could not otherwise have learnt. I would not have those years blotted out. They are my most precious heritage. But if it had continued a little longer I must have died. I needed your lesson{.} (*OSLO*/UCL; J. G. Wood, *The Natural History of Man*, 1868)

1891

n.d. January 1891, Matjesfontein. *To Will Schreiner*: 'Next year if my novel is done I mean to be flowing in riches.' (*OSLO*/UCT)

n.d. January 1891, ?Matjesfontein. *To Mary Sauer*: 'Yes, dear{,} life is small & inexplicable if we take only our own individual lives, they are not a whole{,} they mean nothing. How shall one explain all the crushed out hope, the suppressed emotions, the little value or use of our own lives, until we are able to see in them nothing but tiny parts of a great whole which is being worked out beautifully in ways we cannot understand. No human being lives alone, we are just parts of the great human race reaching slowly the condition in which the far thinking deep feeling man or woman are possible. Of my own life I never think anything but that which in an infinitesimal way may help the men & women who come after me; humanity grows better just by the little {…} in each individual who makes it. And after all love & knowledge in themselves are ends. Just to have loved something, just to know & reason & think make life worth living.' (*OSLO* New Letters section/RLSC)

n. d. February 1891, Matjesfontein. *To Mary Sauer*: 'I've got so many stories but I don't think any of them have sensational name, I've never that {I} know told them to any one. One is called "New Rush, a Diamond Field Story" & one is "Jan van der Linden's wife", & one "Saints & Sinners" but I should have to call it something else if ever I publish it, because there is another book published under that name.' (*OSLO*/NLSA; the second mentioned story did not see the light of day)

n.d. July 1891, Cape Town. *To W.T. Stead*: 'I am always going to write that long letter on the sex question, but I think my next novel will be the best explanation of my views. I think they are too complex to be stated shortly.' (*OSLO*/NASA)

1892

n.d. March 1892, Matjesfontein. *To W.T. Stead*: 'As soon as I can find anyone in England who will undertake arrangements with publishers I shall send home much work = my five articles on South Africa, which will form a large book, & a thing dealing with the whole subject of sex, as far as my ten years' work at that subject have yet brought me, & a large novel.' (*OSLO*/NASA)

2 April 1892, Matjesfontein. *To Mary Sauer*: 'I'm as well as possible & working hard now. Yesterday something came right {in} my big book that I've been thinking over for years. I was so glad. {…} I worked 13 hours yesterday, not counting the time I took for my meals.' (*OSLO*/NLSA)

13 September 1892, Matjesfontein. *To Will Schreiner*: 'I am sending down my Boer article to get it published in Cape Town before I send it home. & then I really shall reread "From man to man" & have that & the Buddhist Priest's Wife ready to take home with me in April.' (*OSLO*/UCT; the latter was still at this stage envisaged as a book rather than as a short story)

29 October 1892, Matjesfontein. *To John T. Lloyd*: 'When I think over your position as shown in your letter, & mine, the chief difference between your view & mine seems to be, that for you the universe is not so Unified as it is for me. I have never been able to conceive of God, & man & the material universe as distinct from one another. The laws of my mind do not allow of it. {…} When I was a little child of five & sat alone among the tall weeds at the back of our house, this perception of the unity of all things, & that they

were alive, & that I was part of them, was as clear & over powering to me as it is today. It is the one thing I am never able to doubt.

'The agony of my childhood, especially from the time I was 9 till I was fourteen, was the impossibility of reconciling this direct perception from which I could never shake myself free, with what I was taught. When at fourteen or fifteen I began to study physical science, this agonizing disorganization ended for me. I was like a child walking about with one half of a puzzle in its hand, into which nothing will not fit {i.e. will fit}: then I found the other half; and it fitted. Since then religion has been to me the one unending joy.

'If you ask me what is my religion, it is hard for me to answer, because we humanbeings have not framed speech for the purpose of expressing such thoughts—but if I must put it into words I would say the Universe is one, & it lives:—or if you would put it into older phraseology, I would say;—there is nothing but God. {...} If you ask me what is the practical effect of this feeling, it is to make all life very precious to me, but also to rob death of all its horrors. There is something beautiful & sacred to me in assisting at the birth of a little baby, in studying the facts of embryology, in watching a little plant seed germinate; there is also something to me wonderful & sacred in death, but it is hardly more overpowering & wonderful to me than birth. {...} I think I first had this feeling with regard to death clearly when my favourite little sister died when I was nine years old. I slept with her little body until it was buried, & after that I used to sit for hours by her grave & it was as impossible for me then, as it is impossible for me now, to accept the ordinary doctrine that she was living on somewhere without a body. {...} I used to love the birds & animals & inanimate nature better after she was dead; the whole of existence seemed to me more beautiful because it had brought forth & taken back to itself such a beautiful thing as she was to me.

'{...} The only man to whose moral teaching I am conscious of owing a profound & unending debt is John Stuart Mill; when I got home to Europe & found men & women whose views exactly coincided with indifference to his works or ridiculing them as old-fashioned, it was keenly painful to me; because they had been the channels through which most of the spirit of current modern science reached me.

'Personally I owe nothing to the teaching of Jesus: except the 5th & 6th chapters of Matthew. No part of his teaching morally ever touched me, as a child, & from the time I was fourteen when I ceased to read the bible or go to church, Christianity has been almost non-existent for me; I have lived to an extent you would hardly understand, in another world; & the name so dear to you brings back to me nothing but sad & depressing memories. But as a great, rare soul, whom doubtless we should love better if a fuller record had been left of him, by his followers, I always wish some record had been left of {...} his life between 20 & 30; those years the most important & intense in which amid agony & temptation his view of life was forming. I think among great religious teachers he does not quite draw me as Buddha & others, because {...} his teaching stops short with the human world; it is to me doubtful whether he ever caught sight of that larger unity; whether he ever realized the divinity in plant & animal, as well as man. {...} Nothing tortured me so in Christian teaching as the scorn for the animal world, & the hatred of matter. But if we knew really what the beautiful soul of Jesus thought & felt, we should find it loved wider & deeper than its followers left us any record of.

'This is a poor answer to send you to your beautiful letter. But except in my own language of parables, I cannot express myself. {...} Words are very poor things. It almost pains {to} write as I have been this afternoon, because what one wants to say one cannot. (*OSLO*/NLSA)

1893

n.d. April 1893, Matjesfontein. *To Cron Cronwright-Schreiner*: 'You know I have so many books written, all the real work done, needing only patient revising, and that I can only give when my nature is alive and intense; I dare not touch my work at a lower mood than the mood I wrote it in, or I shall spoil it.' (*Life*, 251)

n.d. April 1893, Cape Town. *To Cron Cronwright-Schreiner*: '{Planning} to leave London in August for some little German or Italian town and settle down there quietly and steadily to copying and revising eight or nine hours a day, then, in about a year and eight months from now, either *The Buddhist Priest's Wife* or *From Man to Man* or one of my big books will be ready. I shall then be independent.' (*Life*, 254; by 'one of my big books' she presumably means one of the books already named, as in 'at least *one* of these big books', or else she may be referring to the afore-mentioned 'scientific' book, which—in shortened form—became *Woman and Labour*, as well as to another unnamed book unnamed here, but perhaps New Rush or Jan van der Linden's Wife, referred to elsewhere in her letters. SCCS transcribed this letter slightly differently in his 'Genesis'; see Unwin, 26; and Harper, xxv)

27 October 1893, ?Cape Town. *To Will Schreiner*: 'You know Will you have more the qualities of a great & wonderful administrator than those that go to make a politician. You have none of the vices that are almost indispensable to the successful politician, & your virtues are not virtues which will tell. You would make a superb judge, & I believe you would make a fine administrator of a district or Governor of a Colony. {...} (I really shouldn't be afraid of being tried by you if I were a Kaffir!) & you would try to hold

the balance evenly & understand all classes, I believe{,} if you were a governor.' (*OSLO*/UCT)

November 1893, Cape Town. *To Cron Cronwright-Schreiner*: 'I have read {Tolstoy's} the *Kreutzer Sonata* to-day. Ellis was right when he said that if I read it I would find all my own views in it. But I differ from him much in some points; he doesn't seem wide enough or full enough. {...} When I was nine years old I had a little imaginary boy Charles, to whom I told all my stories, with whom I argued and talked; and, when I was sixteen, Charles had changed and was the ideal man whom I should some far off day meet and who would help me to attain to all that was noble and strong; when I did a wrong or impure thing, I always shrank from it because it would divide between me and Charles, who would be so noble and strong. Tolstoy sees the hideousness of the conventional sensual ideal of "love"; but the nobler holy possibility beyond he does not see; his nature never thirsted for it because in his youth he had sullied sex feeling in himself. {...} {H}e does not see the ideal sexual intercourse as a sacrament to be partaken of between two souls; not only for the production of children, but sometimes going even further and consecrating the two who partake of it to a life—the highest fellowship in production, mental and spiritual, of the highest good and beauty. To me sexual intercourse would have failed, if it were not something both tried to be pure and great enough to be worthy of, and which did not stimulate and strengthen them for a holier, broader, more unselfish love.' (*Life*, 259–60; *The Kreutzer Sonata* was translated into English in 1890)

1894

February 1894, Middelburg, Eastern Cape. *To W. T. Stead*: 'Neither on the subject of Christianity nor of sex have I gone from the standpoint of *An African Farm*, as people will understand if ever I publish one of my larger books.' (*Letters*, 213)

1895

28 February 1895, Kimberley. *To Cron Cronwright-Schreiner*: 'While you are at Rondebosch go for a walk in my dear wood and see that old Summer House. That part is the scene where *From Man to Man* is laid. Rebekah lives there when she is married and always walks in those woods.' (*Letters*, 217–8)

24 May 1895, Kimberley. *To Betty Molteno*: 'Modern Political Economists, such as Karl Marks {i. e. Marx} have gone much further than Mill in the analysis of economic fact, & as far as mere technical knowledge of logic goes other writers will {...} now reproduce for you all Mill stated, but the

spiritual, the pure soul searching after the truth which is God, seeking to know nothing, to seek nothing, to discover nothing but truth, that, just that you will find no where else as in following & watching the mind of Mill work! I never read a page of Mill but I seem to #enter a higher holier atmosphere, even Plato does not affect me in the same way. I have owed spiritually singularly little to other people; but to Mill my debt can never be paid.' (*OSLO*/UCT)

30 September 1895, Kimberley. *To Mary Brown*: 'I am working very hard. I shall have my book on South Africa {*Stray Thoughts on South Africa*} out early next year, and the big novel copied and revised before the end if I keep so well.' (*Life*, 276)

1896

25 May 1896, Kimberley. *To John X. Merriman:* 'Your speech was without any doubt the most brilliant & powerful that has been made in the Cape Parliament—but this is not a time of day in South Africa when any speech, reason, or argument, counts:—it is the day of money. {...}

'There are two & only two questions in South Africa, the native question, & the question—Shall the whole land fall into the hands of a knot of Capitalists. The Dutch & English question, as you have yourself said, is nothing—in fifty years it will not be. But the native question & the capitalist question are in their infancy now, will loom right over the land in fifty years' time, & unless some mighty change set in, will deluge the land with blood.

'{...}It is beginning to become clear to me that if Rhodes ever comes back to power, it will be partly by the aid of his money, but mainly through the Bond; he will regain his power over the retrogressive element in the country by throwing the native to them to be torn in pieces.

'For the Boers as a whole I have the {...} most intense personal sympathy & admiration. For five years in my early girl-hood I was a teacher among them, & I know them as perhaps few, I might say, no, cultured Englishman in South Africa, knows them—& I love them. Their love for personal liberty—for themselves—is to me little short of being divine—but on the native question we have to fight the main body of them to the death for the next 20 years. Yes, they have had no Job; but they have had no language in which a Job could express his thoughts! Has Australia had a Job or America even? The greatest American, Emerson, is even not quite a Job! {...} I love the Boer—let us deal justly, generously by him as by the native: but let us not give one inch to his cardinal vice.' (*OSLO*/NLSA; the Afrikaner Bond, founded in 1880, was intent on a white-supremacist federation of the four South African states independent of British rule; the reference to Job is presumably to the stoic endurance in the face of injustice expressed in the biblical Book of Job, which is generally regarded as the high point of the Old Testament for grandeur of conception and language)

29 June 1896, Kimberley. *To John X. Merriman*: 'I have been struck by the fact on some farms I have been on, that, while the Kaffirs, who seem to me such a much more noble folk, are treated with scorn & severity, the Half-caste servants, or some of them, are petted & spoiled. {...} In one family I was struck by the way in which an old coloured woman of 70 & her daughter of 40 seemed to dominate & govern the mistress #& the house. I found out afterwards that the old woman had actually born {i.e. borne} several children to the grand father in the old slave times {...} In many cases where there is of course no personal relation between the master's family & the coloured servants there is still a racial connection. {...}

'I do not think I over state the painful position of the Halfcaste {...} I could recount to you if there were time, several instances in which coloured women have poured out a flood of bitterness at their position, when a few words of indirect sympathy had showed them that I felt kindly towards them. I know also one highly cultured & intellectual woman, in a good social position{,} who has one 8th of Hottentot blood. She has declared that if she had had any conception of what her children would have to go through she would never have given one of them birth. Her hatred towards her grand father for the misery he has caused his descendants is something almost savage! She certainly is the only person in upper ranks of life, who has ever spoken frankly to me of their position; but I have not the slightest doubt that thousands who do not speak, feel just as bitterly.

'{PS} No, I have never read {Robert Louis} Stevenson, strange as it may seem I have a most peculiar antipathy to novels. I love the Mill on the Floss and Turgannieff's Fathers & Sons & a dozen others, but I think I like them because they are science or poetry, not because they are novels!!! I have often tried to analyze why it is that I have this intense horror of ordinary novels, while the all ({i.e. all the} folks of this age from Huxley & Darwin to servant girls find pleasure in them, & benefit too. They are so dry!' (*OSLO/* NLSA; George Eliot's *The Mill on the Floss* was published in 1878, and Ivan Turgenev's *Fathers and Sons* was translated into English in 1867)

n.d. December 1896, Kimberley. *To Constance Lytton*: 'There is a great tragedy in the lives of modern women that women of the old style perhaps know nothing of. It is the tragedy which arises when a man cannot really love a woman because she is too much his superior; intellectually and emotionally she moves in a higher world than that in which he can move. It would kill him to live always in her atmosphere. A sparrow cannot live up in the air where an eagle breathes easily! That is the tragedy which lies as the key note of my two unpublished novels. In the first the woman marries & then for ten years you have a picture of her life, "trying to be more what he would like, than what she is", & then in the end even that mighty passion for the man is worn out, & her soul is free. The other novel is just the story of a woman who loves a brilliant & immensely wealthy politician, & the reason why, though he loves her (in his way), she can't marry him. I would rather be the second woman than the first. Perhaps you will say all this has nothing to do with you but I think it has.' (*OSLO*/LFP; the second novel referred to is the projected novel *The Buddhist Priest's Wife*, which in S's final corpus appears simply as a short story)

1897

12 November 1897, Kimberley. *To Betty Molteno*: 'If ever I get my big novel copied out, we'll buy a big farm & perhaps you & Miss Green {her partner, Alice Greene} will come & open a big school there. (*OSLO*/UCT)

16 December 1897, Kimberley. *To Betty Molteno*: 'Under the surface there is a strong feeling against this tyranny & corruption that is eating the heart of the country out, what is needed is some strong leader to give expression to it. But all that happens in the Colony seems to me such a small thing compared #to what has gone on in Mashona & Matabele land. Did I tell you of the educated Christian Kaffir who came to see us the other day? I fancy I did. He had been up in Matabele-land talking to the chiefs & indunas there. I asked him what they gave as their reason for fighting. He said, "They say they fought for death." I asked what he meant; & he said that they had never any hope of conquering the white man or driving him out, but their treatment was such that death was the one thing they desired. The Chartered Company are trying to drive them down into the fever swamps to live where they all must die by inches. Ah my dear friend, it is these things that are so terrible to me. I sometimes feel ashamed to look at a black man. But we can but each live out our little life, doing the best we can with the little fragment of strength that is given us. (*OSLO*/UCT; 'induna' is the Xhosa term for a senior figure in the chief's service)

1898

n.d. February 1898, Kimberley. *To Mary Sauer*: 'I'm working very hard. I've just bought a type writer to help me copy out my big novel. It's nice when life is so happy, you wish it could always go on just so! That's how I feel now.' (*OSLO*/NLSA)

10 November 1898, Johannesburg. *To Betty Molteno*: 'I suppose no one understands just how one feels to one's work—#that it's a kind of religion to me. That it lies in a region where neither praise nor blame {...} can ever

touch it as far as one's own feelings are concerned. I have said good bye to my work, & I can burn all my MSS (I have passed through that struggle & given it up) but I couldn't publish a line till I was satisfied.

'I have left it in my will that all my MS are to be burnt when I die. Did I ever send you a little Prelude to read called "The Child's Day"? I like it best of all the things I have written. I will send it you to read, if I haven't shown it you before. It's the #prelude to my big novel "From Man to Man". I know whatever the doctors say I shall never live to revise any of it, & I have three big books written{,} only wanting a few months of health to revise them. It was a great struggle a few months ago to give it all up. That was my real death. My physical death when it comes will be nothing. My soul is really here under the table in the box of manuscripts that will all have to be burnt when I die.' (*OSLO*/UCT; the other two 'big books' are *Woman and Labour* and perhaps the projected *A Buddhist Priest's Wife*)

15 December 1898, Johannesburg. *To Betty Molteno*: 'I'll send the little #prelude, but you must remember it's not revised; it's the first rough cast.' (*OSLO*/UCT)

1899

28 June 1899, Johannesburg. *To Will Schreiner*: 'I think & think the matter over, & I cannot but feel that the immediate thing is to work for peace, but it is possible that in after years one will see that war now was our last chance against the enemy. Don't think I would not do all I can on the side of peace, that what little I can do is done on that side, "give them all they want rather than fight,"—but the doubt will come!! If we had the natives on our side it might perhaps be better to make the stand now, we will have to make it one day—but our birds are coming home to roost. Every act of injustice against the black man, is tying our hands to-day. If the name Boer was a name to conjure by among the natives of South Africa, if we knew they would stand by us we could meet the Capitalist now. As it is, war would be a catastrophe, so awful that one feels it an imperative duty to put it off as long as possible. What you men have to do is sail on, & as close to the wind as you can, & never give them a change of *turning you out*.' (*OSLO*/UCT)

25 July 1899, Johannesburg. *To Havelock Ellis*: 'I shall never be a mathematician, nor a man of science making vast discoveries, nor a great leader of the people bound to them in love & sympathy & giving them voice, I shall never be the mother of ten children, creating them and feeling their dear soft hands on me; I shall never find out if I have the power for music I have always felt I have, shall never know if that craving to paint I have had since I was a little child was the craving of power, in my poor little handful of life, which consists now mainly of cooking & house cleaning, I shall know few

things, I am only a broken and untried possibility—but this I have{:} that I can sympathize with all the lives{,} with all the endeavours, with all the accomplished works; even with all the work attempted & not accomplished of <u>other men</u>.' (*OSLO*/HRC)

18 September 1899, Karree Kloof Farm, near Rustenburg, Karoo, Northern Cape. *To Betty Molteno*: 'If I can revise my big novel next year, I shall get several thousands for it, & be able to buy a farm & escape from Johannesburg to a country life. Every thing seems possible when I feel #so strong & get a little sleep.' (*OSLO*/UCT)

1901

31 January 1901, Hanover, Karoo: *To Betty Molteno and Alice Greene*: 'I am glad you got the MS all right. I've a curious tenderness for that little bit of writing. It always seems to be the incarnation of my own childhood, that seems so far now, & yet is nearer & more real than anything else in the world. {...} The novel which follows is the life of Rebekah & her little sister.' (*OSLO*/UCT)

14 November 1901, Hanover. *To Alice Greene*: 'I am sending you <u>registered</u> by this post an MS of mine. The revised copy is destroyed with all my other MS at Johannesburg. Please send it to my sister-in-law{.} I want to ask my brother to put it in his safe as I don't want it destroyed. I love it so much{,} it's the Prelude to my big novel. The revised copy was the thing I love best of all I have ever written: You can read it if you like but it's only the first rough draft dashed down, then I wrote it out carefully. I have only the rough first draft of the novel left but I could write it out again from memory if I had time. I would like to live to do it.' (*OSLO*/GFP)

25 December 1901, Hanover. *To Ettie Schreiner*: '"What we desire in youth, that we have in old age," Goethe said {in *Poetry and Truth*, 1812, part 2}. I am sure it is true with regard to spiritual matters, because slowly the ideal which we strive after must shape itself within us but, I think it often happens with other things. At least it is my dream that it will so happen. {...}

'I hope you got the little MS of mine safely. I wrote it fifteen years ago in Italy. I like it almost better than anything I ever wrote because it came to me such a curious way. I wrote the novel to which it is the prelude years before, when I was Africa. I was sitting one day writing an article on the Bushman, & suddenly in an instant, all the scenes in that little prelude seemed to open themselves before me, one after the other in a flash, like when you open one of those folded series of views & draw them all open quickly. I saw the little girl at the back-door, & on her flat stone, & in the garden under the tree making storie{s} & repeating poems right to the end, & curious, it was only when I sat down to write it out that I saw how it bore on the story that was coming & which I had written so long before. All my stories come to me that way. I never consciously try to make one, but none except Peter Halket {i.e. her 1897 novella, *Peter Halket*} ever came so completely & at once, they are sometimes only in bits for months before they are ready. {...}

'{PS} I sent mother that little prelude to read 10 years ago when I first came out from England. If she's forgotten it & would care to read it again you might give it her, but I don't want others to read it. (*OSLO*/UCT)

1902

20 March 1902, Hanover. *To Betty Molteno*: 'I'm copying out my long novel by bits as I'm able & will send you some to read when I'm half through. My hands & feet are very much swollen, & walking is almost impossible to me further than just about the house to do my house work.' (*OSLO*/UCT)

25 May 1902, Hanover. *To John Brown*: 'I've been able to work a little at my 6th chapter the last days again, & hope I shall get on a bit, if this fine weather continues.' (*OSLO*/UCT; this is the chapter entitled 'How Baby-Bertie went a-dancing')

4 June 1902, Hanover. *Journal*: 'I am revising the 6th chapter of *From Man to Man*.' {A few days later} 'Have been copying out all the evening chapter 7 of *From Man to Man*.' (*Life*, 347, 348; SCCS does not provide the date of the second excerpt)

1903

23 June 1903, Hanover. *To Ettie Schreiner*: 'About the typing. I have only a very little bit ready{,} would take a good typist about one day or less, & I copy out so slowly that it may be months before I have any more (I may never ever finish the book at all!){...}I have a splendid typewriter of my own & could do it myself but it hurts my chest so.' (*OSLO*/UCT)

22 October 1903, Hanover. *To Ettie Schreiner*: 'You will see how I deal with just this point in my novel. There is I believe a real physical basis for this difference in men & women's memories as regards sexual emotions & relations. In the fact lies one of the grand points about which the tragedy of human life centres. The man does simply not remember what he thought & felt with regard to sex emotions—& the woman forgets nothing! A man remembers quite as well as a woman, the day he was top of his class & got the prize, he never forgets that through life. But the day he said good bye to the little school girl he loved, & how he wept when he said good bye to her, that he quite forgets.' (*OSLO*/UCT)

1904

13 May 1904, Cape Town. *To Havelock Ellis*: 'I made Rebekah say, years ago when I was a young girl (and it's a curious thing as showing how instinctively one knows things one can't have experienced) that in youth, though one longs for love and sympathy, one's master passion is for the intellectual knowledge of truth and for experience; but when one grows older, though one still loves knowledge, one's master need is for human relations of love and sympathy.' (*Letters*, 244–5)

10 June 1904, Hanover. *To Alice Greene*: 'There is going to be a terrible native war before long & we (you or I) are quite powerless to do anything. I have thrown away 10 years of my life in trying to stop the inevitable. What iota of good have I done? Was one Matabele kept alive by Peter Halket {i.e. the novella}? Was one English shot arrested by all my writing with regard to the Boer war? (*OSLO*/UCT; the references are to *Trooper Peter Halket of Mashonaland* and to the newspaper articles she collected for an *English South African's view of the Situation*, 1899)

19 June 1904, Hanover. To Alice Greene: 'All goes on here as ever. I & the meerkats & Neta {her dog} & the little Kaffir boy form the world to each other.' (*OSLO*/UCT)

19 November 1904, Hanover. *To Alice Greene*: 'You know my dream has always been that one could knock about the world when one was young, but when one got older settle down to a large broad sort of home life. A household with plenty of people of all sorts & kinds who love each other & have some sort of need of eachother—as Rebekah does in my novel.' (*OSLO*/UCT)

1905

15 February 1905, Hanover. *To Cron Cronwright-Schreiner*: 'I suppose you hadn't time to read my bit of MS.? It's difficult for me to judge at it apart from the whole book. I know it as part of the whole only, & you could judge it apart. In the book as a whole it is the first sort of indirect intimation of the life Rebekah is leading & her husband's disloyal act to her, & I'm not sure whether it does not pull it out of the artistic shape.' (*OSLO*/NLSA)

10 May 1905, Cape Town. *To Betty Molteno*: '{PS} When I get back to Hanover I'm going to leave every thing & try to get my novel revised even if I only do ten lines #each day.' (*OSLO*/UCT)

1 July 1905, Hanover. *To Betty Molteno*: 'I am revising my novel. {...} If there is any public fight which will be worth fighting in this country it will be in defence of the #natives & the Chinese. The poor, dear, old Chinamen are having an awful time. {...}

'{PS} Perhaps I shall get one of my books ready after all & I can buy the farm & you come & live there.' (*OSLO*/UCT)

11 July 1905, Hanover. *To Will Schreiner*: 'I am working a bit at one of my books copying out & revising: if I could get it done, say in two years' time I might go {to Nauheim, for heart treatment}! I am feeling very strong & if it were not for the noises in my heart should be fine.' (*OSLO*/UCT)

31 August 1905, Hanover. *To Betty Molteno*: 'The thing that is hardest for me not to be troubled about now is these Chinese. They are practically slaves{,} flogged & ill treated in the mines, & when by any chance they manage to escape there is no hope for them{,} every man's hand is against them. They must starve & die or be captured & sent back to the mines {...}. I would write on the question if I saw the slightest use; but it is not {--} things must play out to their own terrible end.' (*OSLO*/UCT)

24 September 1905, Hanover. *To Fan Schreiner*: 'Cron will be coming to Cape Town again on the 18th of next month for ten days. It will be his third visit to Cape Town since parliament. But I have no money to come. I am working hard at my book to try & earn some, but those publishers are so bad I may get nothing after all.' (*OSLO*/UCT)

31 October 1905, Hanover. *To John X. Merriman*: 'It was rather strange that your letter should have come just when I was thinking I must write & ask you whether you had read a book called the Souls of Black Folks {i.e. Folk}, & to advise you to get it at once if you have not. It's by a coloured man, I should say from his photograph nearly a full blooded Negro, called du Bois & son of a slave. It's a book I have long been seeking & waiting for, in which some native should give true expression, not to what he feels it's politic & wise to express to white men, but to what he really feels. This book is just what I have wanted. The chapter I like best is the one called "The passing of the first-born" where he speaks of his child, with its "proud" little curly head who died before he ever learnt what he was {...}.

'{...} At present I am reading for about the 10th time Don Quixote. A friend in England has sent me an ideal little copy in four tiny volumes & I read myself to sleep with it every night, & I've never enjoyed it so much before.

'South African politics & public matters are to me simply heart breaking at the present time, & I am trying to forget them in revising one of my old novels that I wrote many years ago. It is simply the lives of two women, one very intellectual & complex, the other very simple & unintellectual, but both equally beloved: it's just the story of all they thought & did & felt, & how it ended with them both. I should like to think I was leaving it ready for publication when I died, but don't make much progress with it because one can only do good work except at high pressure {i.e. one cannot do good work except at high pressure} & one daren't sometimes put the pressure on.' (*OSLO*/NLSA; W.E.B. Du Bois, *The Souls of Black Folk*, 1903; Miguel de Cervantes' *Don Quixote* was translated by Tobias Smollett in 1770)

1906

24 June 1906, Cape Town. *Journal*: 'I am revising Rebekah's letter to her husband.' (*Life*, 349; see Ch. XVIII; SCCS's 'Genesis' in Unwin and Harper mistakenly gives Hanover as OS's address at this time)

10 October 1906, Matjesfontein. *Journal*: 'I went for a lovely walk in the afternoon to my koppie, Rebekah's. I'm so happy' (*Life*, 349; the only specific koppie referred to is in Ch. IX, and relates to Bertie's story, not Rebekah's)

17 October 1906, Matjesfontein. To *Cron Cronwright-Schreiner*: 'I've got half a chapter done since I came here.' (*OSLO*/NLSA)

26 October 1906, Matjesfontein. *To Cron Cronwright-Schreiner*: 'I'm not bad dear, but my heart is very weak. My eyes seem to make everything faint before me sometimes. Perhaps I wrote too much of my book: it is exacting work. I do so want to finish that book, dear. Can you understand?' (*OSLO*/NLSA)

3 November 1906, Matjesfontein. *To Cron Cronwright-Schreiner*: 'I slept last night, the first night for two weeks {. . .} Oh love, it is wicked of me, the thing I can't give up is the hope of finishing my book.' (*OSLO*/NLSA)

20 November 1906, Matjesfontein. *To Cron Cronwright-Schreiner*: 'I wrote at my book all the morning.' (*OSLO*/NLSA)

21 November 1906, Matjesfontein. *To Cron Cronwright-Schreiner*: 'At the end of two years perhaps I shall have got better & done my book!!! It's strange how hopeful my nature is. I never seem quite able to give up all hope. I only want one small ray of light to make me go on, like a donkey after straw.' (*OSLO*/NLSA)

24 November 1906, Matjesfontein. *To Cron Cronwright-Schreiner*: 'I wrote to Ellis some time ago suggesting he should write a book or one or two books on sex in its normal, beautiful manifestations. Show for instance the wonderful effect of sex love in stimulating & raising the intellectual faculties, as in the case of the Brownings {Robert, and Elizabeth Barrett Browning) who both produced nearly all their best & greatest work during their intensely happy married life, & Mill's case & a great many others. Also to write on the strange & beautiful blending of maternal feeling with sexual love—in almost all normal women when they have been married to a man

a few years. {...} To me study of sex in its higher manifestations, where it becomes in men & women the stimulus to noblest self sacrifice & the highest intellectual activity, is far more interesting than the fact that a certain unhappy abnormal man is only in love with the digestive organs of dogs! But with Ellis it is just the other way. To a certain extent Ellis is a true decadent; that is why he has a sympathy with Oscar Wilde's writings & Symonds's &c which I never can have. (*OSLO*/NLSA; the references are to Oscar Wilde (1854–1900) and John Addington Symonds (1807–1871), both of whose writing pursued a philosophy of sensual pleasure)

24 November 1906, Matjesfontein. *To Cron Cronwright-Schreiner*: 'I don't know when I've ever for years been so well as to-day. I've worked & written from this morning till now, 10.30 p.m. {...}. The whole morning still writing at my book.' (*OSLO*/NLSA; given the fragmentary nature of both this and the above extract and their shared date may mean they are from the same letter)

25 November 1906, Matjesfontein. *To Cron Cronwright-Schreiner*: 'I went out to buy a pot of ink to go on with my writing, but it was too lovely, I had to go for a little walk down to my old #kunnie tree at the drift. Now I am going to go on with my writing.' (*OSLO*/NLSA; see Chs. III and IV, pp.74 and 93, for references to kunee trees, a.k.a. kuni-bush)

5 December 1906, Matjesfontein. *To Cron Cronwright-Schreiner*: 'Yes, I think {Alfred, Lord} Tennyson was a poet and a true poet, but not a very great one. {...} I think some of his little lyrics will live as long as the English language lasts, "Tears, idle tears", for instance, is immortal. He was not a man with a great intellect, & then the range of matter over which he could be a poet & seer was small. He was a poet of pensive sweetness, moods of human life & expression like all others, by the poet who supremely feels them, but there is no new note of intensity, of reckless force, of passions, in all his works. "Come into the garden Maude" is infinitely sweet & tender, but it has no breath of fierce passion. {Robert} Browning, who had felt what the hunger for truth & knowledge was, could write the "Grammarian's Funeral", pouring into human speech for all time the pure deep saying {i.e. deep-saying} longing of the noblest human intellects for truth & knowledge; Tennyson couldn't, because he hadn't the intellect to hunger for them, but he could write a poem, a true poem, about the old uneducated grandmother thinking over the days of her youth. (*OSLO*/NLSA; see her characterization of John-Ferdinand, via Tennyson, in Chs. III and VI)

12 December 1906, Matjesfontein. *To Cron Cronwright-Schreiner*: 'I'm copying out the chapter of my work now, ready to have it type written.' (*OSLO*/NLSA)

1907

5 January 1907, Matjesfontein. *To Cron Cronwright-Schreiner*: 'I'm getting "fine" with my work.' (*OSLO*/NLSA)

16 January 1907, Hanover. *To Cron Cronwright-Schreiner*: 'I'm so well today. Tomorrow I'm going to try to get to my writing.' (*OSLO*/NLSA)

c. 18–20 January 1907, Hanover. *To Cron Cronwright-Schreiner*: 'I always feel that sexual instinct pure & simple is much maligned: that the worst & meanest vices of life do not arise from sexual passion pure & simple but rather from a petty vanity & love of admiration. {...} I am really keeping so splendidly well: I don't need more than the little girl. Emotional companionship, some one who loved me tenderly & whom I loved I do need; but it is useless to long to find that in the ordinary coloured girl. If I could have a little wild Kaffir boy or girl—yes! I'm really getting on splendidly' (*OSLO*/NLSA; dated 20 January in *Letters*, 262, where SCCS adds "[servant]" before the first mention of "girl")

22 January 1907, Hanover. *To Bob Muirhead*: 'I am living alone here. Just now I haven't a servant at all so I & Ollie the dog & the three meerkats have the world of this little house & yard all to ourselves; & you may picture me going every evening to the village pump for water. I'm trying to write at my book too, a bit.' (*OSLO*/UG)

9 February 1907, Hanover. *To Edward Carpenter*: 'I've not eaten meat or soup practically now for one year & a half, & never taste it when I'm in my own home, live principally on sour milk & a very very little dry biscuit (bread & sugar are worse for me than meat). {...} My objection to meat eating is & remains the horror of eating one's animal brothers. I never pass a flock of sheep, or cattle with their dear large restful eyes but I get a stick in my heart. {...}

'{PS} {...} I'm writing at my book.' (*OSLO*/SCL)

20 February 1907, Hanover. *Journal*: 'I am just finishing "You Can't Capture the Ideal".' (*Life*, 350; this is Ch. XVIII)

25 February 1907, Hanover. *To Cron Cronwright-Schreiner*: '{I}f a thing be true, it must come to thousands of minds, it must live in millions of hearts; & that makes the use of a writer: not that he expresses what no one else thinks & feels, but that he is the voice for what others feel & can't say. If only the powers that shape existence give me the strength to finish this book, I shall not have that agonised feeling over my life that I have over the last ten years, that I have done nothing of good for any human creature. I am not sure of the book's artistic worth: to judge of that from the purely intellectual standpoint one must stand at a distance from one's own or any

one else's work. But I know it gives a voice to what exists in the hearts of many women & some men, I know I have only tried to give expression to what was absolutely forced on me, that I have not made up one line for the sake of making it up.' (*OSLO*/NLSA)

26 February 1907, Hanover. *To John X. Merriman*: 'Fortunately (or unfortunately!) for myself I was born with such a firm constitutional build in one certain direction, that unless I violated myself I should have to keep on in one course. I was a republican, a feeler of the injustice of woman's position, an opponent of all <u>hereditary</u> rights to govern others, a believer in the primary moral importance of defending the weak, animals or men, against injustice of oppression &c &c when I was ten, just as I am today & must be when I'm eighty unless I sell my soul. But I know & believe there are numbers of person more gifted {&} more valuable than myself, who have not been born with a kind of constitutional mandate {...}

'{...} But I really fix little hope on this incoming government or any other. The first thing they are trying to do is bring down wages. Really enlightened men & women must be in this country for the next 50 (perhaps 30! only) years as the voice of one crying in the wilderness. I am now as an old Boer would express it "full up to my throat" with South Africa. I have not lost my faith in the glorious forward march which humanity is still going to take upon earth; for "I doubt not through the ages one increasing purpose runs" but here in South Africa we are the crest of a wave & there will be an awful sweep down wards before we mount on the other side;—hideous native wars, injustice & greed riding rampant,—with always the protesting few of course. Do not think I am despairing over human life & things generally; I am more full of hope than ever; but just as I saw in England in '88 that there was a long terrible downward dip before us, so I see it here today. {...} The subject of the decay & death of nature & empires has so interested me all my life that I have brought in a whole chapter on it in my big novel—which doesn't sound promising for the novel!—but it really <u>had</u> to come in, because the woman in the book was so interested in it.' (*OSLO*/UCT; see Ch. VII; the earlier quotation comes from Tennyson's "Locksley Hall": "Yet I doubt not thro' the ages one increasing purpose runs, / And the thoughts of men are widen'd with the process of the suns.")

2 March 1907, Hanover. *To Cron Cronwright-Schreiner*: 'I'm beginning to copy my chapter, but I'm not a quick writer when I write properly.' (*OSLO*/NLSA)

4 or 5 March 1907, Hanover. *To Cron Cronwright-Schreiner*: 'I sat up writing at my book very late.' (*OSLO*/NLSA; this is dated 14 March in *Letters*, 265)

5 March 1907, Hanover. *To Cron Cronwright-Schreiner*: 'I am so absorbed & interested in my book. I don't like to think of anything else.' (*OSLO*/NLSA)

20 March 1907, Hanover. *To Cron Cronwright-Schreiner*: 'You will see that if you read my novel all other matters seem to me small compared to matters of sex, & prostitution is the most agonising central point. Prostitution, especially the prostitution of men of themselves to their most brutal level{,} can't really be touched till man not only says but feels woman is his equal, his brother human to whom he must give as much as he takes; & the franchise is one step towards bringing that about.' (*OSLO*/NLSA)

22 March 1907, Hanover. *To Will Schreiner*: 'I haven't added a line to my book for six weeks. {...} One of the dreams of my life is that I should finish my book & be able to do something for {the young sons of an old friend}; but oh Laddie I fear it won't be; the difficulty in breathing grows greater & greater. The thought that I might finish that book & so feel I had been of some use in the world is the only thing that makes me wish to put off the end, for I would not willingly live over again the last 12 years of my life, as I would not willingly live #over the first twelve—all the between part I would live over & over again if I could, in spite of all the shades & pains that are incident to all human life.' (*OSLO*/UCT)

26 March 1907, Hanover. *To Julia Solly*: '{W}e want some one organization in which <u>all</u> women can unite. {...} {I}t is a root question of justice & freedom. There is no other question in the world on which I feel so strongly & which I have studied so much. If ever I have the strength to finish the book I am working at now you will understand how deeply I have felt on this matter.' (*OSLO*/UCT; OS's emphatic 'all' gives particular relevance to the direction being taken by *From Man to Man*)

24 April 1907, Hanover. *To Edward Carpenter*: 'I'm feeling much better just now & am writing hard at my book so of course I'm never lonely.' (*OSLO*/SCL)

28 April 1907, Hanover. *Journal*: 'I like Rebekah's letter; it's too long, all to have been written in one night, but <u>that</u> doesn't matter.' (*Life*, 350)

14 May 1907, Hanover. To *Alice Greene*: 'I am getting on a little with my book, I work every minute I'm well enough.' (*OSLO*/UCT)

c. 17-20 May 1907, Hanover. *To Cron Cronwright-Schreiner*: 'I am going to get the big tin box in & pack away my papers this morning{.} Of course you may read them all & go over them if you like if I die first; there is nothing of mine I don't like you to see. This afternoon I am going to try &

go on with {a} new chapter of my book, & also to copy out the last one, {...} so that I have one to keep & one to send to England to typewrite.' (*OSLO*/NLSA)

23 May 1907, Hanover. *To Cron Cronwright-Schreiner*: 'Oh, I wish I could get my book done before I die. It may not be any good; but I feel {I} have to do it. I used to feel I couldn't die till it was done; that fate wouldn't let it be {...} If one has done one's best, that is all...?' (*OSLO*/NLSA; see *Letters*, 269, which excludes the question mark SCCS initially transcribed)

27 May 1907, Hanover. *To Cron Cronwright-Schreiner*: 'That one chapter is longer than *Peter Halket*. Now come two little chapters; then a very long one; & then the first, & much the longest, part of the book is done; then comes the shorter second part, but which I love. Oh, if I could be under conditions to finish it... I've set my heart so on finishing it before the end comes. I could do so much work now if I was strong & could get fresh air. My brain has never been so clear & strong in one way. I tried to go out for a walk yesterday but I came staggering back & am only now recovering from it.' (*OSLO*/NLSA; the first-mentioned 'longer' chapter is probably Ch. IV, the 'two little chapters' Chs. V and VI, and the 'very long one' Ch. VII)

c. June–August 1907, Cape Town. *To Caroline Murray*: 'Everything connected with politics in South Africa is very distressing to me & I'll just try to forget it & stick to working at my novel.' (*OSLO*/UCT)

25 September 1907, Hanover. *To Cron Cronwright-Schreiner*: 'I had a delightful journey here as far as sun & sunlight went. I began to breathe as soon as I got on the rise above De Aar {...} I am going to try to get a whole long chapter finished in this fortnight... I feel how much I have gained by the change. I have no shortness of breath & no cough. I'm quite well.' (*OSLO*/NLSA)

3 October 1907, Hanover. *To Cron Cronwright-Schreiner*: 'I've read the volumes of Theal since I came here. How utterly he has changed this edition since he got in tow with Rhodes & the Bond! He has the face to say people may wonder at the changes he has made but he has entirely changed his opinion! A funny thing for a man to do who has been making a study of South African history all his life! He used to be a great friend of the native; now he even attempts to defend slavery. It is very sickening.' (*OSLO*/NLSA; see *Letters*, 273; of George McCall Theal's 11-volume *History of South Africa*, only the first 5 volumes were published by this time, in 1888–1893, with volumes II–IV revised between 1907 and 1910. OS's reference would be to Theal's treatment of the period 1505–1795)

4 October 1907, Hanover. *To Cron Cronwright-Schreiner*: 'I am very very well now it's cold. Wrote at my book till 12 last night.' (*OSLO*/NLSA)

22 October 1907, De Aar. *To Adela Villiers Smith*: 'The most important event of my childhood was the birth of a little sister {Ellie}, and my love for her has shaped all my life. It was her death, when I was about nine, which first made me realise the falsity of what I had been taught and made a freethinker of me. She only lived eighteen months, but for that 18 my life was entirely in and through her, and I watched her die. The novel I am revising now is dedicated to her, and the opening chapter is about a little girl's feeling when her new little sister is born. I sometimes think my great love for women and girls, not because they are myself, but because they are not myself, comes from my love to her.' (*Letters*, 274)

n.d. 1907, De Aar. *To Ettie Schreiner*: 'People think when people drop dead suddenly of heart disease they have died easily; they don't know the years in which they have struggled hand over hand with death, by day & by night. I would be so willing to die, but oh I wish so to get just a little well to finish my book. Then I could die easily & think I had left something to comfort & help some other women perhaps.' (*OSLO*/UCT; curiously, the letter opens with the words, 'My dear Ellie')

4 December 1907, De Aar. *To Ursula Schreiner*: 'I have got the asthma remedy Dad spoke about. {...}

'I am working hard at my book {...} I'm nearly half way through so perhaps in 1909 I'll go to England {...} I'll be a blooming millionaire when my book's done!' (*OSLO*/UCT)

4 December 1907, De Aar. *To Isie Smuts*: 'I am working very hard at my book, all the time I can. {...} {The} new asthma remedy from England, Dr. Tucker's cure, {...} is not only helping my asthma but relieves my heart greatly.' (*OSLO*/NASA)

1908

9 February 1908, De Aar. *To Will Schreiner*: 'I am trying to get on with my book, but the heat in this little room makes working slow.' (*OSLO*/UCT)

n. d. 1908, De Aar. *To Mary Brown*: 'Have you ever read a little story of Kipling called "The end of Passage". It is often in my head now as I lie here. Last night I went down to the camp {the Railway Camp at De Aar where Schreiner's husband had a business} for dinner thinking it would be good to see the people walking about. When we came back we found the house had been burgled. {...} Tonight Cron has gone down to dinner but I am not going as I didn't like to leave my ms. Tonight if it gets cooler & I feel able I am going to pack them all into a bag & take them to the bank.

I don't think the conditions of life here will ever be such that I can finish my book{s}, but still I cling to them. They seem the one thing left that still relates me to life & my fellow human beings.' (*OSLO*/NLSA; Rudyard Kipling's story, "At the End of the Passage", was published in his volume, *Life's Handicap: Being Stories of My Own People*, 1891)

24 February 1908, De Aar. *To Will Schreiner*: I'm trying hard to get on with my book, "the encyclopedia" as Cron calls it, "that is going to be finished in the next century". My heart is getting quickly worse & worse, & yet if I could live under more possible conditions than I have lived under for the last 14 years I might perhaps finish it{.} I cling to it as the only thing I have left in life; the thought that if I finish it before I die perhaps some day some soul in the dark will read it & find help in it, & all these last years of my life will not have been utterly thrown away. But here in de Aar it is a hand over hand fight to live at all.' (*OSLO*/UCT)

24 March 1908, Matjesfontein. *To Will Schreiner*: 'I only want to live many years more if I can work, if not I'd rather die today. I'm getting to the last end of the money Fred {her eldest brother} left me, & yet even when I'm better as I am the last three days I can't put pressure on myself or the pump stops working & sticks. You see all creative work of any kind, even original thought on impersonal matters, if it's your own & comes from you, has to be done under a certain amount {of} emotional & intellectual pressure, & that means physical heart pressure. I think I broke down at de Aar in the way I have just because I did write a chapter & a half shut up in that little room with the temperature inside from 85 to 95 day & night. I am going to make a good beginning for the new year by getting out all my papers today, & tomorrow!' (*OSLO*/UCT)

9 April 1908, Matjesfontein. *To Adela Villiers Smith*: 'It's funny to me to think of your having the little son christened. It's to me quite as savage an institution as a Kaffir witch-doctor weaving a spell to keep away the evil eye: and so un-Jesus-like. But then all Christianity, so called, is. To me Jesus was a poor working-man socialist of genius, a sort of Keir Hardie! (*Letters*, 27; Keir Hardie, a trade-unionist, founded the British Labour Party in 1906)

11 April 1908, Matjesfontein. *To Cron Cronwright-Schreiner*: 'I sat up writing at my book till one last night & did a lot of work. I would finish my book in a little more than a year if I were always living here & had nothing but writing to do.' (*OSLO*/NLSA)

8 May 1908, Matjesfontein. *To Will Schreiner*: 'Wait till my book's done & then see me in a robe from England & a three guinea hat!' (*OSLO*/UCT)

18 May 1908, Matjesfontein. *To Cron Cronwright-Schreiner*: 'I wonder if you would some day perhaps have time on a Sunday afternoon or morning, say, to do something for me: To read over my little chapter "Fireflies in the Dark", & tell me quite truthfully, without fear of hurting me, if you find it interesting. I am so afraid I have become so subtle in my modes of thought, I have thought so much about some impersonal things & care so much for them, that others may find them very uninteresting [...] I live so much alone & think so much that I am afraid sometimes I have lost touch with the intellectual artistic reader.' (*OSLO*/NLSA; see Ch. XII)

23 May 1908, Matjesfontein. *To Betty Molteno*: 'I am working a little at my book with great pleasure & am much stronger.' (*OSLO*/UCT)

4 June 1908, De Aar. *To Will Schreiner*: 'Second rate men can easily do the Prime Ministry of this country or can even work officially at its Federation. That is a thing which will be accomplished if there were only third rate men in this country. But the work that calls for great men & women here, & that none but they can accomplish, because it is a work requiring devotion to a high ideal & self obliteration, is the wise ordering of our native question. That calls for the largest, the sanest, the widest intellects & hearts the world has seen.

'In my small way I am doing what I can. If it were typewritten & easy to read I would {send} you a chapter of my novel I'm just finishing. The colour question comes in quite naturally there, because one of the centre points of the story is that the wife has adopted & brings up as her own among the legitimate children a little half-coloured child who is her husband's by a coloured servant. He never suspects the child is his till the end of the book, when he attacks his wife with bringing up a coloured child with his white children. You will of course see how this opens up the whole question of our relation to the darker races, & the attitude which says "they are here for our interest{,} for our *pleasure*, & to hell with them when they aren't that!" If only I could live to finish that book, I would feel satisfied, though it was perfect failure.' (*OSLO*/UCT)

27 June 1908, Cape Town. *To Adela Villiers Smith*: My heart feels so tender over a baby girl because of all the anguish which may be before it. I always think of it when I touch and hold in my arms the dear little female bodies; which no love can shield from the anguish which may be waiting for them. I have done all I can to help to free women, but oh it is so little. Long ages must pass before we really stand free and look out on a world that is ours as well as man's. The poor little political franchise is just a tiny, little, wee step towards it. I don't think you can understand a little how I love those suffragettes in London, those that I do know, and those that I don't. They are

women who have freed themselves spiritually fighting for freedom: we, here, have in our little movement only slaves clanking their little chains along as they go, asking for their little franchise. You know when I was a young girl and a child I felt this awful bitterness in my soul because I was a woman, because there were women in the world. I felt [like] the wonderful Kaffir woman, who once was talking to me and said, "There may be a God, I do not say there is not; but if there is he is not good—why did he make woman?" During those ten or twelve happy middle years of my life the bitterness went; I realised the evils of woman's position but I was so full of infinite hope. Every thing seemed coming right quite soon just on the other side of the hill. I loved all my beautiful men friends in England and the Kingdom of Heaven on Earth seemed just here. Now, especially during the last eight years, I seem struggling with more than the old bitterness; it seems choking me, suffocating me sometimes. I try to fix my eye on the future but the future seems so far. It wouldn't matter a bit that one will never reach it if one knew it were coming <u>soon</u> to others. These dear suffragettes are just making life possible to me. It's not what they are trying to <u>get</u>, it's what they are becoming—they <u>are</u> breaking free!! (*Letters*, 280–1)

28 June 1908, Cape Town. *To Fred Pethick-Lawrence*: 'I am working at my novel now.' (*OSLO*/UCT)

3 October 1908, De Aar. *To Emily Hobhouse*: 'No one needs me here now except the natives—& that is indeed hard & stern works that calls to all the bravest souls in South Africa for many years to come.

'{...} We shall have an uphill fight here to rouse & educate our women to their public duties. You see, we are just 60 years behind Europe in this, as in so many other matters. (*OSLO*/HT)

1909

3 January 1909, Matjesfontein. *To Minnie Murray*: 'I do so want to get my novel done before I die. I feel that that, & not even speeches & working at a society is the <u>real</u> work I can do for women. I feel I should be quite happy when I was dying if I had done that. My dear friend Miss Molteno thinks I am so wrong not to go to Europe where I am so much better & could finish my work, instead of staying here in this hot climate which doesn't suit me. She doesn't realize I <u>can't</u> leave my husband & go where if he were ill or in need of me I couldn't get to him. {...} I don't think any woman who is not married can realize all a woman feels to her husband.' (*OSLO*/NELM)

c. 1 January–28 February1909, Matjesfontein. *To Isie Smuts*: 'I am writing at my novel, but one can't write all the time, in fact when I have written for a couple of hours I have to go & lie down & it rests one's brain to have something far removed from your work to think of.' (*OSLO*/NASA)

26 February 1909, Matjesfontein. *To Betty Molteno*: 'The way in which the natives are treated here is too abominable.' (*OSLO*/UCT)

n.d. July 1909, De Aar, *To Betty Molteno*: 'I am soon publishing a book on "Woman" {*Woman and Labour*}. It is ready but I can't find an agent to do the business part of making the business arrangements with the publishers for me yet. I want to find some practical business woman; the men cheat you too much. I must get something for this book as I'm come pretty well to the end of my stock. If only I was in England to go round to the publishers with it I know I should do well. {…} If I can get it published satisfactorily perhaps I may yet come to England when my novel is done! The air is nice & cool here now & I am able to work.' (*OSLO*/UCT)

25 July 1909, De Aar. *To Adela Villiers Smith*: 'Before I was born my mother lost two children, a little son of five about six months before, and a little one of two years three months before I was born. My mother never cared for her children especially her daughters as soon as they were older, say eight or nine. But of her tiny babies and children she was passionately fond. She was almost distracted when the little one died three months before my birth, and said she found no comfort in anything but walking up and down by herself behind the church which stood near the little mission house in which I was born. It's curious, as all my life since I was almost a baby of two or three, I've always had such a passion for walking up and down. One of the first things I can remember, when I can't have been more than three, was walking up and down in a passage with cocoanut matting on the floor and making stories to myself: and I can remember the other children laughing at me and my mother telling them they were to leave me alone.' (*Letters*, 287)

n.d. October 1909, Cape Town. *To Fred Pethick-Lawrence*: 'I have not been working at my book. Running a house with one little coloured girl to help you, you can't get any time for mental work, but I am going to try to get on with it while down here.' (*OSLO*/UCT; the suggestion in *OSLO* is that the reference may be to *Closer Union* or to the US edition of *Dream Life and Real Life*, but given that the former had already appeared as newspaper articles in 1908, and that the latter would not either seem to warrant the term 'working at', it seems likelier to be *From Man to Man*.)

n.d. October 1909, Cape Town. *To Adela Villiers Smith*: 'On the other end of the table is a huge brown paper parcel which contains my novel that I love so, much of it unrevised and no good if I died. I've been sorting my papers to-day and it's made me feel so hopeless, all that mass of half finished work. All my life seems such a failure, but I've lived and I've loved many beautiful things; and had even more love than I was worthy of. […]

I am sending you the little Prelude. Send it back when you've read it. I've got to revise it yet. It's just as it came to me many years ago one day on the Riviera. I know you'll understand it. I love it specially because it came to me in such a curious way. I wrote the rough draft of this novel years and years ago when I was quite a young girl before I went to England. In England I was too absorbed in social problems ever to read it over even. One day, I think it was in the winter of 1888, I was on the Riviera at Alassio; I was sitting at my dear old desk writing an article on the Bushmen and giving a description of their skulls;—when suddenly, in an instant, the whole of this little Prelude flashed on me. You know those folded up views of places that one buys; you take hold of one end and all the pictures unfold one after the other as quick as light. That was how it flashed on me. I started up and paced about the room. I felt absolutely astonished. I hadn't thought of my novel for months, I hadn't looked at it for years. I'd never dreamed of writing a Prelude to it.—I just sat down and wrote it out. And do you know what I found out—after I'd written it?—that it's a picture in small, a kind of allegory, of the life of the woman in the book!! It's one of the strangest things I know of. My mind must have been working at it unconsciously, though I knew nothing of it—otherwise how did it come? Don't show the Prelude to anyone, and don't tell anyone about it. It's only for you.' (*Letters*, 290–1; see also letters dated 12 June 1890 to Havelock Ellis and 25 December 1901 to Ettie Schreiner for references to this inspirational moment; although OS writes that in the winter of 1888 she had not looked at *From Man to Man* 'in years', letters written in 1886 and 1887 contradict this)

14 December 1909, Muizenberg. *To Adela Villiers Smith*: 'Did you get my little Prelude? Please return it, darling. In the novel, when the little girl grows up she spends some of the most important moments of her life at Muizenberg close to this spot. It's so curious that I feel as though some great tragic events of my own life had taken place here. I walk again and again to the spot where years ago "Farmer Peck's" little thatched house used to stand, and think "Yes, here Rebekah walked". I don't think any one else can have an idea how real and how "out of oneself", something not made up by oneself but which one simply knows, all these people are.' (*Letters*, 291–2; OS's reference is perhaps to Ch. VIII)

1910

5 May 1910, De Aar. *To Adela Villiers Smith*: 'Every woman who is thirty or over ought certainly to have her own "little foot of earth".

'{...} I am reading Milton a little as I've nothing else to read. I read him a great deal when I was a child aloud to my mother while she was cooking and doing needle work, and got to love him even when I couldn't understand all. I think one should always try to let children read and learn by heart the best poetry while they are quite young. One loses one's taste for inferior things if once one has known the best, and children feel so much more and understand so much more than people dream; most people grow stupid and blunt off between eleven and eighteen. There is many a man who would have got to love and understand Milton at ten who couldn't possibly understand him, reading him for the first time at twenty. If I had a child I should mainly educate it up to ten or eleven on the best poetry.' (*Letters*, 293–4; John Milton's epic poem, *Paradise Lost*, 1667, is just one of his many works OS would have read)

31 July 1910, De Aar. *To Anna Purcell*: 'I love little baby girls with a peculiar tenderness—but it's so sad to bring a woman into the world, till better times come. You can shield her during her childhood—but what then?' (*OSLO*/NLSA)

18 October 1910, De Aar. *To Fred Pethick-Lawrence*: 'The passage in "Rebel Women" I think so fine is that of the poor drudge who speaks of her sorrow at the thought of bringing another woman into the world. The "idea" is common enough. The genius-touch is in the cry breaking out in that seemingly soulless drudge. It is like when many years ago a Kaffir woman suddenly poured out to me all the sorrow and anguish of being a woman in the most unsurpassed language. It is something one never forgets.' (*OSLO*/UCT; Evelyn Sharp's *Rebel Women*, a collection of suffrage stories, was published in 1910; for references to this incident, see Schreiner's draft Wollstonecraft introduction and also *Woman and Labour*)

22 December 1910, Portlock, near Graaff-Reinet. *To John X Merriman*: 'It is sad—but not strange—that almost every attempt at legislation during the last session has {been} in the direction of retrogression. The attempt to make legal marriage impossible between coloured & white, is but a small indication of the tide that has set in.' (*OSLO*/NLSA)

23 December 1910, Portlock. *To Isie Smuts*: 'I am up here among these high mountain tops {...} The cool air after the terrible heat of de Aar soon revived me, & I am much better. For the first time for more than a year I've been able to get to my writing again really which is a great comfort. {...} I still have a dream of someday being able to finish my novel & buy a little farm up in the mountains where we {she and her husband} could live together—but I guess it's only a dream.' (*OSLO*/NASA)

1911

31 January 1911, Oudeberg, near Graaff-Reinet. *To Edward Carpenter*: 'I'm working a bit at my book. If ever I should finish it perhaps I'll bring it home

to England myself to publish but I don't think I ever shall finish it—but I mean to try to the end. {...}

'I'm full of thought about that invention of his {Bob Muirhead's, a mutual friend and correspondent}. I hope it's something to do with "wings". I've hungered for wings ever since I could desire anything. One day they will discover a way of condensing force in some convenient way, & you'll fasten the container onto your back between your shoulders & then spread two beautiful butterfly wings on each side—& away you'll fly. I've always known people must fly, some day, just as there must be perfect love & fellowship on earth sometime. Our dreams are prophetic because we are part of life.' (*OSLO*/SCL)

28 April 1911, De Aar. *To Edward Carpenter*: 'No I like my long sentences—when they come! There are things you want to present short off & blunt; and there are other things {that} don't present themselves to your mind so. {...} It's the way things come to you that is their spirit. If they came in a different shape they'd be different things!

'{...} I've been having the most blissful joy reading Gilbert Murray's translations of Euripides' plays. They are glorious. For the last 20 years all the books that have given me the most pleasure are the translations of Greek & Latin writers. Jowet's Plato & all the prose writers one has been able to get at, but Gilbert Murray is the only man who has made Greek poetry live in English. I like Euripides more even if be possible than our sweet Will Shakespeare{,} he seems closer to me—but it's ill judging between the dear Gods—they each sit on their own throne with a crown of eternal glory on their heads.

'Edward, do you hate Well's books as much as I do? The note of that type of modern book is that the writers seem to have lost all sense of the existence of such a thing as loyalty—even to oneself!' (*OSLO*/SCL; Murray's translations included *Andromache* (1900), *Fabulae* in 3 volumes in (1901, 1904, and 1910), *Hippolytus* (1902), *The Bacchae* (1902), *The Trojan Women* (1905), *Electra* (1905), and *Medea* (1910); the prolific science fiction and realist writer, H. G. Wells, had published ten novels by this time; for Jowett, see letter to Isaline Philpot, n.d. August 1887)

18 May 1911, De Aar. *To Mary Drew*: 'I shall some day publish those articles in book form but I've two large novels I want to revise before I march. It seems to me they ought to come first, but months & months pass when I can't put pen to paper, & even writing a note is difficult for me sometimes.' (*OSLO*/BL)

12 December 1911, Cape Town. *To Havelock Ellis*: 'There is my friend {...} who thinks it's wrong for people even if married to have any sex relations

with each other except just when they want to make a child. She says her husband feels just the same! I would base all my sex teaching to children & young people on the beauty & sacredness & importants {i.e. importance} of sex—sex intercourse is the great sacrement {i.e. sacrament} of life—he that eateth & drinketh unworthily eateth & drinketh damnation to himself, but it may be the most beautiful sacrement between two souls without any thought of children{,} I feel. (*OSLO*/HRC; the biblical quotation comes from 1 Corinthians 11:29, and continues with a reference to the importance of 'discerning the Lord's body')

1912

20 January 1912, Milnerton, near Cape Town *To Will Schreiner*: 'Oh laddie it {is} hard not to be able to work when I think of how much I could do for others, not only for myself{,} if I could finish some of my work. A stab goes through my heart whenever I look at my great portmanteau of unfinished work. {...} It's not sudden death we have to fear, that's beautiful—it's the many years of struggling to work when the power is gone, to feel you are no more of any use in the world.' (*OSLO*/UCT)

25 April 1912, De Aar. To Minnie Murray: 'It is not by hanging around members of Parliament sending petitions, & begging for the vote - but by labouring to rouse & enlighten ourselves & to fit ourselves for using it, that it seems to me we shall be best doing our work in S.A. today. {...} What we want today is an evangelist movement, rousing & touching the women of S.A.{,} not a mere little political movement centering round the parliament house in C. Town. When the mass, or even a very large mass of women & men in S.A. feel it is right that women should have their share in guiding the state, & that is wrong & an injustice injuring the nation to withhold it from {them,} the politicians will move at once.

'The most important point of all is how we are educating & influencing our young girls, who in ten years' time will be the women of S.A. guiding its destinies—teaching them to be brave, to fear nothing; to desire freedom for themselves & all other women on Earth:—trying to make them feel they have a duty to themselves & also to the world at large.' (*OSLO*/NLSA)

n.d. May 1912, De Aar. *To Havelock Ellis*: 'My father was infinitely tenderer to us as children and had a much greater heart than my mother. A woman loves her own little babies with a selfish animal instinct, but as children grow up it is continually the father who gives the widest, most sympathetic love. And as for other people's children, are not the words step-mother and mother-in-law the two bitterest words in the world? Who farm little babies and starve them to death? Women in most cases and not men. Who keep brothels and betray young children and girls into a life which means disease and generally early death, without motherhood or wifehood or love? Women! [...] I don't for one moment believe in the moral superiority of women.' (*Letters*, 307)

7 August 1912, De Aar. *To Havelock Ellis*: 'I got the *Freewoman*. I think it ought to be called the *Licentious Male*. Almost all the articles are by men and not by women, and the whole tone is unlike even the most licentious females or prostitute. It is the tone of the brutal self-indulgent selfish male. There is something that makes one sick, as if one were on board a ship. It's unclean. And sex is so beautiful! It can be discussed scientifically, just as simply and straightly as one discusses the use and function of the eye and stomach, the latter with its wonderful function of turning organic and inorganic matter into flesh, bones, nerves, and muscles. One can discuss it philosophically, noting the yet wholly mysterious and marvellous place it holds in the life of the globe. You can talk of it from the poetic standpoint, as Shelley, Keats, Euripides, and all lofty souls see it, and it is divine. {...} The difficulty seems to me, with a thing so beautiful, wonderful, mighty, all-pervading, a thing so bound up with the deepest and noblest emotions of our nature, to talk of it in any way that is not noble, or at least clean and rational: but the *Freewoman* and the *New Age* make it coarse and repulsive every time they touch it. To say that the *Freewoman* is the expression of all we are going to fight for is a lie. It is the expression of exactly that which we are going to fight against, that we may free ourselves and the world from that brutality and selfishness that degrades and tarnishes the divinity of sex.' (*Letters*, 313)

11 August 1912, De Aar. To John X Merriman: 'No, I do not take a sorrowful view of life generally; nor above all of the condition of the world at the present day. {...} The clear minded impartial looker on knows perfectly well, or ought to, when things in his country or any other (of which he has intimate knowledge) are going, from his standpoint{,} forwards or backwards. Sometimes of course the backward movement is permanent, & means death. This was the case when the Roman Empire decayed; when Greece in third century & second century began to fail. Far seeing souls did then see the decay, & did see all it meant; & were surely sorrowful. But there are smaller waves of backward movement & of forward. In 1880 when I went to England a strong (from my standpoint) forward movement was setting in. It continued till (roughly speaking) about '89 {or} '88. Then we who there were working in the heart of things, felt a change becoming to come; subtle, but wide, & unmistakable. We all felt it. In 1890 when I left England to visit South Africa, {...} {t}here was from the liberal & advanced stand point a distinct & vast back-wash setting in: & it was to go on till it

produced the Jameson Raid & the Boer War. When I went back to England {...} things had reached a much lower level than when I left in 1890. A dead pall rested over the whole life of the people—it was ghastly! The upper class—'society'—under the growing influence of the then Prince of Wales, Edward, was becoming rotten to its core. {...}

'The "nonconformist conscience" that Rhodes so hated & feared was dieing {i.e. dying} in the middle classes, a passion for dress, luxury & gain was eating it up. The saddest of all to me was the change among my own section{,} the working classes & democratic organizations. The noble impersonal enthusiasm which had played such a large part among us in the early '80s was dead or at least torpid. A lifeless striving after gain for themselves had taken its place. {...} The whole press almost was in the hands of the capitalists—because they represented the spirit of the nation. Literature was dying{.} In place of the giants who were passing{,} William Morris, Browning, Tennyson, Huxley, Darwin, we had our idol Rudyard Kippling—& he gave voice to the soul of the people when he thirsted for a land—

> "Where the best is like the worst,
> And there ain't no ten commandments,
> And a man can slake his thirst!"

'{...} You say, I am needlessly depressed when I say I perceive a steady downward & backward movement in South Africa, which it seems to me, must go on for twelve, fifteen, or even twenty years; & you say, "Things are never so bad as they seem." Not only are they sometimes as bad, but they are sometimes much worse!

'We, who between 1888 & 1890, felt the great backward wave creeping over us in England, knew that many & evil days were coming; but even in our most farseeing moments did we never picture anything so morally shameful & nationally degrading as the wave of greed & Imperial lust that was to sweep over England, {...} to end with the connivance of Rhodes, Chamberlain & Edward the 7th in the Boer war; which all but brought England onto her knees. It is true that in the last years England has been rudely awakened again; & is now moving forward slowly—but evil bears fruits which long poison the soil on which it falls.

'{...}We are narrowing our social & political rights—we are trying to withdraw even educating advantages from the mass of our people, who are our natives. In our defence force we are going to tax the nation to inaugurate a vast power for evil & blood shed, & civil war; which will begin with the native but not end there. When we have had our big native wars & dispossessed the native of his land, we may get cheap labour for the mine owner & the farmer, but we shall have created such a terrible proletariat as will be our ultimate undoing. {...} The mere fact that our politicians have been able to give themselves incomes of three & four thousand a year in a poor country like South Africa {...} & {that} the nation has taken these things sitting down, shows to me the direction in which we are moving.' (*OSLO*/NLSA; Kipling's poem 'Mandalay' is in his 1892 volume, *Barrack-Room Ballads and Other Verses*)

5 October 1912, De Aar. *To Alice Greene:* '{Regarding} manly & womanly qualities {...} I know of none such. (Have any men on earth ever shown more courage than the often little frail women who are enduring the horrors of imprisonment & forced feeding in battling for their ideal? As a powerful man said to me last week "There isn't a social reform on earth for which I would go through what those women are going through.")

'{...}The Baby-farmers, procurers, step mothers, & women slave owners are just as cruel, & false & cowardly as men. What are the manly qualities & the womanly apart from early training in the home? (*OSLO*/UCT; the reference to 'women battling for their ideal' is to their campaign for the abolition of discriminatory passes in South Africa)

1913

March 1913, Muizenberg. *To Emily Hobhouse*: 'It isn't the pain and weakness one minds, it's the not being able to work. My one novel especially I would have liked so to finish. I feel that if only one lonely struggling woman read it and found strength and comfort from it one would not feel one had lived quite in vain. I seem to have done so little with my life.' (*Letters*, 321)

13 April 1913, De Aar. *To* Caroline Augusta *Rhys Davids*: 'The reading of Gilbert Murray's translations of Euripides lately has been a revelation of joy to me. The wonderful thing to me is that any man could have written of women as he does. But genius has no limit of sex or race. It's curious to sit here in this little house in the karroo veld and feel that perhaps the thing nearest to you in the world is the brain of that old Greek dead now these two thousand years. We who can't read Greek should be so grateful to Gilbert Murray for giving him to us. I'm so glad I didn't die before I had him.

'{...} Such works as Wells's *New Machiavelli* illustrate the ghastly condition which arises where the old laws of relation between the sexes are broken down and a high code of perfect Truth, openness and loyalty in all sex relations has not taken its place. But one need not grieve that one's own little world has been lost, because such a law is writing, and will and must write, itself in the hearts of the noblest men and women and spread slowly from them to others.' (*Letters*, 323–4; H. G. Wells's *The New Machiavelli* was published in 1911)

25 April 1913, De Aar. *To James Henderson*: 'I fear my day dream of visiting Lovedale will not soon be realize{d}. To me the solution of your native question is Education, Education, Education! {...} There are some points touching the education of native women on which I should much like to have your opinion, but am not now able to write.' (*OSLO* New Letters/CL)

12 September 1913, De Aar. *To Will Schreiner*: 'What I propose is this{.} I have an MS. The Prelude of my big novel. I have been offered £300 for it & refused it because I always have had a hope I might be able to get better & finish my novel. But it's quite complete in itself. If I die there will be a boom in me & my writings for a little time as there always is, & you will get more than £300 for it. Will you let me send it to you, you drawing up a little business like document saying I have given it to you, to be published after my death. But that if before my death I am able to return the £200 & want it to print with my novel you will return it me. If after my death it fetches more than £200 divide the money{,} give the money for a little scholarship for girls at the South African College, a prize for the best essay on English literature for example. Will you let me have the £200 on these terms. I shall not want all the money at once{,} you can give me £50 when I sail in December; & send the rest when you hear from me that I've got safely over the voyage.

'Oct 15th. 1913

'Dear I began this letter a month ago, but I have not sent it because I've been so ill it has seemed impossible to me I should ever need the money. {...}My lungs are completely broken down & hardened by the #life-long asthma. The doctors here say I am not breathing with my left lung at all, & only with part of my right. Through these lungs the heart has to force the blood & I don't see how anything can really be done. If I had a place in Africa that suited me {...} I would just stay on quietly here in Africa & wait for the end, but I have no where to go. I have never recovered from my last year's stay at Muizenberg. My lungs have been much worse ever since. I feel I #must go to Europe{,} especially if the end is coming because there are nursing homes & places where I can stay & trouble no one. I don't see what is to become of me in this country.' (*OSLO*/UCT)

1914

15 January 1914, Alassio. *To Havelock Ellis*: I haven't written because I've been six days in bed. Those terrible internal pains came on suddenly as never before. I sent for an Italian doctor here; he said it was stone in the kidneys. For two days nothing but blood, due to the edges of the stone, he said, tearing the walls. {...} He was afraid of the heart failing and so would not give me the large doses of opium the Cape Town doctors gave me. (*Letters*, 329)

16 March 1914, Florence. *To Havelock Ellis*: 'I cling to the thought of Nauheim as my last hope. If I can't get better and work I would so much rather die. The terrible thing is that I may not, and may live on year after year to be a burden to others. I can't even read or write a letter without exhaustion any more.' (*Letters*, 332)

15 June 1914, Bad Nauheim. *To Cron Cronwright-Schreiner*: 'We went first to see Goethe's old house where his father and mother lived to the end. {...} You know it brought back all my own youth in such a strange way, the time when I was a little governess & Goethe was more to me than any writer except Mill, & how I used to long to see that house & dream of it. It's just as I pictured it.' (*OSLO*/NLSA; dated 26 June 1914 in *Letters*, 335)

21 August 1914, London. *To Havelock Ellis*: 'To me this is the most sordid war in which England has ever engaged. She is backing Russia, not because she loves Russia but because millions of her money are invested there, and millions more in France, whose money system will break if the Russian autocracy falls. She fights Germany, not to set the Germans free from military rule, but because she is her trade rival whom she must crush.' (*Letters*, 338)

13 October 1914, London. *To Havelock Ellis*: 'War is Hell. Though people like the English who have always made it in other peoples' countries have never realised [it]. It's when it comes to your own land that its full horror bursts on you.' (*Letters*, 340)

13 October 1914, London. *To Edward Carpenter*: '{PS} I wish I could feel with you that this war is going to bring the #Kingdom of heaven. I feel it is the beginning of a half a century of the most awful wars the world has seen. First this—then another war of probably England & Germany against Russia, then as the years pass with India, Japan & China & the native races of Africa. While the desire to dominate, & rule & possess #Empire is in the hearts of men there will always be war.' (*OSLO*/NELM; see *Letters* 340–1, which dates this letter 'October' and places it after 16 October)

16 October 1914, London. *To Havelock Ellis*: 'Yesterday at Durrants Hotel a boy brought a note. It ran: "Madam, When Mrs. Smith took the room for you she did not mention that your name was Schreiner. As we find that is either an Austrian or a German name you will please leave our Hotel at once." Of course I took a taxi and my things and left at once.' (*Letters*, 340)

n.d. November 1914, London. *To Samuel Cronwright-Schreiner*: 'I have never before in my life been so lonely. Sometimes I don't seem to be alive at all, but only creping {i.e. creeping} about in a ghastly dream. No one wants me. #I've no relation with life or thought in England or Africa or anywhere else. What I do feel a little hard is that people should now turn on me—twenty five years ago when I wrote "The Sunlight Lay Across My Bed" they all (my friends) approved & admired it. I am only holding the same views now! Hell & Heaven are exactly to me what they were then. Rhodes understood it perhaps better than other people: he told a man he hated it more than anything he'd ever read! (*OSLO*/NLSA)

13 December 1914, London. *To Havelock Ellis*: 'Oh Havelock I do hope so this is my last year. I don't know why I am writing so to you, life is sad enough for you. You know I could bear all in my personal life; if it wasn't for this terrible exhibition of what humanity is. It isn't ever the fighting & the hating, it's the lying. There is no truth on earth. I have always loved humanity & believed in it: now a great cry comes into my heart, why doesn't God take up a sponge & mop us all up & squeeze us into space.' (*OSLO*/HRC; letter dated 14 December in *Letters*, 344–5)

1915

n.d. 1915, London. *To Emily Hobhouse*: 'If the Imperialists were severely [?beaten] in German West and in Egypt peace would probably come very soon, but as this is most unlikely to happen, it won't. I don't think that feebly gushing over the war does any good. To combine, as the Labour Party under Keir Hardie and some Social Democrats are doing in Germany, to protest against the action of their own government, is immense good. If women could combine—which they won't—in their millions to defeat the politicians of their own country at the next elections, and to prevent their husbands and sons from enlisting, that would do good, and anything one individual ever does to diminish this hideous nation-hatred does do good.' (*Letters*, 347)

n.d. March, 1915, London. *To Emily Hobhouse*: 'If war is ever to be stopped on earth it will be only by the passing away of the ideals of empire, national supremacy, and the search after national wealth as the first object in life.' (*Letters*, 347–8)

23 April 1915, London. *To Samuel Cron Cronwright-Schreiner*: '(When I was coming out {of a Beethoven concert at Queen's Hall} two fine looking young men were walking beside me who had been to the Concert & they were talking Cape Dutch. I turned to them & said in Cape Dutch, "I suppose you are students from the Cape? I am from the Cape too." They said very politely "No, we are Belgians." I said in Dutch, "You must excuse me, but the language you were talking was exactly African Taal". They said, "Oh, yes, they are quite the same!")' (*OSLO*/NLSA)

n.d.?1915, London. *To Adela Villiers Smith*: 'No, the only feeling I have about my life is that I have thrown it all away, done nothing with it. I have only two excuses, that I started with everything against me, and that I have always done at the time what I felt to be the right thing. But I doubt me whether I have been right; I have always felt, do the nearest duty first; so one sacrifices all the larger ends. (*Letters*, 348)

1916

22 March 1916, London. *To Havelock Ellis* (postcard): 'I had to get the doctor in the night the other day. He injected morphine & strycnine {i.e. strychnine}, which gave relief, says it's neuralgia of the heart.' (*OSLO*/HRC)

4 July 1916, Llandrindod Wells. To Havelock Ellis: 'Did you get my letters asking you about destroying all my letters. {...}

'The curse of Hintonism is that its false; that it doesn't look the facts of human nature in the face. That it makes out you can freely & recklessly play with the gratification of sex instinct—it's like teaching a child you can strike matches & throw them down just werever {i.e. wherever} you think good. Advance on the matter of sex means in the future more & more a sense of the awful importance of sex feeling; & the need for its absolute control by the higher centres of the mind, the reason, sense of duty. {...} 'I am a little better, but only able to live while I am lying down flat with my feet higher than my head; as soon as I sit up all vitality goes. The doctors say it {is} because my heart is too weak to pump the blood up to my head when I'm upright.' (*OSLO*/HRC)

5 October 1916, London. *To Georgiana Solomon*: 'I have not read Platje's book but will get it from Mundie's. You know I am a pacifist, & from what I hear he advocates the natives coming over here to help kill. I think it the greatest mistake.' (*OSLO*/NLSA; the references are to Sol T. Plaatje's *Native Life in South Africa*, 1916, and to Mudie's Lending Library and Subscription Library)

1917

29 March 1917, London. *To Will Schreiner*: 'I am completely broken down{,} the stone in the kidney being even worse than the heart. I was just feeling at the worst of everything when my landlady came in & said she would want my room at the end of the week. I just felt in despair as I am too ill to go about looking for rooms. But my doctor told me of a place where on her recommendation they would take me. They are too expensive for me to keep but I shall go in there on Monday, till I am well enough to look about. With a German name it is practically impossible to get rooms.' (*OSLO*/UCT)

n.d. May 1917, London. *To Georgina Solomon*: 'I know you {...} won't forget me if at any time you should hear of rooms anywhere {...} high up in Hampstead but near a bus. I seem choaking {i.e. choking} down here in the fog. One large bedroom would be enough if I couldn't get a sitting rom {i.e. room}. The bedroom is the only thing that matters to me. I could climb to the second floor, but not higher.

'{PS} Poor Platje looked so tired!' (*OSLO*/UCT)

n.d. August 1917, London. *To Will Schreiner*: 'I know of course you won't agree at all with this {...} view in this little allegory—but I'd like to know if you don't think the word wae even if of my own invention! is good where it stands! Of course I can't publish anything now. I just write them.

'{...}I tried to get through to you on the telephone the night of the great raid but couldn't. But I knew from the sound the bombs were not down your way. I am not afraid at all for myself. Life has become for me so much unbroken physical anguish, that I have no fear of the great stranger. If I could really work, I would not mind anything—but I am broken. I'm no good to any one any more.' (*OSLO*/UCT; for the word 'wae', see her allegory, 'Who Knocks at the Door', first published in *Fortnightly Review*, 1917, and then in *Stories, Dreams and Allegories*, 1923: 'my heart was *wae* for the great desolation I had seen—that men with their own hands should tear down that which with so much toil they had reared')

n.d. August 1917, London. *To Will Schreiner*: 'I am trying to write a little book called "the Dawn of Civilization" "Stray Thoughts on Peace & War {...} homely personal confession of a believer in Human Unity." Rather a long name! But I am seldom well enough to do anything. If I should not finish it I wish the part that is written to be published.' (*OSLO*/UCT; a section of the 'little book' was published posthumously, in *Nation and Athenaeum*, 1921)

2 December 1917, London. *To Betty Molteno* (postcard): 'I went yesterday with a deputation to the House of Parliament about the Indian woman's franchise. A kind woman helped me up the stairs.' (*OSLO*/UCT; the Women's Indian Association, founded in Madras in 1917, demanded equal rights for women, including the franchise and access to education)

1918

n.d. 1918, London. *To Will Schreiner*: 'I am sending you with this the introduction, a Prelude {to} a little book I've been trying to write, but no doubt will never be well enough to finish. I know you won't agree with my out look in the Preface & Prelude, think it foolish & sentimental. But I'll want you to understand a little how I feel. Don't criticise & discuss it, because I know you won't like it. But I should like you to tell me if it seems uninteresting {to} you. One may dislike a thing very much & yet not finding it uninteresting. The book if ever it were published I think you would find interesting, however little you agreed with it.' (*OSLO*/UCT; the Preface is not extant)

n.d. 1918, London. *To Adela Villiers Smith*: 'Would you, some time, tell me something: when you read that little "Prelude" to my book I showed you the other day, did you think it was a made up thing, like an allegory, or did you think it was real about myself? Please tell me, because if I haven't made it clear, I must. I thought it was quite clear, but the only other person to whom I've shown it didn't understand.' (*Letters*, 358)

19 October 1918, London. *To Havelock Ellis*: 'I've been very ill. That's why I've not written. Three weeks ago I thought the end had come. I've had two doctors & been X rayed four times {…}. The doctors have done nothing for me, there seems nothing to do{.} The pictures show that I had had thysis {i.e. phthisis} tuberculosis some years ago when I was a young girl, there are big holes in the lungs that have got healed up. It must have been when I was a young young girl & broke that blood vessel, I have always had a pain under my shoulder. The{y} say every organ in my body is misplaced by the lifelong asthma. My heart is twice the size & the point two full inches from where it ought to {be} & the blood flows back into it with each beat through the defective valves. I have "arteroid sclerosis" of the blood vessels, & a floating kidney which presses against the colon & I have a stone in the kidney; & my stomach is very much enlarged & quite misplaced because the diaphragm has broken down, but {…} the most serious thing is the enlargement of a gland in the middle of the chest; it is this which gives me such agony now & prevents my eating. I used to have {an} attack of angina once in several weeks or even months, but in the last 9 weeks, I have continual attacks all day, whenever I move or try to eat, & even in the middle of the night I wake up in the midst of an attack. They don't of course think I can be cured {…}.

'{…} I've read Jane Austin again & again & Pickwick Paper{s}, & George Eliot and {Sir Walter} Scott, it's no use my reading them any more. I often read the bible, the language is so beautiful, but it's very depressing, all the horrors & tortures of the old Jewish tribal life. Have we got much further today? {…}

'{PS} I haven't told my Husband or my brother how bad I am as I don't want them to be troubled. {…} I've told you. Because I fear you may misunderstand my not writing.' (*OSLO*/HRC; the term 'tuberculosis' came into being as a synonym for 'phthisis' around the 1840s; OS refers at other times to Jane Austen and Sir Walter Scott, but not to particular novels; Charles Dickens's *The Posthumous Papers of the Pickwick Club,* a.k.a. *The Pickwick Papers*, 1837, appears to have been a favourite)

1919

26 January 1919, London. *To Cron Cronwright-Schreiner*: 'When I sit here alone in the dark day after day, I know more & more & more certainly that nothing matters much in life but love and a great pity for all our fellows. We in this world full of agony & torture & wrong have to bring into being the only God we shall ever know, by love and pity. It is so terrible to be human creatures, the universe is so awful, we must make it beautiful. It's ten days since I've spoken to any one except the girl who brings up my coals & water; & now I can't ride of {i.e. on} the tops of omnibuses any more, my life is so walled in. One comes so dead face to face with the deep facts of existence.' (*OSLO*/NLSA)

n.d. late 1919, London. *To Adela Villiers Smith*: 'Just fancy, to-day I got an invitation to a dance! The first invitation to a dance I have ever had in my life. I have never even seen a dance, or been in a ballroom. All the dancing I've seen has been that of naked Kaffirs, which was splendid though terrible, the real war dances, and Boers leaping about in their heavy boots. All the dancing I've done has been alone in the veld, when I've jumped in the air and thrown up my arms and shouted with the mere joy of living.' (*Letters*, 364)

n.d. late 1919, London. *To Havelock Ellis*: I've been reading a new book [*Night and Day*, by Virginia Woolf] they say is like Jane Austen. It's no more like Jane Austen than {SCCS deletes the name}. All that glorious simplicity and directness of language and effect, which is in all great works of art, seem always wanting in twentieth century art. You laugh at my reading Dickens? Well, just that one description of the old inn in *Barnaby Rudge*: one sees the inn, smells it, knows it, one could go up to the north of London to look for it, feeling so sure it does exist—that's art. Dickens was not an intellectual man, not an educated man in the bookish sense—but an artist: so his work will live. When the whole of our middle-class life as lived today, when all London slums and their poverty and sorrows have passed away, men will still find them in Dickens's work. He never painted a lady or a gentleman—he couldn't, but he painted much more important things. The world is full of great men of genius and ability now. A greater genius than Lenin has not appeared in these last hundred years—unless it was Karl Marx. And the ability of the age goes into science, into medicine, chemistry, etc; art and fine writing are in this age secondary. {...} When Rome was burning, Nero was fiddling.' (*Letters*, 363; *OSLO*'s reproduction of this letter excludes SCCS's reference to Woolf's *Night and Day*, which was published on 20 October 1919; Charles Dickens's *Barnaby Rudge* was first published in serial form in 1840-41 and then in book form in 1841)

December 1919, London. *To Havelock Ellis*: 'We are a race of devils—shooting the Indians, starving the Russians and Germans, trying to crush the Irish—and so pleased with ourselves! If the Germans had done in Alsace what we have done in India we should all rise up with a howl.' (*Letters*, 365–6)

1920

10 November, Wynberg. *To Betty Molteno*: 'The strike {of municipal workers} was to have taken place in Port Elizabeth tomorrow but I think the natives will drop it. The right to strike is only a white man's privilege in this country: they will only be shot down if they strike. {…}

'I don't know whether you'll be able to live in this country dear. If I could still walk even as much as I could when I left Africa, I would be quite happy here; but shut up absolutely without the means of getting out{,} life is a stiff order. In England one had the buses, & one had books & newspapers. I have never seen a magazine since I came here. I have subscribed to the library, but can get none. {…} It's so terrible in this supreme hour of the fate of the human race on earth, never to know what is going on in the world of human life. {…}

'It would be supremely interesting to be in South Africa now if one could travel about & *really* learn to know what the natives are feeling & thinking. I wish I could go to Basutoland & Kaffir land.' (*OSLO*/UCT)

Recipients of letters

John Brown (1842-1929) was a Scottish medical doctor, and for a time worked as the district surgeon in Fraserburg, where Olive Schreiner met him and his wife Mary Brown (see below) in 1873. They encouraged Schreiner to publish *The Story of an African Farm* as well as to pursue a medical training (this was short-lived because of her ill-health). Schreiner's friendship with them continued through her life, sometimes involving personal visits, and she corresponded with them sometimes as a couple, sometimes singly, although mostly with Mary.

Mary Brown, née Solomon (1847–1935), the niece of the Cape parliamentarian, Saul Solomon, was active in social and charity work in England, and in South Africa was involved with the Women's Christian Temperance Union, the Women's Enfranchisement League, and the National Council of Women. Schreiner dedicated the second edition of *The Story of an African Farm* to her, and regarded both her and her husband, John Brown, as among her dearest friends.

Edward Carpenter (1844–1929) was a British writer, anthologist, socialist and New Age philosopher and pioneering gay rights activist. Schreiner met him through Havelock Ellis (all three were members of the Fellowship of the New Life) and sometimes stayed with him at his co-operative farm in Millthorpe, near Sheffield. Carpenter published, among many other books, *Love's Coming of Age* (1886) and *Angels' Wings: A Series of Essays on Art and its Relation to Life* (1898).

Erilda Louisa Elizabeth Cawood, née Buckley (1842-1903) lived with her husband and family on the farm Ganna Hoek in the Cradock district. During the 1870s Schreiner often visited there from the next-door farm where she was a governess. Her friendship with Erilda was almost fatally threatened by the latter's reaction to *African Farm*. Later, Erilda introduced Schreiner to Samuel Cron Cronwright.

Samuel Cron Cronwright-Schreiner (1863–1936) was Olive Schreiner's (unofficially estranged) husband. Because Schreiner's asthmatic condition worsened in certain Karoo areas, he sold his farm after their marriage and entered business and legal practice, also working with Schreiner politically and on some writing projects. In 1902 he was elected to the Cape legislative assembly, and remained a member until the formation of the Union of South Africa in 1910. After Schreiner's death he produced *The Life of Olive Schreiner* and *The Letters of Olive Schreiner*, as well as editing several of her writings. He adopted her name on marriage, but later returned to his own: his father, born Samuel Cron Wright, had formally changed the family's name to Cronwright in 1884 (the year Cron turned 21).

Caroline Augusta Rhys Davids, née Foley (1857–1942) was a British scholar and translator. In 1894 she married Thomas Rhys Davids, a prominent Pali scholar, and founder of the Pali Text Society. She studied at University College, London; held a lectureship at the University of Manchester; served as president of the Pali Text Society, and published widely on Buddhism. She dedicated to Schreiner her *Psalms of the Early Buddhists* (1909), translated from Pali. She was also active in reform causes involving children's welfare, women's suffrage, and the alleviation of poverty.

Mary Drew, née Gladstone (1847–1927) was a British writer, political secretary and an active feminist, and opposed to the Anglo-Boer War (1899–1902). Her father was the British Prime Minister, William Gladstone. It is not clear when and how often Schreiner met her but they corresponded on political and religious matters, and exchanged some of their writings.

Henry Havelock Ellis (1859–1939) was a British physician and sexologist, and author of the multi-volume *Studies in the Psychology of Sex* (1897–1910), among many other influential scientific studies. He and Schreiner met in 1884 after Ellis wrote to her praising *The Story of an African Farm*.

He was the secretary of the Progressive Association, and a leading member of the Fellowship of the New Life, and Schreiner's most important, regular, and long-term correspondent as well as a close friend (given the intimacy and intensity of their letters critics speculate on the nature of that closeness). While Schreiner was in South Africa, Ellis acted as her informal agent with publishers, and continued in this role with Cronwright-Schreiner after Schreiner's death.

Richard Garnett (1835–1906) was an influential librarian at the British Museum from 1851 to 1890, and a prolific writer, editor and translator; in 1888, for example, he published a collection of short stories, *The Twilight of the Gods*, and *The Life of Ralph Waldo Emerson*. Schreiner's slight correspondence with him was occasioned primarily by his gifts of books and pamphlets.

Alice Matilda Greene (1858–1920) was a British schoolteacher who took up a position at the Collegiate School for Girls at Port Elizabeth from 1887 to 1890, where she met Betty Molteno and became her life partner. Schreiner met the couple in the early 1890s, and they visited one another periodically, both in the Cape and when they lived in England. See Elizabeth (Betty) Molteno, below.

Frank Harris, né James Thomas Harris (1856–1931) was a British journalist and editor of the literary *Fortnightly Review* from 1886 to 1894, and it is in this capacity that he and Schreiner occasionally corresponded. He later became notorious as the author of *My Life and Loves* (1931).

Rev. Dr. James Henderson (1867–1930) was principal of Lovedale Missionary Institution from 1906 to 1930, a non-sectarian and non-denominational theological seminary and school, founded in 1841 by the Glasgow Missionary Society to promote higher education for Africans.

Emily Hobhouse (1860–1926) was a British social reformer and social welfare worker, who became known to Schreiner through her protest against the Anglo–Boer War (1899–1902) and her active engagement with its victims, particularly in the concentration camps established by the British. She published *The Brunt of the War: And Where It Fell* (1902) and *War Without Glamour: Women's War Experiences Written by Themselves 1899–1902* (1924).

Philip Kent (1841–1901) was a British literary reviewer and translator. Schreiner wrote to thank him in February 1883 for his review of *The Story of an African Farm*, and there followed occasional correspondence about publishing and other literary matters, Schreiner sometimes seeking his advice.

Lady Constance Lytton (1869–1923) was a leading militant suffragist and cousin to Adela Villiers (later Smith; see below). Schreiner met her in the early 1890s during her visit to the Cape and continued their friendship through correspondence, dedicating *Woman and Labour* to her in 1911.

John Xavier Merriman (1841–1926) was the last Prime Minister of the Cape Colony (1908–1910) before the formation of the Union of South Africa. Schreiner's correspondence with him started in 1896, after he had been forced out of his cabinet position in Cecil John Rhodes' government on account of his opposition to Rhodes, and continued until 1913, when he failed to vote against the 1913 Natives Land Act.

Elizabeth (Betty) Molteno (1852–1927) was the daughter of Sir John Molteno, Prime Minister of the Cape Colony (1872–1878), the sister of Caroline (married name: Murray; see below), and one of Olive Schreiner's closest friends. Their prolific correspondence dates from early 1891, after their first meeting in the Cape. She was the headmistress of the Girls Collegiate School in Port Elizabeth from 1890 to 1899, and active thereafter in Cape Town (with her partner Alice Greene; see above) assisting Boer women and children in British concentrations camps, as well as in anti-racist political activism. She and Alice contributed to the collection of anti-imperial and anti-war poems, *Songs of the Veld* (1902), initially banned in South Africa. Schreiner made some use of her London flat at 9 Porchester Place from 1917 to 1920.

Robert (Bob) Franklin Muirhead (1860–1941) was a British mathematics teacher active in the Glasgow Socialist League and a friend and colleague of Edward Carpenter's whom Schreiner met at Millthorpe. He and Schreiner became friends and corresponded from late 1888 to 1920.

Caroline Murray, née Molteno (1853–1937) was one of Sir John Molteno's daughters, and sister to Elizabeth (Betty) Molteno (see above). Their correspondence was occasional and fairly formal, and mostly had to do with the Women's Enfranchisement League.

Minnie Murry, née Parkes (1865–1929) lived with her husband, Haldane Murray, on their farm Portlock, near Graaff-Reinet, where Schreiner sometimes stayed. She set up a local branch of the Women's Enfranchisement League in the area, earning Schreiner's increasing respect although differences arose between them in relation to the racial franchise.

Sir Henry Wylie Norman (1858–4939) was a British journalist (later, a politician) whose review of *The Story of an African Farm* for the *Fortnightly Review* in 1883 was the only occasion for correspondence from Schreiner.

Karl Pearson (1857–1936), a British mathematician and pioneering statistician, was Professor of Applied Mathematics at University College London, from 1884. He and Schreiner met in 1885 at the Men and Women's Club in London, of which he was a founding member, thereafter becoming good friends and intellectual companions for a short time. He published the influential *The Ethic of Freethought* in 1888 and *Grammar of Science* in 1892.

Frederick (Fred) William Pethick-Lawrence (1871–1961) was married to the prominent British suffragist, Emmeline Pethick Lawrence (1867–1954); they shared names on marriage. Schreiner's correspondence was either to him alone or to them as a couple, and was precipitated by his ownership of the radical newspaper, *The Echo*, and its denunciation of the Anglo-Boer War. He was a campaigner for women's suffrage and a pacifist and, later, a British Labour politician.

Isaline Philpot, née Needham (1852–1925) lived with her husband Dr J H Philpot in London where Schreiner came to know them during the 1880s; the couple also became friends with Cronwright-Schreiner when he travelled in England protesting the advent of the Anglo-Boer War.

Anna Purcell, née Carnbier Faure (1870–1943) was married to William Frederick Purcell, an etymologist who held a senior position in the South African Museum in Cape Town, and lived on a rural estate called Bergvliet on the outskirts of Cape Town. She was engaged in relief work for Boer women and children during the 1899–1902 Anglo-Boer War and later in the Cape Women's Enfranchisement League. In 1909 she edited a set of extracts from *The Story of an African Farm* and *Dreams*, under the title Olive Schreiner's *Thoughts about Women*. After her husband's death in 1919 she lived until 1923 in London, where she typed the last seven chapters of *From Man to Man*, and re-typed the 1911 TS.

Mary Sauer, née Cloete (1863–1937) married the Cape politician Jacobus Wilhelmus Sauer in 1884 (he was later responsible for introducing to Parliament the 1913 Natives Land Act). She and Schreiner met in 1889 and became close friends; their letters are marked by an intimate and passionate intellectual and emotional engagement.

Henrietta (Ettie) Schreiner (1850–1912) was Olive's deeply religious sister. She married the Rhodesian mining engineer John Stakesby Lewis in October 1891 in London. From 1878 she devoted herself to the Templar temperance movement, becoming widely known in South Africa as a public speaker during the 1880s and 1890s and, later, as a social worker.

Frances (Fan) Hester Schreiner, née Reitz (1852–1931) was Olive Schreiner's sister-in-law. Her father was the progressive Cape farmer and politician F W Reitz, and her brother the President of the Orange Free State and then State Secretary of the Transvaal. She married Will Schreiner in 1884, later becoming an active member of the Cape Women's Enfranchisement League.

Catherine (Katie) Whitby Schreiner (1838–1898) was Olive's eldest sister. She married a trader, John Findlay, in 1860 (when Olive was five years old), later settling with him in Fraserburg.

Ursula Hester Schreiner (1892–1963) was the younger of two girls born to Will and Fan Schreiner. She worked as a nurse during the First World War, and in 1917 married (in London) Dr Ralph Lester Scott with whom she settled in Cape Town, and had four children. She was a pioneer of family planning in South Africa. In 1963 she donated a large collection of Schreiner material to the University of Cape Town Libraries.

William (Will) Philip Schreiner (1857–1919), Olive's younger, beloved brother (married to Frances Reitz), was appointed in 1893 as Cape attorney-general in Cecil Rhodes's second Ministry and became prime minister of the Cape Colony from 1898 to 1890. After returning to Parliament in 1909, he defended the non-racial Cape franchise and led a delegation consisting of African political leaders to London to protest the proposed racist South Africa Act. From 1915 to 1919 he served in London as South Africa's High Commissioner.

Adela Constance Smith, née Villiers (1872–1956), who married the British MP Sir Francis Smith in 1901, and was Constance Lytton's cousin, met and made friends with Schreiner during an extended visit to the Cape. She is referred to in Cronwright-Schreiner's *Letters* as Mrs Francis Smith, and in *OSLO* as Adela Villiers Smith. Only some of her letters are available in *OSLO*, since SCCS destroyed some of them after reproducing them in his *Letters*.

Alys Whitall Pearsall Smith (1867–1951) was a US Quaker who settled in England, later marrying Bertrand Russell in 1894. She and Schreiner met regularly in England in 1888 and 1889.

Sybella (Isie) Margaretha Smuts, née Krige (1870–1954) married Jan Smuts, prime minister of South Africa (1919–1924; 1939–1948) in 1897. Schreiner and she met some time before 1899, when their correspondence started, and became friends. She was an active member of the Suid-Afrikaanse Vrouefederasie (South African Women's Federation). Their friendship was strengthened over their common hatred of British imperialism, but began petering out with the increasing evidence of their differing attitudes to racial politics.

Julia Solly, née Muspratt (1862–1953) was a British feminist and pacifist who moved with her husband to Kimberley, where Schreiner lived from 1894 to 1898. She was an active member of the Women's Temperance Union and the Cape Women's Enfranchisement League. In 1913 she became a member of the National Council of Women and later one of its vice-presidents.

Georgiana Margaret Solomon, née Thomson (1844–1933), born in Scotland, became principal of the Good Hope Seminary for Girls in Cape Town in 1873 and, in 1874, married the South African politician Saul Solomon (1817–1892). She assisted in pro-Boer activities both during and after the Anglo-Boer war, also helping found the Suid-Afrikaanse Vrouefederasie (South African Women's Federation) in 1904, although at that time living permanently in England. In London she hosted various meetings involving black South Africans and their delegations, including Solomon Plaatje, whom Schreiner heard speak at her house in 1919.

William Thomas (W T) Stead (1849–1912), editor of the *Pall Mall Gazette* from 1880 to 1890, and subsequently of the *Review of Reviews* until his death, was an influential campaigner for social reform. Schreiner was drawn to him particularly on account of his series of essays entitled 'The Maiden Tribute of Modern Babylon' (1885) on the sexual exploitation of under-age girls, as well as his opposition to the Anglo-Boer War (1899–1902), although there were strong differences (e.g. his admiration of Cecil John Rhodes).

T. Fisher Unwin (1848–1935) gave his name to the London publishing house (established in 1882) that was responsible for publishing most of Schreiner's writing in the UK. Schreiner's correspondence with the publishing house was addressed to him personally, and was mostly to do with these publications, although Schreiner occasionally made requests for books or recommended others to him (writers, a translator or typist she was helping promote) . The letter included here is the only one to mention *From Man to Man*. Unwin published *Undine* after Schreiner's death, as well as *From Man to Man*; he also published Cronwright-Schreiner's two books on Schreiner, *The Life of Olive Schreiner* and *The Letters of Olive Schreiner*.

APPENDIX 3

THE PROJECTED ENDINGS

NEITHER of these projected endings can be taken as definitive. They were geared, to some degree, to their respective interlocutors. Moreover, what Schreiner told her husband was either invalidated by later plot developments or lacks the requisite revisions. The letter to Pearson was written even longer before she gave up work on the novel. Yet in various respects this ending seems truer to the spirit of her project, and fits well with another comment (albeit brief) that she made in a letter of 28 January 1889 to her long-term friend, the socialist and gay rights activist Edward Carpenter (in Appendix 2).

Olive Schreiner's Letter to Karl Pearson, 1886[1]

I think I have told you what the story is about often: two sisters grow up on an African farm; the elder reserved & self-contained with a passion for physiology, & Mill's *Logic*[2] as her particular companion. The younger [is] beautiful & sweet, with the clinging, where she loves, self-forgetful nature, incapable of enduring the anger of anyone who is near her, which forms the ideal wife in most men's minds. She becomes a prostitute, not through any evil, but through her sweet fresh objective nature, through her lovingness, & her non-power of opposing the human creatures who are near her. The men whom she comes into contact with, from the first who seduces her to the last who leaves her in London streets, are none of them depraved, they are more or less all of them 'good fellows' in different ways—the only misfortune is that they look upon a woman as a creature created entirely for their benefit. Her noble pure-hearted cousin when he proposes to her, & she tells him of her first lover, says quietly he cannot marry her: a man cannot have an impure wife, & leaves her. No one can blame him.

I make no comment throughout the book, I never speak in my own person, the characters simply act & you draw your own conclusions. Rebekah the intellectual sister marries, because she finds she has exhausted the farm, she wants to see a new life; she wants the new experience of marriage,

[1] The original is held at UCL; my source is the *OSLO* transcript, 11. 14–180, which I have lightly edited. For the remainder of the letter of 10 July 1886, see Appendix 2.

[2] Schreiner first read J. S. Mill's *A System of Logic* (1843) at Klein Ganna Hoek, see her journal entry 19 August 1875, and spoke highly of Mill to Betty Molteno, 24 May 1895 (both in Appendix 2).

why should she live all her life without knowing it?—she has a passionate admiration for the glorious strong cousin Frank.

At eighteen she marries him & goes to live at Cape Town. There is an account of her life there as shown in her diaries.[3] You vaguely see the agony she [is] enduring & the growth that is going on in her, but it is only in the last scene of the book that you have the full key to it. She grows harder & colder & deader to the outer world, more careful in the performance of her outward duties, but finding her life only in her tiny study with her books & her microscope, it is they alone which make the torture of union with an animal nature possible to her.

So far there is nothing in the book which the philistine need much object to: then near the middle of the book there comes on the scene, a man, a traveller from England who has come to the Cape to see his wife who is staying there. You feel that with her hunger for intellectual sympathy, with the fierce suppression of all her desires that has gone on all her life, it is impossible that this man should not become paramour to her. His nature is artistic in type, keen & analytical, properly intellectual, for the first time the woman meets a nature with which she can be alone, to which she has not to bend herself: I paint very shortly the growth of her feeling for him & the battle to hold it down.

Then there is a scene where she sits on the sea shore in Kalk Bay,[4] & he comes to her, & he tells her what she is to him. Then you have the two sides. His view—the right of the individual, the right each human being has to complete & perfect his life, not to have it crushed & warped. He tells her of his married life, why he has ceased to live with the woman who is his wife; he paints the agony that animal physical union was to him (I have sometimes wondered whether I have painted him as suffering more than a man would suffer under such circumstances, but I think not), & the death to his intellectual nature that contact with that placid low-typed nature was. Has society, have our fellow men, all our fellow men a right to say to us, 'Here is your life, your one life; take it, crush it, deform it; I demand it!'? He cries out in passion to the woman.

Then there is her view, she paints all the evil in marriage as it is, the uneven union, framed & held together for the purposes of material life of property, she shows that she feels its degradation & prostitution, then she says—that he is right to leave his wife, but she is not to leave her husband. However clearly we may see the abstract right & truth, there is always this—our duty to the human beings nearest us in our place & time & country. She says that she

[3] In the MS held at HRC, Rebekah's philosophical musings were put into diary form rather than the self-to-self dialogues of the later drafts of the novel.

[4] Between Muizenberg and Simon's Town on the Cape Peninsula.

is strong to live & work out her own life where she is, she can do it: if he could not, then he was right to leave, she knows she has strength to live on to the end. Then in a bitterness of agony & scorn, [upbraiding?][5] her with her weakness & clinging love for husband & children, he leaves her. He goes away from Cape Town & she thinks they will never meet again.

Then there is a scene, she is travelling in an ox waggon; they are 'outspanned' in the sun one hot afternoon; she sits alone looking out over the hills. Over her heart that strange impersonal peace comes that comes into our hearts when we contemplate nature. What does it all matter? All the wild longing that has been feeding on her heart fades away from her. Then comes the Nirvana-like quiet in which all the things of life slip away from her. Then a waggon passes & the driver of that waggon speaks to the driver of hers. Long after it has passed, she hears from the driver that the man she care[6] for was in it.

Then the wild mad waking up again of the human. They 'outspan' in the moonlight: the children go to sleep in the waggon, the driver & leader under it: she lies alone on the front box: on the opposite hill there is a fire burning, she knows what it is. And then she wants to go to him; she wants to go & creep in where he lies asleep, & creep up to his feet & put her face against them—just that, nothing more, while he lies asleep there. Oh, she wants to see him, to hear his voice; she is almost mad.

She beats her head against the waggon chest—she must go to him, she must go to him—he is so bitter against her! Then a horseman stops at the side of the waggon; it is he. He has heard too from his driver who is there. Then she gets quietly down from the waggon & stands by him & talks.—This is the scene that I can't bear to think anyone should read—they do not kiss each other; once he takes her face between his hands, & holds it. He is strong now. Both see their life of work stretching out before them; & both know they will not be alone in it. He creeps into the waggon to kiss her children; with a sudden impulse she cuts off the long black braids of her hair that she has been so proud of, close to her head, & gives them to him when he comes back to her: they stand still, talking in the moonlight, & then he goes. So they are united forever.

Afterwards there is a scene where she finds her prostitute sister. When she is dying Rebekah sits beside her & paints before her the woman's dream of the future, the freedom, the joy, the strength that are to be. Bertie listens but half uneasily; there is to be all this for woman but what of man! True to her old love for them she says uneasily, 'But, Rebekah, we don't want

[5] Only the letters 'ab' appear, followed by a space; 'upbraiding' is Richard Rive's suggestion; see his edition of *Olive Schreiner Letters 1871–1899*, 92, in Select Bibliography, *supra*.

[6] Notably, OS writes neither 'cares for' nor 'cared for'.

anything to happen to men!' And Rebekah kneels down by her, & paints as she sees in that moment of passion & hope the future of love; the time when men & women shall so use their sexual natures & the power they have over each other that they shall be the source of life & strength; when love shall be no more bound down to material conditions; but shall be what it is striving to be now, the union of mind, the foundation of the entire nature; there is no hereafter for the individual, but for the race a glorious future. She paints it as she sees it at that moment.

Afterwards when she is lying with her arms round her sister, the sister dies. ('Grave digger again!' you will say. But to me, there is nothing sad, nothing depressing in that scene. It fills me with joy & exhilaration. What is death!

And yet we thank God ever,
That dead men rise up never;
And even the weariest river,
Winds somewhere safe to sea![7]

It is not the death of the individual that is the sad thing in human life, but the death of the ideal. All we desire is that as long as we live we should keep up faith in it, & the strife after it.[8] One would like to think that after the change of death one's mind's work, like the material of one's body, might form a matrix from which a higher type of existence might spring.)

Then comes the main scene in the book. Rebekah's husband reproaches her with having brought Bertie into the house & buried her openly, when it ought to have been done quietly, so that nobody talked. And then she turns to him; in all her long married life it is the first time she has acted in material things without attention to his pleasure. She asks why she should not take out her dead & bury it in the sunlight—she who for 14 long years herself has been living as a prostitute. Then they talk. Then one sees what her life has been: those first married years when intense passionate love works in her heart for him. When week after week & month after month all life is one long striving to come near to him, one passionate mad determination that at last they shall understand each other, & a spiritual bond be formed between them—then how she finds out his unfaithfulness, & bit by bit the strife dies. Then she turned to her books & lived in them alone. They talk & she tells him of her feeling for the other man.

[7] An adaptation of lines from Charles Swinburne's 'The Garden of Proserpine' (1866), which reads more fully as follows: 'We thank with brief thanksgiving | Whatever gods might be | That no life lives for ever; | That dead men rise up never; | That even the weariest river | Winds somewhere safe to sea.'

[8] A habitual locution in OS. Substituting the phrase 'the striving after it' for 'the strife' would lose the significance achieved here: striving *is* strife.

He thinks she is rather good to have known all about his unfaithfulnesses & kept so quiet. When he finds she has never kissed the man & never writes to him, he laughs & calls it all moonlight folly. When she talks of the work, that is to be done in the future, of the sexual institutions which shall be dragged down & altered, he laughs half kindly & pats her on the head: he says she talks like a fool, he says she mustn't excite herself so, it's not good for her in her condition (she is expecting a child), he tells her to come into the dining room with him; to his brandy & soda. And now she has said all, & there is not a shadow of deception.

The end of the book is two tiny scenes. One is the man she loves dying in the Kaleharee Desert[9] with his Kaffir boy near him. ('Grave digger again'; yes, but I can't help it.) He is dying & in the dim confusion he keeps telling the boy to get up on the waggon chest & see if he doesn't see anyone coming. The boy says 'No'. He says, 'Yes, but a little figure, a little woman figure, do you see nothing coming?' He thinks she is coming to lie by him, now there can be no wrong now.

—Then the last scene. She is sitting alone in the twilight; she has got the letter that day to say that he is gone. She sees before her her life's work & his, that must be done by her alone now. Then her little child comes in & asks her to take it to bed, it is very sleepy. She takes it up in her arms but it says it can walk. She says, 'No, I am not tired: I am very strong.'[10]

OLIVE SCHREINER

A Note by S. C. Cronwright-Schreiner as to the Ending of the Novel[11]

Olive Schreiner told me briefly how this novel was to end.

Drummond, persisting in his search for Bertie, found her in a house of ill-fame at Simon's Town, stricken down by a loathsome and terrible disease. Rebekah took this dearly loved sister to her own house at Rondebosch, where everything that love and medical science could do was lavished upon her. But, alas, the rescue came too late; the ravages wrought in this tender but helpless woman were too far advanced; and her death approaches. Possibly it was after depicting this deeply wronged woman's death that Olive did the 'outburst' on Veronica and Mrs Drummond that 'relieved her so' (*Life*, p. 180). Something of the intensity of the scene and of the 'outburst' may perhaps be inferred from the extract from Olive's letter to Ellis of the 5th April, 1889 (*Letters*, p. 160).

With regard to the death scene, Olive told me what were the last words, or among the last words, of Bertie. Some people were gathered round the

[9] The Kalahari Desert was explored by the Scottish explorer and missionary David Livingstone in 1849, and subsequently crossed by traders and ivory hunters.

[10] The ambiguity of the pronouns may be suggestive to some readers.

[11] In the first edition, SCCS appended this account to the end of Ch. XIII.

dying woman's bed; I do not know all who were present, nor how it came that Mrs Drummond was among them; but that evil woman was there. Baby-Bertie's simple nature had presumably never been troubled by the doubts, still less had it reached the conclusions, inevitable in the case of a cultured modern mind of the calibre of Rebekah's: Bertie had no doubt retained the primitive beliefs implanted early in her mind by her childlike 'little mother'. However that may be, as the end drew near, Rebekah leaned over her dying sister and asked her whether she would like them to pray. It is no great mental effort to remember the very words of the reply, because they seemed to me so terrific and because Olive chuckled over them. She used to style such a cut 'the stroke oblique', and was always pleased, as in this instance, when she got it in at the right moment. 'Let Mrs. Drummond pray,' said Baby-Bertie; 'she is a Christian.' And so one of the two women Olive loved so passionately passed into the Silence.

Rebekah lived on. The sense of full comprehension and close fellowship between her and Drummond increased until they realised mutually the depth and the fitness of the undying love between them. But, as they were situated, a more intimate relationship was unwarrantable to such a woman as Rebekah; for her it was impossible to do anything which could degrade such a love; it therefore became inevitable that she must give up and leave the one man who she felt could be her life's close companion; and so they parted forever. Leaving Frank, she went to Matjesfontein with her children and the little coloured girl Sartje. There she lived, educating the children and rearing Sartje as though a child of her own.

There is a little koppie in the flat at Matjesfontein, some distance west of the lonely Station, towards the bare and rocky mountains Olive so loved. This koppie she often referred to in her letters as 'my koppie'. From the Station, away across the vast and barren flat to the koppie, was a favourite walk of hers. There we see the last of Rebekah. As the sun sets, flooding the Karoo flats with radiance and glowing the brilliant mountains as it disappears behind them, Rebekah stands on the summit of the lonely koppie in the soft effulgence of the evening light, in something of that unutterable beauty of wild nature that suffused the veld and comforted the mind of Waldo of the *African Farm* when he went out 'to sit in the sunshine'.[12]

Of the subsidiary characters I know no more. Possibly, however, this is of little moment. What happens to them does not seem to me to be of much interest after they cease to impinge upon Rebekah and Bertie; and those two women are now, we know, beyond them.

S. C. CRONWRIGHT-SCHREINER

[12] The final chapter of *The Story of an African Farm* is titled 'Waldo Goes Out to Sit in the Sunshine'.

APPENDIX 4

TEXTUAL EMENDATIONS AND LIST OF VARIANTS

General Emendations

The following silent emendations have been made throughout:

Brackets: Cronwright-Schreiner used square brackets in Unwin and Harper to add words surmised in his editorial process. He provides no guide as to whether these additions relate to illegible words or missing words. He sometimes adds a question mark and sometimes not. His square brackets and question mark have been retained only in cases where there has clearly been guesswork. Where necessary, Explanatory Notes explain further.

Capitalization: Capital letters are used, where appropriate, for the following words or phrases: Avenue, Ayah, Bay, City, Clergyman, Father, Flats, Front, Inferior Races, Minister, Mistress, Mother, Pharisee, Sepoys, Town, Universe.

Commas: Schreiner sometimes uses commas between adjectives and sometimes not. Decisions about adding or deleting commas have been made on a case-by-case basis, and generally relate to the rhythm of the sentence and, where relevant, the author's interest in a particular emphasis.

Dashes: OS makes considerable, idiosyncratic use of the dash, often together with a full stop, a semicolon, a colon, or a comma. The use of both together is regarded as unnecessary and distracting. In each such case, I have made a silent decision as to which of the two to keep. Where OS uses an exclamation mark and a dash, or a question mark and a dash, I have kept both. When a dash introduces a quotation, this is generally replaced by a colon, unless the quotation reads as text within a sequence of thinking or talking.

Paragraphing: I have occasionally silently reparagraphed the text to fit with the conventions of dialogue, but have not reparagraphed long paragraphs that would benefit from division.

Past tense verbs: the use of past tense verbs has been regularized in the case of the following: burn, dream, knit, leap, learn, and smell; OS's misuse of 'lay' as past tense is changed to 'laid'.

Prepositions: prepositions have occasionally been emended for clarity or grammatical correctness.

Pronouns: the use of pronouns has been regularized, relating both to individual nouns and to sections that wander between gendered and non-gendered pronouns.

LIST OF GENERAL LEXICAL EMENDATIONS (DEPENDING ON CONTEXT)

each other → one another
for ever → forever
farther → further
good bye → goodbye
handkerchief → kerchief
kapje → kappie
mierkat → meerkat
near by → nearby
O → Oh
Oh → O
on to → onto
one another → each other
relations → relatives
some one → someone
story → storey
to-day → today
to-morrow → tomorrow

List of Variants

The list which follows shows textual variants between the present edition and the editions SCCS produced: Unwin (first impression) 1926 (*U*) and Harper 1927 (*H*).

10.28 as it were] as if it were *H*
16.9 as a bitch looks when] as a bitch when *H*
16.25 raised] raised out *U*, *H*
18.3 pear leaves] pear tree leaves *U*, pear-tree leaves *H*
20.26 got home] got it home *U*, *H*
22.9 sitting] sitting up *U*, *H*
22.10 long-tail] long-tailed *H*
23.23 must just let her] must let her *H*
29.29 swan] swam *U*
30.31 trees round the dam] trees which grew round *U*, *H*
31.19 stramonium] stramonia *U*, *H*
32.38 people] someone *U*, *H*
38.13 and threw its light full onto her [...] and onto her hand with the white frill thrown across it] and threw its light full on her [...] and her hand with the white frill thrown across it *U*, *H*
39.22 stuck out] struck out *U*, *H*
40.7 as one who repeats what they have] as one who repeats what he has *H*

41.1 if you would have let me] if you will let me *U*, *H*
46.38 outstretched wing] outstretched wind *U*, *H*
47.11 since as a boy] since a boy *U*, *H*
48.13 which he ate] which it ate *U*, *H*
51.34 deal table] table *H*
52.21 That scale] The scale *U*
54.16 who I shall find] whom I shall find *U*, *H*
54.27 we two will] shall *H*
54.28 we will look] we shall look *H*
54.31 we two will] we two shall *H*
55.14 fastened in] fastened to *U*, *H*
56.18 the candle] candle *U*, *H*
56.19 breeze] breezes *U*, *H*
56.21 led into] led to *U*, *H*
56.37 so fully on] so fully upon *U*, *H*
58.25 in the fact] from the fact *U*, *H*
59.15 increasing proportions of] increasing proportions in *U*, *H*
60.31 might have had, looking] might have, when *U*, *H*
61.26 to the dam] down to the dam *U*, *H*
62.6 eleven] eleven o'clock *U*, *H*
64.2 the door of] the floor of *U*, *H*
65.31 never had] had never *H*
65.28 though] thought *U*, *H*
66.2 Even] Even then *U*, *H*
66.8 awaking] waking *H*
68.5 coming also] also coming *U*, *H*
69.31 compared to] compared with *H*
69.32 hand] hands *U*, *H*
70.32 safety] safely *U*, *H*
70.32 the father] her father *U*, *H*
72.25 orange trees] orange tree *U*, *H*
74.11 hung down from the trees] hung from the trees *U*, *H*
74.14 use to make] used to make *H*
74.27 tall slender young trees were] a tall slender young tree was *U*, *H*
74.28 between the rocks] between them *U*, *H*
75.2 on the mound] upon the mound *U*, *H*
77.3 made it sparkle] made them sparkle *U*, *H*
79.5 Rebecca stood looking at the lovely face, half turned] Rebecca, looking at the lovely face, half-turned *U*] Rebecca, looking at the lovely face half turned *H*
81.14 personal] the personal *U*, *H*
82.2 hair and] hair, and on *U*, *H*

84.6 thickened] thickening *H*
84.23 listened] listening *H*
84.37 room next to] next room to *H*
85.2 felt she did] felt, *U*, *H*
85.3 her] Veronica *U*, *H*
85.32 in the bath.] in. *H*
87.24 had been grown up and gone] was grown up and had gone *U*, *H*
89.28 pear branches] pear tree branches *U*, *H*
90.10 the old Kaffir man] her old Kaffir man *U*, *H*
91.26 and leaned] leaned *U*, *H*
93.14 her finger] her fingers *U*, *H*
95.2 I will go] I *will* go *U*, *H*
98.0 John-Ferdinand shows his new house] John-Ferdinand shows Veronica his new house *U*, *H*
98.14 down towards the orchard] down the orchard *U*, *H*
98.33 now regretted] regretted *U*, *H*
99.27 morning] mornings *U*, *H*
100.19 has seemed ill] had seemed ill *H*
100.36 as she knew] and as she knew *U*
102.3 so the great oak trees] for the great oak trees *U*, *H*
102.14 placid eye] placid eyes *U*, *H*
103.15 in both] both in *H*
103.26 as bedroom] as a bedroom *H*
105.12 two years before Rebekah was married, with her husband] with her husband two years before Rebekah was married *U*, *H*
105.36 embroideries which] embroideries *U*, *H*
106.4 determined] had determined *U*, *H*
106.4 had helped] helped *U*, *H*
106.16 and in which] and in it *U*, *H*
107.38 to do anything but] to do anything except *U*, *H*
108.30 or ever afterwards] or afterwards *U*, *H*
108.36 vineyard there] vineyard *U*, *H*
109.6 and of] of *U*, *H*
110.16 of the house] the house *U*, *H*
110.30 for] to *U*, *H*
111.4 and she] she *U*, *H*
112.15 and examined] and *U*, *H*
113.1 the father and mother] her father and mother *U*, *H*
113.9 into a smile] in a smile *H*
120.4 had done anything] had not done anything *U*, *H*
122.14 saw to it that] saw that *U*, *H*
123.22 taught herself] taught *U*, *H*

124.29 did she realise] she realised *U, H*
125.32 It had been a long time] It was a long time *U, H*
125.36 as any other] or any other *U, H*
127.30 has been carved] have been carved *U, H*
130.25 mind and matter] mind and water *U*
131.21 that it is] that is vital *U*
134.38 satisfies] insofar satisfies *U, H*
135.29 at second hand, but through them all actually living] at second-hand, but actually, as though living *U, H*
135.32 walked] walked and walked *H*
136.24 been merely dependent] being merely dependent *U, H*
137.2 that in humanity] that humanity *U, H*
141.3 pastoral] pastural *U*
142.3 proves not] proves [? does not prove] *U, H*
142.19 fully developed] full developed *U, H*
142.27 quicker] more quickly *H*
143.4 unendowed with] unendowed in *U, H*
143.8 crushed as undesirable] crushed and undesirable *U, H*
147.34 saying, 'There] saying. 'Their *H*
148.5 surrounded himself with] surrounded himself by *U, H*
148.27 philosophers] philosopher *U, H*
149.5 men drank wine] man drank wine *H*
150.4 debt] debit *U, H*
150.23 back-beat] back-seat *H*
152.6 stupid] and stupid *U, H*
154.34 underlie] underlies *U, H*
154.6 have] has *U, H*
157.17 bass] base *U, H*
157.34 was obliged] man was obliged *U, H*
160.28 predatory] predative *U, H*
161.1 self-defensive] self-defencing *U*, self-defensing *H*
161.30 not allowed by the latter to] not allowed to *U, H*
162.27 might have had] may have had *U, H*
164.17 haphazardly] haphazard *U, H*
166.20 Her] Its *U, H*
166.21 she] it *U, H*
166.21 she] it *U, H*
166.12 her] its *U, H*
166.13 his] its *U, H*
166.22 alit] lit *U, H*
166.24 he] it *U, H*
168.7 this and this is for woman] this and this is for women *H*

169.9 falling softly] falling *H*
178.20 other stocking.] other. *U, H*
182.1 moss] roses *U, H*
182.35 could not see] cold not see *U*
186.25 she moved her hand] she moved his hand *U*
187.32 what with her false hair] with her false hair *U, H*
188.7 dickens] Dickens *U*
192.36 such a one] such an one *U, H*
193.6 blaze of sunshine] blare of sunshine *U, H*
196.37 then I went] than I went *U*
197.9 regarding your politeness] to your politeness *U, H*
198.33 piece them together] piece them *U, H*
203.32 Please tell me] Please to tell me *U, H*
203.33 you] *you* *U*, *H*
205.28 me] *me* *U*, *H*
205.28 Frank] Frank [her baby] *U, H*
205.29 bath] bathe *H*
205.32 so] so [cruel] *U, H*
205.37 so long as] so *U, H*
205.17 he] it *U, H*
208.39 him] it *U, H*
209.27 his] its *H*
211.1 his] its *H*
221.15 he] it *H*
222.4 his] its *H*
224.12 has led woman] has led women *U*
225.12 in spring] the spring *U*
229.20 hê] hè *U, H*
230.1 fingers] finger *U, H*
231.2 by the moment] at the moment *U, H*
231.30 tired, little woman] a tired little woman *H*
232.9 know, of course, it's absolutely ridiculous!] know it's absolutely ridiculous! *H*
233.28 knew!] once knew! *U, H*
238.24 All the family were] All the family was *U, H*
239.30 Their letters] his letters *H*
240.11 invite] invited *U*
254.18 blew] blow *U*
241.19 when she was on] when on *U, H*
243.2 kerchief] handkerchief *U, H*
246.2 farther] further *U, H*
246.19 Christmas] Xmas *U, H*

247.37 was drying out] were drying out *U*
248.20 leaving us] leaving this *U*, *H*
249.15 but the soap] the soap *H*
250.34 put supper ready] get supper ready *H*
252.17 ze] the *U, H*
252.32 had helped] and helped *H*
253.20 mignonettes] mignonette *U, H*
254.11 awoken] waked *U, H*
256.24 over the nek] over the neck *U*
265.16 absent-mindedly] absently *U, H*
268.14 ceiling] roof *U, H*
268.29 zings] sings *U, H*
273.15 milliner's] millinerer's *U*
274.16 began] opened it and began *U, H*
275.24 keys] notes *U, H*
276.7 vill] will *U, H*
287.21 hand on their arm] head on their arm *U*, *H*
287.35 so that] so carelessly that *U, H*
290.20 Bath chairs] bathchairs *U*, *H*
292.37 climbed the steps] climbed the step *U, H*
299.13 Then he brought] When he brought *U*, *H*
301.20 kittens in her lap] kitten in her lap *U, H*
303.31 room door] room *U, H*
303.35 vhy] why *U, H*
305.11 her wrists and fingers] her wrists and finger *U*
305.27 he was sitting] sitting *U, H*
306.4 round] around *H*
308.7 hand-washstand] wash-hand-stand *U, H*
309.1 sat for a moment] sat looking at the street for a moment *U*
310.9 Christmas] Xmas *U*, *H*
312.5 slippers] slipper *U*
313.12 china] China *U*, *H*
313.34 at her sides] at her side. *U, H*
314.9 carry to] carry *U, H*
319.1 Also at] On *U, H*
324.12 our telescopes] out telescopes *U*
325.30 they looked] he looked *H*
326.14 Their pictures] The pictures *H*
331.36 would be right] would [?not] be right *U*, *H*
349.6 there rang out] there rung out *U*
355.13 rested his hand] rested his head *U*, *H*
355.21 up in Africa] in Africa *H*

359.21 where she had found it] where she had found them *U, H*
362.37 Their praise and their blame are] is *U*
367.6 an isolated monad] an isolated nomad *U, H*
374.4 dwarf themselves] dwarf himself *H*
374.5 of their art] of art *H*
374.5 to their thought] to thought *H*

EXPLANATORY NOTES

The following abbreviations are used in the notes:

AF	*The Story of an African Farm* (1883; repr. Oxford: Oxford University Press, 1992)
Afk.	Afrikaans language
DSAE	*Dictionary of South African English on Historical Principles* (Cape Town: Oxford University Press in association with the Dictionary Unit for South African English, 1966)
Du.	Cape Dutch language; or Cape Dutch
Eng.	English
FMTM	*From Man to Man*
Harper	Harper & Brothers (New York, 1927) edition of *From Man to Man or Perhaps Only...*
OS	Olive Schreiner
OSLO	*Olive Schreiner Letters Online*
SAE	South African English
SCCS	Samuel Cron Cronwright-Schreiner
TS	Typescript
TSA	*Thoughts on South Africa* (London: T. Fisher Unwin, 1923)
Unwin	T. Fisher Unwin (London, 1926) edition of *From Man to Man or Perhaps Only...*

All biblical references are to the 1611 King James Version, unrevised (Oxford: Oxford University Press for the British and Foreign Bible Society, 1860). This is the version OS used and later donated to Karl Pearson; it is now lodged in the library of University College London.

Dedication

3 *Ellie*: Helen, or Ellie as the family called her, born on 22 March 1864, the twelfth and last of Rebecca's children. As the eldest child at home (Ettie having been finally sent to school), OS took care of her until she died on 22 August 1865. OS was in fact almost 10 ½ years old at the time. See letter to Adela Smith, 22 October 1907 (Appendix 2), for an account of what Ellie meant to her. The couplet quoted in the dedication is from Emerson's poem, 'Each and All'.

My Only Daughter: the child born to OS and SCCS on 30 April 1895 was taken to the nurse's room for the night, but was found dead the next morning. She had not yet been named. The birth was presided over by a medical doctor and a midwife. See letter to Mary Sauer, 10 May 1895 (in Appendix 2) for an account of this event. On the preliminary page of her 1911 TS, OS included the following line: 'She never lived to know she was a woman'. She crossed out 'never loved' and replaced it with 'did not live', and then crossed out the entire line. For a possible correspondence, see letter to John X. Merriman, 31 October 1905 (Appendix 2).

I Prelude: The Child's Day

9 *the little mother*: a diminutive form used affectionately even if sometimes also patronizingly. The diminutive—applied to a variety of nouns—is far more often used in Afk. than in Eng. Thus the frequent use of the word 'little' throughout this novel will remind readers of OS's deep attraction to Boer culture, despite her increasing political distance from its racial attitudes, and the fact that she generally spoke of England as her home. OS used the expression in letters to her mother; e.g. 'My own little Mother' (letter to Rebecca Schreiner, 27 February 1894, in *OSLO*).

Ayah: from the Hindi *ãyå* and/or Portuguese *aia*; a term noted as 'offensive to some' (*DSAE*, 32); used generally by Europeans to name female domestic servants, and specifically their children's nursemaids, when they were of Indian or Malay origin, although the novel identifies Ayah as Khoi.

Hottentot: now understood as derogatory, the term was generally used (and not necessarily with derogatory intent) by nineteenth-century Europeans to designate people now referred to as Khoi or Khoikhoi.

'O ja, God! Wat zal ons nou zeg?': OS provided the translation in a footnote: 'O yes, God. What shall we now say?' Like most Khoi in the Cape Colony, 'Ayah' speaks Du., which was in the process of transforming into Afk.

Swedenborg: Emanuel Swedenborg (1688–1772), Swedish scientist, theologian and philosopher. See also note to p. 89.

kappie: the large and capacious cloth sun bonnet worn by Du. women, which had a flap to shade the back and sides of the neck.

Kaffir: derogatory; also spelled 'Kaffer' (influenced by Du. and Afk.); from the word *kafir* (meaning 'infidel' in Arabic. OS's contemporary, Katie Makanya (unknown to her), denounced the term as "too much like the Xhosa word *kafula*, which means "to spit upon"'. See Margaret McCord, *The Calling of Katie Makanya* (Cape Town: David Philip, 1995), 34.

kraals: enclosures; from the Portuguese *curral*. A Du. and Afk. term, it has been absorbed into SAE to refer to African villages typically formed of huts within a palisade; also used for animal pens or folds (*DSAE*, 395).

kraal heap: compost heap based on manure (not in *DSAE*).

thorn trees: *Vachellia karroo* (formerly *Acacia karroo*), native to southern Africa. In Ch. I of her 1911 TS, OS includes a footnote identifying the thorn tree as a mimosa: 'The mimosa, generally called thorn tree in South Africa; a tree with a delicate acacia leaf and long white thorns from an inch to three inches in length, and with a sweet-scented yellow honey blossom.' See also note to p. 20.

the flat: from Du. & Afk. *vlakte* ('plain') and *vlaktes* ('plains'), after *vlak* ('flat').

10 *as it were*: That is, Rebekah rearranged her fingers so as to make the hand ('it') look like a mouse. From Cape Du./Afk. *as't ware*.

11 *but a little light*: this phrasing, not uncommon in SAE, is borrowed from Afk., where *maar* ('but') functions as 'only', as in *daar was maar min lig* ('there was only a little light'). As noted in Appendix 4, one may see in OS's practice an imitation in English of Afrikaans speech patterns, more evident here than in the previously mentioned example ('as it were'). Her usage may well have influenced some later South African writing: see J. M. Coetzee, 'Pauline Smith and the Afrikaans Language', *English in Africa* 8/1 (1981), 25.

14 *Bushman*: now widely but not universally considered as derogatory, the term was generally used in OS's day to designate the San, who were—along with the Khoi—the original inhabitants of southern Africa. See also note to p. 69.

fossilised leaf: in her 1901 MS, OS depicted a different fossil: 'a flat slate-coloured stone with the perfect impression of a fossilized creature, something like a frog, but with wings', foregrounding Rebekah's subsequent interest in the 'winged reptile' in Ch. VII, p. 163; see also note to p. 359.

16 *'O Lord!'*: OS's distinction between the exclamation 'Oh' and the vocative 'O' has been regularized in this edition.

'O my God!': the phrase reads similarly in Du./Afk. as in Eng. See also note to p. 9.

Mietje . . . and Katje: familiar Du./Afk. names; in Du./Afk. the *j*-sound is more like *k* than *y*. The name Sartje, first referred to in Ch. XII, also applies.

put you on a clean dress: in using the dative without a preposition, OS represents the Du. influence on the speech patterns of 'old Ayah': *zij moet je een schoon jurkje aantrekken* ('she must put a clean dress on you').

17 *blue flies*: *Calliphora vomitoria*, bluebottle fly, a species of blowfly.

stoep: from the Du. & Afk. *stoep* ('step', 'porch'). Standard in SAE. The footnote on the term in Ch. I (Unwin and Harper) reads: 'Stoep: Stone-flagged veranda.' SCCS attributes this footnote to OS but it is not evident in the 1911 TS. Her 1901 MS reads more fully: 'a raised pavement of stone some feet high, which almost always runs before Cape houses, & which may or may not be covered by a verandah'. OS is mistaken in identifying the veranda with the roof alone. This possibly helps explain her odd use of the phrase 'in the veranda' on one occasion, but it is more likely that SCCS misread her handwriting, and 'in' has been emended in this edition (but not in Unwin or Harper) to 'on the veranda'. See p. 211.

17 *four-o'clocks*: *Mirabilis jalapa*; its flowers open from late afternoon until early the following morning.

18 *Peter and his Pig*: cf. 'my Peter book', p. 40; although the reference is to a particular page, OS gives it the status of a book.

Queen Victoria: that Queen Victoria (mentioned earlier in the Prelude in relation to the child's votive assemblage for the dead baby) inherited the British throne in 1837 at a youthful age may help account for her particular appeal to the child Rebekah. The frequent mention of Queen Victoria in the Prelude and other chapters points up her continuing significance, sometimes ironic (see pp. 47, 272, 308, 310, 311, 337; see also note to p. 33).

South Africa: the Union of South Africa had come into existence only a year before OS prepared her 1911 TS, although the name was sometimes used earlier, as a territorial reference.

19 *Here is a little box of presents . . . even old Ayah*: in OS's 1901 MS, the gift-giving was more limited, and related to rank; in her 1911 TS, she manually added the passage about a more expansive gift-giving.

20 *mimosa pod*: *Vachellia karroo*; see OS's note on 'thorn tree' quoted earlier (note to p. 9). Although the thorn tree belongs to the subfamily Mimosaceae, it is not technically a mimosa. However, older writings from the Cape use 'thorn tree' and 'mimosa' as synonyms. Both have pods.

hand-lamb: a lamb raised by hand, fed with a bottle. Afk. *hanslammetjie* from Dutch *handslammetje.*

21 *"And through . . . around my bed"*: from 'An Evening Song' written by Isaac Watts (1674–1748).

cock-o-veet: *Telophorus zeylonus*; a.k.a. bokmakierie (SAE and Afk.). OS anglicizes the term. SCCS's footnote reads: 'The Bush-shrike, a very handsome bird with resonant call notes of great beauty—a prime favourite of Olive's.' (There are, however, different varieties of bush shrikes.)

so—so!: with this particular use of 'so', OS again introduces Afk. speech patterns into her prose, although this will be more obvious later (see note to p. 102): as in the Afk. *sy maak dit so*, or, in the past tense, *sy het dit so gemaak*.

22 *"O cock-o-veet!"*: here and subsequently OS uses the 'O' not just as a vocative, as indicated earlier, but also as an honorific, in the manner of Rudyard Kipling's *Just So Stories* (1902).

little long-tail monkeys: the 'long-tail' vervet monkey (*Chlorocebus pygerythrus*) is native to Africa; later OS uses the term 'long-tailed' (pp. 45 and 58).

Nam-nams: any of several shrubs of the genus *Carissa* of the Apocynaceae family. The name comes from the Khoi *!num-!num*; 'nam-nam' is a variant spelling (*DSAE*, 512).

Kaffir plums: fruit from the evergreen indigenous tree *Harpephyllum caffrum*; so-called to designate its difference from and apparent inferiority to the European plum (*DSAE*, 343 e).

they gave her of: OS uses the literal translation of the Afk.: *hulle het haar van hul noem-noems gegee*, where *van* means 'from' or 'of'.

tiger: Africa has no tigers; early travellers and settlers often called leopards tigers, borrowing from the Du. term *tijger* ('leopard') (*DSAE*, 721: 1). Ch. I uses the term 'leopard' (p. 46); Ch. XI connects the terms: "they caught a tiger, one of the huge leopards" (p. 301); Ch. XII reverts to 'tiger' (p. 339).

the tiger winked with his eyes: as mentioned in Note on the Text (p. xxxix), the use of pronouns has been regularized; this emendation is also recorded in the List of Variants (pp. 477–84) in the event that readers might wish to consider for themselves the erratic gendered movement within certain paragraphs.

23 *by her*: Afk. *by*, 'next to'. See also 'by the table' (p. 25), where 'by' means 'at'. SAE has absorbed this usage from Afk., whether as preposition (as here) or as adverb (see also note to p. 59).

24 *they caught with*: literal translation of Afk. *met 'n strik gevang* ('caught in a trap'); *met* means 'with'.

make—so: literal translation of Afk. *maak so* ('do it like this'). See also note to p. 102, and Note on the Text, p. xl.

25 *What Hester Durham Lived For*: an illustrated story by Sarah Tytler (1827–1914), published in the British monthly periodical *Good Words* and collected in the annual *Good Words for 1863* (London: Alexander Strahan and Co., 1863), 488–93.

Sepoys: from the Persian word *sipāh* ('infantry soldier') designating British Indian Army infantrymen native to India. The Sepoy Rebellion (1857–8), a.k.a. Indian Mutiny, was sparked partly by the religious insults delivered to the sepoys (whether Muslim or Hindu) by British East India Company officers.

In the picture: a wood engraving by Thomas Morten (1836–66), accessible online on the Victorian Web: www.victorianweb.org/art/illustration/3.html.

"Alone, like a rock . . . stood there": Rebekah is reimagining a sentence taken from the caption of Morten's wood engraving (*Good Words for 1863*, 493) or the story itself: 'They clung around Hester, where she stood like a rock in a stormy sea' (492).

26 *"The Assyrian came down—"*: the opening words of 'The Destruction of Sennacherib' by Lord Byron (1788–1824).

"Like mist . . . on the sea—": the first two lines of a hymn composed by Robert Murray MacCheyne (1813–43). The first stanza reads: 'Like mist on the mountain, like ships on the sea; | So swiftly the years of our pilgrimage flee; | In the grave with our fathers how soon we shall lie! | O children, to-day to the dear Saviour fly!' See *Hymns for Sunday Schools: Youth and Children* (New York: Carlton & Porter, for Methodist Episcopal Church, 1854), 114.

26 "*Rome shall perish . . . hath spilt—*": the lines come from stanza v in 'Boadicea: An Ode' by William Cowper (1731–1800), first published in 1815, with a semicolon after 'spilt'. The stanza continues: 'Perish, hopeless & abhorred, | Deep in ruin as in guilt'. See *The Poetical Works of William Cowper*, ed. Robert Aris Willmott (London: George Routledge & Sons, 1860), 180–1.

"*Rome, for Empire far renown . . . The Gaul is at her gates!*": these lines also come from Cowper's 'Boadicea: An Ode', this time from stanza iv, which in fact reads 'far renown'd', rhyming with 'ground', and is, like the earlier two lines, differently punctuated.

Hymns for Infant Minds: published in 1804 by Jane Taylor (1783–1824), with a second edition in 1810 by Jane Taylor and Ann Taylor (1782–1866). It ran to at least fifty editions. Jane Taylor is best known for her 'Twinkle, twinkle, little star'.

27 *Elijah*: prophet during a critical time in Israel's very early history, the nation having turned from God's word to worship the false god Baal. Elijah represents hope and redemption. See letter from OS to John X. Merriman, 11 August 1912, in *OSLO*: 'There is always Elijah at the door of his cavern in the darkest hour of national degeneracy.' For Baal, see 1 Kings 19.

"*And instead . . . myrtle tree*": 'Instead of the thorn shall come up the fir tree, and instead of the brier [*sic*] shall come up the myrtle tree' (Isaiah 55:13).

Miss Plumptree's Bible stories: probably Helen Plumptre's *Scripture Stories*, or, *Sacred History Familiarly Explained and Applied to Children* (1819); may also refer to her *The History of Joseph* (1822), *The History of Joshua* (1825), *The History of Moses* (1839), or *The History of Samuel* (1842), all published in London by James Nisbet. OS's misspelling of the name in the 1911 TS is retained here, as in Unwin and Harper, for it announces the child's naïve or distanced perspective.

We had two came to visit us once: in her 1911 TS, OS changed the standard English (grammatically correct) phrasing from 'come' to 'came' to achieve the colloquial phrasing she desired.

"*Goody-no-shoes*": probably a play on Goody-two-shoes, used later (see note to p. 54), underlining Rebekah's class position and rural upbringing. The 1901 MS has 'Goody-two-shoes'.

"*Tom-boy*": retained here are OS's estranging capitalization and hyphenation of the term 'tomboy', an English term in use since the mid-sixteenth century (it has no equivalent in Afk.).

"*You tell tale tit . . . Shall have a little bit!*": the opening lines of a popular 'Mother Goose' nursery rhyme which probably first appeared in *Mother Goose's Melody, or, Sonnets for the Cradle* (1765 or 1766).

say it up: OS's rendition of the Afk. *opsê* ('recite').

28 "*Four and twenty tailors . . . snail*": adapted from a nursery rhyme that first appeared in *Gammer Gurton's Garland, or, the Nursery Parnassus* (1784)

and then in James Halliwell's *The Nursery Rhymes of England* (1844), where the first lines read: 'Four-and-twenty tailors | Went to kill a snail'. See Iona Opie and Peter Opie (eds.), *The Oxford Dictionary of Nursery Rhymes* (1951; repr. Oxford: Oxford University Press, 1992), 496.

She paused for a while . . . Now, go to sleep my baby: OS manually inserted this section into the 1911 TS. Rebekah's strong identification with black women is a marked feature of the novel here centred on milk; in this regard, see letter from OS to Havelock Ellis, 22 July 1888, in Appendix 2.

29 *'London's burning! . . . London's burning!'*: this song, generally believed to derive from the Great Fire of London in 1666, was adapted from a version first recorded in 1580 with Scotland as its subject. It was introduced into at least one Eastern Cape mission station after the 1820s, later emerging as a Xhosa song, *Umzi watsha* ('the homestead is burning'; *watsha* is a contraction of the verb form *uyatsha*).

'The swan . . . the swan!': see Opie and Opie (eds.), *The Oxford Dictionary of Nursery Rhymes*, 400. For a slightly different version of this tongue-twister, see James Orchard Halliwell, *The Nursery Rhymes of England* (1842): Swan swam over the sea— | Swim, swan, swim; | Swan swam back again, | Well swam swan.'

When a full-grown woman . . . the still water: OS added this sentence to the 1911 TS, indicating her adult nostalgia for this idealized version.

30 *Long Jan*: from Afr. *Lang Jan* ('Tall John').

lands: tilled land or fields; from Dutch *landerijen*, and, in Afk., *land* and landery (s.) and *lande* and landerye (pl.). The anglicized plural of the term ('Lands for Tillage') may be said to have entered SAE as early as 1731 in an English translation of Peter Kolb's *Caput Bonae Spei Hodiernum* (*Present State of Cape of Good Hope*); see *DSAE*, 412: 1.

burned as black as a Kaffir: cf. the restriction of Lyndall's movements, as a white female child: '"Little one, you cannot go . . . Your little face will burn, and your nice white dress be spoiled"' (*AF*, 155).

31 *stramonium*: OS probably meant *Datura stramonium*, part of the nightshade (Solanaceae) family, commonly known as thorn apple or, in Afk., *stinkblaar or malpitte*, and toxic even to the touch.

he said what he thought . . . with stramonium branches: that is, 'he said he thought the best way of making the roof would be with stramonium branches'.

32 *krinkle*: Afk. *krinkel* ('crinkle').

people: the 1911 TS shows OS replacing 'someone' with 'people', thus achieving an Afk. flavour; cf. Afk. *mense* (Eng. for 'people').

33 *Her heart was beating so she could hear it*: in her use of the word 'so' (see note to p. 102), OS again creates an Afk. flavour: *Sy hart het so geklop sy kon dit hoor*; literally: 'her heart had beaten so [much] she could hear it.' See also Note on Text, pp. xl and xli.

33 *Prince Consort*: Queen Victoria's first cousin, Prince Albert of Saxe-Coburg and Gotha (a German dynasty), whom Queen Victoria married in 1840.

35 *milk house*: Du. and Afk. *melkhuis*. The standard Eng. ('dairy') would have given a different register. Elsewhere in the novel (e.g. p. 47) OS uses the term 'milk room'.

36 *meerkat*: *Suricata suricatta*; a small, burrowing carnivore that lives in groups and is easily tamed, unlike the mongoose with which it is sometimes confused. OS admired them in the wild, and kept some as pets. See also pp. 45, 153 and 163.

'Zij's een snaakse kind!': SCCS, in manually emending OS's TS, translated the Du. sentence into ungrammatical Afk.: *Sy's 'n snaaks se kind'*. OS's use of Du. is correct. Her TS reads *Zij*, which OS also has in her 1901 MS. It also appears that SCCS wrote over the Z to produce *Sij* before turning to the Afk. *Sy*.

37 *Perhaps only God knew what lights and shadows were!*: SCCS used a version of this sentence for the epigraph to his edition of the novel, reproducing a facsimile holograph quotation from a version of the Prelude that is no longer extant, 'Perhaps only God knew what the lights & shadows were.' Neither the 1911 TS nor the 1901 MS include a definite article (nor do the Unwin and Harper editions).

I will—I—will: for many South African readers, given the Afk. flavour already established in this text, the doubled force of each 'I will' may be heard through the Afk. *ek wil*. In both languages 'will'/*wil* means 'want' as well as indicating the future, but in Afk. the emphasis is stronger than in Eng. See also note to p. 95.

38 *and threw its light full onto her . . . white frill thrown across it*: it is evident here that OS was revising carelessly. (She cannot be said to have finished revising the 1911 TS of the Prelude, despite her having sent it to so many of her correspondents.) She emended the 1911 TS to read: 'and threw its full light on her, as she lay with the baby's head on her arm, ^&^ her hand with the white frill ~~was~~ thrown across it'. SCCS, as in Unwin and Harper, rightly understands OS as saying that the candle also threw its light on Rebekah's hand: 'and threw its light full on her, as she lay with the baby's head on her arm, and on her hand with the white frill thrown across it'. However, given the three repetitions of 'on', they do not entirely clarify the sentence in this way, hence their substitution in the present edition, in two instances, by 'onto'. (It must also be considered that, in deleting 'was', OS may possibly have meant: 'and threw its light full on [Rebekah], as she lay with the baby's head on her arm, her hand with the white frill thrown across it'.)

Kaffir beans: the seeds of the boerboon, *Schotia afra*, a.k.a. Karoo boerboon; native to South Africa. Its bean-like seeds are large, flat and brown, and edible, whether green or mature; roasted seeds were used as a coffee substitute (for additional associated references, see pp. 74, 120, and 183).

39 *eh*: 'hey' is the standard SAE spelling for this conventional, emphatic addition to a statement or question. It derives from the Du. and Afk. *nè*

('not so?'), phonetically captured in the vowel sound 'eh'. As so early a South African English novelist, OS has no orthographic model to follow, although *DSAE* finds the first usage of 'hey' in print in 1900 (*DSAE*, 285). However, 'eh' has been retained here as OS uses that spelling in her letters; e.g. 'Eh my darling' (letter to Havelock Ellis, 21 December 1884, in *OSLO*).

etna: usually capitalized, an Etna—named after the volcano—consisted of a cup fixed in a saucer in which alcohol was burnt to heat the liquid in the cup. Unwin and Harper also use a lower-case *e*.

My fatherland's force!: presumably Eng. transliteration of the Afk. expression *My vaderland se vors*, where *vors* from *Vorst* (Du.) or *vors* (Afk.) means 'ruler', 'sovereign', or 'prince'. OS may have heard the expression among the white farmers (Boers) of her governessing years, but from the Khoi domestic servant's mouth it resounds with irony.

41 *old-fashioned*: having the characteristics of a grown-up person. Cf. Charles Dickens's *The Old Curiosity Shop* (1841; London: Folio Society, 1987), where Nell Trent is described as an 'old-fashioned child in her looks and manner' (242).

'Das een snaakse kind!': as earlier in the Prelude (see note to p. 36), SCCS translates OS's rendering of 'Ayah's' Du. into ungrammatical Afk. (*Dis 'n snaaks se kind*), losing the colloquialism OS seems to be striving for. For OS, 'Das' seems to be an acceptable and perhaps old-fashioned elision of 'Dat is' (Eng.: 'that is'), as suggested by her Eng. translation of the elision as ''Tis'.

42 *sleeping well*: In her manual insertions into the 1911 TS, OS turns to Ayah's perspective: 'as she passed out she turned'; 'casting deep shadows into far [corners]'; 'especially that in which the two children lay!'; and 'But they were all sleeping well.'

II The Book: The Woman's Day

45 *beacons*: markers of land boundaries; from the Du. *baaken* (*DSAE*, 53).

velskoen-wearing: according to SCCS's edn., OS provided the following note in Ch. XI (see p. 276): 'Velskoens (skin-shoes) are the home-made shoes of undressed leather generally worn by Hottentot or Bushmen servants at the Cape.' The term derives from the Du. *vel* ('skin') and *schoen* ('shoe'), *velskoen* (Afk.); the standard plurals would be *velschoene* and *velskoene* (*DSAE*, 768).

Tante: Du. and Afr. for aunt; usually capitalized as a title or term of respect.

46 *nek*: Afk. for mountain pass; this has entered SAE (*DSAE*, 400). OS's footnote in her 1901 MS glosses 'nek' as follows: 'The low ridge which sometimes unites two mountains or hills.'

mealie: maize or Indian corn; from Du. *milie* and Afr. *mielie* (see *DSAE*, 451). SCCS changed 'mealie' to its variant 'mielie' (Afk.) but the Eng. variant OS uses in her TS has been restored. See Note on Text, p. xl.

'Calm . . . palm': stanza iii, ll. 1–3 of a hymn composed by Horatius Bonar (1808–89). Elim was one of the camps the Israelites established after their

exodus from Egypt. OS substitutes Bonar's 'like' with 'as'. The final line of the stanza reads, 'Beside her desert-spring'.

48 *kloof*: from Afr. *kloof* ('ravine' or 'gorge'); now standard in SAE (*DSAE*, 380).

49 *rounded except at the point . . . small square tip*: see the description of Isaac in Ch. XI, the tip of whose nose 'was so sharply a four-sided square that it almost suggested that the point had been artificially cut off instead of being the work of nature' (p. 267).

yellow-backed book: developed in England in 1840 to compete with the 'penny dreadful', the so-called 'yellow-back' was marketed as popular reading mostly in fiction, and notably in adventure stories.

50 *ting-ting-kie*: *Cisticola* sp.; from the San *quinqininyq* (*DSAE*, 722); the standard Afk. spelling is *tinktinkie*, translated as dickey-bird in the 1937 *Groot Woordeboek*. OS's original footnote reads: 'The ting-ting-kie is a slight, very lively bird, not much larger than a humming-bird, often seen moving quickly about among the grass and low bushes in South Africa'; and to this SCCS added: '(The Cape wren-warbler)'.

51 *'Ten little nigger boys . . . then there were nine'*: adapted in 1868 from a song composed by the American Septimus Winner in 1864, called 'Ten Little Indians' or 'Ten Little Injuns', this song became especially popular through the Christy-minstrels' visits to Cape Town in 1862 and 1865. See Nigel Worden, Elizabeth van Heyningen, and Vivian Bickford-Smith, *Cape Town: The Making of a City. An Illustrated Social History* (Cape Town: David Philip, 1998), 244. For OS's further use of this offensive term, see note to p. 53.

52 *Come to us!*: in her 1911 TS, OS deleted the sentence following on from this one: 'And we are drawn with an infinite longing, though that which they tell of, we know well, no man ever has seen or ever will!'

Chaldean . . . conception: from Genesis 3:16. See also note to p. 372.

53 *the little niggers*: nowhere in the novel does OS use this derogatory term in the authorial voice. It appears either in quotation, as in the song Frank sings (see p. 51), or in dialogue, as here and on p. 323, or in free indirect discourse, as on p. 233. The term was used authorially in *Undine* and in this chapter in the 1901 MS but was in the latter emended to the conventionally more neutral term 'Kaffir'; this revision is a key aspect of OS's increasing sensitivity to racist terminology.

54 *"geloofje"*: Du. for 'little belief' or 'folk belief' (Afk. *gelofie*). SCCS provides the following note for Unwin and Harper (he implies this is OS's note but it is not in her 1911 TS): 'Superstition.'

Goody-two-shoes: this term, long used to describe a highly virtuous child, was popularized through the publication of an anonymous children's story, *The History of Little Goody Two-Shoes* (1765).

56 *fifty or sixty volumes*: in the 1911 TS, OS explains how the child Rebekah acquired these volumes, before deciding on a deletion: 'volumes, ~~bought~~

~~with the money she had saved by drying peaches and pears and sending them to the market in the town~~'.

Illustrated London News: the world's first major illustrated weekly news magazine (est. 14 May 1842), particularly valued for its fine engravings. Well subscribed to in South Africa, it included numerous articles on South Africa.

Madonna della Sedia: or *Madonna della Seggiola*, painted by the Italian Renaissance artist Raphael (1483–1520), it depicts Mary, Christ's mother, holding her baby, watched by a young John the Baptist.

57 *She*: '~~You~~ ^She^' (1911 TS). Elsewhere OS draws in her reader by using the pronoun 'you', but she decided against it on this occasion.

58 *monkey ropes*: probably *Rhoicissus tomentosa*, a vine native to South Africa with rope-like stems often reaching to the top of 20-metre trees and looping across them. Thomas Pringle refers to one species of 'monkey's rope' (which he explains as the 'colonial name') as 'the native vine of South Africa' in his *Narrative of a Residence in South Africa* (1834), ed. A. M. Lewin Robinson (Cape Town: Struik, 1966), 93.

avondbloem: from the Du. *avond* (evening) and *bloem* (flower), now *aandblom* in Afk. (the Afk. term has several variants; see *DSAE*, 1). SCCS adds a footnote: 'Aandblom: evening flower (a species of hesperantha).' If the aandblom that OS refers to is a shrub, it could be the species *Struthiola* or *Gnidia* in Thymelaeaceae family. *Hesperantha* sp. is appropriate to sweet-smelling flowers that open at dusk.

to advise with: to consult (now obsolete in standard Eng.).

grafts and flutes: the practice known as flute-grafting involves accurate cuts of the stocks to allow surfaces to close easily, preventing disease.

59 *if he was by*: OS uses the Afk. *by* (here meaning 'present'); see also note to p. 23.

'Blessed are the pure in heart': Matthew 5:8.

everlasting flowers: probably *Helichrysum vestitum*, although this is also a general term for various species of plants whose dry papery rays (petal-like parts) retain their colour for years.

61 *'if they love them'*: in the 1911 TS, both here and in Bertie's earlier question to the tutor on p. 60, 'You do love me, don't you', OS changes the word 'like' to 'love'.

62 *'snysels'*: from the Afk. verb *sny* meaning *cut* (*DSAE*, 660). SCCS adds the following footnote: 'Dough cuttings, for soup.'

fountain: natural spring; now archaic in Eng. but preserved in SAE via the Afk. *fontein* (*DSAE*, 235).

63 *the Bay*: 'Port Elizabeth'. The city (in 2023 renamed Gqeberha to honour its Xhosa heritage) spreads around the coast of Algoa Bay, and is still sometimes called the Bay. Port Elizabeth was founded in 1820 by British settlers to the Cape, and named after Elizabeth Donkin, the late wife of the

then acting governor, Sir Rufane Donkin. SCCS attributes this footnote to OS, but it is not evident in the 1911 TS.

64 *saffron root*: OS's use of the term 'root' indicates that her reference is in fact to turmeric (*Curcuma longa*), which often substituted for saffron (derived from the flower of the *Crocus sativa*) in Cape Dutch cooking. Only the former was used medicinally, for its anti-inflammatory properties; in this case for what 'Ayah' supposes may be menstrual cramps.

65 *a faint glow . . . at the far end of the valley*: as another sign of the carelessness of her revision, OS adjusts her phrasing in the 1911 TS: '~~only~~ a faint glow ^only^ lingered at the far end of the valley' but either SCCS or Unwin and Harper rightly adjust this to 'a faint glow lingered only at the far end of the valley'.

Her father . . . muttered: SCCS added the two commas to the first two lines, thus stressing the rhythm of the first sentence, and provided the following note: 'Olive once drew attention to this rhythmic paragraph thus, and commented upon it:

Her father, as he passed her
On his way back from the sheep kraals,
Laid his hand upon her shoulder:
"It grows late and cold," he muttered.'

66 *even though*: SCCS, probably thrown by the semicolon after 'lately' in the 1911 TS, misunderstood OS's logic and changed 'though' to 'thought', as reproduced in Unwin and Harper.

67 *Bushman girl . . . bottle of wine*: this brief comment alludes to a history of social degradation, poverty, and induced addiction to alcohol, using what had already become, and what would for too long remain, a stereotype in white South African culture, that the author recirculates in 'The Problem of Slavery': '[Bushman] mothers readily forsaking their young or disposing of them for a trifle' (*TSA*, 108). OS recognizes in her political writing the damage done to the San. The solution she offers is for 'a millionaire [to buy] up thirty or forty large farms, [. . . and leave] the Bushmen at peace in the territory *not* trying to civilize them' (letter to John X Merriman, 29 June 1896, in *OSLO*). See also note to p. 69, as well as Rebekah's reference on p. 152.

Karroo: from the Khoi term *karo* ('desert-like'), also spelled Karoo (OS uses the variant spelling throughout her writing), a large arid region stretching across much of the Western Cape and Eastern Cape provinces and northwards into what would, between 1854 and 1994, be known as the Orange Free State. In OS's day the Eastern Cape province was known as the Eastern Province. See also note to p. 97.

69 *Bushman . . . Hottentot*: OS believed that there was a racial difference between the Khoi ('Hottentot') and San ('Bushman'). Traditionally the San were hunter-gatherers and the Khoi were pastoralists; nowadays, the distinctions between the two groups are a matter of debate, but are understood by some to be merely cultural, hence the term Khoisan for the

generic group (now said to contain not just two but numerous small groups that bear different names). For OS's own commentary, see 'The Problem of Slavery', in *TSA*, 106–9; and for historical research on the Khoisan, see Nigel Penn, *The Forgotten Frontier: Colonist and Khoisan on the Cape's Northern Frontier in the Eighteenth Century* (Athens: Ohio University Press; Cape Town: Double Storey Books, 2005).

70 *her feet were almost too small for her body*: an allusion to the Chinese practice of foot-binding, metaphorically indicating Bertie's childlike nature. Cf. Rebekah's self-to-self philosophizing: 'We scorn the Chinaman because his women compress their feet, not perceiving how infinitely more deadly and grotesque is the compression of our bodies' (p. 149); and 'We fit our sphere as a Chinese woman's foot fits her shoe, exactly, as though God had made both—and yet he knows nothing of either' (*AF*, 155).

She held them in her hand: 'hands' in Unwin and Harper, but 'hand' in the 1911 TS, followed by a reference her earlier editors should have noticed to 'her free hand' in the following paragraph—an indication of poor editing.

72 *Tennyson's Idylls of the King*: a cycle of twelve narrative poems by Alfred, Lord Tennyson (1808–92). John-Ferdinand may be reading just the first set of four, published in book form in 1859, or the second set of eight, published in book form in 1870 (the complete set was available only in 1889). For OS on Tennyson, see her letter to SCCS, 5 December 1906, in Appendix 2.

the sheep that had strayed in her father's veld: from the Du. and Afk. *veld* ('field'); now standard in SAE to refer to open, undeveloped countryside (*DSAE*, 764: 2) but OS uses it here to refer to 'fields' or 'lands'. The 1901 MS indicates that these are sheep from the neighbouring farm.

73 *Boer biscuits*: rusks; twice-baked dough, often with fermented raisins in the place of yeast (*DSAE*, 82). OS transposes the Afk. *boerebeskuit* (from the French *biscuit*).

ration room: the room from which the domestic servants and farm labourers were allotted food ('rations') as part of, or sometimes instead of, wages.

74 *honey creepers*: probably the wild clematis, a.k.a. traveller's joy, *Clematis brachiata*, a climbing plant which bears masses of small, sweet-scented flowers in late summer and autumn.

kunee trees: the Karoo kuni-bush, a.k.a. koeniebos, *Searsia undulata* (was *Rhus undulata*). Not in *DSAE* print but added to its online version. OS elsewhere describes the kunee tree as characteristic of the Karoo: 'a vast creeper-like tree, whose interlaced branches, touching the ground everywhere, forming beehive-shaped masses, looking like immense Kaffir huts, [and which] often [. . .] forms the foundation of [the] masses [of vegetation]' (*TSA*, 33–4). Cf. 'coonie' (*Undine*, 276).

to make medicine of: the bark of the boerboon roots is used for digestive purposes: to treat diarrhoea, for example (see O. O. Olajuyigbe and

A. J. Afolayan, 'Ethnobotanical Survey of Medicinal Plants Used in the Treatment of Gastrointestinal Disorders of the Eastern Cape Province, South Africa', *Journal of Medicinal Plants Research* 6/18 (2012), 3418).

74 *jasmine shrubs*: the starry wild jasmine, *Jasminium multipartum*, has a scrambling habit and can clump like a shrub; it grows profusely in the Eastern Cape, and is indigenous to South Africa.

sweet-henries: *Plumbago auriculata*; not in *DSAE*. See note below.

75 *plumbago*: OS provided the following footnote: 'Plumbago, or sweet-henry, as the Frontier children call it, has a delicate, pale-blue flower growing on a large partly creeping shrub. It is the great ornament of the Eastern Province bush. Its sky-like flowers are sensitive and curl up if roughly touched or plucked.'

76 *sheep's tail*: a culinary delicacy (fat-tailed sheep were bred in the Cape for the quality of the fat stored in the tail).

Daddy-long-legs: either the spider *Pholcus phalangiodes* (sometimes thought to be venomous) or the crane fly (*Nephrotoma* sp.), which has a thin body and stilt-like legs and often stunts the growth of plants.

77 *Angora goats*: originally from Asia Minor, brought to the Cape Colony in 1838, and the source of mohair. SCCS bred Angoras and published a book about them.

Boer goat: bred from indigenous stock, including from goats owned by the Khoisan, and selected for their meat rather than their milk; hardier and more resilient than Angoras.

79 *Milton*: John-Ferdinand is reading either John Milton's *Complete Poems and Major Prose* (indirectly alluded to in a later chapter, see note to p. 370) or, more likely, his epic poem, *Paradise Lost* (1667), referred to on p. 85. The latter is significant here for its being based on the biblical story of humankind's fall from innocence into shame. OS refers to reading Milton at different times of her life; see her letter to Adela Smith, 5 May 1910 (in Appendix 2).

love-grass: *Eragrostis capensis*, which has heart-shaped spikelets, but is technically not a lovegrass; 'African lovegrass' was the name given to *Eragrostis curvula*; a tufted, often tussocky, perennial grass exported to Oklahoma in the early twentieth century for soil stabilization.

chickweed: *Stellaria media*, native to Europe and introduced into South Africa during the 1700s; some varieties are naturalized in South Africa.

widows: the common blackjack, Afk. *wewenaar* ('widower'), either *Bidens pilosa* or *Bidens bipinnata*; naturalized in South Africa, it has a small, slender black seed with tiny claws at one end.

80 *wild mustard*: *Rapistrum rugosum*, native to various parts of Africa.

81 *an aloe has one flower, once; if you cut that down, nothing more comes*: this feature is not characteristic of the aloe. Rebekah is instead referring to

a species of agave which was introduced to the Cape soon after European settlement, and is now common throughout the Karoo and Eastern Cape. Aloes flower every year whereas agaves, which look somewhat similar, are semelparous; that is, they flower once and then die.

84 *Everyone at the farm seemed to like her except Griet*: in the 1911 TS, OS first emended and then deleted the only direct authorial comment about Griet's dislike of John-Ferdinand: '[Griet] who seemed to feel ^~~intuitively~~^ an even more virulent antagonism towards her, than ^~~that which~~^ to John Ferdinand'.

pumpkins: '~~parsnips~~ ^pumpkins^' (1911 TS).

85 *someone sleeping by her and caring for her*: OS added this last clause to the 1911 TS: 'sleeping by her. ^and caring for her.^'.

and she gave old Ayah, who did her room, a shawl she had knitted: OS added this last clause, without commas, to the 1911 TS.

a wild cry: '~~shriek~~ ^cry^' (1911 TS).

86 *How did . . . as she emptied the bath*: OS added Griet's statement and the clauses that follow to the 1911 TS, replacing 'How Veronica knew she was standing outside the door remained a mystery to her'. The effect is to add voice to Griet's fictional presentation.

aloes: Cape aloes, a juice derived from the succulent aloe leaf, *Aloe ferox* a.k.a. bitter aloe, is 'an effective laxative' (Coates Palgrave 80), besides having a long history of other medicinal use. 'Cape aloes' has no entry in the plant section under 'Cape' in *DSAE* print.

the tops of the tall blue-gum trees about whose homestead were just visible over the nek: OS, who sometimes uses 'about' meaning 'above', had difficulty with the syntax in this phrase, as the various deletions in the 1901 MS also show. It remained in the same muddled form there as in the 1911 TS. She might have reorganized the phrase as follows: 'above whose homestead the tops of the blue-gum trees were just visible when you climbed the nek'. The homestead referred to is on the De Wets' farm; see p. 63: 'We'll get Percy Lawrie to ride over to Mrs de Wet's and bring some blue-gum leaves'.

Algoa Bay: SCCS added the footnote 'Port Elizabeth', attributing it to OS, but no note by her is evident either in the 1911 TS or the 1901 MS. See also notes to pp. 63 and 97.

89 *Swedenborg*: first mentioned in the Prelude (see note to p. 9), as well as on pp. 58 and 262. OS's repetition of the father's reading matter stresses how strong was Swedenborg's influence, via John Wesley (1703–91), on most nineteenth-century Evangelical and missionary movements, especially the Lutherans. Swedenborg's eight-volume *Arcana Caelestia* ('Heavenly Mysteries') and other writings interpreted the Scriptures as the true and immediate word of God, and provided practical guidelines for human conduct, especially care for others, since faith alone was insufficient for salvation. OS's own father had been trained as a Lutheran, employed first

by the London Missionary Society and then by the Wesleyan Missionary Society.

89 *had had put up*: OS's insertion in the 1911 TS ('^had had^ put up') draws attention to the fact that she now, in 1911, wishes to stress the labour of others in this racist, colonial society.

90 *the old Kaffir man she was nursing*: the 1911 TS has 'her old Kaffir man she was nursing' but OS's grammar has been corrected here, whereas it was left as is in Unwin and Harper.

91 *then she loosened herself . . . the bank*: see the word 'lost' creeping into what OS wrote here in her 1911 TS: 'then she ^lostened herself from his arm &^ sat down again on the bank'. This was corrected in Unwin and Harper.

92 *I only have not long ago told you how I love you, only because I thought you knew, as I knew, how you loved me*: SCCS or Unwin and Harper delete the first 'only'; this small change barely improves the clumsy sentence which arguably draws attention either to John-Ferdinand's clumsily awkward thinking, odd though this may be for a man who reads Tennyson and Milton, or to some falsity in his articulation. Had she wished to, OS might have revised the sentence, but the point about John-Ferdinand is made: he is so sure Bertie loves him that he felt no need to articulate his love. The present edition leaves OS's sentence as it is, given the possibility that it was intended to draw attention to some awkwardness or falsity.

93 *the cicadas cry*: while both a reference in the Prelude and later references in this chapter draw attention to the cry of a single cicada (see pp. 12 and 92), the 1911 TS does not include an apostrophe here or in the chapter title; and elsewhere in the chapter, too, the plural is used.

under their feet as they walked: the 1911 TS reads: 'under your foot as you walked', but OS changed 'your' to 'their'.

riems: SCCS added the following note: 'Raw-hide thongs.' The term 'riem', which comes from Du. and Afk. *riem* (s.) and *rieme* (pl.), has entered SAE at least in its singular form; see *DSAE*, 594.

inspan: harness oxen to the wagon, from the Du. *inspannen*; the term has entered SAE (see *DSAE*, 317).

94 *How is this, Bertie?*: OS retains the sense of the mother's Afk. speech: *Hoe's dit?*

though she did not understand what: in the 1911 TS, OS added this final clause to her portrayal of Griet's interiority.

95 *I will go*: 'will' is not underlined in the 1911 TS but Unwin and Harper italicize it. For reference to its Afk. timbre, see note to p. 37.

96 *kerchief*: OS deleted the word 'shawl' in the 1911 TS and, oddly, substituted 'handkerchief', despite the earlier reference to Ayah's 'little shawl' (p. 9). She seems to wish to suggest a lightweight rather than a heavy covering for Ayah's shoulders (such that Bertie is knitting for Ayah, p. 85).

But since handkerchief as we know it would not fit around the shoulders and also since in Ch. VI Bertie dreams of Ayah's 'little yellow shawl' (p. 177), the word 'shawl' may well have been retained here. However, since OS wished to change the word 'kerchief' has been substituted for 'shawl', similar to the substitution of the handkerchief that Dorcas wears around her head (p. 243). Unwin and Harper retain 'handkerchief' here and elsewhere.

'O, ja, Heere!': *Heere* is a variant, like *Here* and *Heer*, of the Du. word for 'Lord' or 'God'.

97 *standing full in the door*: readers might expect 'doorway' here and elsewhere, but OS wishes to use 'door'; see 1911 TS: 'door ~~way~~'.

as the wagon was climbing the nek: OS adds the following footnote: 'In those days there was no railway in the Eastern Province, and persons going to Cape Town were obliged to make the whole journey overland by wagon or cart, taking several weeks; or they might travel by wagon or cart as far as the Bay (Port Elizabeth) and take the steamer round the coast to Cape Town. Even by this route a journey such as Rebekah's would take twelve days or fourteen.' The railway from Cradock to Cape Town was established only in the 1890s. The road distance is about 810 km (503 miles). The road distance across the 'Eastern Province' (now Eastern Cape province) from Cradock to Port Elizabeth/Gqeberha is 250 km (155 miles).

98 *John-Ferdinand shows his new house*: in the 1911 TS, OS retitled this chapter by striking out the name 'Veronica' ('John-Ferdinand shows ~~Veronica~~ his new house').

99 *only a Kaffir cook*: OS's manual change in the 1911 TS (from 'he had no good cook' to 'he had only a Kaffir cook') may have been intended to indicate the mother's racialized perspective.

Night Thoughts: written by Edward Young (1681–1765), *The Complaint: or, Night-Thoughts on Life, Death, & Immortality* was published in nine parts between 1742 and 1745. OS had perhaps seen, or would certainly have agreed with, George Eliot's damning review of Young's volume in *Westminster Review* (1857), 'Worldliness and Other-Worldliness: the Poet Young', in *The Essays of George Eliot*, ed. Nathan Sheppard (New York: Funk & Wagnalls, 1883), 205–56, esp. 236–8.

Keble's hymns: John Keble (1792–1866) was a churchman and hymnwriter, as well as a professor of poetry at England's Oxford University and a leader of the Oxford Movement. Oxford's Keble College is named after him. The reference may be to *The Christian Year: Thoughts in Verse for the Sundays and Holydays throughout the Year* (1827), or *Lyra Innocentium: Thoughts in Verse on Christian Children, Their Ways, and Their Privileges* (1846), or the selection of his hymns in *Hymns Ancient and Modern*.

100 *biltong*: dried meat; from the Du. *bil* ('rump') and *tong* ('strip')

101 *dervish*: a member of one of the various Muslim ascetic orders. The reference here is to what are commonly known as the 'whirling dervishes'. OS

added this detail between 1901 and 1911. In the 1901 MS the chapter ends as follows: 'Griet shouted hurrah, & tossed up her little skirts as the cart drove away; & the little mother said it all seemed like a dream.'

102 *so*: cf. 'so' (1911 TS); 'for' (Unwin and Harper). SCCS again misunderstood OS's use of 'so' and changed it to 'for'. See also Note on the Text, p. xl.

pine plantations streched away up the mountainsides: pine plantations were established on Devil's Peak in 1893 to restore its ravaged slopes, as Carl August Luckhoff notes in his *Table Mountain: Our National Heritage after Three Hundred Years* (Cape Town: Balkema, 1951), 112–13. In the 1911 TS, OS changed 'pine' to 'fir', following a common procedure in which the term 'fir' is wrongly applied to the genus *Pinus*.

Devil's Peak: along with Table Mountain, Lion's Head, and Signal Hill, Devil's Peak forms the mountainous backdrop to Cape Town, and is the closest of the four to the area in Rondebosch where Rebekah lives; see letter to Havelock Ellis, 7 January 1890 (in Appendix 2).

giant: the reference to the mountain as a 'giant' originated in Luis de Camões's *Os Lusiadas* (*The Lusiads*, 1572), which likened Table Mountain to a threatening Greek Titan, Adamastor.

great, godlike, placid eye: cf. 'eye' (1911 TS); 'eye' (1901 MS); 'eyes' (Unwin and Harper). Possibly OS intended the singular term to have the same significance as the negative one-eyed vision Rebekah defined later: 'Are you not, and one-eyedly, perverting the teaching of great minds, as the priestly in all ages pervert and make falsehood of the perception of the great prophets who preceded them?' (p. 154).

one of the little stations: the Cape Town–Wynberg railway line, which passed through Rondebosch and Newlands, was established by December 1864. It extended to Muizenberg in 1882 and to Simon's Town in 1890.

Malays: technically, people of Malayan origin (Malaya was renamed Malaysia in 1946), but the term was used in the British Cape Colony for people from the Dutch East Indies, perhaps on account of the fact that the Malay language was the medium of trade (*DSAE*, 437–8). From the mid-nineteenth century, the Malay language was hardly used at the Cape, and 'Malays' became the term used for Muslims in the Cape, whatever their actual geographical origin.

coloured: a charged and changing term in South African racial history; the general meaning is 'mixed-race'; see *DSAE*, 160; but it was also sometimes used to refer to the Khoisan.

103 *the Peninsula*: the Cape Peninsula.

Cape of Storms: the Portuguese explorer Bartolemeu Dias, who rounded the Cape in 1488, is said by some to have called it both *Cabo das Tormenta*s (Cape of Storms) and *Cabo da Boa Esperança* (Cape of Good Hope). Historical records vary, but see B. W. Diffie, *Foundations of the Portuguese Empire, 1415–1580* (Minneapolis: University of Minnesota Press, 1977), 161.

Avenue: the word, capitalized just on this occasion in the 1911 TS, designates Newlands Avenue, which ran and still runs from the edge of Rondebosch, where Rebekah lives, into and through the neighbouring suburb.

104 *Rebekah had never asked . . . from her sister*: in the 1911 TS, OS added these last two sentences, helping explain the later silence between the two sisters.

106 *glee club*: a musical or choir group.

and now and then she told some gossip . . . sent them out tea and cake: OS added these extensive details to the 1911 TS, from 'Cape Town' to 'cake', replacing a shorter comment in which Mrs Drummond speaks simply 'about the people she knew, and their affairs'.

107 *the saintly John*: after this comment, OS made a significant deletion: '~~I believe he never kissed a woman in his life but his mother or his aunt~~' (1911 TS).

109 *ante-nuptial contract*: until the later twentieth century, under Roman Dutch law practised in South Africa, all marriages were in community of property unless an antenuptial contract specified otherwise. Only with an antenuptial contract was the wife entitled to own or retain ownership of property; even so, she could not sign legal contracts independently of her husband.

110 *She liked the labour*: a comparison of the 1901 MS and the 1911 TS shows that both the presence of the 'coloured boy' and the details about Rebekah's 'labour' are late additions.

surprise for: oddly, but perhaps there is some biographical significance here, SCCS silently replaced OS's 'for' in the 1911 TS with 'to' (Unwin and Harper). OS's original phrasing has been restored.

111 *They spent all the mornings together*: virtually none of the discussion (between Mrs Drummond and Veronica Grey) presented in this section appears in the 1901 MS. OS's correspondence refers over and again to the care she took in revising this and related passages, including earlier than 1901. See Appendix 2 for several references.

all three: the following paragraph makes clear that John-Ferdinand has joined the two women.

112 *the holland cover*: the fine linen used for furniture covers typically came from Holland, and the name stuck.

113 *'"And learn how pure . . . My own wife's face!"'*: not identified.

115 *'"What have I done . . . a wife for me?"'*: not identified. Given the earlier reference to Young's verse, both this and the unidentified verse a little earlier may well be of the author's ironic making; that is, John Ferdinand's sentimental versifying.

117 *to help the maid carry down the packages*: among various other differences between the 1901 MS and the 1911 TS is the presence in the latter of a housemaid assisting with the packages.

118 *tatting*: a traditional handicraft in which cotton or linen is woven with either a shuttle or a crochet hook to make a lacy pattern.

123 *statue of Hercules*: Hercules is the Roman name for the Greek demigod Herakles. The statue is a repeated reference in OS's novel: see also pp. 125, 138, 236, and 371.

Variation of Plants and Animals under Domestication: Charles Darwin's *The Variation of Animals and Plants Under Domestication* (1868). That OS transposed 'Animals' and 'Plants' (left unchanged here) suggests not just Rebekah's priorities, but also her own; see also OS's journal, 26 January 1876, and her letter to Havelock Ellis, 26 November 1884 (in Appendix 2).

Cornwallis Grammar: Caroline Frances Cornwallis, *The General Principles of Grammar* (1847).

Smith's Latin Principia: William George Smith, *Principia Latina* (1863). Studying as a young woman for what she at one stage hoped would become a medical career, OS went 'three times through Smith's Latin Principia by myself!' as she put it later in a letter to Will Schreiner in 1912 (in *OSLO*).

124 *Pre-Adamite Earth*: probably *The Pre-Adamite Earth: Contributions to Theological Science* (1847) by John Harris, who argued that a cosmos predated and anticipated God's creation of man, hence his titular reference to 'pre-Adamite'.

125 *On the brown carpet . . . round the desk*: this image may well stand as an oblique allusion to Charlotte Perkins Gilman's 'streak that runs round the room [. . .] a long, straight, even *smooch*, as if it had been rubbed over and over', in *The Yellow Wallpaper* (1892). See *The Charlotte Perkins Gilman Reader: The Yellow Wallpaper & Other Fiction*, ed. Ann J. Lane (London: The Women's Press, 1981), 15. For a speculative essay on OS's and Gilman's 'mutually international influences' (52), which does not, however, consider this particular fictional congruence, see Judith A. Allen, *The Feminism of Charlotte Perkins Gilman: Sexualities, Histories, Progressivism* (Chicago: University of Chicago Press, 2009), ch. 4.

126 *a visit found*: meaning unclear; SCCS or the typist may have had difficulty deciphering the MS: OS may have written, for instance, 'a visit made' or 'an insect found'.

128 *two opposing intellectual conceptions of the nature of the universe*: see *AF*, 101–18 ('Times and Seasons') for an earlier representation of the opposing conceptions, the former based on religious faith, the latter based on scientific inquiry.

131 *'There is no small sin . . . the will of God is great'*: Rebekah is probably thinking of John Calvin whose *Institutes of the Christian Religion* (1536) departed from St Augustine's teaching in rejecting the distinction between mortal and venal sin. See Jean Calvin, *Institutes of the Christian Religion*, (1563).

innoxious: harmless. 'Innocuous' is more common, but 'innoxious' tends to be used in a medical register, and thus suits the metaphors of Rebekah's thinking.

we know that it is vital: i.e. that the truth is vital.

136 *History of the Ancient World*: probably Philip Smith's *A History of the Ancient World*, 3 vols. (1863–5), the first volume of which has the relevant map at the front.

138 *hetairai*: courtesans. In ancient Greece, *hetairai* (variants: *heterai, heterae*) were educated and talented women who served as paid or financially compensated companions to wealthy or powerful men, actively taking part in symposia, and controlling their own income. Neither necessarily providing sexual service nor being financially dependent on sexual service, they were distinct from both prostitutes and wives.

140 *ignis fatuus*: a.k.a. 'will o' the wisp'; phosphorescent light commonly created by the atmospheric conditions around bogs, swamps, or marshes, and said to lure travellers from their safe paths on to unsafe ground.

142 *The man whose ideal it is . . . snapped off?*: this convoluted sentence, as reproduced in Unwin and Harper, has been left unchanged, but rearranging the word order renders its meaning clearer: 'The man whose ideal it is that human good and justice are finally served by the non-requital of injuries and the large expansion of sympathy even toward those who inflict suffering on himself—does his failure to evoke any response, and his final crushing beneath the hands he refused to strike, prove anything but the solidarity of humanity and that the foremost branch which grows too far beyond its fellows must ultimately be snapped off?'

144 *Shelley . . . Keats*: both favourite poets of OS's, 'lofty souls'; see her letter to Havelock Ellis, 7 August 1912 (in Appendix 2).

poisonous arrows: had OS revised this passage, she might well have replaced 'poisonous arrows' with 'cannon fire', in line with the thinking Rebekah makes evident in the stories she tells the children. See e.g. p. 338. The absence of this revision, along with OS's use of the word 'savage', may help date this section or, indeed, the entire chapter, as written long before Chapter XII, making the latter a late chapter in the compositional history of the novel.

145 *prostitute king*: by this idiosyncratic phrasing, Rebekah does not mean 'pimp', but instead confers on royalty the criminal act of engaging in, benefiting from, or condoning prostitution, or any acts of exploitation in an extractive economy.

146 *Telemachus . . . stop the gladiatorial conflict*: Telemachus tried in 391 CE to stop a gladiatorial fight in a Roman amphitheatre, and was stoned to death by the crowd, after which the Christian emperor banned gladiatorial fights. He is memorialized as a martyr in John Foxe's *Book of Martyrs*. (Odysseus' son is also called Telemachus.)

146 *Barabbas*: the New Testament figure whom Pontius Pilate, under pressure from the crowd, freed from crucifixion instead of Jesus (see Matthew 27:16–22).

147 *Lucrezia Borgia . . . as she glides noiselessly by*: Rebekah's implied comparison is between Lucrezia Borgia (1480–1519), on the one hand, who is a stereotype of feminine promiscuity and treachery, and, on the other hand, outwardly virtuous figures like Veronica Grey and Mrs Drummond.

148 *parvenu*: a recent arrival in an established social class.

superstructure: Karl Marx's term for society's cultural and political structures, which are created through its 'base' structure (labour conditions, property relations, etc.). While there is no direct evidence that OS read his *Contribution to the Critique of Political Economy* (1859), she appears to be using the term in a similar way, and was of course in discussion with her close friend Eleanor, Marx's daughter, and other socialists of the time who were reading Marx.

150 *the Prussians*: Prussia was conquered in the thirteenth century by the Teutonic Knights, a German crusading order, who regarded the pagan Prussian tribes as barbaric.

back-beat: this appears to be OS's own term for an evolutionary return, perhaps used here rather than 'reversion' in order to provide a more positive implication. Other cognate evolutionary terms apparently her own are 'down-drawers' and 'down-draught' in this chapter (see pp. 144 and 147), although used there with negative implications.

151 *the Kaffirs . . . month after month*: in Moorosi's 1879 rebellion in Lesotho, then a British Protectorate, the Baphuti people were held in an eight-month siege by the Cape British forces (the white militia were assisted by Basotho and Mfengu soldiers). The Cape colonial government, in support of white colonists who had been invading Baphuti territory, was forcing Moorosi to submit to its authority in all political, judicial, and cultural matters. Moorosi's mountain fortress (*qhobosheane* in seSotho), south-east of the Orange River, was indeed on 'flat-topped' terrain, and several hundred Baphuti were killed, although there appears to be no record in written historical accounts of starved women and children among the wounded and dead. See Anthony Atmore, 'The Moorosi Rebellion: Lesotho, 1879', in Robert I. Rotberg and Ali A. Mazrui (eds.), *Protest and Power in Black Africa* (New York: Oxford University Press, 1970), 3–35; and Peter Saunders, 'The Moorosi War', in his *'Throwing Down White Man': Cape Rule and Misrule in Colonial Lesotho* (Pontypool: Merlin Press, 2011), 64–81.

152 *Pharisee*: a Jew who observed Mosaic law; in Christianity the term became synonymous with hypocrisy. Unwin and Harper do not capitalize the term, thereby negating its historicity.

153 *Nero*: Roman emperor (37–68 CE); posthumously declared a public enemy by the Senate.

the survival of the fittest: deriving from Herbert Spencer's *Principles of Biology* (1864), this term was taken up by social Darwinists, including OS's friend Karl Pearson. In many ways Rebekah's projected interlocutor reflects Pearson's thinking or its imagined logical extensions.

155 *the sea lion who carries about his young in the bag on his own person*: sea lions are mammals but not marsupial. OS may have imagined that the layers of blubber contained a pouch.

156 *the Swiss who gathered a score of spears . . . for his fellows to . . . win their nation's freedom*: Arnold Winkelried, or von Winkelried, a legendary fourteenth-century hero, whose sacrifice in battle brought victory to the Swiss against the Austrians in the Battle of Sempach (1386).

The legend of the mother: though there are many mythical stories about courageous mothers in history, such a story linked to a 'bird of prey' has not been identified.

157 *bass notes alone*: struggling with OS's handwriting and, indeed, her meaning, SCCS added the following footnote: 'After "alone", the MS (insofar as it is legible) runs: "Without the . . . and the air and the . . ., which alone gives it form and life," is like, etc. This sentence is omitted.' SCCS did not speculate in his footnote on what OS might have written, but we may do so, depending on SCCS's deciphered words. Given the word 'bass' (which SCCS mistook as 'base'), and our knowledge of OS's and Rebekah's view of the unity or harmony of life as both sociological and spiritual, OS may have continued Rebekah's musical metaphor about a man who defines life only through its 'destructive element' or its 'bass notes alone': 'To attempt to explain and sum up life by considering this element only [the destruction of the weak by the strong] is like the man who should attempt to represent a great musical symphony by playing its base notes alone, without the upper notes and the air [i.e. tune] and the harmony, which alone gives it form and life.'

158 *the mighty jaw and the almighty claw*: cf. Tennyson's 'Nature, red in tooth and claw' in his *In Memoriam* (1850), lvi. 15.

''Tis love . . . go round!': the exact quotation has not been identified, but see 'Love makes the world go round' in the *Oxford Dictionary of Proverbs*. OS may well have come across it in ch. 9 of Lewis Carroll's *Alice's Adventures in Wonderland* (1865), in the Duchess's voice. The dictum appears to be older than that, however, since in 1788 James Hurdis, professor of Poetry at Oxford, parodied it in his 'The Village Curate': ''Tis drink | And only drink, that makes the world go "round".'

between species and species and distinct groups: OS may have intended to write, 'among species and between species and distinct groups', but the meaning remains unclear. SCCS's version, as in Unwin and Harper, is reproduced here.

162 *the possible Shakespeares we might have had*: cf. 'some mute inglorious Milton' in Thomas Gray's 'Elegy Written in a Country Churchyard'

(1751) and the limited opportunities open to Shakespeare's imagined sister in Virginia Woolf's 'A Room of One's Own' (a lecture delivered in 1928 and published in 1929).

to poach on deer in the green forests: Rebekah alludes to the legend that Shakespeare was once caught poaching on an estate in Warwickshire; see Samuel Schoenbaum, *William Shakespeare: A Documentary Life* (Oxford: Clarendon Press, 1975), 82–7.

163 *osseously*: concerning bone structure.

165 *no man liveth to himself and no man dieth to himself*: 'For none of us liveth to himself, and no man dieth to himself' (Romans 14:7).

166 *Spirit of the Ages*: OS's essay 'The Boer' explains the term: 'That complexus of knowledge and thought, with its resulting modes of action and feeling, which for the want of a better term we are accustomed to call "the spirit of the age," and which binds into a more or less homogeneous whole the life of all European nations, is created by the action of speech and mainly of opinion ossified and rendered permanent, portable, in the place of literature' (*TSA*, 93). Cf. William Hazlitt's *The Spirit of the Age* (1825), and other nineteenth-century discussions of zeitgeist in, e.g., Thomas Carlyle's *Sartor Resartus* (1833–4) and Matthew Arnold's *Literature and Dogma* (1873).

alit: (archaic) alighted.

When the Spirit of the Ages . . . desolate spot: in this section of the paragraph, OS's pronouns become erratic: the Spirit is first called 'he' and then becomes 'it' before returning to 'he'; the woman is first called 'it' before becoming 'she'. Unwin and Harper reproduce the erratic pronouns but they have been regularized in this edition, starting with 'her eyes' instead of 'its eyes', and ending with 'he cried' rather than 'it cried'.

168 *strong and hard and shaped like a man's*: cf. Darwin: 'We thus see that in many, probably in all cases, the secondary characters of each sex lie dormant or latent in the opposite sex, ready to be evolved', in *The Variation of Animals and Plants Under Domestication*, in *The Works of Charles Darwin*, ed. Paul H. Barrett and R. B. Freeman (London: William Pickering, 1988), ii. 23.

169 *mix on*: from the Afk. *aanmaak* ('mix'), *aan* providing OS's 'on'.

170 *chatelaine*: a hook or chain worn at the waist for holding keys and other items in daily use.

172 *bobotie*: 'A traditional dish (probably of Malay origin) made of lightly curried minced meat baked with a savoury custard topping' (*DSAE*, 79: a). The term is part of SAE.

the patriarch Jacob . . . or was it Job?: according to the Old Testament, Jacob had twelve sons and one daughter, born of four women (see Genesis 29:32–30:23 and 35:17–18), whereas Job had one wife, and seven sons and three daughters (see Job 1:2 and 42:13).

Brownlee's: this name stands as the only mention of Frank's social circle other than references to the 'glee club'.

173 *Japanese lanterns*: these change on p. 175 to 'Chinese lanterns'. In either case, they are made of paper or silk.

174 *tore from the waist to the bottom*: this echoes the figurative language used in Ch. IV, p. 93: 'tore it from top to bottom'.

'Oh the torture . . . cannot follow thee': from the popular American Civil War song titled 'Just after the battle, Mother'. OS's second line is slightly different from the version in 'America Singing: Nineteenth-Century Song Sheets' (accessible online from the Library of Congress website).

175 *She turned into the next avenue . . . at Rebekah's gate*: understanding the position of Rebekah's house in relation to the avenues in Newlands reveals Bertie's endeavour not to be seen re-entering the house. Bertie runs through the area called the 'great avenues' (see p. 102), and then down Newlands Avenue ('now in the great avenue') but does not take the front entrance to the property, instead turning the corner in order to arrive at its side entrance, whereupon she needs to cross the veranda to enter the front door of the house. That the house is on a corner formed by two avenues is confirmed by the later reference to 'the front avenue', which is Newlands Avenue (see p. 213).

181 *black boy*: this is OS's first use of the word 'black' in this context. In Cape Town in the 1880s there were few Africans. Further on in this chapter, the same character is referred to as a 'coloured boy' (p. 184; see also p. 360). The terms 'black' and 'coloured' were not generally used interchangeably in South Africa in the late nineteenth or early twentieth centuries, but OS may be adopting a term used in the USA.

182 *Simon's Town*: established in 1680 as a water anchorage for ships of the Dutch East India Company. Lying in False Bay, on the Indian Ocean side of the Cape Peninsula, it is roughly 44 km (27 miles) from Cape Town.

185 *the Flats*: the Cape Flats was the name given to a flat, sandy area bridging the Cape Peninsula and the mainland (for further mentions, see pp. 201 and 207).

186 *five o'clock in the morning*: the time is 'half past four' on p. 185, and Rebekah has been listening for Frank for over fifty minutes. In character, Frank exaggerates the earliness of the hour.

187 *jackass-fool*: a jackass is, literally, a male ass or donkey.

Norfolk jacket: loose, belted, single-breasted jacket with box pleats at the back and front. Designed originally as a comfortable shooting jacket, it was fashionable in the 1860s.

192 *octopuses . . . would drag you down and absorb you*: Rebekah may be thinking of the mythic monsters of Victor Hugo's *The Toilers of the Sea* (*Les Travailleurs de la mer*, 1866) and Jules Verne's *Twenty Thousand Leagues*

Under the Sea (*Vingt mille lieues sous les mers*, 1870), although the tentacles of the giant Pacific octopus *Enteroctopus dofleini* may possibly sometimes extend to this length; see William L. High, 'The Giant Pacific Octopus', *Marine Fisheries Review* 38/9 (1976), 18.

198 *Somerset Strand*: a seaside resort 50 km (31 miles) from Cape Town, situated on the eastern shore of False Bay, and just over 20 km (12 miles) by land from Muizenberg.

199 *Robertson and Worcester*: according to SCCS, OS added the following footnote: 'Worcester is 109 miles inland from Cape Town on the main line; Robertson is 30 miles farther, on a branch line; both are in an opposite direction from Somerset Strand. In those days there was no train to them.'

Muizenberg: according to SCCS, OS added the following footnote:

> Muizenberg is a seaside place 15 miles from Cape Town, now connected by rail, but in those days only to be reached by a lovely veld drive; after you left Wynberg you came to few houses except Rathfelder's Hotel and some scattered farms among vineyards and cultivated fields; for the rest, there were wild trees and shrubs.
>
> At Muizenberg itself, where now red-brick hotels and lodging houses alternate with tin or whitewashed shanties, and the railway whistle screams, and rows of bathing houses cover the shore, and half- clad children, not rising to the simple dignity of the nude or maintaining the convention of ordinary clothing, paddle on the sand— at Muizenberg there was then one solitary farmhouse known as Farmer Peck's, with a thatched roof and mud floors, where travellers might put up their horses and obtain a simple meal. Above towered the mountain from whose crags an eagle might still sometimes be seen rising, casting its long shadow on the unsullied slopes; and below stretched the long, long curve of white sandy beach, unflecked, except where, here or there, a jelly-fish or a 'Portuguese Mariner', thrown by the long smooth waves, decked the shore. Far out the white breakers curved in long unbroken lines, and to the right, where the sand and the curve of the bay ended, great rocks which through the ages had fallen from the crags above lined the water, and the waves ran singing in and out among them. As far as the eye could reach there was no living thing, but it might be the eagle from the crags, or the white seagulls hovering over the water, or the little dots of glittering life upon the sand.

Given the reference to 'Portuguese Mariner', what OS calls a jellyfish is probably a bluebottle, *Physalia physalis*, usually known as 'Portuguese man-of-war'.

200 *Farmer Peck's*: the inn was built in 1825 as a halfway house between Cape Town and Simon's Town. See OS's footnote reproduced on p. 199. See also letter from OS to Adela Smith, 14 December 1909 (in Appendix 2).

great white seagulls: probably the kelp gull, a.k.a. Southern black-backed gull (*Larus dominicanus*), which measures 60 cm (23.5 in) from the tip of the bill to the end of the tail.

201 *aigrette*: the tufted crest of the egret, used as a plume to adorn the head or a hat; it may also have been made of gems.

203 *hipped*: preoccupied by, obsessed with.

206 *jellybag*: a style of hat or cap, usually of wool, worn snugly around the head.

207 *Adderley Street*: originally Heerengracht, a major residential street in old Cape Town, it was renamed in 1850 and became the city's commercial hub.

208 *blockhouse*: one of three small, isolated forts on the slopes of Devil's Peak, built by the British in the first occupation of the Cape in 1795, as an extension of existing Dutch fortifications.

silver trees: *Leucadendron argenteum* a.k.a. *Protea argentea*, native to the Cape Peninsula and found mostly on the lower slopes of Table Mountain from Lion's Head to Devil's Peak. The dense velvety hairs on the leaves produce a distinctive silvery sheen.

213 *because I was a woman*: see note to p. 109. See also letter from OS to Adela Smith, 5 May 1910 (in Appendix 2).

216 *nothing mattered to me . . . show me that they knew*: OS might have clarified her meaning by writing instead: 'nothing mattered to me, not even if people would come and talk to me of you and show me that they knew' or 'nothing mattered to me, as long as people didn't come and talk to me of you and show me that they knew'.

stripes: lashes.

220 *vleis*: ponds or low-lying marshy ground, from the Du. or Afk. *vallei* (valley). See *DSAE*, 775.

221 *terrier of no full breed*: in his *Life of Olive Schreiner* (London: T. Fisher Unwin, 1924), SCCS writes of 'a little fox-terrier [. . .] intensely loved by Olive' as a child (74).

222 *And, sometimes, I have asked . . . your fingers*: pronouns have been regularized in this paragraph. In Unwin and Harper they remain erratic.

227 *the little brown history*: possibly William Walker's *Paroemiologia Anglo-Latina*, or, *A Collection of English and Latin Proverbs* (1672), which includes the proverb Rebekah thinks of.

228 *'Wat wil jij hê?'*: OS added the following footnote: 'Literally, "What do you want?" But the pronoun "*jij*" is in Cape Dutch, the only language of the coloured people of the West, and is the most extreme insult when applied to a superior. It is used only to children or servants. Even equals avoid its use as much as possible.' By 'West', OS means the Western Cape.

234 *Caledon*: situated about 100 km (62 miles) east of Cape Town in a farming district, Caledon was named after the second Earl of Caledon and first

British governor of the Cape (1806–11). Established in 1810, it was by 1870 a thriving community, famous for the hot springs that had been long used by the Khoi who populated the region.

235 *Sea Point*: a suburb of Cape Town, Sea Point is loosely used here to indicate the Atlantic suburbs more generally. Cricket matches were usually played on Green Point Common in Green Point, the suburb adjoining Sea Point.

239 *red karroo*: ochre-coloured soil is characteristic of the region.

the town where Aunt Mary-Anna lived: SCCS added a footnote: 'Cradock'. Proclaimed a township in 1814 (formalized by title deed in 1818) in the Eastern Cape region of the Cape Colony, Cradock functioned largely as the centre of an agricultural community until the establishment in 1880 of the railway connecting it to Port Elizabeth, which postdates the narrative action in this chapter and in Ch. IV (see note to p. 97). As a young woman OS began her writing career in Cradock, living there or close by for nearly ten years. For further reference to the town and surrounding district, see note to p. 360.

river bed: SCCS provided a footnote: 'Fish River'. A.k.a. the Great Fish River, it runs through the Eastern Cape; during the nineteenth century, it formed the border of the Cape Colony.

a human corpse: the image may help date the narrative: there was mostly peace on the frontier between 1853 and 1877 in a period otherwise marked by the Cape Frontier Wars (also called the Xhosa Wars) of 1779–1879.

buck-wagons: large, strong transport wagons with a frame projecting over the wheels; from the Afk. *bokwa* (the first syllable referring to the body of the wagon, and *wa* meaning 'wagon'), according to *DSAE*, 118. Alternatively, the Du. and Afk. word *bak*, which translates as 'body of the wagon' and is pronounced like 'buck', seems more likely as a source. SCCS's poem 'A Song of the Wagon-Whip' opens with the words, 'The great buck-wagon'; for the poem, see *A Centenary Book of South African Verse*, compiled by F. Carey-Slater (London: Longmans, Green, 1925), 61–3.

hotel at the corner: SCCS's footnote reads: 'The Victoria Hotel.' Built in 1840 as Victoria Manor, and incorporated into a row of townhouses, it advertised as a hotel in the early 1850s, and not only still stands but also helps host an annual Schreiner Karoo Writers Festival.

Cobb and Co.: a transport company also mentioned in *AF*, 157; Lyndall travels in one of its coaches.

Diamond Fields: SCCS added the following note: 'Now Kimberley'. The Diamond Fields, the source of the diamonds procured by the Jewish figure introduced later in this chapter, were established in the 1870s; Kimberley was formally founded in 1873 (see also note to p. 254). For histories of Kimberley, see Robert Vicat Turrell, *Capital and Labour on the Kimberley Diamond Fields, 1871–1890* (Cambridge: Cambridge University

Press, 1987); and William H. Worger, *South Africa's City of Diamonds: Mine Workers and Monopoly Capital; Kimberley, 1867–1895* (Johannesburg: Ad Donker; New Haven: Yale University Press, 1987).

240 *'Nagmaal'*: Communion service for the Holy Sacrament in the Dutch Reformed Church, usually held four times a year, and attended by a large congregation from the remote farming districts. Many Boer families moved away from Cradock in the 1830s, leaving the area in a show of discontent at British rule and the abolition of slavery in order to trek northwards, but they often returned for *nagmaal*. The Afk. term derives from the Du. *nacht* ('night') and *maal* ('meal').

ironstones: sedimentary rock containing a substantial proportion of iron minerals; sometimes banded on account of the sedimentation.

Kaffir Location: while the earliest recorded South African application of the word 'location' was related to dwellings used by the British 1820 Settlers, this word (like 'township') developed in a different, ethnically specific direction, as indicated in John Nixon's memoir, *Among the Boers* (1880): 'The natives are not allowed to live in the town, but reside in a "location" assigned to them outside it' (quoted in *DSAE*, 425).

241 *Dorcas*: see Acts 9:36 ff.

242 *sosatie*: SCCS added the following note: 'Roasted curried meat.' From the Javanese *sesate* ('skewered meat'), the meat may alternate with vegetables on the skewer, and may be spiced rather than simply curried (*DSAE*, 663).

'Our little cook . . . turn out': the use of the third person is characteristic of the Afk. language in the context of Afrikaner patriarchy, with its old-fashioned respectfulness and distance within family relations.

244 *'London's Burning! Fire! Fire!'*: see note to p. 29. That (as Bertie recalls) Rebekah sings this song to her little sister to wake her out of a nightmare (this might well be a nightmare of social shaming) bears an uncanny relation to SCCS's statement to Havelock Ellis that OS's letters and diaries (had he not destroyed them) 'would have set the Thames on fire'.

246 *brace*: OS presumably means one of a pair of leather braces, commonly used in the nineteenth century to hold up trousers, and often worked with silk.

250 *the Fields*: SCCS added a footnote: 'The Diamond Fields were in those days known simply as "the Fields".' See also note to p. 254.

whatnot: a set of open shelves often used for display.

251 *His face . . . proclaimed him at once a Jew . . . a moneylender . . . at a high rate of interest*: OS's stereotyping of her Jewish characters in this chapter and Ch. XI jars with her 'Letter on the Jew', *Cape Times*, 2 July 1906, as well as with her claim that it is as impossible to 'sum [. . .] up' the Englishman as it is 'the Jew' (*TSA*, 321). Her refusal to dignify with a name the figure she calls 'the Jew' is of a piece with her use of the terms 'Ayah' and 'old Ayah' to replace a name, betraying the stereotyping that lies behind it.

251 *frikkedel*: SCCS added a footnote: 'Minced meat ball, "rissole".' OS uses a variant of the more common Afk. spelling *frikkadel*, derived from the French *fricadelle* (*DSAE*, 278).

252 *'And ze young lady, vill she not see too?'*: whatever its (unpleasant) comic effect, OS's persistent rendering of his speech as foreign, through syntax as well as pronunciation, entrenches 'the Jew' not as a complex, particularized character but as a type. For extensive discussion of 'the Jew' as allegorical, see Anna Snaith, *Modernist* Voyages, in Selected Bibliography, *supra*.

253 *East End garret*: the widespread pogroms in Russia during the nineteenth century drove many thousands of Jews to flee to Austria and Germany, where they lived in overcrowded conditions, general deprivation, and increasing anti-Semitism, e.g. the considerable 'Jew-baiting' in Germany in 1819, as Schmeul Almog puts it in *Nationalism and Antisemitism in Modern Europe, 1815–1945* (Oxford: Pergamon, 1990), 8. Many migrated to London (the first massive migrations were later, in the 1860s); in this case, to the East End, where 'they could take advantage of some of the cheapest—and humblest—living accommodation that the world's most expensive city had to offer'; see Jerry White, *London in the Nineteenth Century: 'A Human Awful Wonder of God'* (London: Jonathan Cape, 2007), 155.

'Old clothes! Old clothes!': see Jack London's description of a 1902 visit to an old-clothes shop in London's East End, in his *People of the Abyss* (New York: Macmillan, 1904), 9–10. Selling old clothes became less viable after 'mass production of ready-made clothing got under way in the 1880s'; see Jerry White, *London in the Nineteenth Century: 'A Human Awful Wonder of God'* (London: Jonathan Cape, 2007), 153.

254 *River Diggings . . . New Rush*: from the alluvial diggings on the banks of the Orange River on the northern frontier of the Cape Colony, where diamonds were first discovered in 1867, diggers 'rushed' to New Rush, lured there in 1871 by the discovery of a large diamond. OS lived at New Rush from 1872 to 1873, in what was then Griqualand West; it was annexed to the Cape Colony in 1877, and New Rush was renamed Kimberley, as SCCS notes in his footnote: 'Now Kimberley.'

with a gait like his own: the imagery of physical degeneracy prevalent in this chapter and Ch. XI extends to Martha and her son; OS's reference to the apparently characteristic Jewish gait has its antecedent in her early essay 'Diamond Fields': 'a little second-class Jewish diamond-buyer, easily known by his nose & his shuffling gate' (16).This reference perhaps puts paid to what would otherwise seem to be implied: that Martha's son is the unacknowledged son of 'the Jew'.

259 *caddis-worm creeping out of its case*: the larva of a caddisfly typically constructs cases out of silk woven with sand. Given the garment that Bertie makes for Dorcas (patterned with red butterflies; see p. 243), it is impossible not to hear the metonymies at work. See, for instance, OS's

letter to Karl Pearson, n.d July 1886, which identifies the chrysalis with the creative imagination (in Appendix 2).

262 *as blind as an earth-snake*: possibly the Cape legless skink a.k.a. blindworm, *Acontias meleagris*, or else a giant earthworm, *Lumbricus terrestris*, fairly common in certain parts of the Karoo. OS may be recalling the witches' chant in *Macbeth* (IV. i. 16) or the spell-casting in *A Midsummer Night's Dream* (II. ii. 12), where Shakespeare refers to the blindworm native to Eurasia (*Anguis fragilis*, often mistaken for a snake).

263 *orbits*: eye sockets; archaic.

outspan: remove the oxen's harnesses, from the Du. *uitspannen* (*DSAE*, 531–2), now standard in SAE.

267 *there was nothing to recall the Jew*: again, the novel hints at but does not settle any question about whether or not Isaac is his unacknowledged son.

the point . . . work of nature: Isaac's nose is strangely similar to Percy Lawrie's: 'rounded except at the point, where it seemed to have been sliced off, leaving a small square tip' (see p. 49).

268 *the wrist . . . a little hairy*: cf. Charlotte Brontë's *Jane Eyre*, where the figure of Bertha is also described in conventionally unfeminine terms.

270 *Bond Street*: this street, in London's West End, had been fashionable for shopping since the eighteenth century.

[?eight]: SCCS's query and addition, in Unwin and Harper, has been retained here.

271 *they burned harpuis bushes*: in his footnote, SCCS glossed 'harpuis' as 'resin'. The term derives from the Dutch *hars* ('resin') and *puisje* ('pimple') to refer to the resin exuding from the stem and branches of the harpuis bush (*Euryops* sp.). This is one of the daisy family, and common in the Cape Peninsula, but around Cradock, the plant type is likely to be *Euryops floribundus*. The bushes were burned as weeds.

273 *sovereigns*: gold coins valued at one pound sterling each. In the 1880s, a sovereign (a gold coin valued at one pound sterling) would have covered a worker's wages for one or two weeks.

276 *"vastrap"*: OS added the following note: 'The vastrap is a kind of wild Highland fling danced by Hottentot or Bushmen servants at the Cape.' It was also danced in rural Boer communities. The word derives from the Dutch *vast* ('firm') and *trap* ('tread'). Now called a *riel* (Afk.), it is danced competitively in Cape communities.

280 *the Strand*: a major thoroughfare in central London.

Seven Dials: a junction formed by the convergence of seven roads, in Covent Garden. In *Sketches by Boz* (1836) Charles Dickens refers to it as a slum area, and, according to *The Victorian Web*, it was 'a breeding ground of vice, disease, and crime'; <http://www.victorianweb.org/>, accessed 2 January 2024.

283 *In Cape Town . . . no theatre . . . two domestic little plays very badly set*: Cape Town offered little serious theatre at the time (the popular Good Hope Theatre was founded only in 1893): Bertie may have seen the two domestic plays at Cape Town's Drawing Room Theatre founded in 1855, or (perhaps) at the first of the two Theatre Royals, founded in 1860 but burned down in 1868 (the second was founded in 1875). The Opera House opened only in 1893. See Worden, van Heyningen, and Bickford-Smith, *Cape Town: The Making of a City*, 190–3, 241.

284 *'Aren't they women?'*: given the rest of Bertie's question, OS may well have written: 'Aren't these women', followed by the rest of the question. Still, there is a certain poignancy and outrage to Bertie's question, as if to say: How can women perform in this way?

the glass of wine: earlier in this chapter, the doctor 'ordered [...] a glass of stout before she went to bed' (p. 283).

286 *'Mudie's Select Library, New Oxford Street'*: Charles Edward Mudie (1818–90) founded his immensely popular lending library in the 1840s, when books cost more than most middle-class English people could afford.

287 *when you pull a string and shake their heads and jaws*: Bertie may be describing shadow theatre, in which two-dimensional images of figures are back-projected on to a white screen, the figures being jointed and capable of being moved by strings in the hands of the puppeteer(s). Alternatively, she may have witnessed a moving image extension of the stereopticon, operated by string. The stereopticon, a slide projector or 'magic lantern' that made use of two lenses, was a popular form of entertainment in the nineteenth century until the invention of movies.

289 *St Leonards-on-Sea*: near Hastings in East Sussex, St Leonards was established in the early nineteenth century as a seaside settlement for the relatively wealthy. OS stayed there at various times during the 1880s; her brother Fred lived in nearby Eastbourne.

290 *esplanade*: the pier would be completed only in 1891.

Bath chairs: named after its origin in Bath, and invented by James Heath in the early nineteenth century, the Bath chair was an early form of the wheelchair, mounted on three or four wheels and equipped with a folding hood.

Dresden figures: Dresden (in Saxony, part of present-day Germany) began manufacturing high-quality porcelain in 1872, and registered its trademark in 1883.

291 *the fish was crimped*: to crimp a fish is to gash it with a knife to make the flesh firmer and crisper when cooked.

292 *headland*: Bertie is probably looking south-west towards Beachy Head, just west of Eastbourne. It is the highest chalk cliff in the United Kingdom but would look small from that distance. Schreiner might have known that Beachy Head became a common spot for suicide from the 7th century on.

294 *'This . . . is country'*: Bertie and Isaac have walked east from St Leonards, with the sea on their right, in the direction of Fairlight. The area is part of the High Weald, a ridge of sandstone and clay.

point lace: lace made with buttonhole stitching, using a needle on a paper or parchment pattern.

298 *worsted ball*: i.e. of wool.

307 *mizzle*: light, mistlike rain (regional, colloquial term in England and Scotland).

310 *the little face*: this seems to refer to an excised plot element, and perhaps one that gives the mound (so often referred to) its particular significance. For a speculative source, see Helen Bradford, 'Olive Schreiner's Hidden Agony', in Select Bibliography, *supra*.

311 *Polly is my sweetheart, Polly is my darling*: not identified exactly, but the words appear to come from the chorus or refrain of one of the many variations on the traditional Scottish song 'Charlie is my darling', which celebrated Prince Charles Edward Stuart, the 'Young Pretender' of the Jacobite Uprising, who was defeated at Culloden in 1746. The poet Robert Burns wrote a particularly bawdy version in 1794. The American Union Army produced yet another version, 'Johnny is my darling'.

My Grandfather's Clock: composed in 1876 by Henry Clay Work, this song became a standard of British brass bands. Bertie hears parts of the alternating refrain.

318 *when her youngest boy was born*: SCCS added the following helpful footnote: 'Rebekah's children, in order of birth, are Charles, Frank, Hughie and Bertie.' He does not mention the adopted child Sartje, born at the same time as the youngest boy, Bertie.

she: Unwin and Harper have 'it' in the place of 'she', but the present edition makes a change, notwithstanding OS's positive use of a non-gendered 'it' in her dreams and allegories of a future ideal.

319 *wizen*: variant of wizened, used earlier, in relation to the baby boy, Bertie; see p. 237.

but it was there: that is, the likeness was there. OS stresses the two children's inherited likeness, as well as what is perceived to be their difference. The opposition 'alabaster' and 'clay' recalls Robert Browning's poem 'Old Pictures in Florence', which OS had been rereading during the late 1880s (see her letter to Havelock Ellis, 30 March 1887 (in Appendix 2), and which she was perhaps alluding to at the time of writing this passage. In Browning's stanza xvi, the speaker contemplates marble statues: 'They are perfect—how else? they shall never change: | We are faulty—why not? we have time in store. | The Artificer's hand is not arrested | With us; we are rough-hewn, nowise polished: | They stand for our copy, and, once invested | With all they can teach, we shall see them abolished.'

320 *Grey boy*: either a reference to the boy's family name or an allusion to the boy's fictional school. Two elite boys' boarding schools were named after Sir George Grey, governor of the Cape Colony from 1854 to 1859 and 1860 to 1861, a figure much admired by OS, presumably for his helping found the Healdtown industrial school: Grey College in Bloemfontein; and Grey High School in Port Elizabeth. OS approved of George Grey's what were for the time liberal attitude towards Africans; and perhaps the reference to his name relates to Rebecca's efforts to educate her sons against current racist attitudes.

Oh Goy!: to use the Yiddish term for Gentile constitutes a startling exclamation from Frank, who replicates his father. Possibly OS wrote an illegible 'Oh boy!', a standard exclamation in South African English.

321 *Titania, the Queen of the Fairies*: a character in Shakespeare's *A Midsummer Night's Dream*, who flouts the orders of her husband, Oberon, by taking charge of an Indian changeling boy.

322 *the Robber Baron . . . in the dark*: Rebekah creates a tale in stark contrast to, for instance, A. J. Foster and E. E. Cuthbert, *The Robber Baron of Bedford Castle* (London: Thomas Nelson and Sons, 1903), in which men storm a castle to free a woman held captive, 'entertained in the lady's bower, as befits a damsel' (ch. xx).

324 *They were human*: this is of course a tale for children, but the terms 'people' and 'human' hardly fit the scene. These terms are repeated through the story as Rebekah continues to tell her children about these human beings' wings.

325 *little worms*: silkworms.

326 *gorra-gorras*: variant of *gorah* or *gora*. Probably from Khoikhoi *Xkora*, *Xgora*, or *qgora* (*DSAE*, 261): a bow-like musical instrument, with a flattened piece of quill or reed interposed between one end of the string (or strings) and the point of its attachment to the bow; blowing on the quill or reed causes vibrations in the strings.

witchdoctors who mumble over bones and make charms: Rebekah's examples cover the range of applications of the term 'witchdoctors' indicated in the cultural and literary quotations supplied by *DSAE* (see esp. 797): from healers and diviners to those in charge of the processes of 'smelling out' referred to later in this chapter, p. 335.

327 *we could not really fight them*: in 1838, in the Battle of Blood River (Zulu: *iMpi yase Ncome*), an estimated 3,000 Zulus were killed under fire from Boer guns and cannons. Three Boer Voortrekkers were lightly wounded.

328 *'The dream ends there'*: in *Closer Union* (1908, first published in newspaper form), OS sees South Africa in terms of a temporal cusp (a bright future/a bleak one): 'If we raise the dark man we shall rise with him; if we kick him under our feet, he will hold us fast by them' (31). She was deeply concerned in the 1910s about the dangers of armed revolt for Africans. Her letter to Will Schreiner, 29 July 1919, speaks of a 'civil war [that] will begin with the native and not end there', for the 'big native wars' will do

no more than further dispossess the African of his land and create 'such a terrible proletariat as will be our ultimate undoing'; see Liz Stanley and Andrea Salter (eds.), *The World's Great Question*, in Select Bibliography, *supra*.

But we cannot say so of any men or women living: the sentence is obscure, but OS seems to mean that we cannot say the same thing about (i.e. ask the same question of) the men and women who inhabit earth; while we share a common humanity that permits this kind of similarity, there is no such connection between earthlings and these intruders.

329 *ringed stones*: ironstone; see note to p. 240.

331 *as it would be right they should treat us*: SCCS wrongly inserted '[?not]' after 'would' (see Unwin and Harper). He misread Rebekah's logic, which is to pursue the following line: that it would seem as right for us to despise them as it would be for them to treat us as the savages we once were.

332 *small English boys*: readers may be startled to hear Rebekah refer to her sons as 'English'.

333 *spinnies*: probably a contraction of the term 'Spinning Jenny' (an eight-spindle spinning frame invented in 1764).

335 *one old writer*: not identified; the denigrating comments are possibly derived from an account given by the historian Tacitus (*c.* 56–118), whom OS read (see her letter to F. S. Lewis, 25 December 1897, in *OSLO*), perhaps in the translation produced by Alfred J. Church and W. J. Brodribb, *The Agricola and Germania of Tacitus* (London: Macmillan, 1879). Tacitus might have been recounting Roman attitudes, as he himself was quite admiring of the Britons.

"smelling out": finding out those assumed to be evildoers.

Bo tree: the Bodhi tree under which Buddha, the great Indian spiritual leader, achieved enlightenment.

"He prayeth well . . . great and small": from Samuel Taylor Coleridge, 'The Rime of the Ancient Mariner' (1798).

336 *Be Thanks*: 'Thanks be!' is the usual expression. OS probably recalls the phrase from a prayer or hymn such as 'To God on high be thanks and praise | For mercy ceasing never' in *The Anglican Hymn Book* (London: Novello, Ewer, 1868), 268; the hymn was translated by R. C. Singleton from the German of Nikolaus Decius, 1485–1541.

camel thorn trees: *Vachellia erioloba* (formerly *Acacia erioloba* or *Acacia giraffae*); very like the thorn tree (see note to pp. 9 and 20). The camel thorn tree is to be found in the north-west Cape but is more common in Central Africa (see p. 355); the name is derived from the early colonists' confusion of the Dutch *kameelperd* ('giraffe') and *kameel* ('camel'). Before settling on 'Perhaps Only—', OS chose 'The Camel Thorn' as the title for this novel, after speaking of it as 'From Man to Man' (see 1911 TS, and SCCS in Appendix 1, p. 378).

336 *[?beginning]*: the (presumably) illegible or missing word that SCCS surmises was possibly 'pinnacle', which better fits Rebekah's sense. For a related passage, see 'The Psychology of the Boer': 'Dark and blinded beyond the average of human souls must have been the old fore-trekker, who [...] could cry, "I, *I* am the centre of this life! The earth is mine, and the fullness thereof!"' (*TSA*, 288).

337 *this: the man—that, . . . the nation—that,*: the punctuation in Unwin and Harper ('this. The man, that, [...] —the nation; that') has been slightly adapted here to clarify the syntax.

I built a high wall right across Africa: see OS's 1901 introduction to *TSA*, where she speaks of her own early desire for such a wall, at a time in her childhood when she felt 'as much insular prejudice and racial pride as it is given to any citizen who has never left the little Northern Island to possess' (*TSA*, 15). Though speaking in that instance of her early attitude to the Boer, she immediately segues into 'making believe that I was Queen Victoria' and ordering 'all the black people in South Africa to be collected and put into the desert of Sahara, and a wall built across Africa shutting it off' (*TSA*, 15). This reads as an oblique comment on the queen of the British Empire quite as much as upon herself.

338 *the Front*: one of the battlefronts in the continuing struggle by the Xhosa to retain their land, livestock, and autonomy; during the Ninth Frontier War (1877–9), which is a possible allusion here (see notes below), the 'Front' would have been the Kei River. The Xhosa fought 'for one hundred years [...] through nine wars of gradually increasing ferocity for their territorial birthright'. See Noel Mostert, *Frontiers: The Epic of South Africa's Creation and the Tragedy of the Xhosa People* (New York: Knopf, 1992), 252. To the east was an independent Xhosa territory (known to the Europeans as Kaffraria, a.k.a. Caffraria). The western lands were placed under British rule in 1847 (British Kaffraria) and incorporated into the Cape Colony in 1866.

assegais: according to SCCS, OS added the following footnote: 'An assagai [*sic*] is the spear used by the Kaffirs in war.' The assegai, from the Dutch *hassegaai* (originally an Arabic term; called *umkhonto* in Xhosa) may be either short, for stabbing, or long, as here, for throwing. By the Seventh Frontier War (1846–7), the Xhosa forces had started to supplement this weaponry with modern firearms, but the massive technological imbalance remained through the Eighth Frontier War (1850–3) and the Ninth.

only a few got away into the bush again: OS may be transposing to Rebekah's childhood an event that occurred while she was working as a governess in the Cape Colony at the time of the Ninth Frontier War, a.k.a. the War of Ngcayechibi, when—on 29 September 1877, in the battle of Ibeka (Xhosa: Ibika)—a female doctor-priest led and encouraged a force of 8 000 Gcaleka (Xhosa) warriors against an outpost at Ibeka. These warriors, along with the woman, were 'mowed down by our shells and rockets', as one of the white victors put it. Quoted in John Milton, *The Edges of War:*

A History of Frontier Wars, 1702–1878 (Cape Town: Juta, 1883), 259. See also Arthur Augustus Thurlow Cunynghame, *My Command in South Africa* (London: Macmillan, 1897), 320–1. Regarding OS's portrayal of a female warrior handing out assegais, no such event appears to be reflected in the historical records.

340 *"Is it not perhaps then best you should go?"*: see OS's 1901 introduction to *TSA*: 'In truth, I am unable to conceive of the varieties and species into which the human race has divided itself as other than varied flowers in the garden of the gods on earth, of which the loss of one would be heavy. In my own garden I desire to see grow all species and kinds of flowers, the rose, the rhododendron, the violet and the orchid and the cactus on the rocks. And I love the purple-eyed periwinkle as well as any plant; only if it spreads inordinately and threatens to choke all the others do I say, "It is a weed; pull it up and circumscribe it!"' (*TSA*, 25).

341 *given place to*: given expression to.

I fthrow them wifth stones!: OS again provides an Afk. flavour here, *met 'n klip gooi* being the concise translation of the Eng. 'to throw a stone at someone and hit them with it'.

342 *It is a finer thing to be a "man" than either of you can know now*: cf. Rudyard Kipling's poem 'If', published in *Rewards and Fairies* (1910) and drawn, he said, from the character of Leander Starr Jameson, the leader of Cecil John Rhodes's notorious Jameson Raid of 1895/6; see C. Carrington, *Rudyard Kipling: His Life and Work* (London: Macmillan, 1955), 382. On their annual visits to the Cape from 1901 to 1908, the Kiplings stayed in The Woolsack, on Rhodes's estate, near where Rebekah and Frank live. OS speaks of meeting the Kiplings in Kimberley (see her letter to Betty Molteno, 30 March 1898, *OSLO*/UCT).

343 *little Yed Yiding Hood*: this European fairy tale, 'Little Red Riding Hood', was published in Perrault's *Tales of Passed Times, by Mother Goose* (1697) and in different versions in the various editions of Jacob and Wilhelm Grimms' *Children's and Household Tales* (commonly known as *Grimms' Fairy Tales*) between 1812 and 1857.

344 *to have her face enamelled*: 'Composed of arsenic or white lead and other ingredients [and] made into a semi-paste [...] an ordinary coating [of enamel] will last for a day or two, but to render the operation of permanent value, the process must be repeated once or twice a week'. See George Ellington, *Women of New York: or, The Under-World of the Great City* (New York: New York Book Co., 1869), 85 n. 35.

345 *that wonderful farm of yours*: see p. 213 for OS's first reference to the farm.

the close season: the season when hunting is officially forbidden.

349 *lappet*: flap.

358 *one quite white rose where all the rest are pink*: in *Variation of Animals and Plants*, Darwin writes: 'Many cases have been recorded of a whole plant, or single branch, or bud, suddenly producing flowers different from the

proper type in colour, form, size, doubleness, or other character. Half the flower, or a smaller segment, sometimes changes colour' (i. 351).

359 *dicynodont's*: dicynodonts are the most abundant therapsids (the stock that gave rise to mammals) from the geological layer known as the Beaufort Group. OS excavated dicynodont remains at Lelie Kloof in the Karoo; see her letter to Havelock Ellis, 8 April 1886 (in Appendix 2). See also note to p. 360.

krans: OS's footnote: 'cliff'. Also spelled *krantz*, and naturalized into SAE, the term comes from the Du. *krans* ('coronet'). It is a more specific rock formation, typical of the Karoo, than the word 'cliff' can suggest (*DSAE*, 398). Elsewhere, OS glossed 'krantzes' as 'precipices' (*TSA*, 17 n. 20).

winged reptile fossil: see 'winged reptile' on p. 163; see also note to p. 14.

360 *great piles of notes and writing on Woman*: the bulk of Ch. VII and part of Ch. XII may well be seen as OS's own 'writing on Woman'. She was composing *FMTM* at the same time as what she called her 'great sex book', *Woman and Labour* (1911), as well as drafting an introduction to a reissue of Mary Wollstonecraft's *Vindication of the Rights of Woman* (1792) and writing her two-part essay 'The Woman Question', *Cosmopolitan* (New York) (November and December 1899). See her letter to Karl Pearson, 13 May 1886 (in Appendix 2).

the little son: cf. Afk. *seuntjie* (boy, son, with affectionate diminutive, very commonly used). OS gives Drummond's speech a South African flavour even though he is from abroad. Usage by the English and Scottish would likely be 'sonny' and 'laddie' respectively.

Midlands: a.k.a. the Cape Midlands or the Eastern Cape Midlands (Cradock lies at the centre of the Midlands). OS worked as a governess at Lelie Kloof from mid-1879 to early 1881, an area rich in fossils and five hours' cart drive from Cradock (see Cronwright-Schreiner, *Life*, 138).

361 *scot and lot*: tax revenue.

362 *lymphatic*: having the characteristics of sluggishness. Sluggishness was formerly believed to be an excess of lymph in the system (lymph being a clear fluid carried back by the lymphatic vessels to the heart for recirculation).

he took it out. . . . : the ellipsis in SCCS's edition (reproduced differently in Unwin and in Harper and differently in the present edition too) indicates his uncertainty about the correct page order or perhaps missing text; see Appendix 1, p. 381.

chaffer: haggle about price.

363 *my Chinaman*: the novel's only reference to South African Chinese, who immigrated mostly from the 1870s onwards, although there were Chinese residents in Cape Town as early as the 1770s; see Worden, van Heyningen, and Bickford-Smith, *Cape Town: The Making of a City*, 54, 65–6. The Chinese were subsequently discriminated against through, inter alia, the Cape Immigration Act of 1902 and the Cape Chinese Exclusion Act (1904), and very badly treated as mineworkers.

364 *the Kalahari*: a large desert occupying almost all of present-day Botswana, the eastern part of present-day Namibia, and a small northerly section of South Africa's Northern Cape province.

Lake Ngami: in present-day Botswana, north of the Kalahari Desert. OS spoke repeatedly in her letters of her desire to visit this general area in order to research social customs; see her letter to W. T. Stead, 12 July 1890 (in Appendix 2).

a description of Bushmen . . . the exact measurement of some skulls: from the late nineteenth century, skulls were being collected and measured in order to chart the route of evolutionary development, some early anthropologists believing that the skull revealed a difference between the 'Bushmen' and the 'Hottentots' (the former generally seen as more 'primitive'). Some Cape Dutch farmers believed that the 'Bushman' skull was distinguished by having no suture down the middle of the frontal bone, and in the early twentieth century the director of the South African Museum helped organize a collection of skulls from cave sites to send to London for craniometric analysis. See Saul Dubow, *Scientific Racism in Modern South Africa* (Cambridge: Cambridge University Press, 1995), 36–9. OS may or may not have known of the late nineteenth-century objections made by the eminent Prussian scientist Rudolf Virchow (1821–1902) to the measuring of skulls. For her early interest in the 'Bushmen', see the references in *SAF* to San cave-paintings as well as her essay 'The Problems of Slavery', first composed in 1892, published in 1896 (*Fortnightly Review*), and later collected in *TSA* as 'The Problem of Slavery'. See also p. 69.

with a flash one after the other: OS draws here from her own experience; see her letters to Havelock Ellis, 12 June 1890, to Ettie Schreiner, 25 December 1901, and to Ettie Schreiner, October 1909 (in Appendix 2).

365 *Socrates . . . Demon*: during the time she was working intensively on *FMTM*, OS was reading Jowett's translations of Plato, published in 1871; see her letter to Isaline Philpot, August 1887 (in Appendix 2). Defining intuition as a mysterious power held by the poet, who is inspired by a divinity that is then passed on to others, Socrates says to Ion: 'God himself is the speaker, and [. . .] through [those he inspires] he is addressing us'. See *The Dialogues of Plato*, trans. Benjamin Jowett (1871; repr. Oxford: Clarendon Press, 1953), i. 108. The standard Eng. spelling is 'daimon' or 'daemon'.

I noticed it when I was a little child: in his 'Apology', Plato refers to his daimon as 'the will of divine power' manifesting as 'a kind of voice [that] first began to come to me when I was a child'. See *The Dialogues of Plato*, trans. Jowett, i. 358 and 356 respectively.

366 *Winged Victory*: in the Victorian era, the Winged Victory (Nikē) of Samothrace, became 'a crucial metaphor for security' in the public imagination, and—among suffragists, for example—'a cipher [. . .] of winning through against the odds'. See Marina Warner, *Monuments and Maidens: The Allegory of the Female Form* (London: Weidenfeld & Nicolson, 1985), 145 and 143 respectively.

367 *"And with twain they covered their face and with twain did fly"*: OS draws here from Isaiah 6:2: 'Above it [the Lord's throne] stood the seraphims: each one had six wings; with twain he covered his face, and with twain he covered his feet, and with twain he did fly.'

369 *the copy within*: Socrates to Phaedrus: 'the true way of writing [is], in the first place, the word which [the writer] finds in his own bosom; secondly, the brethren and descendants and relations of his idea which have been duly implanted by him in the souls of others'. See *The Dialogues of Plato*, trans. Jowett, iii. 188.

the desire to incarnate is instinctive: in *The Descent of Man*, which OS read in 1873, Darwin wrote: 'The imagination is one of the highest prerogatives of man. By this faculty he unites, independently of the will, former images and ideas, and thus creates brilliant and novel results. [...] Dreaming gives us the best notion of this power; as Jean Paul [Richter] says, "The dream is an involuntary art of poetry".' See *The Descent of Man, and Selection in Relation to Sex* (1871), in *From So Simple a Beginning: The Four Great Books of Charles Darwin*, ed. Edward O. Wilson (New York: Norton, 2006), 804.

the dream-god of the Semitics: the Semites' (Jews') idea of God as reflected in the Old Testament.

370 *which would be quite justified, if their opinion were asked*: the word 'which' refers to the statements about like or dislike rather than to the public's advice.

not to let the thing die: an echo of the wording used by Milton in 'The Reason of Church Government' (1641), in *Complete Poems and Major Prose*, ed. Merritt Yorkes Hughes (Indianapolis: Hackett, 2003): 'I might perhaps leave something so written to aftertimes, as they should not willingly let it die' (preface to Bk 2).

"Shall I call to the birth and not cause to bring forth?" saith the Lord: Again, OS is drawing from Isaiah (66:9): 'Shall I bring to the birth, and not cause to bring forth? saith the Lord.'

371 *the bearded face smiles down at it*: this is the first full description of the statue referred to earlier (see note to p. 123). A copy of the original (no longer extant), which is attributed to the Greek sculptor Lysippos (380–310 BCE), is held in the Louvre and shows a vine-wreathed Silenus with the infant Dionysus in his arms (in Greek mythology, Silenus is Dionysus' companion and tutor). Dionysus a.k.a. Bacchus is a mythic deity associated with agriculture, fertility, wine, and ecstasy. OS uses this image to represent the mother-love that men may experience and exhibit.

372 *Ancient Chaldea*: Babylon or Mesopotamia. The Chaldeans were regarded by the Persians as expert readers, writers, and astronomers.

the thing we love should live on its own life: in OS's handwriting, 'in' can easily be mistaken for 'on', and she may well have written 'live in its own life'. However, the phrase is probably best understood as 'the thing we love should live on, in its own life'.

375 *the three young ones*: Hughie, Bertie, and Sartje.

MORE ABOUT **OXFORD WORLD'S CLASSICS**

The Oxford World's Classics Website

- Browse the full range of Oxford World's Classics online
- Sign up for our monthly e-alert to receive information on new titles
- Read extracts from the Introductions
- Listen to our editors and translators talk about the world's greatest literature with our Oxford World's Classics audio guides
- Join the conversation, follow us on Twitter at OWC_Oxford
- Teachers and lecturers can order inspection copies quickly and simply via our website

www.oup.com/uk/worldsclassics

MORE ABOUT **OXFORD WORLD'S CLASSICS**

American Literature

British and Irish Literature

Children's Literature

Classics and Ancient Literature

Colonial Literature

Eastern Literature

European Literature

Gothic Literature

History

Medieval Literature

Oxford English Drama

Philosophy

Poetry

Politics

Religion

The Oxford Shakespeare

A SELECTION OF **OXFORD WORLD'S CLASSICS**

JOHN BUCHAN	**Huntingtower** **The Thirty-Nine Steps**
JOSEPH CONRAD	**Heart of Darkness and Other Tales** **Lord Jim** **Nostromo** **The Secret Agent** **Under Western Eyes**
FORD MADOX FORD	**The Good Soldier**
JOHN GALSWORTHY	**The Forsyte Saga**
JAMES JOYCE	**A Portrait of the Artist as a Young Man** **Dubliners** **Occasional, Critical, and Political Writing** **Ulysses**
RUDYARD KIPLING	**The Jungle Books** **Just So Stories** **Kim** **War Stories and Poems**
D. H. LAWRENCE	**The Rainbow** **Sons and Lovers** **Women in Love**
WYNDHAM LEWIS	**Tarr**
KATHERINE MANSFIELD	**Selected Stories**
ROBERT TRESSELL	**The Ragged Trousered Philanthropists**
VIRGINIA WOOLF	**Flush** **The Mark on the Wall and Other Short Fiction** **Mrs Dalloway** **Orlando: A Biography** **A Room of One's Own and Three Guineas** **To the Lighthouse**
W. B. YEATS	**The Major Works**

A SELECTION OF **OXFORD WORLD'S CLASSICS**

	Travel Writing 1700–1830
FRANCES BURNEY	Cecilia Evelina
ROBERT BURNS	Selected Poems and Songs
JOHN CLELAND	Memoirs of a Woman of Pleasure
DANIEL DEFOE	A Journal of the Plague Year Moll Flanders Robinson Crusoe
HENRY FIELDING	Jonathan Wild Joseph Andrews and Shamela Tom Jones
WILLIAM GODWIN	Caleb Williams
OLIVER GOLDSMITH	The Vicar of Wakefield
SAMUEL JOHNSON	The History of Rasselas
ANN RADCLIFFE	The Italian The Mysteries of Udolpho
SAMUEL RICHARDSON	Pamela
TOBIAS SMOLLETT	The Adventures of Roderick Random The Expedition of Humphry Clinker
LAURENCE STERNE	The Life and Opinions of Tristram Shandy, Gentleman A Sentimental Journey
JONATHAN SWIFT	Gulliver's Travels A Tale of a Tub and Other Works
HORACE WALPOLE	The Castle of Otranto
MARY WOLLSTONECRAFT	Mary and The Wrongs of Woman

A SELECTION OF **OXFORD WORLD'S CLASSICS**

	Late Victorian Gothic Tales
	Literature and Science in the Nineteenth Century
JANE AUSTEN	**Emma** **Mansfield Park** **Northanger Abbey** **Persuasion** **Pride and Prejudice** **Selected Letters** **Sense and Sensibility**
MRS BEETON	**Book of Household Management**
MARY ELIZABETH BRADDON	**Lady Audley's Secret**
ANNE BRONTË	**The Tenant of Wildfell Hall**
CHARLOTTE BRONTË	**Jane Eyre** **Shirley** **Villette**
EMILY BRONTË	**Wuthering Heights**
ROBERT BROWNING	**The Major Works**
JOHN CLARE	**The Major Works**
SAMUEL TAYLOR COLERIDGE	**The Major Works**
WILKIE COLLINS	**The Moonstone** **No Name** **The Woman in White**
CHARLES DARWIN	**The Origin of Species**
THOMAS DE QUINCEY	**Confessions of an English Opium-Eater and Other Writings** **On Murder**
CHARLES DICKENS	**Oliver Twist** **Barnaby Rudge** **Bleak House** **David Copperfield** **Great Expectations** **Nicholas Nickleby**

A SELECTION OF **OXFORD WORLD'S CLASSICS**

CHARLES DICKENS	**A Christmas Carol and Other Christmas Books** **Dombey and Son** **The Old Curiosity Shop** **Our Mutual Friend** **The Pickwick Papers** **Tale of Two Cities**
GEORGE DU MAURIER	**Trilby**
MARIA EDGEWORTH	**Castle Rackrent**
GEORGE ELIOT	**Adam Bede** **Daniel Deronda** **The Lifted Veil and Brother Jacob** **Middlemarch** **The Mill on the Floss** **Silas Marner**
EDWARD FITZGERALD	**The Rubáiyát of Omar Khayyám**
ELIZABETH GASKELL	**Cranford** **The Life of Charlotte Brontë** **Mary Barton** **North and South** **Wives and Daughters**
GEORGE GISSING	**New Grub Street** **The Nether World** **The Odd Women**
EDMUND GOSSE	**Father and Son**
THOMAS HARDY	**Far from the Madding Crowd** **Jude the Obscure** **The Mayor of Casterbridge** **The Return of the Native** **Tess of the d'Urbervilles** **The Woodlanders**
JAMES HOGG	**The Private Memoirs and Confessions of a Justified Sinner**